European Decolonization

The International Library of Essays on Political History

Series Editor: Jeremy Black

Titles in the Series:

European Decolonization

Edited by

Martin Thomas
University of Exeter, UK

ASHGATE

Published by
Ashgate Publishing Limited
Gower House
Croft Road
Aldershot
Hampshire GU11 3HR
England

Ashgate Publishing Company
Suite 420
101 Cherry Street
Burlington, VT 05401-4405
USA

Ashgate website: http://www.ashgate.com

British Library Cataloguing in Publication Data
European decolonization. (The international library of
   essays on political history)
   1. Decolonization 2. Europe–Colonies –History–20th
   century
   I. Thomas, Martin
   325. 3'4

Library of Congress Cataloging-in-Publication Data
European decolonization / edited by Martin Thomas.
      p. cm. – (The international library of essay on political history)
   ISBN-13: 978-0-7546-2568-1 (alk. paper)
   1. Decolonization–History–20th century. 2. Europe–Colonies–History–20th century.
   I. Thomas, Martin, 1964–

   JV151.E87 2007
   325'.3094–DC22

                                                                            2006050104

ISBN 978-0-7546-2568-1

Printed in Great Britain by TJ International Ltd, Padstow, Cornwall

Contents

Acknowledgements

The editor and publishers wish to thank the following for permission to use copyright material.

Academy of Political Science for the essay: Steven Metz (1984), 'American Attitudes Toward Decolonization in Africa', *Political Science Quarterly*, **99**, pp. 515–33.

Cambridge University Press for the essays: Matthew Connelly (2001), 'Rethinking the Cold War and Decolonization: The Grand Strategy of the Algerian War for Independence', *International Journal of Middle East Studies*, **33**, pp. 221–45. Copyright © 2001 Cambridge University Press; Chen Jian (1993), 'China and the First Indo-China War, 1950–54', *China Quarterly*, **133**, pp. 85–110. Copyright © 1993 China Quarterly; Patrick M. Boyle (1995), 'School Wars: Church, State and the Death of the Congo', *Journal of Modern African Studies*, **33**, pp. 451–68. Copyright © 1995 Cambridge University Press; Karl Hack (1999), '"Iron Claws on Malaya": The Historiography of the Malayan Emergency', *Journal of Southeast Asian Studies*, **30**, pp. 99–125.Copyright © 1999 National University of Singapore; Ritchie Ovendale (1995), 'Macmillan and the Wind of Change in Africa, 1957–60', *Historical Journal*, **38**, pp. 455–77. Copyright © 1995 Cambridge University Press; Frederick Cooper (1996), '"Our Strike": Equality, Anticolonial Politics and the 1947–48 Railway Strike in French West Africa', *Journal of African History*, **37**, pp. 81–118. Copyright © 1996 Cambridge University Press; Robert Blackey (1974), 'Fanon and Cabral: A Contrast in Theories of Revolution in Africa', *Journal of Modern African Studies*, **12**, pp. 191–209; Tony Smith (1978), 'A Comparative Study of French and British Decolonization', *Comparative Studies in Society and History*, **20**, pp. 70–102.

Canadian Association of African Studies for the essay: Cora Ann Presley (1988), 'The Mau Mau Rebellion, Kikuyu Women, and Social Change', *Canadian Journal of African Studies*, **22**, pp. 502–27.

Oxford University Press for the essays: John Flint (1983), 'Planned Decolonization and its Failure in British Africa', *African Affairs*, **82**, pp. 389–411. Martin Thomas (2003), 'The Colonial Policies of the Mouvement Républicain Populaire, 1944–1954: From Reform to Reaction', *English Historical Review*, **118**, pp. 380–411; Richard C. Crook (1986), 'Decolonization, the Colonial State, and Chieftaincy in the Gold Coast', *African Affairs*, **85**, pp. 75–105.

Sage Publications for the essays: Jean-Philippe Peemans (1980), 'Imperial Hangovers: Belgium – The Economics

of Decolonization', *Journal of Contemporary History*, **15**, pp. 257–86; Anita Inder Singh (1985), 'Keeping India in the Commonwealth: British Political and Military Aims, 1947–

49', *Journal of Contemporary History*, **20**, pp. 469–81; Anthony Kirk-Greene (2001), 'Decolonization: The Ultimate Diaspora', *Journal of Contemporary History*, **36**, pp. 133–51.

Taylor and Francis Limited for the essays: John Darwin (1984), 'British Decolonisation Since 1945: A Pattern or a Puzzle?', *Journal of Imperial and Commonwealth History*, **12**, pp. 187–209; Petra M.H. Groen (1993), 'Militant Response: The Dutch Use of Military Force and the Decolonization of the Dutch East Indies, 1945–50', *Journal of Imperial and Commonwealth History*, **21**, pp. 30–44; Ronald Hyam (1988), 'Africa and the Labour Government, 1945–51', *Journal of Imperial and Commonwealth History*, **16**, pp. 148–72; David Goldsworthy (1990), 'Keeping Change within Bounds: Aspects of Colonial Policy During the Churchill and Eden Governments, 1951–57', *Journal of Imperial and Commonwealth History*, **18**, pp. 81–108; Patrick Chabal (1983), 'People's War, State Formation and Revolution in Africa: A Comparative Analysis of Mozambique, Guinea-Bissau and Angola', *Journal of Commonwealth and Comparative Politics*, **21**, pp. 104–25.

Every effort has been made to trace all the copyright holders, but if any have been inadvertently overlooked the publishers will be pleased to make the necessary arrangement at the first opportunity.

Series Preface

This series focuses on key episodes and issues in political history and does so by bringing together essays selected from journals that exhibit careful analysis of political history. The volumes, each of which is edited by an expert in the field, cover crucial time periods and geographical areas, particularly Europe and the USA. Each volume represents the editor's selection of seminal essays on political history in his particular area of expertise, while an introduction presents an overview of the issues in the area, together with comments on the background and significance of the essays chosen.

The strength and nature of political beliefs reflect, to a great extent, the degree to which ideologies provide a sense of identity, value and purpose to both individuals and the community. Like all important questions about recent and modern society, this is one that can be answered in a different way by commentators and by readers. Secular ideologies over the last 250 years tended to rely on the notion of progress and the desire of humans to improve their condition, and thus rejected the Christian lapsardian view of human existence with its emphasis on sin and humankind's fallible nature. Although they varied in the political, economic, social and cultural analyses and prescriptions, such ideologies shared a belief that it is possible, and necessary, to improve the human condition and that such a goal gives meaning to politics and society. In short, reform was seen as an end in itself and progress as something attainable.

There was only limited support for continuity and stability, as opposed to reform, as public goals. For an institution or government to pledge itself to inaction would have been extraordinary. Instead, as with Islamic and Christian fundamentalism, conservative politics were propounded primarily in terms of a return to an earlier situation (true or mythical), and thus as reform through reaction, against a perception of the present, rather than as a static maintenance of the present. Commitment to change rested on prudential considerations, especially the need to modernize in order to compete successfully on the international scene, but also on powerful ideological currents. Reform, as a means and goal, was the foremost secular ideology and one that was shared by governments with very different political outlooks. There is no sign that this will change. However, across the world, reform meant very different attitudes and policies and focused on both improving and abandoning the past. This was true not only of domestic policies but also of those abroad, both foreign and colonial policy. Thus, reform could entail the development of empires and also their dissolution. Like 'freedom', 'liberty' and 'justice', 'reform' was a value-laden term. It could mean both more and less government intervention and this helped to contribute to controversy.

Politics was not only a matter of ideologies and government initiatives. As volumes in this series indicate, it is also important to consider the extent and consequences of popular participation in politics, the nature of accountability and the conception of the public: from corporatism to individualism.

Any selection of what to include is difficult. The editors in this series have done an excellent job and it has been a great pleasure working with them.

JEREMY BLACK
Series Editor
University of Exeter

Introduction

Europe's modern colonial empires disintegrated in a thirty-year period from the end of the Second World War in 1945 to the final collapse of Portugal's grip over its southern African territories in the mid-1970s. It was a remarkably rapid end to empires that had been centuries in the making. And the rapidity and near totality of Europe's withdrawal from empire was certainly not foreseen either by governments and colonial political elites or by their anti-colonial opponents. But can this decolonization be so neatly compartmentalized? After all, even approaching the end of the twentieth century, a few colonial outposts endured, principally island territories and trading ports governed by international treaty, Hong Kong pre-eminent among them. Nor was decolonization as finite as the rather arid exercises in constitutional 'transfers of power' would have us believe. The political, bureaucratic and military structures of colonial rule were gone, but numerous informal imperial networks remained. Colonialism bequeathed a significant, and often bitterly contested, cultural heritage evident across a wide societal spectrum from language, religion and the arts, to legal and educational systems, architecture and the urban environment of post-colonial states. As newly independent states, former colonies faced lasting, and ongoing, cultural and political difficulties in reconciling their sense of national identity with the colonial past that shaped it. The first generation of rulers in these countries often sought to define that national identity in opposition to their own struggles with the former colonial power. However, the apparent rupture with former colonial masters was sometimes belied by economic realities. Former colonial dependencies were handicapped by patterns of industrial and agricultural output, restrictive currency alignments and trading partnerships established under European rule. These would, in turn, make trade dependency, crippling loan payments and chronic deficits a common feature of political economy in the developing world. Elsewhere, the former colonizers withdrew only to return in the guise of political and scientific advisers, military missions and aid providers, bankers and lenders of last resort. Sovereignty for many former colonies was sometimes more apparent than real.

Several important essay collections on national experiences of decolonization have highlighted the marked local variation in the ways and means by which transfers of power occurred (Gifford and Louis, 1982 and 1988; Ageron, 1986; Ageron and Michel, 1992; Coquery-Vidrovitch and Georg, 1992; Lloyd-Jones and Costa Pinto, 2003). So, too, work on the policing of disorders, 'emergencies' and wars of decolonization points to the inadequacy of any mono-causal explanations for the outbreak and duration of colonial conflict (Rioux, 1990; Anderson and Killingray, 1992; Holland, 1994, Ageron, 1997). Others reject the idea of any transfer of power out of hand as factually inaccurate and inherently patronizing, implying as it perhaps does that freedom from colonial dependency was something that could be granted or withheld at the whim of the imperial powers (Furedi, 1994). The theoretical shortcomings of the high political 'transfer of power' approach are essentially those of agency and of Orientalism. The transfer of power idea, much like the concept of a decolonization process, once favoured by Marxist structuralists and political scientists, leaves no room for consideration of Africans and Asians as authors of their own destiny. In other words, abstract models of decolonization typically deny much space for individual local initiative – or agency – in shaping the course of events. In this reading of decolonization, colonial peoples are typically discussed in terms of abstract forces rather than as individuals, groups and communities with distinct ideas about how to bring colonial rule to an end. Similarly, Edward Said's construction of 'Orientalism' as a means to explain the proclivity of Western elites to project their own cultural stereotypes about non-Western societies should give us pause when discussing colonial, or indeed contemporary, policy formulation, whether in Western capitals or in colonial territories. Sensitivity to signs of Orientalist-type thought among policy-makers and Western publics may help us understand their unspoken assumptions, prejudices and actions in regard to empire problems and colonial peoples (Said, 1979; Lockman, 2004).

It is also quite feasible to argue that in some cases a more or less orderly transfer of power did occur, while in others colonial withdrawal was either more chaotic or less definitive (Butler, 2002). As the editors of a key recent work on colonial cultures remind us, 'Any effort to compare different imperial systems – or even parts of a single empire – raises questions about what it is that we should be comparing: similar chronologies across different colonial contexts, or disparate chronologies but similar patterns and rhythms of rule?'(Cooper and Stoler, 1997, p. 29). Numerous disjunctures become apparent when we try to compare various methods and outcomes of colonial domination. And whatever imperial powers may have wished to believe about the central direction of colonial withdrawal, the collapse of empire was as likely to be influenced by events at the colonial periphery as by executive decisions at the administrative heart of government. The most impressive surveys of decolonization therefore engage with the long-running historical debate over the relative importance of imperial 'centre' (sometimes referred to as the 'metropole') and the colonial 'periphery' before venturing general conclusions about how and why empire was abandoned (Brown and Louis, 1999).

Further analytical problems arise when considering European decolonization as a whole rather than as the national experience of Europe's major imperial powers and their individual overseas possessions. Are there necessarily any causal links between them? How sensitive were individual imperial powers to the successes and failures of their European neighbours? How far did anti-colonial nationalists draw inspiration and encouragement from the precedents set by their counterparts in other colonial territories? In short, is there a domino effect to African and Asian decolonization, something perhaps indicated by the close chronological proximity of the three major waves of colonial pullouts – in the late 1940s, in the late 1950s, and in the first four years of the 1960s?

At a more global level, how can one link the specificity of contest within colonies to the periodicity of European history and cold war conflict? It is, for example, commonly asserted that the two World Wars were decisive events in the march towards decolonization, as much because of their impact on the major European states involved as because of their effects in the colonial world. But was this equally true of all Europe's imperial powers – as applicable to neutral Holland and Portugal as to the combatants, Britain, France and Belgium? In similar vein, the extent to which the emergence of a new international system characterized by the bi-polar cold war rivalries of East and West affected patterns of colonial withdrawal is all too often painted with too indiscriminate an historical brush. The strategic, economic and ideological ambitions of the rival super powers, complicated, from 1949, by the more strident anti-colonialism of Communist China, can all too easily relegate the ideas and actions of Europe's imperial powers and their colonial opponents to walk-on roles in a cold war epic. This, however, is to misunderstand the more complex interplay of decolonization and cold war, and to under-estimate the capacity of European imperialists and extra-European anti-colonialists to exploit East–West conflict in fulfilment of their local objectives. It is also to reduce the super powers themselves to ideologically driven stereotypes. American, Soviet and United Nations interest in colonial affairs was critical in some areas, but, it seems, of limited importance elsewhere. And if, in general, the tendency for late colonial disputes and anti-colonial protests to become caught up in cold war tensions increased over time, it bears emphasis that the super powers were quite capable of acting in ways that seemed at variance with their declared ideologies, if not their national interests. Witness Stalin's perfunctory interest in early African anti-colonial struggles and the Soviet Union's changing outlook towards Israel and the Arab world either side of the Suez watershed in 1956. Witness, too, John F. Kennedy's readiness to sup with leftist insurgents in Algeria or America's protracted courtship of the non-aligned movement despite the avowed neutralism and 'new-left' tendencies of several non-aligned states. And remind ourselves of the persuasive argument, propounded above all in the work of William Roger Louis, that America's gradual usurpation of Britain's global role was generally more consensual than confrontational (Louis, 1978 and 1984; Louis and Robinson, 1994).

The idea that Britain acquiesced in its imperial eclipse thanks in large measure to its overriding acceptance of America's strategic and economic predominance may help explain why decolonization caused relatively little disruption to British society (Ovendale, 1996; Darwin, 1991). When compared with France or Portugal, the domestic ramifications of Britain's colonial withdrawal were slight. Admittedly, Prime Minister Anthony Eden's ignominious fall after the disastrous Suez intervention in late 1956 bucks this trend, but this was less a purely imperial affair than a foreign policy crisis in the Western alliance. Eden fell from office because he misunderstood the clash between British and US strategic objectives in the Arab world and had dared to think he could act in direct contravention of Washington (Kyle, 1991; Scott Lucas, 1991; Louis and Owen, 1989). From 1957 to 1963, Eden's successor and party colleague, Harold Macmillan, who had been decidedly hawkish over General Nasser's nationalisation of the Suez Canal, took greater pains to integrate likely American reaction into his thinking on decolonization (Aldous and Lee, 1995; Ashton, 1996; Goldsworthy, 1970). Suez aside, the fact remains that other, more momentous changes in the British Empire from Indian independence in 1947, through Britain's 'dirty wars' in Kenya, Malaya, Cyprus and elsewhere in the 1950s, to the final rash of colonial pullouts from sub-Saharan Africa, the West Indies and from East of Suez in the 1960s occasioned neither constitutional crises nor major public protests in Britain itself. On the one occasion where such a crisis threatened – Southern Rhodesia's Unilateral Declaration of Independence in November 1965 – the Labour Government faced greater condemnation from African Commonwealth countries than from a British public aware that Harold Wilson's administration had scant room for manoeuvre against Ian Smith's diehard Rhodesian Front. Ardent British imperialists were not hard to find, even at this late stage in decolonization, but as their French counterparts knew only too well, it was impossible to demand loyalty from a settler community that brooked no compromise in its defence of white racial privilege. In any event, what popular British attachment to Empire remained by the early 1960s was more a matter of nostalgia, of sporting rivalries, and of hackneyed, racist complaints about Britain's declining standing in a world 'gone to the dogs' than of serious political commitment to reverse an inevitable trend (Ward, 2001). After all, even the official arguments enunciated immediately after the Second World War in favour of phased constitutional reform and slower colonial withdrawal were hardly compelling (Flint, Chapter 7). Instead, once India and its South Asian neighbours completed their early transition to independent nationhood, outright opposition to decolonization appeared increasingly unrealistic, anachronistic and reactionary, at variance with the pragmatism seen by many as the redeeming feature of both British-style governance and the British corporations keen to do business with the new rulers of Africa and South East Asia (Stockwell, 2000; White, 1996).

Over the subsequent decade from 1948 to 1958 Britain resisted colonial insurgencies, not to maintain an indefinite hold over colonial territory, but to impose its will over the terms and timing of withdrawal. This, of course, might appear the ultimate excuse for an imperial power: hiding the wish to remain in political control behind the claim that order must first be restored before their departure could take place. It is nonetheless difficult to make straight comparisons between Britain's wars of decolonization and those of its European counterparts precisely because, with the unique exception of Cyprus, British officialdom regarded eventual self-government as the logical outcome of victory. Moreover, colonial withdrawal became ever more closely associated with economic retrenchment. By the time the Wilson Government announced its intention in January 1968 to complete Britain's military pullout from East of Suez within three years, the overriding need to cut defence costs in the wake of sterling devaluation foreclosed discussion of whether Britain should maintain a global role (Pickering, 1998; Darwin, 1991, p. 28). If economics dominated Britain's strategic choices in the late 1960s, the financial arguments for or against continued imperial connections had by then been played out anyway. As Saki Dockrill has argued in the context of the East of Suez decision, immediate economic circumstance only added a further dimension to more long-term strategic and political factors pushing the Labour Government towards withdrawal (Dockrill, 2002). As European economic co-operation deepened in the late 1950s and Britain belatedly turned its attention to membership of the Common Market in the early 1960s, so former economic justifications for colonial connections weakened. The sterling area, so critical to Britain's post-war economic recovery, declined in economic and strategic importance after 1956 (Schenk, 1994; Hinds). There was still much lucrative trade to be done with erstwhile British dependencies, but formal colonial ties had become a hindrance and not a help to the development of similar trading relationships with the emerging export economies of the Middle East, sub-Saharan Africa and South East Asia.

Britain, it seems, got off lightly along its road to decolonization, escaping the domestic traumas that accompanied colonial collapse in France and Portugal (Kahler, 1984; MacQueen, 1997). Its former colonial subjects were not so lucky. British imperial withdrawals were not, in general terms, the direct result of armed insurgency. That said, recent studies indicate that after 1948 the containment of rebellion among Malaya's Chinese immigrant community was neither as clear-cut nor as politically neutral as is suggested by those who regard it as the optimum example of a colonial 'hearts and minds strategy' (Hack, 2000; Ramakrishna, 2001). It is also apparent that dirty war practices, including systematic torture and cursory legal process, were integral to British suppression of the Mau Mau uprising that broke out among Kenya's Kikuyu population in 1952 (Anderson, 2005; Elkins, 2005). In other colonial environs inter-communal bloodletting frequently occurred immediately British officials and armed forces pulled out. Such was often the case where sovereign control over territory was disputed between different ethno-religious communities, as in the Indian sub-continent, Palestine and, at a later stage, Nigeria and Cyprus. This is not to suggest that the British should have remained. Rather, it is merely to indicate that their departure released pent-up inter-communal tensions, many of them directly attributable to previous colonial policies, which had been poorly addressed in the last days of imperial rule. First and foremost, it is the comparative aspect to European decolonization, and certainly not the pattern of events in the immediate aftermath of colonial withdrawal, which makes the British experience seem more orderly and less violent. Dutch, French and Portuguese decolonization are all more readily identifiable with last-ditch resistance to colonial insurgencies.

Between 1945 and 1949 the Dutch colonial authorities used force in an attempt to re-impose political control over the Netherlands East Indies. So-called 'police actions' were twice undertaken against the Republican administration established in Java following the nationalists' unilateral declaration of the independence of Indonesia on 17 August 1945 (De Groen, Chapter 5). Just as Japan's wartime occupation of Indonesia undermined Dutch colonial authority and facilitated efforts by Sukarno's Indonesian nationalists to win broader popular support, so in French-ruled Vietnam the actions of a quisling pro-Vichy regime beholden to the Japanese military enhanced the legitimacy of Ho Chi Minh's Communist-led Vietminh coalition as the legitimate voice of Vietnamese national resistance to foreign occupation. Another obvious parallel between the Indonesian and Vietnamese paths to decolonization was the prominent role played by foreign powers, the United States and Communist China above all. Strengthened by its role as the provider of Marshall Aid to the Netherlands and France, America's intervention was central to the outcome of Dutch and French decolonization from South East Asia, but in diametrically opposed ways. American economic and diplomatic pressure pushed the Dutch from Indonesia in 1949 at precisely the moment that the victory of Mao's Communists in China convinced President Truman's administration to bankroll France's continuing war against the Vietminh (MacMahon, 1981; Wall, 1991; Lawrence, 2005; Jian, Chapter 17). In both cases, the intrusion of cold war geo-politics into local colonial conflicts transformed the stakes involved. Increasing United Nations interest in the fate of colonized peoples, sharpened by UN-based ideas of trusteeship as well as the gradual emergence of an influential bloc of non-aligned states in the UN General Assembly, added to the gamut of international pressures faced by intransigent imperial powers. Although the UN would come into its own as a catalyst of decolonization in the 1950s and 1960s, Indonesia was an early test case of the capacity of member states to cajole a reluctant European nation towards colonial evacuation (MacMahon, 1981.)

With former colonies likely to be strident opponents of colonialism as newly admitted UN member states, the General Assembly would become the most significant multilateral forum through which anti-colonial nationalists could convey their message to the wider world. None were more successful in doing so than Algeria's Front de Libération Nationale (FLN), which successfully exploited the UN and other international organizations to win the propaganda war against their French opponents (Connelly, 2002 and Chapter 19). The Algerian war of 1954–62 was, of course, the most violent, costly and divisive of all France's late colonial conflicts. But it was not the first of France's protracted wars of decolonization. As one historian of French colonial withdrawal has noted, 'French decolonization was marked much more by turbulence, by the onrush of opposing forces into a political vacuum, than that of other nations ... the near paralysis of national government, the often impetuous action of colonial officials on the scene and the intensifying discontent of the local populations mark French decolonization more pronouncedly than that of any other such national retreat.'(Betts, 1991, p. 3) It is tempting to suggest that impetuosity among colonial officialdom and popular discontent were hardly the sole preserve of the French Empire. But France, along with Portugal, fought hardest, longest and dirtiest to keep parts of its colonial patrimony intact. Both of these imperial powers were notionally committed to the assimilation of key overseas territories, a factor that made them more unwilling to cede control over key territories. Algeria in the French case, Angola and Mozambique in the Portuguese, were, in theory, constitutionally and culturally integrated with the motherland, their large settler communities forming part of a greater metropolitan population.

Again, we must be wary of generalization. South of the Algerian Sahara in the French West African federation, assimilationist policies were only selectively applied in the oldest urban settlements of French Senegal (Hargreaves, 1988, pp.46–47). Across francophone sub-Saharan Africa, European settlement was limited, economic interests more diffuse and less intractable, and the cultural distance between these colonies and France much greater than in the case of French Algeria (Coquery-Vidrovitch and Goerg, 1992; Hodeir, 2001; Lefeuvre, 1997). A comparison of the two principal capitals of French North and West Africa illustrates the point. Dakar was an important colonial hub, but it was less Europeanized and did not have the emotional resonance of Algiers, the city that would become the cockpit of French resistance to decolonization and the arena for the bitterest struggles in France's end of empire (Çelik, 1997; Jordi and Pervillé, 1999). In French West Africa, the major threat to French colonial hegemony came not from armed insurgents or settler diehards, but from organized African labour and trans-colonial political parties whose influence extended throughout the region (Cooper, 1996, and Chapter 6; Schachter-Morgenthau, 1964). Much like their British counterparts in West Africa, eventual French accommodation with the 'constructive nationalists' of French West Africa owed much to the mutual preference for negotiation over conflict and a shared recognition that long-term economic and strategic interests were best served by a smoother transition to self-government. In the French West African case especially, these accommodations were also the product of the deep-rooted cultural and political ties that linked the indigenous political elites of Senegal and Ivory Coast to France. If France could lay some claim to 'successful decolonization' from West Africa, it was a very different story elsewhere (Chafer, 2002).

Assimilation was never an option for either French Indochina or French Madagascar, the two territories that witnessed the most intense French colonial repression in the late 1940s. In these instances, it was the intransigence of the commanders on the spot, combined with the 'near paralysis of national government,' and the distractions of post-war reconstruction at home that made such violence possible (Devillers, 1987; Tronchon, 1986). The political stand off between the Vietminh-led Democratic Republic of Vietnam in Hanoi and the Saigon colonial administration became more explosive once the chain of command between the Paris Government and the Saigon authorities eroded. If French government was not quite paralysed, the accountability of ministers and colonial officials was certainly subverted by those in favour of a military solution in Vietnam (Shipway, 1996). In March of the following year, 1947, senior politicians and colonial bureaucrats manipulated the available evidence and bypassed collective decision-making procedures in order to ensure the vigorous repression of Madagascar's leading nationalist movement, the MRDM (Shipway, 1996b). Once again, the escalation of colonial conflict into wholesale military violence was bound up with the inter-party dynamics of coalition government in the French Fourth Republic (Thomas, Chapter 10). The Indochina War would further escalate into the first major proxy war of the early cold war. The subtleties of French political objectives for Vietnamese, Cambodian and Laotian self-government within the framework of the French Union were gradually subsumed beneath a widening war fought by large-scale conventional forces supplied by US and Chinese backers. By the time Vietminh forces laid siege to the French army fortress at Dien Bien Phu in early 1954, the question was not whether France would be defeated, but when and with what consequences. By contrast, the Madagascar rebellion was quickly suppressed, but the punishment meted out by the French state to senior MRDM leaders was one among many instances of colonial injustice to arouse passionate intellectual engagement with decolonization in France (Sorum, 1977). If matters of conscience played a more prominent role in the metropolitan debate over decolonization in France than elsewhere, this was substantially because the uncomfortable juxtaposition of colonial occupier and military oppressor was more keenly felt by a society still traumatized by its Second World War experience of Nazi cruelty (Schalk, 1991).

If Madagascar and Indochina provoked the initial intellectual engagement with decolonization, only the Algerian war of independence caused deep and lasting fissures in French society, so much so that the entire constitutional and party political edifice of the Fourth Republic crumbled away in the May Crisis of 1958 (Le Sueur, 2001; Rioux, 1990). Until recently, the socio-political divisions in France laid bare by dirty war, army rebellion and the fate of Algeria's settlers tended to obscure the extent to which the FLN and Algeria's Muslim population secured their freedom by their own efforts. It remains understandably difficult for French or Algerian historians to view the Algerian conflict as more than a domestic upheaval, a war of dreadful cruelty, or a popular struggle for national liberation. Torture, in particular, continues to exert a horrible fascination, sharpened by a number of sensational legal cases in France and by Algeria's tragic descent back into savage internal conflict after 1992 (Branche, 2001; Roberts, 2003). Conversely, it is that much easier for historians from the English-speaking world to interpret the war as an exemplar of the interactions between cold war and the internationalization of decolonization (Connelly, 2002; Wall, 2001; Thomas, 2000). Yet these approaches have much in common, their essential pre-occupation being with the savagery of asymmetric warfare and the ultimate inability of democratic states to cope with unrestrained use of their military capacity (Merom, 2003).

Only Portugal can rival France in the intensity of its colonial wars, the impact of decolonization on metropolitan society, and the long-term destabilization of former colonial states (MacQueen, 1997). At state and inter-state level, the violence of decolonization in lusophone Africa was precipitated by the escalation of local rebellions, first into proxy wars on Southern Africa's cold war frontline, and then into civil wars between rival nationalist forces still supported by their external proxies, most notably Communist Cuba and Apartheid South Africa (Gleijeses, 2003; Schneidman, 2004; Jaster, 1988, part III). But at local level, the violent disintegration of Portuguese Africa reflected the brutal colonial intransigence of the Salazarist regime. This was, in turn, compounded by the rapaciousness of a colonialism predicated on the coercive extraction of wealth from predominantly agrarian peasant societies (Bender, 1978; Vail and White, 1980; Isaacman and Isaacman, 1983). In this respect, the nature of late colonial rule in Portuguese Africa shared much in common with nearby Belgian Congo. Here, too, the apparatus of the colonial state was configured to facilitate the exploitation of natural resources – predominantly minerals and hardwood timber. In both Portuguese and Belgian Africa, Catholic Church and other missionary agencies also played a prominent role in educational policy and public health provision, and in the differential treatment of particular ethnic groups. Sometimes this took place in conjunction with state bureaucracy and sometimes as a substitute for it. But, as Mahmood Mamdani has argued, the different ethnic constructions placed by these state or Church authorities upon particular sections of a colonial population bred profound inter-communal resentments that could explode into violence during the decolonization process and after it (Mamdani, 1996).

Belgium's abrupt withdrawal from tropical Africa in 1960–61 left a political vacuum soon filled by contending political, ethnic and regional groups in the former Belgian Congo, Rwanda and Urundi. The brutal death of Congolese national leader Patrice Lumumba, and the unfolding saga of Belgian complicity in his murder, shady CIA involvement in the Belgian Congo's violent transitional politics, and United Nations intervention in the Congo Crisis of 1960–63 drew more immediate international attention and lasting political controversy. But the worsening political polarization between Hutu and Tutsi communities in Rwanda, apparent in the aftermath of the Belgian departure, was even more significant in the long term. It was during these critical years from 1959 to 1964 that the inter-communal hatreds, which culminated in the 1994 genocide, assumed more concrete form. First, the establishment of a Hutu-dominated republican government in Rwanda, and then the development of an oppositional Tutsi exile insurgency operating from nearby Uganda, demonstrated that the inter-ethnic rivalries previously fostered by the Belgian authorities in Stanleyville would set the pattern for Rwanda's post-colonial politics. That these animosities would escalate into civil war and, ultimately, genocide could not perhaps be foreseen. But whatever the case, the connections between colonialism, the precise circumstances of decolonization, and the 1994 massacres of the Tutsi cannot be dismissed as secondary to the more proximate causes of the genocide (Mamdani, 2001, chapters 2 and 3). The colonial roots of this most tragic of late twentieth-century events are still only dimly understood and cry out for our attention.

Next to Belgium's rapid exit from Central Africa, Portugal's apparent resolve to remain appears all the more remarkable. In this context, Portuguese intractability calls to mind French and not Belgian comparisons. Ultimately, Portugal's messy withdrawal from sub-Saharan Africa after the 1974 overthrow of the Lisbon regime originated in the same inter-weaving of domestic and peripheral pressures that characterized the eventual French retreat from Algeria. In Portugal's case, as in France's, it was a colonial army railing at the inadequacy of metropolitan political leadership that brought about a change of regime. But, whereas in the French case the army rebels hoped to secure a renewed political commitment to victory, the leading officers of Portugal's Armed Forces Movement were anxious to break the political logjam preventing decolonization. Their views found a receptive audience within Portuguese society where opposition to the one-party state meshed with hostility to unending colonial war and recognition that Portugal's economic and political future lay with the European Community. We should, however, remember that in Lisbon and Algiers military leaderships felt compelled to intervene in the domestic political process owing to the determined resistance of the nationalist insurgents they faced. In this sense, events at the colonial periphery remained as pivotal to the end of empire as ever.

All this leaves us with a more complex picture of decolonization, one in which, as suggested earlier, formal 'transfers of power' can tell only part of the story. Yet this is hardly surprising in light of the number of countries and peoples involved, the variety of non-state actors engaged by colonial breakdown, and the impact of decolonization on the modern international system. It would surely be more surprising to find that an abstract theoretical model of decolonization could be generically applied without regional variation or concession to individual circumstance. Such might be comforting to the hard-pressed researcher, but it would not be historical.

The essays that follow offer numerous different perspectives on European decolonization. Their approaches vary. Some focus on the high politics of inter-governmental negotiation or the internationalization of decolonization as foreign powers and the United Nations involved themselves more directly in the end of empires. Others examine the situation at the colonial periphery, highlighting the role of the peoples most concerned in achieving their own national independence, whether through political engagement, public protest or taking up arms against the colonial power. Still others consider the role of particular interests – political parties, business groups, settler communities, or the armed forces – in determining the executive decisions made about colonial withdrawal and post-colonial relationships with newly independent states. Finally, some of the essays assess the gender dimension to decolonization, considering the particular contributions of women to anti-colonial protest and resistance.

The twenty-one essays collected here have been grouped into six discrete parts. The justifications for doing so relate either to their similar thematic focus, their treatment of overlapping problems, or the comparative perspective that emerges when the essays in question are placed alongside one another. The contributions in the first of these six parts, 'Long term perspectives', take a broad view of colonial collapse and imperial withdrawal. The American historian Tony Smith (Chapter 1) contrasts the domestic political processes and differing political motivations that affected the courses and outcomes of French and British decolonization. Jean-Philippe Peemans (Chapter 2) takes a different approach, placing economic factors at the heart of colonial breakdown. His is a metropolitan view, considering the role of the Belgian Congo and eventual withdrawal from it in Belgium's economic and industrial development. Robert Blackey (Chapter 3), by contrast, focuses on the role of revolutionary ideology in decolonization. Focusing on the colonial periphery, he assesses the thought and actions of two leading thinkers of people's revolution in Africa, the Martinique-born psychiatrist Frantz Fanon, and Amilcar Cabral, inspirational leader of the leftist insurgency in Portuguese Guinea-Bissau. The result is an interesting examination of the importance of African adaptations of Marxist-Leninism to national liberation movements. The final essay in this opening section takes a more global view of decolonization. John Darwin (Chapter 4) tackles the vexed question of whether decolonization should be regarded as an ordered process, an enforced retreat, or a combination of accident and design. Focusing on the grand sweep of British imperial policies in the twenty years after 1945, he examines the issues – economic, social and party political – that shaped decision-making in London, highlighting the similarities and contrasts between Labour and Conservative governmental policies.

The second part, 'Post-war problems and confrontations', is more narrowly focused on the late 1940s. Each of its four essays discusses key events in European decolonization, all of which were linked in some way with political or social changes either precipitated or accelerated by the Second World War and its immediate aftermath. Petra Groen (Chapter 5) examines why the Dutch authorities opted to use military force in an effort to regain the political initiative in the Dutch East Indies after the territory's nationalist leadership declared

Indonesian independence at war's end in August 1945. The Dutch experience in Indonesia between 1945 and 1949 demonstrates that deployment of troops, whether as a coercive force, an instrument of repression, or as a political lever to extract political advantage in negotiation could easily backfire, particularly where the strategic interests of major cold war allies were at stake.

If armed insurrection was less common in black Africa than in South East Asia, popular protest was not. Frederick Cooper's discussion (Chapter 6) of the railway workers' strike in French West Africa during 1947 and 1948 illustrates the central role of organized African labour in accelerating decolonization. Increasing labour militancy and the proliferation of trade unions in post-war Africa owed a good deal to wartime economic conditions and the limited reforms conceded by the governments of post-Liberation France. Cooper's contribution provides us with a classic example of African agency – in this case, direct strike action – in undermining the structures of colonial power. The pivotal role of local non-state actors in shaping the course of events in late colonial Africa is also a theme that runs through John Flint's essay (Chapter 7). His analysis of the failure of Colonial Office schemes for a gradual transition to African self-government highlights the extent to which Whitehall planning for colonial reconstruction and reform – much of it undertaken in the latter stages of the Second World War – could be overtaken by popular pressure for more rapid social and political change. Finally, in this part, Anita Inder Singh (Chapter 8) describes how British strategic objectives in India changed the closer the sub-continent came to independence and partition. In this instance, policy adaptation to imminent decolonization was more successful than in the French case, albeit thanks in large part to the conciliatory attitude of India's post-independence government. But the more established constitutional framework of the Empire-Commonwealth also made the British task of accommodating India easier than equivalent French efforts to build a viable post-war imperial system in tandem with the restoration of republican democracy at home.

The third cluster of essays, grouped under the heading 'Decolonization and party politics', ranges over the years 1945 to 1960. In this part, our focus is primarily upon high politics in general and party politics in particular. Ronald Hyam's masterly survey (Chapter 9) of the African imperial policies pursued by Clement Attlee's Labour Government reminds us of the sheer scale of the empire problems confronting Britain's first post-war administration. Whether keeping empire intact or facing up to eventual decolonization, colonial affairs demanded an extraordinary breadth of vision, the more so as the clouds of cold war gathered, sometimes obscuring the importance of local developments in the process. At the same time as the Labour Government in Britain was tackling problems of colonial reform in Africa, the coalition ministries that dominated post-war politics in France's Fourth Republic confronted incipient colonial breakdown across much of the French Empire. Martin Thomas (Chapter 10) highlights the central role of a single political party, the Christian Democrat *Mouvement Républicain Populaire* (MRP), in the colonial choices made. A new centrist political grouping rooted in wartime resistance to German occupation, the MRP soon became the most intransigent opponent of either fundamental colonial reform or imperial withdrawal. By 1947–48 its senior leaders had assumed control of policy formulation in Indochina, Madagascar and North Africa. Their hard-line opposition to colonial pullouts helped ensure that France's road to decolonization would be marked by conflict and violence.

If the MRP provides an example of a decisive party political shift in the central direction of imperial policy, David Goldsworthy's measured assessment (Chapter 11) of Conservative Party interest in colonial affairs in the early 1950s suggests that metropolitan changes in political direction were not always as radical as might be assumed. If Conservative ministers were sometimes more hostile to decolonization and colonial reform than their Labour predecessors, their reluctance to countenance the end of empire was not as complete a barrier to transitional change as might be imagined. It is, however, the subsequent Conservative administration led by Harold Macmillan that is more readily associated with decolonization. Nowhere more so than in black Africa from which the major part of Britain's colonial withdrawal occurred 'on Macmillan's watch', if not always at his behest. Ritchie Ovendale's reconsideration (Chapter 12) of the background to, and consequences of, the British Prime Minister's famous February 1960 speech to the South African Parliament in Cape Town is instructive. It provides a case study of a decisive political intervention with tangible effects on the subsequent course of decolonization. And it demonstrates the equally critical importance of more intangible qualities; in this case the changing mind-set and underlying assumptions among Britain's political elite in regard to the speed and desirability of colonial withdrawal.

Part four contains four chapters that variously examine the impact of violence and political confrontation on the course of European decolonization. Karl Hack (Chapter 13) reviews recent historical treatments of British military policy and political action during the so-called Malayan 'Emergency'. Obviously important in its own right, the British military and police response to the Communist-led uprising centred within Malaya's Chinese ethnic minority has acquired wider significance among historians and strategic analysts as an example of apparently successful counter-insurgency. Hack's essay places this more favourable interpretation of British military strategy in Malaya in context, illustrating that in this locale, as in so many others, a counter-insurgency policy built on the ethos of winning 'hearts and minds' was far more coercive than might be thought. Richard Crook's view (Chapter 14) on Britain's post-war abandonment of the system of indirect rule through favoured tribal chiefs in the Gold Coast is not directly concerned with political violence. Rather, it considers colonial changes in elite co-operation intended in large part to prevent the collapse of order in a West African territory moving rapidly towards political confrontation with the British colonial state. The prospect of united mass opposition to British rule, bringing with it a breakdown in control over the Gold Coast's cocoa export economy, brought the colonial authorities face to face with an uncomfortable choice. Either they relinquish a system of rule based on a favoured elite or they accept the possibility of escalating protest and civil breakdown. In Crook's interpretation of post-war events in the Gold Coast, decolonization was substantially driven by the strength of African civil society in opposing the outdated structures of colonial rule.

The emergence of a vibrant civil society in the Belgian Congo had for years been stifled by the exactions of colonialism and by the limited resources of the Belgian colonial state. As a result, historians have tended to describe Belgium's vast African colony as being at the mercy of 'an unholy trinity' of state authorities, the Catholic Church and the trading companies that controlled the lion's share of the Congo's exports. The apparent haste and civil disorder that characterized eventual Belgian withdrawal has thus been widely interpreted as consequential upon the collapse of these three pillars of colonial control. However, as Patrick Boyle (Chapter 15) demonstrates, the 'unholy trinity' concept cannot alone explain the form that decolonization took in the Belgian Congo. Focusing on educational provision before and after independence, Boyle shows that the so-called 'triple alliance' between state, church and trading companies was never as solid as sometimes claimed. Nor was the eclipse of Belgian authority quite as abrupt or total as often portrayed.

The violence that attended decolonization in the Belgian Congo was replicated many times over in Portuguese Africa as shown in Patrick Chabal's comparative survey (Chapter 16) of revolutionary anti-colonialism in the territories of Mozambique, Guinea-Bissau and Angola. The presence of large settler communities in Mozambique and Angola invites comparison with other settled-related decolonization conflicts in Africa, from French Algeria to British Kenya and Southern Rhodesia. Nevertheless, perhaps the most critical factor in explaining the outbreak and duration of political violence in Portuguese Africa as a whole was the sheer intransigence of the colonial power. Salazarist Portugal's refusal to negotiate an end to empire ensured that armed struggle against colonial domination was as much a practical decision as an ideological one.

Chapters 17 to 19 in the fifth part explore 'the internationalization of decolonization'. Their focus is on the parts played by key states and the United Nations in bringing an end to European colonial empire. Chen Jian's contribution (Chapter 17) charts the role of Mao's China in supporting the Vietminh's war of liberation in Vietnam. The creation of the People's Republic of China in October 1949 and the subsequent escalation of cold war tensions in Eastern Asia quickly spread to the Indochinese Peninsula, already the scene of a bitterly fought struggle between French and Vietminh forces. Just as Vietminh and Chinese Communist leaders were quick to cement their co-operation, so, too, successive French governments of the early 1950s would come to rely more heavily on the United States to support the military costs of the Indochina war. As Jian shows, the highpoint of this internationalization came with the Geneva Conference of 1954. The conference convened to negotiate the terms of French withdrawal and Vietnamese independence, but, in fact, marked only the beginning of a descent to another war in Vietnam, this one even more devastating than the last. The United States may have allowed itself to be sucked into a quasi-colonial war in Vietnam, but elsewhere the vestiges of its traditional anti-colonialism remained stronger. Steven Metz (Chapter 18) investigates the gradual evolution of American official attitudes towards African decolonization from the last years of Harry Truman's presidency to the short-lived Kennedy administration of the early 1960s. He highlights greater subtlety and continuity in US foreign policy approaches than conceded by those who characterize American attitudes as either rigidly Euro-centric in the pre-Kennedy years or stridently Africa-centric during Kennedy's term of office. Once again, we are forced to reassess widely held assumptions about decolonization, this time regarding America's role and purpose in supporting African nation building. Finally, in this section, Matthew Connelly (Chapter 19) sets the Algerian war of independence firmly in an international context. Rejecting the image of a purely Franco-Algerian conflict, Connelly demonstrates how and why the war became increasingly internationalized. Indeed, his argument can be taken further: internationalization of the Algerian war was fundamental to the FLN's strategy for victory. Algerian nationalist guerrillas could never match French army firepower and instead confronted an increasingly sophisticated and ruthless military opponent. In these circumstances, exploitation of various international forums and the cultivation of sympathetic international allies were vital to the FLN's ultimate success. This was not simply internationalization of decolonization caused by the pressure of cold war; it was internationalization deliberately manipulated by one of the warring parties at the expense of the other.

The book's final part, 'Forgotten constituencies?' brings together two essays dealing with quite separate themes. What unites them is the light they shed on sections of society long dismissed in historical assessments of colonial collapse. Insofar as the role of gender issues has been addressed in histories of decolonization, attention has tended to centre on indigenous women as victims of colonialism and on white women in the colonies as occupying, at once, a superior place in the prevailing racial hierarchy and a subordinate place in the hierarchy of gender. Cora Ann Presley (Chapter 20) illustrates how far the Kikuyu women of Kenya were integral to the development of opposition to the British colonial state. Kikuyu women's political activism and their support for the Mau Mau rebellion of the 1950s were products of the constraints imposed upon them both as indigenous Africans and as women by the racial, political and gender hierarchies of colonialism. As a result, their struggle against British rule was motivated by the rejection of a social order in which they faced multiple forms of discrimination.

If the gender dimension to decolonization deserves more attention, so, too, do the social and cultural legacies of colonial withdrawal. One way to chart these is by investigating the histories of those for whom decolonization meant either an unwelcome return to Europe or an enforced exile in the land of the former colonial power. Fittingly, perhaps, in the final essay of this collection, Anthony Kirk-Greene (Chapter 21) looks at a sometimes neglected, but quite distinct constituency. He concentrates on the British colonial officials, high and low, for whom decolonization meant an abrupt change in lifestyle. Albeit not as traumatic as the plight of refugee communities, the end of colonial careers marked only the beginning of a sense of abandonment and misrepresentation. Whether typecast as 'colonial oppressors' or, less melodramatically, as complicit in an imperial project considered embarrassing or ethically indefensible, 'the thin white line' of former colonial civil servants have had relatively little say in explaining their own perspective on decolonization. Theirs is a neglected voice. It nonetheless rings louder than that of the many thousands who either died in the cause of anti-colonial struggle or who were merely caught up in its terrible violence. The silence of so many victims of European colonialism reminds us that the collection of chapters presented here, no matter how vivid and thought-provoking they may be, can only present a partial picture of the end of empire.

References

Ageron, Charles-Robert (1986), *Le Chemins de la décolonisation de l'empire française 1936–1956* Paris: Éditions CNRS.

Ageron, Charles-Robert (ed.) (1997), *La guerre d'Algérie et les Algériens 1954–1962*, Paris: Armand Colin.

Ageron, Charles-Robert and Michel, Marc (eds) (1992), *L'Afrique noire française: l'heure des Indépendances*, Paris: CNRS Éditions.

Aldous, Richard and Lee, Sabine (eds) (1995), *Harold Macmillan and Britain's World Role*, London: Macmillan.

Anderson, David M. (2005), *Histories of the Hanged. Britain's Dirty War in Kenya and the End of Empire*, London: Weidenfeld and Nicolson.

Anderson, David M. and Killingray, David (eds) (1992), *Policing and Decolonisation. Nationalism, Politics and the Police, 1917–65*, Manchester: Manchester University Press.

Ashton, Nigel John (1996), *Eisenhower, Macmillan and the Problem of Nasser: Anglo-American Relations and Arab Nationalism, 1955–1959*, London: Macmillan.

Bender, Gerald J. (1978), *Angola under the Portuguese. The Myth and the Reality*, London: Longman.

Betts, Raymond F. (1991), *France and Decolonisation 1900–1960*, Basingstoke: Macmillan.

Branche, Raphaëlle (2001), *La torture et l'armée pendant la guerre d'Algérie, 1954–1962*, Paris: Gallimard.

Brown, Judith and Louis, Wm. Roger (eds) (1999), *The Oxford History of the British Empire. vol. IV: The Twentieth Century*, Oxford: Oxford University Press.

Butler, L.J. (2002), *Britain and Empire. Adjusting to a Post-Imperial World*, London: I.B.Tauris.

Çelik, Zeynep (1997), *Urban Forms and Colonial Confrontations. Algiers under French Rule*, Berkeley, CA: University of California Press.

Chafer, Tony (2002), *The End of Empire in French West Africa. France's Successful Decolonization?*, Oxford: Berg.

Connelly, Matthew (2002), *A Diplomatic Revolution. Algeria's Fight for Independence and the Origins of the Post-Cold War Era*, Oxford: Oxford University Press.

Cooper, Frederick (1996), *Decolonization and African Society. The Labor Question in French and British Africa*, Cambridge: Cambridge University Press.

Cooper, Frederick and Stoler, Ann Laura (eds) (1997), *Tensions of Empire. Colonial Cultures in a Bourgeois World*, Berkeley, CA.: University of California Press.

Coquery-Vidrovitch, Catherine and Goerg, Odile (ed.) (1992), *L'Afrique Occidentale au temps des français. Colonisateurs et colonisés, c. 1860–1960*, Paris: Éditions la découverte.

Darwin, John (1991), *The End of the British Empire. The Historical Debate*, Blackwell: Oxford.

Devillers, Philippe (1987), *Paris-Saigon-Hanoi, Les archives de la guerre, 1944–1947*, Paris: Gallimard.

Dockrill, Saki (2002), *Britain's Retreat from East of Suez: The Choice between Europe and the World?*, London: Palgrave-Macmillan.

Elkins, Caroline (2005), *Britain's Gulag: The Brutal End of Empire in Kenya*, London: Cape.

Furedi, Frank (1994), *Colonial Wars and the Politics of Third World Nationalism*, London: I.B. Tauris.

Gifford, Prosser and Louis, William Roger (eds) (1982), *The Transfer of Power in Africa. Decolonization, 1940–60*, New Haven, CT.: Yale University Press.

Gifford, Prosser and Louis, William Roger (eds) (1988), *Decolonization and African Independence. Transfers of Power in Africa, 1960–1980*, New Haven, CT.: Yale University Press.

Gleijeses, Piero (2003), *Conflicting Missions. Havana, Washington and Africa, 1959–1976*, Chapel Hill, NC: University of North Carolina Press.

Goldsworthy, David (1970), *Colonial Issues in British Politics, 1945–61: From "Colonial Development" to "Wind of Change"*, Oxford: Oxford University Press.

Hack, Karl (2000), *Defence and Decolonisation in South East Asia, Britain, Malaya and Singapore, 1941–1967*, London: Curzon Press.

Hargreaves, John (1988), *Decolonization in Africa*, London: Longman.

Hinds, A.E. (1987), 'Sterling and Imperial Policy, 1945–51', *Journal of Imperial and Commonwealth History*, **15**, (1), 148–69.

Hodeir, Catherine (2001), *Stratégies d'Empire. Le grand patronat colonial face à la decolonisation*, Paris: Belin.

Holland, Robert (ed.) (1994), *Emergencies and Disorder in the European Empires after 1945*, London: Frank Cass.

Isaacman, Allen and Isaacman, Barbara (1983), *Mozambique from Colonialism to Revolution, 1900–1982*, Boulder, CO.: Westview Press.

Jaster, Robert Scott (1988), *The Defence of White Power. South African Foreign Policy Under Pressure*, London: Macmillan.

Jordi, Jean-Jacques and Pervillé, Guy (eds) (1999), *Alger 1940–1962. Une ville en guerres*, Paris: Éditions Autrement.

Kahler, Miles (1984), *Decolonization in Britain and France. The Domestic Consequences of International Relations*, Princeton, N.J.: Princeton University Press.

Krozewski, Gerold (2001), *Money and the End of Empire: British International Economic Policy and the Colonies, 1947–1958*, London: Palgrave-Macmillan.

Kyle, Keith (1991), *Suez*, New York: St Martin's Press.

Lawrence, Mark Atwood (2005), *Assuming the Burden: Europe and the American Commitment to War in Vietnam*, Berkeley, CA.: University of California Press.

Lefeuvre, Daniel (1997), *Chère Algérie. Comptes et mécomptes de la tutelle coloniale, 1930–1962*, Paris: Société Française d'Hisoire d'Outre-Mer.

Le Sueur, James D. (2001), *Uncivil War. Intellectuals and Identity Politics during the Decolonization of Algeria*, Philadelphia, PA: University of Pennsylvania Press.

Lloyd, Jones, Stewart and Costa Pinto, Antonio (eds) (2003), *The Last Empire: Thirty Years of Portuguese Decolonisation*, Bristol: Intellect.

Lockman, Zachary (2004), *Contending Visions of the Middle East. The History and Politics of Orientalism*, Cambridge: Cambridge University Press.

Louis, William Roger (1978) *Imperialism at Bay. The United States and the Decolonization of the British Empire, 1941–45*, Oxford: Oxford University Press.

Louis, William Roger (1984), *British Empire in the Middle East, 1945–51. Arab Nationalism, the United States and Postwar Imperialism*, Oxford: Oxford University Press.

Louis, William Roger and Owen, Roger (eds) (1989), *Suez, 1956: The Crisis and its Consequences*, Oxford: Clarendon Press.

Louis, William Roger and Robinson, Ronald (1994), 'The Imperialism of Decolonization,' *Journal of Imperial and Commonwealth History*, **22** (3), 462–511.

Lucas, William Scott (1991), *Divided We Stand: Britain, the United States and the Suez Crisis*, London: Hodder and Stoughton.

MacMahon, Robert J. (1981), *Colonialism and Cold War. The United States and the Struggle for Indonesian Independence, 1945–49*, Ithaca, NY: Cornell University Press.

MacQueen, Norri (1997), *The Decolonization of Portuguese Africa. Metropolitan Revolution and the Dissolution of Empire*, Harlow: Longman.

Mamdani, Mahmood (1996), *Citizen and Subject: Contemporary Africa and the Legacy of Late Colonialism*, Princeton NJ: Princeton University Press.

Mamdani, Mahmood (2001), *When Victims Become Killers. Colonialism, Nativism, and the Genocide in Rwanda*, Princeton, NJ: Princeton University Press.

Merom, Gil (2003), *How Democracies Lose Small Wars. State, Society, and the Failures of France in Algeria, Israel in Lebanon, and the United States in Vietnam*, Cambridge: Cambridge University Press.

Ovendale, Ritchie (1996*), Britain, the United States and the Transfer of Power in the Middle East, 1945–1962*, Leicester: Leicester University Press.

Pickering, Jeffrey (1998), *Britain's Withdrawal from East of Suez: The Politics of Retrenchment*, London: Macmillan.

Ramakrishna, Kumar (2001), *Emergency Propaganda: The Winning of Malayan Hearts and Minds, 1948–1958*, London: Curzon Press.

Rioux, Jean-Pierre (1990), *La guerre d'Algérie et les Français*, Paris: Fayard.

Roberts, Hugh (2003), *The Battlefield: Algeria, 1988–2002. Studies in a Broken Polity*, London: Verso.

Said, Edward (1979), *Orientalism*, New York: Vintage.

Schachter-Morgenthau, Ruth (1964), *Political Parties in French-speaking West Africa*, Oxford: Clarendon Press.

Schalk, David L. (1991), *War and the Ivory Tower: Algeria and Vietnam*, Oxford: Oxford University Press.

Schenk, Catherine R. (1994), *Britain and the Sterling Area: From Devaluation to Convertibility in the 1950s*, London: Routledge.

Schneidman, Witney W. (2004), *Engaging Africa. Washington and the Fall of Portugal's Colonial Empire*, Dallas TX.: University Press of America.

Shipway, Martin (1996a), *The Road to War. France and Vietnam, 1944–1947*, Oxford: Berghahn.

Shipway, Martin (1996b), 'Madagascar on the Eve of Insurrection, 1944–47: The Impasse of a Liberal Colonial Policy', *Journal of Imperial and Commonwealth History*, **24** (1), 72–100.

Sorum, Paul Clay (1977), *Intellectuals and Decolonization in France*, Chapel Hill, NC: University of North Carolina Press.

Stockwell, Sarah (2000), *The Business of Decolonization: British Business Strategies in the Gold Coast*, Oxford: Oxford University Press.

Thomas, Martin (2000), *The French North African Crisis. Colonial Breakdown and Anglo-French Relations, 1945–1962*, London: Palgrave-Macmillan.

Tronchon, Jacques (1986), *L'insurrection malgache de 1947*, Paris: Karthala.

Vail, Leroy and White, Landeg (1980) *Capitalism and Colonialism in Mozambique*, Minneapolis, MN: University of Minnesota Press.

Wall, Irwin M. (1991), *The United States and the Making of Postwar France, 1945–1954*, Cambridge: Cambridge University Press.

Wall, Irwin M., (2001), *France, the United States, and the Algerian War*, Berkeley, CA: University of California Press.

Ward, Stuart (ed.) (2001), *British Culture and the End of Empire*, Manchester: Manchester University Press.

White, Nicholas J. (1996), *Business, Government and the End of Empire: Malaya, 1942–1957*, Kuala Lumpur: OUP South East Asia.

Part I
Long-Term Perspectives

[1]

A Comparative Study of French and British Decolonization

TONY SMITH

Tufts University

INTRODUCTION

Despite the historical significance of European decolonization after the Second World War, there has been no serious interpretive account of it as an overall process. A number of excellent case studies exist analyzing specific policies or periods in the imperial capitals or in the colonial territories, and there are several chronologically complete surveys of the decline of European rule overseas. These have neither been directed nor followed, however, by studies attempting to conceptualize synthetically the entire period. In default of a wide-ranging debate over the character of decolonization as an historical movement, a kind of conventional wisdom has grown up attributing the differences in the British and French experiences to a combination of their respective imperial traditions and the governing abilities of their domestic political institutions. As yet, there has been no systematic attempt to separate carefully the chief variables to be analyzed, to assign them weights of relative importance, and to coordinate them in an historical and comparative manner. This essay hopes to open discussion of these questions.[1]

While there were definite political options open to Britain and France in imperial policy after 1945, the historically conditioned realm of the possible precluded the adoption of certain courses of action. The material hardships following the Second World War combined with the clear ascendance of the two 'anti-imperial' powers, the United States and the Soviet Union, and with the increased maturity of nationalist elites throughout Africa and Asia to force a decided retrenchment of Europe overseas. In retrospect, we can

I would like to acknowledge the assistance of the Lehrman Institute and the German Marshall Fund of the United States in the completion of this essay. An earlier version was presented at the Lehrman Institute in December 1975.

[1] In this essay, the word 'colony' will be used to refer to the variety of overseas possessions called, according to their status in international law, protectorates, trusteeships, and condominiums as well as colonies.

see that the truly important political decisions to be made by Paris and
London after 1945 concerned not whether the colonies would be free, but
rather which local nationalist factions they would favor with their support
and over what piece of territory these new political elites would be
permitted to rule. What would be federated, what partitioned, who should
govern and according to what procedures, constituted decisive issues where
the Europeans continued to exercise a significant degree of control. When
the Europeans did not respect the historically imposed limits of their
power, however, their policies were to meet with defeat. Thus, while the
Suez invasion of October–November 1956 constituted a political crisis of
the first order in Britain, it was the only occasion when colonial matters
occupied such a position. In France, by contrast, the interminable wars in
Indochina and Algeria cost not only the lives of hundreds of thousands of
Asians and Africans but eventually brought the collapse of the Fourth
Republic as well.

A comparative analysis of British and French abilities to withdraw from
their empires after 1945 suggests four respects in which the British were
favored. First, there was the legacy of the past in terms of ideas and
procedures on imperial matters, precedents built up over the decades
before the Second World War, which served to orient European leaders
and organize their responses to the pressures for decolonization. On this
score, the British proved to be ideologically, and especially institutionally,
more fit than the French to cope with overseas challenges to their rule.
Second, there was the international 'place' of Britain and France and
especially the different relations maintained by the two countries with the
United States. Third, there was the question of the domestic political
institutions of France and Britain with their very unequal capacities to
process a problem of the magnitude of decolonization. The French
multi-party system with its weak governing consensus clearly was not the
equivalent of the two-party system in Britain. Even had the French system
been stronger, however, it is not evident it would have dealt more
effectively with decolonization, for national opinion, and especially the
'collective conscience' of the political elite in France, was significantly
different from that in Britain. The fourth variable to be analyzed directs
attention from Paris and London to the character of the nationalist elites
with whom the Europeans had to deal. Here, it will be argued that the
situations in Indochina and Algeria presented France with serious
problems that Britain was simply fortunate enough to escape (at least until
Suez). The comparative study of European decolonization depends in
important measure, that is, on the comparative study of colonial nationalism. Since this last factor is frequently neglected in favor of Eurocentric
analyses of decolonization, the second section below will investigate it in
some detail.

I

In terms of colonial ideology and institutions, the British experience prepared London remarkably well for the liquidation of empire after 1945. In a sense, one may mark the first phase of British decolonization as stretching from the Durham report of 1839 relative to Canada to the Statute of Westminster of 1931. By this series of measures, Britain created the Dominion system and institutionalized a procedure for gradually loosening control over her possessions. For a time, to be sure, the final character of the Commonwealth (as it came to be called after the turn of the century) remained in doubt. During the interwar years, however, it became clear that the sometime dream of 'Imperial Federation' whereby London would control the economic, defense, and foreign policies of the several allied Anglo-Saxon peoples would never come to fruition. Instead the measured progress from representative to responsible government and from there to Commonwealth status would culminate in the establishment of fully sovereign states. However grand in theory the ideas of a stronger federal structure may have sounded when proposed by men like Joseph Chamberlain, the experience of the First World War served instead to weaken the alliance. It was British entanglements, after all, which had involved the Dominions in warfare far from home at a cost of over 200,000 dead. It was wiser perhaps for them to imitate the United States and delay involvement in these 'foreign' affairs. Or better yet, the Dominions might make common cause with Washington, which emerged from the war appearing both militarily and economically better suited to lead the Anglo-Saxon world than London. Thus, the Balfour Declaration of 1926 only stated what had already been decided in fact: the sovereignty of the Dominions in all respects. The Statute of Westminster of 1931 served as a confirmation of the Declaration. Although the Ottawa Agreements inaugurating an imperial preference system were signed the next year, they failed to provide economic unity where political unity was lacking. The British Commonwealth of Nations was not to be a federal organization.

In these circumstances, the Government of India Act of 1935 must appear as the first major step in the decolonization process which began in earnest after 1945. For although the Act itself fell far short indeed of according independence to India, it was now undeniable that the 'white' Dominions would eventually be joined in their informal alliance by peoples of other racial stock. To the Indians, of course, this was scant satisfaction since not only the time of their independence but, more important, the politically most crucial features of their emerging state seemed to be outside their ability to control. But in London the Act was in many ways decisive. It reconciled the majority of popular and elite opinion to the eventual independence of this 'crowning jewel' of empire, considered along with the

British Isles themselves to be the other 'twin pillar' of Britain's international rank. Of course there is the mistake, encountered in the works of Britishers especially, of seeing in retrospect a grand design for decolonization that in fact did not exist. Closer inspection commonly reveals the British to have been following Burke's sage counsel to reform in order to preserve: London made concessions more usually to subvert opposition to British rule than to prepare for its demise. So, for example, to see Indian independence in 1947 as necessarily following from the Government of India Act of 1935 which in turn unerringly confirmed the intentions of the Government of India Act of 1919 (itself the natural product of the Morley–Minto reforms of 1909) assumes a British gift for foresight which a detailed examination of the historical record makes difficult to sustain. What is lacking in these accounts is a sense of the conflicts, hesitations and uncertainties of the past and of the attempts to reinterpret or renege on the promise of eventual independence for India.

Nonetheless, the British *did* establish a tradition of meeting colonial discontent by reforms which associated the subject peoples more closely with their own governing. The prior evolution of the Dominion system *did* exert an important influence on the style of British policy towards India. And the ultimate decision to grant India independence and to permit her to withdraw if she wished from the Commonwealth *did* constitute a momentous precedent for British policy towards the rest of the colonies.

How limited, by contrast, was the French experience in handling political change within their empire. When in January–February 1944, a group of colonial civil servants met in Brazzaville, capital of the French Congo, to draw up proposals for imperial reorganization in the aftermath of the war, the many worthwhile recommendations they made—the end of forced labor and special native legal codes, the creation of territorial assemblies and their coordination in a 'French Federation', the representation of colonial peoples at the future French Constituent Assembly—failed to deal with the truly central problem, the possibility of a colonial evolution towards independence.[2] That is, the French are not to be criticized for failing to provide complete and immediate independence to their colonies, but rather for their steadfast refusal to consider even eventual separation a viable political option. As the conference report preamble put it:

The ends of the civilizing work accomplished by France in the colonies excludes any idea of autonomy, all possibility of evolution outside the French bloc of the Empire; the eventual constitution, even in the future of self-government in the colonies is denied.[3]

[2] For a discussion of the conference, see D. Bruce Marshall, *The French Colonial Myth and Constitution-Making in the Fourth Republic* (Yale, 1973), pp. 102–15.

[3] *Brazzaville: 30 janvier–8 fevrier 1944*, published by the Ministère des Colonies, 1944, p. 32.

74 TONY SMITH

Nor were matters to improve with time. Despite the rapid enactment of a host of unprecedented reforms proposed by the Conference over the next two years, there was no thought of conceding political advantages to colonial nationalists which might lead to independence. By the summer of 1947, this had been made clear on successive occasions to the Indochinese, to the Tunisians and Moroccans, to the Malagasies, to the blacks of West and Equatorial Africa, and to the Algerians. Indeed, the matter had become fixed by the Fourth Republic's Constitution in the terms providing for the 'French Union' in its Title VIII.[4]

Experts in jurisprudence have convincingly pointed out the ambiguity and contradictions with which the final text establishing the French Union abounds. Its one central feature stands out clearly enough, however: the authority of France over the Union was beyond dispute. Neither in the immediate present nor in the future would there be a partnership among equals within this 'federation'. The only significant power whatsoever conferred on the Union was that of pooling members' resources for the common defense (article 62). But it was 'the Government of the [French] Republic [which] shall undertake the coordination of these resources and the direction of the policy appropriate to prepare and ensure this defense'. In legislative matters, the Union was totally subordinate to the National Assembly (articles 71–2). Nor could foreign nationalists convert the Union into a platform from which to dislodge France from her overseas possessions, for its key institutions (the Presidency, the High Council, and the Assembly) were safely under metropolitan control (articles 62–6 and 77). What the Union assured, in essence, was that the peoples of the Empire would be neither French nor free.

A variety of reasons may be adduced to explain the French failure to develop before 1945 any mechanism which might have served as a bridge for the transfer of power to their colonial subjects after the War. The most popular explanation has been to assert that the French blindly trusted to their policy of 'assimilation' whereby the colonies would eventually be one with France. Recent scholarship has tended to suggest, however, that the notion of 'association', with its connotations of the eventual separate development of the colonial peoples, had grown increasingly important in French policy circles in the twentieth century.[5] Or again, one might argue that the British experience with 'informal empire' had bred an aversion to direct rule abroad which the French, given their weaker international position, were not able to follow, forced by the logic of things into

[4] Tony Smith, 'The French Colonial Consensus and People's War, 1945–1958', *The Journal of Contemporary History*, October 1974.
[5] See Hubert Deschamps, 'French Colonial Policy in Tropical Africa between the Two World Wars', William Cohen, 'The French Colonial Service in West Africa', and Leonard Thompson, 'France and Britain in Africa: a Perspective', in Prosser Gifford (ed.), *France and Britain in Africa: Imperial Rivalry and Colonial Rule* (Yale, 1971).

annexationist/protectionist policies. But were this a decisive determinant of postwar behavior, one might expect to find the British insistent on maintaining direct rule after 1945, since they no longer enjoyed the power position which made the rhetoric of 'burden of empire' a possibility. The most crucial difference in the British and French imperial traditions would rather appear to lie in the long-established procedures by which London dealt with colonial discontent: progressively representative government tending towards eventual independence. Institutional practices, not ideological penchants, best explain the advantages Britain held over France in terms of the legacy of colonial tradtions to handling the problems of empire after 1945.

Prewar theory and practice did not alone decide postwar imperial policy, however. That the United States emerged after 1945 as the world's dominant power clearly helped the British accept their decline in international affairs more easily than it did the French. Thus, wartime cooperation in the development of the atom bomb had extended into an important place for Britain within NATO where the British held five of the thirteen principal command posts, with seven reserved for the Americans and one for the French. But the most salient aspect of the difference in Washington's relations with Paris and London emerges perhaps from an analysis of the quality of the bonds linking Franklin Roosevelt to Winston Churchill and to Charles de Gaulle. While Roosevelt held Churchill in high esteem, 'He hates de Gaulle with such fierce feeling that he rambles almost into incoherence whenever we talk about him', Cordell Hull reported in the summer of 1944.[6] With the North African landing of November 1942, and the assassination of Darlan a month later, the Americans moved to make General Henri Giraud, and not de Gaulle, head of civilian administration there and commander-in-chief of the surrendered French army of several hundred thousand men. Despite de Gaulle's ability in 1943 to rally behind him the National Liberation Committee (CFLN) and the support of certain resistance groups operating inside France, the Americans continued to oppose his leadership. Even at the moment of the liberation of France, Roosevelt refused to recognize the General's authority, insisting instead that a military administration run the country until the wishes of the population were made known by elections. It was the end of October 1944 before the United States finally recognized de Gaulle's provisional government.[7]

Certainly more than personality factors were at play. For the features of de Gaulle's personality that the Americans and sometimes the British

[6] Cited in Gabriel Kolko, *The Politics of War: the World and United States Foreign Policy, 1943–1945* (Random House, 1968), p. 83.

[7] A. W. DePorte, *De Gaulle's Foreign Policy, 1944–1946* (Harvard, 1968), chaps. 2 and 3. Also *ibid.*, chap. 4.

76 TONY SMITH

found so antipathetic had to do with his determination not to let France be absorbed by her allies during the war and relegated to a satellite role deprived of all initiative thereafter. So, early in the struggle, he had protested the manner in which the British occupied Diego Suarez on Madagascar and conducted operations against the Vichy troops in Syria. Similarly, the General had intimations of Roosevelt's plans for the French Empire: that Indochina or Morocco might be made trusteeships of other powers; that British or American bases might be permanently established on New Caledonia or at Bizerte and Dakar; even that a new buffer state might be created between France and Germany, to be called Wallonia and to run from Switzerland to the Channel. De Gaulle's sharp reaction to such considerations was in perfect accord with his ambition to regenerate France as a nation. As he told Roosevelt:

I know that you are preparing to aid France materially, and that aid will be invaluable to her. But it is in the political realm that she must recover her vigor, her self-reliance and, consequently, her role. How can she do this if she is excluded from the organization of the great world powers and their decisions, if she loses her African and Asian territories—in short, if the settlement of the War definitively imposes upon her the psychology of the vanquished?[8]

This wartime experience was to leave a permanent mark on French attitudes towards the United States whenever colonial questions arose. All shades of French political opinion suspected American moves in North Africa after the Allied landing there in November 1942, believing Washington wished to expel the French in order to move in itself. British efforts to pry the French out of the Levant at the end of the war were similarly believed to depend on American support. And the jealousy with which the French tried to protect their monopoly over affairs in Indochina after 1946, despite their reliance on ever-increasing American aid, serves as yet another instance of their suspicion of American designs.[9] One need only reflect on the welcome London gave to American involvement in Greece and Turkey in 1947, and in Iran in 1953, to appreciate the importance of the difference relations with Washington made in the overall process of European decolonization.

Certainly, at times, the British had reason to find the relationship most frustrating. To many, it appeared that the United States would have its own way at every turn, insistent on its rights but reluctant to honor its obligations. America's power, geographic isolation and (as the sentimental

[8] Charles de Gaulle, *The Complete War Memoirs of Charles de Gaulle* (Simon and Schuster, 1967), p. 574.

[9] Anti-Americanism flared in France each time the dependent role became evident: over the Marshall Plan, the E.D.C., the 'nuclear shield', and American funds for the Indochinese War. See, among others, Georgette Elgey, *La république des illusions* (Fayard, 1965), pp. 101, 133, 139–41, 248; and Alfred Grosser, *La politique extérieure de la Ve République* (Seuil, 1965), pp. 17, 47 ff.

liked to feel) immaturity in foreign affairs combined to produce this mixture of righteousness and irresponsibility the British found so taxing. But it was only a minority who argued, as some radical American historians do today, that Washington's moves were in fact premeditated efforts to sap British power in a design to replace her in international affairs. These observers could point, however to American carping during the interwar period at imperial and Commonwealth arrangements which favored the United Kingdom economically as the prelude to a move after 1945 to replace the British in the Mediterranean and the Middle and Far East. Max Beloff nonetheless portrays the dominant mood when he writes 'The degree to which British statesmen and diplomats expected a natural sympathy for British policy to exist in the United States and equated any hostility to or criticism of Britain with treason to America and not merely to Britain can be abundantly illustrated.'[10] Surely the confidence with which Britain relied on American power to fill the vacuum left by the end of her formal and informal spheres of control around the globe is remarkable, especially when contrasted with the French experience. So, to cite but one example, Gabriel Kolko may picture Anglo-American relations over Middle East issues as one of unrelieved antagonism. But Anthony Eden's own account of how he wooed Washington's intervention in Iran against Prime Minister Mossadegh and his evident relief that a consortium arrangement could be worked out which preserved British interests in the area (however much it may have furthered the ambitions of the Americans in the process) makes it difficult to agree that all was cynical maneuvering for advantage between the two Anglo-Saxon powers.[11]

The third of the major differences in the respective abilities of the British and the French to decolonize takes us from international considerations to an analysis of their domestic political institutions. Britain had a 'loyal opposition', a stable two-party system, and a strong executive. France, to the contrary, was plagued by disloyal opposition from both the Right and Left, by a multiparty system, and by a notoriously weak executive. Hence the French were not so able as the British to process a problem the magnitude of decolonization.

To an observer with a background in French domestic politics, surely the most striking thing about the British political system during this period is the manner in which its institutions seemed to function more effectively during crisis. Faced with a challenge to its authority from abroad, the system organized its responses as ranks closed and hierarchies of command asserted themselves. This resilence of British institutions was highlighted

[10] Max Beloff, 'The Special Relationship: an Anglo-American Myth', in Martin Gilbert, ed., *A Century of Conflict, 1850–1950: Essays for A. J. P. Taylor* (Hamish Hamilton Ltd., 1966), p. 156.

[11] Anthony Eden, *Full Circle* (Houghton–Mifflin, 1960), chap. 9.

especially at the time of the invasion of the Suez Canal Zone, the single occasion when matters related to empire focused the concerned attention of the British public and its leaders. It is not a question here of whether the policy was a colossal blunder or whether the fault for its failure lay with Eisenhower and Dulles. The point is simply, as Leon Epstein demonstrates in his careful study of British politics at the time, that the system performed remarkably well.[12]

Not that there was always unanimity. As the most thorough study of party politics during decolonization suggests, imperial issues were perhaps as much a matter of serious bi-partisan dispute during the 1950s as at any time in modern British history.[13] But the discipline of the parties, the institutional strength of Government leadership, and the way partisan conflict tended to increase party solidarity (rather than create centrifugal struggles as was so often the case in France), meant that from the mid-1940s until the mid-1960s, British imperial policy was characterized by coherence, consistency and strength.

The most delicate balance point at this time in British politics was the effort by the Conservatives not to let these issues tear them apart after they came to power in 1951.[14] As David Goldsworthy documents, the Conservatives were the Party of Empire, tied to it emotionally in perhaps their most vital collective myth, the pride in empire, and connected to it concretely through settlers, business interests, and the Colonial Service, all of whom sought their place in its ranks.[15] Yet despite Churchill's return to power, the single serious misstep under their leadership was Suez. A part of the reason for their success was surely that Labour had shown the way by granting independence to the several territories of south Asia and by preparing the road for the future independence of the Gold Coast. In addition, there was luck: Churchill was out of office after the spring of 1955 and so was not able to maintain the mistaken policies he had drawn up, paramount of which was the creation of the Central African Federation in 1953.[16] Harold Macmillan (from 1957) and Iain Macleod (from 1959) proved themselves more realistic leaders. They were substantially aided in the pursuit of their policies by the logic of the British political system which made it quite difficult for the recalcitrant reactionaries in the Party—probably no more than 10–15 percent of its strength, though on specific issues they could rally greater support—to create enough instability in the system for concessions to be made to them. Try as they might, first over Egypt,

---

[12] Leon D. Epstein, *British Politics in thè Suez Crisis* (University of Illinois, 1964).

[13] David Goldsworthy, *Colonial Issues in British Politics, 1945–1961* (Oxford, 1971).

[14] This point is made with particular clarity by Miles Kahler, 'End of Empire: Decolonization in the Politics of Britain and France', unpublished paper, Harvard University.

[15] Goldsworthy, *op.cit.*, pp. 166 ff.

[16] Patrick Keatley, *The Politics of Partnership* (Penguin, 1963), pp. 393 ff.

then over Cyprus, and finally over Central Africa and Katanga, they remained isolated and impotent.[17]

In contrast, if there is one point at which French Socialist politicians, academic observers, and right wing military officers are in agreement, it is that they all hold the manifold structural shortcomings of the governmental system under the Fourth Republic (pejoratively referred to as 'le système') responsible for the terrible trials of French decolonization. Charles de Gaulle expressed with characteristic bluntness the sentiments of many when he replied in 1948 to an interviewer who inquired how he would 'significantly modify the foreign policy of France' should he return to power:

> I will not have to change the foreign policy of France since at present France has no foreign policy. Her regime does not permit it any more than it permits her to have an economic policy worthy of the name, a social policy, or a financial policy, etc. The truth is there is nothing. Thus I will not change this policy which does not exist, but I will make the policy of France.[18]

A general theory of the Republic's weakness could readily almagamate the various criticisms of 'le système' into a unified explanation of its difficulties.[19] Under both the Third and Fourth Republics, the root cause of political weakness was to be found in political division which, although not so serious as to prevent a governing center coalition for France, ¬nonetheless habitually precluded the unity indispensable for effective government. We are told that this political division was the product of the simultaneous playing out of several historical conflicts wracking French society at large (Williams, Hoffmann), of the difficulty of governing against the cynical opposition of those who denied the entire system legitimacy (Aron), of French attitudes toward power which hindered the growth of effective authority relations (Crozier), all aggravated by a form of constitutional government which, with its multiple parties and weak executive, exacerbated these conflicts in the very seat of power (Wahl, MacRae, Barale), and so encouraged the irresponsibility of elected officials (Leites). Inability fed upon inability until the default of government authority reached such proportions that, at the first serious threat of military insubordination, the regime totally collapsed.[20]

[17] *Ibid.*, part 5; Goldsworthy, *op. cit.*, chap. 8 and pp. 352 ff; Rudolph von Albertini, *Decolonization* (Doubleday, 1971), pp. 245–7.

[18] Charles de Gaulle, *La France sera la France* (F. Bouchy et Fils, 1951), p. 193.

[19] The following comments are drawn from Smith, *op. cit.*

[20] Philip Williams, *Crisis and Compromise: Politics in the Fourth Republic* (Anchor, 1966); Stanley Hoffman (ed.), *In Search of France* (Harper and Row, 1965); Raymond Aron, *Immuable et changeante: de la IVe à la Ve République* (Paris, 1959); Michel Crozier, *The Bureaucratic Phenomenon* (Chicago, 1964); D. MacRae, *Parliament, Parties and Society in France, 1946–1958* (St. Martin's Press, 1967); Jean Barale, *La Constitution de la IVe République à l'épreuve de la guerre* (Librarie Générale de Droit et de Jurisprudence, 1963);

80   TONY SMITH

At first reading this seems to make good sense of the French experience and contrast meaningfully with the case of British domestic institutions. But on closer analysis this account shows serious problems, since it neglects to point up the stubborn colonial consensus which held from the Socialists to the Right and which contributed as much to the ineffectiveness of the political system as this, in turn, made a sound policy impossible to agree upon or implement. For as a review of the Indochinese policy of the Blum and Ramadier governments in 1946–7 and of the Algerian policy of the Mollet government of 1956–7 demonstrates, it was unity, resolution, and action which at these critical junctures of Socialist national leadership emerge as the hallmarks of the regime. What typified these truly decisive periods of Socialist leadership was not so much the shortcomings of the political system through which they had to govern as their own unrealistic, tenaciously held positions on colonial matters. Admittedly the French political system was a weak one whose divisions clearly complicated the reaction to colonial nationalism. But it is all too tempting to use the system as a scapegoat and so to forget the dedication of the Fourth Republic to an image of France which found its highest expression with de Gaulle: that to be internally stable, France required international greatness, and that to obtain this rank she must count on her empire since in this enterprise she had no certain friends.

Time and again throughout the history of the Fourth Republic, beneath the invective of political division, one finds a shared anguish at the passing of national greatness, a shared humiliation at three generations of defeat, a shared nationalistic determination that France retain her independence in a hostile world—all brought to rest on the conviction that in the empire they would 'maintenir'. Thus the Socialists shared with most of their fellow-countrymen an image of France, a kind of collective conscience, born of the political paralysis of the thirties, the shame of the Occupation, the stern prophecies of General de Gaulle, the fear of domestic communism, and the initial expectations and ensuing disappointments of the Resistance. With most of their fellow-countrymen, they too experienced the loss of Indochina as the failure not of an historically absurd colonial policy first launched by de Gaulle but as the failure of a regime. They feared, then, that the decline of France to second-power status marked not so much an inevitable phase of world history, but the inner failing of a people. The charges of being a 'bradeur d'empire' raised more profound self-doubt in the National Assembly than did charges of 'scuttle' at Westminster.

It was, therefore, not only the political institutions of France and Great Britain which were dissimilar, but perhaps more importantly the national

Nicholas Wahl, 'The French Political System', in Samuel Beer and Adam Ulam (eds.), *Patterns of Government* (Random House, 1962); Nathan Leites, *On the Game of Politics in France* (Stanford, 1959).

moods or psychologies of these two countries. Where, for example, does one find in the annals of French leaders anything equivalent to the entry in the journal of Hugh Dalton, assistant to Lord Mountbatten in negotiating the independence of India, dated February 24, 1947? 'If you are in a place where you are not wanted and where you have not got the force, or perhaps the will, to squash those who don't want you, the only thing to do is to come out. This very simple truth will have to be applied to other places too, e.g., Palestine.'[21]

One may object that this analysis fails to disaggregate sufficiently the constituent forces in each country. How important was it, for example, that Labour was in power immediately after the war and so could set an example in Britain of how to deal with colonial nationalism? Doubtless the influence of the Fabian colonial bureau and the work of Arthur Creech-Jones as Colonial Secretary from late 1946 until 1950 had their positive impact. But it should be recalled that the Socialists led the government in France as well in the crucial years 1946–7, when the decision to fight nationalism in Southeast Asia was made. Thus, at the very time the British Socialists were deciding to hasten the withdrawal from India, the French Socialists were staging emotional appeals in the National Assembly in favor of supporting military action in Indochina.[22] The leaders of both parties wore Socialist labels, but they were more clearly to be recognized by their national than their party memberships.

Nor is it convincing to argue that differences in civilian control of the military adequately explain divergences in French and British decolonization. For military insubordination in France was far more a reflection of the national crisis than it was the cause. That is, the French military came to see itself as an interest group with claims to make against the state only after the state had created the situations where these interests could be formed.

It is similarly difficult to argue that economic interests offer more than a partial explanation of the different patterns of decolonization. To be sure, settler interests weighed heavily in deciding policy in Kenya and Algeria, and there is evidence that mining interests initially made their voices heard in favor of efforts to keep the Central African Federation under European control. Elsewhere, however, business groups appear either divided (Morocco), disinterested (much of sub-Saharan Africa), or unable to stem the political tide (India). Of course it is possible to find the hand of business wherever one wishes in theoretically, if not historically, logical terms. So economic interests are damned if there is federation (in Nigeria, it is

---

[21] Hugh Dalton, *High Tide and After: Memoirs 1945–1960* (Frederick Muller Ltd., 1962), p. 211.

[22] For the very different attitudes of Prime Ministers Attlee and Ramadier, see the excerpts of parliamentary debates of 1946–7 reprinted in Tony Smith, *The End of European Empire: Decolonization after World War II* (D. C. Heath, 1975).

sometimes alleged, this allowed for more rational exploitation by outside groups) and equally damned if there is decentralization (in French West Africa, so one hears, these same interests would balkanize to divide and rule). But so long as colonial nationalists were not communists or, unlike Mossadegh in Iran and Nasser in Egypt, did not appear to represent threats to basic European overseas economic concerns, leaders in Paris and London could realistically hope to count on the pressures of economic development to create a working arrangement with European business. Indeed, in some instances a strong, leftist nationalist was to be preferred to a compliant but incompetent collaborator.

In short, disaggregation of the 'nation' into its constituent political forces offers insights into specific periods or cases but does not appear to have conditioned the overall pattern of European decolonization. For the factors of general relevance, it is aggregate national characteristics which emerge as the most decisive. But as the last point above suggests, an important determinant of the style of European decolonization had to do not so much with political structures and considerations in London and Paris as with the character of nationalism in the overseas empire.

II

However thorough a comparison might be made between the policies of Paris and London, such an approach focuses the study of decolonization too narrowly on the imperial capitals, neglecting the decisive role played by the peoples of Asia and Africa in their own liberation. For it is possible to trace the history of decolonization not in terms of European, but of Asian and African, developments. The victory of Japan over Russia in 1904; Lenin's rise to power in 1917 and his subsequent aid to national elites striving to reduce European influence in their countries; the triumph of Mustafa Kemal in Turkey after the First World War; the rise of Gandhi to leadership of the National Congress Party of India in 1920; the increasing importance of Cairo in Arab affairs following the defeat of efforts at Arab unity in the First World War and the emergence of modern Egyptian nationalism under Saad Zaghlul Pasha; the rapid growth of colonial economies during the interwar period with corresponding shifts in local social and political structures; the Japanese conquest of European colonies east of India and the hardships suffered by colonial peoples in all other parts of the globe during the Second World War; Kwame Nkrumah's return to the Gold Coast in December 1947; Mao Tse-tung's entry in Peking in January 1949—all these developments offer an alternative way of charting the course of history and analyzing its decisive movements. From this perspective, concentration on the formal boundaries of empire or on events deemed significant at the time in European capitals risks obstructing our vision of those determining processes of history which occurred silently within colonial territories giving a local pedigree to nationalism, or which took place regionally without respect for imperial frontiers on the basis of communication among Asians or Africans. Looked at from this angle, history ran by other clocks whose timing mechanism synchronized only occasionally with the pacing of events in Europe. In order to form a just appreciation of the colonial problem facing Paris and London, our attention must turn from these capitals to Hanoi and Delhi, to Cairo and Algiers, to Accra and Abidjan.

Where comparative analyses of colonial nationalism have been undertaken, they generally tend to advance typologies of nationalist leadership ('liberal-separationist', 'traditional-nativist', 'extremist-radical' and the like), to compare them to their local opponents (the 'liberal-assimilationists' and 'traditional-collaborationists'), and then to analyze the content to the various ideologies of nationalist mobilization (indigenist, religious, or socialist). Unfortunately for comparative purposes, such constructs show serious problems on closer inspection. Any effort to propose ineluctable stages or types of nationalist development must fail given the variety on historical record. Thus the drive for national liberation may be preceded (Tunisia), accompanied (Morocco), or followed (Nigeria) by the political predominance of traditionalist leaders and ideas. Or again, the same man (Ferhat Abbas) or movement (the Indian Congress Party) may be successively advocates of assimilation, separation, and revolution while in other cases these various positions may be assumed instead by rival men and groups (Algeria). Or again, the same movement may contain quite heterogeneous members spanning the liberal-traditionalist-radical spectrum (the Indian Congress Party) or the same individual may alone espouse the whole gamut of ideological appeals (Sukarno with his mixture of nationalism, Islam, and communism officially proclaimed as NASAKOM). Such typologies only give us a false sense of security which even casual reference to the historical record must easily disrupt.

We are on surer ground when we turn from a study of values and the penchant for ahistorical categories to an analysis of structure, and see that the decisive question in the comparative investigation of colonial nationalism has to do with the character of the rural–urban alliance. For whatever their values, what Bourguiba, Ataturk, Sukarno, Nkrumah, Nyerere, Ho Chi Minh, Gandhi and Houphouet-Boigny all shared was their leadership at the moment of national independence over groupings both traditional and modern in values and structure with a scope so broad that the split between the countryside and the city was overcome. Obviously such nationalist alliances varied enormously among themselves depending on the interests represented, the solidity of the party apparatus aggregating anti-colonial forces, the relative power of local groups outside the nationalist fold, and the international dangers which a young independence movement had to face. But it is, I believe, through an analysis of these forces that we can best elaborate a typology of colonial nationalism and so understand the contribution of the peoples of Asia and Africa to the character of the decolonization process.

A comparison of reactions in Black Africa and Madagascar to postwar French colonial policy with those of nationalists in Algeria and Indochina offers a good illustration of the importance of local conditions in determining this historical movement. For it is important to emphasize that *French policy was essentially the same throughout the empire*: political reforms were granted only so long as they could be seen tending to preserve French rule. Demands for change which might ultimately destroy the French presence were immediately to be squelched. De Gaulle was the chief architect of this plan and he made its terms clear to the Vietnamese by his Declaration of March 25, 1945, which his successors in power reaffirmed in their negotiations with Ho Chi Minh at Fontainebleau in the summer of 1946. The Second Constituent Assembly adopted the same stand with the Algerians, and the first legislature of the Fourth Republic confirmed it in the terms of the Statute of Algeria voted in the summer of 1947. General Juin took the message to Morocco after having delivered it in Tunis. Marius Moutet, the Socialist colonial minister, was relying on the same view when he called for a boycott of the extraordinary conference called at Bamako, Soudan by the Black Africans under French rule in October 1946.

The French subsequently demonstrated the seriousness of their resolve. In November 1946 they shelled the port of Haiphong, taking the lives of several thousand Vietnamese in their determination to rid the city of the Vietminh. In March–April 1947 they responded to a nationalist raid on an army base on Madagascar with a repression which by official estimates killed 86,000 natives. Since the Sétif repression of May 1945 had momentarily cowed the Algerians, rigged elections commencing in the spring of 1948 kept the peace in North Africa. But shortly thereafter, the French felt obliged to launch a concerted repression south of the Sahara against the Africans of the Rassemblement Démocratique Africain (RDA).

If the policy was the same, the results were not. Within a month of the French attack on Haiphong, the Vietminh had replied by an attempted coup in Hanoi. While the Sétif repression effectively fragmented the Algerian political elite for a time, a revolution willing to give no quarter finally broke out in 1954. But in Black Africa the policy succeeded. A closer analysis of the situation there and a review of the variables mentioned earlier may suggest why: the ability of a nationalist party to buckle together the alliance of the forces it represents; the relative strength (actual or potential) of this party's local opponents; the need of such a party for aid from the international system to maintain its local predominance. Thus to understand the process of European decolonization means to put some order into the variety of colonial situations which it concerned, since a French policy anachronistic in certain areas proved well suited to master the events in others. Why did French policy succeed so well in Africa when it failed so totally elsewhere?

Immediately after the Second World War, African nationalism in the French territories found its most advanced expression in Senegal and the Ivory Coast. But as we shall see, it was the Ivory Coast which was quickly to emerge as the key territory in French policy south of the Sahara. Here the leading political formation was Houphouet-Boigny's Parti Démocratique du Côte d'Ivoire (PDCI) which was founded on the base of the coffee and cocoa planters' voluntary association, the Syndicat Agricole Africaine (SAA). As President of the SAA, Houphouet had been elected to the French Constituent National Assembly, and there, in the spring of 1946, had proved instrumental in passing the legislation which ended the bitterly hated forced labor regulations in effect throughout French Africa under the Third Republic and intensified under Vichy. By this legislation, Houphouet was able in one stroke to secure a decisive blow for his own class against the European planters in coffee and cocoa (who could not compete with the African without the help of cheap, requisitioned labor) and to enlist the support of the great mass of the territory's inhabitants who were subject to these terrible regulations. So Houphouet-Boigny, the largest planter in the Ivory Coast, became in the words of Ruth Morgenthau 'a hero and liberator. This achievement was the beginning of a myth around Houphouet, the first truly national Ivory Coast tradition.'[23] By October 1946, the PDCI had 65,000 members and was the largest party in French tropical Africa.

At the very time the Ivory Coast was securing an initial measure of national unity behind Houphouet, the country was finding itself in increasing turmoil with the French administration. The economic aspect of the problem was familiar throughout the postwar world: shortages and inflation. But it was aggravated in the Ivory Coast by the sharp decline in world market prices for coffee and cocoa which together constituted 75–92 percent of the country's exports between 1947 and 1957.[24] In the Territorial Assembly, at the same time, a number of political issues served seriously to divide the PDCI from the settler delegates and the colonial administration. What brought these local issues to the intense concern of Paris, however, was the alliance which had grown up between the PDCI and the French Communist Party, and the increasingly dominant role the

[23] Ruth S. Morgenthau, *Political Parties in French-Speaking West Africa* (Clarendon Press, 1964), p. 181.
[24] Aristide Zolberg, *One Party Rule in the Ivory Coast* (Princeton, 1969), p. 163.

PDCI was playing throughout the Federation of French West Africa (AOF).

In the first French Constituent Assembly (October 1945–May 1946), the African deputies had recognized both the Socialist and Communist parties as their allies in the effort to secure liberal reforms in colonial rule. Although the leaders of the Provisional Government assured the Africans these reforms would not be modified whatever the fate of the first draft of the constitution, the promise was not kept. The combined pressures of settler lobbying, de Gaulle's warning that firmness must be displayed, and the need to come to some unequivocal stand in the negotiations with the Vietminh during the summer of 1946 worked together to produce a text in which the second Constituent Assembly (June–October 1946) defined the French Union in terms distinctly less liberal than those earlier proposed.[25] In response, therefore, some 800 delegates from French Africa assembled at Bamako in October 1946 to coordinate their efforts to secure liberal reforms. In an effort to sabotage the congress, Colonial Minister Moutet used his influence inside the Socialist Party to convince affiliated Africans, most notably the Senegalese, to boycott the meeting. In the absence of the well-organized Senegalese, the PDCI with Houphouet at its head emerged as the unrivaled leader of both French West and Equatorial Africa through the creation of the interterritorial party, the Rassemblement Démocratique Africain (RDA). Several years later this was to prove critically important when the issue of attaining independence as a federation arose and the unionists within the RDA found themselves cut off from their Senegalese allies outside and so less able to thwart what came to be Houphouet's goal of breaking the federation into sovereign states. At the time, a boycott on the part of the French parties which had also been invited to the conference as observers meant that the Africans responded favorably to the one metropolitan party in attendance, the PCF. It was hardly surprising, then, that the newly formed RDA would affiliate itself (*apparentement*) with the Communists in the first legislature of the Fourth Republic elected in November 1946.

With the exclusion of the Communists from the French Government the following May, and especially with the railway strikes in West Africa in the fall of 1947, Paris began to anticipate the need to deal with the same firm hand in West Africa that it had already shown in Indochina, Algeria, and Madagascar. In January 1948, Socialist deputy Paul Béchard was appointed Governor General of AOF and Orselli was named Governor of the Ivory Coast. Initially these men pursued a somewhat conciliatory policy, trying to woo the RDA and the PDCI away from the Communists. But when this showed no signs of progress, Orselli was replaced by Laurent Péchoux and the administration cracked down to rid the territory of the

[25] Marshall, *op. cit.*, chaps. 5, 7, 8; Morgenthau, *op. cit.*, chaps. 2, 3.

RDA by the time of the elections to the second legislature in 1951. Naturally this repression (as it was frankly called) fell most heavily in the Ivory Coast. PDCI officials were imprisoned en masse, villages favorable to the Party found their taxes raised, even pilgrims to Mecca were prohibited from leaving if they were members of the Party. In a move familiar in all the French territories after the war, administrators reorganized electoral districts and rigged election results to favor their hand-picked candidates. The repression did not go unanswered. Between February 1949 and January 1950, the Party responded in kind to these measures. Hunger strikes, mass demonstrations, acts of civil disobedience, and actual street fighting took the lives of several score Africans while hundreds were injured and thousands arrested.[26]

For our concerns, the most striking thing about these developments is that ultimately the policy achieved its aims. Unlike the situation in Algeria or Indochina, but like the case of Madagascar, force worked. From the spring of 1950, when Houphouet-Boigny met with François Mitterrand in Paris and determined to break with the Communists, until the present day, France has had no better friend in Africa. Here, then, is the signal success of French decolonization, the exemplar of the policy of reform within order designed to guarantee a continued French presence in the overseas territories. It raises the obvious question of what factors were present in the case of the Ivory Coast which were lacking in Indochina and Algeria.

The most serious problem immediately facing Houphouet-Boigny in the period from February 1949 to January 1950 was the inadequacy of his party organization. Relative to other political formations in French Africa the PDCI may have seemed a potent force, but it simply could not tolerate the pressures put on it by the French administration. It should be recalled that the PDCI only came into existence in 1946 and that it built on the foundation of the SAA created just two years earlier. While it is true that the SAA associated tribal chiefs with commoners and that Houphouet had important credentials both as a planter and as the scion of a leading chiefly family, this simply did not constitute strength enough to oppose the French. The root weakness of the Party seems to have been the tribal structure of the country (indeed, wherever we turn in colonial situations these 'primordial divisions'—to use Clifford Geertz's term—constitute the basic obstacle to party formation regardless of whether the society is 'tribal' or 'peasant'). The PDCI was in fact an 'indirect party' in the sense that its structure depended more on the loyalty of elites who had their bases independent of party control than on authority the Party could muster on its own account. Beneath its upper levels, Party structure mirrored rather than bridged the cleavages within society at large. Once the top split, the Party, devoid of horizontal linkages at lower levels, simply fragmented into

[26] Zolberg, *op. cit.*, pp. 131 ff; Morgenthau, *op. cit.*, pp. 188 ff.

88 TONY SMITH

its constituent parts. As Aristide Zolberg puts it, '. . . the structures created in 1947 helped maintain ethnic ties even when economic and social change might have diminished their importance . . . basic party units coincided with ethnic wards, and party life also reinforced ethnicity. . . . Those who were particularly responsible for party organization knew that its machinery was adequate only for electoral purposes.'[27] What occurred under French pressure was, quite simply, the disaggregation of this elite as some succumbed to hopes for personal gain while others responded to fears of personal loss.

This alone, however, cannot explain Houphouet's capitulation to the French. Other parties at other times have been fractured by repression only to arise more powerfully thereafter. Is it not conceivable that Houphouet could have appealed over the head of his fellow party leaders to the people, retired to the bush and begun a war of national liberation against the French? If a West African specialist may balk at the idea, certainly a student of Asian politics would not. Houphouet was, after all, widely agreed to have charismatic personal qualities, and the election results after his reconciliation with France suggest that in the eyes of the people his opposition served to heighten his prestige. But this is not the course of action Houphouet chose and while the reasons may seem apparent to the Africanist, they may be illuminating for a comparative study of decoloniza-tion attempting to encompass the Middle East and Asia. In a word, as the largest planter in the Ivory Coast, Houphouet-Boigny realized the obvious: the future of his class and thereby of his people lay with France. Mobilize the peasantry? Conduct guerrilla warfare? Nothing seems less probable. As this Catholic, this traditional chief, this leading spokesman of the African bourgeoisie put it to his compatriots at the opening of a fair in 1953: 'If you don't want to vegetate in bamboo huts, concentrate your efforts on growing good cocoa and good coffee. They will fetch a good price and you will become rich.'[28]

To promote these export crops, the Ivory Coast of the early 1950s needed the cooperation of France. For the country produced only 3 percent of the world's output and this an inferior variety making it especially vulnerable to price fluctuations on the international market. Under a 1954 agreement with France, however, Ivory Coast coffee (accounting in those days for some 57 percent of total exports) received both a quota guarantee and a price floor in metropolitan markets.[29] The growing middle class of African planters, along with their upper-class colleagues on the great

[27] Zolberg, *op. cit.*, pp. 143, 237; Morgenthau, *op. cit.*, pp. 207 ff.

[28] Cited in Zolberg, *op. cit.*, p. 151. Tribal cultivators are, of course, very different from peasants so that for reasons of social structure they may be more difficult to mobilize in revolution.

[29] Elliot J. Berg, 'The Economic Basis of Political Choice in French West Africa', *American Political Science Review*, LIV (1960), p. 290; Zolberg, *op. cit.*, p. 165.

estates, depended for their livelihood on the stability of these contracts.[30]

Houphouet-Boigny and the interests he represented faced another challenge as well: the threat of incorporation into a federal West Africa. Since 1904, French practice had been to finance the entire Federation from indirect taxes levied throughout the area. Wealthier territories perenially complained about this practice in the Grand Council in Dakar, but to no avail. After 1945, the Ivory Coast confirmed a trend begun earlier, so that by the mid-1950s it was the undisputed economic leader of the AOF, accounting for 45 percent of the region's exports. As a result of the Federation's taxing system, the Ivory Coast received an average of only 19 percent of the money it remitted to Dakar. These taxes to the federal authority amounted, in turn, to two or three times the amount collected and retained locally, so that of the total governmental revenue levies in the Ivory Coast, well over half left, never to return.[31]

In order to make good its separation from French West Africa, the Ivory Coast needed the support of France, for throughout the Federation in the early 1950s the mood was for union. Houphouet's preference for decentralization met the opposition of Léopold Senghor from without the RDA, while from within the Party, Sékou Touré of Guinea began to challenge the Ivory Coast leadership. As a result of French support, however, Houphouet could disregard the opinion of his fellow West Africans. The French National Assembly's framework law of March–April 1957 severely weakened the federal authority of the AOF by removing certain of its powers to Paris and devolving others onto the reinforced territorial assemblies, Senghor complained of the 'balkanization' of West Africa and most observers have agreed with him that this was the conscious intention of France.[32] At the Bamako RDA conference held in September 1957, Touré was much more popular than Houphouet (who found his only backing from wealthy Gabon), but the Ivory Coast's Paris connections made it quite invulnerable to African objections.

Before the territorial assemblies had fully assumed their new prerogatives, however, the Fourth Republic fell. The French scheme of things for Africa was now expressed in de Gaulle's idea of the 'French Community'. By the terms of the Fifth Republic's constitution, Africans had two choices: either 'federation' in subordination to France, or independence. In other words, the policy of the Fifth Republic was essentially the same as that of the Fourth so far as African federations were concerned. They could expect no comfort from Paris, for France would not support a gradual evolution

[30] In 1944 there were 40,000 of these farms. By 1956 there were 120,000, while the population total was under 3 million: Zolberg, *op. cit.*, p. 27.

[31] Computed from figures provided by Zolberg, *op. cit.*, pp. 159 ff.

[32] This judgment is shared by Morgenthau, Zolberg, Michael Crowder and Pierre Gonidec, among others.

towards a federal structure for the AOF which reduced metropolitan control. (The contrast with the British in Nigeria at the same time is striking. Here the pressures for decentralization—at least after the Richard's constitution of 1946—came from the Africans themselves, and especially from the Northern Region.)

A comparison of the Ivory Coast with other colonial situations suggests that the key variable to analyze for an understanding of the colonial response to metropolitan policy is the local power position of the predominant nationalist elite. For every war of colonial liberation carries within it a civil conflict so that in fact the nationalist elite is fighting on two fronts: against the imperial power and against other local groups striving to replace it. Dominant elites are therefore prudent to avoid armed confrontation with the imperial authority. This is not only because it is sensible to recognize that, given the great disproportion of military means, it is especially their fellow citizens who will be killed. The elites understand as well that the initial military setbacks they can expect to suffer may well release the centrifugal forces of class and ethnic division which so profoundly mark most colonial societies. Since warfare in the colonial context will almost inevitably be a protracted, decentralized affair, the initially dominant nationalist elite may find their position assumed by rival leaders. It is, after all, a story of nationalist fairy books that nationalism feeds on its own reversals, jumping up from the earth each time more powerful than before until the entire 'people' is united on that great day of liberation. In fact, as closer inspection of virtually any colonial situation will warrant, there are a variety of nationalist movements behind what to the casual observer may seem like a single wave of nationalism, and these diverse groups are frequently seriously at odds.

Thus civil war lurks in the heart of every movement for national liberation. So, shortly after the signature of the Anglo-Irish Treaty of 1921, serious strife broke out within Ireland lasting for two years before the Provisional Government was able to bring it under control. The terms of the dispute continued to mark Irish life for decades thereafter. Again, in the very midst of fighting the Dutch effort to regain the Netherlands East Indies, the Communists attempted a coup against the Hatta–Sukarno government (the Madiun Rebellion of 1948) which the Indonesian Army never forgot. In the case of Tunisia, Bourguiba found his agreement to 'internal autonomy' as a prelude to eventual independence hotly contested by Salah ben Youssef, Secretary General of the Destour Party, who secured important backing within the country as well as from the Algerians and the Egyptians. Only because his leadership of the nationalist movement was so undisputed could Kwame Nkrumah accept the 1950 constitution for the Gold Coast which offered him a good deal less than independence. What he must certainly have feared was that his continued recalcitrance would prompt the British to support the separatist movement in Ashanti and the Northern Territories (as they might easily have done). 'We have no program but independence' declared the Moroccan Istiqlal Party in the early 1950s. This made good sense indeed for a party representing landed interests in a country where 60 percent of the rural population was landless and the nationalist movement divided into three autonomous forces. It was the same slogan adopted by the Wafd Party in Egypt on the occasion in 1951 of their unilateral abrogation of the Anglo-Egyptian Treaty of 1936. But the Wafd quickly saw things pass out of its hands with the mobilization of the Muslim Brotherhood and the Free Officers and the coup against the monarchy in 1952. More wisely than the Wafd, Ho Chi Minh avoided confrontation with the French until it was literally forced upon him, realizing that whatever the apparent strength of the Vietminh, Indochina was far from secure in its hold in 1946. In the case of the Ivory Coast, there is a slight variation in this pattern. For what Houphouet-Boigny had to fear was not so much local as federal interference with his position. That is, other forces in the AOF played the functional equivalent of an internal threat to his leadership.

Yet however reluctant virtually any nationalist elite may be to enter into war against the imperial authority, such confrontations do occur and we must investigate further to see the possibility of establishing categories of nationalist leadership, determining in each case its likelihood of heading a militant insurrection. Dominant groups *least likely* to mount a sustained challenge to the colonial order are those which recognize the fragility of their control locally and the interest they well may have in a European connection. A particularly clear case of this, as we have seen, is the Ivory Coast. Here local factors—the threat of the AOF to incorporate the territory—combined with international considerations—the preferential treatment given in French markets to coffee and cocoa production, the economic basis of the ruling class—to dictate a policy of prudence towards Paris. Not that an elite based on export revenues is necessarily a willing collaborator with European interests; Colonel Quadafi of Libya is evidence enough of this. But even in the case of Quadafi, it should be recalled that petroleum products have demonstrated a special immunity to international pressures, and that even this is true only of the present period, as the experience of Prime Minister Mossadegh testifies. The royal court of Cambodia provides another instance of elite collaboration with the Europeans. The Cambodian king welcomed the French return since this promised to destroy the anti-monarchical forces the Japanese had fielded before their defeat and to return to his rule the territory seized by Siam during the Second World War. Royal courts do not make the best collaborators, of course, since economic development tends to throw up classes whose attitudes undermine their legitimacy. European interests are most effectively represented instead by what may be called an import–export elite whose capacity to develop economically, even if only within certain limits, allows it to cooperate usefully with the international system and at the same time assure domestic stability. The history of Latin America from the mid-nineteenth to the mid-twentieth century (and beyond) demonstrates this.[33]

What I have presented is, of course, an ideal type to which there are important historical exceptions. Thus, fragile nationalist elites will not always recognize where their interests lie in the manner of Houphouet-Boigny. Just as the Czar was extremely ill-advised to tangle with Japan in 1904—and even more mistaken to back his Slavic brothers in Serbia in 1914—so the Wafd Party of Egypt unwittingly committed suicide in October 1951, when it chose to abrogate the Anglo-Egyptian Treaty of 1936 in a vain attempt to recover the Sudan and the Suez Canal. What occurred, quite simply, was that in undertaking policies which exceeded their power internationally they fell prey to local opponents. Nor can one assume that the imperial power will always understand the needs of its foreign collaborators. Britain inadvertently threatened the Jordanian monarchy by its invitation to join the Baghdad Pact in the spring of 1955. And Britain ultimately destroyed the regime of its faithful Iraqi friend Nuri Pasha as Said as one of the prices it paid for the invasion of Suez. On the other hand, groups one might not expect to lead determined nationalist movements do succeed, as the survival of the Moroccan monarchy attests. In this case the explanation seems to be that the king could count on the divisions among his local opponents to neutralize each other in his favor, while towards the French (and later the Americans) he was most conciliatory. These apparent exceptions to the ideal type seem rather to confirm the likelihood that rulers basing their power on traditional legitimacy or import–export revenues will be least ready to mobilize their peoples for wars of national liberation.[34]

In light of the foregoing analysis, what sorts of nationalist elites may be expected to enter into violent conflict with an imperial regime? Three situations tend to produce such leaders: where an elite dependent on the foreign power has never been created; where an elite once created is destroyed; where such an elite has been displaced by the rise of a rival political formation.

In the case of Algeria, a Muslim elite was simply never created which

[33] Colin Leys argues that the British effectively created such an elite in Kenya in the few years before their departure. See his *Underdevelopment in Kenya: The Political Economy of Neo-Colonialism, 1964–1971* (University of California, 1974).

[34] This suggests that Elliot Berg's influential analysis of the economic limits on political choice in French West Africa after 1945 (article, *op. cit.*) is too narrow since it fails to distinguish the political and social variables of poverty. Were he correct, were economic need so decisive politically, Algeria would never have had its revolution.

depended for its position on the good favor of the French. The role of local native elite was pre-empted by the settlers. As a result, the rise of an important Frenchified Muslim class failed to occur, and it became increasingly likely as the twentieth century progressed that the terrible grievances of the Muslim peasantry would be directly expressed against the French instead of being mediated by a native bourgeoisie. To be sure, there were the various bourgeois movements associated with Ferhat Abbas and Doctor Bendjelloul which had a certain activity from the mid-1920s until the mid-1940s. But these never created any ties with the masses. In retrospect, they must be seen as highly visible but politically insignificant compared to the efforts of Messali Hadj and the Reformist Muslim Ulama who gave a popular base to opposition to the French. Once the revolution began in November 1954, the French sought desperately for some group with authority with whom they could negotiate a settlement on better terms than those held out by the National Liberation Front (FLN). None was found, partly because the history of rigged elections served to stigmatize any Algerian who worked with the French as their puppet, but more importantly because the class of people who might have seen their future interests tied to France and who might have feared a radical peasant uprising just did not exist in any important number.[35]

In the case of Indochina, a nationalist elite which might have had an interest in cooperating with the French after 1945 was destroyed. Here the decisive factor was the Japanese Occupation. As George M. Kahin and John W. Lewis write:

Japan's role in Indochina was radically different from her occupation of any other Southeast Asian country. In the rest of the colonies there, the Japanese realized the advantage of working through the native elites, whom they regarded as more satisfactory instruments of administration than Western colonial civil servants. In order to secure the support of the educated indigenous groups in these other areas, the Japanese were obliged to grant them concessions. . . . The one great exception was Indochina. There the pro-Vichy French administration was willing to come to terms with the Japanese. . . . Thus, during the war the major channel open to those Vietnamese who wished to free their country from Japanese, and ultimately French, control was an underground movement where Vietnamese communists already had a strong and entrenched position.[36]

Other developments contributed to making it difficult to find a local counterweight to the Communists after 1945. Economically, the French presence in the 1930s had rested on the investments of a number of large capitalist firms like Michelin, the activities of a Chinese merchant class (with their families totaling perhaps 4 percent of the country's population),

[35] Tony Smith, *The French Stake in Algeria, 1945–1962* (Cornell University Press, forthcoming, 1978).

[36] George M. Kahin and John W. Lewis, *The United States in Vietnam* (Dial Press, 1967), pp. 14–15.

94 TONY SMITH

and the influence of a few thousand wealthy landowners whose property for the most part was located in the Mekong Delta.[37] In addition, between 1929 and 1932, the French had liquidated the most important non-Communist opposition to their rule when a combination of the Tan Viet and the Viet Nam Quoc Dan Dang had risen against them. Despite the simultaneous suppression of Communist insurgents in Nghe-Tinh province in 1930–1, the ICP proved far more resilient than their fellow Vietnamese nationalists. Thus the economic base on which a collaborating nationalist elite might stand was exceedingly narrow, while politically the French repressions of the thirties and the Occupation of the early forties worked to the advantage of the Communists.

While these considerations suggest that the French presence in Southeast Asia would have to be drastically modified after 1945, one is not warranted to conclude immediately that a Communist-sponsored peasant revolution would necessarily triumph there ultimately. For the congeries of political forces existing in Vietnam that the Communists did not control—the Catholics, the Cao Dai, the Hoa Hao, and perhaps even the Buddhists—might have been welded together with other potentially anti-Communist forces to split the union of communism with nationalism. Thus, had the French seriously backed Bao Dai in 1947 and granted his demands for the unity and independence of Vietnam as they apparently debated doing, Cochin China might effectively have been denied to Ho Chi Minh and in the process the Cambodian monarchy preserved. Paris could have counted on the threat from the north to persuade Bao Dai to limit his claims to sovereignty in favor of a veiled French presence. However much one may admire the Communist-led Vietnamese Liberation Movement, it does not do justice to its achievement to assume its victory was somehow inevitable. In Malaya, where admittedly the Communists were in a more difficult situation for a variety of reasons than their counterparts in Vietnam, a crucial part of the final British success was their willingness to respect the independent power base of Tengku Abdul Rahman, head of the Alliance Party associating Malays with Chinese, in order to crush the insurgents. Perhaps the 'Bao Dai formula' would have failed whatever the French position, for as the preceding analysis showed the social structure there was not favorable to the French return. But one must be cautious not to confuse the political predispositions of a particular structure with a necessary historical outcome.

A comparison of Indochina with Indonesia is instructive at this point since the chief differences between the two areas seem to be more political than economic or social if one is interested in evaluating the possibilities for a Communist-led revolution there. For Indonesia in the 1930s had, if

[37] John T. McAlister, Jr., *Viet Nam: The Origins of Revolution* (Knopf, 1969), chap. 6; and Joseph Buttinger, *Vietnam: a Political History* (Praeger, 1968) chap. 9.

anything, a greater percentage of landless peasants than Indochina, while
the Dutch plantations and Chinese merchant class effectively stifled the
growth of an indigenous middle class.[38] Moreover, Communism had come
to Indonesia earlier than to any other country of Asia and Africa, and had
quickly made an important place for itself in local politics.

The obstacles to Communist success in Indonesia as compared to
Indochina seem to me to have been essentially political. First, the
Indonesian Communist Party (PKI) showed very bad timing in the
uprisings it staged. Whereas in Indochina it was especially the non-Communist nationalists who destroyed themselves in rising against the French
before the Second World War, the PKI revolt of 1926–7 effectively set the
Party back for over a decade while other nationalist organizations, more
reluctant to use force, were gathering strength. During the war, the PKI
entered into a United Front with other nationalists against both the Dutch
and the Japanese. But their attempted coup against the Hatta–Sukarno
Government in the fall of 1948, at the very moment a large Dutch force was
preparing an offensive against the nationalists, earned them the perpetual
mistrust of many of their erstwhile allies. Second, Tokyo's toleration of
Indonesian nationalism during the Occupation denied the Communists
hope of controlling through the underground resistance either the
country's great nationalist hero Sukarno or, more important, the bulk of
those Indonesians given military training first by the Dutch and then by the
Japanese. After the defeat of Japan, therefore, non-Communist Indonesian
nationalists enjoyed an autonomy in organizational and military terms
unknown to their Indochinese counterparts. Finally, after a determined
effort to reoccupy the Islands, the Dutch accepted United Nations, and
especially American, pressure, and in 1949 conceded independence to the
area. Had the Indonesians been obliged to fight as the Indochinese were, it
is conceivable the PKI might have been resurgent.[39] To sum up this
argument, Communism in Indonesia was not defeated by the predispositions of the country's social structure, which rather encouraged its
development, so much as by a series of fortuitous political developments.

[39] I have been unable to find a comparative study of Communist organization in
Indonesian and Vietnamese villages.

[38] George Kahin estimates that by 1925, perhaps half the families on Java and Madura
(together accounting for two-thirds of the country's population) were landless and that this
percentage increased during the 1930s. Françoise Cayrac-Blanchard puts the landless there at
60 percent of the population in the early 1970s. Apparently a combination of communal
mutual aid, strong patron–client relations, and the existence of two opposed tendencies of
Islam combined to discourage class conflict at the village level. See Kahin, *Nationalism and
Revolution in Indonesia* (Cornell 1952), pp. 17 ff; Cayrac-Blanchard, *Le parti communiste
indonesien* (Colin, 1973) pp. 33–4; Clifford Geertz, *The Religion of Java* (Chicago, 1960), pp.
127 ff; Ruth McVey, 'The Social Roots of Indonesian Communism' (speech published by the
Centre d'Etude du Sud-Est Asiatique et de l'Extrême-Orient, l'Université Libre de Bruxelles);
and Rex Mortimer, 'Class, Social Cleavage, and Indonesian Communism', *Indonesia*, no. 8,
October 1969 (Cornell).

96 TONY SMITH

Had the French been able to engineer a functionally similar set of circumstances—and it does not seem to me beyond the realm of the historically possible that this might have happened—Cochin China and Cambodia might have been kept from Communist control with relatively small involvement on the part of the French and Americans.

There is a third type of situation in which a nationalist elite may be expected to oppose the colonial order on the basis of its local power position. This is the case of a national manufacturing bourgeoisie whose rise displaces the previously dominant elite in the name of tariffs to protect their young industries and for the sake of more rational agricultural production to feed the urban proletariat and increase rural demand for manufactured goods. Such a situation is illustrated by India. Here the alliance of the peasantry and the rising urban bourgeoisie brought about by Gandhi after 1920 through the vehicle of the National Congress Party created the force which eventually would evince the British.[40] The roots of this manufacturing bourgeoisie lay in the 1850s in the textile mills of Bombay and the jute industry of Calcutta. The *Swadeshi* movement beginning in 1905 over the British decision to partition Bengal involved a boycott of British goods in favor of domestic products, so demonstrating to this bourgeoisie in tangible terms the utility of nationalism. But the period of greatest expansion for this group began after the First World War when the British permitted the first important protective tariffs for India since it was increasingly the Japanese who were profiting from the subcontinent's low custom duties.[41]

At the same time the Indian manufacturing bourgeoisie was gaining strength, Gandhi was effectively extending the nationalist creed to the Indian peasantry. His greatest success initially was his 1920 program of 'full non-cooperation' with the constitution of 1919, but he gained still wider support in the early 1930s with his world famous campaigns of civil disobedience. However much Gandhi may have inveighed against the evils of the modern world, preached the rights of Untouchables, and promoted the interests of factory workers, Barrington Moore, Jr. seems correct to stress that his respect for property rights and insistence on non-violence gave the Indian industrialists no serious cause for alarm. At the same time Gandhi provided the ideological vehicle whereby the peasantry and manufacturing elite could join forces.[42]

Indian specialists seem agreed that had the British not granted independence to the subcontinent within the first few years after the end of

[40] The significance this alliance for the political development of India is given central importance by Barrington Moore, Jr., *Social Origins of Dictatorship: Lord and Peasant in the Making of the Modern World* (Beacon, 1966), pp. 370 ff.

[41] Angus Maddison, *Class Structure and Economic Growth: India and Pakistan since the Moghuls* (George Allen & Unwin Ltd., 1971), chap. 3.

[42] Moore, *op. cit.*, pp. 373 ff.

the Second World War, there would have been a revolution.[43] The
Congress Party declared its militancy clearly in its 1942 Quit India
Resolution, and the incidents of the interwar years combined with scattered
disturbances in the military immediately after the surrender of Japan to
make British minds turn once again to memories of the Great Mutiny of
1857. India would be done with the British.

Nevertheless, it is not clear that the organization of interests which
ultimately brought India to independence would have maintained their
hold on the country had an intense revolution of long duration been
necessary. For not only was there the serious problem of minorities,
especially the Muslims, there was a destitute class of peasants as well whom
revolution would doubtless rouse to political activity. An official study of
landholding in India (exclusive of Pakistan) in 1953–4, found that 23
percent of the rural households were landless, another 24 percent owned
less than one acre, while 14 percent owned between 1 and 2.5 acres.[44] One
may legitimately speculate in these circumstances on the fate of the 3.5
percent of the population which was reported (in what was certainly an
underestimate of their property since the census was part of an effort to
reduce large holdings) to own 36 percent of the land. As it was:

India has been governed since independence by a coalition consisting of the
bureaucratic-military establishment, which implements policy, the big business
groups, which have backed Congress financially, the rank and file politicians who
mainly represent the rural squirearchy and richer peasants, and the intellectuals
who articulate policy . . . [Nehru] was a leftist flanked by conservatives who knew
from experience that it was not worth opposing progressive resolutions or
legislation which were not likely to be implemented.[45]

The case of India presents us, then, with a nationalist elite which would
surely have hesitated long before launching into revolution but which gave
every indication of pursuing such a course should the British prove
obstinate and refuse to grant independence. It is to the credit of British
statesmen that they could view the changed status of such an important
possession so realistically and attempt as best they could to harmonize their
interests with the future of a country which for over a century had been the
base of their foreign policy from the Mediterranean to China.

The foregoing case studies offer examples of a spectrum of colonial
responses to the maintenance of European rule after 1945, ranging from
militant revolutionary opposition to the call for independence within the
framework of a continuing European presence. They are not intended to
establish rigid, predicitve models for the likelihood of colonial uprisings,

---

[43] See, among others, Francis Hutchins, *India's Revolution: Gandhi and the Quit India Movement* (Harvard, 1973).

[44] Maddison, *op. cit.*, p. 106; Moore, *op. cit.*, pp. 368 ff.

[45] Maddison, *op. cit.*, p. 89; Moore, *op. cit.*, pp. 385 ff.

98   TONY SMITH

but to establish instead a heuristic typology. The factor which this study suggests should be most closely analyzed is the place the momentarily predominant elite occupies in respect to the double challenge it faces: from the international system and from local rivals. Import–export elites and traditional rulers are threatened in both respects and are well-advised to moderate their nationalist demands in order to assure continued foreign support for their regimes. On the other hand, a national manufacturing elite allied with rural forces representing more than a handful of great landlords is clearly more able to press its autonomous claims. But it must avoid if possible the radical suggestion to push for an all-out war of national liberation since it should recognize that the radicals intend to take advantage of popular mobilization not only to oust the foreigners, but to create a revolution from below and be done with them as well. By this same token, the most militant elite will be one which fears no local rivals—since none exists to any politically significant degree—and at the same time sees the outsiders with whom it must deal as the inveterate enemy of its most essential demands.

In this respect, Algeria and Indochina were idiosyncratic in the challenge they posed to France. These two colonies simply had no genuine parallels in the British experience. Kenya might be thought comparable to Algeria, but in essential respects this was not the case. For how could this relatively insignificant East African land be the equivalent to the British of what Algeria meant to France: the home of more than 2 percent of the national population; the location of badly needed petroleum resources; and a strategic outpost of France whose capital, Algiers, was only 500 miles southwest of Marseille? It was largely because Kenya was so unimportant that the British could arrange for the sale of the European farms at full value to the Africans and so create, virtually overnight, an export elite on whom they could base their post-independence relations.[46] In Algeria, on the contrary, the incomparably more powerful settler presence negated any attempt to create a politically important Muslim bourgeoisie. Nor could the French copy the example of the Republic of South Africa and cut themselves off from their North African territory. This was not because of 'centralizing traditions', but because, unlike South Africa, Algeria was far too poor for a small minority of the population to maintain its rule without constant aid from the outside. For these reasons—which had to do with Algeria and not with France—withdrawal was especially difficult. Had the French had the experience and institutions of the British it is not evident they would have responded to the crisis more ably.

The comparison between Indochina and Malaya is more ambiguous. But the relatively greater strength of the non-Communists after 1945 in Malaya combined with a British willingness to work with them to weld

[46] Colin Leys, *op. cit.*

them into a nationalist force capable of beating the insurgents. The British started with more advantages than the French and worked with them more skillfully.

The one celebrated instance where British policy failed was with Nasser. This is generally interpreted in the literature as a release of pent-up emotions over Britain's declining world role, but perhaps instead it is the one case where London shared the bad fortune plaguing Paris and found itself up against an anti-colonial leader with whom it could not strike a bargain. Indeed the major setback to Britain in decolonization occurred in relation to its 'informal empire' in the Middle East. The first challenge had come when Prime Minister Mossadegh nationalized the British petroleum holdings in Iran. 'He had never been very amenable to reason, and lately it had been necessary to humor him as with a fractious child', writes then Foreign Secretary Anthony Eden in his memoirs about this 'megalomaniac', 'Old Mossy'.[47] In this confrontation, Britain had ultimately got its way, but not before being obliged to call the United States to its rescue and paying a certain price in the form of a condominium agreement on Iranian oil.

Nasser's seizure of the Suez Canal in 1956, three years after the fall of Mossadegh, seemed if anything more menacing to Eden who had now become prime minister. 'A man with Colonel Nasser's record could not be allowed to "have his thumb on our windpipe",' Eden declared:

Some say that Nasser is not Hitler or Mussolini. Allowing for a difference in scale, I am not so sure. He has followed Hitler's pattern, even to concentration camps and the propagation of *Mein Kampf* among his officers. He has understood and used Goebbels' pattern of propaganda in all its lying ruthlessness. Egypt's strategic position increases the threat to others from any aggressive militant dictatorship there.[48]

The greatest threat Nasser represented was the undermining of the weak, Western-oriented Arab elites of the Middle East—Libya, Saudia Arabia, Iraq, Jordan and Lebanon as well as the sheikdoms of the Persian Gulf—so monopolizing the region's petroleum reserves. Eden felt that this also would permit Russia a foothold in the area, and even endanger the British territories in East and Central Africa.[49] Whatever the reality of this belief, Suez—and indeed the decline of British fortunes in the Middle East altogether—was the most damaging of its global withdrawals.

It is, then, not enough to compare policy formulation in London and Paris in order to explain the pattern of postwar European decolonization. Whatever the advantages held by the British in terms of international place, domestic political institutions, and the legacy of imperial traditions and

---

[47] Anthony Eden, *op. cit.*, p. 230.   [48] *Ibid.*, pp. 474, 481.

[49] Elizabeth Monroe, *Britain's Moment in the Middle East, 1914–1956* (Johns Hopkins, 1963) chap. 4; Harold Macmillan, *Riding the Storm: 1956–1959* (Macmillan, 1971), chap. 16.

procedures, a comparative analysis must be made as well of the colonial situations over which the Europeans ruled after 1945 in order to conceptualize this historical process adequately. For the pattern of decolonization was decisively shaped by the character of the nationalist elites the European presence helped to produce in their overseas territories.

CONCLUSION

This essay has maintained that if a host of factors conspired to force an end to European overseas empires after 1945, the Europeans could nevertheless significantly influence this process in most cases by their attention to grooming their successors. For virtually every nationalist movement harbored a civil war whose divisions allowed the colonial authority a strong voice in local affairs. By deciding with whom they would negotiate, by what procedure they would institutionalize the transfer of power, and over what territory the new regime would rule, Paris and London decisively influenced the course of decolonization.

In order to exploit the genuine power they had in these circumstances, the Europeans had to have the experience and the institutions to maneuver adroitly in the colonial setting, and the political wisdom to respect the limits of their abilities, to know what they could not hope to accomplish. In this respect, the British had substantial advantages over the French in four regards: their imperial traditions had given them a preference for 'informal empire' and had furnished them with an established procedure for the devolution of power; their close links with the United States let them view the changing world order with guarded optimism; their domestic political institutions demonstrated an ability to handle issues of this magnitude with relative dispatch; and, except for Suez (where intervention by the United States and the Soviet Union could be blamed) their use of force was restricted to situations where it could be realistically expected to achieve reasonable ends.

If it is possible to conceptualize separately these influences on the process of decolonization, it is nonetheless their close interrelationship which becomes apparent as soon as a specific case is studied. Consider, for example, the conflicts in French Algeria and Indochina. Even though, as we have seen, the social structures of these two countries predisposed them to a revolutionary break with France after 1945, it was surely not inevitable that local factors would preclude a peaceful devolution of power: France was not locked into conflict by some iron law of structural necessity. In regard to Indochina, the French might have decided not to return in force to Southeast Asia, but to make arrangements with Ho Chi Minh for the orderly transfer of sovereignty with special safeguards for certain French interests in the area. Or, alternatively, Paris might have pursued the 'Bao

Dai formula' more realistically and so had a reasonable chance of preserving its authority in a new form in Cochin China and Cambodia. By way of comparison, British Malaya and especially the Netherlands East Indies had structural predispositions roughly comparable to Indochina, yet a combination of political factors discouraged Communist takeovers there.

A similar argument can be made for Algeria. In retrospect, it appears evident that Algeria would have become independent of France sometime after 1945. The economic, social and political history of the country was tending in this direction since the turn of the century, and international events served to confirm the process. But is it absurd to speculate that had the French been able to maneuver more wisely—had, for example, the Algerian Statute of 1947 been a genuine home-rule bill somewhat along the lines proposed *at the time* by the Muslim bourgeoisie and the French Communist Party—the base might have been laid for a ruling elite there eager to work in collaboration with Paris?

In other words, it is conceivable that the Indochinese and Algerian revolutions might have been avoided. Although an analysis of the structural features of the two countries internationally and internally shows them to have been particularly prone to a revolutionary break with France after 1945, the room for political artistry in the immediate aftermath of the war seems to have been adequate to permit other developments. Admittedly all things were not possible: a political break with France was well-nigh inevitable. But the form this break would take and, in consequence, the nationalist elite independence would tend to confirm in power, might have been different. That these alternate paths were not taken by the French sends us back to the other factors under consideration: to their imperial traditions, to their international place after 1945, and to the logic of their political institutions and the opinions of their political elites.

The multiplicity of factors entering into the course of postwar decolonization calls forth a last remark. There can be the terrible temptation to try to simplify such a multiform process, either by exalting one consideration over all others or by trying to force the particular case into what seems to be a general movement or pattern. Certainly decolonization acquired an international momentum, and it is possible to isolate certain variables which seem to have had a marked influence on its progress regardless of time or place. But the various colonial areas were not dominoes responding to some inevitable 'historical tidal wave of nationalism' any more than the European governments had a set response to every colonial challenge whatever its nature. Nationalism in each case had its local pedigree and its own internal tensions composed of unique constellations of class, ethnic and regional alignments. So, too, different governments in Paris and London acted in noticeably different fashions. In this sense, there were

102   TONY SMITH

multiple decolonizations, whose discontinuities, ambiguities, and uniqueness must be respected, however much they may interfere with the desire to
reduce history to a crystalline pattern, to discover a single formula which
makes sense of its complexity. If this essay has been an attempt to arrive at
some general propositions about postwar decolonization, it has also been
written with the knowledge that from the position of the specific case,
generalizations always run a bit too smoothly. But the model for the
analysis of the end of European overseas empire may be taken from the rich
and ever-growing literature on its earlier expansion. Here particular case
studies are informed by a generally recognized body of more comprehensive propositions which in turn are constantly reevaluated in light of new
information. The historiography of decolonization today lacks this fruitful
exchange. Its present task is to elaborate a comparative framework for
historical analysis and so to tie specific cases to the general movement of
European decolonization.

[2]

Imperial Hangovers: Belgium — The Economics of Decolonization

Jean-Philippe Peemans

The following essay tries to assess the impact of the decolonization process on what could be called the 'Belgian power structure', that is to say, the specific type of equilibrium between social and political forces which is a feature of that country and also has economic roots. This already difficult task is further complicated by the absence of a synthetic study on the historical development of Belgian society.

It is true to say that 1960 saw the end of an era. But at the same time, contrary to some forecasts which exaggerated the economic importance of the Congo to the metropolis, the decolonization process had no economic consequences for Belgium. The colony was very important, but at a more subtle level. For example, despite its weakness in trading relations with the metropolis, it contributed significantly to the massive profits made by joint stock companies in Belgium itself. This leads to the question of how much influence was exerted by the colonial system upon the structures of economic power inside Belgium. And from there, one is led to examine the interplay between that economic power and other social and political powers.

To this end it is necessary to outline how, in turn, the colonial system, the decolonization process and post-colonial relations influenced or altered the interplay between the different elements of the Belgian 'power structure'.

The colonization of the Congo was a rather hazardous answer to general problems stemming from the contradictions in the in-

Journal of Contemporary History (SAGE, London and Beverly Hills), Vol. 15 (1980), 257-86

dustrialization process. If Belgian industrialization got off to a very quick start, it was because of an extraordinary combination of factors: the ability to transfer the labour-saving techniques of the British 'industrial revolution' to the continental country with the lowest level of wages due to an unlimited supply of cheap labour, the availability of a European market thanks to its integration within the French Empire, which was itself at the same time a large buyer for military purposes, and a large supply of the raw materials required by current technology.[1] Thus from the beginning there was a contradiction, because the element, cheap labour, which was favourable for profit and rapid accumulation, was at the same time unfavourable to the development of a mass demand and a large national market for finished products. It resulted in a heavy dependency on foreign markets and in specializing in exports of semi-finished products.[2]

So on one hand, Belgian industry developed with capital-intensive enterprises in the mining and metal industries, located mainly in the southern part of the country (around 1900, 1 percent of enterprises, mainly joint stock companies, employed 50 percent of the workers), and on the other hand, there was an overwhelming majority of small-scale enterprises, using labour-intensive techniques, and largely oriented to the national market.[3]

The disparity between these two types of industries was still more accentuated by the heavy financial backing given to the large enterprises. Most of them were controlled by financial holdings, which monopolized the credit system, hampering the growth of small-scale enterprises. The greatest of these holdings, the *Société Générale de Belgique*, with its subsidiaries, controlled 40 percent of bank assets from 1850 to 1914.[4]

There were, of course, links between these features of the economic structure and certain elements of the socio-political structure. At the time of independence, the State was controlled by an alliance of the different factions of the francophone bourgeoisie in a system where less than five percent of the adult population had the right to vote. If there was a certain amount of agreement between these factions in order to maintain their privileges and common control of the State, there were also differences expressed in the rivalries between Catholics and Liberals. The catholic bourgeoisie, which was very conservative and strongly opposed to the ideas of the French revolution, was mainly a traditional, land-owning bourgeoisie, close to the nobility, and opposed to a rapid industrialization which could endanger the social order. They largely controlled the countryside, both as landowners and also through the Church, which was in effect an organ of the State, and controlled the education and welfare networks. The liberal bourgeoisie was largely industrial, influenced by the moderate tendencies of the French Revolution, and advocated a policy of free trade and complete economic liberalism.[5]

Ideological conflicts were important in terms of power politics. Understandably the Catholics, who controlled the popular masses through their existing authoritarian and paternalistic social institutions, unlike the liberals who had almost no such power base, were fiercely opposed to any measure which would encroach upon their control over potential popular votes, while the Liberals tried to extend State action in the fields controlled by the Catholics in order to weaken this monopoly. In that struggle for influence, it was the political future of these different sections of the bourgeoisie which was at stake. These ideological struggles continued while those in the field of economics gradually died out between 1850 and 1870, a period of rapid economic growth, during which financial investment in the large industries increased, mainly through the *Société Générale*. Many of its old and new stockholders, most of whom belonged to landed families, thus became less resistant to an accelerated industrial growth, as it was for them an alternative means of increasing the return on their capital, as opposed to investing it in agriculture. At the same time, the increase in the industrial area controlled by the holding company progressively brought together the interests of stockholders, managers and entrepreneurs, Catholic as well as Liberal.[6]

Thus by 1880, there was some tendency towards fusing the economic interests of the Catholic and Liberal sections of the bourgeoisie, but the ideological conflict continued to play an important part, mainly because the Catholic ruling classes retained their nostalgia for the 'golden age' when they had had a monopoly over the cultural and social life of the masses.[7]

In the last twenty years of the nineteenth century, the dominant but conflicting partnership of two sections of the bourgeoisie began to be challenged in the economic as well as in the political field. It was a period of difficult economic adjustment marked by a high rate of technical progress in the industries launched by the first industrial revolution. Belgian traditional industries had to struggle to maintain a normal rate of profit in a context of high international competition and low prices. This development occurred at the precise moment when newly-organized trade unions and workers' movements were trying to increase their level of wages and better their living standards. Despite a fierce resistance to these movements, the entrepreneurs were obliged to make concessions with consequent pressure on profits on capital investment.

There were two ways in which profits could be maintained or increased. The first way was to manufacture new products using new techniques. This path was followed in some countries then entering the second Industrial Revolution and able to accelerate their capital accumulation. Belgian industries largely missed that turning-point, probably because it required risky long-term investments. On the contrary, the financial groups tried to minimize risks, as the majority of their stockholders looked to industrial investment for greater security than could be obtained from land investment and also because their managers were mainly skilled engineers attached to the techniques and industries they had traditionally mastered.

The second way was to find a more favourable environment in which to exploit the old techniques; for example, in places with lower wages, and in countries trying to develop the techniques already mastered by Belgian industry. In both cases there were new opportunities to improve profits. That second method was largely followed by the Belgian financial groups which sponsored new investments in railways, mining and metallurgy in Russia, China and the Middle East.

It was in this search to find new fields of profitable investment that the colonization of the Congo took place. It is very clear that to start with this colonization did not obey any economic logic, as that part of Africa was looked on as an enormous vacuum by the financial groups interested by the new developing countries. There was absolutely no encouragement from them for the colonization of that part of Africa. The Congolese adventure began as a political initiative undertaken by King Leopold II, who was both a monarch anxious to defend the vital interests of his country which he ruled with scornful benevolence, and a man who regarded the new continents with the eyes of a merchant adventurer of old. He was indeed a kind of business tycoon well adapted to the problems of his time.

This is not the place to study in depth the role of a man who is still a figure of controversy and who aroused so much fascination and so much hatred. Nevertheless, his role was crucial if only because he built a state apparatus in the colony which had all the features of the mercantilist epoch (monopoly of exploitation of the natural resources, extreme harshness of the methods used to mobilize manpower resources, confusion between private and public uses of State money), while at the same time he largely utilized resources provided by that policy of 'primitive accumulation' to lay down the infrastructure which prepared the ground for profitable investment. After twenty years of rather painful efforts, he had financed not only the external economies required by further investments, i.e. the construction of railways and the use of waterways, but he had also largely financed the expeditions which led to the discovery of rich deposits of non-ferrous metal in Katanga.[8]

From that moment onwards Belgian financial groupings actively participated in the colonial undertaking. They were granted very large privileges, though always in close partnership with the State. It is interesting to note that in 1910, less than four years after the large penetration of these financial interests in the colonial economy through the founding of the UMHK and other large companies, State monopolies were suppressed. After a short period of hesitation about which plolicy to follow, a very clear tendency of close cooperation between the colonial administration and the finance companies progressively emerged after the first world war. The administration used its full powers, through different kinds of constraints and pressures in order to undertake large public works, to mobilize a large volume of cheap manpower for the mines, the large plantations, and to foster exports. There was indeed a systematic bias in policy, which limited and hampered the development of petty traders and settlers in order to keep the manpower resources available for undertakings sponsored by the State or by the finance companies.

During that period, the latter completely reversed their attitudes towards operations abroad. Investments in other parts of the world, which were so important before the first world war, vanished almost completely. The reasons were evident: e.g. the experience of the Russian Revolution, Chinese instability in the twenties, and gave an impression of great insecurity, which constrasted sharply with the oasis of peace prevailing in the colony.[9] At the same time, the control of mining, plantations and transport in the Congo provided high returns which also contrasted with the difficulties and slow growth of the traditional metropolitan industries. Thus the financial interests, through their holding companies, were able to

262   *Journal of Contemporary History*

compensate between low and high profit undertakings which alleviated some of the problems of the aged Belgian industrial structure. Increasingly, these financial groups developed activities inside the colony and dominated its economy completely. At the beginning of the thirties it was estimated by a Senatorial commission that three-quarters of the assets of the colony belonged to four Belgian holding companies. Among them, the *Société Générale* held almost two-thirds of these assets.[10]

However, the economic dominance of these holding companies and the benefits therefrom were not separated from other features of the colonial system. This system as it developed in the interwar years was one in which de facto power stemmed from a narrow cooperation between three agents of social control: the colonial administration, the large enterprises sponsored by the finance houses, and the Catholic Church. Together, they devised a development policy which closely related the defence of their own particular interests with the elaboration of a rather complicated colonial doctrine, supposedly aimed at promoting the indigenous society to a state of 'civilization', which they had the right both to define and impose. That right was indeed the root of their de facto power, because the de jure power of control, that is to say Parliament, the Government and especially the Ministry of Colonies, recognized their special ability to master the specific problems of colonial policy. The colonial administration was the base of this triangle. In it was invested the right to control the indigenous population; the Catholic Church was recognized as having a special role in the field of morality and in the education of the colonized population, even by its adversaries in the metropolis; and finally, the finance companies, not least for the profits accruing to the metropolis, were given a free hand to control resources which were of vital interest to the colonial power.[11]

From this collaboration and the de facto acceptance of the autonomy of administration, Church and finance companies in the colony, there emerged a specific colonial social order which was jealously guarded and insulated from the social and political norms that applied in the metropolis. There was also a high degree of mobility between the administration and business interests. The fact that high-ranking colonial civil servants could expect to end their careers with a position inside one or other of the finance companies cemented the bonds between these two institutions. The third one, i.e. the colonial Church, was greatly strengthened by the fact that a large majority of the colonial élite were Catholics.[12] Catholics had an influence in the colonial system which was proportionately much greater than their influence at home.

A consequence of this situation was the Church's tendency to apply to the colonial situation the principles of the authoritarian paternalism its predecessors had longed to impose in the nineteenth century to solve the 'social question' inside the metropolis. All the features of that ideology were present and reinforced in the colonial context: the limitation of teaching to elementary and professional schools, the promotion of civic and moral behaviour through work and discipline and healthy leisure activities, the training of women for household tasks to protect the family, etc.[13]

The aim was to apply this model to society as a whole, but the lack of means limited its application to only some social groupings like the large mining enterprises. But there it was propagated at a high level of 'totalitarian' paternalism; the education of individuals, the regulation of social life all being closely linked with the search for higher productivity from the workers. That interplay of the economic, social and political elements of the colonial power system was all pervasive, and the colony was a privileged area insulated from all the movements which, in the metropolis, had progressively reduced the hegemony of the traditional ruling classes. The colonial system of power also prevented the development of trade unions, even among European workers. Similarly, it was largely able to eliminate competition from small and middle-scale settler enterprises. It is noteworthy that this supremacy of the finance houses upon the colonial economy was denounced for the first time during the thirties, precisely by those parliamentary representatives of middle-ranking enterprises, especially Flemish ones, who at the same time criticized the monopoly exerted on the credit system in Belgium itself by these finance houses.

This well illustrates one of the effects of the colonial system on the metropolitan social and political arena. Because the colony was an insulated region free from the political pressures brought about in Belgium by the rise of working-class movements, an area where capital could be accumulated with a minimum of institutional constraints, it strengthened, socially and politically, those groups in the metropolis which controlled the colonial system. They benefitted both indirectly and directly from the higher profits realized from the colonial economy.

They exerted total economic and political control in the Congo, and justified their untramelled power in terms of the needs imposed by the 'colonial reality'. The same justification could be and was advocated in the metropolis in order to foster a sense of colonial responsibility. Such a responsibility implied not only that the colony had to be protected from reforms which were socially and politically divisive inside the metropolis itself, but also that the defence of colonial interests required unity in the metropolis, especially united support for those actively engaged in the colonial adventure.

In short, its control of colonial affairs meant that the traditional right, mainly francophone, Catholic and unitarian, could maintain a dominating influence in Belgium, far greater than otherwise would have been the case. This occurred precisely at a time when its power was being challenged on many fronts, not only from the socialists, but also from the rising new Flemish bourgeoisie, which at the end of the twenties tried to assert its financial autonomy and to conquer leading positions in the State apparatus.[14]

It was in fact a very subtle struggle of power. The francophone Catholics, from the beginning of the 1920s a political minority in the southern part of the country, in face of the rising of the Socialist party, needed the support of the Flemish Catholics who controlled the majority of the popular votes in Flanders, through their populist programme aimed at defending the Flemish community as a whole against francophone supremacy, without class distinction. Such a programme was a powerful tool in the hands of the rising Flemish bourgeoisie which was at the same time an ally and a new rival for the control of the State. In this difficult struggle, the defence of the colonial heritage with its patriotic overtones was a good card to play to promote the status quo in a unitarian state structure.

The second world war reinforced the autonomy of the colonial power system, as the State had almost no means of exerting control, neither through its metropolitan administration, nor through its government in exile in London. The first period following the second world war did not reduce that large autonomy. At the same time, during most of the fifties, Congolese enterprises continued to provide an average rate of profit higher than their metropolitan counterparts controlled by the same financial holdings.[15] Thus they masked the deep structural problems of Belgian industry. Consequently, the control of colonial assets continued to give the finance companies greater facilities for the accumulation and distribution of profits than the situation of their metropolitan enterprises would normally have allowed.

Coming now to the process of decolonization between 1955 and 1960, it is essential to emphasize the great importance that their control of the colonial resources still had for the big financial holdings in Belgium.

The most remarkable feature after the second world war was that these financial groups could simultaneously secure highly profitable investments in the Congo and yet protect that privileged area from the interference and political rivalries of the metropolis. They were at least to maintain that situation during the ten years from 1945 to 1955.

To achieve this, a new development policy was established inside the colony after the second world war. This policy was undertaken by the 'enlightened' wing of the colonial administration, which recognized the reality of the 'social question' inside the colony, i.e. that section of the administration which was sensitive to the sharpening of social tensions among different categories of the African population at the end of the war, because influential in the decision-making process. Its objective was to eradicate the most salient features of the harshness of the manpower mobilization system (compulsory cultivation and too low agricultural prices, compulsory manpower recruitment, labour migration and too low wages), and to undertake the long-term stabilization of the colonial system.[16]

The new policy had three objectives. The first was the improvement of the living conditions of at least a section of the workers in the main cities and in the most important industries. The second was the development of a petty bourgeoisie of clerks, low-ranking civil servants, and teachers in the primary schools. They were supposed at the same time to become the instrument of an increasing apparatus of State control of the whole colonial society, and to have an increasing stake in the maintenance and development of the colonial system.[17] This urban petty-middle class would be complemented by the promotion of some peasants to the rank of small independent farmers, differentiated from the rest of the rural communities and encouraged to produce an agricultural surplus.[18] The third objective was the realization of a rather ambitious plan for a new infrastructure aimed at modernization and at sustaining the economic activities of the private sector for export or for the domestic market.

The achievement of these ends required an increase in the role of the colonial state and in the finances at its disposal, via increased taxes and borrowing. The framework was laid out in the first Ten Year Plan for the colony which appeared in1949. Its implementation was made easier by the huge increase in resources due to the booming Western demand for Congolese exports, up to the mid-fifties. This initiative by the colonial administration was not resisted by its two other partners and traditional pillars of the colonial order: the finance houses and the Catholic Church.

The finance houses were attracted first of all by the stabilization of the colonial system in order to ensure maximum security for their investments, and shared the conviction that the promotion of an indigenous middle class was the surest way to realize that goal. This is a conviction deeply entrenched in the consciousness of the Belgian bourgeoisie and was worked out in the metropolis itself from the end of the nineteenth century. At the same time, the promotion of an army of African workers and clerks was seen as a tool to maintain low costs in a growing economy which required more trained people, and as a device to check the pressures made by the European skilled workers, employees, and civil servants to improve their economic position, including the repeated efforts to organize trade unions aimed at the exclusive defence of European labour.

The finance houses were not opposed to an increase of direct and indirect labour costs, firstly because their industrial operations were more and more capital intensive, secondly because they were convinced that productivity increases required an improvement in the quality of labour. Their fear was that change might be too rapid, and they were ready to give support only to policies which kept a tight control over the pace of change, i.e. they wished to continue along their paternalistic and authoritarian way. There was again some parallel with the policy which had been pursued in Belgium: there, the protection of a stabilizing middle class could not lead them to compete with the activities controlled by the financial groups. The new conception gave fresh perspectives for action to the third traditional partner of the colonial order: the Catholic Church. Many missionaries had persistently criticized the crude system of manpower exploitation prevailing before, and they saw the legitimization of their presence and role in the colonial society precisely in terms of the promotion of a paternalistic mode of economic and social progress for the African masses. The new policy gave new opportunities for the development of social and educational services largely controlled by the Church. Thus, the policy received support from the main partners of the colonial system of power, and it was favoured by the excellent conditions prevailing on the international markets for Congolese exports.

The ten years following the war saw a large increase in the value of mineral and agricultural exports, which fostered an enlargement of the domestic market, sustained also by the increase in public spending: therefore there was a place for the beginning of an import substitution process for consumer good industries, and some intermediary goods. But this type of growth was heavily dependent on external factors, as many obstacles limited the expansion of mass demand. Among these obstacles the most important was, of course, the very uneven distribution of income between the European and African sectors of the colonial society. These disparities were increased by the acceleration of the accumulation, as is usual in such cases. At the same time, the gap was also widening between cities and rural areas. In the cities, growth was mainly the result of the European settlers and companies relying on an unlimited supply of cheap labour. They were the main sources of employment increases, as the growing capital intensity in the mining and industrial activities provoked a huge increase in productivity and sharp reductions in the employment levels. At the same time, most of the African rural sector was stagnant, despite the ambitious programme of the Administration.[19] The latter, in fact, encountered fierce resistance from the settlers in the rural areas, who were opposed to any measure which could improve the position of the African peasantry, because they feared that such improvement would reduce the manpower available, increase wages and create unfair competition for them. This crisis of the African peasantry tended to support a permanent migration to the cities, at a time when employment opportunities for unskilled labour were diminishing. But the tendency toward structural unemployment was not reflected in wage levels, because these were artificially protected by the Administrative measures.

Thus, underlying an apparent prosperity were deep structural problems, which, if not tackled in time, threatened serious social tensions and disruption. And in fact the Administration could not cope with the problem, pre-occupied as it was with the maintenance of a growing but stable administrative system. Even at that level, problems were new and enormous. The main problem was the mode of integration of the low-ranking African civil servants promoted since the end of the war. These people hoped that the system would be more and more open to their aspirations, and work on the basis of qualification without any race barriers.[20] They wanted to be integrated and recognized as indispensable for the development of the Congo.[21] Their hopes for promotion and respectability were nourished by official speeches about the future role of the indigenous élites in a very long process of modernization, which would finally lead to a kind of 'Belgian-Congolese Community'. This vaguely-defined concept was used at the beginning of the fifties to indicate that in the very distant future, some kind of association would exist between the metropolis and its colony. Neither the nature of this relationship nor the type of organization which would prevail in the Congo were precisely defined.[22] The idea was vague enough to sustain the hopes of promotion by the emerging African petty-bourgeoisie and at the same time provoke a reaction from the European minority to protect its privileges for the future. It also began to claim the attention of the metropolitan social and political groups, who became aware that they had to have some kind of presence in the colony. If the situation was evolving slowly toward a type of association, it could, of course, have consequences in Belgium itself: for instance if it was moving in the direction of a kind of parliamentary representation of the colonies in the metropolitan power system 'à la française'.

Thus in the Congo, there was on one side the European interests, mainly settlers, traders and low-ranking civil servants, who feared any change in the relations between the Europeans and Africans, and whose associations for the defence of European interests flourished under different names and banners, and on the other side there was the penetration of metropolitan organizations. Their action was often able to prevent or diminish the impact of measures aimed at the development and stabilization of an African middle class. Thus, this latter group was more and more frustrated in its hopes for promotion[23] and began to attach more importance to other ways of gaining some power, such as the development of ethnic associations in the large cities, which were at the same time the cradle of grass-roots politics under the cover of cultural activities.

On the other side, there was a slow but persistent penetration of metropolitan organizations inside the colony. That penetration was

Peemans: *Belgium — Economics of Decolonization*   269

made easier by the fact that a growing number of Europeans were entering the colony, not as settlers, but as temporary immigrants. Inevitably they were more sensitive to the patterns of metropolitan social and political life and offered fertile ground for the penetration of the metropolitan rules of the game inside the colony. Trade unions, like the Christian CSC and the Socialist FGTB, were extending their recruitment among the Europeans, even if all kinds of measures, including intimidation, were taken by employers to limit their influence.[24] Political circles inspired by the different metropolitan parties were also active, even if there was no question of their being transformed into political parties inside the Congo. It is typical that at this time, most metropolitan-inspired organizations hesitated between being exclusively reserved for European members or becoming mixed in one way or another.

This penetration of metropolitan politics was greatly accelerated by the measures taken by the liberal Minister of Colonies, Buisseret, to promote the development of the public education network and later, to liberalize the conditions for the creation of associations, among which were trade unions.[25] These measures were very important because, for the first time in colonial history, they openly introduced elements which played a great role in the political life of the metropolis but had been carefully rejected by the traditional partners of the colonial order as threatening the stability of the system. Their immediate application was very restricted, but their potential dynamic was enormous, especially in the perspective of the future development of a Belgian Congolese Community. Thus, the colonial system ceased to be a closed one and became open to external influences and ready to participate in the political interaction which regulated the power structure in Belgium. The decisions themselves clearly now indicated that the colony was a part of Belgian politics, as they could not be efficiently opposed by the traditional pillars of the colonial order. So the rules of the game were, of course, completely transformed, as the former dominant partners were losing their monopoly on the decision-making process and as the colony was no longer insulated from metropolitan political and social influences.

From that moment, the situation in the colony reflected the progressive change in the balance of power. On one side, there was a growing radicalization of the African petty bourgeoisie, more and more frustrated by the resistance of the European vested interests to its full integration into colonial institutions.[26] This radicalization

corresponded with a certain instability in the European community, insecure, but divided, about its future. On the other side, there
was a more and more overt penetration of metropolitan social and
political groupings into the colonial society. Even if for the moment they had no official place in the power structure, they were
developing their influence among the Europeans as well as among
the Africans, in order to be present at the evolution toward what
was seen as a kind of association between Belgium and the Congo.[27]

These movements of course escaped from the control of the traditional pillars of the colonial order, who clearly realized that these
developments threatened their power. Given the international context, the penetration of metropolitan politics was indeed not only
the way toward a possible take-over by the metropolitan social and
political forces, but it could also open the gate to African nationalism. Confronted with this rapidly changing new situation, the
traditional partners of the colonial order could not control
developments nor maintain their former unity of action. The new
situation revealed the fragility of their former power monopoly
which had only lasted as long as the colony was sealed off from
metropolitan social and political influence.

In fact, the three partners of the former alliance did not react in
the same manner to the threats to their power, influence or
economic interest. The Catholic Church saw that its dominant position in the field of education, culture and social assistance was
directly endangered by the facilities given to its liberal or socialist
counterparts.[28] This would inevitably lead in the future to an erosion of its power, as had happened in Belgium, and to the loss of its
predominance in the ideological formation of African élites. It was
further challenged by an external development. From 1956 on, the
Vatican itself realigned its policy toward the acceptance of political
independence in Africa and no longer clung to the defence of the
colonial system, which could threaten its presence in the long run.
From that time onwards, the Catholic media in the colony were
open to the expression of opinions supporting nationalism.[29]

As for the finance companies' attitude, one can assert that they
were extremely opposed to Belgian political influences entering the
colony. For instance, it was only in mid-1959 that the European
employers officially recognized the Congolese trade unions, largely
sponsored by the big metropolitan trade unions.[30] They were also
strongly opposed to the emerging African nationalism, but it seems
they were incapable of understanding the accelerating pace of

change, being prisoners of their own ideology on African affairs. And if finally they accepted the idea of autonomy at some unspecified future date, their passive resistance to the 'Belgianization' of the colony had rendered impossible its implementation as the 'slow and orderly process' they advocated.

As far as the colonial administration was concerned, it was divided, being unable to cope with the rapid pace of change which eroded its power, or to elaborate a strategy which could maintain its dominance and freedom of action. Its former power was rooted in the recognition by the metropolitan government that the 'administration' was mastering the 'colonial sciences' to manage problems which were specifically African. When this specificity was eroded by metropolitan politics or by African nationalism, its power rapidly crumbled. With its experience rendered obsolete and its inability to face the new problems, the administration's fate was sealed. Its power vanished with the riots which broke out in Leopoldville in January 1959, for which it was blamed.[31] In fact, even before these dramatic events, power had definitely shifted into the hands of the Brussels government.[32]

With the weakening of the colonial administration, the Church and the financial groups had to rely on the Brussels government, which passed to a Catholic-Liberal coalition in 1958. The new government was concerned with the Congolese problem, and established a working group to prepare a declaration on the future of the colony. This group and the government hesitated between autonomy or independence as the solution. And after the January 1959 events, when the idea of independence was admitted, there was much discussion on its content and on its timing. The new Colonial Minister, M. Van Hemelrijk, was a Flemish Christian Democrat, opposed to the domination of the colonial French-speaking establishment. He denounced the narrow ties of interest existing between the colonial administration and the financial groups and favoured a quick movement toward independence. He had to give way to the more moderate A. De Schijver who tried to slow down the pace of change and delay independence by three to five years. But after less then three months, confronted with the united front of the Congolese political leaders, he had to concede complete independence for six months later, i.e. the end of June 1960.[33]

This precipitateness appeared hazardous and inconsistent, contrasting sharply with the immobility of the preceding years. But it reflected the deep contradictions of the situation. The shift of the decision-making process to the metropolis was only apparent. In fact, the Belgian government did not have the means to influence the evolution of the colony. The colonial administration had become a ghost while the Church as well as the financial groups were too strongly opposed to a 'Belgianization' of the colonial political and social life to allow Brussels to deal with the fundamental problems of the colonial regime, i.e. the crisis in the rural areas, increasing income disparities, the slowdown of industrialization and a growing social discontent in the large cities. There was simply no machinery to prepare for a slow progress to autonomy or independence through a progressive transfer of the metropolitan political and social institutions, which the Belgian politicians had in mind. This solution, therefore, could not become an alternative to the growing radical nationalism, in which the African petty bourgeoisie was becoming the main agent of change, and from which Belgian politics were excluded. A 'slow and orderly process' would have required costly economic and social investment at the least, to bring about a change in income distribution inside the colony. This, at the same time, would have meant an increase of State intervention, inevitably in the form of a massive penetration of Belgian political structures into the colony, as metropolitan economic and military aid would be needed.

There was no question of waging a colonial war to maintain the system, not only because Belgian politicians would not take the responsibility for it,[34] but also because there was no pressure from the main colonial interests in that direction. The settlers were far too weak to defend their position militarily.[35] The type of development promoted by the colonial State and the finance companies resulted in a privileged position for employees and civil servants in the European population, i.e. temporary settlers in the colony for career purposes and so concerned about their future reintegration into Belgian society. As to the financial interests, they knew perfectly well that, economically and militarily, an armed occupation of the Congo was unthinkable. Confronted with the inevitable loss of their former dominating influence, the finance companies simply tried to minimize the risks in a situation which was getting out of their control, by influencing the main agents of change in the dialogue established from 1959 on, between the Belgian politicians and the emerging Congolese political forces. These companies were not devoid of powerful means of acting on the course of events:

they controlled the basic industrial structure of the Congo, the financial assets and even the commercial channels to international markets. They hoped for a deal with the new African élites, who, though busy taking control of the State machine, would still need their experience, money and techniques. They could find allies from among the majority moderate Congolese leaders, but feared that the radical minority would come to power and threaten their interests and freedom of action through planning or nationalization. Thus they supported any measure which could weaken the future independent State as a powerful unitary structure. They had ties with the supporters of a federalist solution, who, however, lost out to the militant unitarist nationalists.[36] But this short-run defeat did not suppress the strategic aspects of these ties, which appeared of the utmost importance after July 1960, during the secession of the Katanga.

One important change occurred during the period preceding independence in the attitude of the finance companies toward the involvement of the Belgian government in Congolese affairs. As the transfer of power to a Congolese authority was taking place, the nature of the intervention of the Belgian State was also changing. It could no longer have a restricting influence on the position of Belgian businesses inside the Congo, but on the contrary, could only became a useful tool to protect Belgian interests and check the pressures which could be made on them by the Congolese authorities. Thus, the Belgian State and the finance companies were obliged to become partners to face the Congolese authorities and conceived at that moment the idea of what would become 'development aid'. A good illustration of that rapid evolution is the measure that the Belgian government took some days before independence, and which tended to minimize the mounting danger of a unitarist nationalist government. It suppressed the Chartered Companies (CSK, CNKI) in which the Colonial State retained a majority interest and which could thus have given the new Congolese Government the control of the UMHK and most of the investments made in the eastern part of the colony.[37]

So much space has been given to the examination of the decolonization process because of the light it throws on the behaviour of the main partners of the colonial power system, the Catholic Church and the financial groups which were at the same time powerful partners also in the metropolitan power system. At the beginning of the fifties, in close cooperation with the colonial administration, they were at the height of what can be called a specific global power system largely independent of the metropolis. 'Global' because in this system the partners not only defended their particular position and interests, but also had the power to impose a strategy of development in every field of social and economic life in the colony. This was expressed by a typical colonial ideology which not only justified their total power inside the dominated society, but legitimized their role in the face of metropolitan opinion. They had a monopoly of knowledge about Africa and the Africans, and what should be the path of future development. They felt almost completely secure about the future of the colony and about their ability to master its development for the benefit of the 'indigenous populations'.

In fact, as stated earlier, that ideology, authoritarian and paternalistic, was specifically geared toward the control of the African society in the same way as it had prevailed in the nineteenth century to protect the interests of the Catholic bourgeoisie in Belgium itself. In Belgium it had taken almost half a century for that dominance to give way to developing popular movements. In the Congo, the partners in the colonial system had been convinced of their ability to maintain their dominance for an indefinite time, and so refused to compromise as they had been progressively obliged to do inside the metropolis. The result was that the system was shattered to pieces in less than ten years. But if they could not at all forecast the fragility of their global power system, the two main partners, the Church and the financial groups, showed a rather astonishing eagerness to adapt themselves to the loss of their hegemony and to defend their particular positions and interests.

In less than five years, they propelled to the top of their own institutional hierarchy (the Church) or they were lobbying and courting (the financial groups) people whom only recently they had regarded as their dependents. The shift from the 'civilizing mission' to 'cooperation for development' was made as easily as in the other metropolises.[38]

However, the 'civilizing mission' also had a metropolitan face. It had been presented there as a task which required also strengthened national unity to tackle the overseas problem with appropriate energy. As such the colonial enterprise mainly served the interests of the unitary francophone bourgeoisie inside Belgium: the success of the colonization certainly contributed to its long-lasting legality. The meaning of 'unity' was indeed in opposition to any transfer to the colony of social-political questions dividing the Belgians, and by the same token, it reinforced the exclusive power of the groups which largely constituted a kind of 'overseas branch' of the francophone bourgeoisie. The loss of the colony, as a field of exclusive power, thus contributed to curtailing the influence of that social group inside Belgium during the sixties.

With the troubles which followed immediately on independence in July 1960, a large majority of the Europeans in the Congo left abruptly. Most of them were civil servants, and with them the structure of the former colonial administration physically disappeared. In the following months, most of the settlers and their families also left the Congo for ever. This dramatic return of the settlers to the metropolis was to have long-term consequences. Their integration into metropolitan life did not become a crucial political issue in Belgium. The problem was tackled without difficulty by the traditional political parties, a task which was eased by the fact that these parties, like the metropolitan social organizations, had contacts among the European urban population, at least in the last years of the colonial regime. Pensions, allocations, preferential recruitment and other measures were taken to solve the question of the reintegration of the former colonial civil servants. Their representatives behaved in fact according to the social rules prevailing in Belgium rather than as a specific 'colonial' lobby.[39] The settlers' interests themselves were not powerful enough to build a pressure group of expatriates as such, and could only attract the support of marginal circles on the extreme right, without greatly affecting the political process.

The most important consequences of this return arose in fact in the Congo itself, particularly in two directions: the maintenance of a large Belgian presence in the Congo, and its resultant effects in Belgium.

The departure of most of the former civil servants and settlers did not affect all the regions in the same way. In Katanga, the majority of the old colonial hands stayed on for at least two more years. In other regions, mainly the eastern and north-eastern, the Belgian presence vanished almost completely. But in the capital, formerly Leopoldville, another phenomenon did occur: a new wave of Belgian advisers, and even middle-ranking employees, the majority with no previous African experience, progressively replaced

the former colonial structure of European employment. This movement was accelerated with the rise to power of the so-called
'General Commissars' at the end of 1960, who were, in their majority, young people who had just completed their university
studies, and who had some close friends among their former professors and class mates in Belgium.

The years 1960-1965 were years of great political instability: the
colonial State had crumbled, and the different factions of the Congolese petty bourgeoisie fought each other fiercely to gain control
of a State apparatus which was effectively losing its grip on events.
The struggles were extremely complicated including as they did all
elements emerging in a transitional period, i.e. ethnic regional
groups interwoven with new ideological divisions, while a new petty
bourgeoisie tried painfully to emerge from the political and
economic chaos, and succeeded in enlarging its share in the declining national income.[40]

The Belgian presence was pervasive in that difficult process,
especially in Leopoldville and Elisabethville. In one way or
another, this presence was felt in every important event, negotiation, change of government or military operation. They were advised, counselled, lobbied as much under the General Commissars and
the Adoula Government as under the Tshombe Government and
even when diplomatic ties were officially broken. In less than five
years, the Belgian presence completely changed its outlook and
structure, but maintained itself very firmly. Further, despite a
sharp reduction in the absolute numbers of Belgians in the Congo,
compared with the end of the colonial period, the number of people
in Belgium personally concerend with Congolese affairs greatly increased. There was indeed a huge turnover among the people staying for some months, or generally a restricted number of years. A
new generation was also concerned, in teaching, business and
public services, who travelled back and forth, or stayed for much
shorter periods than under the colonial regime.

Strangely enough, it was a 'new frontier' period for young people just leaving the universities. Arriving in the Congo, they were
confronted with a society in complete turmoil, and were forced into
close contact with the changing Congolese society. It was thus a
situation which contrasted very much with the closed, insulated
society, protected by its fragile consciousness of superiority, that
their elders had known some years before. At the same time, many
of them were involved in the international struggles which aimed at

influencing the direction of the new Republic. They were involved in all the manoeuvres which resulted from an increased influence among the western powers, sometimes made at Belgium's expense (in the Katanga affair for instance). They were also in the thick of Third World politics including elements which tried to check Belgian influence: the period of the open UNO intervention in Congolese affairs being the most difficult from that point of view.[41]

This situation certainly contributed to breaking down a certain narrow-mindedness for a lot of people who were living the experience in the field. The 'colony' had been a discovery for a generation at the beginning of the century, but a discovery which led finally to a kind of 'arrogant provincialism'. The Congolese crisis in a Third World perspective was like a new discovery, and for many, it was not only a cultural shock, but also a personal adventure.

This development was not restricted to Belgian expatriates. It also affected Belgian politicians and 'public opinion' in Belgium. In fact, the world of Belgian politics became much more concerned by what was happening in the Congo and its international aspects, than it had been during the colonial period, when Belgium as the colonial power theoretically had its 'civilising mission'. It was a process of 'learning by doing', through which most of the government and members of parliament, as well as the party leaders, discovered unexpected dimensions to Belgian involvement in international affairs.

Another interesting feature was that the main political groupings largely agreed on the policy which had to be followed, that was to participate actively in all western efforts to keep the Congo under Western influence, and at the same time defend Belgian interests as far as possible. That evolution was made easier by the fact that the Minister of Foreign Affairs, P. H. Spaak, was a former Secretary-General of NATO and a leading member of the Socialist Party.

Spaak's role was crucial for two reasons. Firstly, he actively manoeuvred internal Congolese politics. He gave to the Katanga secession a support which, while as discrete as possible, was essential to protect Belgian interests over there, especially when they were threatened by UN pressures. The price paid for this support until the end of 1962 was of course the continuous denunciation of Belgian neo-colonialism by numerous Third World countries, and repeated tensions with the Congolese Government. But at the same time, there was a policy of collaboration with Leopoldville, in order to reinforce the pro-Western moderates, and favour a peaceful reunification, which would at the same time stabilize the country and not be as hostile to Belgian interests, including those in Katanga. Such a policy, given the international context, could only be applied in close cooperation with the United States, and by framing the protection of Belgian interests in a broader Western context. Secondly, he succeeded in softening the opposition to such a policy in Belgium itself. There was opposition from certain Flemish and Socialist quarters, who blamed the finance companies for their political blindness and irresponsibility during the colonial period, and who favoured complete disengagement from the Congo. On the other hand, there were the pressures made by the finance companies to maintain the Katanga secession as long as possible and to help it more overtly. Spaak neutralized the first group by presenting his policy toward the Congo as a part of Belgium's international responsibility stemming from its alliances, and he convinced the financial interests that his policy would better ensure their security in the long run. Finally, he achieved a degree of unity between the Belgian political and business worlds, which became an important element in promoting an active involvement in the political development of the former colony. The Congolese crisis thus had the paradoxical result of promoting unity and cooperation between these two partners in the Belgian power system, in the exact way which had been desired by the financial groups during the colonial period, but not then achieved. This illustrates the fact that the most significant consequences of the decolonization crisis were in the subtle changes in the Belgian power structures and the ways the political élites behaved towards their changing situation in the Congo.

As far as metropolitan public opinion was concerned, there was a complex evolution, through the decolonization crisis, into an understanding of Third World problems, perhaps different from other Western countries. For it was also a 'new discovery of Africa'. All the comfortable views on the success of the Belgian paternalistic colonial system, which had been diffused through the education and the mass media, were of course shattered. At the same time, Belgian public opinion discovered African and Asian nationalism in their most violent expression, making Belgium the target of sharp attacks against its past and present African policy. Newspapers of all tendencies were full of information about the crisis and the space devoted to the situation in the Congo was certainly ten times larger than in the 'gold age' of the colonial period. But there was an evident lack of analytical equipment with which to tackle the problem. Reactions in the mass media reflected a deep malaise and a rather emotional approach. If some papers condemned the 'irresponsibility' of all the partners in the decolonization, most of them also denounced an international plot against Belgium. The first phase faded away rather quickly. Thereafter the media concentrated on the humanitarian aspects of the 'drama', where Belgians as well as the Congolese populations appeared as the victims of an international plot by which Afro-Asian nationalism was preparing the ground for communism,[42] and consequently insisted that Belgium had to accept new responsibilities to compensate for its former 'irresponsibility'. These ideas played a certain part in making easier the framing of the continuous involvement inside the Congolese crisis, in a multilateral Western perspective. They contributed to the approval by 'the silent majority', even of a joint US-Belgium military intervention in Stanleyville at the end of 1964.

That event was nevertheless the start of a new development in public opinion especially among the young and in the universities, where it was seen as an overt neo-colonialist operation. From that moment, Belgian involvement in Congolese affairs was repeatedly denounced as a manifestation of second-hand imperialism. This criticism increased with the years, especially at the end of the sixties, when the Mobutu regime began to repress student protest inside Zaïre universities. But that movement was part of the general radicalization of an active youth minority which occurred in Belgium as elsewhere, and which was focused mainly on the Vietnam war. But it gave birth to a rather impressive number of pamphlets and unpublished papers, which revealed an active sympathy with Third World nationalism and a new spring-board for neo-marxism.[43]

Zaïre's problems, however, never led to mass demonstrations like those which denounced the US intervention in Vietnam. And it was only as late as 1978 that the radical minority could make its voice heard inside the power system, when its theses were more or less repeated by the Chairman of the Flemish Socialist Party in order to denounce the corruption of the Zaïre regime. In terms of power politics, that tendency thus remained rather marginal, and the scene was dominated by the continuation of the policy undertaken by P. H. Spaak.

The rise to power and the consolidation of the Mobuto regime, since 1965, has given new perspectives to the partnership between the Belgian political and business worlds concerning Zaïre affairs. On one side they were confronted with a more stable political power which progressively asserted its independence, sometimes through temporary clashes with the former metropolis, as in the 1966 take-over of the UMHK and its transformation into the *Gecamines*. The finance companies lost the freedom of action they had maintained under the Katanga secession. They had to recognize the full authority of the new regime which asserted its objectives: to use State power and control national resources in order to increase its bargaining power with foreign capital and consolidate the economic position of the small privileged groups linked with the regime.[44] The UMHK affair was very important. Although another subsidiary of the *Société Générale*, the SGM, maintained a large degree of control over its management and its handling of commercial problems, the affair demonstrated that the financial groups could maintain their stake in the country only if they submitted to the objectives of the new regime and recognized it as a full partner in the decision-making process. It showed also that the support of the Belgian State was absolutely necessary in the new bargaining process and that even a close cooperation with the United States and multinational Western institutions was required. The amount of indemnities to be paid to the UMHK had finally been agreed partly under the pressures made by the World Bank and IMF on the Zaïre regime.[45] From that moment onwards, the Belgian political and financial world undertook a policy of close and multiform cooperation with the Kinshasa Government. That cooperation became more and more institutionalized through State to State relations, with the development of loans, credits and the financing of important technical assistance in the civilian as well as in the military field.[46] The largest part of the so-called development aid was devoted to Zaïre, a situation which was strongly approved by Belgian industrial interests.[47] At the end of the sixties, that cooperation reached a climax with a renegotiation of the Zaïre bilateral debt with Belgium and the official visit of King Baudouin.[48] The axis of cooperation was very clear. The State to State relations created a good climate for an involvement of the financial groups in the great projects undertaken by the Kinshasa regime, mainly in the infrastructure.

These projects were realized with large international financing, but they had an important spill-over effect for Belgian industry. For instance, in 1971, orders given to Belgian enterprises in the Inga and Inga-Shaba projects represented 50 percent of orders received by these enterprises from projects in Third World countries. From the beginning of the seventies the Zaïre debt largely shifted from public to private loans granted by multinational bank groups. Belgian groups, mainly the *Société Générale*, were rather well-placed in that movement. The Belgian groups were heavily involved in the Zaïre economy, through State investments or indebtment, and their presence depended largely on the relations existing between Zaïre and Belgium. At the same time, they had less economic responsibility for the operations in which they participated, and which were often denounced as prestige and uneconomic spending. They were thus actively concerned with the type of policy followed by the Zaïre regime which tried to use the country export resources as a tool to promote, through State control, the economic position of a small privileged group linked with State power. However, it is noteworthy that they took no direct risks and made no direct new investments. As other small and middle-sized foreign enterprises also did not increase their own investment, that situation was invoked to justify the 'Zaïrinization' measures of 1973, which took over all that category of foreign ownership.[49] In fact, these measures have struck at the last remnants of the settlers' era, but they have not hit the financial groups as such.

From 1974 onwards, the Zaïre economy drifted into a crisis, due simultaneously to the fall of copper prices, to the deepening of the agricultural crisis, and to mismanagement at all levels of the State structure. The regime saw its bargaining counters with foreign capital weaken one after the other, and it was reduced to a very unfavourable position. Progressively forced to renegotiate its debt from such a position, it had to allow controls on its public spending, so degenerating to a situation in which it came to be almost dependent on multinational Western tutorship. This was a rather new situation, as Western powers tried at the same time to stabilize a country they considered strategically important while putting heavy pressures and constraints on their 'ally'.

Belgium occupied a key position in the difficult discussions between the Western powers and the Zaïre regime. It was not a forefront position, but its intervention was looked upon as absolutely necessary by its Western partners to supervise and even manage the 'reconstruction' tasks. At the same time, the Zaïre authorities often tried to use their 'special relations' with Brussels to get a softening of certain conditions from other Western creditors with less traditional sympathy for Zaïre problems.

To conclude: if the decolonization process has quickly and completely destroyed the social and political system established by Belgium to ensure its domination in the Congo, it has not eliminated the presence of the former metropolis in Central Africa. On one hand, the Belgian power system has been closely involved with the emergence of a regime that was the negation of all the principles and mechanisms that had been advocated to ensure an orderly process of democratization: an authoritarian and corrupt regime using the economic surplus extracted from the export sector to consolidate a social group which could be called an oligarchy as well as a State bourgeoisie, and using the slogans of the most violent nationalism to realize an apparent consensus: all features which are officially distrusted by the Belgian political and economic power circles.[50] On the other hand, this involvement has led not only to a multi-lateral cooperation with this regime, but it has also led to a pragmatic consensus of action between the partners of the Belgian system of power which had never been reached before in the field of colonial policy. And finally, it has given to Belgium an international responsibility, even greater than during the colonial period, as the emerging state was looked on as having a special strategic importance, and as Belgium was recognized as having a 'special' responsibility in this area by its Western allies.

Far from having been eliminated from the international scene because of the loss of its 'Empire', Belgium has thus maintained its role in a changing world largely through its involvement in the evolution of its former colony. It has even been the best school of international power politics for its political class, which has adapted itself rather easily to a kind of pragmatic machiavellianism, to cope as well with the special blend of Third World dictatorship that has developed in Zaïre as with the forces which tried to insert themselves in it. At the same time, the main Belgian financial groups have been able to maintain a large influence on the Zaïre economy and largely to hold on to their interests.[51] Nonetheless, the Zaïre economy is a stagnating one, so that Belgian finance companies there were unable to keep pace with the accelerated movements of international investments or with the rate of growth of output and investment in Belgium itself. During the sixties and the seventies, the stagnation and the rampaging crisis of the Zaïre economy contrasted sharply with the emergence of new industrial nations in South East Asia and Latin America. The maintenance of Belgian interests in Zaïre was thus not a way of keeping pace with the trends of international trade and finance. And it is very clear that during this period, there was absolutely no reshaping of the structure of Belgian investments toward the new growth economics of the Third World. Belgian business was almost absent from that restructuring of the world economy in sharp contrast with the behaviour of the United States, Japan and Germany. Only from 1974 onwards, after the shock of the oil crisis, did Belgian business make a new and successful effort to penetrate the Arab countries, but under the form of sales or contracts with public enterprises and institutions, not under the form of direct investment; in this perspective, today Algeria has replaced Zaïre as the first trading partner of Belgium in Africa.

Since 1960, Belgian investment abroad has mainly followed the direction of the other EEC countries, in enterprises and sectors linked with Belgium's traditional exports, in order to ensure their protection or promotion.[52]

As for the financial groups, they operated mainly in two directions. The companies they sponsored in the mining sector of the colony before 1960 undertook new direct investment in the same sector but mainly in non-Third World countries, Canada and Australia for instance. On the other hand, they largely developed their own banking operation, trying to take up a good position of broker in the field of international financial operations and of investments realized in Western Europe by multinational enterprises. But that movement was not spectacular and simply kept pace with the growing internationalization of the Western European economies. Paradoxically enough, in the last twenty years, the Belgian economy has become more and more European-centred, and there was no overseas substitute for the former importance of the colonial investments relative to the metropolitan assets.

There was thus an apparent discrepancy between the relative importance that Zaïre kept for Belgium in the network of its international relations and the weakening of its economic weight relative to the new dimensions of the Belgian economy. There is probably a link between that diminishing economic importance of Zaïre from a bilateral point of view, and the growing multi-lateral aspects of Belgian economic relations with its former colony. It is more and more in the broader context of the growing financial and

284   *Journal of Contemporary History*

economic interdependence with other Western countries that a
'Zaïre policy' has still a meaning for the formulators of Belgian
policies.

Notes

1. See for example, J. Mokyr, *Industrialization in the Low Countries, 1795-1850*
(Yale University Press 1976).

2. J. M. Wautelet, *Division économique du travail et production élargie du
capital; Belgique 1873-1913* (University of Louvain 1976).

3. Institut National de Statistique, *Recensement économique et social 1937*, vol.
2, 476-479.

4. B. S. Chlepner, *Le marché financier belge depuis cent ans* (Brussels 1930),
21-30, 95-130.

5. P. Delfosse, *La formation des familles politiques en Belgique, 1830-1914*
(University of Louvain 1979).

6. M. Quévit, *Les causes du déclin wallon* (Brussels 1978), 62-78.

7. I. Cassiers, *Réflexions préliminaires par une analyse du rôle de l'Etat en
Belgique, 1880-1914* (University of Louvain 1976); P. Joye and R. Lewin, *L'Eglise
et le mouvement ouvrier en Belgique* (Brussels 1967).

8. J. Ph. Peemans, 'Capital accumulation in the Congo under colonialism: the
role of the state', in P. Duignan and L. H. Gann (eds.), *Colonialism in Africa*, vol.
IV (Cambridge University Press 1974), 164-169.

9. P. Berthe, *Les investissements belges à l'étranger. Reflets et perspectives de la
vie économique*, 17, 2 (1978), 87-100.

10. Sénat, Commission des Colonies, Discussion du budget pour l'exercise 1934,
Documents parlementaires, no. 85 (Brussels 1934).

11. J. Stengers, 'La Belgique et le Congo' in *Histoire de la Belgique contemporaine, 1914-1970, la Renaissance du Livre* (Brussels 1974), 394-400.

12. J. L. Veccut, *The 'classical' age of Belgian colonialism: outline for a social
history, 1910-1940*, unpublished paper presented to the Seminar on Zaïre, SOAS,
London, October 1978.

13. P. Delfosse, op. cit., 14-19.

14. C. H. Höjer, 'Le régime parlementaire belge de 1918 à 1940', *CRISP* (Brussels
1969), 3-62, 313-368; V. Lorwin, 'Belgium: religion, class and language in national
politics', in R. Dach, (ed.), *Political opposition in Western democracies* (Yale University Press 1966), 147-187.

15. See for example, *Bulletin de la Banque Centrale du Congo belge et du Ruanda
Urundi*, no. 11 (1956), 419-430; no. 11 (1959), 435-441; Banque Nationale de Belgique, *Statistiques économiques belges, 1950-1960*, vol. 2, 218-231, 338-340.

16. See J. Ph. Peemans, 'Capital accumulation in the Congo under colonialism:
the role of the State', in P. Duignan and L. H. Gann (eds.), *Colonialism in Africa*,
vol. IV (Cambridge University Press 1974), 192-196.

17. Congrès Colonial National, 6th Sess., *Comptes rendus de séances et rapports*

Peemans: *Belgium — Economics of Decolonization*   285

préparatoires (Brussels 1948); Institut de Sociologie Solvay, *Vers la promotion de l'économie indigène* (Brussels 1956).

18. Guy Malengreau, *Vers un paysannat indigène: les lotissements agricoles au Congo Belge* (Brussels 1949).

19. P. Bouvier, *L'accession du Congo Belge à l'indépendance* (Brussels 1965), 78-83.

20. R. Anstey, 'Belgian Rule in the Congo and the aspirations of the Evolué Class', in P. Duignan and L. H. Gann (eds.), *Colonialism in Africa*, op. cit., vol. II, 1970.

21. J. Stengers, 'Une décolonisation précipitée: le cas du Congo Belge', *Culture et développement*, vol. X, 4 (1978), 533-538.

22. L. A. M. Petillon, Discours d'ouverture à la session ordinaire du Conseil de Gouvernement, Session de 1952, Léopoldville, Conseil de Gouvernement, 1952.

23. C. Young, *Politics in the Congo* (Princeton University Press 1965), 75-86.

24. P. Joye and R. Lewin, 'Les trusts au Congo', *SPE* (Brussels 1961), 190-201.

25. A. J. J. Van Bilsen, 'Bilan de la politique Coloniale d'une législature 1954-1958', *La Revue Nouvelle*, May 1958.

26. See for instance P. Lumumba, *Le Congo Terre d'avenir, est-il menacé?* (Brussels 1961), 66-69.

27. From that moment Belgian political parties repeatedly took up positions over the future of the Colony: le Manifeste du P.S.C. sur le Congo, Information No. 9, 15 April 1956; P.S.B. Un programme pour le Congo et le Rwanda Urundi, rapports présentés au Congrès extraordinaire des 30 Juin et 1er Juillet 56 (Brussels 1956).

28. A. A. J. Van Bilsen, *Vers l'indépendance du Congo et du Rwanda Urundi* (Brussels 1958), 120-121.

29. J. Meynard, J. Ladriere, F. Perin, *La décision politique en Belgique* (Paris 1965), 349-351.

30. Le 20 Mai à Léopoldville: Pacte social? Le train des décisions gouvernementales: des pressions contradictoires qui se neutralisent, Courrier hebdomadaire du *CRISP*, Brussels No. 19, 1959.

31. Rapport de la Commission Parlementaire sur les événements de janvier 1959, Documents parlementaires, Chambre des Représentants, Document 100, 27 March 1959.

32. J. Stengers, 'La Belgique et le Congo. Politique coloniale et décolonisation', in *Histoire de la Belgique contemporaine, 1914-1970* (Brussels 1974), 422-423.

33. J. Meynard, J. Ladriere and F. Perin, op. cit., 355-359.

34. L'envoi de militaires belges au Congo, *CRISP*, No. 40, 1959.

35. *Eurafrica*, Revue de la Fedacol, 1959, No. 1, 6-1; No. 2, 16-22.

36. J. Gérard-Libois and B. Verhaegen, Congo 60, Les dossiers du *CRISP* (Brussels 1961).

37. P. Joye and R. Lewin, op. cit., 288-295.

38. See for instance the speech made by L. Bekaert, President of the FIB (Belgian Federation of Enterprises) and a leading Belgian industrialist, in January 1960, to advocate future cooperation with the Congo (FEB, Rapport annuel, 1973, Brussels, 77).

39. F. Baudhuin, *Histoire économique de la Belgique, 1957-1968* (Brussels 1970), 222-235.

40. J. Ph. Peemans, 'The social and economic development of Zaïre since independence: an historical outline', in *African Affairs*, 74, 295 (April 1975), 154-157.

41. J. Gérard Libois and B. Verhaegen, *Congo 1960, 1961, 1962, 1963, 1964* (Brussels 1961 to 1965).

42. One could read for instance in *La libre Belgique*, 8 November 1965: 'La crise congolaise pourrait mener à un coup d'Etat, l'actuelle confusion politique ne sert que les visées chinoises.'

43. See for example, Comité Zaïre, *La CIA et le Zaïre* (Antwerp 1977); Comité Zaïre, *Zaïre, le dossier de la recolonisation* (Brussels and Paris 1978).

44. J. Ph. Peemans, op. cit., 160-165.

45. R. E. Verhaeren, 'La Société Générale et l'Union Minière', *La Revue Nouvelle* (November 1972), 371-374.

46. B. Piret, 'L'aide belge au Zaïre', *Contradictions*, no. 1 (1972), 111-137.

47. FEB, *La présence économique belge dans le monde* (Brussels 1973), 76-90.

48. J. Gérard-Libois, 'Dix ans de relations Belgique-Congo', in *CRISP*, 29 May 1970.

49. Lutumba Lu-Vilu, 'De la Zaïreization à la rétrocession et au dialogue Nord-Sud, 1973-1975', *OIL* (Brussels 1976).

50. B. Verhaegen, 'Impérialisme technologique et bourgeoisie nationale au Zaïre, Connaissance du Tiers Monde', Cahiers Jussieu, 4, Collection 10/18 (Paris 1978), 347-380.

51. F. Chonneux, 'L'après Congo et le Zaïre', *La Revue Nouvelle* (November 1972), 379-381.

52. *Reflets et perspectives de la vie économique, Présence de l'économie belge dans le monde* (Brussels 1978), 101-112, 125-130.

[3]

Fanon and Cabral: a Contrast in Theories of Revolution for Africa

by ROBERT BLACKEY*

LENIN set the tone for most successful revolutions in the twentieth century when he altered traditional Marxism to suit the conditions of Russia. Mao Tse-tung followed Lenin's example when he too adjusted Marxism (and Leninism) to a Chinese environment. It seems to follow, therefore, that attempts at revolution everywhere should not be mere imitations of previously successful upheavals but should, instead, be tailored to fit specific circumstances. Thus, African revolutions should be made on the basis of African conditions. But such conditions are not, in general, always easy to discern, nor are separate analyses of those conditions certain to be similar. This is especially true of the theories of revolution of two of the most important and influential figures in recent African history: Frantz Fanon (1925–61) and Amilcar Cabral (1925–73).

Although a native of Martinique, Fanon's ancestry was African. He studied medicine in France, became a psychiatrist, and then practiced in Algeria where he soon found himself involved in the Algerian Revolution. Fanon's thoughts on revolution were based mainly upon his knowledge of and experience in much of Africa, especially Algeria.[1] Cabral was the organiser and leader of the revolution in the country of his birth, Guinea-Bissau (formerly Portuguese Guinea). His theories were a result of his experiences, beginning as a student in Lisbon, continuing as an agronomist who surveyed the agricultural resources

* Associate Professor of History at California State College, San Bernardino, and co-editor (with Clifford T. Paynton) of *Why Revolution? theories and analyses* (Cambridge, Mass., 1971).

[1] Fanon's life and thought may be surveyed in the following: G. K. Grohs, 'Frantz Fanon and the African Revolution', in *The Journal of Modern African Studies* (Cambridge), VI, 4, December 1968, pp. 543–56; David Caute, *Frantz Fanon* (New York, 1970); Renate Zahar, *L'Oeuvre de Frantz Fanon* (Paris, 1970); Peter Geismar, *Fanon* (New York, 1971); Pierre Bouvier, *Fanon* (Paris, 1971); Philippe Lucas, *Sociologie de Frantz Fanon* (Algiers, 1971); Paul A. Beckett, 'Frantz Fanon and Sub-Saharan Africa: notes on the contemporary significance of his thought', in *Africa Today* (Denver), XIX, 2, Spring 1972, pp. 59–72; Emmanuel Obiechina, 'Frantz Fanon', in *Ufahamu* (Los Angeles), III, 2, Fall 1972, pp. 97–116; Irene L. Gendzier, *Frantz Fanon: a critical study* (New York, 1973); and L. Adele Jinadu, 'Some Aspects of the Political Philosophy of Frantz Fanon', in *African Studies Review* (East Lansing), XVI, 2, September 1973, pp. 255–89.

of his country for the Portuguese Government, and concluding as a nationalist and revolutionist.[1] Both Fanon and Cabral dealt with many of the aspects of revolution, the former more as an abstract theorist, the latter more as a party organiser. They examined the nature of revolution in Africa, the social structure, the utility of party and leadership, the value of violence, and the rôle of culture, while they also speculated upon post-revolutionary society.

The purpose of this article is to discuss and illustrate the differences and similarities between the theories of these outstanding and original revolutionists. While it will be the task of others to determine where the ideas of one or the other, or of anyone else for that matter, are especially applicable to a given African situation, it is hoped that this attempt at contrast will be a contribution towards understanding African revolutions and the continent's search for identity.

NATURE OF THE AFRICAN REVOLUTION

Fanon and Cabral were essentially men of peace. Neither plunged immediately into the troubled waters of revolution without first trying more tranquil currents. Fanon practised at a hospital in Algeria and tried to work through legitimate channels before he felt compelled to join the rebels. He explained his position in his letter of resignation from the hospital at Blida in 1956: 'The function of a social structure is to set up institutions to serve man's needs. A society that drives its members to desperate solutions is a nonviable society, a society to be replaced.'[2] In the same year a handful of men led by Cabral formed the African Party for the Independence of Guinea and Cape Verde (P.A.I.G.C.) – the Cape Verde Islands are some 600 miles off-shore and considered part of Guinea-Bissau. Earlier attempts at reform had failed, but for three years the P.A.I.G.C. employed peaceful means to gain independence. When this also proved unsuccessful other means had to

[1] Although there is no biography of Cabral his ideas are discussed in the following: Ronald H. Chilcote, 'The Political Thought of Amilcar Cabral', in *The Journal of Modern African Studies*, VI, 3, October 1968, pp. 373–88; Gérard Chaliand, *Armed Struggle in Africa: with the guerrillas in 'Portuguese' Guinea* (New York, 1969); Basil Davidson, *The Liberation of Guiné: aspects of an African revolution* (Baltimore, 1969); Bernard Magubane, 'Amilcar Cabral: evolution of revolutionary thought', in *Ufahamu*, II, 2, Fall 1971, pp. 71–87; Eduardo Ferreira, 'Theory of Revolution and Background to his Assassination', in *Ufahamu*, III, 3, Winter 1973, pp. 49–68; Maryinez L. Hubbard, 'Culture and History in a Revolutionary Context: approaches to Amilcar Cabral', in *Ufahamu*, III, 3, Winter 1973, pp. 69–86; and Charles McCollester, 'The Political Thought of Amilcar Cabral', in *The Monthly Review* (New York), XXIV, 10, March 1973, pp. 10–21.

[2] Frantz Fanon, 'Letter to the Resident Minister' (1956), in *Toward the African Revolution* (New York edn., 1969), p. 53.

CONTRAST IN THEORIES OF REVOLUTION FOR AFRICA 193

be employed. 'In the beginning', wrote Cabral, 'we thought it would be possible to fight in the towns, using the experiences of other countries, but that was a mistake. We tried strikes and demonstrations, but . . . realized this would not work.'[1] At these points both men became revolutionists.

On the nature of the African revolution Fanon and Cabral were in general agreement, differing only over emphasis and detail, some of which, however, is very important. Of the two, Cabral was far more explicit, but both expected revolution to be more than just a struggle for independence. For Fanon, revolution was part of the process of the regeneration of man and society, of self-liberation and rebirth. Only through revolution could a suppressed people undo the effects of colonisation. As a psychiatrist, Fanon was particularly interested in the psychological effects which revolution would have on the colonised man. For true liberation to occur, he asserted, independence must be taken, not merely granted; it must be the work of the oppressed themselves. It was through the actual struggle that liberation would come, restoring integrity and pride, as well as the past and the future. 'True liberation is not that pseudo-independence in which ministers having a limited responsibility hobnob with an economy dominated by the colonial past. Liberation is the total destruction of the colonial system.'[2] The oppressed must bring all their resources into play because the struggle is at once total and absolute.

The African revolution, and the larger liberation struggle of colonial people everywhere, is the fundamental characteristic of the advance of history in this century, according to Cabral.[3] Such a revolution means the transformation of life in the direction of progress which, in turn, means national independence, eliminating all foreign domination, and carefully selecting friends and watching enemies to ensure progress. 'The national liberation of a people is the regaining of the historical personality of that people, its return to history through the destruction of the imperialist domination to which it was subjected.'[4] A people must free the process of development of the national productive forces. Thus the struggle is not only against colonialism, but against neo-colonialism as well.

[1] Quoted in David A. Andelman, 'Profile: Amilcar Cabral', in *Africa Report* (New York), May 1970, p. 19.

[2] Fanon, 'Decolonization and Independence' (1958), in *Toward the African Revolution*, p. 105.

[3] Amilcar Cabral, 'Guinea and Cabo Verde Against Portuguese Colonialism' (1961), in *Revolution in Guinea: selected texts by Amilcar Cabral* (New York, 1969), p. 14.

[4] Cabral, 'The Weapon of Theory' (1966), in ibid. p. 102.

194   ROBERT BLACKEY

Cabral possessed a vision that encompassed the broad spectrum of revolution; he had an appreciation of the crucial everyday work of the struggle that Fanon lacked. He stressed that revolutionists must not fight for ideas alone, but for material benefits, improved conditions, and a better future for children. The fight must not be merely for abstract ideas of liberty and independence, but for local and pressing grievances and problems.

National liberation, the struggle against colonialism, working for peace and progress, independence – all these will be empty words without significance for the people, unless they are translated into real improvements of the conditions of life. It is useless to liberate a region, if the people of the region are then left without the elementary necessities of life.[1]

In other words, it is through gaining supporters by arguing for local grievances that revolutionists will open the prospect for a better future wherein the more abstract ideas could be incorporated.

Proceeding further, Cabral emphasised that although the goal of national independence was unquestionably vital, the struggle itself, to be truly successful, must continue on three levels: political action, armed action, and national reconstruction. This means: (i) that political work must be maintained at all levels of society to establish and preserve national unity; (ii) party organisation and discipline must be strengthened and adjusted to the evolution of the struggle to correct mistakes and hold leaders to proper principles and goals; (iii) the armed forces must be strengthened and the enemy isolated; (iv) liberated areas must be defended, kept tranquil, and developed for the benefit of the people there; (v) more cadres of complete revolutionists must be trained to be able to go out in the countryside and educate the people; and (vi) ties must be strengthened with other African nations, and with anti-colonialist and anti-imperialist forces everywhere.[2]

Cabral was thorough as he linked the revolution to the daily needs of the people. But this might have come to nothing without sufficient education and preparation beforehand. Here Cabral's contribution to the concept of revolution is especially valuable and, perhaps, unique. He used his position as a government agronomist during 1952–4 to travel about his country and acquire an intimate knowledge of the life of his people, thus laying the groundwork for a later time when he would combine the theory and practice of revolution: 'nobody has yet made a successful revolution without a revolutionary theory',[3] he said, echoing

---

[1] Cabral (1965), quoted in Lars Rudebeck, 'Political Mobilisation for Development in Guinea-Bissau', in *The Journal of Modern African Studies*, x, 1, May 1972, p. 3.

[2] Cabral, 'The Development of the Struggle' (1968), in *Revolution in Guinea*, pp. 125 f.

[3] Cabral, 'The Weapon of Theory', p. 93.

CONTRAST IN THEORIES OF REVOLUTION FOR AFRICA 195

Lenin. Before the armed struggle was launched, Cabral and his fellow leaders made a careful analysis of their society; they came to understand the position of the tribal chiefs *vis-à-vis* the villagers; they examined the social structure in the towns; they investigated the views of those who lived without chiefs; and they studied the ways in which Portuguese colonial exploitation actually affected the every-day life of the population. This earlier political preparation made the struggle possible. The tireless work of listening and talking, of directing and explaining, of relating the P.A.I.G.C. to the people, and vice versa, was what apparently made the difference between success and failure.

By 1960 P.A.I.G.C. members were out in the countryside explaining their aims and mobilising the people; Cabral had come to believe that their struggle would need massive rural support before the revolution began. The small guerrilla band, or *foci*, as espoused by Che Guevara and Régis Debray, would not have been enough to spark the struggle. Instead, a period of two years preparatory political work was undertaken. This was especially difficult since Guinea-Bissau had an illiteracy rate of some 99 per cent, a shockingly small number of university trained men (only 14 prior to 1960), and no military academy to teach tactics and strategy. A political school was founded in Conakry (in the neighbouring Republic of Guinea) in which, at first, party members received political instruction and were trained how to mobilise the masses. Then those peasants and youths who had been recruited went to the school, whereupon they embarked on an intensive education programme so that they too could return to the countryside to convince others to join the struggle. The attempt to gain followers avoided generalisations and pat phrases, using instead questions and information that would relate directly to those involved.

We started from the concrete reality of our people. We tried to avoid having the peasants think that we were outsiders come to teach them how to do things; we put ourselves in the position of people who came to learn *with* the peasants, and in the end the peasants were discovering for themselves why things had gone badly for them.[1]

This political preparation was probably the hardest work of the revolution, but it was also the most useful. By 1962–3 the P.A.I.G.C. was ready to fight, and the years of preparation proved invaluable.

Fanon, as indicated above, paid little attention to the details of making a revolution; he was more interested in encouraging their occurrence. Analysis for the sake of analysis was for intellectuals; Fanon wrote to arouse, to anger, and to warn against the dangers of

[1] Cabral, 'Practical Problems and Tactics' (1968), in *Revolution in Guinea*, p. 159.

exploitation. But he expected the African revolution to proceed along two stages. First, there would be a period of physical struggle during which a national programme has to emerge to act as a unifying element in order to achieve independence. (This was no easy task, and Fanon, unlike Cabral, did not give it much attention.) Secondly, after independence the energies of the revolutionists must be directed into building a socialist state. Fanon did not encourage a chauvinistic type of nationalism; as a pan-Africanist he recognised that it was necessary to hold a people together. But he did favour a nationalism based upon the genuineness and individuality of the indigenous culture which would, in turn, unite with other anti-colonial and socialist movements; such a nationalism, however, has proved elusive.

Fanon's affinity for socialism was, like Cabral's, primarily the result of circumstance; he was not doctrinaire about it, nor did he feel that traditional Marxism–Leninism was completely suitable to Africa. Specifically, neither Marx nor Lenin dealt with the question of race, probably because it never occurred to them. Fanon took aspects of Marxism–Leninism and injected the race factor: 'you are rich because you are white, you are white because you are rich'.[1] Although he did not consider himself a Marxist he was sympathetic with the Marxist approach to revolution. But Fanon emphasised 'underdeveloped countries' as the agency for change, not 'social class'. Moreover, not only did Fanon wish to be free from capitalism, but also from any institutionalised form of communism as well. In fact, it was with sanguine – though it seems unrealistic – expectations that he looked to the Third World to create a humanistic society, apart from and independent of capitalism and communism.

Cabral similarly did not consider himself a Marxist and modified Marx on the subject of class in a way only slightly different from Fanon. 'We agree that history . . . is the result of class struggle, but we have our own class struggles in our own country; the moment imperialism arrived and colonialism arrived, it made us leave our history and enter another history.'[2] Therefore, while the class struggle has continued it has done so in a modified way. Africa's struggle is against the ruling class of the imperialist countries; this has given the class struggle another connotation, and has meant a different evolution for the African people. 'In colonial conditions no one stratum [or class] can succeed in the struggle for national liberation on its own, and

---

[1] Fanon, *The Wretched of the Earth* (New York edn., 1968), p. 40.

[2] Cabral, 'Brief Analysis of the Social Structure in Guinea' (1964), in *Revolution in Guinea*, p. 68.

CONTRAST IN THEORIES OF REVOLUTION FOR AFRICA 197

therefore it is all the strata [or classes] of society which are the agents of history.'[1] Thus, in colonial countries traditional Marxism does not work; the class struggle does not command history – the entire colonial state does.

CLASS STRUCTURE

It is in their analysis and discussion of classes where we find the sharpest contrasts between Fanon and Cabral. It is here that their fundamental differences lie, and where students of the African revolution must devote most of their attention, not only in order to make or understand revolutions, but also because of the foundation 'class' provides for post-revolutionary society.

There is no doubt that in Africa the peasantry comprises the largest single group in society. For most of recorded history, as well as for traditional Marxism, peasants have been the poorest revolutionists. Fanon recognised their conservatism, and accepted the premise that in industrial countries they were, generally, the least aware, the worst organised, and the most reactionary class. Even in the Third World the peasants were often retrograde and prone to religious fanaticism and tribal warfare. But in the twentieth century, especially in China and Vietnam, the peasantry has become revolutionary when provided with an appropriate ideology, capable leadership, and efficient organisation. Fanon was aware of this, and believed that under stress or provocation the peasants were capable of uncontrollable rage. Peasants, he said, had 'bloodthirsty instincts' and were capable of brutality and violence. Because of this Fanon concluded that they must be an integral part of the African revolutionary élite since they were the only true and spontaneously revolutionary force. 'It is clear that in the colonial countries the peasants alone are revolutionary, for they have nothing to lose and everything to gain.' Peasants would answer the call of revolution, thinking of their liberation only in violent terms. 'The starving peasant, outside the class system, is the first among the exploited to discover that only violence pays. For him there is no compromise, no possible coming to terms.'[2]

Fanon also selected the peasants as part of the revolutionary élite because, in the absence of a significant African proletariat, they were in

[1] Ibid. p. 69.

[2] Fanon, *The Wretched of the Earth*, p. 61. For an evaluation of his views on the peasantry, as well as on class in general, see B. Marie Perinbam, 'Fanon and the Revolutionary Peasantry – the Algerian Case', in *The Journal of Modern African Studies*, XI, 3, September 1973, pp. 427–45; and Martin Staniland, 'Frantz Fanon and the African Political Class', in *African Affairs* (London), LXVIII, 270, January 1969, pp. 4–25.

the majority. In addition, the other classes had to be evaluated and utilised in terms of the peasantry, whose thinking is 'pure' and un-hampered by the inconsistency and compromise of the urban pro-letariat and bourgeoisie. For Fanon, even in the post-revolutionary society the peasants must be central and pivotal; when they become the politically decisive arm of the revolution the nation will become a living reality to all its citizens.

Like Fanon, Cabral recognised the importance of the peasants because their very numbers provided the main strength of the opposi-tion to foreign domination. Experience taught the P.A.I.G.C. that the rural masses would 'be the principal force in the struggle for national liberation'.[1] Also, more than other groups, they have kept their culture and identity intact. But the peasants in Guinea-Bissau proved to be most difficult to convince that they were being exploited. Therefore, although the struggle must be based upon the peasants, Cabral did not see them as a revolutionary force *per se*. Here he distinguished between a physical force, which the peasants are, and a revolutionary force, which they are not. Admittedly, they comprise most of the population, control most of the nation's wealth, and do most of the producing. But to convince them to fight was difficult because, unlike in China, the peasants of Guinea-Bissau had no tradition of revolt and therefore did not welcome the revolutionists readily.[2] Thus, Fanon and Cabral both saw the peasants as perhaps central to any African revolutionary movement although, as we shall see, unable to lead a revolution them-selves. Where they differed, however, was in the relative faith each had in the peasants: Fanon saw them as a spontaneous revolutionary force, whereas for Cabral they were a vital, but difficult to persuade, physical force.

The two men also differed concerning the rôles played by the pro-letariat and the *lumpenproletariat*. (Since they did not consider them-selves Marxists, it is doubtful that they used these words, along with 'bourgeoisie', because they believed in them. Rather, it is suspected, they employed them symbolically as a basis for comparison with European revolutionary theory and because they were writing, in large measure, to a western audience familiar with such terminology.) The urban or colonial proletariat Cabral preferred to call 'wage-earners'. Although they were hardly a traditional proletariat, many became committed to the revolution because, in comparing their

---

[1] Cabral, 'At the United Nations' (1962), in *Revolution in Guinea*, p. 38. Also see Cabral, 'Identity and Dignity in the National Liberation Struggle', in *Africa Today*, XIX, 4, Fall 1972, p. 47.

[2] Cabral, 'Brief Analysis of the Social Structure', p. 61.

CONTRAST IN THEORIES OF REVOLUTION FOR AFRICA 199

status to that of European workers doing the same job but earning more, they developed a consciousness of their exploitation.[1] They are a 'little proletariat' and helped to make up the backbone of the revolution. Nevertheless, the cities themselves are strongholds of colonialism, and revolutionary activity there must be of a limited and clandestine nature.[2] Fanon, however, had absolutely no use for the colonial proletariat; in fact, he was contemptuous towards African workers who, he insisted, were like the bourgeoisie in industrial countries: a favoured class. 'In the colonial territories the proletariat is the nucleus of the colonized population which has been most pampered by the colonial regime.'[3] They were in a 'comparatively privileged position', and thus reluctant to attack a system which both created them and guaranteed their existence. 'In the colonial countries the working class has everything to lose; in reality it represents that fraction of the colonized nation which is necessary and irreplaceable if the colonial machine is to run smoothly.'[4] To rely on the proletariat, said Fanon, is to try to transpose European conditions on Africa.

Fanon and Cabral are equally far apart on the question of the *lumpenproletariat*. Marx thought this group was incapable of any constructive action. Cabral agreed to the extent that they were not to be trusted because of the assistance they usually give to the colonialists. But Cabral distinguished between two categories of *lumpenproletariat*. He expected nothing from the traditional *déclassés*, the beggars, prostitutes, pimps, and petty criminals. But the other group of *déclassés* are those 'young people who are connected to petty bourgeois or workers' families, who have recently arrived from the rural areas and generally do not work'.[5] This group is astute enough to compare its standard of living with the colonialists and, with the close relations it has with both the rural areas and the towns, has the potential for revolutionary consciousness.

Fanon did not draw a similar distinction between categories of *lumpenproletariat*. After beginning in the countryside, he said, the African revolution would filter into the towns through the *lumpenproletariat*, 'that fraction of the peasant population which is blocked on the outer

---

[1] Ibid. pp. 62 f.

[2] Cabral, 'At the United Nations', p. 37.

[3] Fanon, *The Wretched of the Earth*, p. 108.

[4] Ibid. p. 109. Fanon's position on the proletariat, especially in its relationship with the peasantry, has made subject to criticism by Marxists. See Nguyen Nghe, 'Frantz Fanon et les problèmes de l'indépendence', in *La Pensée* (Paris), 107, February 1963, pp. 22–36; and Jack Woddis, *New Theories of Revolution: a commentary on the views of Frantz Fanon, Régis Debray, and Herbert Marcuse* (New York, 1972), pp. 25–175.

[5] Cabral, 'Brief Analysis of the Social Structure', p. 59.

fringe of the urban centers, that fraction which has not yet succeeded in finding a bone to gnaw in the colonial system'. Once politicised this group would be the 'urban spearhead' of the revolution. 'For the *lumpenproletariat*, that horde of starving men, uprooted from their tribe and from their clan, constitutes one of the most spontaneous and the most radically revolutionary forces of a colonized people.'[1] Unlike Cabral's more precise analysis, Fanon's discussion here is highly romanticised. He expected 'the pimps, the hooligans, the unemployed and the petty criminals . . . all the hopeless dregs of humanity' to be able to 'recover their balance, once more go forward, and march proudly in the great procession of the awakened nation'.[2]

The final class to be evaluated by both men as they formulated their theories of revolution was the bourgeoisie (i.e. the merchants, business-men, civil servants, professional people, and a few agricultural land-owners). To Fanon it was a useless, parasitical class, not even a true bourgeoisie, but a 'greedy caste, avid and voracious . . . It remembers what it has read in European textbooks and imperceptibly it becomes not even a replica of Europe, but its caricature.'[3] And unlike in Euro-pean countries, the bourgeois phase in the history of underdeveloped countries is a useless one, not even promoting an economy to make a socialist revolution possible. The national middle class which takes over power at the end of the revolution is underdeveloped itself, and is in no way commensurate with the bourgeoisie of the mother country. It is engaged neither in production, building, nor labour. 'It is completely canalized into activities of the intermediary type. Its innermost vocation seems to be to keep in the running and to be part of the racket.'[4] Because the national bourgeoisie

is strung up to defend its immediate interests . . . sees no further than the end of its nose, [and] reveals itself incapable of simply bringing national unity into being, or of building up the nation on a stable and productive basis . . . [it] should not be allowed to find the conditions necessary for its existance and growth.[5]

The bourgeoisie only tries to replace the colonial class that had been removed by the revolution, whereas for Fanon the aim is to redistribute the productive energies of the nation, not to substitute black bourgeoisie for white.

Fanon wrote that the bourgeoisie must betray its classical rôle and not act like selfish, national bourgeoisie; it must think of the nation

---

[1] Fanon, *The Wretched of the Earth*, p. 129.
[2] Ibid. p. 130.   [3] Ibid. p. 175.
[4] Ibid. p. 150.   [5] Ibid. pp. 159 and 174 f.

CONTRAST IN THEORIES OF REVOLUTION FOR AFRICA 201

above itself and join with the revolutionary forces 'to repudiate its own nature in so far as it is bourgeois, that is to say in so far as it is the tool of capitalism, and to make itself the willing slave of that revolutionary capital which is the people'. But Fanon was not hopeful that the bourgeoisie would 'follow this heroic, positive, fruitful, and just path; rather, it disappears with its soul set at peace into the shocking ways . . . of a traditional bourgeoisie'.[1] Therefore, it must be replaced since by exploiting the country it is endangering the future.

Fanon resented the national bourgeoisie for another reason. As a pan-Africanist he was ambivalent towards nationalism which he viewed as a tool of liberation only. He wanted revolution to overflow national boundaries to create a new humanism in all of Africa. But the national bourgeoisie, he feared, put obstacles in the path of his dream. 'This is why we must understand that African unity can only be achieved through the upward thrust of the people, and under the leadership of the people, that is to say, in defiance of the interests of the bourgeoisie.'[2]

Cabral saw the same alternative facing the bourgeoisie – i.e. joining the revolution or betraying it – but he expected different results. Fanon's 'national bourgeoisie' is Cabral's 'native petty bourgeoisie'. This group emerges out of foreign domination and is indispensible to the system of colonial exploitation. It stands midway between the masses and the local representatives of the foreign ruling class. Even though it is native, the petty bourgeoisie strives to be like the foreign minority and become integrated with them. But the colonial system is such, observes Cabral, that this is impossible. Those of the African middle class 'do not succeed in overcoming the barriers thrown up by the system. They are prisoners of the social and cultural contradictions of their lives. They cannot escape their role as a marginal class.'[3] The petty bourgeoisie is the class which inherits power as a result of their European education and service to the colonial régime; their rôle in the African bureaucracy is indispensable. From this situation a feeling of bitterness and frustration develops which leads to them questioning their marginal status and rediscovering their identity. This group among the petty bourgeoisie (as opposed to those committed to, or compromised with, colonialism) is the only one capable of leading the revolution, since the peasants are a non-revolutionary force and the working class is in an embryo state.

The revolutionary petty bourgeoisie must then return to the masses

[1] Ibid. p. 150.
[2] Ibid. p. 164.
[3] Cabral, 'Identity and Dignity', p. 42.

and completely identify with them. This process is slow and uneven, with many among the bourgeoisie being indecisive. But it is only through the struggle that they can hope to identify with the masses; from the African bourgeoisie there arises 'the first important step toward mobilizing and organizing the masses for the struggle'.[1] With the success of the struggle the petty bourgeoisie must continue to lead. 'The moment national liberation comes and the petty bourgeoisie takes power we enter, or rather return to history, and thus the internal contradictions break out again.'[2] When this happens 'the petty bourgeoisie can either ally itself with imperialism and the reactionary strata in its own country to try and preserve itself as a petty bourgeoisie or ally itself with the workers and peasants'.[3] This, finally, means that for the petty bourgeoisie to fulfil its rôle in the revolution it 'must be capable of committing suicide as a class in order to be reborn as revolutionary workers, completely identified with the deepest aspirations of the people to which they belong'.[4] This, said Cabral, is the dilemma of the petty bourgeoisie in the struggle. It is also the fulcrum upon which turns the success of the revolution.

Thus, although both men could agree on the nature of the dilemma facing the indigenous bourgeoisie, the results of their respective analyses pointed in opposite directions. Fanon's bourgeoisie would fail the revolution and try to use the struggle for its own selfish ends; other groups would have to ensure the success of the struggle. But Cabral's bourgeoisie, in sufficient numbers, would – no, must – join forces with the masses, and become reincarnated in the condition of workers and peasants to bring about a successful revolution. This is one of the most important differences between their theories.

PARTIES AND LEADERSHIP

Lenin made a distinctive contribution to the theory and practice of revolution when he substituted party for class as the motive force. The party, he said, showed the masses the way.[5] Virtually all revolutionary theorists since then have utilised Lenin, in one way or another, in their analyses of parties and leadership. Fanon and Cabral each recognised

---

[1] Ibid. p. 47.

[2] Cabral, 'Brief Analysis of the Social Structure', p. 69.

[3] Ibid. p. 70.

[4] Cabral, 'The Weapon of Theory', p. 110.

[5] For a discussion and evaluation of Lenin's theory on, and contribution to, the concept of revolution, as well as those of others, see Robert Blackey and Clifford T. Paynton, *Revolution and the Revolutionary Ideal* (Cambridge, Mass., forthcoming).

CONTRAST IN THEORIES OF REVOLUTION FOR AFRICA 203

the value of efficient leaders for a successful revolution but, as with the other factors we have surveyed, there are both similarities and differences in their considerations.

Fanon, as emphasised above, recognised the conservative nature of the peasants, as well as their potential for collective and spontaneous violent action. But peasants lack adequate intellectual leadership without which the revolution would fail. Such leadership, according to Fanon, will come from the revolutionary élite in the cities who otherwise have no base for action. It is crucial for revolutionary leaders to intervene at the precise moment when peasant hostility erupts against the colonial force. With outside leadership, momentum can be maintained and the insurrection of the peasants can be transformed into a revolution.[1] Thus, Fanon hoped to turn peasant violence into an angry awareness of injustices by merging it with revolutionary leadership. When peasant revolts occur it is the duty of revolutionary leaders to move in and direct them.

What Fanon found wrong with most national political parties in colonial countries was that they were reformist and alienated from the peasants. He opposed single-party régimes as 'the modern form of the dictatorship of the bourgeoisie, unmasked, unpainted, unscrupulous, and cynical'.[2] Instead, he urged the more radical and militant members of those national parties to join with the peasants, and together become the basis for the political organisation of the revolution. Although he was not especially specific regarding this organisation, he did develop the idea of a minority or illegal party, composed of the urban radicals acting as the ideological vanguard and the masses as their numerical base.[3] This illegal party, then, is led by deviant nationalists who have reacted against the enclosed character and limited nature of the traditional national party. They are pushed out of the city to the countryside where they discover that the peasants, unlike the urban proletariat, are not indifferent. In this way the rôle of the peasants in the illegal party is crucial; the party is the product of the fusion of the peasants with the urban revolutionary élite (to which the galvanised *lumpenproletariat* are later added).

Perhaps because he was in more of a central leadership rôle in his revolution than Fanon was in Algeria, Cabral employed greater precision in discussing the rôle of party and leadership. Like Fanon he shared a fear of élites but the P.A.I.G.C. had a real structure that

[1] Fanon, *The Wretched of the Earth*, 'Spontaneity: its strength and weakness', passim.
[2] Ibid. p. 165.
[3] Ibid. pp. 125–8.

14

Fanon's vaguer illegal party lacked. 'In our circumstances the Party equals the State because there is no other means of making the State a truly national, truly liberating organism',[1] wrote Cabral. He sought a government that would emerge during the struggle, grow from village roots, and avoid the perils of becoming a privileged minority or an oligarchical network. 'The Party is the people', said Cabral. 'For us the people's opinion . . . is extremely important, because the Party is fighting for the people.'[2] Cabral's study of the social structure of his country indicated that for victory to be achieved *all* the groups of Guinea-Bissau would have to be united, and not just Fanon's peasants, *lumpenproletariat*, and urban leadership. Therefore, one of the primary functions of the P.A.I.G.C. would be to minimise the conflicts and contradictions among the various groups and classes making up the struggle. Only a politically aware, revolutionary party can distinguish between true national independence and fictitious political independence, and then make it known, through the struggle, to the masses.[3]

During the struggle, liberated areas must be organised so that colonial rule can be replaced effectively. Autonomous regions must be eliminated to prevent local potentates from exercising power, selfishly, over the people. Everything must be tied to the party's central organisation, with military leadership a part of (and not separate from, nor superior to) the political. But military effectiveness is vital because the revolutionists must show the masses that they are at least as powerful as the colonial army; otherwise they might lose the support of the masses. Therefore, the party must also train and organise forces to follow-up the political groundwork. Simultaneously, care must be taken to keep the guerrillas in contact with the masses and to encourage local participation. All this is the task of the party for Cabral.

REVOLUTIONARY VIOLENCE

Fanon is probably best known for his views on violence and revolution, a subject about which there is considerable debate.[4] Although he was not especially consistent in his pronouncements on violence,

---

[1] Quoted in Davidson, op. cit. p. 138.
[2] Quoted in Chaliand, op. cit. p. 68.
[3] Cabral, 'The Weapon of Theory', p. 105.
[4] See A. Norman Klein, 'On Revolutionary Violence', in *Studies On The Left* (New York), VI, 3, 1966, pp. 62–82; Barbara Deming, 'On Revolution and Equilibrium', in *Liberation* (London), XII, 1, February 1968, pp. 10–21; Louis Coser, 'Fanon and Debray: theorists of the Third World', in Irving Howe (ed.), *Beyond the New Left* (New York, 1970); Horace Sutton, 'Fanon', in *Saturday Review* (New York), 17 July 1971; Gendzier, op. cit.; and Jinadu, loc. cit.

CONTRAST IN THEORIES OF REVOLUTION FOR AFRICA 205

much of what he said can be understood if *all* of his views are considered. Cabral's thoughts on the subject were somewhat similar, although he was not as preoccupied with violence as Fanon.

During the revolutionary process of seizing freedom, violence, according to Fanon, is necessarily applied because the very structure of colonialism is fundamentally violent.

Decolonization, which sets out to change the order of the world, is, obviously, a program of complete disorder . . . [Colonialism] is violence in its natural state, and it will only yield when confronted with greater violence.[1]

Decolonisation involves 'vomiting up' foreign values and this produces new men. Through violence Africans come to realise that the colonialists are no different from themselves, that their lives and their skins are the same. This discovery, according to Fanon, 'shakes the world in a very necessary manner. All the new, revolutionary assurance of the natives stems from it.'[2] Thus, violence 'makes it possible for the masses to understand social truths and gives the key to them. Without the struggle . . . there's nothing but . . . [the masses], still living in the middle ages.'[3] Violence and revolution are not only rewards in themselves, but means to a greater end as well.

Yet, Fanon admitted that other means may be appropriate if the situation dictates it. 'If need be, the native can accept a compromise with colonialism, but never a surrender of principle.'[4] A colonised people must win their war of liberation, he insisted, 'but they must do so cleanly, without "barbarity" . . . The underdeveloped nation that practices torture thereby confirms its nature, plays the role of an underdeveloped people.'[5] The rest of the world, in order to accept a colonised nation setting itself up as an independent nation, must see the colonised people, in every one of its acts, as lucid and self-controlled.

Because we believe one cannot rise and liberate oneself in one area and sink in another, we condemn, with pain in our hearts, those brothers who have flung themselves into revolutionary action with the almost physiological brutality that centuries of oppression gave rise to.[6]

An explanation for this apparent inconsistency may lie in the North African context in which Fanon found himself, and in the emotional nature of much of his writing. In Algeria the French were deeply entrenched with a large *colon* or settler population, and were determined to hold on, whatever the cost; the Algerian revolutionists had no

[1] Fanon, *The Wretched of the Earth*, pp. 36 and 61.
[2] Ibid. p. 45. [3] Ibid. p. 147.
[4] Ibid. p. 143. [5] Fanon, *A Dying Colonialism* (New York edn., 1965), p. 24.
[6] Ibid. p. 25.

206   ROBERT BLACKEY

alternative to violence. Therefore, when Fanon wrote of violence as 'a cleansing force . . . [freeing] the native from his despair and inaction ',[1] he was probably referring to Algeria only; he was not celebrating violence *per se*. In fact, he acknowledged that while 'in Algeria the test of force was inevitable . . . other countries through political action and through the work of clarification undertaken by a party have led their people to the same results'.[2] Thus, Fanon wrote only of a reactive violence that was an integral part of justice and non-compromise.

Cabral did not devote very much attention to violence, though like Fanon he realised that it was the essential instrument of imperialist domination. Revolution and national liberation, he believed, cannot occur

without the use of liberating violence by the nationalist forces, to answer the criminal violence of the agents of imperialism . . . Imperialist domination implies a state of permanent violence against the nationalist forces. There is no people on earth which, having been subjected to the imperialist yoke (colonialist or neo-colonialist), has managed to gain its independence (nominal or effective) without victims.[3]

Violence needs to be used not only in response to the violence of imperialism, but also to ensure true national independence. Compromises with imperialism, as experience taught Cabral, do not work. But, as opposed to the French in Algeria, who were well settled, there have been other colonialists who have not been interested in establishing that kind of colony. Therefore, in such a situation, as in Guinea-Bissau with the Portuguese, terrorism need not be employed. A military struggle is often enough.[4]

RÔLE OF CULTURE AND FUTURE PROSPECTS

As with most of the components of revolution we have considered, especially where the two theorists tend to share similar ideas, Cabral was more organised and attentive to detail than Fanon. But when both men defined the rôle of culture in a revolutionary situation, and speculated about the future, the differences between them are less pronounced. Each employed more generalisations than usual – though Cabral still less than Fanon – and each was essentially optimistic.

One of the greatest evils of colonialism, according to Fanon, is that 'it turns to the past of the oppressed people, and distorts, disfigures,

[1] Fanon, *The Wretched of the Earth*, p. 94.
[2] Ibid. p. 193.
[3] Cabral, 'The Weapon of Theory', p. 107.
[4] Cabral, 'Practical Problems and Tactics', p. 135.

CONTRAST IN THEORIES OF REVOLUTION FOR AFRICA 207

and destroys it'. It warns Africans that if the settlers depart then they 'would at once fall back into barbarism, degradation, and bestiality'.[1] Colonialism had 'generously' lightened their darkness. But this negative situation can only be countered when the native turns backwards towards his unknown roots – then he 'turns himself into the defender of his people's past; he is willing to be counted as one of them, and henceforth he is even capable of laughing at his past cowardice'.[2] The purpose of culture is to utilise the past to open the future, to be an invitation to action and a basis for hope. 'To fight for national culture means . . . to fight for the liberation of the nation, the material keystone which makes the building of a culture possible. There is no other fight for culture which can develop apart from the popular struggle.'[3] Thus, culture aims not only to counteract the evils of colonialism but to construct the future.

A national culture is the whole body of efforts made by a people in the sphere of thought to describe, justify, and praise the action through which that people has created itself and keeps itself in existence. A national culture in underdeveloped countries should therefore take its place at the very heart of the struggle for freedom which these countries are carrying on.[4]

Culture is a vital part of a people's identity in its struggle for freedom.

Cabral agreed. In fact, he went so far as to assert that it is impossible to create and develop a revolution unless a people keep their culture alive in the face of continued organised repression of their way of life. 'It is cultural resistance which at a given moment can take on new forms – political, economic, military – to fight foreign domination.'[5] Cabral further observed that in the colonial situation the cultural influence of the imperial power is limited to the capital and other urban centres, and then only to small numbers of petty bourgeoisie and urban workers. As for the masses, they are either completely or almost untouched by the culture of the colonial power. Since foreigners are not even interested in promoting culture for the masses, the latter, in turn, 'find that their own culture acts as a bulwark in preserving their identity'.[6]

The future, to Fanon's mind, would be bright. Every victory in the revolutionary struggle 'is a defeat for racism and for the exploitation of man . . . [inaugurating] the unconditional reign of Justice'.[7] Fanon

---

[1] Fanon, *The Wretched of the Earth*, pp. 210 f.
[2] Ibid. p. 218.   [3] Ibid. p. 233.
[4] Ibid.   [5] Cabral, 'Identity and Dignity', pp. 40 f.
[6] Ibid. p. 41.
[7] Fanon, 'Algeria Face to Face with the French Torturers' (1957), in *Toward the African Revolution*, p. 64.

did not elaborate upon what would happen after the success of the revolution. His emphasis was on redistribution rather than upon material creation. Moreover, he viewed the struggle for liberation as part of a larger African-wide movement for a democratic and social revolution. But in pursuing this goal, Fanon warned, none of the African nations could afford to imitate western and capitalistic ways of life; in fact, none should *dare* imitate the West because it would only lead to a similar moral and spiritual debasement. He tried to minimise the differences between Arab Africa and Black Africa because they, as well as the other divisions of the continent, in no way reflected tribal differences, geographic realities, or economic and social factors. They were, instead, the 'gift' of Europe to Africa. Fanon believed that common interests should bring Africans together in order to 'try to set afoot a new man'.[1]

Cabral also believed in looking to the future, beyond the struggle for national liberation, to the economic, social, and cultural evolution of the people on their road to progress. He, too, opposed 'narrow national-isms which do not serve the true interests of the people' and favoured instead an 'African unity, on a regional or continental scale, inasfar as it is necessary for the progress of the African peoples'.[2] Although he expected tribal differences to disappear with the success of the struggle as they were absorbed by the new social order, he still recognised that everyday conditions must also be changed. The most important thing of all, he said, 'is an understanding of our people's situation . . . We must assure [them] that those who bear arms are sons of the people and that arms are no better than the tools of labor.'[3] The purpose and goal of the revolution is to protect the man with the tool.

EPITAPH

Fanon was more concerned with making the revolution than with predicting the future in much detail. His writings were intended to be a part of the war against colonialism and imperialism. He saw hope for Africa in all the people of the continent coming to grips with the problems of unity and solidarity, so that they could collectively pursue the best interests of all concerned, especially those of the masses, in the quest for total liberation. Fanon was a brilliant propagandist of revolu-tion, a prophet of hope for the oppressed.

[1] Fanon, *The Wretched of the Earth*, p. 316.
[2] Cabral, 'Guinea and Cabo Verde Against Portuguese Colonialism', p. 17.
[3] Quoted in Chaliand, op. cit. p. 35.

CONTRAST IN THEORIES OF REVOLUTION FOR AFRICA 209

Less emotional than Fanon, Cabral was also a prophet of hope. He, too, was primarily concerned with making the revolution, but he placed it under the microscope of analysis in a way Fanon did not. More than any other revolutionist in this century, with the exception of Lenin and Mao Tse-tung, Cabral lived, breathed, and thought through his people's revolution as a unique event. He was laying down a cardinal principle when he said that 'it is necessary for each people to find its own formula for mobilizing for the struggle'.[1] Each country entering upon a path of revolution must look to its own internal contradictions and problems.

Our own reality – however fine and attractive the reality of others may be – can only be transformed by detailed knowledge of it, by our own efforts, by our own sacrifices . . . However great the similarity between our various cases and however identical our enemies, national liberation and social revolution are not exportable commodities.[2]

He was a high-principled but practical and far-sighted revolutionist.

In lieu of Cabral's advice no conclusion that unequivocally decides in favour of either revolutionist would be in order. Fanon, to be sure, is the better known and more widely read. His words pound on the doors of consciences; what he says comes from the heart and swells the body to action. But Fanon, as we have observed, is sometimes contradictory and his generalisations often lack supportive evidence. However valuable Fanon may be, he should not be taken as the sole guide for the African revolution. Cabral is more an excellent companion than an alternative, while their differences can be overcome by following his advice to find the proper formula for a given situation.

Both Fanon and Cabral fell victim to a cancer, the former to the kind medical science is attempting to conquer, the latter to the variety for which revolution seeks a cure. The differences in their theories of revolution are important to evaluate, but it must also be noted that they were seeking a similar future for their people.

[1] Cabral, 'Practical Problems and Tactics', pp. 159 f.
[2] Cabral, 'The Weapon of Theory', p. 92.

Robert Blackey is a professor of history at California State University, San Bernardino and author/editor of several books and articles on revolution, British history, and history teaching and learning. He is a former vice president of the American Historical Association and recipient of a number of local, state, and national awards for academic and service excellence.

[4]

British Decolonization since 1945: A Pattern or a Puzzle?

by

John Darwin

It is scarcely a matter of dispute, or even of serious argument, that by 1945 the British empire was in decline, and British world power ebbing away. The global conditions once so favourable to Britain's colossal empire-on-the-cheap were disappearing one by one with the emergence of the military superpowers, the relative decline of the British economy, the obsolescence of old-style sea-power and the new turbulence of Britain's colonial possessions. It is easy and tempting indeed to regard Britain's international career from 1945 up until her eventual entry into Europe in 1973 as a dismal epilogue to the Second World war, a gloomy saga of lost illusions, lost opportunities and lost causes as the inevitable gradually became the irresistible. From our vantage point in the 1980s we can applaud the realists who grasped the inexorability of declining world status and the futility of resisting it, and regret the wrong-headedness of those who would not read the writing on the wall. From this it has been an easy step to conflate the 25 years after 1945 into a single phase of rapid and predictable decline.

Decline, however, is a treacherously ambiguous phase in the history of empires. The Habsburg empire declined from 1848, or perhaps from 1809, but survived until the last year of the First World War. The Ottoman empire had been in decline since the treaty of Carlowitz in 1699, but survived to inflict 217 years later a series of humiliating defeats on Britain in the Middle East war; the Sick Man of Europe had shown an alarming will to live, perhaps because even sick men will resist being eaten alive. In the same way, though Britain's relative decline as a world and imperial power was a safe bet by 1945, four issues still remained obscure. How rapidly and how completely would British power contract? How swiftly would self-government be conceded to the extremely heterogeneous collection of territories that constituted the imperial system? What would self-government amount to when and if it were granted? And what kind of post-colonial relationship would be established between Britain and her ex-colonies? On each of these questions great uncertainties existed at the end of the war. Yet only by taking these uncertainties into account is it possible to make sense of the calculations of the policy-makers. Unless, that is, we assume that the actual course of British decolonization exactly followed a master plan laid down in Whitehall – an event that would be

188   PERSPECTIVES ON IMPERIALISM AND DECOLONIZATION

unique in British post-war history – or that the policy-makers expected or
intended that events should fall out as they did. That too strains credulity
too far.

I

Of course, from the moment that the British began the transfer of power
in their colonial territories after 1945 they set about constructing a
rationale for their actions plausible enough and ambiguous enough to
satisfy international and especially American opinion, to soothe opinion
at home and to flatter the colonial politicians whose goodwill they
wanted. The task of fabricating an account that would gratify if not flatter
every interested constituency was an heroic one; but it was a challenge
that the British official mind was almost uniquely fitted to meet. To
extract a set of guiding principles from the raw mass of incoherent
political and administrative action, to transform past decisions into the
self-evident prelude for future policy (however contrary), to embalm the
whole in a paste of consistency with a dash of altruism, these were the
tasks for which after all it had been trained and at which the scholar-
mandarins excelled.[1] Circumstances required that the policy-makers
make myths as fast as they unmade colonies, for the creation of new states
and the dissolution of empires was chancy work as the politicians of the
French Fourth Republic discovered. Much flannel was needed to prevent
combustible elements jarring on each other: the unravelling of empire
must appear as an orderly, rational, honourable and, above all, deliberate process – a pattern and not an embarrassing puzzle.

From this necessity was borne what remains perhaps the most influential account of how Britain came to transfer power in her colonial territories after 1945. Its most graceful exponent was Harold Macmillan, a
romancer in the tradition of Disraeli. In his memoirs, Macmillan reiterated what had become the orthodox defence of decolonization. 'There is
a common illusion', he wrote, 'that this story ... is one of weakness and
decay, resulting from the loss of the will to govern inherent in a democratic system. This is an undeserved libel on a people who, twice in my
lifetime, demonstrated their courage and tenacity, as well as against its
leaders.' He went on:

> It is a vulgar but false jibe that the British people by a series of
> gestures unique in history abandoned their empire in a fit of frivolity
> or impatience. They had not lost the will or even the power to rule.
> But they did not conceive of themselves as having the right to
> govern in perpetuity. It was rather their duty to spread to other
> nations those advantages which through the course of centuries they
> had won for themselves.[2]

In this picturesque version, decolonization became not a symptom of
defeat and decline but a crowning achievement of British rule, the goal
towards which, Macmillan insisted, colonial rulers had steadily striven.

Implicit in it is the assumption that British colonial policy after 1945 prescribed the steady introduction of phase after phase of constitutional development, carefully graduated to the individual needs of each colony, until at the end of the day a more rapid acceleration became possible and desirable. The road from colonial subordination to sovereign status lay through the corridors of power in a beneficent Whitehall. Empire itself was presented as a white man's burden, a trust honourably discharged and then deliberately and systematically wound up. Here was Whig history large as life and twice as shameless. Just so might we imagine Lord Grey of the Reform bill telling his great grandchildren that his purpose in 1832 had been to pave the way for universal suffrage.

The low-minded alternative to this grandee history has been to see the decolonizing process as an inevitable response to the collapse of British power. One recent Commonwealth historian has discovered in the period 1941–71 an overarching *Pax Americana* and a Britain reduced at the end of the Second World War 'almost to protectorate status'.[3] It is easy in this perspective to see the sloughing off of colonial possessions as the progressive shedding of intolerable burdens at the earliest possible moment. Here decolonization was the conscious recognition that since Britain's days as a great power were numbered, it was essential to speed the transfer of power if disaster was to be avoided. Hence, in rapid succession, representative government, self-government and then independence were offered to grateful colonial politicians, and Britain escaped, as the policy-makers had always intended, unscathed by colonial conflicts that were as futile as they were unwinnable. A modified version of this is represented by those historians who see post-war British colonial policy as a deliberate step-by-step retreat in the face of the floodtide of colonial nationalism, a staged retreat the pace of which was dictated less by British decay than by the rapid growth of political organization and mass politics in the dependencies.[4]

Finally, there are those accounts of post-war British policy which base themselves chiefly upon the memories of civil servants or ministers of the time, or, as in the recent official study of colonial development, upon privileged access to the plans and blueprints of the policy-makers.[5] The result is an uplifting chronicle of sagacity and foresight, of careful adaptation to new circumstances, of enlightened and sympathetic response to the aspirations of colonial populations, of dignified understanding that Britain's role must change with the times. In this version, too, decolonization proceeded in orderly fashion at a pace dictated not so much by the urge to share Britain's democratic heritage, nor by fears of catastrophe, nor by timidity in the face of the nationalist tiger, but rather as a consequence of judicious appraisal, a careful weighing of ends and means, a desire to be helpful and constructive. This, of course, is mandarin history, a version of decolonization of which Sir Humphrey Appleby would approve, and might have written: decolonization as an ordered sequence of memoranda, minutes and masterly inactivity.

Common to all these versions is the assumption that decolonization

190   PERSPECTIVES ON IMPERIALISM AND DECOLONIZATION

should be seen as a consecutive sequence, that the British adopted broadly consistent policies across the whole face of their imperial system, and that even if they sometimes changed gear or shifted from the brake to the accelerator and back again, the makers of policy were always moving deliberately in the same direction. The trouble is that the more closely we peer at the actual course of Britain's retreat from empire, the more difficult it is to see any ordered pattern. The notion that post-war decolonization was a long-matured act of benevolence is belied by the record of British rule in much of the pre-war British empire, especially in Africa where the system of indirect rule conserved power precisely in the hands of those whose democratic instincts were least developed.[6] The building of an independent deterrent and the Suez expedition are curious enterprises for a power reduced 'almost to protectorate status'. The onslaught on the Malayan Communist Party, Mau Mau, EOKA or the Front for the Liberation of South Yemen scarcely resemble a staged retreat in the face of nationalism. As for the omniscience of the mandarins, the record of British policy in other spheres, for example, in economic policy or towards Europe, suggests that the predictive powers of the official mind should be measured in hours rather than decades. Moreover, it would have required exceptional clairvoyance to have predicted in the late 1940s that decolonization would follow the course and yield the results that it has.

The fact is, of course, that British foreign and colonial policy after 1945 was riddled with extraordinary and baffling inconsistencies. The independence of India and Pakistan in 1947 took a form precisely contrary to that intended by British policy-makers almost until the last moment. The reluctant concession of self-government to Burma and Ceylon was contrasted with the simultaneous brusque imposition on Malaya and Singapore of a unitary colonial constitution to which local leaders were bitterly opposed and which then had to be abandoned. Colonial withdrawal in South Asia was matched by the uncompromising reassertion of colonial rule in Hong Kong.[7] In 1949 India was admitted to the Commonwealth as a republic. A year earlier, London had refused precisely that concession to Burma which then left the Commonwealth. In Africa between 1948 and 1958 the disparities were no less striking. The Gold Coast and Nigeria were conceded self-government in doses after 1948. But in East Africa African political activity in Kenya was firmly repressed in the 1950s, and an indefinite prolongation of colonial rule envisaged. In Tanganyika, the British tried to impose a multiracial constitution the effect of which was actually to enlarge the influence of immigrant communities – at the expense of Africans – through the new representative institutions. In Central Africa, the centrepiece of British policy was the construction of a white-ruled federation into which the protectorates of Northern Rhodesia and Nyasaland were thrust regardless of the wishes of their African populations. With its telescope clapped firmly to its ear, London declared that opposition could be neither seen nor heard.

Even after 1958, as the scramble out of Africa got under way, British policy remained a jungle of quirks and quiddities. As late as the spring of 1959, the date of Kenya's independence was pencilled in as 1975.[8] The decision to share the benefits of Britain's political tradition with Mr Kenyatta was, to put it mildly, a sudden one. In 1963, the British eventually, and reluctantly, closed down the Rhodesian federation on the grounds that the majority of Africans in the northern territories were opposed to membership. But also in 1963 Aden was gerrymandered into a South Arabian federation after a Legislative Council vote from which most of the elected members (elected anyway by only 10 per cent of the population) were absent.[9] Further east methods were no less proconsular. After a two-month tour of North Borneo and Sarawak in 1962, the Cobbold Commission concluded that although most of the interior population had little idea what the scheme for a Malaysian federation entailed, it could be assumed that the majority favoured it.[10] Plainly, in both cases the wishes or even the interests of the inhabitants were at best a secondary consideration. Nor can it be assumed that even after London became fully committed to the transfer of power in the African colonies and elsewhere, that British policy-makers had quietly resigned themselves to a European destiny or meekly accepted the status to which Britain's relative economic decline condemned her. As late as 1965 the British intended to remain in Aden as the guardians and patrons of a gimcrack South Arabian state, just as they were already of Malaysia, and to use the two great bases. The deployment of the army and navy east of Suez was markedly increased after 1960. As late as 1965 Harold Wilson – that latterday Curzon – made his celebrated assertion that Britain's frontiers were on the Himalayas. (The discovery two years later that they were really on the Rhine was one of the fastest strategic withdrawals in modern times.) Meanwhile, at home, amid a series of financial hurricanes, the Labour Government grimly sought to defend sterling's role as a reserve currency and to preserve the Sterling Area as the economic proof of world power.[11] Not until the dual crisis over devaluation and withdrawal from East of Suez at the end of 1967 did the old imperial reflexes cease to twitch.

Indeed, far from suggesting a staged and deliberate rundown of Britain's overseas commitments and imperial responsibilities, the leaps and lurches of British policy after 1945 form a set of baffling contradictions, indicating neither a gracious manumission of deserving subjects, a headlong retreat in the face of rampant nationalism, nor the cool assessment of Britain's changing interests. What are we to make of it?

During the Second World War, the British had come to recognize that major changes would have to be made in their empire to meet local aspirations, to reflect new social and economic needs and to conciliate American opinion. The necessity for change was most pronounced in Asia where all British colonies had felt the impact of war and conquest. Above all, there was the question of India.

Before 1939 the British had planned to bring India towards dominion status by slow and indefinite stages once the federal constitution laid down in the 1935 India Act had become fully operational.[12] Whatever chances this programme had of success were wrecked by the outbreak of war.[13] Congress denounced India's involuntary participation in an alien conflict and withdrew from government in the provinces. After a series of fruitless negotiations about how much control Indian politicians would be allowed over India's war effort, culminating in the Cripps Mission of 1942, Gandhi launched the abortive 'Quit India' campaign in August 1942. British counter-measures were decisive. The Congress leaders were gaoled and the Congress machine proscribed. But the British remained desperately anxious to secure the support of as many Indians as possible for the Indian war effort and to avoid ruling India by decree. Various politicians were co-opted into office. But the crucial step was to acknowledge the hitherto scouted claim of the Muslim League to be representative of all Indian Muslims, in return for its political cooperation.[14] As a result, by the time the war ended in 1945 Indian politics had undergone a quiet revolution. The Congress leadership, gaoled, bitter and resentful, were determined to reassert their authority. The Muslim League had made hay while the sun shone and captured many Muslims from Congress. Their claim to speak for the Muslim community could not lightly be set aside. Finally, the British were saddled with the promise made by Cripps in the desperate days of 1942 that Britain would give India independence at the war's end.[15]

The Attlee government believed that the prompt fulfilment of this pledge would reap a rich reward in Indian gratitude, and that Congress would respond in a spirit of fraternity.[16] They also intended that Indian independence should follow the formula laid down ten years earlier: an Indian federation that would become the Dominion of India. Their reasons were not merely sentimental. A federal Indian dominion, run by sympathetic Indian politicians would, it was argued fondly in London, respect the long tradition of Anglo-Indian strategic partnership in Asia. India would look to Britain to guarantee her vulnerable northern frontier and in return would share the burdens of the weary titan in South East Asia.[17] But to win this prize, it was essential, as the Chiefs of Staff remarked, for India to be 'stable and contented'.[18] India was anything but that. Congress leaders, now out of gaol, demanded immediate independence and threatened insurrection if it were delayed. They were determined to concede nothing to the Muslim League. Briefly, the Viceroy, Lord Wavell, and London toyed with the idea of a further round of repression to force Congress into a reasonable frame of mind.[19] This was fantasy. In the spring of 1946 the Home Member of the Government of India gloomily remarked 'On the whole I doubt whether a Congress rebellion could be suppressed'.[20] From that moment, British policy in the sub-continent was governed by a sense of frightening impotence. The Raj was over.

Nevertheless, the Attlee cabinet was determined that, come what may, some formula should be found to preserve Indian unity and hold both Muslims and Hindus in a federal state. This was the purpose of the

Cabinet Mission of 1946 which drew up a byzantine scheme for a three-tier federation of India that would reserve external affairs and defence – those aspects of Indian political life which interested Britain most – to a central government, and preserve the unity of India's armed forces. The Mission came, saw and failed.[21] By the end of 1946 Wavell, the Viceroy, was warning that, as waves of communal turbulence washed over the sub-continent, Britain's capacity to keep order was melting away.[22] In desperation Wavell proposed his breakdown plan – to force the Congress and Muslim politicians into compromise. British rule, said Wavell, should be progressively withdrawn from province after province, leaving the local politicians to settle between them the distribution of power, until at last British troops and civilians could be evacuated from the main ports and Indian self-government would become a fact.[23] But the Attlee cabinet would not hear of it.

Their reasons are revealing. Wavell's plan, of course, would fracture the unity of India, probably for ever. But a greater danger worried ministers. To put the plan into effect, it was discovered, would require the repeal or drastic amendment of the 1935 India Act with its obligations and responsibilities.[24] The thought of subjecting their policy to parliamentary debate and public scrutiny at such a moment drove ministers into a panic. They also rejected any idea of setting a time limit on British rule fearing, as the Cabinet minutes record, that it might 'be regarded as the beginnings of the liquidation of the British Empire'.[25] Attlee had not become the King's first minister for that. Instead of changing his policy, Attlee, following a sound political maxim, changed the Viceroy instead.

The new Viceroy, Lord Mountbatten, was shrewd enough to extract from a reluctant Cabinet the promise of a public and precise time-limit,[26] and a virtual free hand to find some way of bringing India to independence. But barren as they were of any idea or policy, the Cabinet's instructions directed the Viceroy to strive for a united India and pay full regard to the defence requirements of the Indian Ocean.[27] Once in India, however, Mountbatten quickly realized that the most for which Britain could hope was to withdraw before British troops and officials were caught up in a vast civil war. But every effort to break down Muslim insistence on Pakistan, or find a formula acceptable to both Congress and the League, seemed doomed to fail until at the last moment Nehru and the Congress reluctantly agreed that partition was preferable to the chaos that threatened.[28] Once Congress accepted partition, Mountbatten set out to terminate British rule at breakneck speed. Before even their new boundaries had been published,[29] two new sub-continental states were declared independent in August 1947.

The course of Cabinet discussion right up to the last phase of the Indian problem disposes of any idea that the end of the Raj represented the triumphant reward for long and careful planning. Relief at Britain's fortuitous escape from a disastrous civil conflict which would have had far-flung repercussions on policy and prestige elsewhere disguised the extent to which India's independence was a humiliating reversal of the

hopes and intentions of pre-war and wartime policy-makers. The outcome in India had been dictated not by the blueprint laid down in London
nor even by negotiation between British officials and Indian politicians. It
was the consequence, above all, of local circumstances, while the policy-
makers in London were largely reduced to impatient and nervous onlook-
ers. Even the crucial decision to divide and quit had waited on the
conversion of Congress and could not have been done without its consent.
The same hasty unplanned retreat occurred in Burma where the British
had originally intended to restore their authority and introduce a phased
approach to self-government.[30] By December 1946 the Governor
reported that the means to resist the principal nationalist party, Aung
San's Anti-Fascist People's Freedom League, were lacking.[31] London
agreed on immediate independence.[32] To add insult to injury, nothing
could persuade the Burmese not to adopt a republican constitution
incompatible with the prevailing conventions of Commonwealth
membership.[33] Even in placid Ceylon, demands for parity with India's
status, British fear of growing communist support, and anxiety to preserve the great naval base at Trincomalee resulted in a dramatic acceleration of the island's hitherto leisurely progress towards self-government.[34]
By 1948, Ceylon, like Burma, India and Pakistan, had cast off British
rule.

II

On the face of it, the great bulk of Britain's Asian Empire, once the envy
of her rivals, had collapsed like a mud fort in a monsoon. What an Indian
historian called the 'Vasco da Gama epoch' in Asian history had come to
an end. But the British were curiously reluctant to see the events of
1945–8 in this light. Their strategic thinking, as Phillip Darby has pointed
out, showed little sign of being influenced by the loss of India.[35] Indeed,
London persisted in thinking that once the excitement of independence
had worn off, Indian politicians would recognize how natural it still was to
collaborate diplomatically and strategically with their former rulers. In
early 1949 Sir William Strang toured South East Asia and the Far East to
assess the chances of containing Soviet influence in the region. He
reported:

> In all this [that is, Soviet containment] the Indian sub-continent has
> a special importance .... India in particular has an important role to
> play in peripheral politics – as a Great Asian Power; as a possible
> member of the Commonwealth; as a country with whom the United
> Kingdom now has an opportunity to develop relations on a new
> basis; as a country with political, cultural and economic interests in
> South West Asia which we should try to carry with us in the framing
> of policies and the development of action in that region.[36]

Arguments of this kind, not zeal for the democratic re-definition of the
Commonwealth, led the Attlee government to bow to Nehru's demand to

stay in the Commonwealth with a republican constitution, although Attlee told Nehru, with Churchillian assurance, that a republic was alien to India's traditions.[37] Agreement was grudging and India was clearly treated as a special case. Much the same pragmatic optimism coloured official attitudes to Ceylon. Patrick Gordon Walker, then junior Commonwealth Minister, visited there soon after independence. British ·policy, he reported, had been a great success. Local politicians 'are extremely friendly and want to maintain and deepen the British connexion'. If the British had only the sense to be tactful, nothing of substance would change. 'It is hardly too much to say', concluded this future champion of the Commonwealth ideal, 'that if we treat them strictly as a Dominion, they will behave very like a loyal colony: whereas if we treat them as a Colony, we may end in driving them out of the Commonwealth'.[38] Elsewhere in Asia, however, London had no hesitation in treating its colonies exactly like colonies. Hong Kong, as we have seen, was triumphantly reclaimed from a fate worse than death, as a Chinese city.[39] And in Malaya, the Colonial Office was determined to build a strong centralized colonial state, embracing Singapore, as a far more effective bastion of British rule and influence than the ramshackle colony that had collapsed ignominiously in 1942.[40] Even after the Malayan Sultans had successfully repudiated the Colonial Office's brainchild – the Malayan Union – a new federal structure imposed closer unity than ever before without any indication of early self-government.[41] Indeed, London's response to the breakdown of control in 1948 was to declare an emergency and accept a growing military burden in the struggle against the Chinese Communist guerillas.

These dispositions in Asia scarcely look like a master plan for imperial withdrawal, let alone the progressive application of a graduated programme in self-rule. This impression is confirmed by events further west, in the Middle East.

Superficially, Britain's position in the Middle East was much less disrupted by the war which had swept across the colonies in the East. The war ended with British armies in firm control of Egypt and the principal Arab states. British prestige had suffered no such catastrophe as Singapore. Yet turbulence rapidly broke the surface. In Egypt and Iraq, the war had rekindled local nationalism, and in Egypt the end of the war saw renewed efforts by the Egyptian government to persuade the British to give up the giant Suez base and withdraw the garrison which had arrived with the so-called Temporary Occupation in 1882. In Palestine, a far more painful dilemma was in the making. For here British policy was to limit strictly the inflow of Jewish refugees, to reassure the Arab inhabitants and their sympathizers among the Arab States. Yet the flow of Jewish immigration, with the end of Nazi rule in Europe, was swelling to a torrent, while the American government regarded British efforts to check the inrush as inhumane and anti-semitic.[42]

This would have mattered much less had not Bevin and the government's military advisers been determined to create a new and durable

196   PERSPECTIVES ON IMPERIALISM AND DECOLONIZATION

Anglo-Arab relationship which would give Britain's dominance of the Middle East region since 1918 a new and more attractive look. In pursuit of this, Bevin sought new treaties with Iraq and Egypt, and was ready to withdraw British troops from the latter, provided suitable arrangements could be made for the reoccupation of the Suez base in an emergency.[43] But all these plans had come to nothing. The Egyptians demanded a share in the government of the Sudan – which London would not concede – and Iraqi popular feeling led to the collapse of a new defence treaty with Baghdad in 1948. Worst of all, the Palestine Mandate was by now in flames. This tragedy had a two-fold importance for British strategy. In the first place, while Britain remained responsible for the Palestine Mandate, it was likely that Arab opinion everywhere in the Middle East would hold Britain responsible for the political outcome of the Arab-Jewish political struggle. But secondly, the British had assumed all along that the tactical withdrawal from Egypt would be possible because in any sub-division of the Palestine Mandate they would retain control of a zone for military purposes, as a new *place d'armes* in the Middle East.[44]

By the spring of 1947, the futile struggle to find a formula for the partition or self-government of Palestine which would satisfy both Jews and Arabs, concern at growing differences with the United States, anxiety about Arab relations if Britain should seem responsible for an Arab fiasco, as well as irritation at the financial and military burden of acting the policeman in Palestine, had already converted Bevin to the desirability of surrendering the Mandate and repudiating further British responsibility for the territory.[45] In September 1947 the Cabinet decided that this course was inevitable and necessary. Withdrawal was of course partly a gesture of despair and impotence. But it was also calculated and tactical. Britain, argued Bevin, could not remain behind to administer a partition under United Nations' auspices: 'We should be engaged in suppressing Arab resistance ... and antagonising the independent Arab states at a time when our whole political and strategic system in the Middle East must be founded on cooperation with those states....'[46] To remain in Palestine had become incompatible with imperial strategy. And evacuation *was* possible because the Cabinet, far from being intimidated by Egyptian intransigence, had decided to stand pat in Egypt and keep the Canal base. Nor, having abandoned Palestine, was Bevin slow to seek compensation elsewhere. The British had had their eye on Cyrenaica since the end of the war. Now, Bevin told his colleagues in February 1948, the need for strategic facilities was 'paramount'.[47] Indeed, the British set out to promote a united Libya under their client Idris just as they had promoted a unitary Iraq under Faisal 25 years before.

British determination to retain a dominant position in the Middle East, come hell or Harry Truman, was sharpened by their perception of it as a weak and disorderly zone, by fears of Soviet expansion, by a corresponding desire to retain air bases giving access to southern Russia, and by the Middle East's rapidly growing importance as an oil producer.[48] But as the language of the policy-makers conveys, behind these rationalizations lay an instinct or habit of mind. Regardless of what was happening in South or East Asia, regardless of the growth of the superpowers, regardless of Britain's self-evident economic weakness, the old assumptions about what Leo Amery had once called the 'Southern British World' still held good. Britain's spheres of influence had been shaken and stirred – but in the late 1940s they still seemed tenable and defensible.

Paradoxically, it was Britain's very economic weakness after 1945 which reinforced the tendency to think imperially. When the war ended Britain's export economy was in ruins, her supplies of foreign exchange meagre, her debts – especially to sterling and dollar countries – colossal, while her requirement for food, raw materials and other supplies to aid economic recovery was necessarily enormous. The attempt in 1947 to honour the terms of the Anglo-American loan by making sterling convertible, was a fiasco and produced a huge sterling crisis. The Labour Government's reaction was to revert to a highly insulated imperial economy, in which the countries of the Sterling Area (the dominions excluding Canada, the colonies and certain associated states) traded freely with each other but rigorously controlled purchases from outside, especially dollar goods.[49] From a British point of view this system, constructed by Cripps, had three great merits. It preserved sterling as a world currency. It allowed Britain's sterling debts to be discounted by exports, and it secured markets and supplies for Britain which might otherwise have been lost. More completely than ever before, economics and empire had come together, and as colonies like the Gold Coast or Malaya earned precious dollars with their cocoa, tin or rubber, the White Man's burden had come full circle.[50] The poet of empire, had he lived, might well have penned a new imperial ditty:

> Take up the Dollar problem
> Send forth the best ye make
> Preserve the Sterling Balances
> The Yank is at the gate.

This imperial economic solidarity was accompanied by a marked new emphasis upon colonial economic development – to earn more dollars for London's dollar pool. Urging prompt action in Malaya upon his colleagues in July 1948, the Colonial Secretary reminded them:

> [Malaya] is by far the most important source of dollars in the Colonial Empire and it would gravely worsen the whole dollar balance of the Sterling Area if there were serious interference with Malayan exports.[51]

Economic development was also intended to alleviate social unrest and to supply Britain with urgently needed commodities that could be paid for in sterling and on tick. This was the motive behind the disastrous Ground Nuts Scheme in Tanganyika, which inspired the famous slogan 'Give us the job and we will finish the tools'.

For all the drama of Britain's hasty exit from India, Burma, Ceylon and

Palestine, her evident inferiority in economic resources and potential military power to the United States and Russia, it is doubtful if the late 1940s should be seen as a period in which the long-standing assumptions about Britain's position as a world and colonial power were decisively repudiated. Plainly, no intelligent policy-maker could doubt that the scope and shape of British power and influence would have to be remodelled; that in certain theatres preponderance must be yielded to the United States;[52] that prudence required no headlong confrontation with American opinion; and that, in the disturbed aftermath of the war, political opinion in Britain's colonies and client states would need careful handling. What was at work could best be described as the selective shrugging off of commitments, the enforced retreat from exposed positions, coupled with the hope, more perhaps than the expectation, that the heart of the system was still sound. How little even the abandonment of the *raj* was expected to presage the disintegration of British power may be gauged from the almost instinctive decision that Britain must acquire an independent nuclear deterrent – because a great power *must have* the most advanced weapons.[53]

III

No less than in the early post-war years, British policy towards the colonial dependencies and the spheres of British influence in the 1950s revealed a series of apparently conflicting aims and objects. On one level, the 1950s saw the continuation of the transfer of power begun in India in 1947. The Gold Coast became self-governing in 1951 under the premiership of Kwame Nkrumah – 'Iron Boy', 'Great Leader of Streetboys', as his admirers called him – and fully independent in 1957. The Sudan became independent in 1956. By the late 1950s, too, Nigerian independence was merely a question of time-tabling: at the 1957 Nigerian constitutional conference the British promised that as soon as the new federal government was working properly independence would be given.[54] Malaya too became independent in 1957. Elsewhere in the colonial empire the 1950s saw the steady introduction of new constitutions with wider representation and increasing provision for local participation in the machinery of government. In Kenya, a council of ministers was created in 1954 with some African and Asian membership. Further changes in 1956 and 1958 enlarged African representation in the legislature.[55] Tanganyika was granted a legislative council and then a system of direct election. The old system of 'native authorities' was democratized by the introduction of elected district councils.[56] In Uganda, the Legislative Council was steadily conceded wider powers: an African majority was created among the unofficial members; then a ministerial form of government with five African Ministers; then, in 1958, direct election to the legislature was laid down.[57] In West and East Africa alike, London seemed committed to steady constitutional progress. The emancipation of Africa was in hand. The 1960s would see the completion of the task. And to parallel the forward constitutional moves in Africa, the same steady attenuation of colonial rule could be observed in the West Indies, in the concession of more internal autonomy in Singapore, in the decision to abandon British rule in Cyprus.

But if we are tempted to see in the 1950s a conscious preparation for the great imperial discard of the 1960s, and the recognition of a sharply reduced international status, a number of tiresome inconsistencies have to be explained away. Certainly the British shied away from a struggle with the 'Great Leader of Streetboys' on the Gold Coast. But their willingness to accommodate him may have had much to do with the enthusiasm of the Convention People's Party leaders for a unitary state, a centralizing government and encouraging economic development.[58] Ghana, on independence, remained firmly in the Sterling Area,[59] and it was difficult to see what British interests were damaged by her constitutional progress. In Nigeria the British were obsessed above all with promoting the unification of this vast, valuable but ill-coordinated colony.[60] Although the pressure for more self-government was largely confined to the southern regions, the British energetically promoted constitutional advancement in all as the only way to keep the different parts of the colony in step and offered independence as a bait to persuade the regionally-minded political parties to agree upon the construction of a federal government.[61] Here independence was the horse and unity the cart; the one was meant to pull the other. And as in Ghana, it was hard to see what damage independent Nigeria, bound to the Sterling Area, reliant upon British markets, British capital and British expertise, could possibly inflict on British interests, and easy to see the benefits.[62] In Uganda, the British smiled sweetly upon the representative aspirations of African members in the Legislative Council. But in Buganda where internal self-rule was a living force, and particularist nationalism had growing appeal, the British harassed the Kabaka ruthlessly.[63] Indeed, it is hard not to conclude that the deliberate promotion of the Uganda Legislative Council was not deliberately and chiefly intended to destroy Buganda's Lukiko. Here again, unification and centralization, not self-rule for its own sake, was the centrepiece of British thinking.

The reservations of British policy about the universal desirability of self-government and independence can be easily seen behind the facade of constitutional progress in East Africa. African representation in the Kenya legislature may have been enlarged, but from 1954 until 1960 no African political organization above the level of the district was permitted. Meanwhile, the suppression of Mau Mau and the 'rehabilitation' of its supporters was vigorously prosecuted. The real aim of British policy was to devise a constitution in which the three communities would be obliged to share power, and in which the rules of the electoral game would throw up moderates and throw *out* extremists – of whatever race.[64] Far from swimming with a tide of African nationalism, this was an ambitious effort to outflank and outmaneouvre any demand for universal suffrage and Kenya's independence as a 'black man's country'. Even in April

1959, the success of this bold experiment seemed to require an indefinite British presence. 'I cannot now foresee a date', the Colonial Secretary told the House of Commons, 'when it will be possible for any British government to surrender their ultimate responsibilities for the destiny and well-being of Kenya.'[65] In Tanganyika, a parallel course was followed. As in Kenya, political evolution was to be 'multi-racial'. Thus in the legislature, parity of representation was laid down in a territory where for every European there were four Asians and 430 Africans. Nor was the democratization of local government all that it appeared. The old native authorities had been purely African in membership: the new elected bodies were to have European and Asian members whose influence was, in the nature of things, likely to be considerably greater than their African counterparts.[66] When African opposition to these changes manifested itself it was harassed by government: speakers were banned; branches prohibited. And government itself encouraged the formation of a multi-racial party, the United Tanganyika Party.[67] That this did not flourish may have been partly because its acronym when pronounced meant (approximately) in Swahili 'no bloody good'.

Thus, in East Africa, as opposed to West, London was determined not to concede the principle of independence, nor to recognize Kenya and Tanganyika as 'black man's countries'. The strategic value of Kenya,[68] the size of the settler community and London's belief that, unlike West Africa, economic advancement depended upon immigrant communities, lay behind this resolve. But the supreme example of this highly discriminating attitude to political advancement was to be found in Central Africa.

Until after the Second World War the British had resolutely turned their face against any scheme for the unification of the two Rhodesias and Nyasaland, arguing that their uneven political development ruled out amalgamation or federation.[69] But in the late 1940s, just as the acceleration of constitutional progress in West Africa was accepted, there was a sharp change of approach. A Labour Government blessed, and a Conservative government implemented, a scheme for the federalization of the three territories, two of them British protectorates, the other a self-governing white-ruled colony. The Federation of Rhodesia and Nyasaland was an exotic constitutional beast. The Federal Government was elected on a mainly white franchise and enjoyed wide powers, particularly in the economic field. But internal security in the two protectorates, as well as their constitutional evolution, remained ultimately in the hands of the Colonial Office. And the federation was self-governing but not independent. Here London essayed its most ambitious experiment in multiracial government, for Central Africa was to be the counter-poise to Afrikaner republicanism in South Africa, and an important and dynamic trading partner for Britain. Against such pressing imperial requirements the opposition of African politicians could make, as we have seen, little headway. Moreover, it is clear that the expectation of Conservative Governments in the 1950s was that, when the question was re-examined at the end of a decade of federation, the case for independence would be unanswerable, even if the political life of the federation remained over-whelmingly in European hands.[70] In 1957 London overrode the objections of the local constitutional watchdog, the African Affairs Board, and approved a constitutional amendment which, while prescribing the same proportion of African members in the Federal legislature, made it easier to obtain a two-thirds majority for constitutional change.[71] Under settler pressure, Colonial Office control over Northern Rhodesia was to be reduced by a new territorial constitution, though in an effort to check the surge of *settler* nationalism an elaborate multiracial franchise was devised.[72]

In Central Africa in the 1950s, British policy was in fact far more concerned with taming the aggression of white settler nationalism, while dissuading it from looking South, than with the promotion of African political development, which appeared painstakingly slow. A multiracial dominion in Central Africa under white leadership, not three independent African states, was London's object – and, apparently, the most likely outcome. Further east, the independence of Malaya in 1957 caused barely a ripple. Under the Anglo-Malayan Defence Agreement in 1957, Malaya could continue to call on British military assistance against internal subversion and external attack. In return Malaya consented to remain in the Sterling Area, and to keep its commodity earnings in London's dollar pool.[73] Singapore, meanwhile, remained a great British base, and colonial rule remained in North Borneo and Sarawak. Here too, as in West Africa, independence signalled a new phase of cooperation, not the end of empire.

Against this background of orderly devolution, the Suez crisis stands out like Ayers Rock. It is easy and tempting to treat the operation as a freakish event in post-war British policy, a wild and irrational response to Nasser's urchin impudence, quite out of keeping with the smooth and elegant progression from empire, red in tooth and claw, to common-wealth, fraternal sweetness and light. But there was more to the Suez Crisis than Eden's liver. Like Sarajevo, the crisis over the Canal was the climax to a long period of tension and rivalry – in this case between Britain and Egypt.[74] The British had remained embattled in the Suez base until 1954, as every effort to persuade successive Egyptian governments to sign a treaty permitting re-entry in an emergency came to nothing. Eventually in 1952 the volatile politics of Egypt had erupted and the military regime under first Neguib and then Nasser came to power. With this regime, the British hoped to do business. In 1954 Eden at last concluded with Nasser an agreement to end British occupation of the base provided that re-entry was assured in the event of an external threat to Turkey or any Arab state.[75] Undoubtedly the British hoped by this to improve their Arab relationships; they still had, after all, other bases in the Middle East. Very likely also, they hoped that Nasser would be an Egyptian Ataturk, content to concern himself with the internal transformation of Egypt without challenging Britain's regional influence. Such hopes were ill-

202   PERSPECTIVES ON IMPERIALISM AND DECOLONIZATION

founded. By early 1956 it was clear that Nasser was determined to challenge British influence and especially the pretensions of the Hashemite Kingdoms of Iraq and Jordan, Britain's closest Arab allies.[76]

Eden's policy was to try to isolate Nasser in the Arab world.[77] But Nasser was too daring. In 1955 he began buying arms from the Eastern bloc. His nationalization of the Canal was the last straw – but also a golden opportunity to cut him down to size. Undoubtedly, British protests about the breach of international law were genuine; and the claims that Nasser could not be trusted with what was still, even in 1956, an arterial waterway of considerable strategic value was genuinely felt. But it is likely that, certainly in the early stages of the crisis, the British aim was to score a decisive diplomatic victory over Nasser, deflating his growing influence in the Arab world and also, a not unimportant consideration, serving notice that the Base Agreement of 1954 was not a dead letter. From David Carlton's recent and persuasive account we can see how Eden, in the struggle to reconcile these Middle East objectives with Britain's great power dignity as a founding member of the United Nations and the post-war order, was driven eventually to the hollow charade of 'separating' the local combatants.[78] But if we admit that the original plan of publicly disciplining Nasser through concerted international pressure was *not* doomed to failure from the outset, then the Suez episode loses some of its craziness. It loses still more if we accept further that British leaders of both parties wished and expected Britain to remain a global power;[79] and if we recognize that even in the mid-1950s superpower dominance was far from complete and that in Africa, the Middle East and the Indian Ocean, Britain seemed likely to retain much of her old position, at least for some time.

Suez, its aftermath, and the reaction of British leaders revealed not so much the abrupt collapse of British power, or even of British nerve, although the domestic repercussions must have forcibly impressed on subsequent British Cabinets the very considerable risks attached to such overseas intervention on a major scale. What it did show was that the Middle East was much too rough a region, and British control of it far too vulnerable to the interference of *both* superpowers for indirect methods of dominance to work successfully. But whether the policy-makers deduced from this anything more than that one more region – one which they had briefly contemplated abandoning in 1945 – was lost to British influence is, at least, doubtful.

IV

As a phase in the post-war history of British decolonization the 1960s appear much less enigmatic than the 1950s. The decade opened, after all, with Mr Macmillan's reference to a zephyr of mild adjustment in Africa, and ended with Britain's renunciation of all military power East of Suez, and a third and final application to the EEC. After 1960 the retreat from empire seems too consistent to be accidental, too purposeful to disguise ulterior imperialism. The four major decisions of the 1960s – the accelerated withdrawal from East Africa, especially Kenya; the acceptance of majority rule in Zambia and Malawi and the dissolution of the Central African Federation; the application to Europe in 1961, and again in 1967; and the decision to terminate in 1971 all military commitments East of Suez, suggest an agonizing reappraisal of Britain's place in world politics.

· Notoriously there was from the autumn of 1959 onwards a markedly more flexible attitude in London towards the political advancement of Britain's colonial territories in East and Central Africa. Various explanations have been put forward for this: the freedom which electoral victory gave to a naturally liberal Mr Macmillan to pursue his policy free from obstreperousness on the backbenches or in Cabinet;[80] Mr Macmillan's own argument that the appropriate moment for transfer of power had arrived; and Ian Macleod's claim that the alternative to prompt withdrawal was a series of bloody colonial conflicts.[81] Doubtless some grain of truth may be found in each of these: but the background to British policy in Africa after 1959 was provided by three events which the policy-makers in London could hardly ignore. The first was the wave of disorder in many different African territories in 1959–60, culminating in the disturbances of Sharpeville. The second was the impact of France's decision to concede independence to her African colonies in 1959, and their triumphant entry into the United Nations in 1960.[82] The third was the devastating prospect opened up in 1960 of anarchy and international conflict in the Congo.[83] These events in turn had to be related to the intensifying rivalry between East and West over the future of the Third World to which Macmillan in particular attached enormous importance.[84] In short, a concatenation of events, mostly external, profoundly altered from 1959 the political landscape of the colonial world: the clockwork schedules of the Colonial Office acquired a curiously pre-Newtonian air.

The constitution-makers now lurched into action with greater urgency than before. At breakneck speed first Tanganyika and then Uganda were advanced to self government followed by independence. Both bordered the Congo, and were exposed to its anarchic fall-out. In Tanganyika, the British made no semblance of resistance to TANU and Julius Nyerere. In, Uganda, they abandoned the effort to coerce Buganda into a unitary state and rammed through a new federal constitution, a patchwork quilt of local autonomies whose subsequent history is ample comment on the durability of the arrangements made.[85] Kenya, however, presented a much more complicated problem than either Uganda or Tanganyika where white settlers were far less numerous and powerful. London's tactics in Kenya were, moreover, far from pellucid. The Lancaster House Conference of January 1960 at which Kenya's accelerated advance to majority rule was announced was, it seems likely, the product of London's calculation that, with timely encouragement, Michael Blundell's liberal New Kenya Group would attract support from all three races in Kenya and outflank settler nationalism and black nationalism together.[86] Kenya's new constitution in 1961 was deliberately intended to promote

204   PERSPECTIVES ON IMPERIALISM AND DECOLONIZATION

this.[87] Kenyatta was kept in gaol until August 1961, while the British bent over backwards to enhance the prestige first of NKG and then of the anti-Kenyatta Kenya African Democratic Union into which the NKG merged.[88] In 1962, Kenya's constitution was decentralized through the institution of regional assemblies, as a reward to KADU.[89] As it turned out, however, KADU with its tribal divisions was no match for the Kenya African National Union and Kenyatta, once universal suffrage elections were introduced: and Kenyatta in power rapidly lost his demonic quality. But it is at very best uncertain that the British originally intended their constitutional reforms in Kenya to lead to independence under Kenyatta in December 1963; much more likely that they hoped that a moderate multiracial party would be the beneficiary of their constitution-making, with a successor-state bound closely to Britain. Compared with the constitutional problem in Central Africa, Kenya was child's play.

In Central Africa, the British Government had begun by readily endorsing the coercion of anti-federation African political movements in Northern Rhodesia and Nyasaland in February-March 1959.[91] In Nyasaland this policy backfired badly and created widespread disorder with the result that London felt constrained to appoint a commission of enquiry under Sir Patrick Devlin. This report was the most violent castigation of a colonial administration perhaps since 1900, and an explicit testimonial to the depth of African hostility to the white-ruled federation.[92] It was in these unfortunate circumstances that the British were obliged to despatch the Monckton Review Commission to consider whether the Federation was now ready for independence and what adjustments should be made in its working – a review laid down in the Federal Constitution. The Review Commission, far from being remote, technical and implicitly sympathetic to the federation, was forced to adjudicate on its popularity among Africans and concluded that it had none.[93] But far from recognizing the inevitability of the federation's collapse, the Commission recommended a series of sweeping reforms designed to make it palatable to African opinion.[94] The British Government eagerly followed this line.[95] In the course of 1961 the white politicians of Southern Rhodesia were persuaded to liberalize their constitution – 15 of the 65 seats were to be available to Africans – so as to mollify African mistrust of white federal domination. Nyasaland could not be saved from majority rule but its right to secede from the federation was not admitted.[96] The crucial decision was over what kind of constitution would be introduced in the Northern Rhodesia Protectorate, with its small but vociferous white community and its mining industry – whose complementarity with Southern Rhodesian coal and foodstuffs was the economic rationale of federation. If Northern Rhodesia were granted African majority rule, the Federation was dead.

In 1960–61, London agonized over this problem. Enormous ingenuity was expended devising fancy franchises that would just ensure a pro-federation majority – but not blatantly. The Cabinet could not agree upon African majority rule.[97] Then in June 1961 a constitutional scheme was put forward by the Colonial Office which seemed likely to yield a white majority in the Lusaka legislature.[98] The whites were overjoyed. Violent African disturbances broke out in Northern Rhodesia in the latter part of 1961. London changed its tune, mindful perhaps of Katanga and aware that with the Kuwait operation, few troops were spare to keep order. The sums were done once more. This time an African majority was on the cards.[99] But even now, hope was not abandoned. Butler, as Central African Secretary, struggled unavailingly to prolong the federation.[100] But its fate was sealed not in London but by the electoral triumph in both Rhodesias of parties opposed to its continuation. In March 1963, the British Cabinet merely switched off the life support. Nyasaland and Northern Rhodesia proceeded out of federation and into independence. By London's criteria, the outcome of decolonization here, as in India, was a disastrous reversal of British policy.

Britain's decolonizing policy in Africa in the crucial phase of the transfer of power from 1960–64 was unquestionably influenced by the long tradition of trusteeship in colonial administration and respect for certain political maxims. But it was also the victim of unpredicted circumstances. Above all, it was meant as a vehicle for preserving British influence in a period of rapid political and international change on the continent. Fearful of Soviet blandishments, nervous of unfavourable comparisons with the generosity of French policy, anxious to construct amenable successor regimes, the British found themselves sliding far more rapidly than they had expected towards majority rule almost everywhere.

But this remarkable flexibility in Africa was accompanied by striking new dispositions East of Suez. Successive defence white papers from 1961–65 stressed the importance of Britain's role in the Indian Ocean.[101] At London's insistence the South Arabian Federation was cellotaped together with the promise of independence and a defensive guarantee from Britain. The Malaysian federation was formed, with a similar British promise, and as at Aden, the use of a military base of great regional importance. These commitments were undertaken at a time when British military manpower, with the end of National Service, was contracting and costs rising.[102] As has sometimes been suggested, British policy was a welcome reinforcement to Washington as America's effort to contain communism in Vietnam grew more and more strenuous. But this East of Suez role conformed well with the instinct, common to politicians of both major parties, to retain Britain's great-power spheres of influence – for just a little longer. Even after the decision in 1966 that Britain could not afford the new aircraft carrier to make her eastern naval position viable, the Cabinet, in Richard Crossman's account, turned hither and thither for some means to keep the Indian Ocean a British lake.[103] As his diaries show, it required the devaluation crisis of November 1967, the unlikely alliance of Jenkinsite Europeanists and the Left and the timely defection of Wilson to overcome the last ditch resistance of what Crossman tartly called the 'Great Britain' school in the Cabinet, and to extract the final avowal that the last vestiges of the imperial role were at an end.[104]

206   PERSPECTIVES ON IMPERIALISM AND DECOLONIZATION

V

Much of Britain's experience of decolonization, it might be concluded, confirms the usefulness of Herbert Spencer's law of unintended consequences. Nothing stimulated political mobilization in the British colonies more than London's efforts to encourage economic development. Careful constitutional compromises invariably carried the seeds of their own destruction.[105] Self-government and independence turned out in most cases to be far more real than the British expected; the influence which the British hoped to exercise over their former colonies faded away as their economic fortunes declined.[106] In retrospect, as we have seen, British leaders liked to see their demission of empire as the actions of an enlightened father, wisely conferring responsibility on his boisterous, but essentially good-natured, offspring. In fact, a better image might be that of an impoverished grandee whose hereditary mansion becomes slowly uninhabitable room by room as, in apparently random sequence, the floors give way, the plumbing fails, the ceilings fall in. But however dilapidated the mansion became, it was not to be given up because no other mode of life was tolerable and an address is, after all, an address.

In short, far from there being a planned withdrawal, a considered transformation from empire to commonwealth, what actually occurred from 1945 until the late 1960s was the unpredictable erosion of position after position, foothold after foothold, followed on each occasion by further efforts to hold together the remnants of world power and influence, by one means or another.

Thus, if we search for any logic in the process of Britain's decolonization we may be disappointed. To that extent, the transfer of power and the retreat of British influence followed a baffling wayward course that had little to do with any of the criteria for imperial withdrawal to which British leaders appealed. To that extent it was a puzzle. But a deeper pattern may perhaps be discerned. The pragmatic ingenious adaptation of British policy was geared, above all, to the preservation of British world power in increasingly adverse circumstances. This is neither puzzling nor surprising. It would have made sense to Metternich or Buol. The old equation of world power, independence and prosperity could not be unlearned so easily. Until the end of the 1950s the limits on superpower dominance still seemed to leave much scope for British power. The burdens seemed manageable and the likely benefits substantial. And, who are we, the Falklands generation, to find imperial fantasies so puzzling?

NOTES

1. See W. R. Louis, *Imperialism at Bay 1941–1945* (Oxford, 1977) 140-46; 188ff; 224.
2. H. Macmillan, *Pointing the Way* (London, 1972) 116-17.
3. W. D. McIntyre, *Commonwealth of Nations: Origins and Impact* (Minneapolis, 1977) 341.

4. For example, S.C. Easton, *The Rise and Fall of Western Colonialism* (London, 1964) 370.
5. See D.J. Morgan, *The Official History of Colonial Development*, Vol.5: *Guidance Towards Self-government in British colonies 1941–70* (London, 1980) 183.
6. P. Gifford, 'Indirect rule: touchstone or tombstone for colonial policy' in P. Gifford and W.R. Louis, *Britain and Germany in Africa* (New Haven, 1967) 351-91.
7. C. Thorne, *Allies of a Kind* (pbk edn. Oxford, 1979) 551, 557-8; G.B. Endacott, *Hong Kong Eclipse* (Hong Kong, 1978) 258-80; D.C. Wolf, ' "To secure a convenience": Britain recognises China – 1950', *Journal of Contemporary History* 18, 2 (1983), 299-326.
8. C. Douglas-Home, *Evelyn Baring: The Last Proconsul* (London, 1978) 283.
9. F. Halliday, *Arabia Without Sultans* (Harmondsworth, 1974) 186-7.
10. *Report of the Commission of Enquiry, North Borneo and Sarawak 1962*, Cmnd. 1794 (1962) 30, 42.
11. Susan Strange, *Sterling and British Policy* (London, 1971).
12. A. Seal, 'Imperialism and nationalism in India', *Modern Asian Studies* 7, 3 (1973), 321-47; B.R. Tomlinson, *The Indian National Congress and the Raj* (London, 1976) 30-1; R.J. Moore, *The Crisis of Indian Unity* (Oxford, 1974) 297-8.
13. 'Hitler has rather overset our Indian politics', remarked the Viceroy in March 1940. Linlithgow to Baldwin, 22 March 1940, Baldwin papers box 107, Cambridge University Library.
14. G. Rizvi, *Linlithgow and India* (London, 1978) 206-7, 237-9.
15. R. Coupland, *The Constitutional Problem in India* (Madras, 1944), Part II, 335-7, 273; R.J. Moore, *Churchill, Cripps and India* (Oxford, 1979).
16. Cabinet India and Burma committee 1st meeting, 17 Aug. 1945. N. Mansergh (ed.), *Constitutional Relations Between Britain and India: Transfer of Power 1942–7* (hereafter *TP*) VI, 79. Cabinet 24 (45) 20 Aug. 1945. CAB[inet] 128/1 P.R.O.
17. Cabinet Far East civil planning unit, report 14 Jan. 1946. *TP* VI. 780; Note by Secretary of State for India on proposed contents of Anglo-Indian treaty. 23 Feb. 1946, *TP* VI. 1051-52; Hollis to Monteath, 13 March 1946, *TP* VI. 1167-73.
18. Ibid.
19. Wavell to Pethick-Lawrence (encl.) 6 Nov. 1945, *TP* VI, 451-4; memo. by Secretary of State for India, 14 Nov. 1945, *TP* VI, 482-3.
20. Thorne to Abell, 5 April 1946, *TP* VII, 151.
21. R.J. Moore, *Escape from Empire* (Oxford, 1983).
22. P. Moon (ed.), *Wavell: The Viceroy's Journal* (London, 1973), 367-75; Wavell to Sec. of State for India, 11 Nov. 1946, *TP* IX, 41.
23. *Viceroy's Journal*, 386ff.
24. *TP* IX, 68; *TP* IX, 332, 358.
25. *TP* IX, 427-31.
26. See K. Harris, *Attlee* (London, 1982) 378-9; *TP* IX, 748-52.
27. *TP* IX, 972-4.
28. S. Gopal, *Jawaharlal Nehru*, 1 (London, 1975), 342-3.
29. *TP* XII, 257-76.
30. See N. Mansergh, *Documents and Speeches on British Commonwealth Affairs 1931–52* Vol. II (London, 1953) 762-5.
31. Governor of Burma to Sec. of State for Burma, 7 Dec. 1946, Prime Minister's papers [PREM] 8/412, PRO.
32. Cabinet 9 (47) 17 Jan. 1947, PREM 8/412.
33. Governor of Burma to Sec. of State for Burma, 9 June 1947; Governor-General, Malaya, to Colonial Secretary, 27 June 1947, both in PREM 8/412.
34. Cabinet 44 (47) 6 May 1947, CAB 128/9.
35. P. Darby, *British Defence Policy East of Suez 1947–68* (London, 1973) Chap. 1.
36. Strang's report, 27 Feb. 1949, C.P. (49) 67, 17 March 1949, CAB 129/33. See also Cabinet Committee on Commonwealth Relations C.R. (49) 2nd conclusions, 8 Feb. 1949, PREM 8/950.
37. Attlee to Nehru, 20 March 1949, PREM 8/950.

208   PERSPECTIVES ON IMPERIALISM AND DECOLONIZATION

38. Memo. by P.C. Gordon-Walker, C.P. (48) 91, March 1948, CAB 129/26.
39. See above Note 7.
40. See A.J. Stockwell, 'Colonial planning during World War II: The case of Malaya', *Journal of Imperial and Commonwealth History* 2, 3 (1974), 337; memo. by Colonial Secretary, C.P. (45) 133, 20 Aug. 1945, CAB 129/1.
41. B. Simandjuntak, *Malayan Federalism 1945–63* (London, 1969).
42. M.J. Cohen, *Palestine and the Great Powers 1945–48* (Princeton, 1982).
43. See Cabinet 57 (46) 6 June 1946; 58 (46) 7 June 1946, CAB 128/5. For Iraq, memo by Foreign Secretary, 3 Oct. 1947, C.P. (47) 277, CAB 129/21.
44. Cabinet Defence Committee memoranda, D.O. (47) 3, 6 Jan. 1947, CAB 131/4; and gloomy report of chiefs of staff dated 7 March 1947, ibid.; also Cohen, *Palestine*, 37-41.
45. Cohen, *Palestine*, 222-23.
46. Memo. by Foreign Secretary, 18 Sept. 1947, C.P. (47) 259, CAB 129/21.
47. Memo. by Foreign Secretary, 4 Feb. 1948, C.P. (48) 43, CAB 129/24.
48. In 1939 the Middle East produced about five per cent of the world's oil. By 1949 this had risen to around 15 per cent. S.H. Longrigg, *Oil in the Middle East* (London, 1954), App.II(b).
49. See P.W. Bell, *The Sterling Area in the Post-war World* (Oxford, 1956).
50. Ibid., 56-7.
51. Memo. by Colonial Secretary, 1 July 1948, C.P. (48) 171, CAB 129/25.
52. B. Rubin, *The Great Powers in the Middle East 1941–47* (London, 1980) 47, 64.
53. M. Gowing, *Independence and Deterrence, 1: Policymaking* (London, 1974) Chap. 6.
54. *Report by Nigerian Constitutional Conference May-June 1957* Cmnd. 207 (1957), 26.
55. *Kenya: Proposals for New Constitutional Arrangements* Cmnd. 309 (1957).
56. J. Iliffe, *A Modern History of Tanganyika* (Cambridge, 1979); G.A. Maguire, *Towards 'Uhuru' in Tanzania* (Cambridge, 1969); R.C. Pratt, *The Critical Phase in Tanzania 1945–68* (Cambridge, 1976).
57. D.A. Low and R.C. Pratt, *Buganda and British Overrule 1900–1955: Two Studies* (London, 1960); D.A. Low and A. Smith (ed.), *A History of East Africa* 3 (Oxford, 1976).
58. The Convention People's Party government eagerly taxed the farmers to provide development finance. G.B. Kay (ed.), *The Political Economy of Colonialism in Ghana* (Cambridge, 1973) 47.
59. For Nkrumah's assurances on this to a former Labour Colonial Secretary, Nkrumah to James Griffiths, 14 Dec. 1956, A. Creech-Jones papers 18/4, Rhodes House, Oxford.
60. See memo. by Colonial Secretary, 3 May 1950, C.P. (50) 94, CAB 129/39.
61. See Note 54.
62. For the early post-independence relationship, O. Ojedokun, 'The Anglo-Nigerian entente and its demise 1960–62', *Journal of Commonwealth Political Studies* IX, 3 (1971).
63. Low and Pratt, *Buganda*.
64. Through such devices as parity of representation and the Council of State.
65. *H.C. Deb.* 5s, 604, col. 563.
66. Maguire, 203.
67. Ibid., 179; Iliffe, *Tanganyika*, 521-2, 535.
68. For London's growing interest in Kenya as a main base in the 1950s, Darby, *Defence Policy*, 124, 125, 175, 203-6.
69. The conclusion of the Bledisloe report in 1939.
70. D.C. Mulford, *Zambia: The Politics of Independence 1957–64* (London, 1967) 51; R. Welensky, *4000 Days* (London, 1964) 77.
71. *H.C. Deb.* 5s 578, cols. 808ff.
72. Mulford, *Zambia*, 50-54, 58-60.
73. *Report by Federation of Malaya Constitutional Conference* Cmnd. 9714 (1956) 8-9.
74. See P.J. Vatikiotis, *Nasser and his Generation* (London, 1978); Patrick Seale, *The Struggle for Syria* (London, 1964); Royal Institute of International Affairs, *Great Britain and Egypt 1914–51* (London, 1952); P. Woodward, *Condominium and Sudanese Nationalism* (London, 1979).

75. D. Carlton, *Anthony Eden* (London, 1981) 356-58; A. Eden, *Full Circle* (London, 1960) 259-61; Selwyn Lloyd, *Suez 1956: A Personal Account* (London, 1978) 21-3.
76. Lloyd, *Suez*, 59; Seale, *Syria*, 247-50.
77. Lloyd, *Suez*, 60; Carlton, *Eden*, 403.
78. Carlton, *Eden*, esp. 427-29.
79. Robert Skidelsky, 'Lessons of Suez' in R. Skidelsky and V. Bogdanor, *The Age of Affluence* (London, 1970).
80. D. J. Goldsworthy, *Colonial Issues in British Politics 1945–61* (Oxford, 1971) 365-66.
81. N. Fisher, *Iain Macleod* (London, 1973) 142.
82. W. J. Foltz, *From French West Africa to the Mali Federation* (New Haven, 1965) 68-70; G. Barraclough (ed.), *Survey of International Affairs 1959–60* (London, 1964) Chap. VII.
83. The summer of 1960, mused Macmillan, bore a disturbing similarity to that of 1914: 'Now Congo may play the role of Serbia' (Diary, 4 July 1960), Macmillan, *Pointing the Way*, 264.
84. Ibid., 47, 116-17, 266, 431.
85. D. A. Low, *Political Parties in Uganda 1949–62* (London, 1962); Low and Smith (ed.), *History of East Africa* Vol. 3, 90-105.
86. Perhaps significantly Macleod's brother was a leading figure in the NKG.
87. G. Wasserman, *The Politics of Decolonisation: Kenya Europeans and the Land Issue 1960–65* (Cambridge, 1976) 46ff; G. Bennett and C. G. Rosberg, *The Kenyatta Election: Kenya 1960–61* (London, 1961) 18ff.
88. Wasserman, *Decolonisation*, 85 for Macleod's jubilation at the electoral victory of the NKG and KADU in 1961.
89. *Report of the Kenya Constitutional Conference 1962*, Cmnd. 1700 (1962) Appendix.
91. Benson to Colonial Office in Mulford, *Zambia*, 104-5.
92. *Report of the Nyasaland Commission of Enquiry*, Cmnd. 814 (1959), paras. 42, 43.
93. *Report of the Advisory Commission on the Review of the Constitution of Rhodesia and Nyasaland*, Cmnd. 1148 (1960), para. 27.
94. Ibid., paras. 100, 114, 123, 221.
95. *Lord Home, The Way the Wind Blows: An Autobiography* (London, 1976) 129-31; Lord Butler, *The Art of the Possible* (London, 1971) 210.
96. Not until December 1962 was Nyasaland's right to secede from the federation acknowledged by HMG.
97. Macmillan, *Pointing the Way* (Diary, 4 Feb. 1961) 309.
98. Mulford, *Zambia*, 194-96.
99. Ibid., 210.
100. Butler, *Art of the Possible*, Chap. X.
101. Darby, *British Defence Policy East of Suez, 1947–68* (London, 1973) 192, 218, 276, 283.
102. Army manpower was more than halved between 1956 and 1966. Ibid., 328.
103. R. Crossman, *The Diaries of a Cabinet Minister*, Vol. 2 (London, 1976) 155-6 (9 Dec. 1966).
104. Ibid., Vol. 2, 634-5, 645-7, 649ff.
105. Iliffe, *Tanganyika*; D. A. Washbrook, 'Law, state and agrarian society in colonial India', *Modern Asian Studies* 15, 3 (1981), 649-721.
106. M. Lipton and J. Firn, *The Erosion of a Relationship: Britain and India since 1960* (London, 1975).

Part II
Post-War Problems and Confrontations

[5]

Militant Response: The Dutch Use of Military Force and the Decolonization of the Dutch East Indies, 1945–50

PETRA M. H. GROEN

Looking back we can say that the decolonization of Asia was inevitable. But for the Dutch in Asia and Europe, the Republic of Indonesia's declaration of independence on 17 August 1945 came as a shock, and an unpleasant one at that. The prospective amputation from the Kingdom of the Netherlands was a burning political issue in the ensuing years, both in the colony and at home. The Netherlands sought refuge in a complex cocktail of political, economic and military measures. These military measures were not confined to the two large-scale military offensives that were referred to, euphemistically, as police actions. The use of last force constituted an important instrument of Dutch policy as long as the conflict lasted from 1945 to 1950. In other words the Netherlands did not flinch from repression in an extreme military form during this engagement. Indeed, military force functioned as a pre-eminent instrument of Dutch repression: there were four army personnel to every police official in Indonesia by late 1948.

This paper examines the use of military force as an instrument of policy and repression in this conflict. It was, after all, not a matter of course for the Netherlands to resort to coercion in this decolonization conflict. True, valuable and established economic and political interests were at stake in the Dutch East Indies. However, the creation and maintenance of a huge military organization meant an economic drain on the mother country, itself destitute after the Second World War. Furthermore, the international community was loathe to condone the use of military force in a colonial context and the Netherlands could have followed the example of other powers which solved their decolonization problems in a more peaceful way. Moreover, the use of military power, in the end, was to be of no avail to the Netherlands. On the contrary, the desperate military situation in 1949 was one of the reasons why the Netherlands government consented to a rapid transfer of sovereignty. The question that arises is why and how the Netherlands expected that it would

THE DUTCH EAST INDIES, 1945–50 31

be able to settle 'the Indonesian question' satisfactorily using military means, and why its expectations were confounded. The discussion will first explain how the use of military force was compatible with general Dutch policy in the conflict with the Republic of Indonesia. I shall then look at the question of how the Netherlands wished to deploy this military force and, lastly, how the expectations regarding military potential foundered in practice.[1]

I

To ascertain how the use of military force fitted into general Dutch policy in the conflict with the Republic of Indonesia, one must examine what tasks were allocated to the Dutch military force as part of this general policy. The original response of the Netherlands to the nationalist revolution that took place after 17 August 1945 in Indonesia was 'reoccupation'. It was through military means that the Dutch goal of restoring colonial authority had to be achieved. The revolution was seen as a political aberration: the work of Japanese intriguers and Indonesian collaborators who had manipulated the gullible masses through propaganda and terrorism. Since the Netherlands, immediately after the war, had only a handful of servicemen, the reoccupation had to be entrusted to its allied agents. The Australians did indeed occupy eastern Indonesia in September 1945 without too much difficulty. In Java and Sumatra, the birthplace of the Indonesian Republic, the British encountered more opposition from an improvised Republican army and autonomous armed groups equipped with Japanese weaponry. They needed more than three divisions to create six bridgeheads on both islands. British interests in Asia precluded any further military effort on their part. Instead Britain demanded political consultation between the Netherlands and the Indonesian Republic to find a solution.[2]

As a result of this British pressure, the vitality of the young Republic and, for the time being, Dutch military impotence, the local authorities in the Dutch East Indies and, in their wake, the Netherlands government proceeded to make a volte-face in the course of 1946.[3] A gradual, limited decolonization was to become the goal. In specific terms, this meant that the Netherlands sought to create a federal Indonesian state, which should be granted independence whilst also being joined with the Netherlands in a Netherlands–Indonesian Union. In this way Dutch interests in a semi-independent Indonesia would be secured. It attempted to achieve these goals by peaceful, but also by military, means. From February 1946 onwards negotiations were conducted with the Republic, while in

32   EMERGENCIES AND DISORDER IN THE EUROPEAN EMPIRES

eastern Indonesia an attempt was being made to form an acceptable federal alternative. At the same time, however, a military force was being amassed which, in the course of 1946, relieved the Australian troops in eastern Indonesia and the British in the bridgeheads in Java and Sumatra. It was attempting to restore and maintain Dutch order in these areas by force of arms. It was thus that the Netherlands' negotiating position was to be consolidated and the federal structure in eastern Indonesia facilitated.

At the same time the military build-up was intended to provide leverage in the longer term at the negotiating table or an alternative means for the Netherlands to gain control of the decolonization process. Both in the Netherlands and in the Dutch East Indies the political and military leaders remained convinced that the conflict could be satisfactorily settled, if necessary by military means. There were two plans in circulation. The conservative wing of the Dutch coalition cabinet (Catholic Party) and the Dutch East Indies army leadership, which still regarded the Republic as the construction of an extremist minority, were convinced that salvation lay in a complete reoccupation campaign to liquidate the illegitimate new state. The left wing of the cabinet (Labour Party) and the civilian political leaders in the Dutch East Indies, on the other hand, were in favour of a territorially limited occupation because this would prompt less criticism nationally and internationally. Their preference for a partial occupation also derived from the somewhat different picture of the adversary that they had meanwhile formed. They had become convinced that a nationalist revolution was taking place in Indonesia. However, they distinguished between radicals and co-operative moderates in the revolutionary camp who, they thought, could be separated by military means. They hoped that a territorially limited occupation campaign would suffice to quell the radicals and to come to terms with the moderates.

In mid-1947 the Netherlands had a force of five divisions in Java and Sumatra. The military build-up, however, brought the Netherlands to the brink of financial bankruptcy. When, in addition to this, the negotiations on the details of the Linggadjati treaty concluded at the end of 1946 with the Republic simultaneously deadlocked, the Netherlands government became pressed for time. The cabinet felt itself confronted with the choices of abandoning the territories, canvassing international support or military intervention. They regarded the first alternative as contrary to Dutch interests, the attempt to canvass international support would be too time-consuming and unproductive for the Netherlands. In the end the government decided in July 1947 on a military offensive. At the urging of the left wing of the cabinet, however, a territorially limited campaign was

THE DUTCH EAST INDIES, 1945–50   33

adopted to place the economically most valuable areas in Dutch hands and to move the Republican leaders to compliance.

The fortnight-long Dutch offensive produced territorial gains for the Netherlands; two-thirds of Java and a third of Sumatra were occupied, but it also provoked a wave of international criticism with the Netherlands' 'big brother', the United States, being among the most vociferous, and moreover led to the Republican leaders' radicalism becoming more entrenched. Although negotiations seemed consequently pointless, they were nevertheless resumed in November 1947 under international pressure and supervision. At the same time an attempt was made to construct a politically, socially and economically attractive federal alternative in the newly-occupied territories. To that end the Dutch military force had to create sufficient order in these areas, an objective which was also necessary to consolidate the Dutch negotiating position. In specific terms this meant that the Dutch troops had to bring an end to the guerrilla warfare that the Republicans had been conducting in the occupied territories since the offensive. The military force was also intended to continue to give the Dutch leverage at the negotiating table and to serve as an alternative method, if needs be, to achieve the Dutch decolonization plan. The disillusioned colonial political leaders and the right wing of the cabinet kept a general campaign of occupation to liquidate the republic up their sleeve, a possibility which for the time being was rejected by the left wing for international political reasons.

At the end of 1948 the deployment of military force as an ultimate remedy again became a topical issue. The negotiations had resulted in a repetition of 1946–47. International supervision had afforded the Netherlands no consolation. On the contrary, after the Republican government had nipped an attempted Communist coup in the bud in September 1948, the United States clearly took sides. Progress was ostensibly being made with the federal reorganization. By the end of 1948 five federal states had been created in Java and Sumatra and a blueprint for the new federal Indonesia had been drawn up under Dutch guidance. But the creation of the political, administrative and economic structure in these areas was increasingly being hampered by the Republican guerrillas. Despite Dutch counter-guerrilla action, the Republican troops made their presence fully felt in the second half of 1948.

The fiasco over negotiations, the growing military unrest and the accompanying political and economic problems in the occupied territories were reasons enough for the new more conservative political leaders in the colony, the colonial military leaders and the right wing of the cabinet to express their preference for a fresh military intervention to liquidate the Republic at the end of 1948. This would enable decoloniza-

34   EMERGENCIES AND DISORDER IN THE EUROPEAN EMPIRES

tion along Dutch lines to be completed with the co-operative nationalists. The left wing of the cabinet, weakened during the 1948 elections, inclined less towards military intervention for fear of international reprisals. In the end they consented to the proposal because the survival of the coalition cabinet, the hopelessness of the negotiations and the growing military problems ultimately carried greater weight.

The fresh, three-week-long offensive that was launched just before Christmas 1948 was intended to lead to the occupation of the Republic and the eradication of the Republican government, its army leadership and its armed forces. The attack was a success in so far as the Republican political leaders were taken prisoner and the strategic sites were occupied. Otherwise, the offensive brought the Netherlands only growing political and military problems. The United Nations stood up for the Republic; the United States threatened to exclude the Netherlands from Marshall aid and the pending North Atlantic treaty. The Republican troops were difficult to quell and stepped up their guerrilla activity. Moreover it proved impossible to carry out the federal reconstruction plans without the Republicans.

The imminence of having to continue to conduct a prospectively hopeless military battle, while the Netherlands had been reduced to the pariah of Europe, brought the Dutch government back to the negotiating table again at the end of February 1949. Counter-guerrilla activity was continued until August 1949 to support the Dutch negotiating position, but to little avail. The Netherlands was forced to agree that sovereignty would be transferred at the end of 1949 without any sound guarantees regarding its interests in Indonesia.

We can therefore conclude that the Netherlands in this conflict deployed its military force as a means of consolidating its negotiating position *vis-à-vis* the Republic, as a means of exerting pressure at the negotiating table and as an ultimate remedy for achieving decolonization along Dutch lines. Specifically this meant that territories had to be occupied by military force, that the occupation if necessary had to be extended and that the opponents in the territory had to be eliminated. The tasks carried out by the Dutch military force, alternately or simultaneously, depended on the political developments in the colony, at home and in the international community, the economic circumstances in both Indonesia and in the Netherlands and the problems to which the use of military force had given rise for the Netherlands. The fact is that we can observe that Dutch military force brought its own dynamic into the conflict. The costs involved in the build-up were an important reason for the first offensive; the military problems that subsequently ensued constituted a reason for the second. The last observation prompts the question of why on the

Dutch side the majority continued to have confidence in the possibility of gaining control of the conflict by force, despite the growing military problems. A further analysis of the way in which the Netherlands imagined it could use its military force is required.

II

The military force available to the Netherlands in Java and Sumatra in mid-1947 consisted of five divisions with a strength of almost 100,000 men. In addition 20,000 men were operating in eastern Indonesia. By the end of 1948 the total strength had been raised to around 140,000. On average more than 65 per cent of these were members of the Dutch army and 35 per cent members of the colonial army. The Dutch troops, most of them conscripts, campaigned mainly in Java and Sumatra. The colonial army was dispersed throughout Indonesia. It was made up on average of 60 per cent Indonesian and 15 per cent Dutch and Dutch East Indies regular personnel and 35 per cent Dutch East Indies conscripts.[4] Opposed to this was the more or less regular volunteer army of the Indonesian Republic, 175,000 strong, and about the same strength on the side of the autonomous armed groups.[5]

The question of how the Netherlands would be able to deploy its military force was answered in the first instance by the Dutch East Indies army leaders. To arrive at a partial or complete occupation of the Republican territory in 1946–47 they drew up a so-called spearhead strategy. The key to this strategy was that the Netherlands troops had to eliminate the enemy command centres in a rapid and surprise large-scale regular offensive and take command of vital key positions and communications. It was only after this brief regular offensive that the 'pacification', the elimination of the opponent, was to take place in the occupied areas. This would involve a counter-guerrilla action, given the plans of the adversary to resort to guerrilla warfare if necessary in the event of a Dutch offensive.[6]

The counter-guerrilla doctrine that the army leaders developed for this pacification, in essence, entailed the following. The troops would be dispersed by brigade over the occupied territory. Within this, each battalion would be allocated an area to pacify. To this end the battalion's platoons were distributed among posts in that territory. These detachments were ordered to patrol their posts in groups of at least ten men, by way of a show of force, to protect certain persons or premises, to gather intelligence and to eliminate armed opponents. If the latter were not successful, or not sufficiently so, in this fashion, 'purges' or 'mopping-up operations' were to be undertaken by a number of platoons or companies

36   EMERGENCIES AND DISORDER IN THE EUROPEAN EMPIRES

together, which entailed a territory being cordoned off and searched. This counter-guerrilla doctrine was based on the pre-war colonial military expertise that had been recorded in detailed tactical regulations. With some updating in the field of communications, arms and equipment, these were again being used.[7] As a supplement to these, from 1945 onwards commando tactics were also applied. Originally this was done only by a commando unit, the Corps of Special Troops that was deployed when the ordinary infantry fell short.[8]

The army leaders expected for the first offensive that the enemy's guerrilla activities would not present insurmountable problems to the Dutch troops. As already mentioned, they continued to adhere to the image of the Indonesian revolution, prevailing in Dutch circles in 1945, as an affair of an extremist elite that was manipulating the masses through terrorism and propaganda. According to the army commanders, this picture was also reflected in the Republican military force. This being so, an attack on the enemy command centres would be disastrous for the organization and morale of the adversary. Without their 'extremist' leaders, the Republican fighters would be unable or unwilling to keep up their guerrilla activities. This disorienting and demoralizing effect would be greatest if the enemy's top military leaders were eliminated, according to the army commanders, which would be the case with a complete occupation but not with a partial one. This is why the Dutch army commanders preferred a comprehensive occupation campaign. But even a partial occupation would, it was suggested, not produce any insurmountable counter-guerrilla problems.

The political leaders in the colony and on the home front had little criticism to make of this military strategy. The fact that in 1947 the government chose the military option considered least attractive by the army leaders was mainly the outcome of political considerations. As has been pointed out, the left wing of the cabinet entirely rejected the idea of a complete reoccupation for national and international political reasons and because, having a different picture of the enemy camp, it had more sanguine expectations of the useful political impact of a limited campaign.

When the Netherlands, after the first offensive, was faced with growing counter-guerrilla problems, the army commanders did not seek the cause in their own counter-guerrilla doctrine or the spearhead strategy. They blamed the problems primarily on the fact that the enemy headquarters had been left intact. It was because of this that the guerrillas in the occupied territories could be organized and co-ordinated undisturbed. They consequently left their strategic and tactical doctrine virtually unchanged, even though they knew that their opponent was preparing itself to step up guerrilla activity in the event of a new attack. They continually advocated a second offensive, the initial target of the attack being the political and military leaders of the Indonesian Republic. After that they predicted the Dutch troops would be able largely to settle the guerrilla war within six months.

This plea of the military encountered objections from the left wing of the Dutch cabinet based on international political considerations. However, only one or two individuals expressed any doubts as to the military strategy. It was only when the offensive had been carried out and the military problems had subsequently escalated that the majority of the political leaders in the Netherlands began to question the army commanders' military forecasts. The latter continued to defend their strategy and tactics, although they admitted that the pacification would take longer than the original six months they had set aside.

We can conclude that the colonial army leaders determined to a considerable degree how Dutch military force was to be deployed. Admittedly, their military recommendations sometimes encountered international and national political objections, but the political leaders seemed scarcely to doubt the military wisdom of their opinions, if at all. Or, as the Dutch government put it in 1949: 'the government has left military strategy and tactics to the army leaders with every confidence'.[9]

We can also conclude that the main reason the army leaders chose this military strategy and tactic was their image of the enemy. The supposition was that a radical, political and military group of leaders was inciting and hoodwinking gullible people through terrorism and propaganda. An attack on the leaders would cause the scales to fall from their eyes. But the colonial army leaders also opted for this approach because they felt that it was the best way of exploiting the weakest military aspect of their opponent, that is the minimal capability of engaging in a large-scale regular battle. This weakness had emerged in 1946 during the opponents' vain attempts to dislodge the numerically much inferior Dutch force from the bridgeheads by means of regular offensives. Moreover, it was precisely in this way that the strengths of the Dutch troops could be turned to best advantage. They were superior in regular warfare because of their training, organization, armament and equipment. Pre-war colonial expertise also had an impact, directly or indirectly, on the army leaders' views as to the preferred military method. This had already emerged from the counter-guerrilla doctrine that they had developed. But besides this, traditional views on the combat capability of the different ethnic groups still held sway, while that same expertise had produced a certain contempt for guerrilla tactics. After all guerrilla warfare had failed to help the Indonesians in the past. The colonial army had proved its superiority at the time, albeit sometimes in extremely lengthy counter-guerrilla campaigns.[10]

III

On paper the use of military power might seem to offer the Netherlands sound prospects of bringing the conflict under control, but military practice proved resolutely otherwise. Why did the use of force fail? The problem did not lie in the launching of the regular large-scale offensives. The first attack proceeded entirely according to plan, as did the second for the most part. The difficulties arose in the ensuing counter-guerrilla activities. The problems were most pressing after the second offensive, but essentially they had begun to be manifest after the first.

During and after this first offensive about 30,000 men from the Republican army and an unknown number of combatants from the autonomous groups had taken refuge in less readily accessible territory. Here they formed pockets and carried out guerrilla activity in the occupied area. This guerrilla warfare involved attacks on military and civilian targets: posts, convoys, patrols and communications, civil servants collaborating with the Dutch, police officials, factories and plantations. If it came to a fight, the Dutch servicemen frequently proved to be superior, but the elimination of these guerrilla fighters was like Sisyphus' assignment. The guerrillas were usually able to hide temporarily or take refuge during patrols and 'mop ups'.

The main reason for the counter-guerrilla problems was the attitude of the population to the Dutch and Republican military forces. Here, too, the guerrillas and the counter-guerrillas were fighting for the support of the population. The Republican military force was able to survive and fight as a guerrilla army only if the population was providing it with shelter, recruits and intelligence. On the other hand, reliable intelligence on the guerrilla groups was of vital importance to Dutch military personnel. Without it their patrols and 'mop ups' were shots in the dark. For such intelligence they had to rely on the local population. In other words, for successful counter-guerrilla activity it was necessary for the population to withhold its assistance from the guerrilla fighters and to support the Dutch troops.

Dutch army commanders realised that the backing of the local population was essential to their counter-guerrilla operations. They worked harmoniously together with the Dutch administrators to recruit this support by both peaceful and repressive means. The first aim of the Dutch administrators who had travelled with the attacking columns was to have all Republican administrators transfer to Dutch service. Their co-operation was regarded as essential precisely because they had authority and information on their region. However, only a proportion of them transferred to Dutch service – precise figures are lacking – on condition that they were protected against reprisals. Some refused on conscientious grounds, some from fear of Republican reprisals. These 'conscientious objectors' were replaced, often by pre-war officials who had meanwhile lost some of their standing.[11] In addition, the Dutch administrators attempted to elicit commitment from the population by holding out the prospect of the federal structure, but this was distrusted by many Indonesians on Java and Sumatra as an anti-nationalistic or anti-Republican position and appealed most to sections of the pre-war administrative elite and ethnic minorities.[12] A bid was also made for the people's favour through economic means such as the distribution of food, medicines and textiles.[13]

But repressive measures were not rejected. Administrators instituted numerous prohibitions, implemented checks such as curfews, night passes, organized a political investigation department and a police force. By the end of 1948 this was 35,000 strong.[14] In addition, the military force carried out patrols and 'mop ups', designed to eliminate the guerrillas, to impress the population and to gather information. During the 'mop ups' civilians, too, were interrogated. Blatant assistance to the enemy meant a prison sentence at least. Special courts martial in the field passed judgements on the spot from mid-1948 onwards, including charges against civilians. Nor was excessive violence towards civilians eschewed as a way of extracting intelligence from the population and terrorizing them into submission. Intelligence units and the Corps of Special Troops used extreme violence on a widespread basis. A question still to be answered is how systematically regular units used this method at this phase of the battle.[15]

Despite these measures some of the population continued giving support to the guerrillas, either out of conviction or under duress. To maintain its position the Republican army did not flinch from violence. Primarily because of this popular support the Republican military force could sustain its guerrilla activity and even step it up in the second half of 1948. In sum, the Dutch counter-guerrilla activity was not an unmitigated success in 1947–48, because it proved impossible to prevent the Republicans from being given or exacting the support of a section of the population.

But Republican guerrilla activity displayed major regional differences. Guerrilla fighting was fiercest in the border areas with the Republic and in less accessible districts. The latter indicates that the counter-guerrilla problems also had another cause, which might be described as the

40   EMERGENCIES AND DISORDER IN THE EUROPEAN EMPIRES

'reaction capability' of the Dutch troops. The effectiveness of the Dutch counter-guerrilla actions was determined not only by the quality of the intelligence on which they had been conducted, but also by the rapidity of response to such intelligence. This speed was in turn dependent on the density and the dispersal of the troops and the state of the terrain. The dispersal of the troops was largely determined by the road network on which the troops relied for their supplies. Moreover, such dependence implied that some of the troops were tied up keeping the lines of communication open. Dispersal and the reaction capability of the troops were again adversely affected because the troops were charged with guarding vital public works, economic sites, administrative officials and posts. As a result the further away the Dutch troops became from towns and roads and the more inaccessible the terrain, the thinner their density on the ground and the smaller their radius of action and the greater the intensity of guerrilla activity. The Dutch military authorities did attempt to improve the reaction capability of the troops by stepping up the frequency of patrols and by forming special surveillance units so that the battle units could be released for patrolling duties.[16] The police, too, were charged with surveillance and patrolling responsibilities, and whole villages were moved if problems persisted in certain areas.

But these measures were only stop-gaps, according to the military commanders who took the view that the crux of the problem lay with the political and military Republican leaders. It was their fault that the guerrilla fighters in the occupied territories had not become demoralized and had managed to keep a firm grip on a section of the population through a reign of terror and propaganda. The colonial army leaders remained convinced that only a small minority of the population, mainly the intelligentsia, was Republican-minded. Most of the population, they thought, were willing to co-operate with the Dutch, provided they were offered safety and security. The latter could be achieved only if the Republic were to be 'decapitated', after which the military organization would be bled dry and the pressure on the population alleviated.

But after the second offensive, the military problems for the Netherlands escalated. During the offensive the Republican political leaders had been eliminated, but not the military leaders, and there was no question of a general demoralization and disorganization of the Republican military force. Dutch troops could not prevent their planned withdrawal to areas suitable for guerrilla warfare and their infiltration into territory previously occupied by the Netherlands. Their guerrilla activities grew rapidly, though with major regional differences in intensity.[17] After a few months a military stalemate was reached. The guerrillas managed to put Dutch troops on the defensive in terrain that was difficult to negotiate,

THE DUTCH EAST INDIES, 1945–50   41

but they were still unable to dislodge them from the towns by means of large-scale battles. In more easily negotiable areas, the Dutch troops retained the initiative.

The causes of these military problems were basically the same as those before the second offensive: the support from the population obtained or enforced by the Republican military force and the limited reaction capability of the Dutch troops. But these factors became more pronounced as a result of this new offensive. The international-political effect of the offensive increased the sympathy of the population for the Republican guerrillas. It was clear that the Netherlands was running a losing race in the international arena. Even the federal leaders started to bet on the Republican horse after January 1949. Besides, the number of opponents increased drastically, because the offensive failed to have the demoralizing and disorganizing effect anticipated and the Republican army in the previously unoccupied territories also became involved in the battle. On the other hand, the reaction capability of the Dutch troops was reduced as a result of the offensive. They had to operate over a greater area, while their numbers remained the same. This gave the Republicans more chance to ensure local support, while this became increasingly difficult for the Dutch troops. The same tendency emerged in the attitude of the Indonesian administrators, who until then had been co-operative. They increasingly began to take the side of the Republic, not only for political reasons, but also for personal security and safety.[18] To compensate for the reduced reaction capability, at this phase of the battle greater resort was had to artillery and the airforce. In addition, a 'military counter-terror' was being applied in certain areas by regular infantry to enforce the support of the population, at least according to one battalion commander. But the downward spiral could not be reversed, even by these blunter military instruments.

The fact that the Netherlands' use of military force resulted in a stalemate was basically due to the Republican military power increasingly managing to command the population's support, which enabled it to operate effectively as a guerrilla force, while the reaction capability of the Dutch military force diminished. These developments were in turn attributable to the Dutch strategy; it played into the adversary's hand. But political factors were also at work: international support for the Republic, the appeal of Indonesian nationalism, the unpalatability of Dutch policy. Even after the first offensive, the limits had begun to emerge of what the Netherlands might achieve as part of its decolonization plan in Indonesia, using violent and peaceful means. But the Dutch image of the adversary prevented a proper impression being gained. This explains why a military answer was chosen which only served to exacerbate the military and political problems.

42   EMERGENCIES AND DISORDER IN THE EUROPEAN EMPIRES

IV

Military force constituted an important policy instrument for the Netherlands during the decolonization conflict in Indonesia. It was used as a weapon at the negotiating table but also as a last resort for the Netherlands to gain control over the decolonization process and thus safeguard Dutch interests in Indonesia. Right up to the last stage of the conflict, military leaders and most of the political leaders in the colony and the Netherlands remained convinced that the Netherlands could settle the conflict satisfactorily through military force. Naturally, this affected the negotiating process. As long as the majority of the Dutch government believed that they had a military trump card up their sleeves, they were only partially willing to arrive at a compromise. We can also conclude that the Netherlands fell into a military trap. The build-up and use of military force gave rise to political, economic and military problems that were combated with more military force.

But the expectations of the Netherlands' and colonial political and military leaders as to what the Netherlands could do by military means proved to be too optimistic. The strategic and tactical doctrine developed by the Dutch East Indies' army leaders and applied with the consent of the political leaders came to grief in the face of the military vitality of the Republic. The army commanders overestimated the capability of the Dutch military force to eliminate the opponent. But above all they underestimated the potential and willingness of the Republican military force to survive and to fight as a guerrilla army with the support of the population. This underestimation of the opponent had its roots in the colonial frame of reference of the army leaders and their accompanying impression of the Indonesian revolution. Nor did the political leaders fare much better. Though some of them became more aware of the revolution going on in Indonesian society, they failed to gauge correctly the Republic's political appeal and the support it enlisted. This is why the majority of them continued to believe or hope that the Republic could be subdued by Dutch military force. That hope and belief died only when the ultimate remedy finally brought the Netherlands to an international political and military dead-end. It was only then that the Netherlands was able to extricate itself with the aid of the great powers from the military trap it had created.

THE DUTCH EAST INDIES, 1945–50   43

NOTES

This paper is mainly based on data taken from my thesis *Marsroutes en dwaalsporen. Het Nederlands militair-strategische beleid in Indonesië. 1945–1948* [Dutch military strategic policy in Indonesia 1945–1950] (The Hague, 1991). Where this is not the case or where there is literature available on specific subjects in English this will be indicated.

1. A general survey of the course of the conflict between the Netherlands and the Republic of Indonesia is to be found in G. McKahin, *Nationalism and Revolution in Indonesia* (Ithaca, New York, 1952), and A. Reid, *Indonesian National Revolution 1945–1950* (Hawthorn, 1974).

2. For the British role in the Indonesian question see C.W. Squire, 'Britain and the Transfer of Power in Indonesia' (Ph.D. University of London, 1978), and P. Dennis, *Troubled Days of Peace. Mountbatten and South-East Asia Command, 1945–46* (Manchester, 1987).

3. A survey of the policies of the lieutenant governor-general in the Netherlands Indies is to be found in Yong Mun Cheong, *H.J. van Mook and Indonesian Independence: A Study of His Role in Dutch Indonesian Relations, 1945–1948* (Singapore, 1980).

4. Altogether the Dutch army comprised 20 per cent war volunteers and 80 per cent conscripts. Data on the KNIL have been taken from the first reliable report from 1948. Military History Section, Royal Netherlands Army. Collection Netherlands-Indies 1945–1950, 18/3.

5. For the relations between the regular Indonesian army and the autonomous armed groups, see R. Cribb, *Gangsters and Revolutionairies: The Jakarta People's Militia and the Indonesian Revolution 1945–1949* (Sydney, 1991).

6. For Indonesian strategic planning see Cribb, *Gangsters and revolutionairies*, and A.H. Nasution, *Fundamentals of Guerrilla Warfare* (Jakarta, 1970).

7. *Voorschrift voor de uitoefening van de politiek-politioneele taak van het leger (V.P.T.L.)* [Regulation for the exercise of the political-police task of the army]. Comparison edition Weltevreden 1928, The Hague, 1945; *Aanwijzingen optreden van Nederlandse troepen in Nederlands Indie* [Instructions for the action of Dutch troops in the Dutch East Indies], parts 1 to 5 (Semarang, 1948); *Kennis van het V.P.T.L.* [Knowledge of the V.P.T.L.] (Batavia, 1949); J.A.A. van Doorn and W.J. Hendrix, *Ontsporing van geweld* [Force gone awry] (Dieren, 1983), 163–5.

8. Van Doorn, *Ontsporing van geweld*, 166–70; J. de Moor, 'Het Korps Speciale Troepen: tussen Marechaussee-formule en politionele actie' [The Corps of Special Troops: between constabulary-formula and police action, in G. Teitler, P.M.H. Groen (eds.), *De Politionele Acties* [The Police Actions] (Amsterdam, 1987), 125, 126, 140–2.

9. L.G.M. Jaquet, *Minister Stikker en de souvereiniteitsoverdracht aan Indonesië.* [Minister Stikker and the transfer of sovereignty to Indonesia] (The Hague, 1982), 239.

10. See also the analysis of the 'ideology' of the colonial army leaders in J.A.A. van Doorn, *The Soldier and Social Change. Comparative Studies in the History and Sociology of the Military* (Beverly Hills, London, 1975), 111–30.

11. G.C. Zijlmans, *Eindstrijd en ondergang van de Indische bestuursdienst* [Final battle and demise of the Indies administrative service] (Amsterdam, 1986), 57–60, 182, 183.

12. J. Bank, *Katholieken en de Indonesische Revolutie* [Catholics and the Indonesian Revolu tion] (Baarn, 1983), 327–34; Reid, *National revolution*, 115–19, 162–4; A. Reid, 'The Revolution in Regional Perspective', in J. van Goor (ed.), *The Indonesian revolution* (Utrecht, 1985), 185, 186, 195–7.

13. Zijlmans, *Indische bestuursdienst*, 60–2, 190.

14. Ibid., 60, 61, 76, 190, 209, 210.

15. The Netherlands government had an inquiry carried out in 1968 into the excessive use of violence by Dutch military servicemen in Indonesia. From this it emerged that the Corps of Special Troops and the intelligence units had resorted to excessive violence on a structural basis. *Nota betreffende het archievenonderzoek naar gegevens omtrent excessen in Indonesië begaan door Nederlandse militairen in de periode 1945–1950*

44   EMERGENCIES AND DISORDER IN THE EUROPEAN EMPIRES

[Memorandum on the archives inquiry into data regarding excesses in Indonesia perpetrated by Dutch military servicemen in the period 1945–1950] (The Hague, 1969). The same emerges from a study of the action of the Corps of Special Troops: De Moor, 'Het Korps Speciale Troepen', 121–43. Other army units certainly made incidental use of this method, see Van Doorn and Hendrix *Ontsporing van geweld*. English speakers can find Van Doorn's conclusions in *The Soldier and Social Change*, 133–77, and J.A.J. van Doorn, H.J. Hendrix, *The Process of Decolonization 1945–1975. The Military Experience in Comparative Perspective* (Rotterdam, 1987).

16. Zijlmans, *Indische bestuursdienst*, 76. The plantation guards at the end of 1948 were 18,000 strong.
17. For an Indonesian view on the guerrilla war in 1949 see T.B. Simatupang, *Report form Banaran. Experiences during the people's war* (New York, 1972).
18. Zijlmans, *Indische bestuursdienst*, 89.

[6]

'OUR STRIKE': EQUALITY, ANTICOLONIAL POLITICS AND THE 1947–48 RAILWAY STRIKE IN FRENCH WEST AFRICA

BY FREDERICK COOPER

University of Michigan

THE strike of African railway workers which began in October 1947 was an event of epic dimensions: it involved 20,000 workers and their families, shut down most rail traffic throughout all of French West Africa, and lasted, in most regions, for five and a half months. As if the historical event were not large enough, it has been engraved in the consciousness of West Africans and others by the novel of Ousmanne Sembene, *God's Bits of Wood*. Sembene dramatizes a powerful strike effort weakened by the impersonal approach of trade unionists, by the seductions of French education, and by the greed of local élites. The strike is redeemed by its transformation into a truly popular movement dynamized by women, climaxing in a women's march on Dakar led by someone from the margins of society and leading to a coming together of African community against the forces of colonialism.

Sembene's novel both complicates the task of the historian and lends it importance: the written epic may influence oral testimony, yet the fictional account enhances the sense of participants that their actions shaped history. When a group of Senegalese graduate students and I went to the railway junction of Thiès to begin a project of collecting testimonies, some informants expressed resentment of Sembene for turning 'our strike' into his novel.[1] What needs most to be unpacked is the connection of the labor movement to the independence struggle: the two were both complementary

[1] The quoted phrase comes from an interview with Amadou Bouta Gueye, 9 Aug. 1994, Thiès. Oumar NDiaye, interviewed the same day, made much the same point. These interviews were part of a workshop and field studies program conducted in August 1994, by Dr Babacar Fall of the Ecole Normale Supérieure, Université Cheikh Anta Diop, Dakar, and the present author. A series of training sessions for graduate students was led by Dr Robert Korstad of the Center for Documentary Studies of Duke University, and I accompanied groups of students who interviewed eyewitnesses in Dakar and Thiès. The students participating in these interviews included Aminata Diena, Makhali NDaiye, Oumar Gueye, Alioune Ba, Biram NDour, and Ouseynou NDaiye. I am particularly grateful to Ms Diena for setting up the Thiès interviews and to Mr M. NDaiye, Mr Ba, and Mr Gueye for organizing the Dakar interviews. This workshop in turn was inspired by a visit that Dr Fall and I made to Thiès in July 1990, in which a graduate student working with Dr Fall, Mor Sene, took us to interview two important witnesses to the 1947–8 events. Mr Sene has himself contributed to the historiography of the strike in his master's thesis, 'La grève des cheminots du Dakar-Niger, 1947–1948' (Mémoire de maîtrise, Ecole Normale Supérieure, Université Cheikh Anta Diop, 1986–7). Following the 1994 workshop, students in Dakar will conduct interviews as part of their research on their own theses and dissertations, and will contribute tapes to an archive of contemporary oral history under the supervision of Dr Fall. Tapes of interviews cited here are preserved at the Ecole Normale Supérieure. My collaboration with Dr Fall in the study of African labor history over the last nine years has been a deeply

and in tension with one another. My goal in this article is both to re-examine the question of how to locate the railway strike in the history of post-World War II West Africa and to point to questions that need further research, for the very extensive nature of this social movement – embracing the colonies of Senegal, the Soudan, Guinea, the Ivory Coast and Dahomey and intersecting a wide range of local contexts, communities, and political struggles – means that it contains many histories and requires the attention of many historians. The research begun in Senegal gets at only some of these histories, and time is running out on the lives and memories of the people involved.

The all-too-neat assimilation of social and political struggles is a matter of hindsight: once independence was achieved, all forms of contestation against French rulers and bosses appear to be part of a seamless pattern of ever-broadening, ever-growing struggle. Some sort of connection is not in doubt; the problem is to pry apart its complexities and ambiguities. The strikers were able to hold out for over five months because they were so well integrated into the African communities in which they lived, but their demands, if realized, would have had the effect of pulling them out of close communities into a professionally defined, non-racial body of railwaymen. The union's goal from 1946 onward was the creation of the *cadre unique*, a single scale of wages and benefits for Africans and white Frenchmen alike. Such a system would widen the gap between the life experiences of railwaymen and those of the peasants, pastoralists and merchants among whom they lived. In political terms one can argue the opposite: to the extent that the strike movement drew from anticolonial sentiments that went beyond the workplace and to the extent that the strike gave Africans a sense of empowerment in their confrontations with the French government, anti-colonial politics risked diluting the work-centered goals of the strike movement. The idea of independence would sever the French connection which was the ideological basis for the railwaymen's claims to equality of wages and benefits with French workers, while opening the union's considerable organizational achievements to co-optation by political parties whose primary concerns lay elsewhere.

In fact, the union and the major political movements of the day remained in uneasy relationship. The men who were the ultimate beneficiaries of decolonization – the Senghors and the Houphouët-Boignys – did not make the cause of the strikers their own. Senghor, more so than other party leaders, maintained contact with the union and when the strike was over moved decisively to bring its leaders into his political fold and under his eyes – a process which increased the union's influence and decreased its autonomy. For many strikers, the behavior of politicians was disillusioning, and for the union structure, the very success of the strike left potentially conflicting alternatives between becoming, as one veteran put it, the 'auxiliaries' of a political party or else focusing as a union on the kinds of claims they could make that stood a good chance of success within the framework of industrial relations emerging out of the strike. If the strike, as a popular movement,

gratifying one, and I would like to thank him for all the help he has given me along the way, for his comments on an earlier draft of this article and for his leadership in setting up the 1994 workshop.

THE 1947–48 RAILWAY STRIKE IN FRENCH WEST AFRICA   83

gave thousands of people a sense of collective strength, the strike – as a process carried out through certain kinds of institutions – defined the terrain of contestation in a narrower way.

This article points to the kind of questions that further oral research across the strike zone will illuminate. Among documentary sources it gives particular emphasis to reports by police spies present at numerous strike meetings. They must of course be used with care, since spies have a tendency to see what their superiors want them to see. But it is clear that the strikers earned the grudging admiration of their opponents, who had clear reasons to try to learn something of what was going on among them. Taken together, available sources offer multiple points of access to an extraordinarily complex social movement.[2]

THE CONTEXT: STRIKE MOVEMENTS AND THE MODERNIZATION OF IMPERIALISM

The strike must be understood in the context of a French government anxious to find a new basis of legitimacy and control in an era when social and political movements in the colonies were asserting themselves with new vigor. These two processes shaped one another: as African movements sought to turn the government's need for order and economic growth into claims to entitlements and representation, officials had to rethink their policies in the face of new African challenges. The truly agenda-setting movement of the immediate post-war years was the Senegalese general strike of 1946. Up to that point, the French sociology of Africa admitted to only two categories, *paysans* and *évolués*. Officials hoped to achieve economic growth by eliminating forced labor, reducing the tax burden on peasants, and improving infrastructure devoted to agriculture, and to attain political stability by granting *évolués* a modest degree of participation in the governing institutions of France itself. The strike movement – beginning in the port in December 1945, extending to commercial establishments in January, and turning at mid-month into a general strike – involved everyone from African civil servants to dockworkers to market sellers (with the conspicuous exception of railwaymen). Confessing his inability to control events, the Governor General welcomed a labor expert from Paris who proceeded to make workers a focus of policy. The general strike ended as officials negotiated with individual categories of workers, granting collective bargaining agreements to each one in turn. By February the strike movement was over, and ordinary laborers had won significant wage increases; government workers were getting family allowances based on a percentage of the indemnities granted to the top ranks; unions were recognized; and wage hierarchies were expanded and bonuses granted for seniority.

[2] The spies' reports appear in the archives as 'Renseignements', often with a notation such as 'African source – good'. Most came from the Sûreté at Thiès, where the almost daily mass meetings were held, but reports from other regions are also used. Archival sources from the Archives Nationales du Sénégal include (from the Government General of Afrique Occidentale Française) series K (labor), 17 G (politics), 2 G (annual reports), and (from the government of Senegal) series D (political and administrative files). The series IGT (Inspection Générale du Travail) and AP (Affaires Politiques) are from France, Archives Nationales, Section Outre-Mer, Aix-en-Provence. The abbreviation 'AOF,' for Afrique Occidentale Française, occurs frequently in the notes.

84   FREDERICK COOPER

Out of the strike came a newly empowered Inspection du Travail that sought to use French models of industrial relations to gain a measure of control over an increasingly differentiated labor force and to promote 'stabilization' as an antidote to the kind of mass, boundary-crossing movement they had just faced. There emerged as well a labor movement able to turn officials' hopes for stability and the assimilationist rhetoric of post-war French imperialism into African workers' claims to French wage and benefit scales. Over the next several years, the labor question focused on the details of what stabilization and 'equal pay for equal work' would mean and on efforts of both workers and labor inspectors to devise an empire-wide *Code du Travail* that would guarantee basic rights and bound conflict within a set of legally defined procedures. Family allowances, minimum wages, wage hierarchies, and trade union rights were all the objects of negotiations, mobilization, and strikes.[3]

Politics was meanwhile being changed from above and from below. Seeking to demonstrate that what were once called colonies were now an integral part of Greater France, citizenship was extended from the few acculturated urban centers to all French territory and – with a limited but gradually expanding franchise – elections were held throughout French Africa from late 1945 onward for positions in the French legislature. As old-line politicians like Senegal's Lamine Gueye tried to maintain control of their parties, 'youth' organizations challenged them in cities and rural constituencies were organized, most strikingly by the Société Agricole Africaine in the Ivory Coast, leading to the formation of a cross-territorial political party, the Rassemblement Démocratique Africain (RDA).

In the middle of the ferment within Senegal over both trade unions and politics was François Gning, Secretary General of the Syndicat des Travailleurs Indigènes du Dakar-Niger, headquartered in Thiès. He had led this union of skilled and long-term African railwaymen since the mid-1930s, and he was an active member of Lamine Gueye's socialist party, the Section Française de l'Internationale Ouvrière (SFIO). His union was the most important group of workers to refuse to participate in the 1946 general strike. His socialist affiliations – the socialists were then in the government in France – were a major factor inhibiting his room to maneuver. It was not a popular stance.[4] As early as December 1945, railwaymen at a meeting in Thiès were talking about a strike, in opposition to Gning.[5] This did not come off, but after the Dakar general strike, Gning and his Comité Directeur decided to start a strike fund, part as sensible preparation, part as delaying tactic. He hoped that 'the example furnished by the groups that recently

[3] Frederick Cooper, 'The Senegalese General Strike of 1946 and the labor question in post-war French Africa', *Can. J. Afr. Studies*, XXIV (1990), 165–215 and 'Le mouvement ouvrier et le nationalisme: la grève générale du 1946 et la grève des cheminots de 1947–48', *Historiens et Géographes du Sénégal*, VI (1991), 32–42.

[4] There was considerable discontent on the railway in the period before the Dakar strike. Renseignements, 9, 27 Apr. 1943, 7 Sept. 1944, 27 Feb. 1945, 11 D 1/1392.

[5] Governor General to Minister, 19 Jan. 1946, 17 G 132. The other side of Gning's connections was that, from 1944 until his dethronement in 1946, he had access to the Governor General and negotiated a number of concessions for the railwaymen. Renseignements, Thiès, 30 Aug., 1, 4 Sept. 1944, K 329 (26); Renseignements, 10 Jan. 1946, and Directeur du Réseau, transcript of meeting of Conseil du Réseau, 24 Jan. 1946, K 328 (26).

THE 1947–48 RAILWAY STRIKE IN FRENCH WEST AFRICA 85

went on strike will allow railwaymen to reflect on the gravity of an act which constitutes a two-edged sword'.[6]

Politics and trade unionism came together in the opposition to Gning's maneuverings in the principal railway junction and repair center at Thiès. In April 1946, officials reported agitation among the railway workers, who felt they had not received what they deserved from their restraint during the general strike. In May, security officials learned that a movement to oust Gning was being organized by a group from the Union des Jeunes de Thiès, who were also active members of the railway union. Here developed an extraordinary conjuncture of the political ideals of a group of young, educated men and a workforce that was largely non-literate. From mid-1945, the Union des Jeunes was led by a clerk (Abdoul Karim Sow) and a school teacher (Mory Tall), and included several people with clerical jobs on the railway. Its goals were simultaneously political, cultural and intellectual – to promote our 'general development', one leader recalled.[7] Its meetings brought out a youthful vigor against the perceived lethargy of older Senegalese politicians and a new combativeness toward the French, even though neither it – nor any other significant political group – was at this time calling for independence.[8] Its attacks were highly personal – the Commandant de Cercle at Thiès was a target – and the administration replied in kind by transferring Tall to a remote northern town, where he promptly organized another Union des Jeunes. The organization published a newsletter, *Jeunesse et Démocratie*, and entered a complicated dialogue with the local section of the SFIO, also led by Gning. It alternated between criticism of the doyen of Senegalese socialist politicians, Lamine Gueye, and attempts to make up with him.[9] The aggressive moves of the 'Jeunes' to remake politics within the SFIO at Thiès led Gning to resign in frustration as its Secretary General.[10]

Gning was a Catholic and his mentor, Lamine Gueye, while Muslim like

[6] Syndicat des Travailleurs Indigènes du Dakar-Niger, Circulaire no. 10, 1 Feb. 1946, signed by Gning, in K 325 (26).

[7] Mory Tall, interview, Thiès, 9 Aug. 1994, by Aminata Diena, Biram NDour, Alioune Ba and Frederick Cooper.

[8] Tall told an early meeting of the 'Jeunes' of the need to 'bring about in a short time a complete assimilation in all domains with Europeans and a larger participation of the indigenous element in the administration of the country'. The union apparently began as an offshoot led by the militant Tall against the conservative Gning within yet another of the discussion-cum-political groups of the immediate post-war years, the Comité d'Etudes Franco-Africaines. Renseignements, 26 June 1945, 11 D 1/1396. The Comité faded while the union took off. Chef du 2e Secteur de la Sûreté to Commandant de Cercle, 13 Oct. 1945, 11 D 1/1396.

[9] Commissaire de Police, Thiès, to Commandant de Cercle, Thiès, 22 Aug., 27, 28 Sept. 1945; Renseignements, Thiès, 3 Dec. 1945, 11 Sept. 1946; Commissaire de Police to Chef de la Sûreté du Sénégal, 22 Nov. 1945; Commandant de Cercle, note for Governor of Senegal, 26 Apr. 1946; Chef du 2e Secteur de la Sûreté to Chef de la Sûreté du Sénégal, 20 July, 13 Nov. 1945; Note by Chef de la Police Spéciale du Réseau Dakar-Niger, 7 Aug. 1945, in 11 D 1/1396. The Union des Jeunes established contacts with Léopold Senghor and felt they had his sympathy despite his unwillingness at the time to follow them in criticizing his mentor, Lamine Gueye. Renseignements, 17 May 1946, 11 D 1/1396.

[10] Commissaire de Police to Commandant de Cercle, 28 Sept. 1945, 11 D 1/1396; Renseignements, 22 Sept. 1945, 11 D 1/1392.

86   FREDERICK COOPER

most peasants and workers, was from the old élite of the Quatre Communes, which had long enjoyed French citizenship and were seen to be distant by most rural Senegalese. The leaders of the Union des Jeunes were Muslim, and one of them, Ibrahima Sarr, came from a family with connections to marabouts, the leaders of the Muslim brotherhoods which held great influence in rural Senegal. Sarr was also well educated: a graduate of a leading trade school, *écrivain* in the *cadre local supérieure* since 1938.[11]

Gning, an *évolué* conscious of having earned his privileges, was unable to assimilate one of the basic lessons of the January 1946 strike: that workers of all levels were laying claim to basic entitlements. He would not attack the privilege of the top cadres, thinking it inconceivable that an ordinary worker 'receive the same indemnities as a Governor'.[12]

Following their attacks on Gning in the Thiès section of the SFIO, the militants of the Union des Jeunes spearheaded a 'revolution' within the railway union, attacking Gning's non-combative approach, his failure to join the successful 1946 strike, and his alienation of non-élite workers.[13] After meetings of the Comité Directeur, demonstrations calling for Gning's resignation, and a public meeting of 1,000 railwaymen at Thiès on 23 May 1946 at which he was repeatedly denounced, Gning resigned. Ibrahima Sarr took over, installing a Comité Directeur largely led by other clerks but including representation of all divisions.[14]

[11] On Sarr's background, see Sene, 'Grève des cheminots'. His pre-strike activism in the Union des Jeunes was noted by police informants. See Chef du 2e Secteur de la Sûreté de Thiès to Commandant de Cercle, 9 July 1945, Note by Chef de la Police Spéciale du Réseau Dakar-Niger, 7 Aug. 1945, 11 D 1/1396. Sarr was listed in the latter document as one of the editors of *Jeunesse et Démocratie*. His connection to a leading Mouride marabout and its importance to the strikers was described by a well-informed strike veteran. Mansour Niang, interview, Dakar, 4 Aug. 1994, by Makhali NDiaye, Aminata Diena, Alioune Ba and Frederick Cooper.

[12] Renseignements, 6 Apr. 1946, K 328 (26); Renseignements, 14 May 1946, enclosing transcript of meeting of 4 May 1946 of Comité Directeur, K 352 (26). The director of the railway system, like Gning, thought that a progressive policy aimed at the élite of railway workers had 'produced fruit'. In particular, he argued that reforms of December 1945 which had opened up the *cadre secondaire* to Africans, who could compete for posts 'with equality of credentials or of merit', had contributed to the willingness of this élite to co-operate with the union leadership in keeping the rest of the personnel on the job during the January strike. These reforms had permitted 1,100 Africans (out of 20,000) to be examined for possible promotion into the *cadre secondaire*. Directeur du Réseau, Compte Rendu on the Conseil du Réseau, 24 Jan. 1946, K 328 (26).

[13] 'Revolution' was the word used by a strike veteran Adoulaye Souleye Sarr, interview, Thiès, 22 July 1990, by Mor Sene, Babacar Fall and Frederick Cooper. He pointed to the milieu of Thiès as the incubus of the revolution.

[14] Renseignements, 22, 23, 24, 25 May 1946, 11 D 1/1392. Gning bitterly attacked the 'conspiracies' of certain *écrivains* associated with the Union des Jeunes but accepted the will of the assembly, wishing the union well in trying to find a Secretary General 'more sincere' than he. Sarr had been transferred by the railway administration from Thiès to Dakar because of his activities in the Union des Jeunes, but the railway transferred him back so he could be near the union headquarters at Thiès, and he was promoted to the *cadre secondaire* on 1 Jan. 1947. Commissaire de Police to Chef de la Sûreté du Sénégal, 25 May 1946, 11 D 1/1392. For a list of members of the Comité Directeur, see Renseignements, 19 July 1946, 11 D 1/1392. This narrative and explanation is quite close to that given by informants, notably Oumar NDiaye, Amadou Bouta Gueye (interview, Thiès, 9 Aug. 1994), Mansour Niang (interview, 4 Aug. 1994), and Abdoulaye Souleye Sarr (interview, 22 July 1990).

Sarr's inaugural speech to the committee, in May 1946, printed and circulated to the men, was at the same time an attack on colonialism and a perceptive use and extension of the new French colonial rhetoric against the old. He called for

the liberation of the worker, giving him sufficient means so that he can live honorably and relieving him, above all, of the singular and painful nightmare of uncertainty about the next day, in other words, the abolition of antiquated colonial methods condemned even by THE NEW AND TRUE FRANCE which wishes that all its children, at whatever latitude they may live, be equal in duties and rights and *that the recompense of labor be a function solely of merit and capacity*.[15]

The new union regime had a base to start: Gning's union was the oldest in French West Africa, and his connections to the Socialist Party and the Government General in 1936-8 and 1944-6 had brought some concessions without strikes. But Sarr was promising to remedy the union's greatest limitation since the 1930s. In fact, the most important railway strike in recent memory, at Thiès in 1938, had been conducted over the opposition of the union, and Gning's élitism had put the largest category of railway workers – the auxiliaries – outside of the union's embrace. Auxiliaries often worked for years if not a lifetime and many were highly skilled; but the railway limited the number of its permanent employees, the *cadres*, to increase its control and decrease its costs. In 1938, a dissident union of auxiliaries had challenged Gning as much as the railway. Their aggressive attempts to shut down the railway had ended in military violence and the fatal shooting of six strikers. The tragic incident was quickly exploited by rightists in Dakar and Paris to eliminate officials who had encouraged bargaining with African trade unions, and the labor movement remained all but dormant until the end of World War II.[16] Reviving his old union after the war, Gning soon learned that the world of labor had changed for good.

Sarr promised to bring auxiliaries and cadres into a single organization and a single struggle. The union's demands consistently had two dimensions: to equalize benefits for all railwaymen in the cadres with no distinctions of origin or race, and secondly to integrate all auxiliaries into the cadres. The demands were both about equity in compensation and about dignity, especially the dignity of lower-ranking workers. The ultimate demand was for a *cadre unique*, a single hierarchy defined by skill and seniority that would set aside the old distinctions of colonial/metropolitan and cadres/auxiliary.[17]

Sarr's other major achievement was to forge a French West Africa-wide

---

[15] Renseignements, 28 May 1946, K 352 (26); Sene, 'Grève des cheminots', 46. In July, Sarr and his colleagues, still fearing a comeback by Gning, played out an unpleasant little game: they threatened a strike unless the Direction of the railway transferred Gning away from Thiès. The demand was refused, but Sarr was put off by a promise to arrange a meeting with the Governor General and the moment passed. Renseignements, 27 July 1946, 17 G 527.

[16] Iba der Thiam, 'La grève des cheminots du Sénégal de Septembre 1938' (Mémoire de maîtrise, Université de Dakar, 1972).

[17] A month into his tenure, Sarr was criticized at a meeting of auxiliaries for not doing enough for them, and he responded with a meeting to assure them that he was and made the integration of all railwaymen into the *cadre unique* the main theme of his tour of the lines. Renseignements, 27 June, 2 July 1946, 11 D 1/1392. Abdoulaye Souleye Sarr recalled that in the early days lower ranking workers were called *travailleurs indigènes* rather than *cheminots* (interview, 22 July 1990).

movement. The *coup de main* that overthrew Gning had been very much a Thiès-centered event; a mass meeting was its climax. Thiès was a very special kind of place: residence and workplace were thoroughly integrated, and railwaymen from diverse parts of Senegal and the Soudan shared common conditions in this double sense; the bonds formed at Thiès in turn travelled up and down the rail line that ran from Dakar to Bamako. It was not clear at first that the new leaders had support along the line, let alone in the other systems of French West Africa. But within a month of his takeover, Sarr embarked on a series of visits, beginning with the Soudan in June 1946 and culminating in a tour of the other railway lines on the eve of the 1947 strike. He told everyone of his desire to end the distinction between cadres and auxiliaries, pleaded the common cause of the workers against the Federation-wide railway administration, and encouraged the payment of dues and contributions to the strike fund. The union organizations on the different lines brought themselves together as the Fédération des Syndicats des Cheminots Africains, and ceded central direction to the Comité Directeur of the Dakar-Niger branch, headquartered in Thiès. In February 1947, the Dakar-Niger branch claimed to have added over 700,000 francs to the fund of 92,000 left by the old leadership – it was ready for a test.[18]

All this took place against the background of what police reports often called 'effervescence' at various points in the West African railway system and in other professions as well. Dakar now seemed a center of calm, and the Governor General attributed this to the success workers had already achieved in that city. Short, localized strikes and strike threats were reported in Dahomey, Guinea and the Ivory Coast.[19] In 1947, in French West Africa as a whole, 164 collective conflicts were reported to the Inspection du Travail, although the vast majority was settled without incident and strikes focused on wage disputes. By then, 133 unions in the public sector and 51 in the private had been officially organized. In Dakar, 40 per cent of workers belonged to unions; by the next year, officials believed that 20 per cent of all wage workers in French West Africa had joined a union. The large majority of the unions affiliated to the Confédération Générale du Travail

---

[18] Syndicat des Travailleurs Africains de la Région Dakar-Niger, Transcript of Assemblée Générale of 9 Feb. 1947, K 459 (179); Sene, 'Grève des cheminots', 47–50; Renseignements, 20 June, 2 July 1946, 11 D 1/1392. The politics of the unions in each line remain to be elucidated, as does the obvious question of why they were willing to cede so much control to Thiès. Some powerful personalities, notably Gaston Fiankan in the Ivory Coast, existed in the different lines. The Federation-wide organization paralleled efforts in the same years of individual trade unions to organize confederations first within each territory, then on the level of French West Africa. The Confédération Générale du Travail was the most successful at forging this kind of centralized organization. AOF, Inspection Générale du Travail, Annual Reports, 1947, 1948.

[19] Governor General to Minister 20 Apr. and 19 June 1946, 17 G 132; Renseignements, Dahomey, June, July, Aug. 1946, and Report of the Gendarmerie Nationale, Porto Novo, 13 Aug. and 18 Sept. 1946, K 352 (26); Renseignements, Guinea, 1 July 1947, Aug. 1947, and Gendarmarie Nationale, Conakry, report, 1, 5 Aug. 1947, K 352(26); Renseignements, Soudan, 8 June 1946, 7 July, 3 Aug. 1947, K 352(26); Chef de la Région Abidjan-Niger to Directeur, Chemins de Fer de l'AOF, 20 Sept. 1946, 17 G 591; Ivory Coast, Police et Sûreté, Rapport Politique Mensuel, 3 Oct. 1946, and Renseignements, 6 May 1947, 17 G 139; Report of Commandant du Peloton de Marché d'Abidjan on strike movement at Tafiré (Korhogo), 16–17 Aug. 1946, 17 G 138.

THE 1947-48 RAILWAY STRIKE IN FRENCH WEST AFRICA 89

(CGT), with the African confederation retaining considerable autonomy despite its affiliation with the communist-led, metropolitan organization. But the Fédération Syndicale des Cheminots remained autonomous of any of the central union organizations.[20]

The other side in the rail dispute was also changing, opening up uncertainty about the status of railwaymen as government employees just as civil servants achieved success in the strike of 1946. The railways had been under the Direction des Travaux Publics. Effective 17 July 1946, they were reorganized as the Régie des Chemins de Fer de l'Afrique Occidentale Française (AOF), which would today be called a parastatal organization and which was described at the time as an 'organization of public utility attached to the private sector and constrained to rules of industrial and commercial operations'. It was administered by a director, M. Cunéo, who reported to a Conseil d'Administration chaired by the Secretary General of the Government General and consisting of 16 members appointed by the administration, eight representatives of the Grand Conseil (the elected legislative body of French West Africa), five representatives of the workers (of whom three were named by the unions), and three representatives of the users of railway services. The board was autonomous in its position, but not in its majority membership, while the status of the Régie implied that its own financial condition – and not the resources of the Government General, or by extension, France – constrained its expenditures. The reorganization meant that railway workers would no longer benefit from a *statut*, as did civil servants, but would come under a *convention collective*, like the metal workers, the bakery workers or commercial workers. Railway workers could not automatically claim the gains acquired by the civil service, and railway officials had an excuse for not responding to political pressure. The Régie became a distinct battleground, consistent with the government's overall strategy of regaining initiative after the unified mobilization it had faced in the general strike of 1946.[21]

The Régie's personnel was organized hierarchically, in a manner parallel to the bureaucracy: the *cadre supérieur* was entirely European, the *cadre commun supérieur* mostly so. The *cadre secondaire* was mixed and the *cadre local* was, essentially, African. All the cadres were either housed or received equivalent indemnities; the indemnities of zone and for family charges were highly skewed toward the superior, largely European, cadres. But most important, the auxiliaries did not receive housing or indemnities; they could be fired for minor offences; they were in many respects treated like temporary workers even though most served for years. And they were the large majority of railway personnel. In 1946, the railway employed 478

[20] AOF, Inspection Générale du Travail (IGT), Annual Report, 1947, 56–9; *ibid.*, 1948, 83. One reason the railwaymen shied away from the CGT or other *centrales* was that white railwaymen were mostly in the CGT, and their overt racism and unwillingness to make common cause with Africans was not a strong advertisement for solidarity. Jean Suret-Canale, 'The French West African railway workers' strike, 1947–48', in Robin Cohen, Jean Copans and Peter C. W. Gutkind (eds.), *African Labor History* (Beverly Hills, CA, 1978), 152, n. 8.

[21] AOF, IGT, Annual Report, 1947, 60–1; Sene, 'Grève des cheminots', 16. The importance to strikers of the *statut* issue was emphasized by Mansour Niang (interview 4 Aug. 1994).

Europeans and 1,729 Africans in the various cadres, plus 15,726 auxiliaries.[22] This structure was very difficult to defend in principle – but useful in practice, especially given the precedent set by government cadres in 1946. Government officials, however, did see that a more coherent structure might offer possibilities of reducing the staffing level of the railway. The direction of the railway agreed: they wanted a smaller and more efficient staff – realizing that the days of the derisorily paid multitude were ending – and they wanted the unions to co-operate.[23] There was room for bargaining.

In August 1946 the Fédération des Travailleurs Africains submitted its demands for a *cadre unique* and for the integration, over time, of the permanently employed auxiliaries into the cadre. The Governor General, under current labor law, appointed a Commission Paritaire, in which representatives of the two sides discussed the issues dividing them. Between December and April, twenty rounds of bargaining were held, most of them 'confused, tedious, broken up by stormy discussions'. Unions representing European workers made the procedures more divisive by their overt defense of racial privilege and rejection of the *cadre unique*. In April 1947, the African union, its demands unmet, staged a theatrical coup: it withdrew from the Commission Paritaire and staged a strike at the moment when the President of France and the Colonial Minister – Marius Moutet – were visiting Senegal.[24]

The three-day strike – throughout French West Africa – was a brilliant maneuver, and it appeared to have worked.[25] Under the pressure of Moutet's presence – as well as that of Governor General Barthes, Lamine Gueye, Léopold Senghor, and other luminaries – the parties agreed on the necessity to create a *cadre unique*, but also to reduce the staffing level of the railway, with the layoffs to be worked out by another Commission Paritaire which would consider seniority and skill. The creation of the *cadre unique* would require working out a table of equivalencies, so that people would be slotted into the correct positions.[26]

[22] AOF, Direction Générale des Travaux Publics, Direction des Chemins de Fer et Transports, Annual Report, 1946, quoted in Suret-Canale, 'Railway workers' strike', 152, n. 5.
[23] This was precisely the kind of thinking that emerged from the 1946 general strike. Cooper, 'The Senegalese General Strike'.
[24] Inspecteur Général du Travail, 'La Grève des Cheminots de l'AOF (1/10/47–16/3/48)', IGT 13/2; AOF, IGT, Annual Report, 1947, 60; Renseignements, 19 Aug. 1946, 11 D 1/1392; Suret-Canale, 'Railway workers' strike', 134–5. Sarr, in explaining the withdrawal from the Commission, told an assembly of workers on 9 February, 'The "toubabs", in perfect unity, lined up against us in the Commission Paritaire'. He and others complained of the racist comments continuously made by representatives of European workers in the commission, and warned of 'a battle with the Europeans'. The latter phrase was used by Mody Camara. Renseignements, 1, 10 Feb. 1947, K 377 (26).
[25] Police spies reported on a series of meetings at Thiès in early April at which the strike was planned: leaders calculated that high officials would accept union claims to avoid the embarrassment of having their President witness an ongoing strike. There were also rumors that 3,000 Africans were about to lose their jobs, and the strike thus had a defensive element to it. Renseignements, 11, 13 Apr. 1947, and Gendarmerie Nationale, Thiès, Rapport, 14 Apr. 1947, K 377 (26). For reports on the strike, see telegrams from the Governors of Dahomey, the Ivory Coast, Guinea and the Soudan, 20–23 Apr. 1947, *ibid.*   [26] Protocole de fin de grève, 19 Apr. 1947, K 377 (26).

THE 1947–48 RAILWAY STRIKE IN FRENCH WEST AFRICA 91

The acceptance of this protocol suggests that the highest levels of the government were unwilling to contest the principle of the *cadre unique* and the integration of auxiliaries. They did not want to defend overtly the discriminatory structure of a colonial labor force against the universalistic claim to equality among all workers. In April, the most far-reaching issue seemed theoretically solved. The issues over which the October strike was to be fought were less than earthshaking; the Director of the Régie later referred to them as 'points of detail'.[27] The real issue was power: who was to control the process by which new modalities of labor organization would be worked out?

In the months after April, two developments took place. The worsening economic situation in metropolitan and overseas France led to a renewed attempt by officials to hold down prices and wages throughout the French domains, the first attempt in Africa having failed during the 1946 strike. In late April and May, Governors General were told to avoid a 'general readjustment of wages of a profession'. Despite fears of renewed general strikes, officials on the scene had to push for restraint.[28] The wages of railwaymen were a major factor in the cost of goods exported and imported. In August, the railway claimed that its 1947 budget was in the red and that the integration of around 2,000 auxiliaries into the cadre would more than triple the deficit and require a 130 per cent increase in railway rates in order to bring it back to equilibrium, in lieu of which a subsidy from the government would have to be forthcoming.[29]

Secondly, in May 1947, the coalition governing France changed. The Communist Party was formally expelled, and a Center-Left coalition took power, although Moutet remained Colonial Minister until November. This meant that certain kinds of debates and certain kinds of compromises did not have to take place within the French government. The new Cabinet did not overtly reverse past labor or imperial policy – it remained committed to rationalizing the workplace and working for a Code du Travail – but it was more open to other sorts of imperatives. In metropolitan France, a bitter railway strike promptly ensued.[30]

Although the Conseil d'Administration of the Régie des Chemins de Fer overlapped in membership and personnel with the Commission Paritaire that had negotiated the agreement of April, it voted in August to reject the accord. This kind of contradiction was in fact part of what the creation of the Régie was all about: government-appointed members put on their parastatal hats, pleaded autonomy and fiscal accountability, and sent the agreement into limbo.[31]

For the union, this was nothing less than a betrayal. By summer's end, Sarr was mobilizing forces for a strike, and angry workers were even

---

[27] Note sur la proposition de loi présentée par M Mamadou Konaté tendant à la création d'un cadre unique des chemins de fer de l'AOF, incl. Cunéo to Governor General 30 Mar. 1950, K 43(1).

[28] Circular signed by Secretary General Marat (for Minister) to Hauts Commissaires, 29 Apr. 1947. For warnings of a general strike, see Inspecteur du Travail Combier (Senegal), Note d'étude, 17 Apr. 1947, and letter to Secretary General, 13 May 1947, IGT 13/4. [29] Note sur l'équilibre financier de la Régie, 12 Aug. 1947, K 459 (179).

[30] Marie-Renée Valentin, 'Les grèves des cheminots français au cours de l'année 1947', *Le Mouvement Social*, CXXX (1985), 55–80. [31] Sene, 'Grève des cheminots', 55–7.

criticizing him for not doing so forcefully enough.[32] They had to cross muddied waters to define issues: the call for a *cadre unique* was a dramatic demand for equal conditions of work – linking the feelings of workers who experienced racial discrimination on a daily basis with the assimilationist rhetoric of the French state – but the other side responded by both accepting and rejecting the *cadre unique*. The union's demand that railwaymen of all ranks be paid the indemnity of zone (the supplement to wages intended to offset geographical differences in cost of living) at the same rate rather than at rates favoring the top ranks was met not with denial but with claims that perhaps the indemnity of zone was a bad idea and should be eliminated for all workers.[33] The issue of integrating auxiliaries into the cadres was not contested either, but issues of effective dates and the standards for integration (general versus selective) were pressed by the Régie.[34] Officially, the disputed issues boiled down to: the effective date for integrating auxiliaries into the cadres; how workers were to be reclassified in forming the *cadre unique*; where examination barriers were to be set for promotions; conditions for leaves; which employees would receive housing; and whether the indemnity of zone would be uniform or would depend on rank.

At the beginning of September, Sarr told an assembly at Thiès that 'The colonialist spirit of the Europeans has once again revealed to us its force'. He explained the detailed issues in dispute. With unanimous agreement, a strike date was set for 10 October. He persuaded proponents of an immediate strike that it was first necessary to make the rounds of the railway depots – including the Ivory Coast, Guinea and Dahomey – and he soon set off on his journey. The Ivoirien union leader, Gaston Fiankan, declared that the Abidjan-Niger region would join the Dakar-Niger in the strike, and he was soon holding meetings in various locations in the Ivory Coast to consolidate support. As Sarr went off to prosyletize the Soudan, French security reported 'Up to now, he is getting confidence and unanimity for the strike along the entire line'. Returning from the Soudan, Sarr appeared before another assembly at Thiès attended by, according to police, 7,000 people. Awaiting him, the crowd beat drums, engaged in 'wild dances' and waved three big French flags. He was escorted to the meeting by cyclists and arrived amidst cries of 'Vive Sarr'.[35]

Just before the strike deadline – on October 7 by one account – Léopold Senghor came to Thiès to meet in private with the Comité Directeur. He told them he was with them in their struggle. Lamine Gueye, meanwhile, already had a strained relationship with the current union leadership and had had an ugly confrontation in Thiès with the 'Jeunes' when he tried to reconcile

[32] Renseignements, 25 Aug. 1947, K 377 (26).

[33] Governor General to Minister, 28 June, 16 Sept. 1947, K 459 (179). This indemnity could rise as high as 7/10 of the base wage; it was a *de facto* mechanism for equalizing base wages while maintaining substantial inequalities. The Governor General claimed to be thinking about suppressing this for civil servants – which would set a precedent, although technically no more than that, for railway workers – and replacing it with an indemnity of residence which would apply only to high-cost areas and apply without distinction of rank or origin. The Governor General, however, feared that opening up this issue raised the possibility of a general strike throughout the civil service and railways.

[34] Mémoire of Régie for the Comité Arbitral, 27 Oct. 1947, K 459 (179).

[35] Renseignements, Thiès, 1, 11 Sept. 1947, and Renseignements, Ivory Coast, 16, 18 Sept., 1947, K 377 (26); Sûreté, Synthèse mensuelle, Oct. 1947, 17 G 527.

them with Gning after Sarr's coup in the railway union. Gueye, according to informants, was willing to talk to the union leaders, but he warned them of the dangers of a strike rather than giving his support. The strikers would remember the difference, even though Senghor failed to back the strikers publicly as he had in private.[36]

The Governor General talked to the union leaders on the eve of the strike and tried to intimidate them. The Inspection du Travail made a last ditch attempt at conciliation. The union felt it had fulfilled all the preconditions for a legal strike by virtue of the fact that it had been jumping through hoops for over a year; officials claimed that these were not the hoops prescribed by law and that the dispute should go to arbitration over the listed items in dispute. An arbitrator and the arbitration appeal panel eventually did hear the case and made their rulings later in the month. This action was too little, too late, and without waiting for the hearing, the union began its strike as planned on 10 October throughout all branches of the railway in French West Africa and on the wharfs in Dahomey and the Ivory Coast under the Régie's jurisdiction. The walkout was virtually complete among the 17,000 railwaymen and 2,000 workers at the wharfs, and it remained that way: on 1 November, 38 Africans were on the job.[37]

SOLIDARITY AND SURVIVAL

Reading police reports – several per day during the five and a half months of the strike – reveals some of its remarkable features: the union's largely successful attempt to preserve unity until January, when the Abidjan-Niger region defected, but the other regions held solid; the fear of the administration that the hiring of strikebreakers or other repressive measures would provoke reactions which it could not control, and its delay for a month before it tried – with only marginal success – to reconstitute a work force and increase traffic; the slowness of African politicians and political parties – and the new institutions of the Union Française – to take cognizance of this act of enormous political and economic importance until the strike was three months old; and the way in which the struggle, as it wore on, became more and more about the strike itself, and its ending reflected the fact that each side had proved its toughness and was ready for the next round – and the next form – of contestation.[38]

The most fascinating question about the conduct of the strike – how such a large and diverse body of workers maintained themselves physically and as a coherent force – requires further investigation. Asked this question, informants stress solidarity within the railway community, connections to farmers, merchants and others in a position to help, and good preparation by

[36] I have not seen any mention of the meeting with Senghor in the archives – apparently the police spies missed this one. It was reported independently by two knowledgeable informants in Thiès, Amadou Bouta Gueye and Oumar NDiaye (interviews, 9 Aug. 1994). It is conceivable that the railway union's later support for Senghor is being pushed backwards, but these informants (both *délégués du personnel* at the time) are quite specific about this meeting. On Gueye's clash with the Union des Jeunes, see Renseignements, 27 May 1946, 11 D 1/1392.

[37] Governor General to Minister, 11 Oct. 1947, IGT 13/2; AOF, IGT, Annual Report, 1947, 62.

[38] For a narrative approach to the strike, see Sene, 'Grève des cheminots'.

the union itself (see below). The question obviously puzzled officials – who were predicting the strike's imminent collapse from its first days to its final months – and the most perspicacious official accounts reached a surprising and frightening conclusion.

The security services gradually learned that railwaymen had a complex web of affiliation within the communities in which they lived. A police spy overheard reports to a meeting at Thiès of a strike official's tour of Senegalese depot towns: at Kaolack a 'humble cultivator gives us 400F'; at Tambacounda, the merchant El Hadj Abou Sy gave sheep to the railwaymen, and local notables, marabouts and merchants offered 20,000 francs and ten tons of millet; at Guinguinéo investigation of a rumor that the marabouts were hostile to the strike proved false, and the strikers' emissary found that the entire population 'is with us with no reserve'.[39] In fact, the leading marabouts of the Islamic confraternities of Senegal – who were close to the administration – used their influence against the strike but closer to ground level the religious organization seems to have been more supportive.[40] Informants claim that marabouts would not support the strike in public but that many were either supportive or neutral in private.[41]

Other reports suggested that merchants in Senegal played a particularly important role in providing assistance, in the form of money, food and trucks to transport food. This was particularly so in Thiès where the health of almost the entire business community depended on the custom of railwaymen.[42] The newspaper *L'AOF*, read by many *évolués*, publicized a collection drive to benefit railwaymen: it reached 134,615 francs in late November and 454,555 by mid-December.[43] The union, according to an informant, channelled its strike funds to men with families, figuring that single men could improvise more easily.[44]

In Abidjan, the Ivory Coast railway union issued an 'Appeal to Africans' in late October and asked 'all black associations' to provide material aid. In November, the union was providing 300 francs to any needy striker who asked for it. 200,000 francs had been paid out in Abidjan, 100,000 each at

---

[39] Renseignements, 19 Nov. 1947, K 378 (26).

[40] The Grand Marabout of Tivaouane, Ababacar Sy, told a religious meeting in January 1948, 'France is good and generous', and workers would get satisfaction only if they politely asked their employers after having accomplished their tasks. 'God the all-powerful has said he will never help his "slave" who, in demanding things impolitely and with hatred, puts forward his desire to possess'. Renseignements, 26 Jan. 1948, K 379 (26). The powerful marabout Seydou Nourou Tall also worked against the strike. Renseignements, 29 Oct. 1947, K 457 (179).

[41] Of the leading marabouts, Cheikh Mbacke is mentioned as having been supportive, but the tolerance of lower level marabouts is what was stressed most in interviews. Informants stressed their personal acquaintance with marabouts at the time. Oumar NDiaye and Amadou Bouta Gueye (interviews, 9 Aug. 1994) and Mansour Niang (interview, 4 Aug. 1994).

[42] Renseignements, 14 Nov. 1947, K 457 (179). A list of donors published in *Réveil*, 20 Nov. 1947, also listed a number of local politicians, merchants and union groups in railway towns such as Diourbel and Kaolack, as well as Dakar and Thiès. Informants noted the importance of merchants' help: Oumar NDiaye and Amadou Bouta Gueye (interviews, 9 Aug. 1994), Mansour Niang (interview, 4 Aug. 1994).

[43] *L'AOF*, 25 Nov., 12 Dec. 1947. The newspaper gave considerable coverage to the strike, although its patron, Lamine Gueye, took a hands-off position throughout its course.   [44] Oumar NDiaye (interview, 9 Aug. 1994).

Port-Bouet, Grand-Bassam, Agboville and Dimbokro.[45] Such support was not unanimous – some citizens of Abidjan refused to donate because the strike had deprived them of meat – but it was substantial.[46] At Conakry, in Guinea, the union appealed to Lebanese shop-owners and African civil servants. According to the police, 'The majority of merchants and civil servants (Customs, post and telephone, auxiliary doctors) have contributed sums between 300 and 500 francs'.[47] In Dahomey, the Inspection du Travail thought that the mass did not look favorably on the strikers but they nonetheless were receiving 'loans of considerable magnitude for their strike fund, coming not only from notables or autochthonous groups, but also from certain Europeans'. The Governor thought that the *évolués* were supportive because the claims for equal indemnities with Europeans struck a chord with them.[48]

Railwaymen did a great deal themselves to organize food provisions. Most workers had not cut themselves off from their rural roots. They had family members who farmed and could either provide a place for strikers to return to or directly supply them with grain or fish. Interviews in 1990 and 1994 underscored the importance of the family mechanism in sustaining the strikers.[49] Union leaders told many workers to return to their villages to reduce the burden for feeding those who remained in the depot towns. Near the smaller stations along the lines, railwaymen sometimes had their own fields and could devote their energies to growing their food as the strike wore on.[50]

Women clearly played a major role in the strike, although one female informant distinguished between their participation in the violent strike of 1938 – where she and other women passed stones to male strikers who threw them at police and strikebreakers – and their role in the non-violent, carefully controlled strike of 1947. Testimonies so far collected stress the role of women within family units – their efforts to find food, their work in market-selling or other non-wage activites to sustain family income.[51] They composed songs supporting the strike and its leaders and taunted strike breakers: their position in railway communities created an atmosphere where *défaillants* (strike breakers) would not want to live. This is a subject which requires further investigation, but it appears less likely that women acted as

---

[45] Renseignements, 31 Oct., 7 Nov. 1947, K 379 (26).

[46] Renseignements, 10 Nov. 1947, K 379 (26).

[47] Renseignements, Coyah, 20 Dec. 1947, K 379 (26).

[48] Inspection du Travail, Dahomey, to IGT, 4 Nov. 1947, K 457 (179).

[49] Adboulaye Souleye Sarr (interview, 22 July 1990), Amadou Bouta Gueye and Oumar Ndiaye (interview, 9 Aug. 1994), Mansour Niang (interview, 4 Aug. 1994).

[50] Renseignements, Thiès, 4 Dec. 1947, and Ivory Coast, 9 Nov. 1947, K379 (26); IGT, AOF (Pierre Pélisson), Report on Strike, 24 Jan. 1948, IGT, 13/2; Abdoulaye Soulaye Sarr, (interview, 22 July 1990).

[51] Khady Dia, who sold peanuts by the Thiès train station, compared the role of women in the two strikes. Interview, Thiès, 9 Aug. 1994, by Aminata Diena, Alioune Ba, Oumar Gueye and Frederick Cooper. Abdoulaye Souleye Sarr (interview, 22 July 1990), Oumar NDiaye and Amadou Bouta Gueye (interviews, 9 Aug. 1994) also suggested that Sembene may have elided the role of women in the two strikes. Informants call the 1938 strike 'la grève de Diack', after its leader Cheik Diack, while the 1947–8 strike is known as 'la grève de Sarr'. All informants stress the importance of women's efforts to sustain families during the long strike.

a distinct entity – let alone that such an entity was led by someone from the margins of Muslim society like Sembene's character Penda – than that they acted as parts of families and communities. Sembene's women's march is absent from oral testimonies and the police record. It remains to be seen how much their actions in turn affected the way these structures operated and altered the meanings of gender within laboring communities, as well as the extent to which the increasing value and security of male wage packets changed power relations within households.[52]

The union itself had realized in its preparations for the strike that the supply question would be crucial. There already existed a *co-operative indigène* headquartered at Thiès and Bamako, which constituted a kind of bulk-buying organization for railway workers. On the eve of the strike, the co-operative leaders, close to the union leadership, had stocked their stores. The strike – not by coincidence – occurred at the end of the harvest season when supplies were at their best. During the strike, the co-operative supplied food and other necessaries to strikers on credit – afterward officials reported the co-operative 1,560,000 francs in debt for food delivered before or during the strike. 'During the entire strike the co-operative sustained you', appealed Sarr to union members as he tried to raise money to pay off the debt.[53] A strike committee official boasted to a meeting at Thiès, with a dig at the marabouts of the Mouride brotherhood, about the work of the co-operative: 'Now ... that we have assured our supplies and have for certain a little money, we are like the 'Cheikh Mourides' [Mouride marabouts]; we do not work but we have our provisions; we thus have people who work for us, it is Allah who is with us'.[54]

In January, three months into the strike, Pierre Pélisson, the head of the Inspection du Travail in French West Africa, reached a startling conclusion about the ability of Africans to conduct a long strike: 'Here the means of defense are very different – and singularly more effective – than in the case of metropolitan strikes because the roots of the labor force are deeper and its

[52] It is hardly likely that the extensive network of police spies would have missed a public event like a march of women from Thiès to Dakar. Sembene's account was specifically denied by Abdoulaye Souleye Sarr (interview, 22 July 1990) and Amadou Bouta Gueye (interview, 9 Aug. 1994), and contradicted by Khady Dia (interview, 9 Aug. 1994). There is a report from December 1947 that when eight workers decided to return to work at Thiès 'a band of women and children gathered in front of their (the returnees') homes and began to insult and threaten them', so that the ex-strikers had to wait for the police to disperse the crowd before reporting to work. Gendarmarie Nationale, Thiès, Report, 23 Dec. 1947, K 379 (26). See also Sene, 'Grève des cheminots', 91, who cites an interview with Mame Fatou Diop, on the importance of songs and the taunting of strike breakers. For a literary analysis of women in Sembene's novel, see F. Case, 'Workers' movements: revolution and women's consciousness in *God's Bits of Wood*', *Can. J. of Afr. Studies*, xv (1981), 277–92.

[53] Renseignements, Thiès, 26 Oct. 1947, K 43 (1); Renseignements, Thiès, 17 Sept. 1948, 5 Aug. 1949, 11 D 1/1392; Abdoulaye Souleye Sarr (interview, 22 July 1990); Jacques Ibrahima Gaye, article in *L'AOF*, 17 Oct. 1947, clipping in K 457 (179).

[54] N'Diaye Sidya, quoted in Renseignements, 29 Oct. 1947, K 457 (179). Food supply became part of the struggle between the two sides. The co-operative supplied food only to strikers, not to railwaymen who went back to work, and officials thought this a major reason why few workers went back to work on the Dakar-Niger. The Régie tried itself to organize the delivery of rice from the Soudan to railwaymen at Thiès and Dakar who went back to work. IGT, AOF, to Deputy Dumas, 6 Jan. 1948, K457 (179).

needs less imperious in Africa than in Europe'.[55] Pélisson had been taught an important lesson: the degree of proletarianization was not an accurate measure of the power of strikers, and the success of the strike lay in the integration of the strikers into the strikers' own communities.

PROLETARIANS, POLITICIANS AND MOBILIZATION BEYOND THE RAILWAY

It was in regard to other proletarians that the solidarity of the strike movement was the most ambiguous. Pélisson noticed this too, writing that most wage workers outside the railway distanced themselves from railway-men, and the latter 'have not benefited from their effective support but only from habitual demonstrations of sympathy'. In Dakar, wage workers were in the midst of peaceful negotiations over another round of wage revisions; no general strike movement emerged in support of the railwaymen.[56]

At times, it looked as if the solidarity of the railwaymen would take on an even wider dimension. In early November the Commission Administrative of the Union des Syndicats de Dakar discussed what to do to support the strikers. The leading veterans of the 1946 strike, Abbas Gueye and Lamine Diallo, tried to convince a 'reticent assembly' of the need for a general strike. They pointed out to civil servants in particular that they shared a fundamental interest in a unified indemnity of zone. But other speakers pushed for 'more moderate' approaches, such as protest meetings, collections of funds and delegations to the Governor General, and it was the latter position which prevailed.[57] In Guinea, the Union Régionale Syndicale de Guinée passed a motion of support for the railwaymen, 'whose demands were theirs as well'. But there was no common action for the common demands.[58] In the Ivory Coast in November, the Union Locale des Syndicats, affiliated to the CGT, decided 'that it could not support the action of the railway union because [it was] not affiliated to the CGT'.[59] Around that time, some civil service unions were thinking about a general strike, but they would not act until they heard from the Rassemblement Démocratique Africaine and its leader Houphouët-Boigny. They were to get no encouragement from him.[60]

The trade union movement, in West Africa and in France, did better by the railwaymen in a financial sense. CGT unions in the region contributed, according to a French CGT source, about two million francs. The National Solidarity Committee of the CGT in France gave 500,000, while other contributions came from French railway unions and another CGT bureau. The RDA in the Ivory Coast gave 350,000 – although its support became increasingly suspect.[61]

What other unions and political parties did not do was organize sympathy strikes, stage large demonstrations or otherwise try to turn the strike into a wider social and political movement. The lack of common action is all the more notable because there was considerable trade union anger at the time

[55] IGT, Report, 24 Jan. 1948, IGT 13/2.   [56] *Ibid.*
[57] Report of meeting, 4 Nov. 1947, K 379 (26); Renseignements, 7 Nov. 1947, K 457 (179).   [58] Resolution of Union Régionale de Guinée, 18 Nov. 1947, K 379 (26).
[59] Governor, Ivory Coast, to Governor General, 21 Nov. 1947, K 237 (26).
[60] Renseignements, Ivory Coast, 9 Nov. 1947, K 379 (26).
[61] Suret-Canale, 'Railway workers' strike', 147.

of the strike over the withdrawal by a new Minister of Overseas France of a Code du Travail which Moutet had tried to implement by decree just before he left office in November 1947.[62] But the causes never were linked, the Code protests fizzled, and the Code debate disappeared into French political institutions for another five years.

Some trade unionists in Senegal were reluctant to lend their support to railway workers in 1947 because railwaymen had not helped them during the general strike of 1946. Moreover, the civil service, metal trades, commerce and industry unions were now engaged in regular negotiations through institutions set up as a result of that strike. As the annual reports of the Inspection du Travail make clear, the 1947–8 railway strike stands out in both years, during which disputes were narrowly focused and easily contained within existing negotiating frameworks. The fact that most of the concessions made to civil servants in Dakar were extended to other parts of French West Africa, and the spread of Dakar-type agreements to other key businesses in West Africa changed the politics of labor on a wide scale. Focusing the labor question on union-management relations within each branch of industry, commerce or government and making workers less inclined toward another venture in solidarity had been the Inspection's strategy since January 1946, and Pélisson recognized even in the midst of the railway strike that the strategy was working.[63]

The relationship of the railwaymen to organized politics was equally ambiguous. The RDA, which like the railway crossed territorial borders, maintained its distance. In the run up to the strike, Sûreté thought that the RDA was fighting against the strike call, hoping that its failure would lead to Sarr's ouster and open up the autonomous union to takeover by pro-RDA leaders.[64] In February 1948, the *Voix de la RDA*, published in Dakar, saw fit to rebut a charge that the strike had been called by the RDA by writing, 'Sarr, the federal secretary of the railway union, whose courage and combativity we admire, is not RDA'. The newspaper insisted that it respected 'trade union independence', and that while it agreed with the demands of the union, 'We had the courage to declare to the railwaymen: on the local level we could do nothing. It was the business of the railwaymen and only the railwaymen to take up their responsibilities'. It claimed that the RDA had tried in the metropole to bring pressure on the government to settle the strike and blamed its opponents for the failure of that initiative.[65]

This article probably represented the view of the RDA leadership in

---

[62] At the Grand Conseil, Senghor noted the 'emotion the suspension of the application of the Code du Travail raised among workers' and urged legislative action. *Bulletin du Grand Conseil*, 29 Jan. 1948, 277–8. See also Renseignements, 19, 28 Jan. 1948, K 439 (179); Directeur des Affaires Politiques, Note pour M. le Ministre, 20 Dec. 1947, AP 2255/1. For more on the Code, see Frederick Cooper, *Decolonization and African Society: The Labor Question in French and British Africa*, forthcoming ch. 7.

[63] IGT, Report, 24 Jan. 1948, IGT 13/2. The 1948 Annual Report of the Inspection du Travail for French West Africa (90) termed the railway strike 'the only important collective conflict' of the year. It claimed credit for the 'favorable evolution' of the situation. There were many more disputes registered with the Inspection in 1947, but they had not led to many serious strikes, a fact for which the Inspection also took credit. *Ibid.* 1947, 59.   [64] Renseignements, 1 Sept. 1947, K 377 (26).

[65] *La Voix de la RDA* was published regularly as a special section of the *communisant* Dakar newspaper, *Réveil*. This article appeared in no. 283, 5 Feb. 1948.

Dakar. The leading light of the party, Houphouët-Boigny was playing a more complicated game. Security officials kept hearing reports of Houphouët-Boigny's covert opposition to the strike. In early November, they reported he had told the strike committee 'that the deputies from French West Africa had not been consulted before the breaking out of this strike, inopportune at this time of year, and that as a result he was not going to be mixed up in their affair'. Two weeks later, security reported, 'In his house, last Sunday, the deputy Houphouët had said to his friends that the strikers have not acted skillfully, that they should have accepted the advantages conceded in the course of this strike, gone back to work in order to renew their demands later and obtain the "full rate" (the full indemnity of zone) by successive steps'. At that point, he said he would go to Dakar to see what he could do.[66]

In Dakar he sang a different tune. Houphouët-Boigny told a meeting called by the Union des Syndicats Confédérés de l'AOF on 7 December that he and his RDA colleague Gabriel d'Arboussier pledged support to the railwaymen 'in their struggle against colonialism' and assured them of the 'presence of the RDA beside you to defend their demands which are legitimate'. The pro-RDA newspaper *Réveil* noted the absence at this meeting of the parliamentarians from Senegal (who were not RDA).[67]

But by this time most of the West African parliamentarians, Houphouët-Boigny included, were pursuing a goal which, however worthy, was not quite the same as the anti-colonialist rhetoric implied. At the time of the union meeting, Houphouët-Boigny and other deputies were in Dakar for the December–January meeting of the Grand Conseil de l'AOF, French West Africa's major deliberative body. They took advantage of their collective presence in Dakar to talk to leading officials and to try to persuade the Governor General to intervene. Houphouët-Boigny and his rival counselor, Lamine Gueye, both told Pélisson of 'their concern not to mix politics with an affair that must remain strictly professional and simply to bring their purely obliging support to settling a conflict whose importance to the country is considerable'.[68] The parliamentarians told both the Inspecteur Général du Travail and the Governor General that their concern was to end the strike 'so prejudicial to the economy of the country as well as to the interests of the Régie and of the railwaymen themselves'. They were rebuffed by Governor General Barthes, who refused to call into question the October ruling of the arbitrators.[69] But in any case, these interventions show the tone of the politicians two months into the strike: a sentiment of regret over the hardships caused by the strike and hope for a quick settlement, but an evasiveness about the substantive issues and an unwillingness to support the strikers unambiguously and publicly.

Houphouët-Boigny reported the meetings to the Grand Conseil, but the effort of some members to debate the strike failed, as its president, Lamine Gueye, claimed the Conseil had no say on such a matter. Gueye went on to distance himself from the strikers, noting that while the interests of the railwaymen were affected by the strike, 'those of the entire country are as

---

[66] Renseignements, Ivory Coast, 5, 18 Nov. 1947, K 379 (26).
[67] *Réveil*, no. 268 (15 Dec. 1947) and no. 269 (18 Dec. 1947).
[68] IGT to Governor General, 12 Dec. 1947, K 457 (179). [69] *Ibid.* IGT 13/2.

well'. At a subsequent session in January, a counselor from Dahomey, Apithy, introduced a resolution asking for a delegation of the Conseil to try to get the government to intervene and attacked Lamine Gueye for failing to act. But this merely led to a brief and bitter exchange of accusations between RDA and Socialist deputies. Several delegates opposed intervention on the grounds that the Conseil did not have jurisdiction. Senghor said contacts had been made with the incoming Governor General, whose presence would raise the possibility of compromise in this 'painful conflict'. He added, 'The role of Grand Counselors is not to have a partisan debate here or to tear each other up and thus to tear up Africa, but to study the technical means to bring a solution to the conflict'. Apithy withdrew his resolution. French West Africa's most powerful political actors had failed even to express a collective opinion on the most salient issue of the day.[70]

Meanwhile, Houphouët-Boigny was doing his bit to end the strike in his home territory. The railwaymen of the Ivory Coast broke ranks in early January and gave up the strike. Pélisson wrote, 'According to our information, this result is due to M. the Deputy Houphouët who succeeded in persuading the African railwaymen to return to work despite the counter-propaganda of M. Sarr'.[71] The police reports from the Ivory Coast (see below) reveal a pattern of intrigue in January which resulted in the union's defection; Houphouët-Boigny's influence on some members of the union leadership – although not its leader, Gaston Fiankan – may well have been crucial. None of this should be surprising: the Ivoirien branch of the RDA had emerged from a group of cocoa planters and was rapidly expanding its power in agriculture as much as in politics. The harvest-time strike obviously affected their prospects with particular acuity.

Senghor was among the deputies who joined the settlement initiative in December and January. He was the only major political figure at the time to have given some indication of support – if only in private – to the strikers and he remained in contact. Senghor sent a letter to the minister, enclosing a list of demands of the union as well as a 'History of the Situation' written by Sarr. His own interpretation was truly Senghorian: 'In any case, the claims relative to the suppression of racial discrimination seem to me to be well founded, even if one can dispute the wage rates. In effect, one cannot speak of a *cadre unique* if there is discrimination within the interior of the cadre, discrimination which is moreover condemned by the Constitution of the IVth Republic'. He appealed for a settlement not on the basis of the April accords, but on the 'spirit of the Constitution of the IVth Republic which proclaims that the Union Française is a union founded on the equality of rights and duties, without discrimination based on race or religion'. Avoiding

---

[70] AOF, Bulletin du Grand Conseil, Procès-Verbal, 23 Dec. 1947, 80–1, 31 Jan. 1948, 320–1. The assembly of the Union Française – the deliberative (but nearly powerless) body intended to allow full discussion of issues facing Overseas France among colonial and metropolitan deputies – had a longer debate on the strike, ending in a resolution calling on the administration to 'resolve' the conflict and not to sanction the strikers. The debate is nonetheless notable for the invocation by supporters of the strikers of images of France's unity, on its progressive role in the world, and on the importance of equality within it to justify favorable treatment for African railwaymen. Débats, Sessions of 6, 12 Feb. 1948, 69–74, 78–89.

[71] Pélisson to M le Deputé Dumas, 6 Jan. 1948, IGT 13/2.

the mundane complexities of a labor dispute, Senghor defined the issue as one of constitutional principles and racial equality.[72]

By then, the Comité Directeur of the union had already criticized both Senghor and Lamine Gueye 'for having placed themselves on the side of the Administration and for their support of Cunéo'.[73] When the December discussions among parliamentarians assembled for the Grand Conseil meeting and the meetings with the Governor General got nowhere, Fily Dabo Sissoko, deputy from the Soudan, began to intervene as well.[74] Since the Soudanais railwaymen were crucial to the Dakar-Niger branch, officials hoped that he would have sufficient influence to get one group of workers to give up the strike in exchange only for promises that Sissoko would use his good offices on the union's behalf after railwaymen returned to work. Sissoko and his allies told officials that the Soudanais railwaymen had 'total confidence' in the Deputy of the Soudan, and that his intervention would insure that 'the Soundanais will detach themselves from the Senegalese and it is certain that overall movements similar to the strike of 11 October will not recur'.[75] Sissoko suggested token concessions, such as changing the date on which auxiliaries would acquire permanent status, but the real message was 'about the influence that the Deputy Fily Dabo Sissoko could have on the end of the strike'.[76] The Régie agreed to the date change, insisting that this promise 'is made to you and you alone to help you in your good offices to bring about an effective return to work and would only apply if the return occurred on the date indicated'.[77]

Sissoko talked directly with Sarr, who was frightened of the potential split in the strike movement within the Dakar-Niger. But the Comité Directeur would have none of this: they interpreted the offer as a 'word game' and as 'sabotage'. Sarr was instructed on 29 January 1948 to reject Sissoko's initiatives: 'A scalded cat fears cold water … and we cannot base our return to work on a promise, above all when that promise is stripped of any guarantee'. Sarr showed the telegram to Sissoko, who was angered and gave indications that he would actively intervene to get the Soudanais railwaymen to go back to work.[78]

[72] Senghor to Minister, 26 Nov. 1947, K 457 (179).

[73] Renseignements, 17 Dec. 1947, K 457 (179).

[74] Sissoko had earlier telegraphed the Ministry to remind them of the 'lamentable situation of several thousand families' affected by the strike, of the 'economic perturbation' leading to a 'fiasco' in the 1948 harvest, and of the unfortunate effects of turning the strike into a 'test of force'. Sissoko to Ministry, telegram, 3 Dec. 1947, IGT 13/2. This language was fully consistent with the tack being taken by most of the West African deputies.

[75] Note signed by Pillot, for the Dakar-Niger Réseau, for M le Directeur Fédéral de la Régie des Chemins de Fer de l'AOF, and sent by Cunéo to the President of the Conseil d'Administration, 19 Jan. 1948, K 457 (179). The administration was thinking that they could split off the Soudanais as early as the end of December. Renseignements, Thiès, 27 Dec. 1947, K 457 (179). [76] Note by Pillot, K 457 (179).

[77] Secretary General of Government General, to Sissoko, 29 Jan. 1948, copy enclosed Inspection du Travail, Bamako, to IGT, 7 Feb. 1948, K 457 (179).

[78] Inspection du Travail, Bamako, to IGT, 7 Feb. 1948, Moussa Diarra, on behalf of Comité Directeur, telegram to Sarr, 29 Jan. 1948, and Renseignements, 4 Feb. 1948, K 457 (179). Another telegram sent by the Comité Directeur at Thiès to the Soudan attacked the entire initiative of Sissoko: 'Regret to put you on guard against the bad propaganda of the Sage of the Soudan who despite promises of devotion to cause attempts

The Inspection du Travail in Bamako reported that Sissoko indeed asked workers to go back, effective 2 February. The union appealed to them to hold fast. And this they did: at Bamako only seven workers returned to work on the day indicated.[79] Sissoko's intervention did little more than discredit him, although it may have made the union leadership nervous enough to look more favorably on the next settlement initiative in early March.

It had taken the leading elected politicians of French West Africa two months to intervene, and their efforts over the next two months accomplished little more than splitting the railwaymen of the Ivory Coast from their comrades elsewhere. Although Senghor, in a private letter to the minister, had assimilated the cause of the strikers to his anti-racist cause, he had done nothing to tap the popular mobilization that was part of the strike. Houphouët-Boigny had invoked the spectre of colonialism in a Dakar speech, but at virtually the same time he was working behind the scenes to end the strike in the Ivory Coast.

In Senegal, Senghor is said to have helped to settle the strike. This perception is more a consequence of what happened after the strike than what he did during it. Senghor realized that the union was one of the most important organized blocks of voters in the territory, and he set about straightening things out.[80] He made Sarr a candidate on his ticket for the Assembly of the Union Française, and he was duly elected in 1953. He is remembered in Thiès for having incorporated the railway workers union into his political movement, but with more than a hint that the workers did more for him than he for them.[81]

The story does not end here. As part of the leadership of Senghor's Bloc Démocratique Sénégalais, Sarr – who did not forget his origins – allied himself with the left wing of the party, and in particular with Mamadou Dia, who became Senghor's Prime Minister after independence. But when Dia and Senghor broke, and Dia and his allies were accused of crimes against the state, Sarr, along with Dia, was imprisoned, a fate he had not suffered at the hands of the French government.[82]

None of this negates the argument – which is the main point of Sembene's fictionalized account – that the struggle itself galvanized a *popular* sentiment

---

negative propaganda of destruction through numerous telegrams and letters addressed to Soudan. Consider intervention of this man as destruction orchestrated with directors of Régie at their visit to Bamako'. Diarra to Moriba Cissoko, 4 Feb. 1948, in Renseignements, Soudan, 5 February 1948, K 379 (26).

[79] Inspection du Travail, Bamako, to IGT, 7 Feb. 1948, K 457 (179).

[80] A month after the strike, as Suret-Canale notes, Senghor finally wrote an article on the subject, in which he in fact mentioned that he 'did not write a single article on the question and ... if I dealt with it at times in my speeches, I did so voluntarily, in measured terms'. He claimed support for the principle of nondiscrimination and, in practical terms, for compromise. The quotation is from *La Condition Humaine*, 26 Apr. 1948, as translated in Suret-Canale, 'Railway workers' strike,' 145.

[81] Mory Tall, Oumar NDiaye and Amadou Bouta Gueye (interviews, 9 Aug. 1994), Mansour Niang (interview, 4 Aug. 1994).

[82] The same thing happened to another leading labor leader of the 1950s, Alioune Cissé. His militant trade unionism never landed him in jail under the French, but Senghor put him there for his role in organizing a general strike in 1968 – an irony he remains well aware of, as he does in the case of Sarr (interview, Dakar, 4 Aug. 1994, by Oumar Gueye, Alioune Ba and Frederick Cooper).

THE 1947–48 RAILWAY STRIKE IN FRENCH WEST AFRICA   103

hostile to the hypocrisies of the colonial regime and led to a sense of empowerment among the strikers whose implications undoubtedly went beyond the sphere of labor. But organizationally, things were not so clear. Neither the major parties nor the major trade union confederations made the railwaymen's cause their own. Neither gave the railwaymen much reason to have confidence in their ability to represent the cause of labor. The strike of 1947–8 was a railway strike of extraordinary proportions, but it began and ended as a railway strike.

THE AMBIVALENCES OF COLONIAL REPRESSION

The government side of the issue leaves its puzzles too: why officials allowed a disruptive strike to drag on so long without being either more repressive or more conciliatory. The government at first had no idea that it would face a long strike: 'The strike will no doubt last a few weeks. It is unpopular in all milieux – merchants, politicians, and workers'. This expectation may be why virtually nothing was done until November to try to maintain railway traffic.[83] And the arrogance of the assumption that the Régie would soon prevail no doubt communicated itself to the well-placed network of spies, who kept telling their bosses that the strike was about to collapse.[84] Self-deception was thus an important element in prolonging the strike.

Although the Régie had conceded the *cadre unique* and the integration of auxiliaries in April, it was struggling for the power to give content to those ideas. Increasingly, the strike itself became the principal issue. On the very eve of the strike, Governor General Barthes, in his last-ditch meeting with union leaders, lectured them on 'the terms of the law and my intention of insuring that it is respected'.[85] He immediately (and in accordance with those terms) sent the dispute to an arbitrator and then to an arbitrational committee – which on 31 October in effect affirmed the agreement of April 1947 and on the whole agreed with the Régie's interpretation of it. From the first, the Governor General and the Régie insisted that the arbitration proceedings alone had legal standing and that negotiation over them was out of the question. The stance led to a virtual loss of contact between Régie and union, and the Inspection du Travail, whose interventions had been critical to settling previous strikes, was largely frozen out of the action.[86] Only in

[83] Directeur Fédéral de la Régie to Directeur de l'Office Central des Chemins de Fer de la France Outre-Mer, 10 Oct. 1947, IGT 13/2.

[84] For example, Renseignements, 25 Oct. 1947, K 457 (179): 'One detects considerable discontent among the strikers who without any doubt did not expect a strike of this length. If it weren't for religious superstition, many would already have returned to work'. A week later, the report was, 'The enthusiasm of the beginning has completely fallen ... the women in particular are starting to get agitated and can expect that 50 per cent at least of the strikers demand to return to work'. Renseignements, 3 Nov. 1947, K 43 (1). Still later, it was the 'profound weariness' of the strikers which gave rise to expectations for a quick end to the strike. IGT to Governor General, 15 Dec. 1947, K 457 (179). The strike still had three months to go.

[85] Governor General to Minister, 11 Oct. 1947, IGT 13/2.

[86] AOF, IGT, Annual Report, 1947, 62. See for example the transcript of the meeting of the Conseil d'Administration of the Régie, 15 Nov. 1947 (K 459 [179]), at which Cunéo remarked: 'Whatever may be the consequences of the strike of African personnel, it seems that respect for the decisions of the judiciary, respect for legality, forbids the opening of new negotiations'.

December were some minor concessions being talked about: making the integration of auxiliaries retroactive to 1 July instead of 15 July, allowing 'individual' reclassifications of some railwaymen in categories where the union had demanded systematic reclassification, and allowing fifteen instead of ten days leave in case of marriages, births and deaths.[87] But it was still on the grounds of the sacrosanct nature of the arbitration decision that the Governor General refused the December initiative of the West African parliamentarians.[88] As late as 3 February, the administration in Dakar claimed that even sending an Inspecteur du Travail to talk to the union would be interpreted as a sign of loss of will, and that it was still necessary that the affair 'end by the total execution of the arbitration ruling'.[89]

Yet at the same time, the administration pulled its punches. At first it did nothing to enforce the arbitrator's judgment: it did not arrest the strike leaders, replace the illegally striking workers with new recruits, or requisition the workers, which would have put them under military discipline. All these options were discussed within the Government General and in Paris, but all were at first considered provocative. Only in the first week of November did the Régie make known its intention to hire replacements for the strikers, and even then the Governor General saw it necessary to explain that 'now, traffic must be assured as far as possible, despite the prolonged absence of African railwaymen'. The minister agreed, but wanted such hiring kept to a 'strict minimum'.[90] Such drastic measures as conscripting strikers into military service were viewed with considerable skepticism at the highest levels of the Ministry. Officials were no doubt reluctant to escalate for fear of going against their own initiatives of the post-war era: to constitute a new approach to labor based on ending forced labor, developing a system of industrial relations, and incorporating trade unions into that system. Measures intended to crush the union and coerce unwilling workers into the workplace would not help the cause. As Robert Delavignette, then head of Political Affairs in the Ministry in Paris, put it 'the strong style directed at the strikers will not itself resolve the problem (one has seen this in the recent past, even in AOF), if the government gives the impression of going back, after a detour, on trade union freedom and on the abolition of forced labor'.[91]

---

[87] The latter concessions were made apropos of an attempt by a deputy and a leader of the Confédération Française des Travailleurs Chrétiens, Joseph Dumas, to mediate the dispute, with the proviso that if the mission failed the Régie would undertake massive publicity of the terms offered in order to induce railwaymen to break with their union and go back to work. IGT to Governor General, 15 Dec. 1947, K 457 (179). The Inspecteur Général du Travail, Pélisson, wanted to let railway workers know that their wages might be revised in parallel with revisions being planned for the civil service, and that he favored giving 'at least partial satisfaction' to the railwaymen, while trying 'to save the face of the Régie'. But the Régie was not interested in saving face, and Dumas was left with narrow possibilities for maneuver, and predictably failed. IGT Note for Dumas, 18 Dec. 1947, K 457 (179).

[88] *Paris-Dakar*, 26 Dec. 1947, and Minutes of Grand Conseil, 24 Dec. 1947, cited in Suret-Canale, 'Railway workers' strike,' 145, 153, n. 25.

[89] Affaires Courantes, Dakar, telegram to the new Governor General, Béchard, 3 Feb. 1948, IGT 13/2.

[90] Governor General to Minister, telegram, 5 Nov. 1947, and Minister to Governor General, telegram, 7 Nov. 1947, IGT 13/2.

[91] Delavignette, 'Grève des chemins de fer et des wharfs en AOF', 13 Dec. 1947, IGT, 13/2. For the context of post-war labor policy – notably the assertion of legitimacy through the abolition of forced labor and the attempt to build a more differentiated,

It was only in mid-November that Sarr was brought to court 'for having ordered the strike in violation of the decree of 20 March 1937 on compulsory arbitration'. Fiankan, the Ivory Coast leader, had been prosecuted earlier and sentenced to three months in prison for interference with the liberty to work, although he was not in fact jailed and his conviction was overturned on appeal. Sarr was sentenced on 11 December 1947 to twenty days in jail and a fine of 1,200 francs for leading an illegal strike, but he never served his sentence: in April, after the strike, the appeals court commuted his sentence to a fine of 100 francs, suspended. Significantly, the prosecutors went after Fiankan again immediately after the Ivory Coast strike was broken and they were anxious to remove him from the scene lest he start it up again. He was convicted of threatening people who returned to work and sentenced to six months in prison on 22 January, but his sentence was later reduced on appeal to two months and a fine, and in the end he was pardoned. There were also some prosecutions in Dahomey and Guinea, most of which ended in acquittals.[92]

Nor did the Régie play another card it had: many of the strikers lived in railway housing, concentrated in various *cités* in key depots. One of the demands of the union was to open such housing to auxiliaries: lodging was quite valuable given the poor infrastructure of colonial towns, and the linkage of housing to job was part of the stabilization strategy of post-war governments. The Régie kept threatening to expel strikers from their homes unless they returned to work, but it did not do so.[93] Perhaps its caution came from the notion – repeated often in reports in the immediate post-war years – that African labor was inherently unstable, all too likely to jump from job to job or return to village life. It was the most experienced and skilled workers who were housed, and it would have been consistent with thinking on the 'stabilization' issue for the Régie to fear that once such workers left the *cités*, they might never be heard from again.

The weapons that the Régie was left with, then, were to manipulate the divisions within the work force and try to get enough manpower in place to run the railway system well enough to avoid economic paralysis. By November, the Régie had started to hire new workers and it kept issuing appeals to strikers – with a mixture of promises and threats – to go back individually. The appeal stressed that the Régie had already agreed (and the arbitration award made this explicit) to the reorganization of the cadres, in some form at least, and to the integration of at least a significicant number of auxiliaries. The poster distributed to the Ivory Coast, for example, pointed out that these measures would mean a 'large raise' for the cadres and

---

stable, manageable labor force – see Cooper, *Decolonization and African Society*. Both policies came to the fore in 1946, as did the new development program, and French officials were eager to demonstrate to a world increasingly skeptical of denials of self-determination that social, economic and political development were at the heart of colonial policy.

[92] Governor General to Minister, 20 Nov. 1947, IGT 13/2; Directeur, Sûreté, to IGT, 15 Sept. 1948, K 458 (179).

[93] Cunéo (Director of Régie) draft letter to all regional directors, 9 Jan. 1948, reminding them that strikers, as of 28 November 1947, had been 'detached' from the Régie and warning them that if they did not return by 15 January they would be dislodged: K 457 (179). For earlier threats, see Renseignements, 19 Nov. 1947, K 378 (26), and Inspection du Travail, Guinea, to IGT, 19 Nov. 1947, K 457 (179).

'a very large raise for qualified auxiliaries'. The threat was that, as of November, strikers had been officially 'detached' from their posts, but that the regime would take them back with seniority intact if they returned immediately and not at all if they held out.[94]

None of this was very effective until the Ivory Coast gave way in early January. As of 1 November, three weeks into the strike, 487 Europeans and 38 Africans were trying to run a railway. By 2 January, 836 strikers had gone back to work and 2,416 new workers had been hired. Even if one accepts the Régie's claim that it really needed only 13,500 men, not the 17,000 it had had before the strike (and after the strike the Régie came up with a new figure of 15,000), the Régie had only recovered little over a quarter of its African workforce. In the crucial 'material and traction' section of the Dakar-Niger line, which included locomotive drivers and other running personnel, less than a sixth of the posts were filled on 2 January. Indeed, the entire Dakar-Niger branch remained solid: 1,125 workers of both races were all there was to do the job of 6,765. The Conakry-Niger line – 1,196 at work out of 2,014 – and the Abidjan-Niger line – 1,424 out of 3,111 – were shakier.[95]

After the return to work in the Ivory Coast, the administration hoped that the other lines would give way, but their most serious attempt, via Fily Dabo Sissoko, to hive off a large section of workers from the union failed. As of 1 February 1948, the active workers as a percentage of theoretical staffing stood at 32 per cent on the Dakar-Niger, 54 per cent on the Conakry-Niger, and 16 per cent on the Benin-Niger. Overall, this meant that 34 per cent of staffing needs were being met.[96]

Officials thought that the union was able to prevent hiring through its influence in the railway centers.[97] Even where new workers were signed on, they did not necessarily work well. This was particularly the case at the wharfs in the Ivory Coast where a mixture of European and African strikebreakers, plus a detachment from the Marine Nationale flown from Dakar to the Ivory Coast, had been put to work. 'The results have not lived up to our hopes, because the detachment which was sent was composed of unskilled workers who had never driven the equipment that was confided to them and which was relieved at the end of a month on the scene just when the Marines began to get used to the material they were using'.[98]

---

[94] Annex to Renseignements, Ivory Coast, 30 Dec. 1947, K 379 (26). Boldface and underlining in original.

[95] IGT, AOF, to IGT, Paris, 8 Jan. 1948, IGT 13/2; AOF, Inspection du Travail, Annual Report, 1947, 62. In February, Africans *en service* for the Régie founded a new Professional Association, headed by none other than François Gning. The call to its first meeting stated, 'We speak to you here with a French heart for the true France'. Its goal was to 'constitute in the heart of the Régie a true family of railwaymen where love of work will be the uniting trait between management and staff'. Even at this meeting, objections were made to Gning's leadership. The Association would give rise to a union, which would contest Sarr's union after the strike, but without a great deal of success. Renseignements, 8 Feb. 1948, K 457 (179).

[96] On these three lines, 839 workers had returned to their posts (including a few who had never left them) and 2,155 had been hired. Situation de la Régie au 1er Fevrier 1948, K 457 (179). [97] Governor General to Minister, 21 Nov. 1947, IGT 13/2.

[98] Directeur Général de l'Office Central des Chemins de Fer de la France Outre-Mer, Note, 15 Dec. 1947, IGT 13/2. Similar disappointment was felt with strike-breaking labor on the wharf in Dahomey. Dahomey, Inspection du Travail, Annual Report, 1947, 33.

Traffic had plunged after the strike and had only partially been restored. In mid-February, passenger traffic on the Dakar-Niger was at 12 per cent of its recent average, goods traffic at 43 per cent. On the Conakry-Niger, passenger traffic was at 20 per cent, goods at 48 per cent. On the Benin-Niger, passenger traffic stood at 10 per cent, goods traffic at 30 per cent.[99] Its effects were felt not only in the damage it was doing to the French campaign to resupply the metropole, but also in the scarcities of goods that were occurring throughout French West Africa and which threatened the painful effort that was being made to provide incentives to peasants to grow marketable crops and workers to work.[100] In fact, the timing of the strike was crucial in this sense: France had with fanfare launched a 'development' initiative in 1946, and the railway strike served both to undermine its economic goals and take the luster off its ideological intervention.

At the end of January, about 300 men from the French railways were sent to Dakar to provide skilled labor, particularly in the troublesome Traction division. Some white CGT leaders and the anti-colonial press urged them not to act as strike breakers, and apparently some asked to be taken back to France or else subtly undermined their own presence by pretending that their equipment was not properly functioning. The fact that the French locomotive drivers were not familiar with the steam locomotives still in use in Africa – and which African drivers knew intimately – may have contributed to the subsequent decision to accelerate dieselization of the system.[101]

However much the administration's actions fell short of all-out combat, the union's achievement in holding together for so long stands out. There is no question that leadership played a big part in it: the strike had been extensively discussed within railway communities in advance and scrupulously planned. Sarr had made the rounds of the depots and cemented a personal identification of the cause with himself and with the strike committee. He ordered his followers to 'stay home and not to indulge themselves in any outside demonstration or any sabotage' – an order which was by all indications followed.[102] In Thiès, the strikers held daily open meetings, where doubts and concerns were aired, but peer pressure was maintained. Whenever there were signs of wavering along the Dakar-Niger line, Sarr went on tour and reaffirmed the personal ties and the group loyalties. Security officials were convinced that this direct approach was effective: 'Before the passage of Sarr, many of them were getting ready to return to work; afterwards, they have again decided, more so than ever, to continue the strike'.[103] Fily Dabo Sissoko – in the midst of his effort to get

[99] Affaires Courantes, Dakar, to Minister, 14 Feb. 1948, IGT 13/2.

[100] Inspection du Travail, Guinea, to IGT, 19 Nov. 1947, K 457 (179); Delavignette, 'Grève des chemins de fer...', 13 Dec. 1947, IGT 13/2.

[101] Gendarmerie Mobile, Rapport, 15 Nov. 1947, K 43 (1); Suret-Canale, 'Railway workers' strike', 140; Abdoulaye Soulaye Sarr (interview, 22 July 1990); Sene, 'Grève des cheminots', 117.

[102] Renseignements, 25 Oct. 1947, K 43 (1). His warning was later published in *Réveil*, 20 Nov. 1947. The orders against demonstrations were passed out in the Soudan as well. Renseignements, Bamako, 11 Oct. 1947, K 43 (1).

[103] Renseignements, 13 Nov. 1947, K 457 (179), in regard to Sarr's trip to the Soudan. There are extensive reports from police spies of meetings at Thiès and elsewhere. See, for example, Renseignements, 29 Oct., 25 Dec. 1947, *ibid.* and Renseignements, 16 Oct. 1947, K 43 (1).

108   FREDERICK COOPER

the Soudanais back to work – told French officials that 'The Soudanais considered themselves bound to the union Leader by a pact which it would be dishonorable to break'.[104]

However impressive the leadership, collective and personal, it was clearly rooted in railway communities – in towns like Thiès and Kayes, where railway workers and their families lived together as well as worked together, and where they were part of broad networks linking them to merchants and farmers in the area. In any case, Pélisson, the Inspecteur Général du Travail noted a crucial aspect of solidarity on the railway: it crossed all ranks.

It is important to observe that the [strike] order was followed not only by the agents of the permanent cadre and the auxiliaries eligible to be integrated into it, the only people with an interest in the agreement under discussion, but also by the mass of ordinary auxiliaries – manual laborers for the most part – and by the personnel of the wharfs whose situation was not at all in question. Led into this behavior by a limitless confidence in their leaders and their directions, undoubtedly as well by fear and at times by concern to keep their word, the African railwaymen have until now kept up, calmly and with respect for public order which is much to their credit, a strike whose prolongation seemed, however, more and more like a dead end.[105]

DEFECTION, DEFIANCE AND AN AMBIGUOUS RESOLUTION

The strike broke first in the Ivory Coast. Pélisson attributed this to the behind-the-scenes machinations of Houphouët-Boigny, but it is also clear that a second tier of union officials staged a kind of coup while Fiankan, the Secretary General of the Abidjan-Niger railway union, was out of the country. The Ivory Coast union was clearly divided, and the officers whom Fiankan had replaced when he became Secretary General had, as early as November, intrigued against him. Fiankan for a time wavered in his support of the strike. Houphouët-Boigny had reportedly told the union leaders of his disapproval of the timing of the strike and their failure to consult him. When the news of the failure of the intervention of the deputies in December reached Abidjan in a telegram from Sarr on 30 December, it led to a tense meeting of a hundred railwaymen, presided over by Djoman, the Adjunct Secretary. Sarr's telegram was pessimistic, but argued that the only way for railwaymen to keep their jobs was to carry the strike to a successful conclusion. Maitre Diop, a lawyer and member of the Grand Conseil just returned from Dakar, confirmed the failure of the Dakar initiative. The Regional Director had shrewdly timed an offer (quoted above) to rehire all workers on the Abidjan-Niger who returned to work at that time, promising wage increases that would flow from the reclassifications approved in the arbitration ruling. The meeting divided between those who favored a return to work and those who wanted to await the return of Fiankan.[106]

The next day, Fiankan was being blamed for his absence (he was in

---

[104] Sissoko therefore saw convincing Sarr as the key. He miscalculated the nature of the union leadership, however, since the strike committee ordered a wavering Sarr not to give in. Governor, Soudan, to Governor General, 12 Jan. 1948, K 378 (26).

[105] IGT, Report, 24 Jan. 1948, IGT 13/2.

[106] Renseignements, Ivory Coast, 14, 15 Nov., 30 Dec. 1947, K 379 (26). On Houphouët-Boigny's role, see Renseignements, 5 Nov. 1947, *ibid.* and IGT to Deputy Dumas, 6 Jan. 1948, IGT 13/2.

THE 1947–48 RAILWAY STRIKE IN FRENCH WEST AFRICA 109

Dakar), and the supporters of the strike were rapidly becoming discouraged. Over the next few days, the failure of the parliamentarians to settle the strike weighed heavily on a divided and depressed group of trade unionists. Sarr was blamed for starting the strike, 'traitors' for trying to end it. Diop and Djoman came out for a return to work. This was decided on 4 January, effective the next day. When Fiankan returned on 5 January, the men had gone back.[107] Meeting with a group of railwaymen at Treichville, Fiankan called them 'traitors to your comrades in Dahomey, Guinea and the Soudan' and demanded why they had gone back. 'It was the Committee in accord with Maitre Diop who gave the order to go back', he was told. Fiankan urged them to strike again. They replied, 'We have suffered enough'.[108]

Leadership was clearly of the utmost importance in maintaining such a strike.[109] The Ivory Coast workers went back essentially under the terms of the arbitration decision, which provided that auxiliaries would be integrated into the cadres in accordance with their qualifications. The members of the cadres were, as promised, taken back to their old posts, but auxiliaries found that the conditions of their return were indeed problematic. The Régie had promised that the strikebreakers hired in the interim – and there were 755 of them out of a theoretical staffing of 3,111 – would keep their jobs, and it was the less senior auxiliaries who would bear the brunt. The Government General in Dakar – despite fear of trouble from the Governor in Abidjan – was content for the laid off auxiliaries to learn that a 'strike always carries risks above all when it takes place outside legal procedures'.[110]

All this served notice that the government was going to play as tough when workers went back as they had when they were out on strike. Perhaps this experience contributed to the determination of the other regions to hold out and to the union's toughness in the post-strike period.

It was only when a new High Commissioner came to French West Africa that further movement took place. Paul Béchard, taking advantage of his arrival, undertook to talk to the principals beginning 26 February. Béchard, as he himself later told it, decided that taking the legalistic line to its logical conclusion – by firing the railwaymen for violation of the arbitration ruling – was 'a brutal solution of rupture with unpredictable political consequences'. He sought a 'last try at conciliation', and he issued a series of proposals based on, but slightly modifying, the arbitration ruling:

(1) In regard to the union's claim to make the integration of auxiliaries retroactive to 1 January 1947, he proposed 1 May 1947 in regard to pay and 1 January 1947 in regard to seniority. The Régie had wanted 1 October and the arbitrator 15 July.

[107] Renseignements, Ivory Coast, 31 Dec. 1947, 3, 4, 7, 8 Jan. 1948, K 379 (26).

[108] Renseignements, 7 Jan. 1948, K 379 (26). At Port-Bouet the next day, Fiankan was greeted with such hostility that he had to leave. *Ibid.*, 8 Jan. 1948.

[109] The strike had not been as solid on the Abidjan-Niger line as on the other lines. On the former, 519 workers had returned to work by 1 January 1948, out of a theoretical labor force of 3,111. On the Dakar-Niger, only 236 out of 6,765 had given up by that date, while only 71 workers on the other two lines combined went back before the new year. IGT, AOF, to IGT, Paris, 8 Jan. 1948, IGT 13/2.

[110] Governor, Ivory Coast, to High Commissioner, telegram, 12 Jan. 1948, and Affaires Politiques, Administratives et Sociales to Governor, Ivory Coast, telegram, 20 Jan. 1948, K 378 (26).

(2) In regard to the reclassification of certain agents in the *cadres secondaires*, Béchard maintained the Régie's equivalence tables, but granted extra seniority to the agents in question.

(3) In regard to where examinations would be required to pass between scales, he placed examination barriers where the Régie wanted them, and also where the union wanted them.

(4) In regard to the union's demand for 15 days annual leave, in addition to a month's vacation, which the Régie had rejected and the arbitrator reduced to ten days, the High Commissioner agreed to 15, but only for family events and only if necessities of service permitted.

(5) In regard to the union's demand for the provision of lodging or a compensatory indemnity to all agents, he agreed with the Régie's position, supported by the arbitrator, that this could not be guaranteed for all.

(6) In regard to the union's demand for a uniform indemnity of zone, at the rate then accorded the highest rank – as opposed to the Régie's and the arbitrator's proposal for incorporating the old, hierarchical indemnities into a hierarchical wage scale and adding an indemnity of residence for places with a high cost of living – Béchard held firm to the Régie's position.

The High Commissioner decided in addition that there would be no punishment for striking, that the Régie would take back all its personnel in the cadres, that all auxiliaries currently at work would be kept on, and that striking auxiliaries would be taken back in order of seniority until the staffing levels had been filled.[111]

The High Commissioner was going along with the Régie on the issues where concessions would be the most costly. In both cases – housing and the hierarchical indemnities – he was not denying an agreed-upon benefit to railwaymen, but preserving the Régie's power to determine the modalities of implementation. In particular, the Régie retained wide discretion to maintain differentiation in emoluments: the incorporation of the highly unequal indemnity of zone into wages would preserve hierarchy, while the smaller and egalitarian indemnity of residence – applied by place and not by rank – would give lip service to equalizing adjustments for variations in the cost of living. Housing would be an emolument that could be used flexibly by the Régie to attract those categories of workers it wanted most. None of these differentials was explicitly racial, nor had any of them been that way in the Régie's offer or the arbitrator's ruling. On the other questions, Béchard's decisions appeared positively Solomonic: each side could claim it got something out of the battle. These proposals, of course, could have been made months earlier.

Union leaders, after discussing the proposal among themselves came back the next day, 15 March, expressing overall acceptance of the proposals but with a single objection: they wanted a guarantee that all auxiliaries would get their jobs back. Béchard later congratulated himself for having 'the intuition that this exigency constituted the stumbling block to the return', for the union had to protect its rank and file. By 4 a.m. he had a compromise: he would still protect those who had returned to work before the negotiated

---

[111] High Commissioner's narrative of strike, 1 Apr. 1948, K 458 (179).

THE 1947-48 RAILWAY STRIKE IN FRENCH WEST AFRICA   111

settlement but agreed to take back in principle all striking auxiliaries. But within a month, and after negotiations between the Régie and the union, a new staffing table – providing for a reduction of the workforce – would come into effect and auxiliaries' rights to keep their jobs would depend on seniority and competence. Striking auxiliaries who had filled, before the strike, the conditions for integration into the cadres would keep the benefits of the transition program. He also made a slight concession on one of the strike issues, easing the examination barriers for passing between certain ranks. Strike days would not be paid. As compensation for the increased cost of living, the Régie was to raise (retroactive to 1 January 1948) wages, expatriation and displacement benefits, and management benefits by 20 per cent, and increase an indemnity of residence for Dakar, Abidjan and other cities. The 20 per cent in this context hardly seemed to be the technical adjustment it was alleged to be but a response to a disciplined strike. Any disagreements over the implementation of the agreement would go to a commission including one representative of the High Commissioner, and two each from the Régie and the union.

The Régie and the union accepted these proposals, and the return to work was fixed for that Friday, 19 March. Béchard concluded his report on the strike, 'It left no victors, no vanquished. Reasons for excessive bitterness for one side or the other have been avoided. Work could be resumed on solid bases, ignoring former divisions, in good order and with confidence'.[112]

Sarr, returning to Thiès after signing the agreement, claimed that the High Commissioner had 'given us concessions which the Régie did not want to give us ... Thus, comrades, our honor is safe and we will return to work having shown that we were men who know what we want'. He did not want strikers to get into disputes with nonstrikers: 'We will resume work calmly, and with discipline'. The end of the strike was celebrated with a long march at Thiès, followed by meetings and dancing. It was an occasion of joy, an expression of confidence in organization and unity. In the years that followed, many children of railwaymen were named after Ibrahima Sarr.[113] The end of the strike is remembered today as a 'magnificent' victory bringing equality and the end of racial discrimination within the labor force, as a 'clear improvement' in the lives of workers, as an achievement won on behalf of the auxiliaries integrated into the cadres.[114]

AFTERMATH

Almost immediately, the two sides plunged into a struggle over the staffing table, over deciding which auxiliaries would be kept and over how integration would take place. The intensity of the disputes must have reminded everyone

[112] High Commissioner's narrative, 1 Apr. 1948, K 458 (179); Protocole de Reprise du Travail, 15 Mar. 1948, IGT 13/2.

[113] Renseignements, 16 Mar. 1948, K 458 (179); Sene, 'Grève des cheminots', 104, 112. The administration feared that auxiliaries, who were still at risk, might try to block the return to work, but Sarr vowed to defend them, and officials noted that 'we must assume that he will not give way on this point'. Renseignements, 16 Mar. 1948, K 458 (179).

[114] Abdoulaye Souleye Sarr (interview, 22 July 1990), Oumar NDiaye and Amadou Bouta Gueye (interview, 9 Aug. 1994) and Mansour Niang (interview, 4 Aug. 1994).

concerned of why the strike had been fought so determinatedly.[115] Management asserted its prerogative to fire people for incompetence or other reasons; the union had the implicit threat of another strike behind its demands.

The discussions over the labor force reduction lasted over two years. The Régie had intended to reduce its 17,000-man force even before the strike began; such a reduction was its quid pro quo during the April negotiations for agreeing to restructuring the cadres and integrating auxiliaries. In the midst of the strike, and probably for political purposes, it claimed it only needed 13,500. But when it came to listing necessary workers, the Régie found it needed to ponder the question – amidst challenges from the union – and then came up with a figure of 14,748 in June 1948. Given the fact that over 2,000 strike-breakers had been hired (not counting the Abidjan-Niger branch) and had to be kept on under the terms of the Protocol, this meant that as many as 5,000 workers could have lost their jobs. But as further delays ensued – including protracted and heated negotiations throughout the summer – many workers left voluntarily, while new works projects and the need to take care of neglected maintenance increased needs, so that by September the number of workers in jeopardy was around 2,500.[116]

Some of the voluntary resignations apparently resulted from union members making life difficult for the *défaillants* or *jaunes*, as strike-breakers were called.[117] From the very start, the union challenged management on so many points that the director complained that his regional directors

find themselves in an annoying situation *vis-à-vis* the unions because of the fact that they are constantly accused of violating the end of strike protocol with threats of informing the Governor General or the Inspecteur Général du Travail. The authority necessary for the execution of a public service is dangerously disturbed.[118]

What was happening was good, hard negotiating, carried out within the new Commission at the federal level (as well as the Conseil d'Administration of

[115] The Inspection du Travail realized immediately that the question of rehiring auxiliaries would be the crucial one in the upcoming weeks. Pélisson thought that the less senior auxiliaries, who were vulnerable to lose their jobs, should be clearly informed of this, so that any who had taken other jobs during their strike could decide if it were advisable to keep them. He thought that Inspecteurs du Travail, not the Régie, should be the ones to break the bad news. IGT, circular to Inspecteurs Territoriaux du Travail, 17 Mar. 1948, IGT 13/2.

[116] These ups and downs are traced in IGT to Inspecteur Général des Colonies, 6 Sept. 1948, K 458 (179), and can be followed in Renseignements, June–September 1948, 11 D 1/1392. The 14,748 figure was agreed to, by a vote of 11–2, at the meeting of the Conseil d'Administration of the Régie, 25 June 1948, transcript in IGT 13/2. At this time, the plan was to fire 2,500 unskilled workers on 31 July, followed by three batches of 850 each of skilled workers. The actual firings turned out to be considerably less drastic.

[117] Inspecteur Territorial du Travail, Dahomey, to IGT, 1 Apr. 1948, IGT 13/2; IGT, Réglement de la grève des chemins de fer africain de l AOF, 24 Sept. 1948, *ibid*. The tension at Thiès was heightened by the presence of the union of nonstrikers organized on the Dakar-Niger by Gning. But for all of Gning's obsequiousness *vis-à-vis* the administration, the latter wanted no part of his union, for it knew where the power lay, and it systematically denied it a place on the bodies which negotiated terms of layoffs and rehirings. High Commissioner to Gning, 15 June 1948, K 458 (179).

[118] Directeur Fédéral de la Régie des Chemins de Fer to Inspecteur Général du Travail, 9 Apr. 1948, K 458 (179).

THE 1947–48 RAILWAY STRIKE IN FRENCH WEST AFRICA 113

the Régie) and within each of the branch lines. The Régie recognized the need to balance its desire to minimize costs with a desire for an 'appeasement policy', and in bargaining sessions the union insisted on 'the social side of the problem'. This meant avoiding brutal layoffs while using the labor force to assure neglected maintenance and the 'modernization of its equipment and its installations', which the Régie had proclaimed its goal. One top official admitted that in the course of 115 hours of meetings, the two sides had come closer together and concessions had been 'pulled out of the Régie', which admitted that its first tables were too theoretical and that more staffing was needed.[119] Then, from June through September, the details of where the axe would fall were negotiated. By this time, attrition had eased the problem somewhat, some of the workers hired during the strike were fired for incompetence and others for faults committed before the strike, and the union negotiated that layoffs take place in three batches, in August, September and October. Lists were generated by trade and seniority, and they were given to the union. Regional commissions heard disputes. Most, according to the Inspection, were settled unanimously. The axe did fall: the August firings consisted of 671 on the Dakar-Niger, 92 on the Conakry-Niger, 112 on the Abidjan-Niger, and 258 on the Benin-Niger, a total of 1,133. In September, 380 workers were fired. At Thiès, where the problem was regarded as 'the thorniest', the Inspecteurs got 348 rehired as temporaries, and encouraged others to seek work as dockers in Dakar or laborers on a development scheme on the Senegal River.[120] In Dahomey and in the Ivory Coast, the union succeeded in getting significant numbers of workers slated for lay off to be reinstated.[121]

The Inspecteur Général du Travail admitted that 'the social malaise remains considerable', particularly the tension between white and black railwaymen. He hoped that the departure of some European railwaymen

[119] Statements of Pillot and Mahé for the Régie and Ousmane N'Gom for the union, Transcript of Meeting of Conseil d'Administration des Chemins de Fer de l'AOF, 25 June 1948, IGT 13/2.

[120] IGT, 'Réglement de la grève des chemins...' 24 Sept. 1948, IGT 13/2. The union's role in establishing lists of workers to be fired was not defined in the Protocol of 15 March, but was apparently offered 'spontaneously' by the Régie when it came up with its staffing table, undoubtedly to insure that the union was complicit in hard decisions that had to be made. This lengthened the proceedings, and let attrition take care of part of the problem. IGT to Sarr, 28 Oct. 1948, K 458 (179). In October, the Régie, with the consent of the union, decided to pension off auxiliaries over 55 years of age, claiming that the life-pensions or layoff indemnities were expensive, but that this would leave a more effective workforce (and would presumably ease the anxieties of younger workers). The rival union, led by Gning, complained about this, but got little more than an explanation of why the main union, Sarr's, and the Régie, had agreed to it. IGT to Gning, 18 Oct. 1948, K 458 (179).

[121] In the Ivory Coast, 342 scheduled layoffs were reduced to 187. Inspection du Travail, Ivory Coast, Rapport sur l'evolution de réglement de la grève de la Régie des Chemins de fer de l'AOF (Région Abidjan-Niger), 28 Aug. 1948; Inspection du Travail, Dahomey, Rapport sur l'évolution de réglement de la grève des cheminots Africains de la Région Bénin-Niger, 25 Aug. 1948, K 458 (179). In the Soudan, most of the laborers laid off were quickly rehired, as were 73 of the 202 skilled workers. The biggest problem was auxiliaries whose skills were specific to railway work. Governor, Soudan, to High Commissioner, 9 Oct. 1948, K 458 (179).

114   FREDERICK COOPER

would ease the way both to hiring more Africans and improving the atmosphere. In any case, Pélisson acknowledged, a bit grudgingly, that the union 'had done its duty in defense of the railwaymen'.[122]

The union had to accept its share of responsibility for the process, but also credit for protecting its own men and inducing strike-breakers to quit. It concluded,

having rid ourselves of the nightmare of staff compression, the situation of all the comrades who remain will be correspondingly improved. All qualified auxiliaries will soon be integrated into the cadre. The agents of the cadre will in several days receive their recalls, fruits of a struggle that will be forever remembered. Thus all will be paid their true value and the frightening number of auxiliaries will diminish considerably by their integration into the *cadre unique* which does not distinguish white or yellow or black, but only workers, period.[123]

But people did get hurt in this process, and in November a group of auxiliaries massed in front of Sarr's home to protest that the union was not looking after their interests and had not accomplished the promised integration of auxiliaries. They accused him of fostering his own political ambitions.[124] Indeed, the process of integrating auxiliaries was slow and partial, and some railwaymen continued to press (unsuccessfully) to regain the status of civil servants while civil servants pressed (successfully) for their own version of the *cadre unique*, with equal benefits regardless of origin.[125]

The concrete gains were significant. The post-strike plan was for 2,500 auxiliaries to be integrated into the cadres. By 1950, the cadres had gone from around 12 per cent of the work force before the strike to over 31 per cent.[126] A financial evaluation of the Régie in 1952 concluded that the cost of integrating auxiliaries was one of the major factors leading to the high freight charges and precarious financial situation of the Régie, as were the substantial raises – estimated at 77 per cent – given auxiliaries since 1948. Officials pointed out in reply that the costs of the 1947 strike were still being paid and that social relations in French West Africa's largest enterprise were important not only in themselves but were 'necessary, as the strike of 1947 proved, for the sound functioning of the Régie itself. I believe that technical progress

[122] IGT, 'Réglement de la grève des chemins...', 24 Sept. 1948, IGT 13/2.
[123] Circular signed Abdoulaye Ba from the union to union subdivisions, apparently intercepted by Sûreté and filed as Renseignements, 8 Sept. 1948, K 458 (179).
[124] 'La vie syndicale en AOF', 31 January 1949, AP 3406/1. There were more protests later in 1949. Renseignements, n.d. [*c.* Nov. 1949] 11 D 1/1392.
[125] Labor reports noted 'malaise' in the civil service and railways. The former received legal assurance of equal pay and benefits from the 'Lamine Gueye Law' of 1950, although its implementation remained a subject of contestation. IGT, 'Rapport: cessation d'application du Protocole de reprise du Travail sur les Chemins de Fer de l'Afrique occidentale française', 2 July 1949, IGT 13/2; Ibrahima Sarr, for Fédération des Syndicats des Cheminots Africains de l'AOF to Inspecteur Général du Travail, 18 Aug. 1952, 18G 163; High Commissioner to Minister, 20 Nov. 1948, Union des Syndicats Confédérés de Dakar, Revendications, 1 May 1949, Secretary General, Services des Etudes, Note pour l'Inspecteur Général du Travail, 18 May 1949, High Commissioner to Minister, 12 Jan., 25 Feb. 1950, all in K 424 (165).
[126] IGT to Inspecteur Général des Colonies, 6 Sept. 1948, K 458 (179); Directeur Fédéral de la Régie to IGT, 30 June 1950, K 43 (1).

THE 1947–48 RAILWAY STRIKE IN FRENCH WEST AFRICA 115

and social progress cannot be separated'.[127] This was a lesson that officials could not forget, and unions would remind them if they did, while rank and file might remind their union leaders if they neglected the human interests that were at stake.

In the aftermath of the strike, its political implications remained to be worked out. The administration had fought the strike as a labor dispute, not as a contest over colonial authority, restraining its authoritarian hand but stubbornly insisting on following its industrial relations procedures. The union had also fought the strike as a labor dispute, restraining itself from public demonstrations more extensive than the regular mass meetings of railwaymen at Thiès. If the rhetoric of Sarr from his first speech in May 1946 onward was filled with attacks on colonialists, it also contained numerous references to the role Africans had played as in the French military, defending French freedom, and this – along with working side by side with French railwaymen – was seen as legitimating the claim to equality of pay and benefits.[128] Similar strategies were used by others to turn the rhetoric of unity and assimilation in the Union Française into claims to entitlements: the veterans' slogan, for example, was 'equal sacrifices, equal rights'.[129] The French reference point was in fact vital to the union's entire argument: the plea for an end to racial discrimination in regard to indemnities, housing and other issues assumed the existence of a unit within which equality could be pursued.

Forty-seven years later, a former railwayman denied that the 'spirit of independence' was behind the strike; the central issue was 'respect of professional value'.[130] Yet the political meanings of the strike are more complicated than that. Equality with French railway workers was a formal demand, yet the spirit of defiance and the anger against French colonial practices could not be so neatly bounded. Nor could the self-confidence gained by the disciplined conduct of a social movement over five and a half months and a vast space be limited to the issues formally at stake. In regard to questions of popular consciousness, the vision of Sembene's novel remains germane to histories of the post-1948 era.

But popular consciousness does not make movements in a vacuum. Organization is a key concern, and here one finds a double ambiguity, in relation to trade union organization and to political parties. The community mobilization on which the strike depended was channelled – in the strike and its aftermath – through the railway union and its Comité Directeur. The very success of its negotiations drew it into a framework of industrial

[127] Mission Monguillot, 'Situation Financière de la Régie Générale des Chemins de Fer de l'AOF', Rapport 93/D, 10 Apr. 1952; Directeur Général des Finances to Monguillot, 5 May 1952, and High Commissioner to Monguillot, 17 July 1952, AP 2306/7.

[128] For example, Sarr told an audience at Kayes in November: 'We have suffered famine and thirst and we have marched naked to defend purely French interests; nothing prevents us to suffer as much today when it is a question of our own interests.' Renseignements, 31 Nov. 1947, K 457 (179). The Comité Directeur included *anciens combattants*, who remained proud of their service to both causes. Abdoulaye Souleye Sarr (interview, 22 July 1990), Amadou Bouta Gueye (interview, 9 Aug. 1994).

[129] Myron Echenberg, *Colonial Conscripts: The Tirailleurs Sénégalais in French West Africa, 1857–1960* (Portsmouth, NH: Heinemann, 1991), 152.

[130] Mansour Niang (interview, 4 Aug. 1994).

relations, modelled on French labor law and French practices. The union, over time, became more of a union.

And whatever the potential implications of the strike to anti-colonial politics, they were in fact channelled through the structures of political parties. The networks created by the union and by the strike as well as the memories and sentiments to which it gave rise were both enlisted in a wider cause and tamed. Senghor was the West African politician who accomplished this with particular acuity. Spending much time as a deputy in Paris and more tending to organizational work in Dakar, Senghor needed a mechanism to get beyond the limitations of the Dakar-centered politics of his mentor, Lamine Gueye. Senghor had not stood publicly by the side of the railway workers. His breakthrough occurred in reaching out to them – as he did to other constituencies via leaders, networks and pre-existing institutions. The Mouride brotherhoods were key constituents in rural areas, labor in the towns. Two of the candidates he kept on his slate after his break with Lamine Gueye in 1949 and his founding of the Bloc Démocratique Sénégalais were Sarr (for the Assemblée de l'Union Française) and Abbas Gueye, one of the heroes of the 1946 Dakar general strike (Assemblée Nationale).[131]

In the memories of participants, there is both pride and bitterness at this process: assertions that the railwaymen's actions set the stage for wider population mobilization, identification with Senghor as a political 'phenomenon'. But one hears from workers as well a disappointment that their own union leaders had become estranged in putting on the *boubou politique* (the robes of politics) and that their interests were being set aside in the scramble for office and the enjoyment of its perquisites. They feared that they would lose the power that derived from their professional focus and become only the 'auxiliaries' of the political parties.[132] By the mid-1950s, the political activities of union leaders would become a source of controversy within the railway union and indeed within the labor movement of French West Africa in general.[133]

CONCLUSION

There remained, in 1948, a great deal for African union leaders to accomplish, on the railroad as well as outside. But in following up the strike, as much as in the strike itself, they had shown that the representatives of African workers would be present where their interests were being discussed. The 1947–8 railway strike was above all a contest over power within a system of industrial relations that had only just been brought to French Africa. No longer willing to defend explicitly and overtly a system of job classifications

---

[131] 'La vie syndicale en AOF au cours de l'année 1948', 31 Jan. 1949, including High Commissioner to Minister, 2 Feb. 1949, AP 3406/1. This report makes it clear that the union remained clear of political involvement during the strike, but that afterward politicians, and Senghor in particular, realized that 'the African railwaymen constitute in effect a very important electoral trump card in Senegal'.

[132] The phrase *boubou politique* was used in an interview by a former government worker and low-level official in a civil service union, while the notion of becoming 'auxiliaries' to political parties comes from Mory Tall. Moussa Konaté, interview Dakar, 8 Aug. 1994, by Frederick Cooper and Alioune Ba. Tall interview, by the *équipe de Thiès*, 9 Aug. 1994.

[133] This theme is discussed at length in Cooper, *Decolonization and African Society*, ch. 11.

THE 1947–48 RAILWAY STRIKE IN FRENCH WEST AFRICA 117

by race or origins, colonial officials were nonetheless willing to fight for power within the structure of bureaucratized industrial relations machinery they had created, over the details of what the wage hierarchy would be and the precise terms of access to different points within it. Hierarchy and differential access to resources were to remain fundamental to the modernized colonialism of the post-war era, and the strike of 1947–8 revealed the impossibility of separating neatly the impersonal structure of a modern institution from the racialized history of colonial rule. In so far as the struggle forced colonial officials to assert ever more vehemently that they did not mean for the new hierarchy merely to reproduce the old, in so far as control of that hierarchy had to be shared with a militant union, officials were made to confront the fact that colonial authority was no longer as colonial as it once was. Such a realization was an important part of the reconsideration by French political leaders and civil servants in the mid-1950s of the strategies and institutions on which French rule depended.[134]

The determination and unity of the African railway workers made clear, for then and thereafter, that their voices would be heard. But the government of French West Africa made its point too: African unions could fight and they could win, but within certain legal and institutional structures. The very battle brought both sides ever deeper into those structures, and neither tried to take the battle outside. The railway workers drew on the strength of their communities – ties of family, commerce and religion within Thiès most notably – whereas proletarian solidarity across occupational lines or a wider African mobilization against colonialism could not be organized. At the end of 1948, a government report, reflecting on a year which had witnessed one titanic labor conflict – and a host of routine disputes and negotiations easily contained within the recently created structures of the Inspection du Travail – applauded the form in which the two sides had joined their conflict: 'Social peace can only profit from such a crystalization of forces around two poles, certainly opposed but knowing each other better and accepting to keep contact to discuss collective bargaining agreements and conditions of work'.[135]

Perhaps. The clearest sign that the terrain of struggle became more closely framed, defined and narrowed was that nothing quite like the general strike of 1946 or the railway strike of 1947–8 occurred again under French rule.[136] For the railway and the government, the strike had a high cost in wages and benefits and a higher one in the lesson learned that the new social engineering strategies of the post-war era would give rise to new forms of struggle and new claims to entitlements. The question this would eventually leave in official minds had profound implications: was it politically wise to use France as a model for Africa and assert that the French empire represented a single entity when that legitimated African claims for a French standard of

[134] This is a major theme of the concluding part of my *Decolonization and African Society*. [135] 'La vie syndicale en AOF', 31 Jan. 1949, AP 3406/1.

[136] The largest subsequent event was a one-day general strike in November 1952 throughout French West Africa, spearheaded by the CGT and intended to bring pressure on the French legislature to pass the Code du Travail. There were co-ordinated strikes in 1953 over the terms of implementation of that code, but while those strikes revealed impressive co-ordination they did not entail the kind of community dynamic of the earlier ones.

living? For African railway workers integrated into the cadres, the material gains of the strike were considerable, but this achievement left open the question of whether African communities would be strengthened or segmented by the higher incomes of a distinctly defined body of men. The strike of 1947 had drawn its strength simultaneously from the communities of the railwaymen and the union's seizure of the institutions and rhetoric of postwar French imperialism as the bases for its demands. The railwaymen now faced the question of whether their strength could serve a broader population or whether in attaching themselves to the cause of national politics the strength would be drawn out of the labor movement and into political institutions where their interests, their sense of community and their visions would be lost.

SUMMARY

This essay is both a reinterpretation of the place of the French West African railway strike in labor history and part of an exploration of its effects on politics and political memory. This vast strike needs to be studied in railway depots from Senegal to the Ivory Coast. Historians need both to engage the fictional version of the strike in Ousmanne Sembene's *God's Bits of Wood* and avoid being caught up in it. Interviews in the key railway and union town of Thiès, Senegal, suggest that strike veterans want to distinguish an experience they regard as their own from the novelist's portrayal. They accept the heroic vision of the strike, but offer different interpretations of its relationship to family and community and suggest that its political implications include co-optation and betrayal as much as anticolonial solidarity. Interviews complement the reports of police spies as sources for the historian. The central irony of the strike is that it was sustained on the basis of railwaymen's integration into local communities but that its central demand took railwaymen into a professionally defined, nonracial category of railwayman. The strike thus needs to be situated in relation to French efforts to define a new imperialism for the post-war era and the government's inability to control the implications of its own actions and rhetoric. Negotiating with a new, young, politically aware railway union leadership in 1946 and 1947, officials were unwilling to defend the old racial wage scales, accepted in principle the *cadre unique* demanded by the union, but fought over the question of power – who was to decide the details that would give such a cadre meaning? The article analyzes the tension between the principles of nonracial equality and African community among the railwaymen and that between colonial power and notions of assimilation and development within the government. It examines the extent to which the strike remained a railway strike or spilled over into a wider and longer term question of proletarian solidarity and anticolonial mobilization.

[7]

PLANNED DECOLONIZATION AND ITS FAILURE IN BRITISH AFRICA

John Flint

Two BROAD interpretations of the movement for decolonization have been put forward. The first of these may be described as 'liberal-nationalist' (some might prefer 'bourgeois') and the second as 'dependentista' or 'neo-colonialist' (though here again some might opt for the epithet 'vulgar Marxist'). Both theses, unfortunately, tend to be heavy with theory but lightweight in their evidential base. Both have originated largely in the speculations of political scientists, though the theories tend to reappear with monotonous regularity in the general historical literature, especially in textbooks. In this article I propose to examine how the decolonization movement originated as a movement for colonial reform in British Africa; what the theoretical assumptions behind this movement were; and how the British proposed, from London, to plan African evolution to self-government. My sources will be, almost entirely, the Colonial Office files for the period after 1938. I make no apologies for this because the dynamic for change, before 1946 at the earliest, lay there, and not in Africa.

I shall devote more space to a critique of the *dependentista* thesis than the the liberal-nationalist theory, because the former is more complex and nearer to reality, while the latter can be somewhat quickly demolished. The liberal nationalist interpretation was itself an ideological by-product of the decolonization process (and essential to it); its evidential base lay in the largely propagandist published sources, both nationalist and imperial, of the time, and the interpretation is largely the stuff of drama and myth. Both need conflict between firmly-drawn characters, a struggle of wills, an unfolding plot and a final resolution of conflict, with hero taking on villain, and a happy ending in which even the villain is mellowed, Scrooge-like, in the contemplation of the final generosity forced on him by the dire warnings of his helpful and enlightened friends and the ghosts of dead empires.

Act I of this drama must surely have been the Second World War (though there was a spectral prologue of forebodings and prophecies from the European catastrophe of 1914–18). As the entire northern half of the world moved through what was to prove the bloodiest period of human history the moral and physical bases of pre-war imperialism collapsed—the Axis Powers rep-

The author is professor of history at Dalhousie Univeristy, Halifax, Nova Scotia, and already a distinguished authority on the earlier partition of Africa through his biography of Sir George Goldie (OUP, 1960). The article was originally presented as a paper at the Australian National University conference on decolonization in August 1982.

resented the ultimate racism, the ultimate irrational autocracy, the ultimate evil. The 'United Nations' (how quickly we forget historical origins!) stood for the ideological opposites—self-determination, the equality of mankind, democracy. The outcome in 1945 was the defeat of Axis imperialism and the triumph of the anti-imperialist Soviet and American super-powers. Western Europe, the historical fountainhead of imperialism, lay in ruins, with France and Britain, the 'greatest' imperial powers, exhausted and weak, dependent on the financial generosity of the USA. The era of European domination had ended; roused by the new *Zeitgeist* the nationalists of the third world (seen as an opposite polarity to colonial rulers) could rally the masses and challenge their masters. The 'struggle' for decolonization had begun. Its victory was inevitable.

Even at a common sense level this story will not hold together. If willingness to decolonize was the result of struggle by nationalists and weakness of the colonial powers then the chronology of declonization makes no sense. By any sensible estimate the British, in 1945, were the strongest of the colonial powers in Africa, with the French next, followed by Belgium and Portugal. These powers should therefore have decolonized in exactly the opposite chronological order. In reality, however, strength represents exactly an index of willingness to decolonize, while political weakness appears to have bred imperialist resistance.

Examination of the documentary evidence undermines the liberal-nationalist myth entirely. It reveals clearly that consideration of policies of decolonization were entirely British in inspiration (with no other colonial power in Africa contemplating such steps before 1958) and that these British ideas antedated the outbreak of the war. They were not the reaction of an 'exhausted' power realizing its own weakness, but contemplated as means of strengthening British economic and international influence. American influence, though exerted, was really of little significance in shaping actual policy, as distinct from public relations.[1] The element of nationalism played no part in these developments until they had reached a relatively advanced stage; we may indeed go further than this and suggest that the emergence of nationalist political parties seeking mass support was the *result* of decisions to decolonize and a creation of imperial policy. Far from nationalists and imperialists standing at opposite poles, they were indeed historically aspects one of the other. No fundamental ideological gulf separated 'nationalists' from imperial policy once colonial reform planning was under way after 1938; the 'struggle' was merely tactical and concerned almost entirely with timing. The 'nationalists' wished to inherit

---

1. Wm. Roger Louis, *Imperialism at Bay: the United States and the Decolonization of the British Empire*, Clarendon Press, Oxford, 1977, deals extensively with this theme. The Anglo-American conflict about colonial goals was very largely a battle of words, with semantic issues looming large. In my work I can find no evidence that the British were willing to trim their sails to an American wind, except in matters of propaganda and drafting. Louis's book seems to suggest that US influence rather stiffened the 'imperial' temper in Britain.

PLANNED DECOLONIZATION AND ITS FAILURE IN BRITISH AFRICA   391

the colonial state, the colonial frontiers and the colonial apparatus of power in all its ramifications.   The British had equal need of 'nationalist' cadres who could carry through exactly such aspirations, and if the nationalists were not there they would have to be created and nurtured.   This argument will be supported through detailed examples later in the context of a critique of the *dependentista* thesis.

The theory which attempts to explain decolonization in terms of under-development theory and the concept of neocolonialism is too well known to require extensive elaboration here.   It has been succinctly summarized by Colin Leys as an outline of the final stages of colonial rule:

> 'new social strata and ultimately social classes were either brought in (through colonial settlement), or created from among the indigenous popu-lation, which had an interest in organizing and facilitating the new economic activities involved (trade, mining, crop production, and so on).   In the course of time these strata or classes became powerful enough to render direct rule by the metropolitan power unnecessary ... the need for the con-tinuous and overt use of force by the government to back up the process of accumulation declined.   This facilitated by replacement of direct colonial administration by 'independent' governments representing local strata and classes with an interest in sustaining the colonial economic relationships'.[2]

The cooption or even creation of a 'comprador' class, followed by the transfer of formal political and administrative power to it, is thus seen by the *dependentista* school as the essential, yet illusory, element of the decolonization process, which may be seen as a kind of mirror image of the earlier phase of partition.

The *dependentista* thesis is certainly more attractive than the liberal-nationalist mythology and it takes care of all the devastating objections which can be raised against the legend of nationalist-imperialist struggle.   Moreover, although it was originally a mechanistic series of theoretical postulates erected on the flimsiest base of historical evidence, when such evidence is examined in detail it lends itself much more to interpretation along *dependentista* than liberal-nationalist lines.

At the outset, however, it should be pointed out that much of this lies in the large element of truism and tautology that runs through the *dependentista* jargon.   It is, for example, impossible to conceive that the decolonizing power had any alternative but to use 'new social strata ... which had an interest in organizing and facilitating the new economic activities' created in the period of formal imperialism; Britain was hardly likely to foster the growth of

---

2.   Colin Leys, *Underdevelopment in Kenya: the political economy of neo-colonialism, 1964–1971*, Heinemann, London, 1975, p. 9.   On the previous page, footnote 13, Leys runs through the major literature on neo-colonialism and underdevelopment published before 1975.

revolutionary communist parties to which it might transfer sovereignty! The only other alternative, the deliberate exclusion of such groups with the objective of returning sovereignty to African precolonial nations controlled by precolonial social elites, an idea favoured in some colonial service circles of Nigeria, was in fact totally impractical, and amounted in fact to a disguised resistance to the very concept of self-government and decolonization.[3]

The crucial element in the *dependentista* thesis, therefore, lies not in the transfer of power to a 'new strata', but in the description of that 'class' as 'comprador'[4] The comprador bourgeoisie is not, cannot be, and must not be, a national bourgeoisie, capable of supporting itself by accumulation from a national economy. It is therefore not fully a capitalist class, but dependent as a class (symbolizing the dependency of the neo-colonial economy) on 'international capitalism' which is seen as dominated by the multinational corporations, generally regarded as linked ultimately to those of the USA. All it can do is preserve, develop and intensify underdevelopment and dependency in the forms of monoculture and raw material production which are the economic legacy of the colonial period. The creation of such a system was the planned purpose of decolonization.[5]

3. See below p. 399. An elaboration of indirect rule institutions could, at most, have led to 'self-administration' of small units and the creation of a permanent need for a cadre of colonial service personnel to co-ordinate these units, maintain transport and technical services and organize relations, economic and political, with the outside world. The concept had a good deal in common with that of the 'Bantustans' in South Africa today.

4. The historiography of empire is, of course, beset with the problems arising from the use of words which carry emotional, instead of rational, overtones. The liberal-nationalist school introduced the emotive terminology of the second world war and the struggle against Nazism in studies of 'resistance' and 'collaboration'. 'Comprador' in its Latin American historical context, appears to carry a more perjorative connotation than 'collaborator', though the terms are often used interchangeably. 'Collaborator', as the memories of Nazism recede, seems to be losing its hateful overtones, with the verbal form coming back into diplomatic and journalistic use to indicate moderation, co-operation and a friendly attitude. This is perhaps why the term 'comprador' is more favoured.

5. The neocolonialist and *dependentista* literature is too vast to summarize here. The above paragraph tries to summarise a number of strains or themes about which most of these theorists are agreed. Paul Baran's *The Political Economy of Growth*, first published in New York in 1957, outlined the view that decolonization hardly affected the realities of formal colonial rule because all the territories were handed over to 'comprador governments'. These were not merely 'fortuitous coincidences' but the result of 'the totality of imperialism' (p. 218). André Gundar Frank emphasized the view that underdevelopment was a systematic purpose of neocolonialism by which the USA (or rather its multinational corporations) intensified 'structural underdevelopment' (*Capitalism and Underdevelopment in Latin America*, London, 1969, p. 336 and *passim*). The writings of Samir Amin (*Accumulation on a World Scale: A critique of the theory of underdevelopment*, 2 vols., New York, 1974 and *Imperialism and Unequal Development*, Sussex, 1977) emphasizes the view that peripheral economies are only partially involved in the world system, which prevents their 'autocentric' development, and fixes them into patterns of transport and monoculture useful to the metropolis. Pre-industrial forms of reproduction thus coexist with incomplete and limited forms of advanced technology; these are fixed and immutable (except to violent revolution) by the dominance of metropolitan multinational corporations who use the comprador regimes to maintain the local order in the system in the periphery. Tautology runs rife through all these arguments; the term 'imperialism' seems to mean nothing more or less than the international capitalist system itself.

It is interesting that Kwame Nkrumah, himself one of the most crucial historical actors in the process of British decolonisation of Africa, was one of the first to elaborate the neocolonial idea and to castigate comprador regimes (though he did not use the Latin American term). He avoids

Footnote 5 continued on next page

In all of these writings there is scarcely any reference to what historians would call primary sources, other than published reports and economic statistics: indeed, the school seems to feed, vampire-like, on the writings of its own members, citing and reciting them monotonously as if they were evidence in themselves.   But the historian can now look at the documentary evidence of British political thinking which lay behind the profound changes in policy which developed steadily after 1938.   In particular we can look at British ideas about the emergence of social classes in Africa, what should be their roles in political and economic life and what should be the relationship between political, and economic and social, change.   Did the British plan the transfer of power to 'compradors', or even to create compradors, in a purpose of perpetuating underdevelopment, peripheral economies and the interests of multinational (or even British national) corporations?

The Colonial Office files certainly do reveal that an almost complete reversal of attitudes towards social change in the British African territories developed in London after 1938.[6]   Before that time the indirect rule philosophy, which had been developed entirely outside the Colonial Office by colonial service personnel, held virtually unchallenged sway, as did the economic doctrine, sacrosanct in the Treasury, that colonies should live off their own resources.[7]   Indeed, if the historian looks for the roots of the 'development of underdevelopment', the fostering of monocultures and metropolitan-oriented transport networks and the creation of 'compradors', they are to be found in the policy of rule through 'native authorities' (truly a 'comprador group' in a state of total dependence upon the British) combined with the concept that infrastructural development to serve the interests of cash-cropping and mining had to be financed from local resources.   Before 1938 reform of 'native administration' could be argued by advocates who wished to improve its effectiveness, but those who argued for its abolition and replacement by some other system

the rather obvious implied question about his own role in the events of 1948–57 in Ghana, then the Gold Coast colony, as well as the strong implication that a continuation of direct colonial rule would have been preferable.   Nkrumah outlines neocolonialism as worse than colonial rule because it left no imperial redress against the corruption, mismanagement and autocracy of collaborationist regimes: '... it means power without responsibility, and for those who suffer from it, it means exploitation without redress.   In the days of old-fashioned colonialism, the imperial power had at least to explain and justify at home the actions it was taking abroad.   In the colony those who served the ruling imperial power could at least look to its protection against any violent move by their opponents.   With neo-colonialism neither is the case.' (K. Nkrumah, *Neo-colonialism, the Last Stage of Capitalism*, London, 1965, Introduction, p. xi.)

6.   The development of a dichotomy of attitudes and thinking between the colonial service in the field and 'London' is a major theme which cannot be dealt with extensively here.   By London in this context I mean not only the officials in the Colonial Office but also other informed groups who helped to shape opinion and attitudes, including members of parliament, the Fabian Colonial Bureau, the British trade unions and interest groups like the Anti-Slavery and Aborigines Protection Society as well as academic and university opinion, especially that which was interested in the development of higher educational institutions in colonial territories.

7.   The two doctrines were closely connected, although the colonial service never embraced the latter with enthusiasm.   Treasury parsimony was at the root of the origins of the indirect rule system, which became codified and dogmatized because it was without doubt the cheapest form of African administration.

were regarded as a lunatic fringe. The aim of colonial rule was seen as the preservation of precolonial social organization. The emergence of 'classes', whether bourgeois or proletarian, betokened a failure of policy. Urbanization was thus frowned upon, migrant labour preferred to settled working men with their families, and the emergence of clerical and professional groups was regarded as an unfortunate by-product, alien in spirit and even in nationality to Africa itself. 'Detribalization' was the ghost which haunted the system.

All these assumptions began to be rather suddenly undermined by quite new attitudes and sentiments which made their appearance in the Colonial Office in 1938–9. The timing is of significance; although the outbreak of war against Nazi Germany solidified these changes and added a strong anti-racist element to them, it is clear that the process began well before the war started. What these changes amounted to, we can now see with hindsight, was the beginning of a movement for colonial reform in which lay the origins of decolonization.[8]

It is interesting to speculate on why these changes should have emerged at that time; Britain was recovering from the long years of economic depression; the strident racism and imperialism of Nazi propaganda was producing reactions of repulsion even on the right-wing of the British political establishment and the German demand for colonial concessions, as well as the Italian conquest of Ethiopia, revived interest in the question of the moral justification for colonial rule and how this might be linked with the values of democratic ideas which were under attack from fascism. But three specific events of the later 1930s were directly responsible for the shift in attitudes in London. These were the widespread riots in the British West Indies during 1937 and 1938, which shattered the complacency of the Colonial Office and in their aftermath destroyed the long held axiom that colonial territories must live off their own resources on *laissez faire* principles; the almost simultaneous publication of Lord Hailey's *African Survey* in 1938; and the appointment in the same year of Malcom Macdonald as Secretary of State for the Colonies.

The new sentiments, taken together, amounted to an almost total reversal of the attitudes of the 1929s and early 1930s. The indirect rule philosophy now came under fundamental and often stridently hostile attack. It was not so much a matter of reforming the system (unless reform could be of such a nature as to alter its very basis and transform it into a system of local government) but of getting rid of its 'traditional' basis and the very concept of 'natural' rulers. Such ideas were linked with a new concern for the role of the educated elements. In January 1939 in a long minute commenting on Hailey's *African Survey* as part of a review of judicial administration in Africa initiated by

---

8. Much ink can be wasted in trying to determine when a policy of 'decolonization' was finally decided. The question, however, is ahistorical. Just as it is nonsense to ascribe to Durham's Report a plan for the creation of independent nations in Australia, New Zealand and Canada, so no one in Britain intended 'decolonisation' in Africa until it actually occurred. Decolonization was envisaged at best as centuries ahead in Africa in the 1940s; in the 1950s it emerged as a 'solution' to problems created by the failure of colonial reform.

Macdonald, the Colonial Office legal advisor, Sir H. Grattan Bushe, declared that indirect rule was doomed. 'My own belief is that given sufficient inertia the system will, sooner in one place and later in another, come to an end.' He implied neglect in the colonial service, where, except in the Gold Coast 'where conditions have passed the possibilities of pretence, serious criticism by any District Officer of the theory or practice of Indirect Rule is not a thing which is done.' 'On the other side of the picture there appears in an ever growing progression the educated African, and he views with extreme distaste the primitive, inefficient and in many cases corrupt institutions of indirect rule. If, like the white man, he need do no more than worship them he might be content. Unfortunately, however, he finds that, unlike the white man, he has to subject himself to them.'[9] The assistant under-secretary, Sir Arthur Dawe, normally staid and conservative, agreed:

'I think that the truth of Sir G. Bushe's remarks . . . is becoming increasingly realised. It is absurd to erect what is an ephemeral expedient into a sacrosanct principle. Things are moving so fast in Africa that the doctrinaire adherents of the indirect rule principle may find themselves out-moded much quicker than anyone would have thought possible a few years ago.'[10]

Beneath these criticisms there were fundamental sociological assumptions which indicated a profound change in attitudes. The preservation of pre-colonial culture was no longer a basic goal (although a minister might still genuflect publicly to the ideal of 'preserving all that is best'[11]). 'Detribalization' ceased to be a ghost, and became an Angel of Progress. 'Classes', whether bourgeois or proletarian, were now to be seen as harbingers of a bright future, fermenting centres of enlightenment in their urban settings, whatever problems this might pose. The business of colonial policy was now the business of social change and the emergence of social classes should be welcomed, not feared or resisted. Everywhere in the colonial empire, Macdonald proudly proclaimed to a Commons Committee, the local populations were

'producing more and more of their own doctors and nurses, their own school teachers and agricultural officers, their own civil servants and lawyers, their own leaders in every walk of life. More and more, also, they are producing their own legislators and their own executive officers and that ultimately is the crux of the matter.'[12]

These assumptions that social classes would gradually replace 'tribal'

9. CO 847/13/47091/2 Min. by Bushe, January 1939.
10. *Ibid.* Min. by A.J.D. 19 January 1939.
11. As did Malcolm Macdonald in the House of Commons Committee on Supply on 7 June 1939, quickly following this with a reference to the need to train colonial peoples in modern science, 'social progress' and 'political thought' so as to become 'full citizens of the modern world'.
12. The quotation is from the same speech as footnote 11 and may be found in CO 847/20/47139.

institutions were not confined to the urban setting; detribalization should be watched and controlled in the very rockbed of rural Africa. Here, it should be noted, it does appear that the British deliberately set their face against the cultivation of rural compradors. The assumption was that British policy must prevent the transformation of traditional chiefs into a great landlord class controlling cash crop exports. At the end of July 1938 J. A. Calder drew attention to what he regarded as the danger of this development, already apparent in Buganda, spreading throughout British Africa in the absence of a firm policy on land use and land law. Calder simply assumed that the aim must be the creation of smallholding agriculture in individual peasant tenure. He pressed for a full-scale study of the problem. Hailey's *Survey* had made the same point. Macdonald took up the suggestion with enthusiasm, held full scale meetings on the question, which he chaired, and sent a circular despatch to all the African colonies two months after the war began, announcing that such a study would be commenced. He stressed that land was the basis of African social structure and that it was 'closely intertwined with issues of future political and economic development'. The matter, he insisted, was urgent, and the British had no policy. African traditions were eroding and governments must intervene. The war would increase the speed of change. 'I am not disposed to adopt a fatalistic attitude of *laissez faire*' and he was ready to use law to fight against peasant indebtedness, while the costs of this would be met from British and not colonial funds.[13]

This commitment to support an independent peasantry and the strong theoretical hostility to the development of an African landlord class is a theme which raises fundamental doubt about the neocolonial interpretation. A mass of peasants, holding legal title to their lands, would hardly appear fertile ground, in the long run, for a class interested 'in sustaining the colonial economic relationships' (to use Colin Leys phrase again) into a post-colonial period. Support for the creation of a powerful landlord class, interested in profits from cash export crops, especially if that class, as in Buganda, could be seen as a 'modernized' and 'enlightened' chiefly élite, would surely have been a better posture, promising the emergence of a conservative yet capitalistic class in command of its mass tenantry and well able to offset any tendencies towards urban radicalism.[14] A further difficulty is presented by the

13. CO 847/12/4708. Mem. by Calder, 23 July 1938; extract of meeting in the S. of S.'s room 27 June 1939; minutes of meeting chaired by Macdonald, 9 October 1939 and F.29, Macdonald to all African governors, 29 November 1939. Hailey's *African Survey* extracts were listed on pp. 3–9 of Calder's memorandum. The great inquiry into land law and policy was a casualty of the period after the end of the 'phoney war' and never materialized. The whole subject of land, land law and land utilization after 1939 and its relationship to political change in Africa is one which well merits serious study.

14. This argument can be applied even more forcefully to white settlers in Africa, who were of course the ideal comprador class (and performed this role historically in Latin America). A truly rigorous neocolonial policy would have seen decolonization to this group throughout east and central Africa, with the concession of responsible government to the Kenya settlers (perhaps forcing them into co-operation with the Indian immigrants and the Baganda elite), an east African federation

Footnote 14 continued on next page

evident strain in London-based thinking, both inside and outside the Colonial Office, which assumed, often with considerable naiveté, that a strong peasantry would prove to be the backbone of a genuine democracy in Africa. The assumption that a democratic system would be the goal of colonial reform was apparently there from the first, was hardly ever discussed in principle, and simply 'emerged' in detailed comment.[15]

The period of the late 1930s also forms a watershed in official attitudes towards the urban African working class, which for the first time began to be recognized not just as requiring official stimulation and protection. Not only was adequate trade union legislation written into the Colonial Development and Welfare Act of 1940 as a condition for the granting of funds, but trade union advisors, generally with British union experience, soon began to make their appearance in the colonies. *Dependentista* theorists have tended to stress the machiavellian aspects of this latter device, and appear to agree with liberal-nationalists in emphasizing that its purpose was to prevent, if possible, the emergence of a 'natural' nationalism among the 'masses'. But if the policy was directed towards the handing over of powers to a comprador bourgeoisie, one is left wondering why the British were at all concerned to prevent the nascent trade unions from falling under the control of politically motivated clerks and literati, or why the trade union advisers stressed the concept of a stable, resident working class and the need for 'economistic' goals, neither of which appeared to serve the interests of international capitalism. The less sophisticated explanation, that the British now wished to foster a stable proletariat, capable eventually of articulation of its economic needs, appears to be more in conformity with the evidence and fits in with the new attitudes to the peasantry and the professional and salaried classes. Colonial Office opinion

centred on Nairobi, the linking of this with a central African settler controlled federation, the welcoming of South African ambitions in 'the north', perhaps leading eventually to a 'United States of South and East Africa'. All these ambitions were strenuously, both covertly and overtly, fought for by the white settlers between 1938 and 1947, and in general were supported by the colonial service personel, especially in Kenya. In 1942–3 the Kenya settlers, with the support of Governor Sir Henry Moore, in effect tried to carry through by stealth the *de facto* creation of a unitary state of British East Africa. British economic and military power was eclipsed by that of South Africa during the war in east Africa, yet the Colonial Office fought, from a weak base, with great skill and effectiveness against all these settler and South African ambitions. In east Africa none of them were realized. Even the Central African Federation, a product of the era in which the colonial reform planning of the 1940s was demonstrably collapsing and leading to decolonization, was so set up as an experiment in decolonization to white settlers that Britain was able eventually to unscramble Malawi and Zambia. As for South Afirca, it came to be regarded as a dangerous rival sub-imperial power, whose influence needed to be resisted. I have dealt with these themes, which are highly complicated and much misunderstood, in a number of unpublished papers which may see print eventually, including 'The Colonial Office and the South African "Menace", 1940–1943'; 'Last Chance for the White Man's Country; constitutional plans for Kenya and East Africa, 1938–43', Parts I and II; and 'Nazi Plans for the repartition of Africa, 1940'.

15. The question of what was meant by 'democracy', on the other hand, was a source of bitter discussion and recrimination from the colonial service side, which constantly attacked the concept of the secret ballot and the Westminster model, regarded as potential instruments for demogagy, corruption and exploitation by rootless parvenu professional politicians. The dire and Jeremiad prophecies bear a striking resemblance to the picture of 'wasteful, corrupt and reactionary comprador regimes' (Baran, *op. cit.*, p. 218) so beloved by *dependentista* writers.

398   AFRICAN AFFAIRS

had come to accept with some enthusiasm that formation of 'classes' in Africa was taking place, and that consequent 'detribalisation'[16] was inevitable, ought to be encouraged, and was 'progressive'.

Given these new assumptions about the inevitability and desirability of social change, had the time come to consider whether these might 'render direct rule by the metropolitan power unnecessary'?

It was Malcolm Macdonald who began to consider these implications. Throughout 1938 and 1939 Macdonald, in public and private, began hammering out a doctrine for an overall and consistent definition of British colonial policy. He was not prepared to defend an implicitly racist position that there could be one policy for the white dominions and another for the colonies.[17] The most articulate statement of what this policy meant was made when Macdonald addressed the summer school on colonial administration at Oxford University on 27 June 1938:

> 'What is the main purpose of the British Empire? I think it is the gradual spread of freedom amongst all His Majesty's subjects, in whatever part of the earth they live . . . .
>
> 'The spread of freedom in British countries overseas is a slow—sometimes a painful—evolutionary process [which had already resulted in the Dominions evolving as "completely free" and "fully sovereign nations"] . . .
>
> 'The same spirit guides our administration of the Colonial Empire. Even amongst the most backward races of Africa our main effort is to teach those peoples to stand always a little more securely on their own feet . . . the trend is towards the ultimate establishment of the various colonial communities as self-supporting and self-reliant members of a great commonwealth of free peoples and nations. The objective will be reached in different places at different times and by many different paths. Before it is reached there may be re-arrangements of political divisions; units at present separate may be combined, others may be split up into component parts. The important thing is to ensure so far as is possible that whatever changes are necessary should be so effected as to be in harmony with the general aim.'[18]

This was the first occasion on which self-government for British African

16. It would be tedious to cite the numerous uses of this concept. I will argue elsewhere that it was fundamentally an erroneous view of social developments which were taking place. That it existed was generally simply assumed by almost all commentators, official or unofficial, African and non-African, at this time. The concept was closely linked to ideas about class formation. For an example see Godfrey Wilson, *The Economics of Detribalization in Northern Rhodesia*, Rhodes Livingstone Institute, 1941, which argued strongly against migrant labour, and for government to follow policy which would recognize and stabilise a permanent urban African working class.
17. *Hansard*, H. C. 30 November 1939, Debate on the Address—'there is no division of imperial policy. We cannot have one policy for the Dominions and a totally different policy for the Colonies. The fundamental principle is the same. They are equal . . . at any given time the peoples of the Colonial Empire shall enjoy the maximum, practicable amount of freedom.'
18. CO 847/20/47139 at folio 1, and CO 323/1868 Pt II/9057 1A.

colonies had been proclaimed as a central purpose of colonial policy.[19] These objectives were announced publicly, though in more guarded terms, in the House of Commons on 7 December 1938.[20] A few days later, in a speech to the Constitutional Club, Macdonald referred to the end of an imperialism which could be seen as 'duping and domineering of weaker people' and proclaimed a 'new imperialism ... the gradual spread of liberty in every part of the colonial empire'.

By mid-1939 Macdonald was linking the idea of political advance with social and economic development by state action. British colonial rule had as its 'main purpose to enable her subjects throughout the Colonies and Protectorates to partake in ever larger measure of the benefits of modern education, of economic well-being, of education, of health and of a full enjoyment of life. We must repay their loyalty by giving back to them the best that lay in our power, the gift of self-government and freedom.' Further speeches in the Commons in June and November reiterated this position.[21]

The Colonial Secretary had evidently begun to contemplate what Leys calls 'the replacement of direct colonial authority by 'independent' governments'. Macdonald would likewise have put 'independent' in quotation marks. Did Macdonald proceed from this to consider which might be the 'local strata and classes' who might eventually man such governments?

Indeed, as we shall see, he did. But put in its *dependentista* jargon the question is naive, crude and conceals some of the most fascinating aspects of the problem.

In effect the disillusionment with indirect rule had pre-empted a choice which had never been a real choice anyway. Some colonial officers continued to argue that 'self-government' would amount to the restoration of sovereignty to precolonial states, but now they were sat upon firmly not only by the Colonial Office, but by governors such as Sir Bernard Bourdillon in Nigeria.[22] The most extreme advocate of this position was Sir Theodore Adams, Chief Commissioner of Northern Nigeria, who maintained that Emirs had 'subjects', that there was 'separate Emirate nationality', tried to insist that emirates

19. Professor Reginald Coupland, who attended the lecture, immediately noticed this, and stressed the point when pumping Macdonald's hand after the lecture. One could, by assiduous scholarship, find earlier references to an ultimate goal of 'self-government' in the writings of colonial servants in Africa, but these are hardly in the line of Macdonald's thought; rather, such writers are considering self-administration of future units which might be considered as protected states, and assume that power would rest in the hands of traditional rulers. It is interesting that Macdonald's words quoted above are almost a paraphrase of the last paragraph of the conclusion to Coupland's chapter on 'The Meaning of Empire' in his book *The Empire in These Days*, Macmillan, 1935, pp. 179–180.
20. *Hansard*, H. C., 7 December 1938.
21. The quotation is from a speech to the British Empire Society given on Empire Day in May 1939, CO 847/20/47139. The Commons speeches are in *Hansard*, H.C., 7 June 1939 and 30 November 1939.
22. Bourdillon, like Sir Alan Burns in the Gold Coast, was, however, hardly typical of the contemporary colonial governor, being much closer to the reforming movement in Britain. For his views on Nigerian politics and constitution plans see my article, 'Governor *versus* Colonial Office: An Anatomy of the Richards Constitution for Nigeria, 1939 to 1945', *Historical Papers/Communications historiques*, Canadian Historical Association, 1981, pp. 125–132 and *passim*.

had the right to all their revenues, argued that they were 'protected states' and asserted that 'The policy of a central African Government is incompatible with the Emirate system. One or other must be discarded.' Bourdillon firmly rejected these claims, which presented 'a grave danger of seriously compromising future political developments . . . If the Emirs cannot learn to see beyond the end of their own noses they are doomed'.[23]

Even given a willingness on the part of the chiefly élites to come together in federations, they could hardly be considered as a strata or class to whom power might ultimately be transferred.[24] Hailey's *Survey* had brought this out clearly. If social change were to be fostered by government action, the 'native administrations' seemed inappropriate and incompetant to undertake such functions so long as they remained under chiefly control. Their maintenance, according to Hailey, was in any case not 'an end in itself' and it was 'not unlikely' that they might even collapse and colonial governments be forced to undertake their functions by direct rule. Hailey raised the question of whether 'native administration' was 'incompatible with the growth of a large educated urban population?' Would the educated African tolerate 'orders from his inferiors in civilization?' He would insist on a system which guaranteed him 'British justice'. There seemed to be few prospects of absorbing the educated African into a chief-dominated system.[25]

It could be argued therefore that the class which would inherit colonial sovereignty—the comprador strata—had been identified beyond doubt as early as 1938.[26] It could only be the English-speaking literate professional group; only they could function in a 'national' setting and command the skills needed to manage a process of social change in a 'modern' state. This being so, following the logic of the neocolonial school, it should have been followed by a restructuring of policy designed to strengthen the bourgeoisie and prepare for the transfer of power. An obvious direction for such change would have been the extension of the elective principle to more urban centres, increasing the number of elected representatives in legislative councils, perhaps supported by the creation of numerous urban governments, elected on a property and educational franchise, and measures to transform 'native administrations' into local government bodies representative of these new elements. The existing West African voting franchise, restricted by property and education

23. CO 847/21/47100/1 *Comments . . . by . . . Bourdillon on Lord Hailey's Report*, Government Printer, Lagos, 1981, Confidential.
24. Unless, of course, British policy had been firmly neocolonial, and had taken active steps to transform the chiefly elite into a comprador landholding class, with sufficient western and technical education to run a neocolonial structure, as in Buganda.
25. Hailey, *African Survey*, pp. 538–42.
26. Always assuming, of course, that the British, for reasons which the *dependentista* thesis seems to be unable to explain, were unwilling to transfer power to existing settler compradors, perhaps with Indian immigrants coopted (an ambition of the East African Indian National Congress, for which they had bitterly fought since its early days) in East Africa, and the transformation of chiefly elites in West Africa, on the Buganda analogy.

qualification, even perhaps liberalized cautiously while excluding rabble, would have admirably suited the purpose of extending the power of a comprador bourgeoisie. At this time no serious critic of imperialism contemplated universal suffrage for African voters, so on that ground such moves would hardly have attracted criticism, but would have been hailed, even by foreign critics, as liberal reforms.[27]

From the documentary evidence, however, it is obvious that not a single person in the colonial establishment, and very few in Britain outside it,[28] were prepared even to consider such a course. Hailey's *Survey* shied away from decisive recommendations, arguing that the problem of 'native administration' needed extensive research and evaluation, but tentatively suggested the development of groupings of native administrations into regional councils which might serve as electoral colleges for central quasi-parliaments. Macdonald, in private discussions with Hailey, pointed out the inconsistency of developing indirect rule further and capping it with a parliamentary body. Hailey, ever cautious and never a man to be impressed with mere logic 'admitted the apparent inconsistency but said that he felt sure that every territory connected with Great Britain would turn towards the Parliamentary model, and that whether Parliamentary institutions were suitable to the country or not, they represented the most educative phase of political development— one through which every country must pass before it can find the political form best suited to its needs'.[29]

These were the desperate times between Munich and the outbreak of war, but in the Colonial Office Macdonald continued to press on with reform. His priority was to implement Moyne's report and pass a colonial development and welfare act, which was quickly drafted. Delayed by Munich and the Treasury Macdonald continued to press for it, successfully intervening with the Prime Minister and arguing, once the war broke out, that it would help to rally

27. Even in Britain universal suffrage was by no means clear until after 1945 in the sense of 'one (wo)man one vote'. Some persons could still not vote because they lacked householder (or housewife) status, and many property owners, as well as university graduates, held more than one vote. In the United States, of course, many states, by legal or other means, prevented blacks from registering as electors. The proposition that illiterates should not be permitted to vote was almost universally regarded as common sense, for in a system of secret ballot with voting papers which listed merely the candidates names without any system for permitting the listing of party symbols, it was not practical for an illiterate to vote. In all the areas of British non-self-governing territory where elective systems were established, literacy was a qualification for voting, with the striking exception of Ceylon, where universal suffrage had been introduced after 1931, with provision to assist illiterates in voting.
28. Coupland pressed the Colonial Office in September 1939 to begin constitutional advances in West Africa, arguing that the urban professionals 'could provide a quota of reasonably competent and public-spirited politicians'. His *The Empire in These Days*, p. 234–238 contains the first serious suggestions for parliamentary self-government in West Africa.
29. CO 847/13/47097. F2 Record of discussions between S. of S. and Lord Hailey, 6 December 1938. This is perhaps the first reference to an interesting concept which constantly reappears later. From the first it was the British who considered that African territories would need to work out specific African forms of 'democracy' and the Westminster model would probably not provide a suitable permanent constitution. Nationalists resisted this firmly. It can be said with some confidence that the emergence of the Westminster model was the result of nationalist insistance and not of imperial imposition.

colonial support for the war effort.[30]   Africa, however, remained high on the agenda.   As early as February 1939 officials were discussing ways to plan political change.   By an almost sacred tradition colonial governors should have been consulted, but several officials were anxious to by-pass gubernatorial opinion.[31]   O. G. R. Williams, head of the West African department, wanted to ask for the views of colonial governors, but opposed any idea of a governors' conference.   Planning, in his view, was urgent.   Britain should initiate change *before* Africans began to demand it 'rather than allow ourselves to be forced into the position of making concessions to the 'clamour of demagogues'[32]   This was a theme that would constantly reoccur in future planning discussions. Meanwhile Hailey's *Survey* was mined as a blueprint for change.[33]

The contradiction between the policy of 'native administration' and the development of legislative councils (which in neo-colonial terms may be seen as the attempt to identify the 'local strata and classes' to whom power might be transferred) had clearly emerged as the central issue of African policy discussion throughout 1939.   It was the theme of the interesting attempt to consult university opinion at a meeting in the Carlton Hotel on 6 October 1939, which revealed the surprising strength of the 'indirect rulers', with only Coupland pressing for constitutional advance on parliamentary lines.   If the 'nationalists' were to be wooed, it was evident that the courtship would fall short of any possibility of breach of promise.[34]

What lay behind this reluctance to identify the 'new strata' to which power could be handed over as part of the colonial reform strategy, given that common sense appeared to have defined the western educated elite as the only acceptable candidate in the long term?   There were two major difficulties, one severely practical, the other theoretical but no less significant.

The practical problem was that in 1939 a 'national' bourgeoisie capable of running a colonial state simply did not exist.   This was literally the case in

---

30.   I hope to develop this point further elsewhere.
31.   e.g. CO 847/13/47100, Min. by Preston 23 February 1939 strongly resisting any consultation with governors, and referring to governors who were 'lacking the necessary leisure or intelligence, or both' to make sensible comments, while chances were 'remote' that they would have views 'of significance or value'.
32.   *Ibid.* Min. by Williams, 7.3.39.
33.   Over 150 extracts were made into separate files of problems for discussion and solution.
34.   This meeting deserves rather more extensive treatment than space permits here.   Besides Macdonald and his senior officials, Hailey and Lugard attended.   That Lugard, the conqueror of northern Nigeria should have been present at the first serious discussion of planning for self-government, is indeed a historical curiosity.   It also is noteworthy that of the academics, all but one, the biologist Julian Huxley, were historians.   Coupland's was the most liberal academic view, and it was sharply contested by his junior colleague from Oxford, Margery Perham, who strongly defended Lugard's demand for regional councils of native administrations, arguing that 'the plane of the tribes' was the African reality, and not the 'plane of our big state system imposed artificially from above ... the intelligentsia are very rapidly acquiring political consciousness and naturally wish to capture the big state system.   We shall probably give in to them too soon.'   In minutes afterwards Perham was condemned as reactionary and representative of the kind of people who had caused much of the trouble in India.   CO 847/17/47135, Record of a discussion held at the Carlton Hotel, 6 October 1939, Minutes by Mahew, 2 November 1939; Keith 3 November 1939; Bushe 7 November 1939 and Seal 11 November 1939.

the eastern and central African territories (unless the British were prepared to accept the white settlers, Indians and Baganda chiefs as such). In West Africa such a bourgeoisie had begun to make its appearance and to articulate a 'nationalist' political philosophy, which was of course essential if the integrity of the colonial political unit and its economy were to be preserved, but it was far too small to be considered capable of manning the administrative system. Much more statistical work needs to be done before we can estimate numbers of the professionally educated with any degree of accuracy, but it is clear that these were extremely small. In the Gold Coast, with the largest educated group in proportion to population of any African colony, there were only 1,000 children in secondary education in 1939, and only 31 at Achimota College, most of whom were preparing for London intermediate BA exams.[35] Only 3,000 electors could qualify for the £100 franchise in Nigeria, and of these it is likely that less than one-third were educated at secondary level.[36] There were a few dozen Africans attending universities in Britain, fewer in the USA, where we know there were twelve university students from Nigeria when war broke out.[37] West Africa alone, therefore, could offer precursors of a coming bourgeoisie, but not a viable class capable of assuming power. The discussion had merely identified a *future* class to which power could *eventually* be transferred.

The way forward was clearly to create such a viable class and this was indeed planned and executed even during the war. The Advisory Committee on Education (ACEC), responding to the reluctance of the West African Governors' Conference to endorse such a development in 1939, made a vigorous counter-attack demanding the immediate establishment of planning for African universities. Their stance was almost completely political; 'a university which fully trains graduates to occupy positions of responsibility' was 'essential to any complete development' and 'progress will be gravely embarrassed unless the essential preliminary steps towards the creation of a university are taken in the immediate future'.[38] This initiative led directly to the creation of the Asquith and Elliot Commissions and resulted eventually in the creation of the university colleges at Legon, Ibadan, Makerere and Khartoum, as well as in the West Indies. Paradoxically, the University of London was given an educational colonial empire as part of the road to decolonization.[39]

35. CO 847/16/47122/1 F8, Minutes of 94th meeting of the Advisory Committee on Education, 18.5.39, comments of Miss Oakden.
36. The property franchise enable many traders to qualify. In Lagos the strong Muslim role in elective politics after 1923 is evidence that the electorate was hardly coterminous with the western educated élite, as many scholars once assumed. See R. Sklar, *Nigeria Political Parties*, Princeton, 1963, p. 46. Sklar is in error when he writes on p. 52 that only 792 voted in the Lagos town council elections of 1938; some 1,500 did so.
37. Sklar, *op. cit.*, p. 73.
38. CO 847/18/47029. Report of the sub-committee of ACEC . . . 4.12.1940, quotations from Part II, pp. 50–1.
39. Secretary of State Stanley's letter to the Vice Chancellor of London University, confidential, of 29 May 1943, soliciting co-operation in the plan, put this paradox very consciously. Stanley

Footnote 39 continued on next page

The ardent neocolonial theorist, at this point, may be tempted to shout 'Eureka!' Having identified their ideal compradors, and finding them lacking in quantity, the British proceeded to create more of them. This is indeed the planning of neocolonialism.

Such a conclusion ignores the other strain of thought which lay behind the reluctance to begin reform along parliamentary lines, the theoretical issue which was referred to earlier. The British were not, in fact, gifted with machiavellian skills and prophetic insights (or their colonial reform movement would not have degenerated into rapid constitutional advance in the 1950s or the scramble for decolonization of the 1960s). They appear to have had no aspirations whatsoever for the role of puppet-masters. A question of the legitimacy of political authority lay beneath all these discussions. From the international perspective Macdonald's statements implied that colonial rule could only be legitimized if its purpose was eventual self-government.[40] Hailey's writings had thoroughly undermined the assumptions of earlier times that indirect rule was self-evidently legitimate, because it was 'traditionally African' and run through 'natural rulers', by insisting that native administrations needed popular acceptance before they could be considered viable. The 'new strata' might well be able, with expansion of their numbers, to run a post-colonial state—but where was their legitimacy? Certainly not in the property and educational franchise, which ensured oligarchy. Nor, as yet, in universal suffrage, which, in the absence of an educated electorate, would produce something worse, oligarchy compounded by demagogy and corruption. The British were indeed looking for inheritors, 'leaders', 'nationalists' and the like, but unless these could be used to develop self-government they could not be made legitimate. At the end of 1939 G. Seel commented that if the time was near for 'Africans who would take part in the deliberations of a national assembly' they must be 'sufficiently representative of the great mass of their fellow Africans... the method of selection will require the most careful

urged the British universities to do their patriotic duty and transform their links with Empire. In the past they had trained and nourished pro-consuls and imperial administrators, now their task would be 'no less vital by taking the form of assistance in the development of Colonial Universities which will rear the local leaders of the future.' The letter is quoted in Eric Ashby, *Universities, British, Indian, and African: a study in the ecology of higher education*, Harvard, 1966, pp. 211–212.
40. There was a strong awareness of the point, which is nowadays discarded into a limbo, that self-government is a much deeper and more fundamentally important principle than sovereign independence of the state. One colonial office official, in a minute resisting American pressure for colonial 'independence', commented that the word independence was 'a political catchword which has no real meaning apart from economics. The Americans are quite ready to make their dependencies politically 'independent' while economically bound hand and foot to them and see no inconsistency in this', CO 323/1858/9057B Min. By Eastwood, 21 April 1943, quoted in W.R. Louis, *Imperialism at Bay*, p. 247. The documents could hardly be mined to find a clearer rejection of neocolonial planning, though many statements along these lines could be found. At the same time Eastwood's futures were wrong; the Americans subsequently did not move to grant independence to their colonial possessions after the war, except in the Phillipines, but integrated them more intensely into the USA, Alaska, Hawaii and Puerto Rico developed self-government and not independence, while as it turned out British Africa in the main ended up with independence but not self-government.

consideration'. It could be 'taken for granted that anything in the shape of direct election . . . will be out of the question for some time to come.'[41] The implications of this kind of thinking were that Britain could not decolonize to mere compradors; the new elite would have to demonstrate that it had genuine support from the masses at large. Ultimately the African elite would discover that this principle was their key to success; by confronting Britain with organized mass nationalist parties the entire house of cards of colonial reform planning could be brought to the ground after 1948.

Thus, in the months before and just after the outbreak of the second world war, a revolution of attitudes had taken place and a mood of colonial reform taken hold. In the economic sphere the doctrine of *laissez faire* had been breached with the Colonial Development and Welfare Act. But in the political sphere, though self-government was now the goal of planning, nothing practical had been decided. The old compradors of settlers and chiefs were losing centre stage, and new 'classes' or peasants, proletarians and professionals being written into the script. But the plot was far from clear. The situation called for the intervention of a *deus ex machina*, and as usual Lord Hailey was expected to fulfill that role.[42]

Towards the end of 1939 Macdonald decided to commission Hailey to undertake a comprehensive study in Africa, and to make fundamental policy recommendations, especially as to how the 'native administration' policy could be harmonized with development of the legislative councils and parliamentary forms. In discussing the task with Hailey Macdonald outlined virtually all the major questions of African policy:

> 'It was time that we got our minds clearer as to the objects of our native policy in Africa. What exactly were we driving at in our policy of 'indirect rule'? What was the next step in advance after we had set up efficient *local* native administrations?
>
> '[Where there was] . . . a considerable European minority, how was govern-

---

41. CO 847/13/47100/f7 Mem., no title, date or signature, but written by Seel sometime before 2 December 1939, on which date he sent it to Boyd.

42. Lord Hailey's rise to an extraordinary position of prominence in Colonial Office influence has yet to be explained. Despite his great age, the fact that his experience was entirely in India as a practical administrator, and that he held only *ad hoc* and advisory positions in the Office, Hailey's was the single most powerful influence on the shaping of policy from 1938 to 1945, after which he became eclipsed by Sir Andrew Cohen. Probably his Indian experience was considered an important asset, for the Colonial Office constantly held the view that British policy in India, and especially relations with the nationalist movement, had been mismanaged beyond repair, and that these mistakes must be avoided in Africa. The lack of systematic and organized research in Africa also gave the *African Survey* an enormous prestige, for there was no other comparable work of reference. Above all, however, Hailey's temperament and attitudes, combining progressive thought and caution, experience and experiment with a sense that 'sound' history could be made by evolutionary stages which tried to keep economics, social change, educational and scientific progress all in tune with each other, admirably suited the mood of the times in Britain, where the idea of 'sound planning' was taking deep root after 1938. His influence on colonial policy can be compared with that of Lord Beveridge in domestic social policy.

ment to be organized *ultimately* so that native interests were not sub-ordinated to European interests and vice versa?[43]

Without general objectives, Macdonald asserted, there was a real danger of taking *ad hoc* steps which could not later be reversed.   In addition, Hailey was asked to visit Southern Rhodesia, to see if any measures could be taken to bring that country's 'native policy' into some kind of harmony with British policy, without which 'Amalgamation (with Nyasaland and Northern Rhodesia) was impossible.'   All the political aspects of his mission would be kept secret; ostensibly it would be announced that he was making further studies of 'native administration'.[44]   The political aspects were made crystal clear in Macdonald's request for Treasury funds for the mission:

> 'The war is likely to create a demand in Africa for a quickening in the pace of development towards self-governing institutions . . . we shall be wise to anticipate this demand (with) . . . carefully thought out plans.   . . . we should pursue a slowly but surely developing policy of training Africans to look after many of their own affairs.'

The problem of the future of indirect rule and how it could be harmonized with the aspirations of 'detribalized natives' was urgent.[45]

Hailey's 1940 visit to Africa was perhaps the last of the epic and eccentric 'travels in Africa' genre, though this frail old man's adventures were in rickety aeroplanes rather than picturesque canoes and steamboats.   In the midst of his inquiries he undertook a brilliantly successful mission to bring the Belgians in the Congo into line with the British cause after the surrender of their King.   His report took a year to complete and was submitted to the Colonial Office in February 1941.[46]   Here only the fundamental lines of the report can be addressed.   From present-day perspectives it is difficult to assess; had it been published in the mid-1950s it would have been condemned by African nationalists as reactionary, but a present generation of young Africans may be tempted to see it as deep and subtle, full of forebodings and warnings of the future.

At the outset of his report Hailey made basic recommendations which were to form axioms of planning for both the Coalition and the Labour governments

---

43.   The underlined words were inserted into the draft record of the conversation in Macdonald's handwriting.
44.   CO 847/16/47100/1/F1 Mem. by S. of S. of a conversation with Lord Hailey, 5 September 1939.
45.   *Ibid.* Macdonald to Sir John Simon, draft at F2.
46.   The original, from which the summary and comments below are taken, is to be found in CO 847/21/47100/1.   This version was published as a C.O. Confidential Reprint for the use of the colonial service as *Native Administration and Political Development in British Tropical Africa* in 1944, but several important passages were omitted from the printed version as a result of governors' objections, especially from Kenya.   It is this version which is republished recently, with an excellent introduction, by A. Kirk-Greene, F. Cass and Co., 1980.

until the collapse of colonial reform after 1948.   Economic and social development must form the base for, and take precedence over, political advance. The former must be regarded as the essence and foundation of reform, while political change was a superstructure which could only reflect the more fundamental changes, and must be in tune with them.   This point was constantly hammered home throughout the report in almost every detailed recommendation in every region.   Hailey saw no problem in reconciling the two so long as, from the first stages, Africans took part in planning and execution of the social and economic developments.   This would entail the transformation of 'native administration' into local government by 'a resolute development of local institutions combined with the progressive admission of Africans to all branches of the government services.'   At the same time this brand of what might be called socio-economic decolonization implied an Indian summer of imperial control, 'until experience has shown us under what constitutional forms the dependencies can move most securely towards the final stages of self-government.'

Hailey then proceeded to endorse all the candidates for the inheritance of imperial power, while doubting the fitness or legitimacy of any.   The Native Authorities were not the 'natural heirs' and he rejected the view that they had inherent rights from traditional African legitimacy.   A future self-governing central government could not be simply a federation of Native Authorities, which were not representative of many facets of African societies, certainly not of the urban areas, and not of some rural areas where indirect rule could not be based on traditional society.   Native Authorities could be used, especially in the 'earlier stages of political development' as electoral colleges for a central legislature and also to form 'regional conferences' to discuss issues before legislative council meetings.   But similar functions could also be allotted to the pan-tribal Unions which had made their appearance in the 1930s, to the urban municipalities and even to professional associations.

The 'intelligentsia' must also be absorbed into the 'advanced institutions of central government' by increased representation in legislative Council, admission to the civil service, and being given extensive experience in urban government, taxation and provision of social services.   Hailey saw the difficulties which would come from the response to such moves by the educated elements, 'unable to read the future in any other terms than the expansion of parliamentary institutions of the normal type', but they must be resisted, for advance along parliamentary lines was irrevocable, while experimentation with other forms was not.   Perhaps by such trial and error experiments in representation, 'full powers' could later be transferred to a legislature 'not constituted in the nomral way'.   Such a body might well be more stable, more truly representative of Africans and more effective than the alien Westminster model.

Hailey's report became a kind of organic blueprint for the colonial reform movement.   Almost every plan, and all the schemes for constitutional advance[47] until the Accra Riots of 1948, bore the stamp of Hailey's ideas. Even the much-trumpeted local government despatch circularized by Creech Jones in 1947 merely carried out the democratization of indirect rule which Hailey would have wished to see inaugurated by stages in 1941.   Throughout 1941–2 Hailey in effect became the Grand Panjandrum of colonial planning in his capacity as Chairman of the Colonial Office Committee on Postwar Reconstruction in the Colonies, seen self-consciously as uniquely forward-looking and ahead of other Ministries, and soon simply referred to as 'the Hailey Committee'.   No one with objectivity who has read the voluminous papers of this committee could leave them and continue to maintain the belief that the British were planning the development of underdevelopment.[48]   By April 1942 the committee had prepared a list of fifty subjects requiring action, or further research and decision.   This document represented no less than a total planning base for a massive scheme of colonial reform in which each item, however detailed, could be planned in an integrated and inter-related fashion.[49]

By this time, however, the British were being forced by American pressures, starting after the signature of the Atlantic Charter but intensifying after America's belated entry into the war, to concentrate not so much on detailed planning, but on public definition of policy and propaganda needs. This phase

47.   It is true that Burns and Bourdillon, governors of the Gold Coast and Nigeria respectively, forced through, against the opposition of the Colonial Office and Hailey, the admission of Africans as members of the Executive Councils in 1942, but the councillors were nominated and the effect was not so fundamental as it might appear.

48.   Indeed, a surprising amount of *dependentista* theory, in different jargon, seems embedded in the committee's papers, especially those dealing with economic problems.   The 'development of underdevelopment' several times seems to be outlined as the dire and probable consequence if the committees plans should *not* be implemented.   As with present-day radical commentators, there was great euphoria, characteristic of all war-time planning, that the boom and slump conditions affecting primary producers would be eliminated by international price planning, state marketing and rigid price controls.   This would form the base for capital formation for industrialization, and the flow of inward imports would also have to be controlled and planned, with rigid fixing of interest rates.   Planned self-sufficiency in food production was essential.   Long range planning had the general objective of 'raising the standard of life in the Colonial Empire itself'.   CO 967/13, Mem. by Clauson on the 'Colonial Economic Problems in the Reconstruction Period'. 31 May 1941. There were numerous discussions of industrialization in the colonies, in great detail, and careful identification of lobbies which would oppose it.   The Committee finally recorded that it agreed as a matter of principle, the development of secondary industry in the colonies should be encouraged in spite of opposition on the part of United Kingdom manufacturers whose interests might be affected.

49.   CO 961/13 is the collection of the papers of the Hailey Committee.   The 50 point list is contained in 'Schedule of subjects for consideration of actions taken', 7 April 1942.   Subjects covered included external relations, a long list of economic matters including marketing, quotas, tariffs, food production, industrialization, financial policy, soil conservation, railway finance, etc.   Constitutional and political change occupied several categories, with individual memoranda on each colony, and was linked to questions of the reorganization of African boundaries, the creation of larger units, future relations with the UK, other Dominions and foreign countries. Other broad categories, often broken down into detailed problems, included social change, broadcasting, airways, land reform, demobilisation, education, health (with a strong plea for priority to the financing of preventive medicine at the expense of curative facilities), the colonial service, the role of women, town and country planning, legislation against racial descrimination (to be introduced in the UK also), the prison system, trade unions, forest problems, and long range speculations on the ultimate objectives of reform.   Only the last item, '50. Eugenics' was not taken seriously; this, it was recómmended, 'should be left entirely to unofficial agencies'.

has been dealt with in great detail in Louis's *Imperialism at Bay*. In the practical sphere the effects of the American intervention were negative, diverting energy to abstract considerations and creating resentment which helped to stiffen conservative attitudes in the Colonial Office, while tipping the scales again towards the indirect rulers in the colonial service. For policy definition, however, the effects were positive (though the result was far from American desires). Churchill's insistence in September 1941 that the Atlantic Charter had no application to the British Empire opened up the field for Labour Party pressure by exposing the absence of well-defined public statements on the goals of colonial reform. Creech Jones, the future architect of West African decolonization, was enlisted to tour the USA and recruited (or infiltrated like the good Fabian he was) important Colonial Office committees on welfare, social and economic development, and education. He and Attlee played an important part in dealing with the Americans, and thus in defining policy.[50] The colonial reform movement had, since 1938, in effect pulled the goals of colonial policy in Africa close to the Labour Party's traditional colonial demands for protection of African labour, encouragement of trade unions, emphasis on social and economic development for Africans, more higher education for Africans, and the building of friendly relations with the educated elite.[51] Such emphases were, in any case, the only sound basis on which to resist American demands. This eventually bore fruit in the public statement which Creech Jones had continued to demand since 1941, when Colonial Secretary Oliver Stanley in July 1943, formally defined the objectives of British colonial policy and declared in the House of Commons that 'we are pledged to guide colonial peoples along the road to self-government within the framework of the British Empire'. This was firmly linked to the obligation 'to build up their social and economic institutions' in harness with an educational policy designed so that 'as quickly as possible people are trained and equipped for eventual self-government'. Economic and social development, and education, would thus parallel political change granting 'further and future responsibilities.'[52] A bi-partisan policy of colonial planning and reform had emerged, and would remain in effect until it foundered in Central African problems in the 1950s.

It soon became clear that this consensus included the West African nationalists as well. As Stanley was delivering his speech, the British Council, prompted by the Colonial Office, was preparing invitations for a West

---

50. In January 1943 formal negotiations began for an Anglo-American Declaration on the future of colonies, with Attlee handling the British end. His draft expressed the essentials of what would become Labour's policy after 1945, stressing the concept that social and economic development, coupled with an educational drive, must first create viable independent economies with just societies, which would be able to assume a real independence 'without danger to themselves and others'. CO 323/1858 Pt II/9057B. War Cabinet paper draft by Attlee, 1 January 1943; sent to US 8 January 1943, final draft to British ambassador in Washington, 1 January 1943.
51. P. S. Gupta, *Imperialism and the British Labour Movement, 1914–1964*, London, 1975 is the best overall treatment of Labour's colonial attitudes.
52. *Hansard*, 13 July 1943 House of Commons.

African delegation of newspaper editors to visit Britain. Given the almost non-existent state of any formal nationalist organizations in West Africa at the time there seemed no other means of contacting the potential nationalist leadership. Nnamde Azikiwe, the future first president of Nigeria, himself drafted the position paper which the editors presented to the Colonial Office— 'The Atlantic Charter and British West Africa'. It was a remarkable document, consistent in all respects but one with the British plan of colonial reform. It stressed 'social equality and communal welfare' and presented a detailed series of demands for social and economic development to form a base for future constitutional development along lines of democratic advance in rural, municipal and central government. This, they agreed, must be planned, gradual and evolutionary. In one respect only did their demands differ significantly from Colonial Office thinking; they boldly suggested a timetable. There should be unofficial majorities in the legislative councils as soon as practicable, and this should be followed by ten years of 'representative government', to be succeeded by five years of 'responsible government' after which each territory should become a Dominion.[53] This was not a bad margin of error, as political prophecies go, even when they are of the self-fulfilling variety.

If such a consensus was achieved as early as 1943, why then was the colonial reform movement in Africa such a colossal failure? For failure it was. Decolonization did not, except in a merely cosmetic sense, proceed by orderly evolutionary stages. It was not a process of finely tuning constitutional arrangements upon a base of fundamental economic and social change. It did not reflect growing self-consciousness of viable 'classes', peasantry, proletarians and bourgeoisie, balancing themselves in a democratic political evolution. No solid bases of rural and urban institutions emerged. The economies did not become sophisticated and self-sustaining. Independence, rather than self-government, triumphed in the end, as did the Westminster model and not a specific unique African form of democracy.[54] The parliamentary British model served only as a temporary expedient, generally collapsing within a few years of independence. In most of Africa the result of decolonization has been to entrench oligarchic government, whether this be military, one party or simple autocracy, in precisely the way which colonial reform planning sought so strenuously to avoid.

To answer this question satisfactorily will need a full monograph on the period from 1945 to 1951. But a number of tentative answers may be

53. N. Azikiwe, *The Atlantic Charter and British West Africa*, Lagos, n.d. (but printed late in 1943). The document was reproduced in the *Pilot*, 13 Sept 1943. It was delivered to Stanley on 1 August 1943. CO 554/133/33732 has the memorandum, and the minutes.
54. The recent constitutional changes in Nigeria may turn out to be an exception to this generalization. Though the new model of federalism is clearly the American constitution, the attempt to reconcile and harmonize precolonial nationalities with Nigerian nationality by the creation of states on ethnic lines displays some interesting and original ideas which do appear to be attempts to create 'freedom' and liberal institutions which could be rooted in an African reality.

suggested.   Fundamentally the whole notion of planning to create nations is profoundly imperialistic.   Its smacks of the *tabula rasa* attitudes towards the humanity of Africa so prevalent in the days of partition.   It is perhaps impossible to forecast human reactions to introduced change, and to herd men like cattle through the gates of a planned history.   Hailey was aware of this in his insistence that Africans should participate in their own planning from the first.

The plan was also over-ambitious, and characteristic of wartime euphoria and confidence.[55]   It assumed a post-war economic and financial capability which Britain did not possess.   British indebtedness and the dollar problem led to the exploitation of colonial export earnings, hoarding of their sterling balances, and reduced real African earnings, which the loyal nationalists were ready to bear in wartime, but which erupted in wide-spread strikes, riots and disturbances after 1945 and formed fertile soil for the transformation of elite reformism into mass nationalism on challenging and not the cooperative lines envisaged by the plan.   In the end this forced a policy of political decolonization to replace that of colonial reform.

London also gravely underestimated the power of resistance in the colonial service, and the difficulties of recruiting new cadres after the war.   Hailey's gradualism, and concept of working upwards by democratization of Native Administration, through regional bodies, to secure representation of 'the masses' at the centre could easily be manipulated into a rearguard action for the preservation of chiefly comprador elites.[56]   Local resistance meant that Africanization of the administrative service in the colonies proceeded at a snail's pace, with only a handful of Africans in service by 1945, despite an acute shortage of personnel.   Racism, officially condemned in London and in governors' circulars to district officers, remained rife and seriously compromised social cooperation with the educated elite.   Even at independence, white churches, schools, clubs, residential areas and beaches were still operating in West Africa.

The social thought which underlay the planning was also deeply in error.   The entire edifice was based on the concept of 'detribalization' and the assumption that class formation was inevitably replacing precolonial ethnicity in Africa.   This, it was believed, would lead inevitably to the politics of social welfare.   Instead, the challenge which the British threw down to the educated elite, that they must demonstrate their legitimacy with the support of the people, led not to leftist and rightist groupings, but to the politics of ethnic reality.   This was perhaps the fundamental flaw, for even had the British, after 1945, possessed the means to undertake a vast scheme of economic and social regeneration, the evidence would now suggest that this would have intensified ethnic consciousness even further.

55.   Paul Addison's *The Road to 1945*, Quartet Books, London, 1977 (first published by Cape, 1975) brilliantly conveys this spirit for British domestic history in the period.
56.   This point is examined in detail in my article, 'Governor *versus* Colonial Office . . .' cited in footnote 22.

[8]

Keeping India in the Commonwealth: British Political and Military Aims, 1947–49

Anita Inder Singh

On 27 April 1949, the Commonwealth Prime Ministers' Conference in London accepted India's request to allow her to remain in the Commonwealth as a republic. The Indian republic would not owe allegiance to the British Crown, which was the keystone of the Commonwealth, and the King would have no place in the government of India. This settlement marked a break with the Statute of Westminster of 1931, which had declared Commonwealth members to be united by 'a common allegiance to the Crown'. Republicanism, in the past synonymous with secession, was now accepted as compatible with full membership.

The resolution passed by the constituent assembly on 22 January 1947 had declared that India would become a sovereign, independent republic. However, in order to facilitate a smooth transfer of power, India agreed to temporary dominion status in August 1947, although no final decision about continuing membership in the Commonwealth was then taken. It was in December 1948 that the Congress passed a resolution expressing the desire of a republican India for continued association with the Commonwealth.[1] India's reasons for wishing to stay in the Commonwealth as a republic have already been analysed by historians.[2] Why the British acceded to India's request has not been detailed so far. Two main questions will therefore be raised in this paper, which is based largely on official British sources made available to scholars only recently under the third year rule. First, how did the British conceive the Commonwealth in the post-1945 era; second, why did they wish to keep India in it?

Partly by accident, partly by deliberation, the Commonwealth had seldom been defined. Lord Rosebery is first said to have used the term in 1884, while assuring an Australian audience that the 'fact of your being a nation need not imply any separation from the Empire...There is no need for any nation, however great, leaving the Empire, because the Empire is a commonwealth of nations.' English socialists apparently liked the idea of a Commonwealth of communities flying the British flag. That ideologue of the Commonwealth, Lionel Curtis, considered

Journal of Contemporary History (SAGE, London, Beverly Hills and New Delhi), Vol. 20 (1985), 469–481.

the word 'empire' a misnomer for self-governing nations within the Empire and conceived of a Commonwealth of nations; while General Smuts preferred to label 'a system of nations. . . a number of nations and states, almost sovereign, almost independent. . . who all belong to this group, to this community of nations. . . the British Commonwealth of Nations'.[3] The birth of the Commonwealth is usually traced to the achievement of dominion status by Canada in 1867. To some, the Commonwealth was synonymous with Empire; to others they were coterminous but implying a distinction between colonies and self-governing dominions within the Empire. The two did not contradict each other as it was assumed that colonies would eventually achieve self-government.[4] Indeed, as Patrick Gordon Walker, one-time Secretary of State for Commonwealth Relations, remarked, 'There could have been no Commonwealth had there not been a British Empire'.[5]

After 1945, protagonists of the Commonwealth showed pride in the common sense of purpose of its members, which they claimed existed precisely because the Commonwealth had no formal constitutional or political machinery. With the British King at its head, the Commonwealth was likened to a family, its members — Canada, South Africa, Australia, New Zealand and Ireland — united by race, culture and language; and family relationships were based on mutual accommodation and under-standing, not on contracts, the successful working of which, in any case, required a spirit of compromise. Formal organization would have destroyed the organic unity of the Commonwealth.[6] Within the family, members would attain self-government as they reached political maturity and were capable of exercising independence of judgement and action. Disagreements might prevail within the family, but all members would stand together in time of need. Since the first world war, the dominions had sought to assert their status as equals of Britain and to follow independent foreign policies, more related to their own interests. The Balfour Report of 1926 and the Statute of Westminster of 1931 defined their equality and autonomy.[7] The dominions had disassociated them-selves from British policy in the Chanak crisis of 1922; they had not endorsed the Locarno treaties of 1925 and the Anglo-Egyptian treaty in 1936;[8] but all had rallied behind the British in the second world war. Each dominion government had secured the support of its parliament to support the British; and the dominions had arrived independently at identical decisions, symbolizing the essential unity of the Commonwealth.[9]

The manner in which the Commonwealth family would function after 1945 would depend largely on the situation in which Britain and the dominions found themselves at the time. The British realized that they were no longer the primary global power, and that the USA was the ultimate bulwark of western security against the USSR.[10] With British resources greatly diminished by war, a White Paper admitted, in 1946, that Britain could not revert to its pre-war imperial role and that regional defence arrangements would be necessary in the future.[11] The British knew that their security was now tied up with that of West Europe; at the same time, West Europe was then taking the first steps to economic recovery and could not be relied upon to guarantee western security.[12] Meanwhile, the Soviet threat to the continent loomed large – in February 1948 the communists seized power in Czechoslovakia and in June 1948 began the Berlin blockade.

Could the Commonwealth play a role in this situation? The British had no doubt that it must serve as 'an independent and strong unit' among the world's chief powers. The Commonwealth was the fount of British power; and it gained strength through the united front it presented to the world. The integrity of each member was the common concern of all, so the defence of the UK was the 'vital concern', not only of the British but also of each separate member of the Commonwealth. Equally, the UK alone without the support of the Commonwealth 'would lose much of its *effective influence and flexibility of power*'. Indeed, the British Chiefs of Staff thought that one of the 'essential measures' required to assure British chances of survival and victory in a war was the maintenance of the united front of the Commonwealth.[13] All dominions shared the British desire to contain the Russians, and none thought it could stand on its own against them. Independent foreign policies and regional interests since 1919 had led the dominions, by the forties, into regional defence pacts to safeguard their security. Australia and New Zealand had signed the Canberra Pact in 1944;[14] Canada and the US had entered into the North American Defence Pact in 1940;[15] and, after the war, Canada sponsored the formation of NATO.[16] So the dominions, like the UK, sought post-war regional agreements with the Americans. What purpose did the Commonwealth then serve? The dominions had no wish to dissolve old family ties, through which they might be able to influence Britain's European policy, thereby enhancing their own international status.[17] On Europe, British relations were, by mid-1948, closer with the US than with the Commonwealth; but as head of the Commonwealth, Britain could envisage herself as the link between the US, Europe and the Commonwealth.[18] And the dominions would realize that the consolidation of West Europe could only safeguard the Commonwealth by building a barrier against the Russians.[19]

What role could India play in this setting? The international situation after 1945 necessitated considerable attention to western defence, but the absence of political co-ordination between Commonwealth countries made impossible any diplomatic or military liaison between them. [20] The British Chiefs had no doubt that India (and Pakistan) would be a 'most desirable addition' to Commonwealth defence. [21] India had been the backbone of British power since the nineteenth century, [22] providing four-fifths of the British defence effort east of Suez during the second world war. [23] Not surprisingly, any discussion on the transfer of power since the forties was usually accompanied by rumination on the participation of an independent India in the imperial defence system. The offer of dominion status with the right to secede from empire, made in the Cripps plan of March 1942, was qualified by the stipulation that power would be transferred to Indians subject to the signing of a treaty to safeguard British interests — and the war cabinet clearly had military interests on its mind. [24] In March 1946, the Labour government intended to accept the recommendation of an Indian constituent assembly for independence only if 'satisfactory arrangements' were made for the defence of the Indian Ocean area. [25] In May 1947, the imminence of partition did not dissuade Lord Mountbatten, then Viceroy, from suggesting to Nehru that India and Pakistan could establish a joint defence headquarters on the lines of the Austro-Hungarian empire before 1914. The Austrian and Hungarian armies had been separate, but there had been a defence headquarters consisting of representatives of both according to their strength, 'with the Emperor at its head'. [26] Military and foreign policy considerations received top priority in official memos and discussions during the negotiations for the transfer of power in 1946–47; and the India Office affirmed, on 8 November 1946, that the military aspect of a future treaty between India and Britain had received most consideration from the British, although it had never been mentioned to Indian leaders. [27] At a time when Britain was experiencing difficulty in raising sufficient forces to meet its international commitments, the withdrawal of more than 20,000 Indians who were manning most of the administrative sections of the SEAC would leave two alternatives to the British — either to replace them with local men — a task time-consuming and expensive — or to introduce British troops in the SEAC; but only at the cost of abandoning their commitments in the Middle and Far East. [28] One of India's main assets was, in fact, 'an almost inexhaustible supply of manpower'; India could produce 'almost as many soldiers as the Commonwealth could mantain'. [29] In October 1949, the Cabinet Defence Committee admitted:

The effect on Army organisation of the granting of self-government to India and Pakistan is often overlooked. For here was a highly trained expandable reserve on which we could count in time of emergency or war. While the cost of this Army to the United Kingdom in peace was relatively small, it was a definite factor in our potential military strength. [30]

The chief advantage of India to Britain was strategic; India was the only base from which the British could sustain large-scale operations in the Far East. If India left the Commonwealth, the British position in the North Indian Ocean would be weakened and oil suplies from the Persian Gulf could not be guaranteed. [31] The British conceived India's participation in a loose organization of Commonwealth defence. The maximum military requirement of India would be that she participate actively in any war in which the Commonwealth might get involved; the minimum was that she accept responsibility for her own frontiers. The British should also try to get Indian assistance in a Middle East war. India should accept only British assistance for maintaining the efficiency of her armed forces, and make available and maintain bases for offence at the required degree of readiness. [32] This conformed with the conclusion of the Commonwealth Defence Conference of 1946 that Commonwealth forces should be standardized and have uniformity of organization and training, and the closest possible liaison should be maintained between officers of dominions, so that collaboration between Commonwealth countries in war would be 'easy and effective'. [33] The British were concerned at Indian approaches to the USA for economic and military assistance; [34] and American diplomats in New Delhi resented British attempts to play off Indians against the US by warning them of the dangers of 'dollar imperialism'. [35]

Political discord and administrative exigency prompted the British to wind up the *Raj* in August 1947 without achieving any of the conditions that would have guaranteed their military and economic interests in an independent India. [36] Nevertheless, the fact that the British contemplated treaties to safeguard their interests in post-independence India, even while they hoped she would remain in the Commonwealth, suggests an attitude to India quite different from that to the old dominions. India owed her position in the Commonwealth to conquest; the 'natural link' of race, culture, common loyalties and instincts — in the words of the *Economist* — 'all that is involved when one people regards another as its own kith and kin' — did not exist between her and Britain. The 'old' Commonwealth could be 'an effective unity' without formal organization and treaties; with the membership of the new dominions of India, Pakistan and Ceylon, it would be difficult for the new Commonwealth to ensure that anything was understood 'unless it is put down on paper'. [37]

India's membership of the Commonwealth would, hopefully, secure for the British the ends they had sought to achieve before the transfer of power, and contrary to some suggestions, [38] neither the bitterness between India and Pakistan arising from the partition riots and their aftermath, nor the outbreak of hostilities between them over Kashmir in September-October 1947, nor even the abolition of the post of the Supreme Commander of the forces of India and Pakistan and India's request that British forces withdraw from her territory by the end of 1947 instead of June 1948, lessened the British desire to keep India in the Commonwealth. Anticipating India's requests for military aid to build up her armed forces after independence, the British thought that any discussions on such issues should be linked to a military treaty between the two countries. A. V. Alexander, then Minister of Defence, advised Attlee in November 1947 that 'our future relationship with the Governments of the two Dominions [India and Pakistan] will be dependent on the success of the proposed defence negotiations. It seems important, therefore, that if this fact is not appreciated by the two Dominions, it should be made quite clear to them now.' [39] The Chiefs of Staff cautioned the cabinet that the British stand in the UN Security debates on the Kashmir issue should not adversely affect the chances of securing defence collaboration with India. [40]

The issue of service conditions of British officers in India provides an interesting illustration of the keenness of the cabinet to encourage India to remain in the Commonwealth, and also to dissuade her from turning to 'foreign powers'. While India had asked for the withdrawal of all British officers by December 1947, the British had anticipated that some would be required to help train the Indian army. Needing British officers far more than India, Pakistan had agreed to a British condition that they would remain under British jurisdiction. India, however, resisted the suggestion that an Indian Commander-in-Chief would not be able to try British soldiers under his command as 'wholly incompatible' with dominion status. The Cabinet Defence Committee decided in November 1947 that acceptance of the British claim would indeed establish 'a colour-bar incompatible with Dominion Status'. The realization that acceptance of the British condition would embarrass the Indian government weighed with the cabinet, and Alexander advised that as the retention of India within the Commonwealth was a 'matter of major strategic importance to us we should not lightly weaken the position of the present Indian administration'. Extra-territorial rights for British officers might also result in recurrent friction 'which might have an important influence on India's ultimate decision whether or not to stay in the Commonwealth'. The British would inform Pakistan of the agreement with India and express readiness to offer Pakistan the same terms. The Indian request for British officers, would, after all, provide the British with the opportunity to co-ordinate India's armed forces with those of other Commonwealth countries, thus achieving the standardization of Commonwealth forces that they sought. [41]

The absence of any written rules made it difficult for the British to define the obligations of Commonwealth membership to India, especially when no regular military or other contribution, such as the British hoped to obtain from India, was forthcoming from the other dominions. No organization existed for consultation in foreign policy and defence, and the cabinet acknowledged that a common foreign policy of the Commonwealth was not susceptible to definition. [42] But even if such a mechanism had existed, the British would have had to contend with Nehru's belief in non-alignment for India; there remained the problem of a republican India in the Commonwealth owing no allegiance to the Crown. By the beginning of 1949, the communist threat to Europe remained; the Middle East was unstable; a communist take-over of China seemed imminent, and Burma and Eire had chosen to leave the Commonwealth. Against this background, the Foreign, Colonial and Commonwealth Relations Offices debated, in January-February 1949, the possibility of keeping an Indian republic in the Commonwealth. The Foreign Office noted that Nehru's emphasis on non-alignment and the abolition of colonialism suggested that he was interested in achieving leadership of an Asia from which all western influence had been excluded, and that this took precedence over the struggle against communism or any conception of Commonwealth solidarity. The aims of India and Britain were therefore somewhat different; but on the other hand, India's adherence to the United Nations and her economic dependence on the Commonwealth — 45 per cent of her total trade was with the Commonwealth and 28 per cent with the UK — implied that it would not be in her interest to break completely with the Commonwealth. The main political advantage of retaining a republican India in the Commonwealth would be the preservation of the size and power of the Commonwealth in 'the eyes of the world, and particularly of potential aggressors'. Such a settlement would be 'a further tribute to the Anglo-Saxon genius for compromise'; and continuing consultation and collaboration would provide the best conditions for the growth of Anglo-Indian attachment and enable the Commonwealth 'to influence the young Indian State during it [sic] adolescence, and would provide opportunities for influencing Indian policy'. It would be 'specially unfortunate' if India were thrust out of the Commonwealth of which she desired to remain a member, if the 'sole basis for her exclusion was the insistence . . . on constitutional forms connected with the Crown'.

On the other hand, a neutral, republican India inside the Commonwealth might suggest the 'material weakness' of the British, which was making them 'so anxious to gain India's goodwill that they were prepared to do so at the cost of undermining the traditional basis on which the Commonwealth has hitherto rested'. It could be argued that a Commonwealth united by the Crown, though smaller, would be more cohesive and exercise a greater influence in world affairs.

The Colonial Office thought that India's presence in the Commonwealth would lessen problems with Indian settlers in British colonies, while her secession would probably have a detrimental effect on relations between Indians and British subjects. Even a friendly treaty relationship with India would fail to check the bad effects of 'India's complete independence . . . on the future of constitutional development in Colonial territories'. It would increase the influence of extreme nationalists in the colonies and reduce that of 'more responsible political leaders who are content that their peoples should remain within the Commonwealth'.

The Foreign Office did point out that a friendly India could have close treaty relations with the British, and if the treaty included mutual guarantees against aggression, the resulting clarification of Anglo-Indian relations would be beneficial, and Anglo-Indian relations might become 'easier than they are under the Commonwealth system, where rights and obligations are undefined and are left to the good sense and good feelings of the different Governments'. Commonwealth countries would be able to treat each aspect of their relations with India 'strictly on its merits'. Under the 'stress of world events', India might actually seek to renew Commonwealth support and offer greater reciprocity 'than she does at present'.

Nevertheless, India's secession from the Commonwealth would have 'world-wide repercussions'. The Soviet Union had voted for the admission to the UN of Burma, which had left the Commonwealth, while vetoing the application of Ceylon, which remained a member, and India's departure from the Commonwealth would probably be 'exploited to the full'. India might well come under Soviet influence and show 'greater intransigence' in world affairs. If India did leave the Commonwealth, the negotiations with her should be conducted so that she did so in an atmosphere of goodwill and with 'intentions conducive to the continuance of a friendly association with the countries of the Commonwealth'. Every effort should be made to avoid a situation which would encourage India to become a 'foreign State' with no close treaty ties with Commonwealth countries. [43]

For the Chiefs of Staff, it mattered little whether or not India remained in the Commonwealth — what was of concern was a friendly India. If India did aim at being the leading nation in South-East Asia, it was 'only reasonable to suppose' that she would desire friendly relations with the Commonwealth. [44] On 14 February 1949, they had suggested that India should be given assistance, even if she left the Commonwealth, to encourage her to take the lead against communism. [45] By the beginning of April 1949, the Chiefs had concluded that India was unlikely to agree to any treaty which demanded 'mutual defence plans' with the British 'for a region of common interest'. They left it to the cabinet to decide whether defence co-operation should grow out of 'the existing friendly relationship' with India. [46]

Among Commonwealth Prime Ministers, opinion on a republican India in the Commonwealth varied. Chifley of Australia and Senanayake of Ceylon favoured India's membership at any cost. Peter Fraser of New Zealand, however, thought that the Commonwealth would be 'weaker with India in than with India out', and preferred to have 'our British peoples prepared to stick together and cut our losses than to have a flabby Commonwealth with no clear guiding principle'. Malan of South Africa believed that Nehru, as an Indian nationalist and 'as an Asiatic will above all' fear the Soviet Union. Therefore 'whether India is in or out of the Commonwealth she will be on the side of the Western powers', while there might be acrimonious exchanges between India and the British on colonialism in Africa and Asia.

The cabinet favoured taking the risk. India in the Commonwealth would be susceptible to Commonwealth influence and the British would maintain 'a solid front against communist domination in the East', and have a better hope of 'true understanding' between East and West. The British might not in reality be able to influence India's foreign policy — 'we shall be making an act of faith', wrote Philip Noel-Baker, then Secretary of State for Commonwealth Relations, 'based on the belief that her contact with us will work a speedy and effective evolution'. The British could hope that India's support for the United Nations would be 'a decisive factor' in formulating her foreign policy, and it was on that basis that the Commonwealth could 'most profitably seek to mould her views and influence her action', and modify the philosophy underlying non-alignment. [47]

So Attlee convened a conference of Commonwealth Prime Ministers at the end of April 1949 to consider India's desire to stay in the Commonwealth as a republic. On 27 April the Prime Ministers unanimously agreed to recommend to the King that an Indian republic should remain in the Commonwealth, which would accept him as its head.[48]

The prestige of a united Commonwealth was expected to outweigh the disadvantages of the Indian republic in the group. In any case, there was never any certainty that even a friendly India would accept all the British terms in a treaty.[49] No obligations were imposed on India as the price of membership; there was only the hope that the Commonwealth would be able to influence in its favour Indian foreign and defence policies. Where other dominions were not involved in British military arrangements in Europe and the Middle East, the British could hardly have demanded this condition of India. India would have refused to pay such a price; and a rancorous 'England versus India' debate would have started anew, with England being accused of imperialist highhandedness at a time when it seemed to her essential that the façade of Commonwealth unity be preserved. Coming less than three weeks after the formation of NATO on 4 April 1949, the Commonwealth decision enhanced its status and that of Britain as head of the Commonwealth. Given Britain's adherence to the Western bloc, India's non-alignment appeared to be coloured by pro-Western hues. It was Malan of South Africa, whose apartheid policies India attacked most vociferously, who summed up the advantages to the Commonwealth of the membership of a republican India:

> ...India is anti-communist and in the present dangerous state of world affairs, that means a great deal to us. Asia — and I am thinking more particularly of China — is becoming more and more overwhelmed by communism. If we lose the goodwill of India, if we lose the co-operation of India, then not only the Commonwealth but the anti-communist Western Powers will lose...an extremely important foothold in Asia...In recent years, certain parts of the Commonwealth have broken away. Ireland has left the Commonwealth, Burma has declared herself an independent republic outside the Commonwealth...India has declared her intention to become a republic. The impression may easily be created...that the Commonwealth is disintegrating, that it is no longer a powerful force in a world...in which there is the possible threat of war...and the threat of aggression from Russia...The decision that was taken at the conference was undoubtedly a decision that will give the world a different impression that the Commonwealth is still a power in world affairs...It was of the greatest importance that the impression that the Commonwealth was collapsing should be removed...[50]

Singh: *Keeping India in the Commonwealth, 1947–49* 479

Notes

1. N. Mansergh, 'Commonwealth Membership', in N. Mansergh et al., *Commonwealth Perspectives* (Durham 1958), 30. For the text of the Statute of Westminster, see N. Mansergh (ed.), *Documents and Speeches on British Commonwealth Affairs, 1931–1952* (London 1953), I, 1.

2. J. D. B. Miller, *The Commonwealth in the World* (London 1958), 137–59; M. Brecher, 'India's Decision to Remain in the Commonwealth', *Journal of Commonwealth and Comparative Politics*, 12, 1975, 62–90; S. Gopal, *Jawaharlal Nehru: A Biography, II, 1947–1956* (London 1979), 43–55.

3. N. Mansergh, *The Commonwealth Experience* (London 1969), 19–22.

4. W. D. McIntyre, *Colonies into Commonwealth* (London 1966), 143–44.

5. P. Gordon Walker, *The Commonwealth* (London 1962), 15.

6. R. G. Menzies, 'The Commonwealth Problem: Union or Alliance', *Foreign Affairs*, 27, 2 (January 1949), 263–73; Lord Altrincham, 'The British Commonwealth and the Western Union', *Foreign Affairs*, 27, 4 (July 1949), 601–17; Earl Attlee, *Empire into Commonwealth* (London 1961), 23 and 26.

7. McIntyre, op. cit., 134–44.

8. Mansergh, *Commonwealth Experience*, 212ff.

9. N. Mansergh, *The Name and Nature of the British Commonwealth* (Cambridge reprint 1955), 16–17.

10. COS Joint Planning Staff paper JP (47) 93, 'Strategic Summary', 16 October 1947, DEFE 4/8; and W. R. Louis, *Imperialism at Bay* (Oxford 1977), 548–50.

11. W. D. McIntyre, *The Commonwealth of Nations: Origins and Impact 1869–1971* (Minneapolis 1977), 347.

12. JP(47)93, DEFE 4/8.

13. Ibid. and Cabinet Defence Committee paper DO(48)12, 'Statement Relating to Defence', 23 January 1948, CAB 131/6. Emphasis mine.

14. Mansergh, *Documents and Speeches*, I, 547–48.

15. Mansergh, *Documents and Speeches*, II, 1157–63.

16. K. Harris, *Attlee* (London 1982), 312.

17. McIntyre, *Commonwealth Origins*, 343–44.

18. Note by N. Charles, 14 May 1948; and CPM(48)5, 'Commonwealth Interest in Collaboration with Western Europe', 5 October 1948, PREM 8/734.

19. N. Mansergh, 'Postwar Strains on the British Commonwealth', *Foreign Affairs*, 27, 1 (October 1948), 129–42.

20. Cabinet Committee on Commonwealth Relations paper CR(48)2, 'Commonwealth Relationship', 21 May 1948; and Cabinet Committee on Commonwealth Relations CR(48) 2nd meeting, 31 May 1948, CAB 134/118.

21. JP(47)93, DEFE 4/8.

22. C. Barnett, *Britain and Her Army* (London 1970), 480; M. Howard, *The Continental Commitment* (London 1972), 17–18.

23. Cabinet Official Committee on Commonwealth Relations, CR(0)(47) 2nd meeting, 8 August 1947, CAB 134/117.

24. War Cabinet Committee on India, 1(42) 2nd meeting, 27 February 1942; War Cabinet Committee on India paper 1(42)5, 28 February 1942; Amery to Linlithgow, (Telegram) 1 March 1942, N. Mansergh (ed.), *TOP*, I, 262, 265 and 273 respectively.

25. A. Inder Singh, 'Imperial Defence and the Transfer of Power in India, 1946–1947', *International History Review*, 4, (November 1982), 570–76.

26. Viceroy's Miscellaneous meeting, 10 May 1947, *TOP*, X, 736.

27. Monteath to Machtig, 8 November 1946, *TOP*, IX, 31.

28. COS Joint Planning Staff paper JP(47)47(Final), 'Withdrawal of Indian Forces', 27 May 1947, DEFE 4/4. See also enclosure in Pethick-Lawrence to Wavell, 26 September 1946, *TOP*, VIII, 598–604.

29. Enclosure 2 in Wavell to Pethick-Lawrence, 13 July 1946, ibid., 57.

30. Cabinet Defence Committee paper DO(49)66, Memorandum by Minister of Defence on 'The Requirements of National Defence: Size and Shape of the Armed Forces 1950–1953', 18 October 1949, CAB 131/7.

31. Enclosure 2 in Wavell to Pethick-Lawrence, 13 July 1946, *TOP*, VIII, 56–57.

32. Enclosure in Hollis to Monteath, 4 October 1946, ibid., 661–62; annex to COS(47)118th meeting, 10 September 1947, DEFE 4/7; and JP(47)93, DEFE 4/8.

33. Mansergh, *Documents and Speeches*, II, 1191–92.

34. COS(47) 141st meeting, 14 November 1947, DEFE 4/8.

35. *Foreign Relations of the United States*, II, 1947 (Washington 1972), 177.

36. Secretary of State to Viceroy, (Telegram) 3 July 1947, L/P&J/10/121; and Cabinet India and Burma Committee paper IB(47)135, 'Defence Arrangements in India', 3 July 1947, CAB 134/136.

37. *Economist*, 9 October 1948.

38. R. J. Moore, *Escape from Empire* (Oxford 1983), 338.

39. A. V. Alexander to Prime Minister, 13 November 1947, PREM 8/930.

40. Secretary, COS to Commonwealth Relations Office, 9 January 1948, annex 1 to COS(48)4th meeting, and minute 2 of same meeting, DEFE 4/8.

41. Cabinet Commonwealth Affairs Committee CA(47)3rd and CA(47)4th meetings, 31 October and 14 November 1947 respectively, CAB 134/54.

42. CR(48)2, CAB 134/118.

43. The following paragraphs are based on Cabinet Official Committee on Commonwealth Relations papers GEN 276/1 to 276/4. Much of the material in these papers was incorporated into GEN 276/6, 'India's Future Relations with the Commonwealth', 22 February 1949, and it is from this that the quotations have been taken. CAB 130/45.

44. COS(49)31st meeting, 21 February 1949, DEFE 4/20.

45. COS(49)25th meeting, 14 February 1949, DEFE 4/19.

46. COS(49)53rd meeting, 8 April 1949, DEFE 4/21.

47. Noel-Baker to Attlee, 20 April 1949, and annexes A and B to same, CAB 21/1824.

48. For discussion on changes in nomenclature, see PREM 8/802, DO 35/2187 and DO 35/2250.

49. Cabinet Committee on Commonwealth Relations CR(49)17, 11 April 1949; note by Secretary (Norman Brook), 'Treaty Relations with India'; CAB 134/119. It is interesting that there is so little emphasis on Indian non-alignment in British official despatches between 1947 and 1949. British interest in military arrangements with an independent India persisted in spite of Nehru's repeated declarations of India's intention to remain non-aligned even before the transfer of power in August 1947 — and continued well after that date. I have been both surprised and bemused that it is not until the beginning of 1949 that the prospect of a neutral India (as distinct from a merely republican India) within the Commonwealth was discussed seriously by British officials, although it was not altogether absent — it is a question of the emphasis in the documents. At the same time, the terms of treaties were drawn up — presumably in case they *did* materialize — and it is curious that the

draft treaties drawn up in 1949 differed very little from those outlined in 1946, when the British thought (mistakenly, as it turned out) that they would be able to make the transfer of power conditional upon their securing satisfactory military arrangements with the Indian constituent assembly. Once it was decided to allow a republican India in the Commonwealth, British hopes of a military treaty intensified. Curiously, British officials tended to blame Indo-Pakistani hostility rather than Indian non-alignment for the absence of defence ties, and it was not until the Korean War that the British High Commissioner in New Delhi affirmed that even if the Kashmir conflict were settled, India would not make any contribution to Commonwealth defence, because she would then want to reduce defence expenditure. The emphasis on the Kashmir conflict was probably wishful thinking on the part of British officials – though it is worth pointing out that they opposed American plans to sign a military treaty with Pakistan in 1951 partly on the ground that it would alienate India and destroy any chances of a similar treaty with *her*. Victor Rothwell (*Britain and the Cold War 1941–1947*, London 1982) has observed that despite British reliance on the USA after 1945, British officials continued to think and to want to act as if Britain was still the primary power; it is possible that while the loss of India in 1947 induced the British to draw up military plans which did not envisage India's participation in Commonwealth defence, they continued to hope that military ties would be made at some future date. Reality, hope and illusion seem to have been interwoven inextricably in the British official mind – and the spate of draft military agreements until 1950 suggests a surprising degree of wishful thinking. Some of these points will be discussed more fully in a paper that I am now writing on post-imperial British attitudes to India.

50. Mansergh, *Documents and Speeches*, II, 862–63.

Anita Inder Singh
is a member of the Research Department of
the Swedish Institute of International Affairs,
Stockholm, and is working on western
interests in India after 1947. Her doctoral
thesis, 'The Origins of the Partition of India,
1936–1947', is due to be published in the
Oxford South Asia series.

Part III
Decolonization and Party Politics

[9]

Africa and the Labour Government, 1945–1951

by

Ronald Hyam

Two quintessential themes dominated the work of the Labour government between 1945 and 1951: economic recovery and Russian expansion. Both problems pointed to an increased interest in the empire in general and in Africa in particular. 'My mind turns more and more', wrote Chancellor of the Exchequer Hugh Dalton in 1947, 'towards a consolidation in Africa'.[1] In October 1949 the Minister of Defence, A.V. Alexander ('King Albert Victorious'), defined the government's three main policy objectives as: (i) securing 'our people against aggression', (ii) sustaining a foreign policy dominated by 'resistance to the onrush of Communist influence' everywhere, from Greece to Hong Kong, and (iii) achieving 'the most rapid development practicable of our overseas possessions, since without such Colonial development there can be no major improvement in the standard of living of our own people at home'.[2] (An astonishing admission! – where now is Lord Lugard? where Lord Hailey?) As far as Foreign Secretary Ernest Bevin was concerned, from the moment that that neo-Palmerstonian took office he saw 'the utmost importance' from political, economic and defence points of view of developing Africa and making its resources 'available to all'. Stepping up the flow of strategic raw materials out of Africa would help to free Britain from financial dependence on America. Bevin's pet projects were to sell manganese ore from Sierra Leone to the United States, and coal from Wankie to Argentina in return for beef. Always dreaming cosmoplastic dreams, he also talked about a new triangular oceanic trade between eastern Africa, India and Australia. But more than this: Bevin feared the Russians would sooner or later 'make a major drive against our position in Africa'.[3] In Attlee's world-picture too, Africa presented the same duality of concern: economically it was immoral not to develop its 'great estates', while politically the Cold War pointed to the necessity of an increasing reliance on African manpower, as well as coming to terms with African nationalism. On the one hand he wanted to increase European settlement in under-populated areas of east-central Africa, but on the other, recognised that in Gold Coast and Nigeria 'an attempt to maintain the old colonialism would, I am sure, have immensely aided Communism'.[4]

Several Labour ministers believed they were called 'to bring the modern state to Africa'.[5] John Strachey – of all people – as Minister of Food foisted the mechanized groundnuts project on Tanganyika to improve the British margarine ration, arguing that only by such enterprises could African possessions be rapidly developed, and 'become an asset and not a liability as they largely now are'. Even Sir Stafford Cripps wanted to 'force the pace' of African economic development in order to close the dollar gap.[6] At the same time, if Britain was to remain a world power, they realized they had to control rising nationalist tension in Africa because, as James Griffiths (the able latter-day Secretary of State for the Colonies) put it in 1950, 'we had to face an ideological battle in the world, especially in the Colonies', and the next ten years would be crucial.[7] 'A glance at Asia', Herbert Morrison declared, was enough to show the kind of troubles which 'could break loose' in Africa if they did not adjust their policies to promote political and economic change as a matter of 'two-way teamwork' between the metropolis and Africans.[8] Beyond that, and for Attlee especially, it was a challenge to statesmanship to meet the susceptibilities of Afro-Asian peoples while maintaining and expanding the Commonwealth. The Prime Minister believed Britain was its 'material and spiritual head', and that it could be a multi-racial international bridge, as well as an effective global barrier against Communist aggression. One of Attlee's principal long-term preoccupations was to prevent newly-independent states seceding from the Commonwealth, since this would be exploited by Russia as a failure and would automatically diminish British influence throughout the world.[9]

The four great axes of Labour's engagement with Africa were political, strategic, economic and racial. Not in any one of these spheres was a simple, straightforward policy possible.

By 1946 the Colonial Office planners were acutely aware of the need for a clear policy based on the political advancement of Africans. There were perhaps five main reasons for this. First, African political consciousness had been stimulated by the war, and the white man's prestige destroyed as an instrument of government, particularly in the eyes (it was thought) of returning black ex-servicemen. Secondly, to carry out the new social welfare and economic development programmes, a new political instrument was required, namely African participation. Thirdly, Colonial Service attitudes had to be reconstructed: morale was bad, the nostrums of Lugard and Cameron were moribund, and officers felt frustrated by newly-emerging African criticisms of them. The men on the spot needed a new sense of 'mission', a fresh constructive goal to work to. A redefinition of policy was thus obviously overdue. Fourthly, it seemed Britain had to retain a positive initiative in the formulation of African policy, otherwise control would pass to 'settler' regimes (South African, Rhodesian and Portuguese), to whom it was a matter of life and death. This would imperil British trusteeship policies; indeed, after the adoption of apartheid in South Africa from 1948, an actual policy-conflict existed. Finally, and perhaps most important of all, international pressures from the United Nations, American and 'world opinion' were (as Secretary of State for the Colonies Arthur Creech Jones said) directing 'the play of a fierce searchlight' over Africa.[10] These outside influences were expected to stimulate the demand for self-government. 'Prejudiced, ignorant and hostile' criticism and interference from 'the anti-colonial bloc' (Communist and Latin American countries, together with India, and, most vocal adversary of all, the Philippines) would be grounded not in trying to reform imperial systems but in abolishing them entirely and instantly as anachronistic. Officials regarded this as a recipe for widespread post-imperial disintegration, as it took no account of fitness for self-government:

> We are just as concerned to see our colonial peoples achieve self-government, but in conditions in which they really can stand on their own, without the risk of subsequently falling under foreign political or economic domination, or under the control of an undemocratic minority seeking power for its own selfish ends.

Britain aimed at establishing stable, effective and representative political systems. This was a delicate operation in which they must not be dictated to by '58 back-seat drivers without responsibility'.[11]

These reasons, internal and international, 'demanded a new approach to policy in Africa' (Ivor Thomas, Parliamentary Under-Secretary at the Colonial Office). A unified, logical, coherent and convincing policy was essential.[12] The process of defining it centred on Andrew Cohen (*'alter ego* of Creech Jones'), head of the African department – he of the purple shirt and spikey handwriting, once a Cambridge Apostle, now 'Emperor of Africa'. Cohen insisted that what was wanted was not another set of platitudinous generalizations but an actual programme of practical policies. 'There will be no question of imposing a stereotyped blueprint. All we can do is to indicate the broad objective. . .'. The first fruit of Cohen's initiative (welcomed by Creech Jones) was a notable State Paper, the famous 'Local Government Despatch' of February 1947. It enjoined the promotion of efficient local government as a priority, and represented the victory of conciliar principles over the Indirect Rule tradition. This was the work of Cohen, G.B. Cartland and R.E. Robinson: Cohen called it 'a joint effort' by the three of them.[13] Robinson – he of the DFC and gravel-voice – was Cohen's special acolyte in the temple of African divination. His most significant job was to make the more conservative governors swallow the new directive, using his historical skills to demonstrate its logical development from previous policy. This most intellectual of Blues ever to think about the Blacks saw the aim of democratizing local government as providing 'some measure of political education'. He stressed the 'transition from local government through personalities to local government based on institutions'. It was no longer possible, Robinson argued, to preserve African societies against change, and British rulers must attempt to see the future. The economic bases of African societies left to themselves were in danger of collapse. Imperial indecision would be fatal: 'No policy of letting sleeping dogs lie is likely to succeed when the dogs are already barking'. (He learned early on that canine metaphors went down well in Great Smith Street.) But young Robinson was optimistic. Communism he thought 'outmoded' and unlikely to have any real future in Africa. Moreover, by constructing a political pyramid with a firm base in local government, there was a good chance that British rulers had 'dug out an adequate system of political irrigation channels before the rains of nationalism have burst into full flood upon them'.[14]

A conference of African governors in November 1947 chewed over the implications of the new local government strategy, not always amicably, together with most other aspects of African policy. A remarkable series of papers was prepared in the Colonial Office for this path-breaking conference. Creech Jones praised them as excellent. The crucial constitutional proposals about the stages of political evolution he did not specifically comment on. The strictly limited nature of this programme (as envisaged by Cohen and Sir Sydney Caine, Deputy Under-Secretary) needs to be stressed, in the light of the wilder misinterpretations which have been placed upon it. Even in the most advanced territory, the Gold Coast, Cohen wrote, 'internal self-government is unlikely to be achieved in much less than a generation'; elsewhere 'the process is likely to be considerably slower'. Accordingly, there must be a long-term plan, 'for 20 or 30 years or indeed longer', for ordered development under continuing British responsibility. Readiness for internal self-government (i.e. the stage attained by Southern Rhodesian whites in 1923) was still 'a long way off'; 'independence' (i.e. control of external affairs, with freedom to secede from the Commonwealth) was not even mentioned.* In his paper Caine assumed merely that 'perhaps within a generation many of the principal territories of the Colonial Empire will have attained or be within sight of the goal of full responsibility for *local affairs*' [my emphasis]. There would be a 'redistribution of power' and friendly association would have to replace 'benevolent domination', but he did not see this as involving the elimination of British power: it should continue to be possible to control the pace and 'influence the main line of policy and, provided the right new techniques are developed, the extent of that influence may remain very considerable'.[15]

Cohen was well aware of the probability that any constitutional programme would need to be radically rewritten from time to time. The crux of the problem was the risk that the demand for self-government ('stimulated by outside influences') might outpace the process of building up local government from below. Nevertheless, 'the rapid building up of local government through the process of devolution . . . is the most important of all the methods by which we must seek to foster political evolution in Africa'. Only thus could the 'evils of a class of professional politicians' be avoided. The Secretary of State agreed: the 'ignorant and gullable [*sic*] majority' must not be exploited by 'unrepresentative oligarchies'. Creech Jones was particularly interested in getting things started. The demand for a share in government responsibility was, he thought, certain to be made with increasing emphasis, and the demand must be satisfied. 'Time was knocking at the door and the art of government had to be learned.' Britain had thus to permit trial and error to Africans, reduce its spoonfeeding, and encourage a virile political self-reliance, without waiting for the educational qualifications it would like.[16]

The strategy of promoting political advancement on local government foundations was a policy to which Attlee was already totally committed. Indeed he noted the 'regrettable failure' in several colonies to develop municipal institutions as 'a first school of political and administrative training'. Politics could not be learned from a textbook. In his view also there was a most serious danger in assuming the Westminster Parliament to be the appropriate objective. Democracy could be fundamentally threatened by the concentration and centralisation of powers in the Westminster model. 'It would have been wiser in India to have followed the model of the United States constitution. . .'. This sort of mistake must not be repeated in Africa. (Has modern Britain ever had so prescient a Prime Minister?)[17]

* The distinction is fundamental. Some historians need to remember what Jim Hacker learned from Sir Humphrey Appleby: 'I *must* be clear on my African terminology, or else I could do irreparable damage' (J. Lynn and A. Jay, *The Complete 'Yes, Minister': The Diaries of a Cabinet Minister, by the Rt. Hon. James Hacker, MP* (London, 1984), 35).

So: *political advancement* of Africans – gradual, smooth and efficiently controlled – was the central purpose of policy. The goal was self-government, but self-government was not something to be hurried on. Demands for it seemed always to arise out of unrest, and invariably created awkward and unwelcome problems. Creech Jones urged the Cabinet to deal with economic and social discontents first, in order to lessen the immediate pressure for constitutional advance, thereby laying firmer foundations for 'liberal and efficient' self-government. Colonies – it was realized – could not be retained against their will, and any attempt to suppress national desires would be a disaster, but there would be no 'scuttling' out of Africa. Azikiwe would not intimidate them. Government must keep the initiative. Ceylon might be the model. Nor would there be any overall blueprint or prepared schedule. The timetable would be left vague. Fitness for political advancement in any individual colony would depend entirely on its own 'social and political viability and capability', and not on any 'extraneous considerations'.[18] Regional variations in Africa would be fully recognized. Cohen stated quite categorically: 'The conception of dealing with Africa as a whole in political questions is a wrong one'. (The Colonial Office accordingly scorned the notion of having a 'secretary of state for Africa'.)[19] The ultimate objective of Commonwealth association must be preserved. To this end, the early nineteenth-century theories of Macaulay and Fowell Buxton were dusted down. A Colonial Office paper on 'our main problems and policies' (1950) declared:

> We are engaged on a world-wide experiment in nation-building. Our aim is to create independence – independence within the Commonwealth – not to suppress it. No virtue is seen in permanent dependence. A vigorous, adult and willing partner is clearly more to be desired than one dependent, adolescent and unwilling. But there is no intention to abandon responsibilities prematurely. Self-government must be effective and democratic. . . .

Above all it must be within a Commonwealth framework, so as to ensure 'an ever-widening circle of democratic nations exerting a powerful stabilising influence in the world'. Premature withdrawal of British responsibility would only create a dangerous vacuum, within which nationalism would be usurped and 'perverted by extremists'. On the other hand, the imperial rulers must accustom themselves to the idea that 'the transfer of power is not a sign of weakness or of liquidation of the Empire, but is, in fact, a sign and source of strength'.[20] A Foreign Office paper on 'the problem of nationalism' (1952) concluded that it was possible to draw the constructive forces of nationalism to the British side and minimise the threatened erosion of British world power. It was a 'dynamic on the upsurge' which could not be stopped, but could be directed and encouraged into 'healthy and legitimate' channels. Destructive, extremist, xenophobic nationalism might be a potent instrument of Communist incitement, but a 'new and fruitful' relationship established with moderate nationalists through a policy of self-government could be the 'best prospect of resistance to Communism'. 'Greater maturity of thought in nationalist peoples and leaders' (without which any form of co-operation might prove temporary and illusory) might be induced by 'creating a class with a vested interest in co-operation', and involving it in social welfare and economic development projects. (The articulation of a 'collaborative bargains hypothesis' was thus well advanced by the time Labour left office.)[21]

All this theorizing was congenial to Cohen. He believed strongly in a continuing firm metropolitan grip on the situation, in being one jump ahead, in controlling and nurturing nationalist movements. This was, he believed, the only possible policy to secure the future stability and viability of territories. The sooner government acted, 'the more influence we were likely to have for a longer period'. In the best reformist traditions of the Colonial Office, he justified their policies as designed to 'strengthen not weaken the British connection'.[22]

In West Africa, the Colonial Office identified three 'political' categories: nationalists (the educated and part-educated), moderates (professional and business groups and the more enlightened chiefs), and rural populations (who were 'not politically-minded'). 'To be successful, policy must satisfy the second class while safeguarding the interests of the third, and going far enough to meet the aspirations of the first to secure some co-operation at any rate from all but the more extreme nationalists'. Accordingly, African representatives should play a major part in working out constitutional reforms. Executives should be re-modelled to give representatives a full share in the formulation and execution of policy. Legislatures should be extended and made 'fully representative of all parts of the country and not merely of the urban and more developed areas'.[23]

When in 1948 the Accra riots broke out in the Gold Coast, Creech Jones, canny and alert as ever, doubted the simplistic theory of 'Communist incitement' initially presented by the local administrators. In any case he was worried that this 'factor in the disturbances may be used so as to obscure or belittle . . . sincerely felt causes of dissatisfaction quite unconnected with Communism', or desires 'to accelerate constitutional development' – at however ill-considered a pace. Creech Jones believed the underlying causes were partly political and partly economic.[24] For him the Gold Coast held the key to future success in Britain's West African policy, and so he set up a commission of inquiry, and appointed Sir Charles Arden-Clarke, the very model of a modern colonial governor, to take over the administration. The new governor was a bit of a showman as well as a shrewd politician, with the reassuring appearance of a dog-lover advertising a good pipe-tobacco. Arden-Clarke's genius was to build on Moscow's known abandonment of Nkrumah as a useful contact, and to treat him as essentially a moderate, no longer 'our little local Hitler'; they were, he thought, in many ways lucky he had become so amenable. Nkrumah's position must be underwritten. The alternative was an inevitable further challenge to British authority, with increasing encouragement from Communist forces outside the country and later perhaps within it. Considerable African participation in the Gold Coast executive was therefore essential. The Cabinet was persuaded by the Coussey Report and Creech Jones's argument that without such progress 'moderate opinion will be alienated and the extremists given an opportunity of gaining further and weightier support and of making serious trouble'. They took a significant step forward, but of course it fell short of full self-government. Ministers refused to say when they would start discussing that.[25] Ideally, Cohen told them, in order to preserve efficient government there should be no further constitutional advance until 1954 or 1955, and it would not be in anyone's interest to have only a short transitional period to responsible government. But Nkrumah was in 1951 asking to take over from the governor the selection of ministers and to be given the title of prime minister.

> It must, of course, be recognised that we may not be able to adhere to an ideal timetable. We may be forced, if we are to keep on good terms with the more responsible political leaders such as Mr Nkrumah and his immediate colleagues and not to force the Gold Coast Government into the hands of extremists, to move more rapidly than ideally we should wish. . . . It would be fatal . . . to forfeit the goodwill of Mr Nkrumah and his colleagues by holding back excessively.

The imperatives of the collaborative mechanism had begun ineluctably to operate. Arden-Clarke diagnosed the salient feature of the situation: there was no alternative to a CPP government, and it could only be replaced by a similar one, or one of even more extreme nationalist tendencies. 'We have only one dog in our kennel. . . . All we can do is to build it up and feed it vitamins and cod liver oil. . . .'.[26]

Nigeria was launched almost automatically on a similar course as a result of Gold Coast developments. Cohen in 1948 quickly alerted Governor Sir John Macpherson to their relevance for neighbouring Nigeria. The principles of Nigerian political advancement were approved by the Cabinet in May 1950: greatly increased Nigerian participation in the executive, both at the centre and in the three regions; increased regional autonomy (within the unity of Nigeria, which was not negotiable); larger and more representative regional legislatures with increased powers. The Cabinet was especially concerned to ensure a smooth transfer of administrative responsibility by speeding up Africanization of the civil service on the lines that had worked well in India.[27] In 1952 Macpherson reflected that Nigeria had obtained a constitution 'in advance of its true capacity', but 'we could not put a ring-fence round Nigeria, and we had to take the initiative, and not wait to be overtaken by events, because of what was happening, and is continuing to happen, in the Gold Coast, the Sudan, Libya, etc, etc,'.[28]

Where had British planners got to in West Africa by 1951? The aim was self-government within the Commonwealth. But this, as Cohen saw it, meant something different for Nigeria and the Gold Coast, 'which can look forward to full responsibility for their own affairs', and for Sierra Leone and Gambia, which were not yet ready for African ministers, and must expect even in the long run to leave defence and foreign affairs to Britain. The Gold Coast was 'very far on towards internal self-government'; Nigeria was only a degree or two behind; but since there was little comparable nationalism in Sierra Leone and Gambia the two of them should be satisfied with a much more limited advance, and remain 'quite content' for 'a considerable time to come'. In all four, the government was trying to provide constitutions based on 'consent and consultation' – under the governor's ultimate authority. Maintaining confidence in British good faith was the essence of it, since this would slow down the pace. Simultaneously local government was being reformed and modernized, and Africanization was proceeding. The theory Cohen discerned behind all these changes was that full African participation provided 'the best defence against Communism', 'the only chance of friendly co-operation' with Britain, and the 'best chance' of persuading an African country voluntarily to remain in the Common-wealth. There could be no question of being deflected from political advancement and administrative devolution by the protests of France and South Africa.[29]

As far as East Africa was concerned, the final forms of government were 'less evident and less near' than in West Africa, but essentially the goal was the same. They would build up and improve the status and experience of Africans (through participation in local and central government) until disparities with Europeans and Indians were removed politically, economically and socially. They could then play a full part in a 'system in which all communities would participate on an equal basis' of genuine partnership. The problem of course was that the settlers objected to this, and indeed disapproved of the speed of African advance in West Africa. To force equality of representation upon the settlers would precipitate a major political crisis. Not that Creech Jones was unduly alarmed by such a prospect: 'whatever privilege they may have had in the past cannot be perpetuated much longer'. Many of the African grievances were, he thought, legitimate, but in such a vast area they ought not to demand exclusive rights, and 'a corrective to their irresponsible nationalism should be applied from time to time'.[30] Viscount Addison (the Cabinet's elder statesman, intermittently concerned with Common-wealth relations) argued the importance of reassuring settlers in order to avoid 'driving them into undesirable alliance with South Africa'. Griffiths, on the other hand, emphasised the necessity of reassuring Africans that ultimate British responsibility would be retained until they had 'narrowed the gap'. Out of these conflicting pressures came a parliamentary statement in December 1950, balancing irreconcilable interests in the well-worn fashion of the declarations of the inter-war years. The goal was 'true partnership' between races, but the immigrant communities had a part to play in the future of Kenya, and were not being asked to agree to 'their eventual eviction'. A certain *stasis* entered East African political advancement as a result. Resolution of the agonizing contradictions of Kenya was deferred, with Mau Mau as the consequence.[31]

North Africa was in many ways acting as the pace-maker for African political advancement. By concentrating on the Gold Coast for the 'beginnings of decolonization' historians have in fact been looking in the wrong place. Independence for Libya (1951) and Sudan (1956) pioneered the way, and arose out of fascinating international constraints. In the case of Libya, J.S. Bennett of the Colonial Office argued (in a series of papers in 1946–47, acknowledged by Cohen to be 'brilliant') that promoting independence would be a useful sop to international opinion and a promising bid for Arab friendship. Elsewhere in Africa, 'rapid political advancement towards independence is not yet in the realm of practical politics, and we are obliged to move more slowly at the price of increasing international criticism'. In Libya, by contrast, the 'prospect of early independence is not unreal'; it was an occupied ex-Italian colony and not a British possession, and thus provided the easiest way in which they could meet the obligations of the Atlantic Charter. A lot of paper about human rights was being generated by the UN: 'Here is a practical test-case, worth any amount of paper'. It was an ideal chance for once to forestall a nationalist protest, 'recognising the inevitable and cashing in on it in good time', instead of waiting to be forced into granting independence 'by local revolt and/or outside pressure'. Britain had some essential strategic requirements, at least in Cyrenaica, especially as a result of uncertainty over its Egyptian tenure, but promoting Libyan independence could be the best way of securing them.[32] Certainly in Sheikh Idris Britain had an 'ideal prefabricated collaborator'. Idris had indicated his willingness to grant bases and generally to allow the British considerable freedom of military action. At any rate the government concluded that the best solution, resolving a complex international tangle, was to back Idris and the Libyan claims for independence under UN auspices.[33]

In Sudan, too, Britain promoted independence. Validated in this case by Indian analogy, it was basically a means of countering the Egyptian claim to sovereignty (Farouk having been proclaimed 'King of the Sudan'). In part it was also a way of pre-empting a UN trust, with its risks of 'letting Russia into Africa'. But if independence would get the Sudan off its Egyptian hook, refusal to sell the Sudanese into Egyptian slavery dashed all Bevin's hopes of negotiating the crucially important new Canal Zone treaty with Egypt. ('I cannot do what I believe to be wrong and retrograde in order to get a quick treaty of alliance'.) This was because the Egyptians insisted on linking the two issues. As to the Suez base itself, Labour policy was to shift its defence on to Anglo-Egyptian co-operation and away from British occupation. Realising that effective use of the base was essentially dependent on Egyptian goodwill, and that ideal strategic requirements would have to be sacrificed in order to ensure it, Attlee in 1946 set the tone for treaty re-negotiation. In a masterly summing-up in Cabinet he declared that Britain could 'not remain forcibly on the ground':

> There was no more justification for this than for our claiming that our neighbours in the Continent of Europe should grant us bases for our defence. Our oil interests in the Middle East were indeed important, but our ability to defend them would only be impaired if we insisted on remaining in Egypt against the will of the Egyptian people and so worsened our relations with the remainder of the Arab world.

The Labour government continued to try to tempt Egypt into some sort of 'equal partnership' in a new Middle East defence scheme, but negotiations remained deadlocked. Attlee was unable to deliver Britain out of its Egyptian bondage.[34] Meanwhile he ruled out the use of force in dealing with the Iranian oil crisis of 1951. This was welcomed by officials as proof that the days were over of 'thinking in Edwardian terms of the use of military and economic power which we no longer possess'. Nationalism, all seemed to be agreed, must be met with diplomacy and publicity, not intervention and force.[35]

Strategically Attlee wanted to give up a 'hopeless' attempt to defend the Middle East oil-producing areas, and to work routinely round the Cape to the east and Australasia, instead of relying on an ever-more problematic Mediterranean route. In addition, he had always been anxious not to get drawn into UN trusteeships for 'deficit areas' in North Africa and the Horn. ('Somaliland has always been a dead loss and a nuisance to us.') His earliest and most iconoclastic initiative as Prime Minister was to demand a strategic reappraisal to take proper account of the atom bomb, the United Nations, and the impending loss of India. He was worried by the costs of continuing Mediterranean commitments he regarded as obsolescent. Nor did he like the idea of supporting the vested interests of a 'congeries of weak, backward and reactionary states' in the Middle East. With impressive 'Little Englander' pragmatism, remorselessly yet reasonably, and with occasional touches of irreverence, he pursued a confrontation with the Chiefs of Staff on these issues through endless committee meetings, and thoroughly rattled them. Attlee was supported by Dalton. This battle of the titans lasted almost 18 months. It ended with a victory for the traditionalist doctrines of the Chiefs of Staff (apparently threatening resignation), backed by Bevin and his formidable Foreign Office team. Their argument was that withdrawal from the Mediterranean route would leave a vacuum, into which Russia (even if not bent on world domination) would move, since 'the bear could not resist pushing its paw into soft places'. This would make a gift to Russia of Middle Eastern oil and manpower, and would dangerously signal to Russia, to America and the Commonwealth Britain's 'abdication as a world power'. Without a first line of defence in North Africa, the Russians would, they argued, rapidly be in the Congo and at the Victoria Falls. They rejected Attlee's concept of a disengagement from a 'neutral zone', putting 'a wide glacis of desert and Arabs between ourselves and the Russians'.[36]

However, despite this fundamental disagreement, there was common ground between Attlee, Bevin and the Chiefs of Staff about the desirability of a strategic base located in Kenya, which Attlee had seen as part of a more general shifting of military resources into less contentious and exposed regions. They all agreed that more use ought to be made of Africa as a manpower reserve, compensating for the loss of the Indian 'British barrack in the Oriental seas', and as a way of relieving the strain in Egypt. East Africa was expected to be more important in a future war, as a result of greater weapon ranges and the weakening of the British position in the Middle East. It would become a major training camp and storage depot. It would also defend 'our main support-area in South Africa'. Work began in September 1947 on the new base at Mackinnon Road, some sixty miles inland by rail from Mombasa.[37] All this tied in with new doctrines of colonial development. The new base in Kenya, Bevin argued, would 'modernise the whole character of our defence as well as our trade and bring into the British orbit economically and commercially a great area which is by no means fully developed yet'. Communications would need to be improved over a wide area. Bevin was keen to develop Mombasa as a major port, and link it to Lagos by a trans-African highway ('passing through the top of French Equatorial Africa', thus enabling Britain, if necessary, to protect the strategic deposits of the Belgian Congo). This scheme the experts pronounced impossible because of the administrative and maintenance costs of African 'all-weather' roads, to say nothing of the difficulty of co-operating with foreign powers. Bevin also campaigned to improve the outlets for Rhodesian strategic minerals to the sea. Railway links to the south were in consequence thoroughly investigated.[38]

A rail link between Rhodesia and Kenya from Ndola to Korogwe was the most favoured project. This would mean unifying the gauges (which ministers thought a strategically valuable exercise), by converting 3,520 miles of East African railways from metre to 3'6" – a five-year task. Tanganyikan authorities naively put their costs at £870,000, while Kenya (with more track and rolling stock) estimated their conversion at £16 million. The new 1,125 mile link itself might be built for £11 million. However, even a 3'6" railway could not carry oversize loads (such as big tanks) and would have to be duplicated by a much-improved road capable of carrying 70-ton weights. (Only a route able to carry heavy equipment would provide any appreciable saving over the shipping routes.) Cohen strongly favoured the 'great advantage of having an all-British railway link from the Cape to Kenya', possibly with a branchline to Kilwa or Mikindani to evacuate groundnuts. (See map.) The project lapsed, however, and for three reasons. There were doubts about the enormous costs and its economic profitability. (Creech Jones was decidedly sceptical – haunted, no doubt, by Labouchère's famous diatribe against

160   HISTORY OF EUROPEAN EXPANSION OVERSEAS

MAP 1   THE PROPOSED RAIL LINK BETWEEN RHODESIA AND KENYA

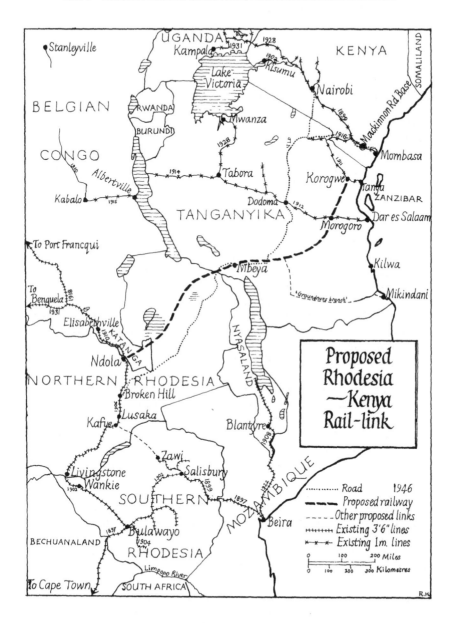

Source: CO 537/1231/102, COS(46)271, report on the development of African communications, 13 December 1946.

the Uganda railway: 'What it will carry there's none can define; . . . It clearly is naught but a lunatic line'.) Then there was the growing difficulty of being seen to co-operate with South Africa. Above all, the Chiefs of Staff decided they did not wish to develop Kenya as a major operational base: it was too far from the Middle East theatre, it had insufficient industrial back-up, and it was impracticable (for racial and political reasons) to import the quantities of white or Indian labour required. The Ndola rail link was accordingly down-graded to being 'strategically desirable but not essential', and at all events not sufficiently important to warrant a contribution from the UK defence vote. 'Cape-to-Cairo' was as far off as ever.[39]

The fate of the railway project was symptomatic of the sheer difficulty of developing Africa. Yet interest in the possible potential and the protean problems of Africa was sufficiently aroused for nine visits to be made by Colonial Office ministers in these years, four of them by secretaries of state. Field Marshal Montgomery (the Chief of the Imperial General Staff) also decided to make a tour of Africa at the end of 1947. ('It is terribly important to check up on Africa'.) He visited French Morocco, Gambia, Gold Coast, Nigeria, Belgian Congo, Union of South Africa, Southern Rhodesia, Kenya, Ethiopia, Sudan and Egypt. The result was an electric 76-page report, containing many a caustic phrase, though his most derisive strictures were reserved for Ethiopia (its 'pathetic Emperor', 'Gilbertian army', 'Addis in Wonderland', and elite of 'Hollywoodian ostentation'). His thesis was the 'immense possibilities' for African development, enabling Britain to 'maintain her standard of living', if not actually to survive, because 'these lands contain everything we need'. However, 'no real progress was being made', and the way was open for Communism. Government should 'think big'. There must be 'a grand design for African development as a whole, with a masterplan for each Colony or nation'. Invoking the spirit of Cecil Rhodes, and roundly condemning the settlers, the African ('a complete savage') and the Colonial Service alike, he demanded that those who said it could not be done should be 'ruthlessly eliminated'. Britain should 'import brains and "go-getters" '. 'Belly-aching will assume colossal proportions; it must be stamped on.' Administrative units should be boldly amalgamated; federations of Central Africa, East Africa and West Africa ought to be established. The High Commission Territories were an anomaly and should be 'abolished'. Eventually South Africa and Central Africa should be linked up. There should be much closer co-operation with other European powers too, and with the Americans.[40]

Despite the staccato tone of the presentation, with its arrogant amateurism presumptuously masquerading as geopolitical genius, senior ministers took this report seriously. Bevin called for its 'urgent study'. Attlee was 'much interested'. With remarkable speed Creech Jones came up with a comprehensive reply, in a 14-page memorandum dated 6 January 1948. (It is the central ministerial document on Labour's African policy, and its preparation must have ruined his Christmas and New

Year.) He agreed that quick and vigorous African development was essential on strategic, economic and political grounds to strengthen Britain and Western Europe; it was also needed to secure smooth African progress in social and political fields, and to help the world supply of food and raw materials. British departure from India and the reduction in its overseas investments generally had still further increased the economic importance of close links with Africa. But the imposition of a centralized 'grand design' drawn up in and directed from London 'would not be practical politics' (words which Attlee underlined in his copy). It would 'conflict with our declared policy of devolution in the progress of building up self-government' and ensuring that Africans attained it as 'part of the western world'. Central direction would not work. It was contrary to all British policy and historical experience. It would not secure the co-operation of local peoples, settler or African, without which effective development could not take place. Developing relationships between peoples over a period of years could not be dealt with on the analogy of a military operation. A blueprint could not be operated by orders in a chain of command, because colonies had powers and responsibilities which would progressively increase. They should be dealt with by devolution, which had worked successfully in India, Ceylon and Sudan. There was in fact no lack of planning. 'We have a clear and well-understood general policy for political and economic development in Africa.' All the territories had 10-year development plans. Montgomery had overestimated the material resources of Africa: 'Africa is not an undiscovered El Dorado. It is a poor continent which can only be developed at great expense in money and effort'. Vast areas were barely self-supporting in food, and could only be made so by a heavy capital expenditure on water, bush clearance, fertilizers and supervisory manpower. The crucial problem was not lack of brains or vigour, but lack of money and the 'pay your way' philosophy, which was now being rectified. African development might well be vital to the survival of Britain, but if so, it must have a much higher priority in supplies and technicians. The present bottleneck was the lack of capital equipment, especially an acute shortage of steel, and a deficiency of consumer goods to provide incentives.

Politically, too, Creech Jones continued, the right means of countering anti-British movements, the real answer to nationalism, 'does not lie in uniformity of policy, or in federation, or in any other imposed measure', but in 'the maintenance and development of our existing friendly relations with the African peoples'; in giving them 'a real part in the constructive work of government', and in building up responsible native institutions. Communists were *not* exploiting the lack of a uniform native policy; it would in fact be easier to exploit such a policy if it were imposed without regard to local conditions. But there *was* a broad overall uniformity, and regional co-ordination was certainly existing policy. Any link-up of African territories with South Africa was out of the question, and the High Commission Territories could not be handed over.[41]

Notwithstanding this drily devastating critique, the Montgomery

Report was a useful weapon in the fight to demand greater attention in Whitehall as a whole for African development needs. Ministers agreed they must urgently have a plan fully co-ordinated and integrated with British domestic economic policy. With some mild breast-beating, they admitted colonial economic development planning to have been defective, because they had not determined on broad lines what proportion of British resources should go overseas, or assessed the relative value of home and colonial projects. For example, there had been no agreed criterion for allocating priorities in agricultural machinery or steel between conflicting British and African demands. All this they would now try to put right. The new Chancellor of the Exchequer (Cripps) said the first thing was to inject a spirit of improvization, and improve the productivity of existing capital equipment, rather than initiating new, large-scale development schemes. The Economic Policy Committee agreed with Creech Jones that, however desirable, a more positive control of the African economic field was not possible, as it would be contrary to the fundamental policy of gradually transferring real power.[42]

Simultaneously with these discussions, Caine submitted a special report on colonial economic development to the Prime Minister. He too rejected the idea of a single centralized plan: they had to work within the Labour policy of 'political advancement'. He called for more liaison, more international collaboration, the allocation of priorities and the mobilization of all available agencies, including private enterprise. All this could be of inestimable value to colonial peoples and to Britain in a few years. They must prepare for the day American aid ran out. 'Prompt action now will mean that we shall by that time be enjoying the first fruits of this new form of colonial investment'. The essential problem was the removal of limitations to development. These were of three kinds: (i) virtually irremovable traditional social barriers (especially land tenure systems), (ii) basic conditions which were remediable in perhaps a generation (soil infertility, scarce labour and insufficient technicians), and (iii) limitations which could in theory be removed at any time by governmental decision (provision of finance, infrastructure and capital goods). Progress could only be gradual, however. Any revolutionary attack on agrarian problems would only cause serious political trouble. Government must therefore work within the limits set by the tolerable pace of social change. In dealing with soil infertility, too, they must be cautious, since they were not sure of the ecological effect of applying Western methods – they must not create a dustbowl even worse than in North America. And the provision of government help was bound to be restricted because of Britain's own needs for basic services and capital goods: iron, steel, machines and cement were all in short supply in Britain itself. A couple of months later Attlee received a report from Hilary Marquand, the Paymaster-General, on his seven weeks' tour of the eastern half of Africa, which reinforced many of these conclusions.[43]

Thus African economic development was faced with multiple

obstacles, clearly identified by the spring of 1948 in a cluster of memoranda. Africa was not amenable to the more euphoric hopes of exploiting it in the common good. Shakespeare and Pliny were equally confounded, as well as Strachey and Bevin: it was not filled with 'golden joys' and it was in fact not easy to conjure anything new out of Africa. The stunning recalcitrance of the environment even to mechanized assault was brought home by the groundnuts fiasco. Inadequate transport was perhaps at the heart of the overall problem. There was maddening difficulty in actually getting essential products out of Africa on an exiguous, congested, war-exhausted rail system; the export of uranium from the Congo, copper from Northern Rhodesia, coal and chrome from Southern Rhodesia, timber from the Gold Coast, and even groundnuts from Tanganyika, were all held up. There were seven different railway gauges in central Africa, yet the high cost of unifying even two of them surprised everyone. It was all very well for Bevin to demand that 'Africa should be as full as possible of transport', but the difficulties were immense. In this as in other sectors, British and African needs were competing. More generally, with the shortage of clothes and bicycles for export from Britain, the African worker could not be given all the incentives he needed. Nutritional problems and debilitating diseases also reduced his efficiency. (The iniquities of the tsetse fly, incidentally, generated more surviving Colonial Office paper than any other subject.) Finally, there was the obvious danger that too concerted a policy of demanding African action to meet Britain's domestic needs (a demand already pushed to the limit by the exigencies of the convertibility crisis of 1947) would be endlessly open to the damaging charge of exploitation, as Bevin was among the first to realize. (The Colonial Office thus sought to distance itself from the work of the new Colonial Development Corporation.) For this reason also international collaboration would remain limited: there must be no hint of 'ganging up' to turn Africa into a hinterland of Western Europe.[44]

Although much thought was given to the ways in which Africa might help to solve Britain's own strategic and economic problems, the empire would not stand or fall on the establishment of a base in Kenya, or poultry farms in Gambia, or the supply of bicycles to Blantyre, or even of peanuts and bananas to Battersea. More fundamental by far was the racial challenge of the stereotypes of Stellenbosch and the precepts of Pretoria.

The advent of the National Party regime in South Africa in 1948, dedicated to apartheid inside its borders and expansion outside them, had worrying implications for the whole of Britain's African policy. Griffiths spoke for all his colleagues when he described apartheid as 'totally repugnant'. South Africa itself, already angry over the perpetual withholding of the High Commission Territories, became alarmed at the Labour government's determination to press ahead with 'arming Africans' (raising troops for the defence of Africa and the Middle East). It was, moreover, outraged by the prospect of the Gold Coast's being turned into 'another Liberia'. Sir Evelyn Baring, the High Commissioner, warned that 'to despise or to ignore the strong and expanding force of South African nationalism in 1951 would be as unwise as it was to decry in March 1933 the power of Hitler to do harm'. Ministers took the point: if Afrikaner racial ideas spread north of the 'great grey-green, greasy Limpopo river' the whole of their African policy might be jeopardized. South Africa might even try to seduce the settlers in Kenya and Rhodesia from their British allegiance.[45] On the other hand, South Africa was deeply involved in, and had useful technical resources for dealing with, transport, soil erosion and disease problems (trypanoso-miasis, rinderpest and locust-plague). Both sides wanted co-operation in these intractable matters, but it was clearly impossible for the British government to agree to extend discussion into the political arena or to be drawn into a local defence pact. Yet they did want South Africa to contribute to a Middle East defence system: this was 'an essential element we could not forgo' (according to P.C. Gordon Walker, Commonwealth Relations Secretary). In Whitehall there were generally held to be four reasons why the maintenance of good relations was important. First, strategically South Africa was a strong country in a pivotal geopolitical position. It had the basis for heavy industry, together with raw materials important in peace and vital in war (uranium, manganese, diamonds, chrome and coal); it was the only African country which could in war provide a large body of trained technicians. The Simonstown naval base was of the 'utmost importance' to Britain; the use of other ports was also required. South Africa would be needed as a transit area, an arsenal, and a troop-reserve for the Middle East. Second, economically Britain was 'in dire need of its gold' (Baring), since the stability of the Sterling Area depended on getting a substantial part of its gold output. It was also a valuable export market – indeed it headed the list of Britain's customers in 1947. Third, trusteeship ('the ethical code of the empire') meant protecting the vulnerable High Commission Territories. Departmentally this was seen as the critical reason for staying on the right side of South Africa, especially in the Seretse Khama case.[46] For many ministers, however, the determining factor was the fourth one: to preserve the Commonwealth. A quarrel with a 'founder member' would be highly embarrassing and 'immensely damaging to British world prestige'. A public dispute might 'break up the association overnight'. Philip Noel-Baker (Gordon Walker's predecessor at the Commonwealth Relations Office) even invoked some emotional (and inaccurate) 'inherited official historiography' about Campbell-Bannerman and Smuts – 1906 and all that.[47]

Unfortunately South Africa had put itself into the international dock by *de facto* incorporation in 1949 of the former mandated territory of South-West Africa, for which it was hauled before the International Court. Britain had at first tried to be friendly and helpful over this, but it was becoming harder all the time. How closely could it afford to side with South Africa at the UN over a case which might be thought weak if not bad? Civil servants were undecided. Some thought the British government was the only one which stood any chance of influencing the attitude of South Africa, but would lose what little influence it had if it 'joined the pack howling against them', so driving them out of the Commonwealth 'into an outer darkness of their own'. Others, while not wanting Britain to be 'tarred with the apartheid brush', thought it was hardly worth while imperilling a South African contribution to Middle East defence ('very nearly the biggest strategic interest of the UK') for the sake of making doubly sure British policy would not be confused with South Africa's. Some felt strategic requirements should be the over-riding consideration. *Per contra*, many officials argued that unless Britain rejected all visible compromise with the Union's native policy, Britain's own African policy would be endangered. (Sir Thomas Lloyd, Permanent Under-Secretary at the CO, complained of 'numerous and growing embarrassments' flowing from the failure to denounce its reactionary policies.) The South-West Africa dispute was formally analysed as requiring the pursuit of three conflicting objectives. Britain needed to preserve good relations with South Africa, but also 'to keep her reputation as a champion of liberal western civilisation', avoiding a conflict with Afro-Asian opinion. Above all, it had to defend its rights as a colonial power *vis-à-vis* the UN, which must not be allowed to establish the right of intervention in non-self-governing territories. If in South-West Africa the UN inserted the thin end of the wedge of a right to dictate policies and decide the future of all African peoples, it would 'bring British authority, peace and good government in Africa tumbling about our ears'.[48]

For the impending Cabinet debate on this difficult controversy, an inter-departmental paper was prepared, signed by Griffiths, Gordon Walker and Kenneth Younger (Minister of State at the Foreign Office). As drafting proceeded, over a period of five months, the recommendation to intervene at the International Court (in order to make British views known) was made stronger. (According to Galsworthy, some aspects of the dispute were 'supremely important' to the Colonial Office.) Griffiths insisted the main issue should be brought out unequivocally: the risk of being misrepresented as supporting South African native policies, as against the threat of the Court's making a decision adverse to British colonial interests. Attorney-General Sir Hartley Shawcross favoured intervention, though acknowledging that the arguments were 'very nicely balanced'; they would attract a great deal of opprobrium, but mostly from those 'who already have a pretty poor view of us in colonial matters'. Presenting the issue to the Cabinet, Griffiths declared himself on balance in favour of intervening, but at the same time he wanted it to be made clear that their appearance before the Court did not imply support for apartheid. Gordon Walker agreed, on 'strict grounds of British interest'. The Cabinet, however, rejected their recommendation. Most ministers felt that representation at or participation in the Court's proceedings would be bound to be misrepresented as implying support for South Africa, and would therefore 'incur political odium'. Indeed, it might actually invite the Court to pronounce on the colonial issues of concern to Britain, in a context most unfavourable to its case, which it could argue more convincingly in future if it had not been present.[49]

Following upon this hardening of opinion and unusual rejection of departmental advice, a Cabinet paper was prepared in the CRO to clarify the more general issues of Anglo-South African relations. Again, this was several months in preparation. It was finally presented by Gordon Walker at the end of September 1950. Indian hostility to South Africa was identified as a significant feature in the equation, since Britain was anxious to enlist India's 'great influence in Asia' to help in the solution of various far eastern problems. Moreover, 'any suspicion that the United Kingdom sympathised in any way with South Africa's native policies would so deeply disturb African and Indian public opinion in our African Colonies as to constitute a threat to their internal security'. On the other hand, it was important to continue to preserve good relations. The 'four reasons' for this were carefully rehearsed. The conclusion was drawn that Britain ought to show that it appreciated South Africa's difficulties, and not simply condemn and antagonise it. Unnecessary polemics should be avoided, and everything possible done 'to retain South Africa as a member of the Commonwealth, preferably as one owing direct allegiance to the Crown'.[50] Gordon Walker spoke to the paper in the Cabinet, emphasizing that strategically South Africa's goodwill was of special importance. Griffiths then examined the other side of the coin, expressing deep concern both about South Africa's expansionist ambitions and about the serious alarm South Africa's policies were arousing throughout black Africa. Aneurin Bevan drew this point out a little more sharply: the time might come when Britain would be forced to consider whether it lost more than it gained by its embarrassing association with South Africa. Other ministers countered this by under-lining the strategic importance of securing South Africa's support in any struggle against Communism, and the 'great value' of the military support she now seemed likely to promise in the Middle East. (Bevin still wanted South Africa to 'look after the east coast of Africa'.) The CRO paper was endorsed. At a subsequent discussion in the Defence Committee, Strachey (now a War Office minister) reluctantly accepted that they must look on South Africa as an ally, but Emanuel Shinwell (now Minister of Defence) remained profoundly unhappy about seeming to give tacit approval to apartheid by any military co-operation. Attlee (who had not yet really turned his mind to southern Africa) summed up correctly if inconclusively: 'it was a matter of great importance'. However, it clearly had been decided that co-operation with South Africa was to remain a prime object of British policy.[51]

But not the only object. Six months later, Gordon Walker produced his own prodigiously thorough and perceptive analysis of the situation, seeking more definitely to balance necessary co-operation by a policy of containing South African expansion. 'This would mean that we do not regard as our sole objective the emancipation and political advancement of the African in all our African colonies.' Of course this would remain a major objective, but 'we must not subordinate all else to it'. A shift towards closer association with Rhodesian settlers had to be faced. There was a real danger that, to avoid domination by Africans (as a supposed consequence of 'political advancement'), white settler communities would throw in their lot with the Union. This was at least as grave a danger as the eruption of African discontent. Containing South African expansion should thus be 'a policy of *equal* weight and importance in our eyes with the political advancement of the Africans in our Central and East African colonies'. If British communities revolted and linked themselves to the Union, the apartheid policies they detested would be established in the heart of Britain's African empire: 'Millions of Africans would be subjected to oppression. Terrible wars might even be fought between a white-ruled Eastern Africa and a black-ruled Western Africa'. They would in the end fatally have 'betrayed our trust to the Africans', who would be 'calamitously worse off'.[52]

This apocalyptic scenario provided the rationale for the Central African Federation. Enthusiastically advised by G.H. Baxter of the CRO and the ubiquitous and utterly pragmatic Cohen, Gordon Walker was the principal ministerial advocate of creating in central Africa a British bloc to contain Afrikanerdom, provided Africans could be persuaded to accept it.[53] He won Griffiths to his side, but Creech Jones and others remained unconverted to this solution, believing other means could be found for achieving its political and economic purposes without upsetting Africans. Attlee fully understood the case for such a federation in principle, but to him, as always, what mattered was 'tide rather than froth'. Drawing on his Indian experience, he believed the vital thing was the long-term trend of growing African nationalism, which, if given insufficient outlet, might go sour from frustration. The fatal flaw he discerned in the scheme of federation as it ultimately emerged was that it froze the progress of African political advancement by stabilizing the whole framework on the Southern Rhodesian model. The Federation thus ran counter to the basic premise of Labour's African policy, and he rejected it.[54]

Retiring as High Commissioner in 1951 after seven years, Baring summarized the three guidelines which had emerged for Britain's South African policy. One, counteract the magnetic new South African nationalist expansion in the north. Two, preserve and develop the High Commission Territories. Three, regularize relations by co-operating as often as possible and always being very careful to avoid sweeping condemnations, which would only 'unite and inflame' all white South Africans behind Malan. There was thus no simple policy for dealing with Afrikanerdom, but a subtle symbiosis of two parallel strategies, co-operation and containment.[55]

In fact there was no simple policy for dealing with any of the problems of Africa. Throughout the continent the Labour government found that the successful adoption of clear new policies was limited by the tension between Cold War strategic imperatives and their ideally required rational disengagements or moral stands. Neither politically nor economically were centralized blueprints possible. Inadequate British resources, and the stubborn facts of the African environment stopped dead in its tracks any striking advance towards an 'economic new deal'. Politically, in principle Attlee was convinced by Indonesia and Vietnam that 'failure to meet reasonable nationalist aspirations led to an ever-worsening position'. But he did not think Africans were as civilized as Asians, and he foresaw a danger in too rapid a transition.[56] The resultant policy was thus not one of wholesale 'decolonization' or 'dismantling the empire'. Labour ministers themselves invariably called their policy merely one of 'political advancement'. And this political advancement was not thought practicable as yet in much of Africa. Progress was uneven. The Gold Coast and Nigeria were seen as exceptions. Attlee lectured the Northern Rhodesian African National Congress about there being 'a long way to go' and 'no short cuts to political maturity'. Political advancement in East and Central Africa was held up by the supposedly immature and irresponsible nature of its nationalism, but also by the presence of white settlers.[57] Fear of driving them into the arms of an expansionist South Africa was a major reason why the Labour government did not take up earlier recurrent proposals (most notably those of Harold Macmillan in 1942) for an assault on the privileges of the Kenya settlers.[58] East and Central Africans themselves were not thought ready to be of use as collaborators in the task of containing Afrikanerdom. Every region indeed had leaders who were seen as mere demagogues, bent only on capturing the colonial state and driving the British out as quickly as possible. This was not at all the kind of future the government intended. In the short term, local government would be used 'to call in the masses to keep the balance', and close control would remain meanwhile. The long-term aim was gradual political advancement towards self-governing states which were broadly-based, stable, viable, friendly, non-Communist, and firmly within the Commonwealth.[59] Labour ministers may well have been involved in a 'controlled colonial revolution' (the phrase is Gladwyn Jebb's),[60] but their emphasis was distinctly on the *control* of the process. This gradualism was essential because they were determined to maintain as far as possible the structure of British global interests in the fight against Communism. Paradoxically, however, as Attlee saw so clearly, 'an attempt to maintain the old colonialism would . . . have immensely aided Communism'. Decolonization was a gigantic footnote to the Cold War.

NOTES

1. Dalton Papers (L.S.E.), I/35/17, Diary, 24 Feb. 1947; CAB 128/10, CM.75(47)5, 9 Sept. 1947.
2. CAB 129/37(3), CP(49)245, Annex A, 18 Oct. 1949.
3. Bevin Papers (P.R.O.), FO 800/435/116, conversation with Portuguese ambassador, 23

Oct. 1948, & 118, minute to Prime Minister, 6 Nov. 1948; FO 800/444/29, minute to Prime Minister, 16 Sept. 1947; CAB 21/2278, minute by Attlee, 16 Sept. 1947; Dalton Diary, I/34/13.

4. CAB 21/2277, minute 29 Oct. 1946, & 2280, minute, 23 Dec. 1949; CAB 134/786, CCM(54)1; C.R. Attlee, *As It Happened* (London, 1954), 189.

5. CO 537/5361, D.R. Rees-Williams (Parliamentary Under-Secretary, C.O.), report on West African tour, 27 Sept. 1948.

6. CAB 129/16, CP(47)10, memo. 4 Jan. 1947; CO 847/36/2/24, speech by Cripps to African Governors' Conference, 12 Nov. 1947 (AGC.22).

7. CO 537/5699/89 A, 16 June 1950.

8. DO 35/4023/62, speech at opening of the African Conference, 23 Sept. 1948. Attlee regarded this occasion as important enough for him to address, but he was prevented by illness (CAB 21/2279, Attlee to Creech Jones, 12 Oct. 1948).

9. Attlee and Gordon Walker Papers (Churchill Archives Centre, Cambridge), ATLE 1/24/1; GNWR 1/7.

10. CO 847/25/7; CO 847/35/6/1 (Cartland memo.) & 7; CO 847/37/1/21.

11. CO 537/4589 (esp. note by Colonial Secretary, Oct. 1949), & 5708, & 5698; CO 936/56/6; CAB 129/24, CP(48)36; FO 371/107032 (UP.134/1), & 107076 (UP.247/10).

12. CO 847/36/1, minute by I. Thomas, 18 Jan. 1947; PREM 8/922, A(49)1.

13. CO 847/35/6, esp. No. 2, memo. by Cohen, 3 April 1946, and minute, 24 Jan. 1947.

14. CO 847/35/9/3, minute by Cartland, 29 Dec. 1947; CO 847/38/3, memos by R.E. Robinson on some recent trends in native administration policy (March 1947). Robinson described the 'pyramid of councils' as 'essentially an organisation for the political education of the rural Africans, and a scaffolding round which territorial political unity can be built' (CO 847/44/3, memo. on the development of British principles of native administration, 1927–47).

15. CO 847/35/6; CO 847/36/1/9, minutes by Creech Jones, 5 May 1947, and report of the committee on the conference of African governors, 22 May 1947 (? by Cartland), esp. Appendix II (AGC.1, 'The general political development of colonial territories', by Caine), and Appendix III (AGC.2, 'Constitutional development in Africa', ? by Cohen). Ivor Thomas wrote that local government would give Africans 'self-government in the matters that really touch them' (minute, 30 May 1947). The most prominent misinterpretation is by D. Williams in *Cambridge History of Africa, vol. 8, From c. 1940 to c. 1975* (Cambridge, 1984), 341, writing about the Gold Coast in 1946: 'independence – perhaps in 15 years' time. This was a sort of date . . . Creech-Jones [sic], or . . . Cohen had in mind'.

16. CO 847/37/5/9, minute 5 of African Governors' Conference, and Cohen to Sir John Hall, 29 Oct. 1947; CO 537/4625, minute by Creech Jones, 1 March 1949.

17. CAB 134/55, CA(48)8, 29 Oct. 1948; CAB 134/56, CA(49)1, 19 Jan. 1949; CO 1015/770/43.

18. CAB 134/55, CA(48)19; CAB 128/15, CM.21(49)5, 21 March 1949; FO 371/73038, speech by Thomas to international study conference on overseas territories of Western Europe, Amsterdam, June 1948.

19. CO 537/7098; FO 371/80130.

20. CO 537/5698/69, & 5699/102.

21. CO 936/217, F.O. study paper, prepared by Permanent Under-Secretary's Committee, 21 Nov. 1952, and Sir Thomas Lloyd to Sir William Strang, 9 Sept. 1952.

22. CO 537/5921/5, & 5929/2, & 5698/66, & 5699/102.

23. CO 537/5698/69, International Relations department secret paper on 'The Colonial Empire today', May 1950, section III, drafted by S.H. Evans.

24. CO 537/3558/122, Creech Jones to Sir G. Creasy, 18 March 1948; CO 96/795, & 796/24 C.

25. PREM 8/924; CAB 128/16, CM.58(49)3, 13 Oct. 1949; CAB 129/36(2), CP(49)199.

26. CO 537/7181/5, Arden-Clarke to Cohen, 12 May 1951, and minute by Cohen, 11 June 1951.

27. CO 537/5787/52, & 7166; CAB 128/17, CM.30(50)6, 11 May 1950; CAB 129/43, CP(50)94; PREM 8/1310.

28. CO 554/298/13, Macpherson to Lloyd, 18 Jan. 1952.

29. CO 936/198/7, memo. 20 Nov. 1951.

30. CO 967/62, Creech Jones to Sir Philip Mitchell, 17 Oct. 1948; CO 537/5698/69; CO 822/114/2, minute, 20 Sept. 1946; CAB 134/1, A(49)2, 5 July 1949. Creech Jones also told Mitchell he had many doubts about the 'essential rightness of some aspects of our past policy, the basic rightness of our being in Kenya, the conditions and distribution of land in Africa'. British past folly and occasional perversity had brought intractable problems, but equally in Kenya difficulties were 'in no small part due to African suspicion and ignorance, and their own failures in social and political development' (and not only to European settlement), and they ought to be more appreciative of the contribution of Western civilisation, 'which they have almost unwittingly enjoyed'.

31. CO 537/5923; PREM 8/1113, CA(50)2; CAB 128/18, CM.76(50)1; CAB 129/24, CP(48)43; CAB 129/43, CP(50)270. See D.W. Throup, *The Economic and Social Origins of Mau Mau* (London, 1987).

32. CO 537/1468, & 1474, minute by J.S. Bennett, 30 May 1946; CO 537/2081, minute by Cohen, 1 Feb. 1947, & 2087, esp. No. 18, Bennett to Brig. Benoy, 31 March 1947; CAB 129/9, CP(46)165, memo. 18 April 1946.

33. CO 537/2088; PREM 8/1231, DO(48)9, 30 April 1948; PREM 8/1478, COS(49)381.

34. PREM 8/946, & 1388/I (1946), Bevin to Lord Stansgate, 31 Aug. 1946; CAB 128/5, CM.58(46), 7 June 1946; CAB 128/19, CM.23(51)6, 2 April 1951; FO 800/435/153, & 457/176, minute by Bevin to Prime Minister, 15 Dec. 1947.

35. CAB 128/20, CM.51(51)2, 12 July 1951, & CM.60(51)6, 27 Sept. 1951; CO 936/217, minute by Trafford Smith, 22 July 1952. See W.R. Louis, *The British Empire in the Middle East, 1945–51* (Oxford, 1984).

36. CAB 129/1, CP(45)144, memo. on future of Italian colonies, 1 Sept. 1945; CAB 131/1; CAB 131/2; PREM 8/515, memo. 19 Feb. 1946; FO 800/475, & 476. Attlee predicted: 'It may be that we shall have to consider the British Isles as an easterly extension of a strategic area, the centre of which is in the American continent, rather than as a power looking eastwards towards the Mediterranean to India and the East' (memo. 19 Feb. 1946).

37. CAB 131/2–5, *passim*, esp. DO(46)99 (COS, 5 Aug. 1946), & DO(46)40, memo. by Bevin, 13 March 1946; CO 537/1883, & 2515; FO 800/451/144, Montgomery to Bevin, 25 Sept. 1947.

38. CAB 131/2, DO(46)40, memo. by Bevin, 13 March 1946; Dalton Diary, I/34/12–13, 22 March 1946; CO 537/1231/102, COS(46)271; CO 537/1233.

39. CAB 131/2, DO(46)48, COS report, 2 April 1946; CAB 131/4, DO(47)27, memo. by A.V. Alexander, 17 March 1947, & DO(47)9/4, 26 March 1947; CO 537/1230, & 1231/102, COS(46)271; DO 35/2373, JP(48)122, & COS(49)6; FO 371/73042, & 73043; CO 967/58. A tentative alternative was a train-ferry crossing the northern part of Lake Nyasa to an outlet at Mikindani, which would get Northern Rhodesian minerals to the coast by the quickest route, but not achieve the Cape-Kenya link (PREM 8/923, Marquand Report).

40. DO 35/2380, memo. 19 Dec. 1947; FO 800/435.

41. PREM 8/923. P.C. Gordon Walker in the CRO welcomed Creech Jones's paper as 'very sensible' (DO 35/2380, minute, 8 Jan. 1948).

42. CAB 130/31, GEN. 210/1; PREM 8/733, & 923, EPC(48)35/4, 9 Nov. 1948.

43. CO 537/3030; PREM 8/923, report by H.A. Marquand on visit to Africa, 2 April 1948, and address to press conference, 18 March 1948.

44. FO 800/435/3, & 444/29; FO 371/73037, & 73038, & 73039; CO 537/3032.

45. CO 537/5896 (Griffiths); DO 35/3140/55; FO 371/76351, & 91171.

46. CO 537/5929; CAB 134/1, A(49)2, CO memo. 5 July 1949; CAB 131/10, DO(51) 17/3, 18 June 1951 (Gordon Walker); DO 35/3140; PREM 8/1284, minute by C. Syers, 22 Aug. 1950. See R. Hyam, 'The political consequences of Seretse Khama: Britain, the Bangwato and South Africa, 1948–52', *Historical Journal*, 29 (1986), 921–47.

47. CO 537/4596; DO 35/3811. Noel-Baker told a deputation led by Tom Driberg, MP, 3 March 1949: 'Our policy is not in the slightest degree influenced by economic, financial, or strategic considerations, not at all. It is influenced by this: 40 years ago

Campbell-Bannerman made a self-governing unit of the Union, to which our Liberal Parliament then agreed. Since then we have worked with them in the Commonwealth on many matters and many South African statesmen have, in our view, rendered great services to the world: we want to go on doing that, we want to keep that co-operation, we don't want to have an all-out quarrel with another member of the Commonwealth in the creation of whose self-government we still take a considerable national pride'.

48. CO 537/5710, minute by W.I.J. Wallace, 19 Sept. 1950; CO 936/123, minute by W.G. Wilson, 12 March 1952; CO 936/125/162; CO 936/217, Lloyd to Strang, 9 Sept. 1952.

49. CO 537/5708, & 5709; FO 371/88560, & 88561, & 88566; CAB 128/17, CM.28(50)3, 4 May 1950; CAB 129/39, CP(50)88. The paper was drafted by Sir E. Beckett, W.G. Wilson and A.N. Galsworthy, together with suggestions from N. Pritchard, and vetting by Cohen, Lloyd, J. Martin, and Sir K.O. Roberts-Wray (the legal adviser); it was then discussed with ministers H. Shawcross and J. Dugdale.

50. CAB 129/42, CP(50)214, 25 Sept. 1950; DO 35/3839; CO 537/5710/142; FO 371/88566. The paper was drafted by G.E. Crombie of the CRO, but a great deal of consultation went into it (e.g. with R.R. Sedgwick, G.H. Baxter, C. Syers, and J.S. Garner), and it was 'much travelled' between departments too, so that in its final form responsibility for it was spread widely. Griffiths for the C.O. and Younger for the F.O. signified their general agreement with it.

51. CAB 128/18, CM.62(50)4, 28 Sept. 1950; FO 800/435/153; CAB 131/10, DO(51)17, 18 June 1951; PREM 8/1284.

52. CAB 129/45, CP(51)109, memo. by Gordon Walker, 16 April 1951, after visit to South Africa, Southern Rhodesia and High Commission Territories.

53. See R. Hyam, 'The geopolitical origins of the Central African Federation: Britain, Rhodesia and South Africa, 1948–53', *Historical Journal*, 30 (1987), 145–72.

54. CO 1015/89/13, BBC talk by Creech Jones, 15 April 1952; CO 1015/144/15, and CO 1015/770, visit of Attlee to Central Africa, August 1952. In this matter Attlee was more far-sighted than Cohen, who had become too personally involved with the federal scheme. Cohen's determination to bring Federation into being was not, however, somehow out of line with his West African policy: there is only a paradox if his commitment to 'decolonisation' is exaggerated. His African policy was consistent: in all parts of Africa he wanted to retain the initiative against extremists, and *control* nationalist movements. He opposed withdrawal of the federal proposals on the ground that it would abandon the field to irresponsible 'outright nationalists', which would only give impetus to European extremists. Africans should therefore, as he put it, be brought round to 'a true realisation of their own interests', confronted as they were by the 'Afrikaner menace' (DO 35/3601/104; CO 1015/59, minute, 31 Oct. 1951; CO 1015/64/36 B, to Sir G. Rennie, 16 Nov. 1951).

55. DO 35/3140/55, & FO 371/91171, Baring's 'final review' dispatch to Commonwealth Relations Secretary, 30 June 1951; see also Gordon Walker Papers, GNWR 1/9, Diary, 2 April 1950.

56. *As it happened*, 191.

57. CO 1015/770/43. Cohen expressly described Northern Rhodesian African opinion as 'immature and unorganised politically' (CO 537/7203/7, memo. 18 April 1951).

58. CO 967/57, Sir A. Dawe's memo. on East Africa, July 1942, and 'Mr Macmillan's counter-proposals', 15 Aug. 1942.

59. CO 847/35/6, minute by Sir F. Pedler, 1 Nov. 1946; CO 537/3561, report on West African tour by Rees-Williams, 27 Sept. 1948.

60. FO 371/107032 (UP.134/1), Sir G. Jebb to Foreign Secretary, 12 Jan. 1953.

[10]

The Colonial Policies of the Mouvement Républicain Populaire, 1944–1954: From Reform to Reaction*

Martin Thomas

HISTORIANS of French imperialism after 1945 grapple with a central question: Why was postwar France so determined to keep its overseas empire intact? The crushing defeat of 1940 and the traumas of occupation and Vichy collaboration were manifestly prejudicial to colonial control. The Vichy-Free French rivalries played out across imperial territory from Africa through Syria to Indo-China amounted to an undeclared civil war. What more obvious evidence of French disunity and inability to govern an empire could there be? Yet within months of the Liberation a new resolve to remain a colonial power had taken root.

Several factors help explain this transition. The first is the nature and outcome of metropolitan liberation. After Vichy's ignominious collapse in July 1944, the differing rates of liberation across southern and eastern France and the provisional nature of republican government prior to the establishment of the Fourth Republic in October 1946 all added to the expectation that reconstruction of the French political system should mark a new beginning – both a deliberate rupture with the wartime past and a cherry-picking of the most attractive aspects of democratic republicanism. The array of new political parties to emerge from the resistance, the long overdue enfranchisement of women, the unprecedented popular appeal of French Communism, the discrediting of much of the French right, and the still untested power of Gaullism suggested that postwar politics would be of a different stripe to the old days of Third Republic immobilism. Perhaps this new political elite would make a better job of the French empire.

Another reason for French imperial confidence in 1945 was less readily admitted, but no less significant. The Vichy state had paid more attention to colonial affairs than the Republic it replaced. This was partly circumstantial. The Vichy regime had freer rein to experiment within colonial territory than in metropolitan France. But ardent Pétainists were also convinced imperialists. Vichy was more assiduous in its colonial propaganda, more fervent in its colonial legislation and more inclined to theorize about the nature and purpose of Empire than its Free French rival.[1] The Vichy years were exceptional. And they had a Gaullist

*The author wishes to thank both the Nuffield Foundation for funding the research for this article, and the journal's referees for their valuable advice.

1. Recent articles on Vichy colonial policy reveal increasing historical interest in the subject. As examples, see Pascal Blanchard and Gilles Boëtsch, 'Races et propagande coloniale sous le régime de Vichy 1940–1944', *Africa*, il (1994), 531–61; Eric Jennings, 'Vichy à Madagascar: La Révolution Nationale, l'enseignement et la jeunesse, 1940–1942', *Revue d'histoire moderne et contemporaine*, xlvi (1999), 727–44; Ruth Ginio, 'Marshal Pétain spoke to Schoolchildren: Vichy propaganda in French West Africa, 1940–1943', *International Journal of African Historical Studies*, xxxiii (2000), 291–312.

equivalent: a republican mirror-image colonialism which, although in direct opposition to Vichy itself, shared many of its underlying imperial values. The success of Free France as an external resistance movement had an obvious colonial dimension. On both sides of the Vichy-Free French divide then, imperial attachments acquired a new material and symbolic importance.

The civilian population living under occupation does not fit easily into this picture of popular imperialism. Did the young *maquisards* evading labour service in Germany, the wives of prisoners of war or the families struggling to make ends meet really care much about empire one way or the other? An answer to this question lies in what historians D. Bruce Marshall and Charles-Robert Ageron have termed the 'colonial myth'. Ageron offers a balanced solution; Vichy's propagandizing had not turned France into a nation of empire enthusiasts, but during 1944–45 the French public endorsed provisional government plans to keep the empire intact. Hence the colonial myth: control of empire, it was assumed, would enable France to reclaim its rightful place on the international stage. French colonial thinking appeared so 'frozen' because most French politicians were haunted by the prospect of French decline and a fear of imperial collapse. Only worsening colonial violence in 1947 led the legitimacy of empire to be seriously questioned.[2]

War in Indo-China, the *Parti Communiste Française*'s (PCF) withdrawal from government, the Madagascar rebellion and rising nationalist dissent in Morocco and Tunisia destroyed the postwar fiction of a French empire reborn.[3] Prior to this, policymakers traded on the disinclination of French voters to engage with imperial problems. Political disputes over the constitution of the French Union centred upon the officials, the legal experts and the political actors within the key advisory commissions charged with the formulation of detailed proposals.[4] Colonial withdrawal was not just out of the question, it was not even in the public mind. If anything, ignorance of actual conditions across the empire was a more potent force for popular imperialism than the more deeply rooted colonialism that Vichy had tried to foster. This brings us to the final aspect of the imperial optimism in France at war's end. This was the anticipation that metropolitan and imperial constitution-making would proceed hand-in-hand. As the provisional government and the first and second Constituent Assemblies made plans for France's new republic, so they also produced a new schema for a more unified empire. Fourth Republic and French Union would be launched

---

2. D. Bruce Marshall, *The French colonial myth and constitution-making in the Fourth Republic* (New Haven CT., 1973); Charles-Robert Ageron, 'La survivance d'un mythe: la puissance par l'empire colonial (1944–1947)', *Revue française d'histoire d'Outre-Mer*, lxxvii (1985), 388–97.

3. Marshall, *The French colonial myth*, pp. 312–14; Alain-Gérard Marsot, 'The Crucial Year: Indochina 1946', *Journal of Contemporary History*, xix (1984), 337–54.

4. James I. Lewis, 'The French colonial service and the issues of reform, 1944–48', *Contemporary European History*, iv (1995), 157–69.

382 COLONIAL POLICIES OF THE MOUVEMENT REPUBLICAIN

together in October 1946. The democratic legitimacy of the former was supposed to enhance the enlightened reformism of the latter. Old-style colonialism was dead, long live a new French imperialism grounded in the concept of federal partnership between metropole and dependent territories. The contrast between warm words and limited practical deeds exposed the actual French refusal to contemplate decolonization.

This article examines the French political party that best exemplified the new imperialism of postwar France: the Christian Democrat *Mouvement Républicain Populaire* (MRP). It traces the evolution of MRP colonial policies from the party's foundation in November 1944 to the Geneva settlement of the first Indo-China war a decade later. Why did this new party become so conservative in colonial affairs when, at its inception, it had neither a strong imperialist tradition nor the ties to commercial, military and bureaucratic interests that usually came with it? In the ten years to 1954, MRP ministers, the party's annual conferences and its overseas federations were identifiable with the worst of colonial repression in the North African Maghreb, black Africa, Indo-China and Madagascar. Yet the organizing principle of French Christian Democracy was a reformist social catholicism that initially facilitated co-operation with parties of the left less reconciled to colonial rule or neo-colonialist dominance.

Unlike their Socialist ministerial partners in the 1944–47 period of tripartite government, MRP supporters were untainted by association with the failure of colonial reform in the late 1930s. Unlike the Radical Party and the *Union Démocratique et Socialiste et la Résistance* (UDSR) – both of which tended to vote with the MRP on colonial matters – the MRP was unencumbered by long-standing links with reactionary settler lobbies. Local Radical Party federations were the most powerful of the major metropolitan party organizations in postwar Algeria. The UDSR's many colonial federations from Algeria to Tahiti were overwhelmingly European-controlled. They remained so after the spectacular 1951 volte-face of Félix Houphouët-Boigny's *Rassemblement Démocratique Africain* (RDA).[5] As a result of this, the RDA, the most powerful of the political parties in francophone black Africa, aligned with the UDSR.

By 1945 the MRP wrestled with its own colonial problem, distinct from that facing its Socialist colleagues in government. The SFIO was slow to abandon its traditional preference for gradualistic colonial

---

5. Archives Nationales (AN), Fonds UDSR, 412AP, box 34/dossier 8, UDSR Tunisia federation letter to party secretariat, 5 Oct. 1951; box 31/dossier 4, Roger Perriard (Algiers) to UDSR secretary-general, 30 June 1953. The UDSR was formed in June 1945 by the fusion of five non-communist resistance groups. From April 1946 the UDSR cooperated with the Radicals in the *Rassemblement des Gauches Républicaines* (RGR), an anti-communist federation that included key conservative deputies of the Third Republic.

reform justified on humanist grounds. By contrast, the MRP could pick its colonial policies off the shelf. In doing so, the party made confusing choices. The strident imperialism of the MRP executive *Comité National* was always at odds with the theoretical support for progressive reform and higher spending on colonial development proposed by the MRP's leading foreign policy specialist, Robert Schuman, among others.[6] Where the Radicals were the key parliamentary defenders of French colonialism in the 1930s, the MRP would assume this role in the Fourth Republic albeit supported by other, less powerful parties of the centre and moderate right. This has led one historian to restate the theory of a postwar French 'colonial consensus' first advanced by Tony Smith in 1974. Where Smith focused upon the SFIO, James I. Lewis contends that the MRP was the most doggedly colonialist of the governing parties in postwar France. In imperial policy at least, in 1945–46 the MRP filled the void left by the sharp electoral decline of the Radicals. Senior MRP figures tipped the balance within the council of ministers against meaningful democratic reforms and colonial self-government during deliberations over the restructuring of the empire as the French Union.[7] Ultimately, as Lewis has suggested, the party clothed its colonial conservatism in the tricolour of French nationalism, insisting that France's imperial connections were fundamental to the nation's postwar recovery. By the time tripartism broke down in May 1947, it was clear that the centre-left would not provide the impetus for imperial withdrawal.[8]

The puzzle of the MRP's colonialism has long exercised historians. Ronald Irving's pioneering studies of French Christian Democracy and of the Indo-China war explored the contradictions within the MRP's attitude to empire and the limitations of its support for 'progressive federalism' in the French Union. Jacques Dalloz also investigated Indo-China and MRP leader Georges Bidault in separate studies, synthesizing his conclusions in a key article in 1996.[9] Frédéric Turpin and, above all, Martin Shipway have exposed the MRP's pivotal role in the descent to war in Indo-China during 1946. Most recently, Turpin and James I. Lewis have stressed the MRP's part in restricting the constitutional reforms within the French Union project and the 1947

6. Charles-André Julien, *L'Afrique du Nord en marche, nationalisme musulman et souveraineté française* (Paris, 1972), p. 166.

7. Lewis, 'The MRP and the Genesis of the French Union, 1944–1948', *French History*, xii (1998), 276–314; Tony Smith, 'The French Colonial Consensus and People's War, 1946–58', *Journal of Contemporary History*, ix (1974), 217–47.

8. Lewis, 'The MRP', 277, 298–302; 'The French colonial service', 176–8; Odile Rudelle, 'Le vote du statut de l'Algérie', in *L'Année 1947*, ed. Serge Berstein and Pierre Milza (Paris, 2000), p. 317.

9. R. E. M. Irving, *Christian Democracy in France* (London, 1973), and *The First Indochina war. French and American policy, 1945–1954* (London, 1975); Jacques Dalloz, *The War in Indo-China, 1945–54* (Dublin, 1990), and id., *Georges Bidault. Biographie politique*; id., 'L'opposition M.R.P. à la guerre d'Indochine', *Revue d'histoire moderne et contemporaine*, xliii (1996), 106–18.

384 COLONIAL POLICIES OF THE MOUVEMENT REPUBLICAIN

Statute for Algeria.[10] Emile-François Callot, Henri Descamps, Pierre Letamendia and Richard Vinen have also explored the party's popular appeal, the social origins of its membership and the reasons for its dramatic loss of electoral support in the early 1950s.[11] This article uses the MRP archive to suggest that the MRP's organizational structure, its dwindling membership and the leadership's efforts to define a coherent imperial position to disarm the challenge of Gaullism contextualize the rightward shift in MRP colonial policy first highlighted by Irving in the early 1970s. To the domestic and international pressures of Cold War and French dependency on the United States examined by diplomatic historians[12], we must add the dynamics of party politics in the early Fourth Republic to explain the MRP's imperialism.

Assessment of the MRP's colonialist outlook must also take account of the party's vision of France's postwar imperial identity. Here, a different strand of historical work provides essential background. In the past decade cultural historians and social anthropologists have done much to redefine the nature of French colonialism. In doing so, they have also extended the boundaries of the social history of empire.[13] Ann Laura Stoler, Herman Lebovics, Alice Conklin and Owen White have all highlighted a growing conservatism in the cultural construction of French imperial policies during the inter-war period. Ann Laura Stoler has traced official efforts to demarcate more rigid social and sexual boundaries between colonial *fonctionnaires* and indigenous peoples.[14] Herman Lebovics has illustrated the emergence of a more hegemonic and culturally-exclusive concept of 'Frenchness'. This, for example, determined the new imperial discourse of 'Greater France' which

10. On Indo-China: Frédéric Turpin, 'Le Mouvement Républicain Populaire et la guerre d'Indochine (1944–1954)', *Revue d'Histoire Diplomatique*, cx (1996), 157–90; Martin Shipway, *The Road to War: France and Vietnam, 1944–1947* (Oxford, 1996), chs. 7–9, and 'Creating an emergency: metropolitan constraints on French colonial policy and its breakdown in Indo-China, 1945–47', *Journal of Imperial and Commonwealth History*, xxi (1993), 1–16. On Algeria: Frédéric Turpin, 'Le Mouvement Républicain Populaire et l'avenir de l'Algérie (1947–1962)', *Revue d'histoire diplomatique*, cxiii (1999), 171–203; James I. Lewis, 'French Politics and the Algerian Statute of 1947', *Maghreb Review*, xvii (1992), 147–72; 'The French colonial service', 153–88 (note 4); and 'The MRP and the Genesis of the French Union', 276–314 (note 7).

11. Henri Descamps, *La Démocratie Chrétienne et le MRP: de 1946 à 1959* (Paris, 1981), livre 3, pp. 171–223; Pierre Letamendia, *Le Mouvement Républicain Populaire. Histoire d'un grand parti français* (Paris, 1995), pp. 151–251; Richard Vinen, *Bourgeois Politics in France, 1945–1951* (Cambridge, 1995), ch. 10.

12. Excellent treatments of MRP foreign policy include: John W. Young, *France, the Cold War and the Western Alliance, 1944–1949: French foreign policy and post-war Europe* (Leicester, 1990); Irwin M. Wall, *The United States and the making of postwar France, 1945–1954* (Cambridge, 1991); *La puissance française en question (1945–1949)*, ed. René Girault and Robert Frank (Paris, 1988); *Le MRP et la construction européenne*, ed. Serge Berstein, Jean-Marie Mayeur and Pierre Milza (Paris, 1993); William I. Hitchcock, *France Restored. Cold War Diplomacy and the Quest for Leadership in Europe, 1944–1954* (Chapel Hill, NC, 1998).

13. This new field is highlighted by Frederick Cooper and Ann Laura Stoler in the introduction to their edited collection *Tensions of Empire. Colonial Cultures in a Bourgeois World* (Berkeley, 1997), pp. 1–37.

14. Ann Laura Stoler, 'Sexual Affronts and Racial Frontiers: European Identities and the Cultural Politics of Exclusion in Colonial Southeast Asia', in *Tensions of Empire*, pp. 198–215.

legitimated the subordination of colonized peoples within the highly centralized and modernizing vision of empire portrayed at the 1931 Exposition Coloniale.[15] Alice Conklin has gone furthest, precisely measuring the retreat from radical social engineering in French West Africa towards a more conservative associationist ideology that reaffirmed the distance between French rulers and their subject populations. She detects a new emphasis in French colonial rhetoric on the extent of differences between colonizers and colonized, and a more racialized evaluation of the need to maintain the social, cultural and political boundaries between them. Influenced by eugenist thinking, by 1930 administrators in French West Africa endorsed the hierarchical structure of tribal society the better to contain popular pressure for emancipation and economic improvement.[16] In similar vein, Owen White has used French political, cultural and educational responses to miscegenation, and the changing conceptualization of a '*métis* problem' in French West Africa, to indicate the hollowness of French colonial liberalism before the 1950s.[17] These works reveal that by the 1930s the official construction of republican imperialism had abandoned the assimilationist ideal of gradually imparting the cultural and political benefits of French civilization to dependent peoples. The brief interlude of Popular Front colonial reform only partially bucked the trend.[18]

The racialized authoritarianism of Vichy colonial rule was already inherent in the imperial system. Nor did it disappear with the restoration of republican democracy in France. Any colonial ideology, whether based on the eventual adoption of metropolitan culture by colonized populations or on the preservation of traditional societal structures in the colonies themselves, is racially hierarchical and authoritarian. The MRP was quick to grasp this. From 1944 the irony was that reforms devised to increase colonial loyalty to France through gradual democratization and the steady improvement of living standards crystallized local political demands that France refused to meet. As ever, the essential contradiction of imperial reformism remained: no matter how liberal a reform might seem, it could not be truly democratic if it presupposed the continuation of colonial control. The 'liberal universalism' espoused by the architects of the French Union was at variance with social exclusion of subject peoples from the highest levels of political office.[19]

---

15. Herman Lebovics, *True France. The Wars over Cultural Identity, 1900–1945* (Ithaca, 1992), ch. 2.

16. Alice Conklin, *A Mission to Civilize. The Republican Idea of Empire in France and West Africa, 1895–1930* (Stanford, 1997), chs. 5 and 6.

17. Owen White, *Children of the French Empire. Miscegenation and Colonial Society in French West Africa* (Oxford, 1999).

18. The gulf between the limited effectiveness and the lasting impact of Popular Front colonial reform is reassessed in *French Colonial Empire and the Popular Front. Hope and Disillusion*, ed. Tony Chafer and Amanda Sackur (London, 1999).

19. The roots of this tension are discussed in Uday S. Mehta, 'Liberal Strategies of Exclusion', in *Tensions of Empire*, ed. Cooper and Stoler, pp. 59–86.

386 COLONIAL POLICIES OF THE MOUVEMENT REPUBLICAIN

Reluctant to cede genuine political power to colonial representatives, French Ministers and officials took refuge in a more clearly defined economic determinism. Even though France was to regulate African political life, the material benefits of increased life expectancy, falling infant mortality rates, better education and long-term infrastructural development justified the continued *présence française*. Reform should increase inter-dependence between metropole and colony, not pave the way for French disengagement.[20] Even here, an inexorable logic of decolonization endured. If the postwar justification of empire rested squarely on improving the lot of Africans or Vietnamese, then surely this was a finite process? If, as Colonial Ministry officials insisted, colonial peoples had yet to acquire the political skills, the level of mass education and the socio-economic sophistication necessary to run their own affairs, what could possibly justify colonial domination once reform conferred these very benefits? The wider political engagement of a subject people within a colonial system was bound to undermine it.

The MRP did not set out to assume a mantle of conservative imperialism previously defined by the French right. But MRP supporters were not immune to a recent imperial past which had obfuscated the contradictions between colonial control, republican ideals and individual rights.[21] Only gradually did this become apparent. When the MRP was launched in late 1944 its attitude to colonial questions was unclear. Not until 1950 did a minority on the left of the party question the boundaries between colonial rulers and indigenous subjects.

In 1944, French Christian Democrat leaders considered the reconstitution of the inter-war *Parti Démocrate Populaire* (PDP). This was rejected. Instead, the MRP executive modelled its new movement on the coalition of Catholic resistance groups from which the bulk of the senior leadership derived. As the MRP's first Secretary-General, André Colin, put it in November 1944, the Movement should be a broad coalition, 'un grand Rassemblement politique groupant tous les démocrates'.[22] Anxious to place clear water between the reactionary clericalism of Vichy and the social catholicism of its supporters, the MRP's basis in wartime resistance was a rallying point to patriotic voters appalled by the Communist Party's attempt to hijack the resistance heritage. The MRP commitment to social reform conferred a progressive image in the left-dominated years of the *après-libération*. Its defence of Catholic values, individual freedom and 'sound' finance eased its rightward shift in the years of third force government after 1947. From this position it

20. Keith Panter-Brick, 'Independence, French Style', in *Decolonization and African Independence. The Transfer of Power, 1960–1980*, ed. Prosser Gifford and Wm. Roger Louis (New Haven, 1988), p. 73.

21. Lebovics, *True France*, p. xiii.

22. AN, Fonds MRP, 350AP1, Dossier: 1MRP2/Dr1, 'Commission P.D.P. et M.R.P., réunion du 8 novembre 1944'.

was only a small step into the right-dominated cabinets of March 1952–May 1954.[23]

If politically active at all before the war, most members of the future MRP's *Comité National* had supported the Movement's inter-war predecessors, the PDP and Marc Sangnier's *Jeune République*. Others contributed to the more liberal Catholic newspapers or were members of Catholic workers' groups, notably the *Confédération Française des Travailleurs Chrétiens*.[24] A similar organization, the *Jeunesse Ouvrière Chrétienne* (JOC) founded in 1925, targeted young Catholic workers aged between fourteen and twenty five. Neither the precursors of the MRP nor the Catholic press of the 1930s took much interest in colonial reform. Rarely close to high office, the PDP never confronted France's imperial problems. It opted instead to support a humanistic colonialism, similar to that of the Socialists. The PDP's few contributions to colonial debate stressed the promotion of French culture, the achievements of the Catholic missions and greater investment in colonial education and social welfare.[25] Catholic worker groups, too, only made their mark in colonial politics after 1945. The JOC set up branches in Senegal, Ivory Coast and Guinea between 1937 and 1939. But JOC membership took off owing to the rapid growth of West African urbanization between 1945 and 1956.[26]

The majority of the MRP leadership came to prominence through outstanding resistance activity. Jean Letourneau helped run the resistance group *Liberté* in southern France before working closely with Georges Bidault in the *Conseil National de la Résistance* (CNR) from 1943. Pierre-Henri Teitgen also worked within *Liberté* prior to his capture and torture by the Gestapo in June 1944. Within French North Africa, Paul Coste-Floret led the Algiers section of *Combat-Empire*. Claude Mont, a future MRP representative within the French Union Assembly, had reorganized Catholic trade unionism in Morocco after

23. Letamendia, *Le Mouvement Républicain Populaire*, pp. 56–63, 80; Descamps, *La Démocratie Chrétienne*, livre 2, pp. 95–167.

24. Oscar L. Arnal, 'Catholic roots of collaboration and resistance in France in the 1930s', *Canadian Journal of History*, xvii (1982), 88; William Rauch Jr., 'From the Sillon to the Mouvement Républicain Populaire: Doctor Robert Cornilleau and a generation of Christian Democrats in France, 1910–1940', *Catholic Historical Review*, (April 1972), 43–66. Founded by Auguste Champetier de Ribes in 1924, the *Parti Démocrate Populaire* failed to make a major electoral breakthrough in the inter-war period. For a profile of MRP deputies, see Emile-François Callot, *Le Mouvement Républicain Populaire. Origine, structure, doctrine, programme et action politique* (Paris, 1978), pp. 241–4, 420 table 3.

25. Danièle Zeraffa, 'La perception de la puissance dans la formation Démocrate Chrétienne', *Revue d'Histoire Moderne et Contemporaine*, xxxiii (1984), 644–5; Jean-Claude Demory, *Georges Bidault 1899–1983* (Paris, 1995), pp. 50–3; Descamps, *La Démocratie Chrétienne*, p. 78; Letamendia, *Le Mouvement Républicain Populaire*, p. 347.

26. Roger Pasquier, 'La Jeunesse Ouvrière Chrétienne (JOC) et la formation d'une élite en AOF', in *AOF: réalités et héritages. Sociétés ouest-africaines et ordre colonial, 1895–1960*, ed. Charles Becker, Saliou Mbaye and Ibrahima Thioub (Dakar, 1997), pp. 376–9.

the Torch landings in 1942.[27] The party's first electoral programme in November 1945 borrowed heavily from the CNR Charter. It advocated a federal imperial system based upon the gradual introduction of representative democracy and eventual autonomy 'aux territoires plus évolués'. The phrase was significant. It asserted the inherent superiority of French rule and reaffirmed the orthodox conception of racial hierarchy in colonial societies.[28] Official statements insisting that the pace and scope of colonial reform should reflect the level of political and cultural sophistication in an individual overseas territory employed what Frederick Cooper and Ann Laura Stoler term 'the grammar of difference'. The ruling elite justified imperial rule by stressing the gulf between French and colonial society.[29]

MRP organizers largely drawn from the Catholic resistance movements made much of a cultural heritage that placed France at the heart of the Catholic world. What Colin Nettelbeck has identified as the 'systematic conflation of Christianity and Frenchness' had implications for the formulation of MRP colonial policy. The case for empire was easier to make if French rule promised moral authority as well as material reform.[30] Dr Louis Aujoulat was among the first to link Christian Democratic ideals and colonial ideology. Aujoulat was a missionary based in Yaoundé who founded the *Action catholique du Cameroun* in 1937 and served as a deputy for the territory between 1945 and 1956. In a report to the third MRP national congress in March 1947, he insisted that the party's humanistic values and respect for individual dignity imposed an obligation to pursue social and economic reform within the French Union.[31] Christian Democracy could not reinvigorate the more archaic concept of a civilizing mission but, to its supporters, its Catholic idealism validated imperial control. In Ronald Irving's words, 'Paris was to be to the French Union what Rome is to the Catholic Church, both spiritual home and supreme authority.'[32]

Christian Democrats by definition linked their religious values to the social reforms and republican values they promoted. Even so, the MRP's social catholicism did not translate readily to a colonial setting. Christian Democratic doctrine made respect for the individual citizen

27. AN, Fonds MRP, 350AP76, Dossier: 4MRP6: 'Election des conseillers de l'Union française', July 1952; Irving, *Christian Democracy*, pp. 75–8.

28. AN, Fonds MRP, 350MRP1, 1MRP1/Dr 2, 'Programme du M.R.P.', 8 Nov. 1945; André Nouschi, 'Modernisation au maghreb et puissance française (1945–1948)', in *La puissance française*, ed. Girault and Frank, p. 256.

29. Frederick Cooper and Ann Laura Stoler, 'Between Metropole and Colony. Rethinking a Research Agenda', in *Tensions of Empire*, pp. 3–4.

30. Colin Nettelbeck, 'The Eldest Daughter and the *Trente glorieuses*: Catholicism and national identity in postwar France', *Modern and Contemporary France*, vi (1998), 450.

31. AN, Fonds MRP, 350AP124, Aujoulat report on the French Union to MRP National Congress, 13–16 March 1947, cited in Turpin, 'Le Mouvement Républicain Populaire et l'avenir de l'Algérie', 171–2.

32. Irving, *Christian Democracy*, p. 200.

POPULAIRE, 1944–1954: FROM REFORM TO REACTION   389

an organizing principle of a just, pluralist society. It acknowledged that industrial capitalism tended towards class formation and closed governing elites. Equally, the MRP stressed the citizen's moral responsibility to pursue individual self-improvement.[33] Neither the MRP's emphasis on citizens' rights and democratic pluralism, nor its belief that individuals should be free to realize their own potential, were compatible with colonial domination. The MRP secretariat escaped this dilemma by insisting that the cardinal tenet of the French Union was its provision for wider citizenship. As late as October 1953 the secretariat tried to prove the growth of democratic participation within the empire by gathering statistics on citizenship applications, the franchise and electoral participation in black African territories.[34]

Social Catholic doctrine may not have offered solid foundations for a distinct colonial philosophy but it clearly influenced the choices made by MRP supporters anxious to find immediate justification for colonial rule. As a result, the MRP's colonialism was a hybrid. It mimicked the Socialists' humanistic defence of reformist imperialism. But it was also indulgent towards the Christian universalism inherent in all French colonialist theory and apologia for colonial control. Conquest of empire had been in Paul Clay Sorum's phrase, 'an effort of Roman Catholic proselytism' supported by intense missionary activity.[35] By 1945 there were some 1.1 million Christians in French black Africa, most of whom were served by missionary priests. The figure was higher still in the Indo-China federation. In 1931 the Société des Missions Etrangères estimated 1.3 million Catholics among the total Vietnamese population of 15 million. Vietnam's Catholics would face stark choices during the Indo-China war. The country's Catholic bishops denounced the Vietminh's atheistic communism, and Vietminh attacks on priests and Church property increased from 1949 onwards.[36] The MRP soon emerged as the party most committed to the defence of Christian observance in the empire. Between 1945 and 1948 MRP ministers also supported closer ties between the Papacy and the Catholic Church in French Africa.[37]

The educational provision and charity networks of such organizations as the *Société des Missionnaires d'Afrique* (colloquially known as the '*Pères Blancs*') and the *Soeurs de Saint-Joseph de Cluny* were readily

33. Ibid., pp. 52–64.

34. AN, Fonds MRP, 350AP7, Dossier: 1MRP6/Dr.2, Secretariat memo., 'Les colonies à l'Union française', n.d. October 1953. The territories selected were Guinée, Togo, Cameroon, French Congo and Madagascar.

35. Paul Clay Sorum, *Intellectuals and Decolonization in France* (Chapel Hill, 1977), pp. 21–2.

36. R. P. Claude Lange, 'L'église Catholique au Viêtnam', in *Les Chemins de la décolonisation de l'empire colonial français 1936–1956*, ed. Charles-Robert Ageron (Paris, 1986), pp. 181–7.

37. Paule Brasseur, 'L'église catholique et la décolonisation en Afrique noire', in *Les Chemins de la décolonisation*, pp. 56–9.

endorsed by the MRP.[38] It was surely no coincidence that once the MRP broke with their PCF coalition partners in 1947, the West African Catholic daily newspaper *Afrique Nouvelle*, a fierce critic of colonial injustice, began denouncing the Communist-affiliated RDA as an atheistic seditionist movement.[39] Unlike the French left, the MRP could support missionary evangelism if not the missions' historic antagonism to republicanism. Yet, thanks to its own republicanism, the MRP was also more at ease with the Jacobin nationalism that had alienated much of the Catholic right from previous imperial expansion. In 1947, for example, Bidault pressed the Vatican and selected French Catholic missions to point out the benefits of imperial rule in an effort to win over American Catholic opinion.[40]

During 1946, the structure of the French Union was discussed within the second Constituent Assembly's constitutional commission. MRP supporters with a particular colonial or legal expertise made a greater impact in these debates than their ministerial colleagues.[41] The MRP leadership did, however, secure the backing of the right-wing *Parti Républicain de la Liberté* over colonial issues. This was crucial to defeat Socialist and PCF pressure for greater colonial autonomy within a revised French Union scheme. The MRP executive feared that their partners in government would cede excessive power to elected colonial representatives. MRP leaders even voted against proposals modified according to their wishes because of their refusal to accept a unicameral French Union Assembly. The MRP's spoiling tactics drew diverse criticism. In April 1946 the Gaullist Jacques Soustelle, the left-wing progressive Pierre Cot and the UDSR leader René Pleven were sharply critical of the MRP's role.[42] On the other hand, Henri Laurentie, director of political affairs at the Ministry for Overseas France, shared MRP reservations. His own proposals for a federal French Union scheme preserved the hierarchical distinctions between territories at differing stages of political and economic development. Laurentie's ideas played a decisive role in shaping MRP policy towards black Africa and Indo-China.[43] The party leadership was also buoyed up by rank-and-file support for a politically restrictive colonial policy.

38. On mission activities in French West Africa, see Paule Brasseur, 'Les missions catholiques à la création de l'AOF, leur développement et leur gestion', in *AOF* tome II, ed. Becker, Mbaye and Thioub, 825–35; White, *Children*, pp. 43–6.

39. R. P. Joseph Roger de Benoist, 'L'hebdomadaire Catholique Dakarois *Afrique Nouvelle* et la décolonisation de l'A.O.F.', in *Les Chemins de la décolonisation*, pp. 531–7.

40. Annie Lacroix-Riz, *Les protectorats d'Afrique du Nord entre la France et Washington du débarquement à l'indépendance. Maroc et Tunisie 1942–1956* (Paris, 1988), p. 28.

41. Shipway, *The Road to War*, pp. 93–4.

42. Paul Isoart, 'L'élaboration de la constitution de l'Union française: les Assemblées constituantes et le problème colonial', in *Les Chemins de la décolonisation*, p. 27.

43. Lewis, 'The MRP', 282–98 *passim*. The clearest treatment of Laurentie's views is in Shipway, *The Road to War*.

Faced with complex constitutional alternatives, press treatment of colonial reform tended to reduce the alternatives to the tightening or the loosening of imperial connections. The MRP newspaper, *L'Aube*, and the party members' journal, *Forces Nouvelles*, circulated from Dakar amongst the party's overseas federations, were therefore unusual. Each stood out in its detailed critique of the electoral regime proposed in Algeria and the black African colonies in 1946.[44] But once MRP ministers secured their preferred version of a more centralized French Union without universal citizenship, common suffrage rights or powerful colonial legislatures, party interest in black Africa waned. Even in 1946 itself, the MRP parliamentary group's weekly *bulletin d'information* contained virtually no references to francophone Africa, excepting a report on the likelihood of an international trusteeship in the Cameroon Mandate.[45] Detailed consideration of the doctrinal implications of differing constitutional schemes remained the preserve of a handful of party specialists. Two of the most influential were Louis Aujoulat in Cameroon and Algiers deputy Paul-Emile Viard.[46]

Aujoulat and Viard represented settler communities that felt particularly embattled in 1945. Cameroon was the heartland of the reactionary lobby group, the *Etats généraux de la colonisation française*. Established in the port of Douala in September 1945 to represent the interests of settlers in French West and Equatorial Africa, the *Etats généraux* were animated by their hostility to emergent African nationalist parties, the RDA above all. Settlers in Cameroon hoped to emulate the success of their compatriots in the Ivory Coast. In August 1945 the settler community in Abidjan persuaded the Ministry of Colonies to engineer the replacement of Governor André Latrille. The Governor's indulgence towards the new African political parties galvanized a vituperative settler campaign against him. Following MRP gains in the elections to a second Constituent Assembly in June 1946, the *Etats généraux* found a more receptive audience in Paris.[47] On 3 August 1946, in a rare acclamation of the pre-war regime, the *Etats généraux* implored the new government to recognize the achievement of the Third Republic in building a strong, unified empire.[48] Stripped of its rhetoric, this was a demand for the maintenance of settler privilege. Although a single electoral college

44. Lewis, 'French Politics and the Algerian Statute', 171–2, n. 37.

45. AN, Fonds MRP, 350AP76, Dossier: 4MRP9/Dr. 1, Bulletins d'information, Groupe Parlementaire MRP, 1946, no. 7, annex 3, 6 March 1946.

46. Shipway, *The Road to War*, p. 93.

47. The *Etats généraux* were built around pre-existing Chambers of Commerce networks in Douala, Dakar, Conakry and other major trading ports, see United States National Archives (USNA), Department of State decimal files, RG 59, 851T.00, French West Africa, Political 1945–49, box 6326, AMCONGEN, Dakar, to State, 3 Nov. 1945. Regarding Latrille: Timothy C. Weiskel 'Independence and the Longue Durée: The Ivory Coast "Miracle" Reconsidered', in *Decolonization and African Independence*, pp. 361–3.

48. Christian Bidegaray, 'Le tabou de l'indépendance dans les débats constituants sur les pays de l'outre-mer français: 1945–1958', in *L'Afrique noire française: l'heure des indépendances*, ed. Charles-Robert Ageron and Marc Michel (Paris, 1992), p. 195.

392 COLONIAL POLICIES OF THE MOUVEMENT REPUBLICAIN

would be established in AOF for elections to the National Assembly, in other black African territories the constitutional provisions of the French Union guaranteed *colon* dominance by preserving a dual college system in national and local elections.

Meanwhile, in Algeria the battlelines between the Muslim population and the settler community were brought sharply into focus by the Sétif uprising in eastern Constantine. Between 7–9 May 1945 over a hundred settlers and local officials were killed in a wave of Muslim violence stimulated in part by French plans to deport Algerian nationalist leader Messali Hadj. French vengeance upon the local Muslim population was immediate and massive. Army free-fire tactics and settler vigilantism left several thousand Muslims dead.[49] Viard, Dean of the Algiers Law School and vice-president of the MRP parliamentary group, typified the hardline mood in the aftermath of Sétif. He made it abundantly clear to the MRP leadership that the settler community was not about to relinquish its grip on Algerian politics by sanctioning any form of federal power-sharing with the Muslim majority.[50]

The MRP was uniquely receptive to its new constituency of settler support during the constitutional debates of 1946. Over subsequent years, growing MRP support for European federalism informed the party's approach to the economic development of the French Union. In December 1948 MRP members in the French Union Assembly sponsored the creation of a federalist group to lobby in support of closer ties between metropolitan France and French Union territories.[51] Rather than marking a systematic reassessment of the politico-economic links between metropole and periphery, this support for imperial federalism simply crystallized opposition against any relaxation of colonial control. Respected party imperial specialists, such as French Union Assembly members Max André and Daniel Boisdon, were arch traditionalists in colonial affairs.[52] Their conservatism dressed up in federalist clothing endured. In July 1958, months after the MRP's final decisive split, party members regrouped in a *Comité national d'entente pour la Démocratie Chrétienne*. The *Comité* condemned reactionary colonialism and nationalist 'fanaticism' in Algeria. Yet it defended French rule in Algiers as an economic imperative.[53]

49. Rapport du général Henri Martin, 14 Nov. 1946, in *La Guerre d'Algérie par les documents* tome I, ed. Jean-Charles Jauffret (Vincennes, 1990), pp. 206–17; Section d'Afrique 2e bur. rapport, 5 June 1945, Aff. pol., C2116/D2, ANCOM.

50. Turpin, 'Le Mouvement Républicain Populaire et l'avenir de l'Algérie', 172–4.

51. AN, Fonds MRP, 350AP7, Dossier: 1MRP6/Dr2, Albert Gortais (secretary-general) letter to François de Menthon (president of MRP parliamentary group), 27 Dec. 1948.

52. Marc Michel, 'L'Empire colonial dans les débats parlementaires', in *L'Année 1947*, 194–5. Max André was president of the MRP group in the French Union Assembly; Daniel Boisdon became president of the Assembly itself in December 1947.

53. AN, Fonds MRP, 350AP76, Dossier: 4MRP8/Dr.2, 'Déclaration du Comité National d'Entente pour la Démocratie Chrétienne', enclosure by Pierre Ceccaldi, n.d. July 1958.

The MRP's colonial 'doctrine', such as it was, contained few specific policy pledges. Instead, the party's failure to sustain its early electoral success drove the MRP leadership to take colonial policy positions defined in relation to their major party rivals. Few prominent Christian Democrats had strong personal connections with the empire. The one notable exception was Paul Coste-Floret, former leader of *Combat-Empire*. Most of his ministerial colleagues faced imperial crises as relative novices. Lack of colonial experience differentiated MRP ministers from their Socialist partners. The SFIO nominated several placemen as colonial governors during the Popular Front era. Three senior Socialists with a hand in colonial affairs – Léon Blum, Jules Moch and Marius Moutet – all returned to office after the war. Their party included well-established colonial federations, particularly that of Senegalese deputy Amadou Lamine-Guèye, a member of the SFIO executive committee from September 1946.[54] In practice, however, the party found it increasingly difficult to sustain popular support in the empire. Guy Mollet, Blum's successor as SFIO leader, faced the rapid erosion of Socialist support in black Africa. In September 1946 Félix Houphouët-Boigny led a group of African deputies that demanded French implementation of the reforms promised under the first draft of the French Union that had been rejected in May. They held a congress in Bamako, French Soudan, on 19–21 October to unite differing black African parties into an inter-territorial grouping, the *Rassemblement Démocratique Africain* (RDA). Backed by the French Communist Party, the RDA quickly emerged as the major political force in French black Africa. Only Senegal and the French Congo retained strong links with the Socialists.[55]

If the foundation of the RDA signalled the decline of Socialist influence in black Africa, it presented a clear opportunity for the MRP to win influence among the RDA's African and settler opponents. The French Union Assembly, the largely ceremonial imperial parliament set up under the French Union, became a stronghold of MRP support. Capitalizing on the Socialists' difficulties, the MRP articulated the revitalized 'colonial consensus' in Fourth Republic politics more forcefully than any other party. As Cold War attitudes hardened in France during the course of 1947, official hostility to the RDA escalated. A political organization affiliated to the PCF, stretching across two colonial federations and with subordinate national parties in individual colonies, presented a serious threat. Once the French Communists left the

---

54. Eighteen of France's thirty colonial governors were replaced by the Blum government in 1936–37, see Irwin M. Wall, 'Socialists and Bureaucrats: The Blum Government and the French Administration, 1936–1937', *International Review of Social History*, xix (1974), 338–9; B. D. Graham, *Choice and Democratic Order. The French Socialist Party, 1937–1950* (Cambridge, 1994), p. 358.

55. Ruth Schachter-Morgenthau, *Political Parties in French-Speaking West Africa* (Oxford, 1964), pp. 90–4; Florence Bernault-Boswell, 'Le rôle des milieux coloniaux dans la décolonisation du Gabon et du Congo-Brazzaville (1945–1964)', in *L'Afrique noire*, pp. 288–9.

394 COLONIAL POLICIES OF THE MOUVEMENT REPUBLICAIN

tripartite coalition in May, a crack-down against the RDA became inevitable. The SFIO, reeling from its loss in influence in black Africa, was no friend of the RDA. But MRP ministers holding the portfolios of defence, foreign affairs and overseas France seized the initiative, entrusting repressive measures to selected colonial appointees. Tried and trusted colonial tricks were employed. In 1948 Upper Volta was abruptly declared a separate West African territory largely to detach it from the RDA-dominated Ivory Coast in readiness for elections in June 1948. Here and in other territories, French officials and MRP supporters pushed African deputies to serve as independents. Their efforts soon achieved results. In September 1948 Senegalese deputies broke with the Socialists and joined former RDA supporters from Dahomey, Upper Volta and Togo to form a new parliamentary bloc, the *Indépendants d'Outre-Mer* (IOM).[56] Strongly encouraged by Aujoulat, this grouping affiliated with the MRP. Soon afterwards the newly promoted Governor of Ivory Coast, the Socialist Laurent Péchoux, set about the destruction of the RDA in its heartland. Official repression peaked in 1950. Violent clashes were followed by the widespread imprisonment of RDA activists.[57]

The Socialists failed to adjust to the development of mass politics in black Africa. As Péchoux's drive against the RDA gathered momentum between 1948 and 1950, Mollet was aghast at MRP and UDSR success in appealing to African politicians who had previously seen the Socialist Party as their natural metropolitan ally. The UDSR became the leading non-communist, left-wing progressives in colonial affairs. And the MRP, which drew increasing support among colonial administrators, emerged as the party of colonial order.[58] Leading lights in the Socialist Party such as Paul Ramadier, Moutet and Mollet wrestled with the contradiction between theoretical support for colonial liberalism and the practical consequences of attachment to assimilationist ideals.[59] The beginnings of a similar crisis of confidence only emerged at the MRP's annual party congress in 1950. Prior to this, the MRP executive considered economic and constitutional reforms conditional upon prior respect for French rule. For those on the right of the party, violent colonial unrest only hardened this conviction. It was order before reform.[60]

The growth of MRP influence in French colonial politics was certainly linked to declining Socialist fortunes. It would, however, be misguided to see this as the key inter-party dynamic in the MRP's

56. Yves Person, 'French West Africa and Decolonization', in *The Transfer of Power in Africa. Decolonization, 1940–1960*, ed. Prosser Gifford and Wm. Roger Louis (New Haven, 1982), p. 155.

57. Weiskel, 'Independence and the Longue Durée', 366–70.

58. Danièle Doumergue-Cloarec, 'Le soutien de l'UDSR et de la SFIO aux partis politiques d'Afrique occidentale française (1951–1958)', in *L'Afrique noire*, pp. 114–17.

59. Jacques Valette, 'Paul Ramadier et l'Union Française', in *Paul Ramadier. La République et le Socialisme* ed. Serge Berstein, (Paris, 1990), pp. 350–2; Quillot, *La S.F.I.O.*, pp. 257–68.

60. See Pierre-Henri Teitgen, *Faites entrer le temoin suivant* (Paris, 1988).

formulation of colonial policy. As the party's core supporters were in many ways deeply conservative, the MRP was always more exposed to a loss of support to other right-of-centre parties. Of these, Charles de Gaulle's *Rassemblement du Peuple Français* (RPF) posed the greatest challenge.

Immediately after the Second World War the MRP drew strong support from recently enfranchised women voters. This had little colonial dimension. The party's religious credentials seemed far more significant. Numerous local federation surveys convinced the party secretariat that women voters were primarily attracted by the MRP's distinctiveness as a confessional party committed to the advancement of Catholic interests.[61] The party had little to offer women seeking an escape from domesticity. Party newspaper *Forces Nouvelles* affirmed MRP opposition to women seeking full-time paid employment, which it even considered adequate grounds for divorce.[62] Yet the MRP was second only to the Communists in attracting women supporters during 1944–46. Existing Catholic women's groups, notably the *Union féminine civique et sociale* and the *Ligue féminine d'Action catholique* assisted the process, as did the MRP executive's initial willingness to integrate women members into the party structure.[63] The nine women elected as MRP deputies to the first Constituent Assembly in October 1945 made few inroads into colonial policy debates. They stressed their own gender specificity over party difference and made most impact in discussion of social issues, notably food distribution and family policy. It was left to Alice Sportisse, PCF deputy for Algiers, to highlight colonial discrimination against women by demanding citizenship rights for Muslim war widows in francophone Africa.[64]

MRP strength among conservative, provincial, and predominantly Catholic voters went into decline within two years of the party's foundation. Even so, the MRP kept a tight grip on government within the 'third force' coalitions of 1947 to 1951 alongside Socialist and centrist party ministers, principally drawn from the Radical Party, the UDSR and the conservative moderates (*modérés*). In office but losing members fast, the MRP's grassroots support was eroded by its key rival among self-consciously Catholic voters – the RPF launched in April 1947. In speeches at Bayeux and Epinal in June and September 1946 de Gaulle attacked those parties supportive of the proposed new constitution. After the constitutional referendum in October, Gaullist antagonism

61. AN, Fonds MRP, 350AP7, Dossier: 1MRP5/Dr. 6 'Sondage (3)'. Departmental MRP federations were sub-divided into *sections cantonales* and *sections communales*.

62. Eric Alary et Dominique Veillon, 'L'après-guerre des femmes: 1947, un tournant?', in *L'Année 1947*, 506–7.

63. Hanna Diamond, *Women and the Second World War in France, 1939–1948: Choices and Constraints* (Harlow, 1999), pp. 186–7, 192.

64. Hilary Footitt, 'The First Women *Députés*: "les 33 Glorieuses"?', in *The Liberation of France. Image and Event*, ed. H. R. Kedward and Nancy Wood (Oxford, 1995), pp. 132–5; AN, Fonds UDSR, 412AP, box 1/dossier 2, *Journal Officiel*, 23 Aug. 1946.

396 COLONIAL POLICIES OF THE MOUVEMENT REPUBLICAIN

towards the Fourth Republic system focused on the MRP, singled out as the party most synonymous with the new regime. On 15 May 1947 de Gaulle chose a ceremony in Bordeaux with a decidedly imperial flavour to attack the government's failure to prevent colonial breakdown. Speaking in commemoration of the Free French colonial governor Félix Eboué, de Gaulle affirmed that the RPF would preserve the empire intact. The underlying message was clear: the French Union would be safest in Gaullist hands.[65]

To make matters worse, the RPF leadership was determined to sustain the fiction that their movement was not a mere political party but a unifying movement or 'Rally'. Electors could thus vote for the RPF without technically leaving their own party for another. In the secrecy of the ballot booth, during French municipal elections in October 1947 numerous MRP members deserted the party for the RPF without formally renouncing their MRP membership. The RPF won over 40 per cent of votes cast, more than the combined MRP and Socialist vote. France's thirteen biggest cities came under RPF control. Here was sweet infidelity indeed. MRP supporters could remain faithful to their Party and yet vote for de Gaulle when it counted. Jubilant Gaullists jibed that the MRP newspaper, *L'Aube* (The Dawn) should be renamed *Le Crépuscule* (The Twilight).[66]

Understandably, MRP organizers became acutely sensitive, almost obsessional, about the RPF's capacity to steal their thunder. Local MRP federations monitored RPF activities at departmental level and appreciated the scale of the threat.[67] The MRP hoped to take votes from the Gaullist movement. But it was far more likely to lose them. Although they shared prestigious resistance origins, the MRP lacked the military élan of imperial 'grandeur' so important to the self-image of the RPF. Between 1947 and 1952 eight Generals served the RPF at national level either as members of its *Comité exécutif* or its *Conseil de direction*. Several, including Generals Charles Catroux, Joseph Monsabert and Georges Billotte, were best known as imperial commanders. RPF membership rolls also indicate that 4 to 5 per cent of RPF members were serving in the armed forces.[68] The RPF's greater success in maintaining

65. Guy Pervillé, 'Le RPF et l'Union Française', in *De Gaulle et le RPF 1947–1955* ed. Fondation Charles de Gaulle (Paris, 1998), pp. 521–3.

66. Irving, *Christian Democracy*, pp. 14–15; Vinen, *Bourgeois Politics*, pp. 159–60; Philip Williams, *Crisis and Compromise. Politics in the Fourth Republic* (Oxford, 1964), pp. 104, 133–4.

67. Bernard Lachaise, 'La création du Rassemblement du peuple français', in *L'Année 1947*, 329. MRP anxiety about the RPF was reflected in the close monitoring of Gaullist literature, rallies and voter recruitment. See AN, Fonds MRP, 350AP76, Dossier: 4MRP8/Dr 4, 'Renseignements communiqués par les fédérations sur le R.P.F. Note schématique', 23 April 1947; 'Meeting R.P.F. au Vélodrome d'Hiver', n.d., 1947. During April 1947 alone MRP federations submitted reports on RPF organization in the Côte d'Or, Haute-Loire, Loire Inférieure, Indre-et-Loire, Ille-et-Vilaine, Moselle and the Nord.

68. Bernard Lachaise, 'Les militaires et le gaullisme au temps du Rassemblement du peuple français (1947–1955)', in *Militaires en République 1870–1962*, ed. Olivier Forcarde, Eric Duhamel and Philippe Vial (Paris, 1999), pp. 456–7.

rank-and-file loyalty during its years in opposition helped account for the sharp decline in the MRP vote from its initial peak of 4,780,908 in the November 1945 Constituent Assembly election to 2,369,778 in the June 1951 election of a new Chamber of Deputies (in which there were 120 RPF deputies to the MRP's 82).[69] The fluidity of the MRP's parliamentary alliances was out of step with the conservative bedrock of its electoral support. Electors who regarded a vote for Bidault as a 'vote against Thorez' were likely to see de Gaulle as a stronger anti-communist option. Gaullism also drew upon a Catholic cultural heritage. And RPF social and economic policies were sufficiently interventionist to woo more liberal MRP voters.[70]

On every issue, from social catholicism to economic policy and leadership in Europe, the RPF threatened to outmatch the MRP. From the luxury of opposition Gaullists could criticize the fudges of coalition politics without restraint. A firm stand on colonial issues seemed essential to avoid presenting an additional target to RPF critics. After all, one consequence of de Gaulle's abrupt resignation as premier in January 1946 was to leave MRP ministers to carry the can for France's humiliating evacuation from Syria and Lebanon.[71] It was therefore with potential Gaullist criticism much in mind that during 1947–49 the MRP secretariat worked to reconcile party enthusiasm for European federalism with a strong defence of the commercial interests of French Union member states. The party's standing foreign policy study group insisted that closer European economic cooperation should not disadvantage colonial producers. It advocated instead a new variant of the *pacte colonial*. As integration proceeded, greater European financial and technical resources would become available to underpin rising colonial prosperity.[72]

If the MRP's anxiety about the RPF was primarily tactical, by 1946 its hostility to the Communists was almost pathological. Unlike the few left-wing renegades of the *Union des Républicains et Résistants* (URR) led by Emmanuel d'Astier de la Vigerie and Pierre Cot, PCF opposition to the Indo-China war was less a matter of conscience than of strategy. This only confirmed the suspicions of MRP ministers about the tactics of their PCF 'partners' in government during the tripartism period. Belief

69. AN, Fonds MRP, 350AP2 Dossier: 1MRP2/Dr. 3/Doctrine, Session Nationale de formation politique, 5–10 April 1960, Memo. by François Garcia, 'Tableau des Partis Politiques Français'. After the collapse of the MRP vote in 1951 it remained almost static even as the party split in 1958. The MRP won 2,374,000 votes in the January 1956 election and 2,378,788 in November 1958.

70. Philippe Portier, 'Le général de Gaulle et le Catholicisme. Pour une autre interprétation de la pensée gaullienne', *Revue Historique*, ccxcvii (1997), 537–49.

71. *Resistance, the political autobiography of Georges Bidault* (London, 1967), first published as *D'une résistance à l'autre* (Paris, 1965), pp. 109, 120–1. Regarding MRP-RPF rivalry, see Odile Rudelle, 'Le rôle du retour du général de Gaulle', in *Le MRP et la construction européenne*, ed. Berstein, Mayeur and Milza, pp. 293–8.

72. AN, Fonds MRP, 350AP71, Secrétariat note, 'Aspects politiques du fédéralisme', 6 July 1948; Section d'Etudes affaires étrangères, 'Note proposée pour servir à l'étude des rapports entre l'Union française et l'Union européenne', 1 Feb. 1949.

398 COLONIAL POLICIES OF THE MOUVEMENT REPUBLICAIN

in Communist malevolence was fed by bitter memories – from the Communists' 'proferred hand' to French Catholics during the Popular Front years to PCF behaviour in the aftermath of the Nazi-Soviet pact.[73] For senior MRP parliamentarians, their resistance experience cemented their hostility to the Communist left and fed their contempt for collaboration among the French right. This extended to those sections of the Catholic episcopacy identified with Vichy's *Révolution Nationale* and a lacklustre opposition to Nazi occupation policies.[74] Within weeks of de Gaulle's January 1946 resignation, MRP deputy premier Francisque Gay complained to Socialist prime minister Félix Gouin that PCF and Socialist ministers systematically blocked MRP proposals. Gay noted that MRP candidates for colonial governorships, the Moroccan Residency and the United Nations secretariat were all turned down in Cabinet.[75]

The resurgence of Christian Democrat-Communist antagonism during 1946 was sharpened by the marked decline in the Socialist vote in the two elections of that year. After the SFIO's share of the vote fell to 21.06 per cent in June and 17.87 per cent in November, the Socialists could no longer mediate – albeit unfairly, according to Gay – between the MRP and the PCF. There were fewer Socialists in key ministerial posts and MRP federation restiveness over participation in the tripartite coalition was increasing.[76]

Shared anti-communism helped conceal the rifts within the MRP leadership over the party's response to the RPF challenge. The MRP co-founders, Bidault, Pierre-Henri Teitgen and party president Maurice Schumann, disagreed over de Gaulle.[77] Once the RPF was formally launched in 1947, the MRP matched the Gaullists' robust defence of French colonial sovereignty. An emphasis on the common colonial ground between the two groups suited MRP leaders still hopeful of future reconciliation with de Gaulle. It also helped postpone the definitive moment of choice for the party members tempted to vote RPF.[78]

73. On 'the proferred hand' (la main tendue): John Hellman, 'French "Left Catholics" and Communism in the Nineteen-Thirties', *Church History*, xlv (1976), 507–23.

74. Descamps, *La Démocratie Chrétienne*, pp. 91–3, 96–8; Maurice Larkin, 'The Catholic Church and politics in twentieth-century France', in *French History since Napoleon*, ed. Martin S. Alexander (London, 1999), pp. 162–3.

75. AN, Fonds MRP, 350AP76, Dossier: 4MRP8/Dr. 4, Francisque Gay letter to Félix Gouin, 28 Feb. 1946. MRP failure to secure its nominees to prefectural and colonial posts provoked a wave of complaints from local party federations.

76. Public Record Office, London (PRO), Foreign Office general correspondence, FO 371/67680, Z1995/58/17, Duff Cooper to Ernest Bevin, annual report on France, 1946, 24 Feb. 1947. Graham, *Choice and Democratic Order*, pp. 310–14, 366–7. The November 1946 election gave the SFIO 101 deputies against 169 PCF and 163 MRP.

77. P[ublic]R[ecord]O[ffice], FO 371/67680, Z170/58/17, Duff Cooper memo., 'Constitution of the Fourth Republic', 6 Jan. 1947; Letamendia, *Le Mouvement Républicain Populaire*, pp. 76–81.

78. Letamendia, *Le Mouvement Républicain Populaire*, pp. 70–1, 99–100.

A mixture of fear and respect for the Gaullist movement was mirrored among local MRP federations within the colonies. In Senegal, for example, the MRP's national secretary, the former mayor of Dakar, Alfred Goux, aligned with the RPF during the October 1947 municipal elections in order to combat the Socialist challenge directed by the Senegalese deputy, Lamine-Guèye. But immediately after these elections, MRP and RPF organizers in Dakar became rivals once more. In general terms, MRP federation activists, persuaded that RPF supporters might yet be tempted into supporting Christian Democracy, pushed the party rightwards on colonial issues between 1947 and 1954. This was attenuated by the MRP's choice of coalition partners. In the four years of third force coalitions between May 1947 and July 1951 the MRP and the Socialists looked to the Radicals, the UDSR and conservative *modérés* to form a working majority. Ministers selected from these smaller parties opposed accelerated colonial reform. This rightward shift also reflected changes in the composition of the MRP membership in the National Assembly. In 1946, the MRP's stature as the voice of social catholicism was boosted by the adhesion of twenty-nine supporters of the smaller client movement, *Jeune République.* During the later third force years, twenty-one MRP deputies defected, mainly to the RPF and the *modérés.* Hence, between 1947 and the general elections of 1951 the MRP executive paid more attention to its right flank than its left.[79]

The MRP framed colonial conflict within the wider setting of the Cold War and the internecine parliamentary struggle with the PCF. MRP policy statements adopted the language of US containment doctrine to disarm the Truman administration's criticism of French colonial rule.[80] Hostility to Communism and a tendency to regard colonial issues from a nationalist perspective reinforced by the developing Cold War hardly amount to a distinctive imperial policy. But when added to the MRP's rigid federalism and its susceptibility to a loss of electoral support to Gaullist and centre-right rivals, it explains the party's inflexibility on colonial issues.

Once the Radical Party and the UDSR joined Paul Ramadier's administration in January 1947, the MRP's blanket commitment to uphold French imperial control became stronger still. The Socialists followed these parties in attempting to form a third force centre alliance. But the SFIO was reluctant to make a stand on the defence of empire, anxious to avoid a repetition of Ramadier's bruising clash with the PCF

79. AN, Fonds MRP, 350AP1, Dossier: 1MRP2/Dr 1/Doctrine, 'Résolutions du Comité Directeur des 31 août et 1 septembre 1946'; Williams, *Crisis*, pp. 31–41. MRP deputies who joined the RPF included former Armed Forces Minister, Edmond Michelet, and MRP executive member, Louis Terrenoire. Algiers deputy Paul-Emile Viard was among four MRP deputies who defected to the *modérés.*
80. Annie Lacroix-Riz, 'Puissance ou dépendance française? La vision des "décideurs" des affaires étrangères en 1948–9', in *La puissance française*, pp. 58–9.

400 COLONIAL POLICIES OF THE MOUVEMENT REPUBLICAIN

in a vote of confidence over Indo-China policy in March 1947. The SFIO national council also faced powerful internal opposition to any definitive rupture with the Communists in pursuit of a centrist alliance with the MRP. The electoral interests of the MRP and the Socialist Party were now diametrically opposed. A firm colonial policy strengthened the MRP hand against the Gaullists, but it laid the Socialists' open to PCF criticism and bitter internal division.[81] This tension became more important as the war in Indo-China intensified.

In 1946, an MRP-directed inter-ministerial committee on Indo-China sanctioned the hardline adopted by Admiral Georges Thierry d'Argenlieu, French High Commissioner in Saigon.[82] Working closely with the French secret service, the Indo-China committee had emerged as the key policy-making forum over the spring and summer of 1945 when plans were finalized to re-establish French civil and military rule across the Vietnamese territories once Japan surrendered.[83] Hô Chi Minh's Vietminh resisted the re-imposition of colonial control. Abortive discussions took place with Vietminh representatives at Fontainebleau in July 1946. The French negotiating team was led by Max André, an MRP supporter appointed by fellow party member, Armed Forces Minister Edmond Michelet. André was advised by Léon Pignon, chief political counsellor in Saigon. Close to Henri Laurentie, Pignon was another expert colonial official whose opinion MRP ministers were inclined to trust. Pignon's advice helped convince Bidault to back d'Argenlieu. The High Commissioner faced bitter parliamentary criticism after a French bombardment of Haiphong on 23 November 1946 confirmed the collapse of dialogue with the Vietminh.[84] Léon Blum's all-Socialist government sanctioned military operations against the Vietminh in December 1946. But Socialist qualms about the war in Indo-China soon increased. SFIO Secretary-General Guy Mollet's left-wing supporters sympathized with PCF objections to the conflict. And in March 1949, the deputy Paul Rivet, the one Socialist delegate within the MRP-dominated delegation at the 1946 Fontainebleau talks, revealed that the discussions were a sham, intended to undermine the Vietnamese negotiators.[85]

During 1947–48 the MRP responded harshly to the widening fissures within the French empire. In January 1947, it fell to Henri Laurentie,

81. Lewis, 'The MRP', 306–13; Graham, *Choice and Democratic Order*, pp. 369–70.

82. PRO, Saigon Consular reports, FO 959/14, E.W. Meiklereid to FO, 17 Dec. 1946.

83. Ministère des Affaires Etrangères (MAE), série Asie, Indochine vol. 31, Direction Générale des Etudes et Recherche, note 221/POL, Comité de l'Indochine memo. for Direction Asie-Océanie, 14 June 1945; Comité de l'Indochine, 'Compte-rendus des nouvelles 21–27 Juillet 1945'.

84. Shipway, *Road to War*, pp. 205–7, 231–2, 245–6; Edward Rice-Maximin, *Accommodation and resistance. The French left, Indochina and the cold war, 1944–1954* (Westport, 1986), pp. 42–3; Jacques Valette, 'La conférence de Fontainebleau (1946)', in *Les Chemins de la décolonisation*, p. 236.

85. Daniel Le Couriard, 'Les Socialistes et les débuts de la guerre d'Indochine (1946–1947)', *Revue d'Histoire Moderne et Contemporaine*, xxxi (1984), 336–9.

Director of Political Affairs in the Ministry of Overseas France, and the High Commissioner in Tananarive, the Socialist Marcel de Coppet, to set the proscription of Madagascar's *Mouvement démocratique pour la rénovation malgache* (MDRM) in train. Renowned as colonial reformers, neither Laurentie nor de Coppet were well suited to devise the repressive measures demanded by the island's influential settler population. Both men did, however, convince ministers in Paris that the MDRM did not represent a genuine unitary nationalism but instead served the sectarian interests of Madagascar's dominant ethnic group, the Merina. Indeed, in planning Madagascar's role within the French Union, Laurentie proposed a federalist scheme based on separate administrative systems in the Merina and non-Merina territories of the island. Detailed schemes such as this made a strong impression on Bidault. He and other senior MRP figures only formulated clear ideas about Madagascar after being persuaded that the MDRM was a seditionist movement.[86] MRP policy proceeded on the assumption that the major force in Malagasy politics was unrepresentative and elitist.

In spite of MDRM instructions to the contrary, rebel attacks on French installations across Madagascar began on the night of 29–30 March. The French responded savagely. By the time the rebellion fizzled out in February 1949, upwards of 89,000 Malagasy had been killed, largely by Foreign Legion and colonial military units. The MRP executive committee's endorsement of this murderous repression reveals as much about the party's determination to suppress colonial opposition in black Africa as it does about MRP support for 'their man' in Tananarive, de Coppet's replacement as High Commissioner, Pierre de Chevigné.[87] The MRP shared the new High Commissioner's determination to smash the MDRM. In an effort to undermine support for the party outside the capital Tananarive, de Chevigné's administration lent support to the MDRM's more moderate rival, the *Parti des déshérités de Madagascar* (PADESM). The PADESM newspaper received government subsidies and transport facilities were made available to party activists during elections. Meanwhile, Pierre-Henri Teitgen urged the government to treat the MDRM as a 'formation fasciste', a demand which typified the MRP's blinkered attitude towards African colonial dissent.[88]

The MRP's hardline over Madagascar reflected three facets of the party's colonial policy-making. First, on issues where the party had no clearly articulated view, MRP leaders were generally responsive to the

---

86. Martin Shipway, 'Madagascar on the eve of insurrection: The impasse of a liberal colonial policy', *Journal of Imperial and Commonwealth History*, xxiv (1996), 80–1, 88–94.

87. Jacques Tronchon, 'La nuit la plus longue . . . du 29 au 30 mars 1947', in *Madagascar 1947 La tragédie oubliée*, ed. F. Arazalier and J. Suret-Canale (Paris, 1999), pp. 118–26.

88. Raymond Delval, 'L'histoire du PADESM ou quelques faits oubliés de l'histoire malgache', in *Les Chemins de la décolonisation*, pp. 283–4; Michel, 'L'Empire colonial dans les débats parlementaires', 202.

expert opinions of Ministry of Overseas France officials, in this instance, Laurentie above all. Second, the MRP treated settler grievances with more respect than did their coalition partners. Madagascar's large settler population, many with long-standing family ties in both Madagascar and nearby Réunion, were a vocal element within the *Etats généraux de la colonisation française* whose influence on the MRP we noted earlier. Third, the MRP leadership was quite willing to sanction repressive measures provided that those in charge of its implementation in particular colonies were sympathetic to the party and could be publicly identified with it.

Parallels can thus be drawn between MRP action over Madagascar and its policy in the trust territory of French Cameroon. As we have seen, in 1945 the cities of Douala and Yaoundé became organizational centres for the *Etats généraux*, largely because settler predominance in Cameroon politics was threatened by the emergence of nationalist political parties and African trade unions. Hostility between settlers, the established tribal population of Douala, and the growing numbers of economic migrants in the port soon generated violence between them. In September 1945, scores of striking African workers and unemployed African rioters were shot down in Douala by powerfully armed white vigilantes.[89] Four months later in January 1946, Clement Attlee's government agreed to place Tanganyika, and the British-administered sections of Cameroon and Togoland under UN trusteeship. French Foreign Minister Bidault was reluctant to follow suit. He argued that a prior decision on trusteeship status for French Togo and Cameroon would complicate plans for the French Union. Behind this excuse lay deeper objections to the idea of UN monitoring or the stronger US intervention in African affairs that might accompany it.[90]

The prospect of unwelcome international scrutiny shaped the French governmental response to the September clashes. The subsequent appointment of Robert Dalavignette, director of the Ecole Nationale de la France d'outre-mer, as Cameroon High Commissioner drew enthusiastic MRP support. Delavignette was an outstanding administrator and a renowned theorist of colonial rule. During his tenure in Cameroon in 1946–47 he contained political unrest. Forced labour was abolished, a labour inspectorate was set up and economic development projects were

89. Richard A. Joseph, 'Settlers, Strikers and *Sans-Travail*: The Douala Riots of September 1945', *Journal of African History*, xv (4) (1974), 669–87; Catherine Coquery-Vidrovitch, 'Emeutes urbaines, grèves générales et décolonisation en Afrique française', in *Les Chemins de la décolonisation*, pp. 494–6.

90. Marc Michel, 'Le Togo dans les relations internationales au lendemain de la guerre: prodrome de la décolonisation ou "petite mésentente cordiale"? (1945–1951)', in *Les Chemins de la décolonisation*, pp. 95–107. On US intentions in the region: USNA, RG 59, 851T.00, French West Africa, Political 1945–49, box 6328, A. B. Scott, Brazzaville Consul, memo., 'Post-War prospects in French Equatorial Africa', 14 July 1945.

initiated.[91] Delavignette was no friend of settler interest. But he also kept a tight rein on nationalist party organization. It was this restriction of nationalist activity, strongly supported by Louis Aujoulat, the MRP's one acknowledged Cameroon expert, that the MRP would continue to advocate after Delavignette's departure from Cameroon in 1947. As in Madagascar, when confronted with a genuinely radical African nationalist movement, the MRP opted for harsh proscription of political activity. Admittedly, after 1947 the MRP was by no means alone in its support for colonial order. But it was none the less instrumental in alienating Cameroon's major nationalist party, the *Union des Populations du Cameroun*, which ultimately pursued a campaign of guerrilla violence against French control.[92]

The unprecedented prominence of colonial problems in French parliamentary affairs between March–September 1947 gave MRP deputies ample opportunity to prove the party's determination to keep the empire intact. In March alone, five Assembly sessions were devoted to the war in Vietnam. The Madagascar uprising was discussed on four occasions between April and June. And the Statute for Algeria was debated on eleven occasions during August and September. The fact that so few metropolitan deputies attended these debates only highlighted the large proportion of MRP representatives who took part. This helped offset the MRP's dismal electoral performance in the overseas territories themselves. Far from fulfilling its claim to be 'le grand parti de l'Union française', the MRP performed badly in the November 1946 elections across the French Union. Only five of the seventy deputies elected from the overseas territories were MRP supporters.[93]

No MRP politician ever ran the French Interior Ministry. The post, which conferred responsibility for Algerian administration, was instead dominated by more seasoned Radical Party figures. Yet the MRP left a lasting impression in Algeria by pushing through the Statute which determined electoral representation and the distribution of fiscal powers within the colony in August 1947. In late August 1946, the Constituent Assembly discussed autonomy proposals formulated by Ferhat Abbas's *Union démocratique du Manifeste algérien*. Georges Bidault, then Premier and Foreign Minister, defended the more limited administrative reforms pursued in Algeria by Yves Chataigneau's government-general. As Odile Rudelle has shown, Bidault's insistence that agreement on an Algerian Statute should be postponed until after the October 1946

91. *Robert Delavignette on the French Empire. Selected Writings*, ed. William B. Cohen (Chicago, 1977), pp. 81, 100–107.

92. Richard Joseph, 'Radical Nationalism in French Africa: The Case of Cameroon' in *Decolonization and African Independence*, pp. 328–46.

93. Michel, 'L'Empire colonial dans les débats parlementaires', pp. 191–2. Two of the MRP overseas deputies were elected from Algeria, two from Cameroon and one from Oubangui-Chari. Thirteen deputies from overseas territories supported the SFIO, the largest single block. Ten backed the PCF, as did RDA representatives. Even the UDSR could claim more support than the MRP with eight overseas deputies elected.

404 COLONIAL POLICIES OF THE MOUVEMENT REPUBLICAIN

constitutional referendum had profound consequences. The intervening period allowed time for the mobilization of settler opposition. The loudest protests came from the Radical Party's Algerian federations. Their leader, René Mayer, deputy for Constantine, agreed with MRP president Maurice Schumann on three core demands. The final Statute should preserve a double electoral college, French control over budgetary allocations and the Governor's executive power. The Fourth Republic constitution also affirmed Algeria's status as three French departments. Algeria would not be treated on nationalist or Communist terms as a republic in the making. Bidault's original postponement of the debate on the Statute until after the new constitution was in place served the MRP purpose by setting narrow confines to the scheme proposed. Infuriated by this constraint, all the Algerian deputies abstained in the final Statute vote.[94]

MRP ministers also lent strong support to the Socialist Minister of Interior, Edouard Depreux, who stipulated that greater Muslim involvement in national administration was not a prelude to Algerian autonomy. And Bidault's ministerial cabinet at the Quai d'Orsay stressed that administrative reform in Algeria should not exceed the measures planned for the neighbouring protectorates of Morocco and Tunisia. Instead, the reforms enshrined in the September 1947 Statute for Algeria ensured the perpetuation of settler control.[95] Passage of the Statute was a triumph of MRP parliamentary manipulation. The party's Algiers and Constantine federations did not see it that way. Its members pressed the leadership to adopt an even more hard-line policy. Led by Paul-Emile Viard, party members in Algeria rejected even the narrow concessions proposed by the executive. Sponsored by Jacques Fonlupt-Espéraber, MRP deputy for the upper Rhine, the final vote on the Algerian Statute decimated MRP support within the colony.[96] Yet the perpetuation of a two college electoral system ensured settler dominance of an Algerian national assembly. Led by Georges Le Brun-Keris, who succeeded Viard as the MRP's main Algerian voice, the MRP federations in Algiers, Constantine and Oran stood for little more than settler prerogative.[97]

94. Odile Rudelle, 'Le vote du statut de l'Algérie', in *L'Année 1947*, 312–15.

95. MAE, Algérie, vol. 2, Depreux to Bidault, 19 Aug. 1946; Direction d'Afrique-Levant au Cabinet du Ministre, 'Statut de l'Algérie', 3 June 1947; PRO, FO 371/60048, Z8121/2830/17, Duff Cooper to Bevin, 12 Sept. 1946. The principal reform enshrined in the Statute for Algeria was the creation of a 120–member Assembly with power of budgetary supervision, elected on a dual college system. Jacques Fonlupt-Espéraber led a commission of MRP deputies which denounced the abuse of the Statute in April 1949: see Letamendia, *La Mouvement Républicain Populaire*, p. 355.

96. MAE, sous-série Algérie, vol. 2, Sûreté Nationale section d'Afrique du Nord, 'Activité politique en Algérie', 22 Jan. 1947; Lewis, 'French Politics and the Algerian Statute', 159–67; Letamendia, *Le Mouvement Républicain Populaire*, p. 355.

97. For details, see Papiers MRP, 350AP85, Dossiers: 5MRP2/Drs. 1–2, including Pflimlin letter to Le Brun-Keris, 25 March 1958.

MRP intransigence over Algeria was of a piece with party policy towards French North Africa as a whole. During 1946, Paul Bergognon, MRP organizer in Marrakech, orchestrated a brief campaign to give the party's supporters in the Maghreb a greater say in North African policy-making. In Georges Bidault they found a champion. As protectorates with their own indigenous system of government, neither Morocco nor Tunisia could join the federal structure of the French Union. Still, the MRP's Maghreb federations advocated a more integrationist policy, arguing that French North Africa should be treated as a single economic and strategic unit.[98] In 1946, Bidault exploited these calls from within his own party in order to coax the Moroccan and Tunisian governments into acceptance of a new constitutional settlement for the protectorates. The French Union scheme put forward alongside the initial Fourth Republic draft constitution was in key respects vague and self-contradictory. French voters rejected the draft constitution in May 1946. As a result, plans for the French Union were rewritten. These revisions remained unclear prior to the publication of the new French Union scheme in October. Uncertain of what was to come, the sultanate administration was receptive to French reforms which acknowledged Morocco's protectorate status.[99] The spectre of an all-embracing French Union also cowed the beylical administration in Tunis. Tunisia's nationalists were less malleable. Both factions of the divided *Destour* Party reacted by calling for outright independence. This drew a prompt response. On 23 August 1946, during the MRP national congress, Bidault's government sanctioned the arrest of senior *Destour* leaders.[100]

The MRP ministers who joined Paul Ramadier's administration in late January 1947 faced internal party pressure from the North African federations to set tighter limits on reform in the protectorates.[101] Grass-roots hostility to reform strengthened Bidault's hand as Foreign Minister in his dealings with well-organized Moroccan and Tunisian nationalist movements anxious to secure prompt concessions. In mid-April 1947, Quai d'Orsay Secretary-General Jean Chauvel advised Bidault that the French position in Tunisia was being steadily undermined. The country was in the grip of a severe drought. The focal point of nationalist opposition, Habib Bourguiba's *Néo-Destour*, was well organized and worked closely with the Arab League in Cairo. Most important, Ramadier's government had yet to decide with whom to negotiate. Tunisia's head of state, Sidi Lamine Bey, commanded little

98. AN, Bidault papers, box 112, René Guyomard, MRP Centre National, to Falaize, cabinet du ministre, 2 April 1946; box 115, Guyomard to Falaize, 22 Feb. 1946; AN, Fonds MRP, 350AP85, Dossier: 5MRP2 Dr. 3 Algérie (3), Jean Fonteneau note to Georges Le Brun-Keris, 6 June 1956.
99. AN, Bidault papers, box 112, no. 736, Charles Mast to Bidault, 30 March 1946.
100. MAE, Tunisie vol. 380, Michel Debré memo., 6 July 1946; Bidault papers, box 112, Sous-direction/protectorats, 'Note pour le président du gouvernement', 9 Sept. 1946.
101. AN, Bidault papers, box 112, Sous-direction des protectorats note, 31 Jan. 1947.

406 COLONIAL POLICIES OF THE MOUVEMENT REPUBLICAIN

public respect. His predecessor, Moncef Bey, enjoyed national popularity but had been deposed by the French authorities in 1943 on charges of collaboration. Restoration of Moncef Bey promised to kick-start the reform process.[102] After consulting Tunis Resident-General Jean Mons, Bidault opted for Sidi Lamine Bey, the more conservative alternative. The MRP executive agreed, insisting that talks on Tunisian self-rule would snowball beyond control. The result was political stalemate in Tunis.[103]

Just as the Foreign Ministry was something of an MRP fiefdom, so too was the Ministry of Overseas France. From this office, Paul Coste-Floret shaped French colonial policy in the early years of third force government during 1948–49. His MRP colleague Jean Letourneau then added to the party's colonial influence as minister responsible for relations with the associated states of Indo-China between 1950–53. Their major pre-occupation throughout was Vietnam. In November 1947, Coste-Floret was well placed to judge the scale of the Vietminh threat. He moved to Overseas France following a nine-month spell as War Minister. As the key protagonist of the unification of the Vietnamese territories under Emperor Bao Daï, Coste-Floret had a vested interest in presenting him as a viable alternative leader to Hô Chi Minh.[104] The MRP leadership ruled out talks with the Vietminh. Any such dialogue would cut across French efforts to recover their military position in northern Vietnam. Differing attitudes to negotiations lay at the root of argument within the council of ministers over the war. The MRP could tolerate Bao Daï as a quisling head of state where the Socialists could not.[105]

Tension between the Socialists and the MRP over the war in Vietnam mounted steadily. Influenced by Delavignette, by then his senior ministry adviser, Coste-Floret tried to keep colonial legislative reform off the parliamentary calendar for fear of its divisive impact on the governing coalition.[106] These tactics backfired. In December 1947, Coste-Floret provoked uproar in the French Union Assembly by prohibiting Emile Bollaert, High Commissioner for Indo-China, from appearing before an Assembly committee to explain government policy.[107] In the following year he blocked SFIO-sponsored attempts at mediation with the Vietminh. Only after Léon Pignon replaced Bollaert as High Commissioner did Coste-Floret concede that Alain Savary, the

102. AN, Bidault papers, box 112, Jean Chauvel to Bidault, 15 April 1947.

103. AN, Bidault papers, box 112, Foreign Ministry, 'Aide mémoire sur la situation en Tunisie', 18 April 1947; Bidault to Teitgen and Chauvel, 18 April 1947; box 115, Présidence du conseil, 'Notice technique de contre-ingérence politique – création du comité de libération de l'AFN', 4 Feb. 1948.

104. PRO, FO 959/19, Frank Gibbs, Saigon Consul, to FO, 11 May 1948.

105. Service Historique de l'Armée, Vincennes (SHAT), série 4Q, Archives de l'état-major de la défense nationale, 4Q119/D8, Comité de l'Afrique du Nord compte-rendu, n. d, Nov. 1946; Maréchal Alphonse Juin, *Mémoires, II: 1944–1958* (Paris, 1960), pp. 186–7.

106. Lewis, 'The French Colonial Service', 186–8.

107. Michel, 'L'Empire colonial dans les débats parlementaires', 213.

Socialists' leading colonial specialist, should be permitted to contact the Vietminh leadership in southern Vietnam in February 1949. Savary's numerous semi-official mediation efforts in Vietnam between 1950–54 made plain the SFIO's mounting disenchantment with the war and its willingness to accept a cease-fire and direct negotiations with the Vietminh executive.[108]

Unlike the Socialist Party, whose departmental federations could exert pressure on the party leadership through the SFIO executive and the party conference, the strongest of the MRP's local federations (from Brittany and Alsace) were not proportionately represented within either the 187-member MRP national committee or the party conference. This representational structure was intended to prevent accusations of MRP regionalism. But it also diminished the scope for rank-and-file opposition to leadership policies.[109] The party's executive commission met fortnightly to review policy in the light of national committee decisions. In practice, it delegated policy-making authority to a more workable thirteen-member Bureau dominated by the strongly imperialist party leaders.[110] Again, unlike the Socialists, this highly centralized decision-making system was not counter-balanced by distinct colonial committees within the MRP's national party headquarters. By September 1947, the SFIO had established both a *Commission nationale d'outre-mer* and a *Bureau de l'Union française*.[111] By contrast, the only specialist colonial group within the MRP's central structure was an '*Equipe Union française*'. Staffed by George Le Brun-Keris, Yvon Razaa and Kenneth Vignes, the *Equipe* liaised between the party secretariat and local federations. It did not, however, develop into a major advisory group.[112]

In April 1948, Coste-Floret reorganized the inter-ministerial committee on Indo-China to oversee the implementation of the Bao Daï solution. The committee's quartet of initial members were all MRP ministers – Coste-Floret, Schuman, Bidault and Teitgen. In Paris at least, Indo-China policy was essentially an MRP affair.[113] The politicization of the restyled Indo-China committee set it apart. A parallel French North Africa committee was different in purpose and structure.

108. Jacques Dalloz, 'Alain Savary, un socialiste face à la guerre d'Indochine', *Vingtième Siècle*, (January 1997), 42–54.

109. Williams, *Crisis*, pp. 91–3, 106–7. The power of the departmental federations within the reconstructed SFIO was evident at the Party's first two postwar Congresses in 1945 and 1946, see B. D. Graham, *Choice and Democratic Order*, pp. 263–6, 274–89, 314–65 *passim*.

110. AN, Fonds MRP, 350AP7, Dossier: 1MRP6/Dr. 2, Secrétariat Général 'Note sur l'organisation du M.R.P.' n.d.

111. Michel, 'L'Empire colonial dans les débats parlementaires', 195.

112. AN, Fonds MRP, 350AP7, Dossier: 1MRP6/DR1, André Colin letter regarding Secretariat Equipes, 22 Nov. 1951.

113. PRO, Fo 371/69654, F6302/255/86, Ashley Clarke, Paris, to P. F. Grey, 22 April 1948. This echoed the position in late 1946. Although the Socialist, Marius Moutet, was then Minister for Overseas France, Bidault headed the interministerial committee during the final stages of the 1946 negotiations: Shipway, *The Road to War*, p. 201.

408 COLONIAL POLICIES OF THE MOUVEMENT REPUBLICAIN

From 1945 it served as a forum for civil-military dialogue. Its member-ship included the North African Governors and the chief of the national defence staff. They curbed the influence of partisan ministers.[114] By contrast, even Vincent Auriol, head of state and president of the French Union, complained that the Indo-China committee members did not inform him of their decisions.[115]

Policymaking increasingly centred on this closed ministerial sub-committee. In the absence of harmonious coalition partnership, effec-tive civil-military liaison or clear executive accountability, only sustained non-governmental pressure might have forced a re-assessment of the MRP's Vietnam policy. But this too was missing.[116] Wider public interest in the 'professional soldiers' war' in Southeast Asia, and in the empire more generally, was also fitful. Three years after its creation, in 1949 less than half of those asked by pollsters could offer even an approximate definition of the French Union.[117] MRP leaders only faced episodic party dissent when the army suffered major reverses such as in 1950 and 1953–4. Neither the failure of negotiations in 1946 nor MRP indulgence towards d'Argenlieu, and Rivet's later accusations about the Fontainebleau discussions, aroused significant protest from local MRP federations.

Ironically, where the protests from the MRP's North African federations encouraged MRP ministers towards the restriction of reform in the Maghreb, the absence of effective local federation pressure gave the MRP leadership leeway to pursue the war in Vietnam. As later events would prove, the party executive was attuned to colonialist pressure from the rank-and-file but turned a deaf ear towards more liberal MRP dissenters. The centralized MRP party structure described above helps account for this. So too does the MRP's falling membership. By 1948, the ideal of a mass Christian Democrat movement transcending sectarian party politics was fast receding. From a peak of 230,000 members in 1947, MRP numbers tumbled to 50–80,000 in the years 1950–58. Disillusioned MRP supporters were not short of party alternatives to choose from. The rapidity with which MRP membership and electoral performance declined indicates that party loyalism was never strongly rooted. Since dissenters generally left the MRP rather than challenging the leadership from within, little wonder that the

114. SHAT, 4Q78/D3, Comité de l'Afrique du Nord, IV session, 21 Feb. 1946. The premier chaired the French North Africa committee. Five ministers usually attended (Foreign Affairs, Interior, National Economy, Overseas France and War). The government Secretary-General, the head of the national defence staff, the North African Residents-General and the Governor-General of Algeria were also members.

115. Entry for 12 Feb. 1948, *Vincent Auriol. Journal du septennat, 1947–1954, tome 2, 1948*, ed. Edmond Mouret and Jean-Pierre Azéma (Paris, 1978), pp. 89–90.

116. PRO, FO 371/69655, F7186/255/86, Saigon Consul to FO, 10 May 1948.

117. Charles-Robert Ageron, 'L'Opinion publique face aux problèmes de l'Union française', in *Les Chemins de la décolonisation*, p. 47; Alain Ruscio also discusses French opinion of the war in his *Les communistes français et la guerre d'Indochine, 1944–1954* (Paris, 1985).

party's colonial policy-makers remained unresponsive to spasmodic criticism from below. Typically, André Denis, MRP deputy for the Dordogne, failed in his attempt to persuade delegates to reject Coste-Floret's defence of the party's Indo-China policy at the May 1949 party congress.[118]

French backing for Bao Daï's Vietnamese regime was confirmed by parliamentary vote in January 1950. Responsibility for the implementation of this policy had passed to Coste-Floret's MRP replacement as Minister for Overseas France, Jean Letourneau. He brought with him a loyal ministerial *Cabinet* headed first by Jacques d'Avout and then by Jean Aubry. Both men had built their careers through working with Letourneau, from his first ministerial post at the PTT, through brief spells as Minister of Commerce and then Reconstruction, to his move to the Ministry of Overseas France. This close-knit group fitted well with the clannish MRP policy-making style.[119] The further internationalization of the conflict in Indo-China after the outbreak of the Korean war in June 1950 stiffened the resolve of Letourneau's *Cabinet* to defeat the Vietminh rather than concede negotiations.[120]

In the absence of sustained parliamentary or public demands for a shift in policy, the MRP rank-and-file acquired added importance as a possible source of dissent. But, as we have seen, the party structure did not facilitate such pressure from below. During 1950, sections of the Catholic press, notably *Témoignage Chrétien*, took up the left's campaign against dirty war methods in Indo-China. This was indicative of a wider crisis of conscience among a vocal minority of MRP supporters.[121] At governmental level, these protests were drowned out by the clamour from Washington for a more vigorous military campaign in Vietnam. General Jean de Lattre de Tassigny's spectacular, if fleeting, success as expeditionary force commander in 1951 encouraged even Robert Schuman to press the case for a more intensive war effort against the Vietminh.[122]

Renewed repression in the Maghreb also sparked opposition from Catholic liberals within the MRP already critical of the war in Vietnam. *Témoignage Chrétien* joined the Socialist and Communist press in attacking government actions in North Africa. And an undercurrent of liberal hostility to 'la politique de fermeté' in the protectorates would

118. Dalloz, 'L'opposition M.R.P. à la guerre d'Indochine', 106–18.

119. AN, Fonds MRP, 350AP76, Dossier: 4MRP7: Cabinets ministériels, 'Liste générale des anciens collaborateurs', n.d.

120. Irving, *Christian Democracy*, pp. 208–9; Chen Jian, 'China and the first Indo-China War, 1950–54', *China Quarterly*, cxxxiii (1993), 85–110.

121. Dalloz, *War in Indo-China*, pp. 124–5. On later Catholic protest against the Algerian war, see Françoise Kempf, 'Les Catholiques français', in *Les Eglises chrétiennes et la Décolonisation*, ed. M. Merle (Paris, 1967), pp. 166–79.

122. AN, 363AP/C28, René Mayer papers, Schuman letter to Dean Acheson, 25 Aug. 1951.

410 COLONIAL POLICIES OF THE MOUVEMENT REPUBLICAIN

register strongly at the MRP's 1952 congress in Bordeaux.[123] Schuman and future MRP leader Pierre Pflimlin were more sensitive to this than other senior MRP figures. Within weeks of leaving the Quai d'Orsay, in March 1953 Schuman made his exasperation clear in an article devoted to the North African situation in the trimonthly review *La Nef*. Reactionary settlers, insubordinate administrators and French corporate interests in the Maghreb were the real barrier to peaceful negotiation. Other leading Catholic intellectuals agreed, notably those grouped in the *Comité France-Maghreb* chaired by François Mauriac. The writer even admitted that his support for the MRP and his sympathy for its anti-Communism had blinded him to colonial injustice in French Africa. The worsening French repression in Morocco during 1953 transformed his outlook. Using his column in the weekly magazine *L'Express*, Mauriac was also a vocal supporter of the Committee for the Release of Colonial Political Prisoners organized by Louis Massignon, professor of Islamic Studies at the Collège de France. But their lobbying for the release of the three MDRM deputies convicted of inciting the Madagascar revolt made few inroads among senior MRP politicians. The deputies were only released following the election of Guy Mollet's Socialist-led government in 1956.[124]

During 1953–54, the Socialists and Radicals, former third force partners of the MRP, faced up to the likelihood of defeat in Indo-China and independence for the North African protectorates. The MRP leadership warned instead of a domino effect culminating in imperial collapse and violent retribution against French settlers and loyal colonial subjects. The MRP's distinctiveness here lies less in its conservatism than in its linkage of French strategic interest with the defence of settler rights. The final twist was the party executive's abiding fear that equivocation would worsen the haemorrhage of electoral support to the RPF. Elections to the French Union Assembly in July 1952 added to their anxiety. The RPF emerged as the largest party block with 104 candidates elected. The MRP lagged behind the Socialists and the PCF with only eighty-four deputies.[125] MRP colonialism brought few rewards.

The MRP never fulfilled its early promise as an engine of liberal reform. Nowhere was this more apparent than in imperial affairs. The bankruptcy of the Bao Daï solution and the MRP's frustration of reform in Morocco and Tunisia lend weight to the Communist jibe that the MRP represented 'Mensonge, Réaction, Perfidie'. As historian Pierre Letamendia observed, to the MRP's opponents the party was a barrier to structural change. It opposed the Gaullists' attempt to alter the

123. Georges Oved, *La gauche française et le nationalisme marocain 1905–1955*, II (Paris, 1984), pp. 269–81 *passim*.

124. Tony Judt, *Past Imperfect. French Intellectuals, 1944–1956* (Berkeley, 1992), pp. 282–3; Sorum, *Intellectuals and Decolonization*, pp. 52–3, 57, 64–5.

125. AN, Fonds MRP, 350AP76, Dossier: 4MRP6, 'Election des Conseillers de l'Union Française', n.d. July 1952.

constitution; it blocked the economic reforms of the Pinay 'experiment' in 1952; it attacked Mendès France's colonial initiatives in 1954–55. In this sense, the MRP's hostility to decolonization fitted a wider resistance to change commensurate with the party's central place in the political order of the Fourth Republic.[126]

After the collapse of tripartism in 1947, and the concurrent emergence of a strong electoral challenge from the RPF, MRP federations were divided between those willing to govern alongside the Socialists and those reluctant to accept the break with Gaullism. Within third force coalitions between late 1947 and June 1951 the MRP consolidated its power relative to the Socialists through its control over colonial policy. Other third force parties, the Radicals and the UDSR especially, backed the MRP line over Indo-China and so muffled Socialist criticism of it. As with economic and financial policies, Socialist capacity to direct colonial affairs declined abruptly after 1947.[127] During 1951–54, the MRP's defence of empire helped bind it to its new coalition partners. As the French war effort in Indo-China collapsed and popular demands for reform in the North African protectorates grew stronger, the MRP's grass-roots membership responded more rapidly than the party leadership. Unfortunately, the distinctive structure of the party hierarchy muted this internal opposition. Furthermore, the MRP executive was slow to grasp that their Gaullist rivals and their former Radical and UDSR colleagues had grown more amenable to imperial reform owing to the expense and unpopularity of colonial conflict. The Gaullists gradually moderated their colonial conservatism over long years in opposition. By contrast, the MRP defined its colonial conservatism while in office. MRP ministers resisted reform on grounds of national and western alliance interest. A pillar of the Fourth Republic establishment, the MRP failed to move with the times. As a result, the collapse of French imperial power and the fate of the MRP were wholly intertwined.

University of the West of England   MARTIN THOMAS

126. Letamendia, *Le Mouvement Républicain Populaire*, p. 98.
127. Graham, *Choice and Democratic Order*, pp. 380–2; Williams, *Crisis*, p. 112.

[11]

Keeping Change Within Bounds: Aspects of Colonial Policy during the Churchill and Eden Governments, 1951–57*

by
David Goldsworthy

One way of periodizing the history of British decolonization between 1945 and 1964 is to think in terms of successive British administrations. At a purely descriptive level, typical thumbnail sketches would look something like this. In 1945–51, the Labour government made numerous charter decisions and set major precedents. It managed the transfers of power to India, Pakistan, Burma, Ceylon, Israel and Libya. It generated many new ideas about the governance and long-term political destiny of colonies proper (for of the countries just named, only Ceylon was a charge of the Colonial Office). And it presided over the 'second colonial invasion' of experts and advisers, which itself reflected the significance quite recently attached to colonial development policy. Between 1951 and 1957, Churchill and Eden presided over Conservative governments which, while broadly following these precedents, certainly did not seek to accelerate the pace of change and in some ways seemed more interested in holding the line. It was a time during which white settlerdom was given greater power in Central Africa and not a single Colonial Office territory attained independence. The only country to do so was the Sudan, a charge of the Foreign Office, and the timing of its independence (1 January 1956) reflected not the fulfilment of some process of tutelage but rather the exigencies of Middle Eastern policy. Territories that gave trouble – Malaya, Kenya, Uganda, British Guiana, Cyprus – were peremptorily dealt with by *force majeure*. The period was brought to an abrupt end by the Suez invasion, the culminating expression of a particular ('conservative') view of Britain's imperial role and, with hindsight, a climacteric event in Britain's imperial life. From 1957 to 1964, and especially after 1959, the Conservative governments of Macmillan and Douglas-Home hastened the end of formal empire with a flurry of decolonizations in south-east Asia, Africa, the Caribbean and the Mediterranean. In the process, colonial development was transformed into 'technical co-operation'.

There is now a substantial literature devoted to explaining these movements in policy. British decolonization emerged from an interplay of metropolitan, colonial and international factors, an interplay of such complexity that there remains wide scope for differing interpretations; indeed there is 'a new historiographical debate' on the subject.[1] With reference to the metropolitan view of things, however, one theme provides an enduring ground-bass. Like any other area of government activity, British colonial policy reflected, very substantially, considerations of strategic and economic self-interest. The Labour government, Hyam argues, had two great preoccupations – Cold War strategy and the state of the economy – and policies towards empire could not be understood without reference to these.[2] He might equally have been referring to the Conservative administrations which followed. For these governments, too, colonial policy was in the first instance 'a gigantic footnote to the Cold War'.[3] In the early and middle 1950s the British determination to crush guerrilla Communism in Malaya, to overthrow the leftist government of British Guiana (in the American hemisphere), to hang on to Cyprus and, of course, to invade Suez, must all be seen partly in this light; while Macmillan in his time was fully alive to the relevance of decolonization in the redefinition of Britain's diplomatic and strategic posture as a would-be independent ally of the United States in the post-Suez age. As for economic self-interest, the early 1950s saw a massive continuation of Labour's efforts to harness colonial commodity production and colonial transactions with the dollar area to the tasks of defending sterling and rebuilding the domestic economy (Malaya was critical in this respect too); while for the Macmillan government, considerations of cost-effectiveness, along with the desire to build up economic links with the world's industrial north rather than its rural south, further propelled the movement towards decolonization.[4]

In short, changing governmental assessments of how best to promote Britain's strategic and economic interests were major determinants of the character of colonial policy. Sometimes these assessments produced an impulse towards accelerating the rate of change, as in Macmillan's later years; at others, their main thrust was towards containment, a tighter assertion of British control. It will be argued that in 1951–57 the British government's world-view was much more conducive to the containment than to the promotion of change in colonies.

To stress the significance of broader interests in this way is not to dispute that numerous 'other factors' had their effect upon policy: colonial nationalism, American pressure, and so on. Nor is it to deny that the policies and plans put together on a day-to-day basis by officials and ministers had an internal dynamic of their own, premised on notions of what colonial policy was *intrinsically* about such as 'good government' and 'development'.[5] This discussion does not aim to assign precise weightings to such diverse variables. It does, however, reflect a belief that while causation is necessarily complex, a discussion which focuses like this one on the view from Whitehall and the cabinet room must maintain a particular sensitivity to governmental perceptions of broader national interest.

Why concentrate on the Churchill and Eden governments? Largely because, of the three periods sketched in miniature above, this one has been relatively neglected by historians of colonial policy-making (though not by historians of foreign policy, and certainly not by historians of Suez). Why this should be is not hard to see. The fascination of the Attlee period lies in its distinctiveness as a time of major initiatives in colonial policy, and the PRO files covering the period have been open for some time now.[6] For its part, the Macmillan government brought the decolonization process to a climax – a sufficient reason for interest.[7] The intervening period has suffered by comparison, appearing of lesser interest than the palpably significant eras of 'initiative' and 'climax' which bracketed it. Yet the Churchill–Eden era was certainly a complex and distinctive one in colonial policy-making, as this article attempts to show by offering a series of impressionistic sketches. It is a treatment of the subject based upon a preliminary perusal of PRO sources, and very much open to the risk (inherent, perhaps, in PRO-based work) of becoming entangled in the thickets rather than seeing the wood for what it is. Even so, it may help to bring out both something of the character of the time and, more specifically, some of the answers which occurred to policy-makers as they contemplated the colonial empire and asked themselves the perennial question: what is to be done?

I

As Prime Minister *revenant*, Churchill himself took little direct interest in this question. One of his early administrative decisions was to abolish the cabinet committee on colonial development which had been active under Attlee,[8] and he frequently did not bother to read Cabinet papers on colonial subjects.[9] Clearly he did not regard colonial policy in general as important enough to warrant his personal attention. But there was more to his attitude than that. Churchill was out of sympathy with the devolutionary aspects of post-war policy, carrying as they did the slow demise of older imperial values, and accordingly seemed to prefer – once the matter had been delegated to a strong and reliable minister – not to be over-involved in what was going on. Several clues to this attitude can be cited. When, on the advice of Andrew Cohen, Oliver Lyttelton agreed to make an initial statement reassuring the colonies that the new government would not reverse Labour's policy, Churchill declined to 'agree with' the statement as requested by Lyttelton; he merely 'noted' it.[10] In February 1952, Lyttelton secured Cabinet's agreement that Kwame Nkrumah should take the title of 'Prime Minister' of the Gold Coast; after the cabinet meeting Churchill drafted a telegram to the Prime Minister of South Africa seeking to exculpate the government: 'I hope you recognize that the decisions taken about the Gold Coast are the consequences of what was done before we became responsible'.[11] And late in 1954, in a brief for Churchill on future decolonization policy, Sir Norman Brook wrote this revealing comment: 'I recognize that this policy may be unpalatable to you. But . . . however much we may sigh for the past, we have to live in the present – and to plan for the future.'[12]

Only two specific areas of policy occasionally aroused Churchill's active concern, mainly for their extra-colonial implications. One was the issue of colonial defence and security, in all its aspects: the military tactics to be used in the Malayan and Kenyan emergencies; the need to upgrade security in colonial territories against the risk of Soviet-inspired subversion; the need to improve colonies' capacity for self-defence so as to reduce pressures on the British Army; the loyalty or otherwise of Africans promoted to officer rank in colonial armies.[13] The other was the issue of black migration to Britain from the West Indies, about which he was calling for urgent reports as early as 1952.[14]

Both as Foreign Secretary and as Prime Minister, Eden, too, seems to have found the devolutionary aspects of policy rather unpalatable. In an early minute he observed: 'I have no first hand knowledge of these territories, but some well-informed, and by no means reactionary, people think that we have been moving at a pretty dangerous political gallop there [West Africa] lately'.[15] Yet he too took very little interest in the substance of policy. The index to *Full Circle*, his volume of memoirs covering 1951–57, is virtually innocent of references to colonial – or even Commonwealth – affairs. His personal interest was engaged only when colonial matters touched on wider issues of strategy and foreign policy: Britain's standing in Washington or the United Nations, for example, or relations with Greece and Turkey (over Cyprus) or with South Africa (over the pace of constitutional change in colonial Africa).[16]

Both Churchill and Eden, in short, were much less closely involved in the direction of broad colonial policy than either Attlee before them or Macmillan after them. Perhaps this is one part of the reason why colonial policy in the period seemed to lack that relatively clear and positive sense of direction which subsequent historiography has tended to attribute to the Attlee and Macmillan periods. But in so far as the leadership had an 'attitude', it can be summarized thus. The inevitability of colonial change was recognized but there was little enthusiasm for it. It was not a high priority, and the framework of thinking was rather negative, based on considerations of how to preserve Britain's influence and to keep change within bounds. In fact, this general prime ministerial attitude was quite consonant with views held by most of the senior ministers.

Keeping change within bounds meant, broadly, two things. The first was that Britain must remain always in full 'control' of colonial events, and demonstrably so. When in October 1955 Eden decided at last to set up a standing cabinet committee on colonial affairs, he did so because too many colonial crises were catching ministers and their department unawares; thus he charged the committee 'to assist the Cabinet in *controlling* constitutional development in Colonial territories'[17] (emphasis added). No less indicative was Cabinet's decision two months later that the word 'independence' should no longer be used in references to the constitutional development of colonies, since this word might give unnecessary encouragement to the idea that territories could in due course secede from the Commonwealth. Only the term 'full self-government' would be used.[18] Thus Britain's overriding control of events would be semantically confirmed.

The second and more basic meaning of 'keeping change within bounds' was that Britain's international interests – strategic, diplomatic, economic – must on no account be compromised by movements in colonial policy, especially movements designed to accommodate nationalism. Probably the clearest statement of this view lay in the document 'The Problem of Nationalism', prepared at top level in the Foreign Office in mid-1952 and circulated to cabinet ministers with Eden's endorsement at the end of that year. The aim of this paper was

> to suggest means by which we can safe-guard our position as a world power, particularly in the economic and strategic fields, against the dangers inherent in the present upsurge of nationalism. On the economic side we have to maintain specific British interests on which our existence as a trading country depends. In the field of strategy we have to ensure our own and Commonwealth security within the larger framework of our obligations as a leader of the free world.

Nationalism, including colonial nationalism, was in effect an 'attempted sapping at our position as a world power by less developed nations', and British policy must aim to anticipate and forestall 'nationalist demands which may threaten our vital interests.' In adopting policies 'we shall have to take into account United States opinion, world (e.g. UN) opinion, and our own public opinion, probably in that order.' The specific measures that might be used ranged from 'domination by occupation' through 'threat of inter-vention' to 'creating a class with a vested interest in co-operation'.[19]

The most consistent hard-liner among the senior ministers was Lord Salisbury. A former Colonial Secretary and Commonwealth Relations Secretary and long-time associate of Churchill's, Salisbury as Lord President of the Council from 1952 to 1957 commented freely and frequently on the tendencies in colonial policy which disturbed him. 'These small countries inhabited by primitive peoples . . . are in fact not adult nations', he wrote in early 1953; '. . . If we allow ourselves to be hustled, not only shall we lose the black countries, but the white as well [from the Commonwealth]'.[20] In a Cabinet paper written in May 1956 he argued, in quite lapidary prose, that governors must be given much greater powers than they already had to control disorder, so as to keep colonial change under the tightest possible rein.[21] (Ten months later he resigned from Macmillan's Cabinet; for this highest of High Tories, the decision to release Archbishop Makarios was the final straw.)

Also concerned to keep things tight, though for bureaucratic and economistic reasons rather than ideological, were the Chancellors, R. A. Butler (1951–55) and, interestingly, Harold Macmillan (1955–57). Macmillan's ready absorption of Treasury-mindedness showed through when, chiefly on financial grounds, he vigorously opposed the Colonial Office's plan to convert an increasingly demoralized Colonial Service into a more widely based Overseas Service.[22] In 1956 he also tried hard to cut spending on colonial development.[23] In these attitudes may be seen, perhaps, a clue to his later pragmatic determination to weigh up the costs and benefits of colonial empire with a view (quite simply) to getting out if the costs, including economic costs, seemed too high.

As for the Colonial Secretaries themselves, neither Oliver Lyttelton (October 1951–July 1954) nor Alan Lennox-Boyd (from July 1954) originated on the liberal wing of the Conservative Party. The records show that Lyttelton in particular sometimes demanded extensive redrafting of official papers in order to tighten up the Colonial Office line, especially in economic and security matters. He was also a strong proponent of the Central African Federation (it was the subject of his first Cabinet submission), and very much a hardliner in coping with colonial disturbances. Yet in the context of the attitudes just described, both Colonial Secretaries sometimes found themselves rather in advance of general Cabinet sentiment on the quintessential colonial-policy issue of constitutional change, especially in West Africa. This was, in a sense, inherent in their very role as Colonial Secretary. Fundamentally, movement towards an ultimate demission of power was settled policy, at least for major (and non-strategic) territories. Thus from time to time the Colonial Secretary had necessarily to argue that now was the moment for a further instalment of devolution. And it needs to be said that on all the occasions when such matters came up to Cabinet level in 1951–57, the Colonial Secretary got his way. With whatever reluctance in some quarters, including prime ministerial, Cabinet accepted that the judgement of the responsible minister had to be respected.

Of course both ministers relied heavily upon their senior officials in what was always an extraordinarily complex and wide-ranging portfolio, and almost invariably followed their departmental briefs very closely. But there was an important reciprocity: the fact that both were strong ministers was valuable for the officials, since it helped compensate at Cabinet level for the Colonial Office's lack of bureaucratic clout in Whitehall. In practice, the Office seldom had a very easy time of it in the interdepartmental dealings by which policy submissions to Cabinet were worked out. Once again this followed to some extent from given roles. Just as CO ministers had sometimes to sell the case for liberalization to a conservative Cabinet, so the CO officials – Lloyd, Poynton, Barnes, Jeffries[24] – found themselves cast as the liberals in Whitehall, in part because it was their role to argue for colonial innovation and the commitment of ever greater metropolitan resources to colonial development. Equally in the nature of things, they met bureaucratic resistance having its roots in the different responsibilities of other departments. Thus Commonwealth Relations Office men such as Sir Percivale Liesching, Sir Gilbert Laithwaite and G. H. Baxter were more concerned to look after the South African connection and more sympathetically disposed towards the Huggins-Welensky government in Central Africa than the CO men ever were. Foreign Office officials seemed to think that the Colonial Office lacked an understanding of Realpolitik (such as inspired the 'Problem of Nationalism' paper,[25] or Foreign Office policy on the Sudan). In Defence, Sir Harold Parker believed that far too much money was spent on 'social uplift' in colonies and far too little on intelligence and security, with the result that, as Malaya, Kenya and British Guiana demonstrated, 'the Colonial Office gets into a mess and then asks the Army to help it out. Experience shows that this is a long and expensive business'.[26] The Home Office firmly resisted Colonial Office notions that it might take over responsibility for Malta on the Channel Islands model.[27] And Treasury officials such as Sir Alexander Johnston and A. E. Drake (of the Imperial and Foreign Division) were always somewhat sceptical of 'colonial development' (which *qua* ideology, was indeed pretty much restricted to the Colonial Office).[28] Nor did they think that colonies, however distressed they might be financially, could have any privileged claim on the Exchequer, especially in a time of domestic stringency, rearmament and acute dollar shortage. In the Treasury view it should in fact be a major aim of policy to wean colonies off British government funding altogether.[29]

Presiding over a high proportion of the committees in which inter-departmental confrontations took place, including the official committee on colonial affairs that had been set up to service the Cabinet committee, was the ubiquitous figure of Sir Norman Brook. The Cabinet Secretary had in effect the final say on many of the colonial policy papers that went up to Cabinet, and was the principal author of at least two of the most important ones: on the future of the Common-wealth in 1954, and the future of the smaller territories in 1955.[30] It was also Brook who in 1956 convened a top-secret committee on counter-subversion in colonial territories, and who convened the committee on colonial costs and benefits which reported to Macmillan in 1957.[31] Brook's role in colonial policy-making has yet to be given its due, and certainly merits a separate study.

Out of such ministerial and bureaucratic interplays was policy made. The rest of this article will discuss some illustrative preoccupations of

88   THE JOURNAL OF IMPERIAL AND COMMONWEALTH HISTORY

the period in more detail. It looks in turn at the Gold Coast as prototype; at the salience of the South African factor in the working out of policies for other parts of Africa; at the implications of the political evolution of colonies generally for the future of the Commonwealth; and at the strategic imperative as it affected colonial policy, especially for Cyprus. In discussing these themes – and they are only a few of the many that could have been chosen – the article will relate them, where appropriate, to the overriding high-policy concerns identified above: the desire not to lose 'control', and the wish to avoid any compromising of broader strategic, diplomatic and economic interests.

II

The Gold Coast was not 'first'. Several countries have already been mentioned, including two in Africa, which attained independence during the decade before the Gold Coast became Ghana in March 1957. The Gold Coast did however meet the Colonial Office's own organizational need for a territory to which it might apply its particular notions of tutelage, formulated in some detail as from the late 1940s. To judge by the relevant PRO files, the Office was not greatly interested in learning from those earlier exercises in the transfer of power in which it had itself played no part. The major cases of India, Pakistan and Burma provided precedents in the very broadest sense, but they were not seen in the Office as providing usable blueprints for handling the politics of transfer in the very different circumstances of West Africa. The same applied to Israel and Libya, each *sui generis* in its own way. Ceylon, being a former ward of the Office, was seen as rather more relevant. But study even of the Ceylon files was confined mainly to Sir Kenneth Roberts-Wray's legal department, where the primary concern was with the wording of legal instruments rather than the broader skills of devolution. Most relevant of all was the Sudan, which through the early 1950s appeared to be approaching independence at much the same rate as the Gold Coast. The Sudan was in certain respects an African pace-setter: Churchill himself observed that 'of course, what happens here will set the pace for us all over Africa and the Middle East'.[32] Accordingly, the Colonial Office did keep a careful watch on what the Foreign Office was doing in the Sudan. Yet this was less because the Colonial Office wished to emulate the Foreign Office's methods than because it felt that events in the Sudan might induce politicians in West Africa to raise the political stakes and thus complicate the Office's task of political management there. In short, notwithstanding the precedents, the Office did tend to treat the Gold Coast as a pioneer, as a test case for Colonial Office methods; which is also how it was generally perceived in the rest of Whitehall and beyond.

A great deal of hope was riding on the Gold Coast, and there was a patent concern in the Office to get things right. On the whole Sir Charles Arden-Clarke's dispatches from Accra were sanguine, and they were used by the Office to assure other departments that the policy of dyarchy and power-sharing was well-advised. Correspondingly, British ministers generally adopted a confident tone in their biennial briefings of the Commonwealth Prime Ministers who would have to pass judgement on Ghana's fitness to join their club.[33] The independence date was being forecast quite accurately in Colonial Office memoranda from about early 1954. All this suggests a government not only committed to its goal but also reasonably sure of the devolutionary stages by which to get there.

Within the government, however, hope was much tempered by reluctance, doubt and even anxiety. The Cabinet meeting of 12 February 1952 was the first occasion on which Churchill's government had to decide whether or not to make a constitutional concession to the Gold Coast (indeed, to any colony): specifically, to retitle the Leader of Government Business 'Prime Minister' and the Executive Council 'Cabinet' and to require the governor to consult the Prime Minister on choice of ministers. Lyttelton 'could not welcome' these changes. But 'with great reluctance' he felt obliged to recommend them, first because his Labour predecessor had bound Britain with a moral and practical pledge, secondly because Arden-Clarke himself saw them as politically necessary. Cabinet approved this unenthusiastic recommendation on the understanding that the changes conferred no more than 'an appearance' of greater authority on Nkrumah.[34] Even so, Churchill brooded on the prospect that in the governor's absence Nkrumah himself might chair the Gold Coast Cabinet, and issued an instruction that if the governor were away the deputy governor must always be present 'short of sudden death or some other equally valid excuse'.[35]

When the Gold Coast next came before Cabinet in May 1953, it was because Arden-Clarke had advised that something more than token concessions were now required 'if the Gold Coast was to continue to be governed by consent'; he and the Colonial Office proposed the transfer of responsibility for finance and perhaps justice to African ministers. The tenor of cabinet discussion was much as before. Negotiations were authorized because they appeared 'inescapable'. Churchill assured Lyttelton of Cabinet support in 'resisting any pressure' for further concessions. The view was 'strongly expressed' that if Gold Coast politicians insisted on responsibility for, say, external affairs and defence, they should be 'left under no illusion' that their country could remain in the Commonwealth.[36]

If Arden-Clarke was regarded as a very good man on the spot, it was not least because he was thought to have the necessary ability to keep firm command of a political situation which might otherwise degenerate into volatility and disorder. Lyttelton assured Cabinet that the governor was 'one of the aces in the Colonial Office pack . . . he has obtained a great personal hold over Dr. Nkrumah and the African Ministers'.[37] At one stage, Nkrumah made various ambitious political demands while Arden-Clarke was on leave in Britain; his intemperateness was seen in London as evidence that the Acting Governor, R.H. Saloway, was 'allowing things to slide, seriously'. Saloway was reprimanded by Lloyd, and there was lingering unease until Arden-Clarke returned.[38]

Lyttelton explicitly preferred to conceive of the evolving Gold Coast constitution as a 'stucco facade' and the African ministers as 'nominal' ministers who should be denied access to sensitive information such as intelligence reports. During the 1953–54 negotiations with Nkrumah he insisted on certain 'sticking points: . . . (1) Governor's reserve powers to be intact (2) Police to be outside political control (3) Safeguards for the public service (4) External affairs to involve reference here etc. These are the bare essentials and cannot on any account be conceeded [sic]'.[39] He was especially adamant on the 'operational control' of the police. In September 1953 Arden-Clarke proposed a degree of power-sharing in this area; Lyttelton refused to countenance dilution of the governor's executive authority.[40] Between the extremes of an overriding power of control over the police in British hands and full operational control in African hands he could apparently envisage no workable arrangements, and hence found it difficult to accept proposals for 'graduated' transfer, for example by way of a police commission on the British model. Certainly the Colonial Office shared ministerial worries about the future of the police; not because the Office anticipated armed take-overs of government – there is no evidence that it foresaw this particular post-colonial phenomenon – but because it feared that post-colonial governments might become authoritarian and use the police politically, creating 'police states' rather than 'policed states'.[41] Through the early 1950s Jeffries and other officials grappled with the problem of how to instil the British 'police idea' – that the police were there to maintain law and order while remaining operationally independent of ministers – and hunted about, without much success, for suitable administrative devices.[42] There was nevertheless a major difference between officials and the minister. The officials believed that the longer the governor retained overriding power of control, the more likely it was that successor politicians, having no other model, would aim to do likewise; since delay would worsen the problem, the nettle should be grasped sooner rather than later. For his part, the minister was not inclined to grasp it at all.[43]

The imperative of 'control' naturally carried greater weight in the areas of defence and internal security than anywhere else. Indeed, in these areas it largely nullified the declared policy of devolving responsibility by degrees. Thus the critical problem in any devolution policy – how and when to pass the point of no return on such important powers – was kept on the shelf during most of 1951–57; which for the Gold Coast meant until the end of the dyarchy. In mid-1955, for example, Lennox-Boyd was still refusing to contemplate allowing

Gold Coast ministers to take part in international discussions of African defence.[44]

There were two related yet distinct issues underlying all this. The first was the issue of Britain's own interests. Judgements about where British interest lay strongly influenced decisions not only about how and when to devolve power, but about what sorts of powers to devolve. One reason for agreeing to political change in the Gold Coast, according to Lloyd, was to avert the possibility of a 'major collision'. As he explained to the Governor of Nigeria, Britain could if necessary apply 'sanctions' to a rebellious Gold Coast but certainly did not wish to do so – not least because it would raise the political temperature in other colonies such as Nigeria, and Britain had a clear interest in preventing that. Hence Britain's 'acquiescence (though it would not be tame acquiescence) in what we all of course recognise to be, theoretically, over-hasty political advance'.[45] Or again, it might appear important to appease Gold Coast ministers in Britain's economic interest; a departmental brief for Lyttelton on proposals for further constitutional change in September 1953 suggested that in the future 'Gold Coast co-operation in the trade and monetary policies of the Sterling Area' might not survive British rejection of such proposals.[46] On the other hand, constitutional change should be resisted when, from the point of view of British interest, the threshold of acceptable risk was clearly exceeded. This is one way of interpreting the ministerial hard line on defence and security issues. Since there could be no guarantee that Gold Coast ministers would behave with complete discretion, giving them defence and security powers, and especially access to intelligence, could well have seemed likely to work to Britain's strategic detriment. There was also the more specific matter of whether the Gold Coast might be, or might become, susceptible to Soviet influence. On the whole the Colonial Office thought not, at least in the earlier 1950s. Arden-Clarke was credited with having steered Nkrumah well away from Communism, and the Office briefed Lyttelton – and Lyttelton in turn advised Cabinet – to that effect.[47] But as independence loomed closer, the Foreign Office in particular, and to some extent the Commonwealth Relations Office, became agitated at the prospect of Soviet influence spreading from Egypt into the Sudan and across to West Africa.[48] If this was seen chiefly as a problem for the post-independence era, it still dictated a policy of maximum vigilance by Britain on security issues for as long as direct British responsibility remained. It was at this time that the official committee on counter-subversion in the colonies was set up under Sir Norman Brook.

The second issue was simply that of readiness. Was the Gold Coast going to be 'ready' for independence? Doubts were felt quite strongly in Whitehall and perhaps nowhere more so than in the Commonwealth Relations Office, accustomed to the civilities of dealing with the old Dominions and now having to look forward to dealing with Ghana. In 1956 F.E. Cumming-Bruce, seconded from the CRO to advise the

Gold Coast on setting up a foreign service, sent back some extremely critical secret reports on the corruption, incipient authoritarianism and lack of ministerial calibre which he saw in Nkrumah's government.[49] His reports were read up to ministerial level, and caused much concern. The Commonwealth Relations Secretary, Lord Home, was deeply worried by these and similar reports and carried his worries right through to Ghana's independence, minuting to Lennox-Boyd in July 1956 'I am frankly unhappy lest we should be taking too optimistic a view', and to his new Prime Minister, Harold Macmillan, in January 1957, 'I am full of foreboding about the whole Gold Coast experiment'. Macmillan responded: 'I agree'.[50]

It might well be asked, of course, whether there was really such a thing as readiness for independence in the way that British governments liked to conceive it: 'stability', 'viability', 'maturity', and so forth. Jeffries was one official who rather doubted that there was. In one of his think-pieces, written late in 1955, he made his point with a metaphor that could not have been more literally paternalist: 'I think there is too much tendency to consider whether these places [the smaller territories] are "ready" . . . Of course they are not, any more than the Gold Coast is "ready" for independence, or than one's teenage daughter is "ready" for the proverbial latch-key'. Supporter though he was of the traditional policy of devolution by stages, Jeffries could see the force of the counter-argument that the policy could at best 'only maintain a state of uneasy equilibrium. Colonial politicians tend to concentrate attention on securing the next constitutional change instead of getting on with the job. Constitutions are in a state of continual flux and there is no stability'.[51] In other words, the lack of readiness might be in part a function of the policy itself.

If so, government would have to base its decisions about decolonization on criteria other than supposed readiness, as it had been traditionally understood. And some few years after Jeffries wrote, that was indeed the manner in which the formal business of empire was concluded.

III

South Africa had a powerful yet contradictory presence in London's thinking about British Africa. On one hand, as a wartime ally, Commonwealth country, still closely linked to the sterling area, trading partner, and the continent's predominant state economically and militarily, South Africa had always to be taken into account and sometimes into consultation. The close 'empire' bonding of the Smuts era was already some years in the past by 1951; but Conservative ministers such as Lord Swinton (Commonwealth Relations Secretary 1952–55) felt that key South Africans such as Forsyth, the permanent head of the Foreign Affairs department, and Havenga, the Finance Minister, were broadly pro-British and that the basic relationship was still good.[52] The negotiation of the Simonstown naval-base agreement of 1955, by which Britain relinquished control of the base to South Africa while retaining the right to use it, was perhaps the most tangible expression of the 'alliance' aspect of the relationship.

On the other hand, British authorities had always feared that South African expansionism would erode their own power in the continent; whence 'a British strategic tradition, stretching back to the 1870s, concerned with reinforcing structures to thwart Pretoria's authority'.[53] Ismay (Commonwealth Relations Secretary 1951–52), Swinton and Lyttelton, no less than their predecessors, were observing this tradition when they accepted the argument that Central African Federation would provide a barrier to Afrikaner imperialism; maintained the policy of keeping Seretse Khama in exile; and resisted South African pressures for the incorporation of the High Commission Territories.[54]

The contradictory forces shaping the relationship could be seen most clearly in the area of regional defence. Both sides wanted defence co-operation, but each balked at the other's key desideratum. South Africa would not meet Britain's request that it commit itself explicitly to providing troops for Middle Eastern defence if required; and Britain would not accept South African proposals for an African Defence Organization in which South Africa and the colonial powers would jointly police the continent.[55]

Here, however, we are concerned primarily with the issue of de-colonization. Trying to assess how South Africa might react to the emergence of self-governing black states was a quite major pre-occupation in the Whitehall of the 1950s. Malan had already signalled to Attlee his perturbation at the pace of change in the Gold Coast. Churchill's telegram of February 1952, noted above, was never sent, but successive Commonwealth Relations Secretaries invested diplomatic effort in explaining Britain's West African policy to Pretoria.[56] From early 1952 it was thought also that the prospect of Sudanese self-government could become a delicate issue with the South Africans, especially if Sudanese politicians raised the possibility of applying to join the Commonwealth – something to which South Africa 'would certainly not agree'.[57] Whitehall was characteristically divided on these matters. Some Foreign Office officials thought it important to avoid 'arousing the wrath' of South Africa over colonial policy.[58] In the Colonial Office, Cohen was 'horrified' by this attitude, while Jeffries minuted: 'My own view is that the U.K. is already committed to the policy of a parti-coloured Commonwealth, and that if we have to choose between going back on that policy or losing South Africa from the Commonwealth we must face the latter. I would therefore rather see the Sudan in than out'.[59]

But it was not the Sudan that forced the issue; it was the Gold Coast. Wishing to preserve South Africa's membership of the Commonwealth but also to propose the Gold Coast's admission, Cabinet decided late in 1955 that the time was ripe to sound out the new Prime Minister,

Strijdom.[60] Britain had at least one diplomatic card to play. As Prime Minister of Southern Rhodesia, Sir Godfrey Huggins had been attending Commonwealth Prime Ministers' Conferences 'in his personal capacity' since 1934. After the Central African Federation was created in 1953, Liesching and other CRO officials had proposed that Huggins as federal Prime Minister (and his successors) should attend 'as of right', even though the Federation was not yet independent.[61] Swinton, a staunch admirer of Huggins, had willingly accepted this suggestion; he noted that the arrangement might not seem 'altogether logical', but 'British constitutional affairs are, fortunately, illogical and elastic'.[62] And once this idea had won general approval in the government, it became possible for Britain to contemplate giving Huggins his 'right' at the 1956 Prime Ministers' meeting (that is, before the Gold Coast's independence), thus establishing at least a formal precedence for the Federation over Ghana within the Commonwealth. It was hoped that playing the federal card in this way would help to satisfy the South Africans and bring them into the Commonwealth consensus on the Gold Coast's admission.

In December 1955 it fell to Liesching, by then the British High Commissioner in South Africa, to make the official approach to Strijdom. It at once appeared that the federal card would be important, as expected; for Strijdom's first remark at their meeting was that 'he could hardly contemplate a situation in which the Federation with a comparatively large established European community should be called upon to take a place behind a purely native African state'. Liesching, in diplomatic response, 'went as far as I could to assure him that this particular problem would be properly looked after'.[63]

Strijdom, however, remained enigmatic about his intentions for the Commonwealth Prime Ministers' meeting; 'his final attitude cannot be taken for granted', Lord Home noted in March 1956.[64] And this meant that both issues, Federation and Gold Coast, had to be left to be settled at the meeting itself. On 5 July, in plenary session, Eden proposed Huggins's admission as of right, confident of South African acquiescence. To his – and the entire government's – astonishment, Strijdom proceeded to oppose, on the grounds that countries should not be represented as of right until their governments 'exercised complete sovereignty over their own affairs'.[65] Further, he carried the meeting.

True indeed that Strijdom could not be taken for granted; not for him Swinton's 'illogical and elastic' device. Weeks later Whitehall was still speculating about his motives. Probably the best guess was that voiced by R. W. D. Fowler of the Commonwealth Relations Office: 'We were more than a little surprised . . . But no doubt his main concern was to guard against the possibility of territories which are still properly "colonial" being admitted to Membership before they are fully self-governing'.[66]

As for the Gold Coast issue, Strijdom had privately told Eden after the opening session of the conference that he would accept the Gold Coast as a Commonwealth member 'contingently' but 'was most reluctant that the matter should be discussed in Plenary Session'. Eden, advised by Brook, decided to take the hint: to keep the matter off the agenda and to collect the individual prime ministers' views in writing.[67] Home was not happy at being pressured by Strijdom; but he could not change the decision, and his office proceeded to draft a circular letter for Eden's signature.

The letter drew a fine distinction between 'self-government within the Commonwealth' and 'membership of the Commonwealth'.[68] This was an important distinction in CRO doctrine of the 1950s, although few outside the British government claimed to be able to grasp it, and even CRO officials occasionally allowed that it was somewhat metaphysical.[69] The point was meant to be that whereas Britain had sole responsibility for bringing colonies to the former status, a decision on 'full' membership, entailing the right to attend Prime Ministers' meetings, had to be taken by all existing members. But Strijdom spotted the potential ambiguity and neatly turned it to his advantage. Since Eden's letter had stated that Britain would indeed bring the Gold Coast to 'full self-government within the Commonwealth', then 'membership' would be a fait accompli which South Africa would feel bound to recognize as such.[70] In this way Strijdom found a means of preserving South Africa's Commonwealth role while absolving himself of any responsibility for Ghana's admission, thus avoiding political odium at home.

Eden, whose personal relationship with Strijdom was poor, was by now enraged at his manoeuvres. 'Strijdom sent me an offensive letter, even an insulting one', he minuted to Home. 'We require no lesson from him in how to treat blacks. We must send a firmer reply. We shall not be respected by these bullies if we do not.' On a subsequent letter from Strijdom he was rather more terse: 'Still obstinate, rude and purblind'.[71] Thus Eden on the eve of Suez: a man frustrated and choleric at being outmanoeuvred by another head of government whom he saw as an adversary, and determined to be 'firm'. But the Commonwealth Relations Office counselled against taking matters any further. Recognizing Strijdom's tactic for what it was, the Office felt that Britain should nevertheless be content with having got Strijdom 'in the bag' with the other prime ministers.[72]

The complexity of Britain's attitude to South Africa, as mentioned earlier, reflected several different and sometimes conflicting interests and concerns – strategic, economic, diplomatic. For the British government of the day, keeping decolonization policy 'within bounds' meant, among other things, that the South African relationship should not be unnecessarily compromised. Like many other interpretations of British interest, this one would change significantly as Britain adjusted to the post-Suez world. The wind of change speech was delivered in Cape Town as well as in Accra, and in the 1960s Britain proceeded to transfer power into African hands in 'settler' and 'indigenous' territories alike, all the way down the map to the High Commission Territories, with no obvious regard to what South Africa – no longer a Commonwealth member – might have felt. But in those final pre-Suez years, as this episode illustrates, sensitivity towards Pretoria's actual and putative views on decolonization was still a significant factor in policy-making.

IV

The accession to independence of India, Pakistan and Ceylon, and in addition India's self-transformation into a non-aligned republic in 1950, had already changed the character of the Commonwealth in important ways. During Churchill's administration British official relationships with India in particular were sometimes quite tense, partly because of India's strongly anti-colonialist rhetoric in the UN and elsewhere.[73] Lord Swinton greatly lamented the acceptance of India into the Commonwealth 'on terms which not only exclude allegiance, but allow a critical neutrality . . . I doubt if we shall ever escape the unhappy results of that fatal decision'.[74]

The growing salience of racial issues was very much a factor. As South Africa's apartheid policies unfolded, Whitehall worried that India might try either to split the Commonwealth, taking the non-white members out, or at least to force Britain to choose between the sides.[75] For some purposes, for example the sharing of military intelligence, Britain by that time had already developed a private and informal notion of 'inner' and 'outer' Commonwealths: Australia, New Zealand and Canada (and less often South Africa) tended to be taken into confidence, the others left out. By the same token, the first three were sounded out well in advance on the racially sensitive issues discussed in the previous section.[76]

In 1952–53, British concerns about 'whither the Commonwealth' were augmented by some quite new factors. The sudden prospect of a Sudanese application for membership concentrated minds wonderfully on the question of whether the Commonwealth might be altered beyond repair by an intake of African members; Cabinet was moved to set up a committee, with Swinton, Salisbury and Lyttelton as the major members, to consider the whole issue of criteria for Commonwealth membership.[77] Shortly afterwards, Malta abruptly demanded to be moved from Colonial Office purview to the Commonwealth Relations Office. Lyttelton explained to Cabinet that the Maltese, 'as a European people boasting a civilisation older than our own, resent their "Colonial" status, more particularly their inclusion in the same constitutional category as the peoples of the African Colonies'.[78] Malta was not perceived in London as a candidate for political independence, chiefly because of the great strategic significance of the Malta dockyards but also because of the island's tiny size. London was, however, well disposed to the idea of making some special arrangement for Malta, and the idea of integration into the United Kingdom, with administration handled by the Home Office, was seriously considered. But this issue served also to widen the concern about the Commonwealth's future, since it raised in acute form the question of what to do about the whole range of small, supposedly non-viable territories. Thus the possibility of developing some sort of multi-tiered Commonwealth structure to accommodate different 'classes' of member became a dominant item on the agenda of Swinton's committee and the supporting committee of officials under Brook.[79] The whole exercise provides another study in the government's felt need to maintain control (in this case, of a Commonwealth which clearly it still regarded proprietorially) and to prevent possible damage to British interests arising from the centrifugal forces that were beginning to emerge.

Swinton himself was much taken with the idea that the best way to preserve the essence of the old Commonwealth (and to keep South Africa in) was to create a lower form of membership for the lesser lights: 'a special class of Commonwealth country, which has complete control over all its internal affairs, but which leaves the United Kindom Government responsible for its external affairs and its defence'. Lyttelton too favoured the idea of 'some sort of "mezzanine" status', and told Swinton's committee that the colonies, or at least the political moderates therein, were unlikely to object strongly since they were 'principally interested in self-government. It was unlikely, for example, that the Gold Coast would wish to conduct its own foreign affairs.' And Henry Hopkinson, Lyttelton's Minister of State, was also attracted to the notion of what he called 'a Purgatory between . . . the Hell of the C.O. and the Paradise of the C.R.O. . . . it would not satisfy the Gold Coast very long. But it might be a useful place to put lesser aspirants more or less permanently, particularly if the idea of Home Office rule for Malta and Gibraltar were to fall through'.[80]

At the official level, the Colonial Office and Commonwealth Relations Office toyed with a variety of formulae that might accommodate these ministerial wishes and, it was hoped, satisfy the aspirations of the second-class members: they could be grouped under a special committee of the Privy Council, they could become 'States of the Commonwealth' or a 'Colonial Council'.[81] Other departments were sounded out, and, in time, came up with predictable views on the criteria for first-class membership. For the Treasury, a country could be a full member only if it was not financially dependent on another member. For the Ministry of Defence, a full member should be willing and able to undertake some external defence commitment, such as the provision of a brigade 'for use in a major war'. Within the Colonial Office itself, one official felt that full membership should depend upon the attainment of sufficient probity in public life.[82]

This long-drawn-out exercise was certainly revealing of contemporary attitudes. Even at the time, however, there were several who perceived it as quite unrealistic. Most of the senior officials were dubious of the two-tier idea from an early stage. Brook's official committee decided firmly against it in July 1953, chiefly on the ground (and with the Gold Coast much in mind) that 'to announce an inferior kind of membership would certainly cause resentment' and might well lead to countries preferring to take their independence outside the Commonwealth.[83] Further, there would be many countries which did not clearly and obviously belong in one category rather than the other; distinctions in such cases would be even more invidious.

Officials then set out to persuade their ministers, on the basis of an interim report written by Brook. Lyttelton accepted fairly quickly. He had by then perceived that the West African politicians were after all 'showing an unwelcome interest' in defence and foreign affairs,[84] and could see that it would be impossible to exclude them from these areas after independence. Swinton held out for a good deal longer – to be precise, until 6 April 1954.[85] His reluctant surrender at a meeting with CRO officials on that date left the way clear for Brook to write a lengthy final report that was essentially a recognition of the inevitable: Britain would simply have to live with a formally egalitarian Commonwealth having a majority of non-white members. But no doubt Britain would continue to work more closely with partners of its own choosing at an informal level.[86]

In December 1954 Cabinet devoted an entire meeting to this report. It is clear from the record of proceedings that there was deep disquiet:

> In discussion several Ministers said that they greatly regretted the course of Commonwealth development which was envisaged . . . The admission of three Asiatic countries to Commonwealth membership had altered the character of the Commonwealth, and there was great danger that the Commonwealth relationship would be further diluted if full membershp had to be conceded to the Gold Coast and other countries . . . It was unfortunate that the policy of assisting dependent peoples to attain self-government had been carried forward so fast and so far.[87]

But in the end Cabinet accepted the report's recommendations, and it is fair to see this as symbolically quite significant: a rare moment of acknowledgment by the Churchill government that this aspect of the old imperial order, to which so many of them were so firmly attached, could not be prolonged.

Well-reasoned and in some ways far-sighted, the 1954 report remains a document of considerable interest. It too deserves a study of its own. One thing that it did not provide, however, was a way out for those territories for which independence of any kind was not thought possible; since they could not become second-class Commonwealth members, they would have to remain as perpetual wards of a (possibly renamed) Colonial Office. It was thought that there would be about twenty such territories; for example, Cyprus, Malta, Fiji, the Gambia, Somaliland and Aden.

In another four countries (Kenya, Tanganyika, Uganda and Sierra Leone) the future course of political development was 'uncertain'. That left the territories considered certain to attain full independence. The list of these was a strikingly modest one, and with reference to two of them the report was not far-sighted at all. In anticipated order of independence ('over the next ten or twenty years'), the list comprised the Gold Coast, Nigeria, the Central African Federation, a Malayan Federation, and a West Indian Federation. The inclusion of the third and fifth of these clearly reflected a continuing belief that there was much that Britain could still achieve by fiat. That such federations should prove to be among the most non-viable of all Britain's colonial creations was another of the realities that would not be fully perceived until Macmillan's time, when new conjunctions of political forces at home and abroad would force a much more fundamental reappraisal.

V

The final case can be presented very briefly, since it deals with but a single incident: indeed, a single spoken word. It is a peculiarly appropriate one with which to round off the discussion; for perhaps more vividly than any other single incident in 1951–57, this one exemplifies that strenuous effort to maintain demonstrable control, to contain, to keep developments within bounds, that so characterized the Churchill and Eden governments. Moreover, the aftermath no less vividly exemplifies the point that such an approach must eventually prove counter-productive in the circumstances of late colonialism, when the supposed costs of relinquishing control are being ever more clearly outweighed by the costs of trying to maintain it.

Through the Churchill–Eden period it remained firm doctrine that most of the strategic colonies must remain outside the mainstream of devolution policy. The Chiefs of Staff were periodically invited by Cabinet to offer their appreciation of the strategic role of particular territories (in 1956, for example, Singapore, British Somaliland and Malta).[88] Invariably they reported that the territory in question was, in the current critical circumstances, of greater strategic value than ever and that the British military presence must be maintained.

In December 1952 Cyprus, a naval and military base of long standing, had become potentially the most significant of all when Cabinet decided in principle that Britain's Middle Eastern Joint Headquarters should be transferred there from Egypt. Bolstering Britain's position in Cyprus was a corollary of the proposed withdrawal of British troops from the Suez Canal zone, with the intention of ensuring that Britain's strategic dominance in the Middle East generally would not be reduced. Eden, as Foreign Secretary, told Cabinet that the advantages of the move to Cyprus would be political as well as military: it would please Turkey, a major Western ally on the Soviet perimeter, and it would help to convince Greece that Britain 'intended to stay in the island'.[89] It was also understood that the United States was strongly in favour of Britain maintaining a strong presence in Cyprus. For all these reasons the retention of Cyprus seemed crucial to the preservation of Britain's status as a significant power.

On 28 July 1954, Lyttelton's final day as Secretary of State, his junior minister Henry Hopkinson achieved lasting notoriety as the man who said 'never' to Cyprus. Specifically, under heavy attack in the course of parliamentary debate, he stated, apropos of Cyprus: 'It has always been understood and agreed that there are certain territories in the Commonwealth which, owing to their particular circumstances, can never expect to be fully independent.' As uproar broke out, Hopkinson modified his words slightly but did not actually retract: 'I am not going as far as that this afternoon, but I have said that the question of the abrogation of British sovereignty cannot arise – that British sovereignty will remain'.[90]

Both the Colonial Secretaries of 1954 later argued, although on differing grounds, that Hopkinson had been misunderstood. Lyttelton wrote that Hopkinson had used the word in a conditional sense, meaning that Britain would never abandon its responsibilities until a stable life could be ensured for minorities; while according to Lennox-Boyd, Hopkinson's meaning was that it would be 'always difficult for us to surrender all power of defence or rights to have ships in the harbour'.[91] Hopkinson too felt that the fault (if there was any) was not his. Some weeks after the debate he maintained that the real problem was that Britain had no general plan for the smaller territories. The lack of such a plan 'in the long run will land us in trouble. Even the Cyprus picture would have been different had we had some public statement of policy to base ourselves upon'.[92]

In view of these assorted defences, what should be noted is that Hopkinson was in fact adhering closely, and perfectly properly, to the brief handed down to him from Cabinet. The decision to rule out any possibility of a change of sovereignty was based on a memorandum which was submitted to Cabinet by Lyttelton and Selwyn Lloyd, the Minister of State for Foreign Affairs, and approved at a meeting at which Lyttelton (though not Hopkinson) was present. While proposing a greater degree of internal self-government for the island, the submission stressed that this should in no way be confused with self-determination. The main reason for this recommendation was completely straightforward:

> In 1950 the Chiefs of Staff were emphatically of the opinion that our strategic needs in Cyprus could be met, both now and in the foreseeable future, only if full sovereignty were retained ... We have assumed that the strategic argument for retention of full sovereignty over Cyprus is at least as strong today as in 1950.

Hence, the new statement of policy

> should include a reaffirmation that we can contemplate no change in the sovereignty of Cyprus . . . We must . . . act on the assumption that deterioration in our relations with Greece is the price we must pay if we are to keep Cyprus. A point may even come at which we shall have to decide whether Cyprus is strategically more important to us than Greece.

And again, 'a containment of the Enosis movement is overdue, and . . . this calls for the dispelling of the notion that Her Majesty's Government may allow self-determination for Cyprus'.[93]

It was all there except the one word 'never'. The use of the word was certainly undiplomatic on Hopkinson's part. But it strains at meaning to argue that he meant it conditionally with an eye to minority interests, or that he was merely talking about the right to have ships in the harbour and not about sovereignty, or that he used the word in any other sense than the context suggests. Believing that he was stating agreed cabinet policy based on Lyttelton's own memorandum, Hopkinson might well have felt somewhat aggrieved when Lyttelton later intervened in the debate expressly to argue that his junior minister had not meant what he said.

It would be tempting to dismiss this episode as a storm in a teacup. Sadly, it was not. There is ample evidence that 'this diehard statement . . . contributed to the outbreak of that violence and counter-violence which was shortly to grip Cypriot affairs'.[94] In attempting a firm application of the principles of control and containment in colonial policy, the government on this occasion helped to precipitate disorder. Once again, it was the task of a successor administration to extricate Britain from a colonial imbroglio that was partly of Britain's own making.

VI

These sketches have sought to convey the character of a distinctive period. The first post-war Conservative government was the first to hold office in a world in which Britain had been reduced from the status of first-order power to second-order power. Britain was in financial straits, with an acute balance-of-payments problem and a vast new defence programme to be somehow paid for; it was confronted with international and colonial crises in theatres as diverse as Germany, Korea, Malaya and Kenya, raising the fear that Britain's conventional military resources might be seriously overstretched. To many, a contraction in Britain's overseas role had begun to seem inevitable. Hindsight suggests that the Churchill government's decision to withdraw British troops from the Canal zone was the first important acknowledgment of this, and indeed Selwyn Lloyd's Cabinet submission on the matter was blunt enough: 'A decision on the future of the Canal Zone is urgently needed. We must redeploy our troops. Commitments elsewhere (and the general need for drastic economies) make a rapid and large reduction of expenditure in the Canal Zone essential'.[95] Within this larger framework, hindsight might further suggest, the Conservative government's acquiescence in the policy of transferring the responsibilities of government to indigenous elites in certain categories of colonial territory was natural and rational enough: not just the long-standing 'goal' of colonial policy as ideologically conceived, but the only appropriate policy in an era of readjustment and contraction.

Yet there was another way of looking at things. Policy in this area was being directed by a Cabinet in which old-style imperialists still had major, and sometimes predominant, influence – the last British Cabinet, indeed, of which this was true.[96] If, as suggested at the outset, major determinants of colonial policy (as of other policy areas) lay in the way in which basic strategic and economic interests were perceived, it needs to be said that British interests were still being viewed through the eyes of a government which had lingering pretensions to the role of a first-order power. As already mentioned, Churchill's government preferred to see the Suez withdrawal not as a retreat but as part of a regrouping of forces designed to *preserve* Britain's Middle Eastern role. In Churchill's own words, 'we are not animated by fear or weakness, but only by the need of making a better redeployment of our forces, and . . . in any case we are not going to be in any hurry'.[97]

The government's basic instinct was to hang on; to conserve. And even amid the economic travails and defence dilemmas of the early 1950s, it was in fact quite possible for the government to perceive Britain's international position as not merely strong, but in some ways as relatively stronger than before the war. As John Darwin puts it, the world of 1952 was one in which

> The vast bulk of the empire had been retained, so it appeared, within the ambit of British influence or under British rule. No immediate great power challenge threatened Britain's established imperial positions. And in Europe, the most demanding commitment of all, an American guarantee had been secured which permitted the continuation of Britain's old extra-European activities . . . the implications of the complex changes in global politics since 1945 were by no means yet so obviously unfavourable to British pretensions to remain a great power.[98]

Thus the movements towards decolonization in certain territories – and it was not yet envisaged that such territories would be great in number, as the Brook report of 1954 made clear – were not to be seen as a function of some general decline in British power. Indeed, Britain's military successes against guerrilla forces in Malaya and Kenya in the mid-1950s seemed to confirm that British power still served as the final arbiter of events in the colonial empire.

ASPECTS OF COLONIAL POLICY, 1951–57   **103**

These were the government's perceptions. That they became increasingly at odds with the realities of Britain's position as the 1950s wore on is now conventional wisdom. The Churchill and Eden governments quite frequently overestimated Britain's real ability to achieve its goals against the wishes of others. The shortlived plan to impose a two-tier Commonwealth on nationalist politicians was indicative of this attitude. So was the continuing belief that colonial federations could be created and sustained at will. So was the belief that rebellion in Cyprus could be suppressed indefinitely. Most important of course was Suez. Whether or not the Suez operation decisively terminated Britain's pretensions to global power – and there is nowadays a revisionist view that the impact of Suez on subsequent British policy has been much overstated[99] – the point here is that Eden believed the operation as conceived could succeed, if necessary in the face of American opposition, and that in this respect he seriously misunderstood the forces at work in the larger policy environment.[100]

What is now apparent is that the Britain of the early to mid-1950s could maintain its world position, and the colonial empire that was a significant part of it, only if certain preconditions were met. In Darwin's words again,

> To uphold their spheres of influence and rule, the British needed American cooperation, colonial quiescence and a sound economy at home. Their delicate position, poised between the superpowers, was vulnerable to the extension of superpower rivalry, to the revival of the European states which would erode their own special claim on American goodwill and to an upsurge of colonial discontent.[101]

In the early and middle 1950s there were certainly economic problems at home and occasional outbreaks of discontent in the colonies. But the point was that at no stage up to the time of Suez did *all* these relevant factors come together in a way that might cause Britain serious difficulty in its imperial role. This, it must be said, represented Britain's good luck more than good management. But it did help to reinforce the Churchill and Eden governments' conviction that they were in a position to retain control, and to keep change within bounds.

Monash University

NOTES

*The research on which this article is based has been carried out in connection with the author's engagement as a volume editor for the British Documents on the End of Empire Project.

1. Michael Twaddle, 'Decolonization in Africa: A New British Historiographical Debate', in B. Jewsiewicki and D. Newbury (eds.), *African Historiographies:*

What History for Which Africa? (Beverly Hills, 1986). All the major texts on decolonization in recent years have stressed the multiple causality of the phenomenon, and have sought to locate colonial policy-making in the context of government policy-making as a whole. See e.g. Miles Kahler, *Decolonization in Britain and France: The Domestic Consequences of International Relations* (Princeton, 1984); R.F. Holland, *European Decolonization 1918–1981: An Introductory Survey* (Basingstoke, 1985); J.D. Hargreaves, *Decolonization in Africa* (London, 1988); John Darwin, *Britain and Decolonisation: The Retreat from Empire in the Post-war World* (Basingstoke, 1988).

2. Ronald Hyam, 'Africa and the Labour Government, 1945–1951', *Journal of Imperial and Commonwealth History*, XVI, 3 (1988), 148.

3. Ibid., 169.

4. Two studies that pursue the themes of strategy and economy, respectively, across these years are R.F. Holland, 'The Imperial Factor in British Strategies from Attlee to Macmillan, 1945–63', *Journal of Imperial and Commonwealth History*, XII, 2 (1984), and Yusuf Bangura, *Britain and Commonwealth Africa: The Politics of Economic Relations 1951–75* (Manchester, 1983).

5. J.M. Lee's *Colonial Development and Good Government: A Study of the Ideas Expressed by the British Official Classes in Planning Decolonization 1939–1964* (Oxford, 1967) remains a valuable treatment of this theme.

6. In addition to the relevant sections of the works listed in Note 1, see, e.g. Ronald Robinson, 'Andrew Cohen and the Transfer of Power in Tropical Africa 1940–1951', in W.H. Morris-Jones and G. Fischer (eds.), *Decolonisation and After: The British and French Experience* (London, 1980); J.W. Cell, 'On the Eve of Decolonisation: The Colonial Office's Plans for the Transfer of Power in Africa, 1947', *Journal of Imperial and Commonwealth History*, 7 (1980); R.D. Pearce, *The Turning Point in Africa: British Colonial Policy 1938–48* (London, 1982); Ronald Robinson and Wm. Roger Louis, 'The United States and the Liquidation of the British Empire in Tropical Africa, 1941–1951', in Prosser Gifford and Wm. Roger Louis (eds.), *The Transfer of Power in Africa: Decolonization 1940–1960* (New Haven, 1982); P.S. Gupta, 'Imperialism and the Labour Government of 1945–51', in J.M. Winter (ed.), *The Working Class in Modern British History* (Cambridge, 1983); M.D. Cowen, 'Early Years of the Colonial Development Corporation', *African Affairs*, 83 (1984); D.K. Fieldhouse, 'The Labour Governments and the Empire–Commonwealth 1945–1951', in R. Ovendale (ed.), *The Foreign Policy of the British Labour Governments 1945–1951* (Leicester, 1984); Wm.Roger Louis, *The British Empire in the Middle East 1945–51* (Oxford, 1984); Kenneth O. Morgan, *Labour in Power, 1945–1951* (Oxford, 1984), Ch. 5; A.N. Porter and A.J. Stockwell, *British Imperial Policy and Decolonization 1938–64*, Vol.1, *1938–51* (Basingstoke, 1987); Hyam, op. cit.

7. In addition to the relevant sections of the works listed in note 1, see e.g. W.P. Kirkman, *Unscrambling an Empire: A Critique of British Colonial Policy 1956–1966* (London, 1966); Dan Horowitz, 'Attitudes of British Conservatives towards Decolonization in Africa', *African Affairs*, 69 (1970); Nigel Fisher, *Iain Macleod* (London, 1973), Chs.8–10; J.D.B. Miller, *Survey of Commonwealth Affairs: Problems of Expansion and Attrition 1953–1969* (London, 1974), Chs.7, 9; A.N. Porter, 'Iain Macleod, Decolonization in Kenya and Tradition in British Colonial Policy', *Journal for Contemporary History*, 2 (1975); Dennis Austin, 'The Transfer of Power: Why and How', in Morris-Jones and Fischer, op. cit.; D.J. Morgan, *The Official History of Colonial Development*, Vol.5 (London, 1980), Chs.5–7. Much more work on Macmillan's decolonization policy can be expected as the 30-year rule moves into the 1960s.

8. CAB 134/67, C.D. (51) 18, 29 Nov. 1951.

9. In August 1953 the Cabinet Secretary, Sir Norman Brook, made a special plea to the Prime Minister to read the Colonial Secretary's paper on the Nigerian constitutional conference, even though the relevant Cabinet meeting had already passed, since Lyttelton had written it himself, had tried to make it readable, and

was 'disappointed' at Churchill's indifference. PREM 11/1367, Brook minute to Churchill, 19 Aug. 1953. Hargreaves, *Decolonization in Africa*, 126, writes that this paper 'presumably because of its hard words, is still withheld from public scrutiny'. In fact a copy may be found in the prime ministerial papers at PREM 11/1367; the reason for its being officially withheld would appear to lie in the extremely disparaging judgements passed on the Nigerian political leaders by Lyttelton, which no doubt did assist readability.

10. CO 537/6696, Cohen minute to Lloyd, 31 Oct. 1951; Lyttelton to Churchill, 7 Nov. 1951; prime ministerial minute, 8 Nov. 1951.
11. PREM 11/1367, draft telegram, 12 Feb. 1952. For whatever reason – second thoughts? advice from Sir Norman Brook? – the telegram was not sent.
12. PREM 11/1726F, brief on C(54) 307, 'Commonwealth Membership', 1 Dec. 1954.
13. See e.g. CAB 128/25, CM 85(52)1, 14 Oct. 1952 (tactics); CAB 129/71, C(54)329, 3 Nov. 1954, with covering note by Prime Minister (subversion; relief of British Army); T220/389 p.184, copy of minutes of meeting of Cabinet Defence Committee, 14 Oct. 1953 (loyalty).
14. PREM 11/824 (coloured immigration, 1952–55).
15. FO 371/95757/UP 2434/25, Eden minute on file, 23 Dec. 1951.
16. See e.g. CAB 128/25, CM 93(52)3, 6 Nov. 1952 (Washington; UN); CAB 128/25, CM 101(52)9, 3 Dec. 1952 (Turkey and Greece); DO 35/4673/156, Laithwaite to Liesching, 13 July 1956 (South Africa).
17. CAB 129/77, CP (55)144, 3 Oct.1955.
18. CAB 128/29, CM 44(55)2, 1 Dec. 1955. The Colonial Office was frankly bemused by this Canute-like directive. 'I do not foresee the Gold Coast celebrating "Ghana Full Self-Government Day"', Sir Hilton Poynton drily observed: CO 1032/98, Poynton minute to Lloyd, 14 Dec. 1955. Lennox-Boyd himself soon came to recognize that the idea was impracticable, and gave up trying to implement it.
19. CO 936/217/1, with covering letter by Sir William Strang (Permanent Under-Secretary at the Foreign Office) dated 21 June 1952.
20. DO 35/5056/6, comments on draft paper 'Colonial Territories and Commonwealth Membership', n.d. (probably late Feb. 1953).
21. CAB 134/1202, 'Powers of Colonial Governors to Preserve Order', note by Salisbury to the Colonial Affairs Committee, CA (56)18, 16 May 1956.
22. CO 1017/396/47, Macmillan to Lennox-Boyd, 5 Jan. 1956; CAB 134/1202, 'Overseas Civil Service', memorandum by Macmillan to the Colonial Affairs Committee, CA (56)8, 21 Feb. 1956. This was the first major issue to be contested between ministers in the newly-created committee.
23. CO 1025/75/41, Macmillan to Lennox-Boyd, 10 May 1956.
24. Sir Thomas Lloyd was Permanent Under-Secretary; Sir Hilton Poynton was Deputy Permanent Under-Secretary with responsibility for economic affairs; Sir William Gorell Barnes was Cohen's successor in the Africa division; Sir Charles Jeffries, the other Deputy to Lloyd, acted in these years as something of an ideas man, producing ruminative papers on the future of (for example) the colonial police, the Colonial Service, the smaller territories, and the Commonwealth at large.
25. And indeed the Colonial Office was not much impressed by the Foreign Office's negative approach to nationalism, at least the forms of nationalism manifested in colonies; CO 936/217/4/5, Lloyd to Strang, 9 Sept. 1952. One senior official dismissed the 'nationalism' paper as a 'jejune, misguided and in places slightly horrific document'. CO 936/217, minute by J.S. Bennett (head of the Mediterranean division), 26 Dec. 1952.
26. DEFE 7/415/40, brief by Parker (Permanent Secretary) for the Minister of Defence for a meeting with the Colonial Secretary and the Secretary of State for War to discuss colonial forces, 27 Nov. 1954.
27. CAB 134/1203, 'Future Departmental Responsibility for Malta', memorandum by the Home Office to the Official Committee on Colonial Policy, CA (O)(56)8, 11 May 1956.

106   THE JOURNAL OF IMPERIAL AND COMMONWEALTH HISTORY

28. The mostly unavailing struggle to raise more funds for colonial development –
    from the Exchequer, from the London money market, from American public and
    private investors, from the IBRD – was a major Colonial Office endeavour of the
    time. Much of the story has been told, though in a purely descriptive way, in D.J.
    Morgan, *The Official History of Colonial Development* (London, 1980), esp.
    Vols.3 and 4.

29. T220/314, Drake memorandum to Johnston, 19 Nov. 1954; Johnston minute to
    Drake, 22 Nov. 1954. Johnston believed that the Treasury would have to keep on
    stressing this 'important' point lest the Colonial Office 'try to blur the issue'.

30. CAB 129/71, C (54)307, 'Commonwealth Membership', 11 Oct. 1954; CAB 129/
    77, CP (55)133, 'Smaller Colonial Territories', 27 Sept. 1955.

31. The records of the counter-subversion committee are still withheld; indeed the
    committee's very existence has yet to be publicly acknowledged. There is however
    a reference to it in FO 371/118677/J1023/39G. On the costs and benefits committee
    see Morgan, *Official History of Colonial Development*, Vol.5, 96–102.

32. FO 800/827, Churchill telegram to Eden, 15 Jan. 1953.

33. See e.g. CAB 130/113, GEN 518/6/9a, 'Gold Coast Candidature for Common-
    wealth Membership', briefing paper for Commonwealth Prime Ministers' Meet-
    ing, 13 June 1956.

34. CAB 129/49, C (52)28, 'Amendment of the Gold Coast Constitution', 9 Feb. 1952;
    CAB 128/24, CM 11(52)6, 12 Feb. 1952.

35. PREM 11/1367, Churchill minute to Lyttelton, 13 Feb. 1952.

36. CAB 128/26.I, CM 34(52)6, 27 May 1953.

37. CAB 129/49, C (52)28, 9 Feb. 1952.

38. CO 554/254, T.B. Williamson minute to Lloyd, 19 March 1953; CO 554/254/24,
    Lloyd telegram to Saloway, 20 March 1953.

39. CO 554/254, minute on file, n.d., early Feb. 1953.

40. CO 554/256/140B, Arden-Clarke to Lyttelton, 14 Sept. 1953; CO 554/256/176,
    Gorell Barnes to Arden-Clarke, 17 Nov. 1953; CO 554/256/182, Arden-Clarke to
    Gorell Barnes, 28 Nov. 1953; CO 554/256/184, Lloyd to Arden-Clarke, 8 Jan.
    1954.

41. CO 537/6960, minute on file by Jeffries, 25 April 1952.

42. CO 1037/2/12, 'Report of the Working Party on the Position of the Police in the
    Later Stages of Colonial Constitutional Development', 22 April 1953; CO 1037/2/
    19, 'Minutes of Meeting in Sir Charles Jeffries' Room on 5th November, 1954'.

43. Nor, it should be said, were the assembled (British) colonial police commissioners
    at their annual Ryton-on-Dunsmore conference in 1954. It was hoped in the
    CO that the commissioners would provide helpful advice on the problem of
    transmitting the 'police idea'. Instead, to the exasperation of some officials, they
    merely declared for the status quo: overriding centralized authority to remain with
    the governor. CO 1037/2/13, 'Conference of Commissioners of Colonial Police
    Forces, 13th July 1954: Relation of Police to Government'; CO 1037/2, minute on
    file by J.S. Bennett, 10 Aug. 1954.

44. CAB 131/16, DC (55), third meeting of Cabinet Defence Committee, 10 June
    1955.

45. CO 554/254/10, Lloyd to Sir John Macpherson, 5 March 1953.

46. CO 554/256/138, brief for Secretary of State, n.d., early Sept. 1953.

47. CAB 129/66, C (54)62, memorandum by Lyttelton, 18 Feb. 1954.

48. FO 371/118676 and 118677, 'Soviet Influence and Penetration in Africa', 1956.

49. For an example, DO 35/6172/246A, Cumming-Bruce to Laithwaite, 21 July 1956.
    Cumming-Bruce further regarded the CO as naive about Gold Coast realities.

50. CO 554/1435/8, Home to Lennox-Boyd, 11 July 1956; DO 35/6177/122, Home to
    Macmillan, 29 Jan. 1957, Macmillan to Home, 29 Jan. 1957.

51. CO 1032/55, Jeffries minute to Lloyd, 16 Dec. 1955.

52. CAB 129/61, C (53)169, 'Relations with South Africa', memorandum by Swinton,
    12 June 1953. Swinton confidently expected Havenga to succeed the dour and
    difficult Malan as Prime Minister, which would, he felt, be a good thing for the

Commonwealth (CAB 129/71, C (54)327, memorandum by Swinton, 28 Oct. 1954). The succession of the dour and difficult Strijdom was an unwelcome surprise.

53. Holland, *European Decolonization*, 139.
54. All these issues came before Cabinet in its early days in office: see CAB 129/48, respectively C (51)11, 9 Nov. 1951; C (51)21, 19 Nov. 1951; C (51)49, 17 Dec. 1951.
55. CAB 131/16, DC (55)10, 'Defence Cooperation with South Africa', memorandum, 7 June 1955.
56. PREM 11/1367, Savingram, Secretary of State for Commonwealth Relations to UK High Commissioner in South Africa, 19 Feb. 1952; CAB 129/61, C (53)165, 'Relations with South Africa', memorandum by Swinton, 5 June 1953.
57. CAB 129/57, C (52)452, 'Membership of the Commonwealth: The Sudan', memorandum by Swinton, 23 Dec. 1952.
58. FO 371/90114, draft of R. Allen to C.G. Davies (Sudan Government Agent in London), n.d., early Dec. 1951.
59. CO 537/6696, Cohen minute to Trafford Smith, 10 Dec. 1951; CO 1032/10, minute by Jeffries, 21 Nov. 1952.
60. CAB 128/29, CM 44(55)5, 1 Dec. 1955.
61. Lloyd at the Colonial Office saw 'no reason to object to this proposal' and the Colonial Secretary was briefed accordingly. CO 1032/50, J.E. Marnham minute to J.S. Bennett, 31 May 1954.
62. CAB 134/768, CCM (54)7, memorandum by Swinton to Cabinet Committee on Commonwealth Membership, 16 June 1954.
63. DO 35/6176/9, 'The Gold Coast and Commonwealth Membership – Conversation between the United Kingdom High Commissioner and the Prime Minister of the Union of South Africa', 15 Dec. 1955 (meeting held on the 13th).
64. CAB 134/1202, CA (56)10, memorandum by Home to Cabinet Colonial Policy Committee, 5 March 1956.
65. CO 1032/52/123A, 'Extract from Minutes of the 10th Meeting of Commonwealth Prime Ministers on 5th July, 1956'.
66. DO 35/4673/157, R.W.D. Fowler to M.R. Metcalf (UK High Commission, Salisbury), 19 July 1956.
67. DO 35/6176/45, 'Note for Record' by Laithwaite, 28 June 1956.
68. DO 35/6176/48, Eden to Commonwealth Prime Ministers, 3 July 1956.
69. DO 35/5056, minute by A.F. Morley, 29 April 1954; DO 35/6176, L.B. Walsh Atkins minute to I.M.R. Maclennan, 22 Aug. 1956.
70. PREM 11/1367, Strijdom to Eden, 5 July 1956.
71. PREM 11/1367, handwritten notes by Eden on Home to Eden (draft letter), 6 July 1956, and Strijdom to Eden, 8 Aug. 1956.
72. DO 35/6176, Laithwaite to Home, 23 Aug. 1956; DO 35/6176/70A, Laithwaite to Liesching, 29 Aug. 1956; CO 554/1435, I.B. Watt minute to J.S. Bennett, 21 Aug. 1956: 'it would be wiser not to reply to it [Strijdom's second letter] . . . We have, after all, got Mr. Strijdom in the bag for the Gold Coast, and we'd better keep the string tied'.
73. CAB 129/60, C (53)138, 'Mr Nehru's Speech', memorandum by Swinton, 23 April 1953.
74. DO 35/5056, memorandum by Swinton, 16 Feb. 1953.
75. CO 1032/51, minute by Lloyd, 21 June 1956.
76. CAB 129/71, C (54)307, 'Commonwealth Membership', memorandum by Swinton, 11 Oct. 1954, 8 (on 'inner' and 'outer' groups); CAB 129/71, C (54)327, 'Anglo-Canadian Relations', 28 Oct. 1954, CAB 129/73 C (55)43, 'Commonwealth Membership', 16 Feb. 1955, memoranda by Swinton (consultations with the 'old three' about the Gold Coast and South Africa).
77. CAB 128/25, CM 93(52)4, 6 Nov. 1952 (Sudan); CAB 128/26.I, CM 26(53)5, 14 April 1953 (committee).
78. CAB 129/62, C(53)218, 'Departmental Responsibility for Malta and the Gold Coast', memorandum by Lyttelton, 28 July 1953, 1.

79. CAB 134/786, CCM (53) 1st meeting, Committee on Commonwealth Membership, 7 May 1953; CAB 130/87, GEN 435/1st meeting, Official Committee on Commonwealth Membership, 15 May 1953.
80. DO 35/5056, memorandum by Swinton, 16 Feb. 1953; DO 35/5056, Jeffries to R.R. Sedgwick, 31 March 1953 ('mezzanine'); CAB 134/786, CCM (53)1st meeting, 7 May 1953 (Lyttelton in committee); CO 1032/9, minute by Hopkinson, 3 July 1953.
81. CO 1032/9/2, 'Departmental Arrangements for Handling Commonwealth Affairs', report by Jeffries on discussion with Liesching and Garner of the CRO, 29 June 1953.
82. T 220/314, 'Bearing of Financial Independence on Commonwealth Membership', brief for the Chancellor of the Exchequer, 6 Dec. 1954; CAB 130/111, GEN 501/3, Interim Report of the Official Committee on the Military Implications of General Templer's Report, 15 Aug. 1955; CO 1032/50, minute by T.B. Williamson, 5 Feb. 1954.
83. CAB 130/87, GEN 435/2nd meeting, 17 July 1953.
84. DO 35/5056/47, Lyttelton to Swinton, 2 July 1953.
85. CO 1032/50, minute by M.G. Smith, 7 April 1954. Lloyd later stated that it was Brook's interim report that had changed the ministers' minds; CO 1032/50, Lloyd to Lennox-Boyd, 3 Sept. 1954.
86. CAB 129/71, C (54)307, 'Commonwealth Membership', 11 Oct. 1954.
87. CAB 128/27.II, CM 83(54), 7 Dec. 1954.
88. CAB 129/80, CP(56)97, 'Singapore', 19 April 1956; CAB 129/81, CP (56)109, 'British Somaliland', 1 May 1956; CAB 129/83, CP (56)205, 'The Strategic Importance of Malta', 5 Sept. 1956.
89. CAB 128/25, CM 101(52)9, 3 Dec. 1952.
90. H.C. Deb., 531 (28 July 1954), 508.
91. Lord Chandos, *The Memoirs of Lord Chandos* (London, 1962), 43; Anthony Seldon, *Churchill's Indian Summer: The Conservative Government, 1951–55* (London, 1981), 603, n29 (interview with Lord Boyd of Merton).
92. CO 1032/54, minute by Hopkinson, 31 Oct. 1954.
93. CAB 129/69, C (54)245, 'Cyprus', 21 July 1954.
94. Holland, *European Decolonization*, 252.
95. CAB 129/68, C (54)187, 'Egypt', 3 June 1954.
96. By March 1957 Churchill, Eden, Swinton, Salisbury and Lyttelton had all left the Cabinet and the generation of Macleod, Heath and Maudling was on the rise.
97. FO 800/827/61, Churchill minute to Eden, 14 Dec. 1953.
98. Darwin, *Britain and Decolonisation*, 165.
99. Kahler, *Decolonization in Britain and France*, 141; Darwin, op.cit., 229–32.
100. On the American role in forcing Britain's retreat (and Eden's resignation), see e.g. David Carlton, *Anthony Eden: A Biography* (London, 1981), 458–65, and Holland, *European Decolonization*, 198–200.
101. Darwin, op.cit., 166.

[12]

MACMILLAN AND THE WIND OF CHANGE IN AFRICA, 1957–1960*

RITCHIE OVENDALE

University of Wales, Aberystwyth

ABSTRACT. *Based on the recently released documents in the Public Record Office, London, this article is concerned with examining the reasons behind the shift in the British approach towards decolonization in Africa signalled by Macmillan's 'wind of change' speech to the South African parliament on 3 February 1960. The documents suggest that the British decision to abdicate in Africa was partly due to international considerations, and to Cold War politics and the need to prevent Soviet penetration in Africa. The change from 'multi-racialism' to 'non-racialism' can be attributed to the influence of the commonwealth relations office under Lord Home, and an initiative from the leader of the Africa Capricorn society, David Stirling. The emphasis on the need for Britain to pursue the same policy in all of Africa can also be traced to the commonwealth relations office. Macmillan, himself, was influenced by the 'moral' aspect, by the policies pursued by the Belgians in the Congo, but above all by the failure of French policy in Algeria.*

What lay behind the British decision to abdicate in Africa, at the time signalled by the address of the prime minister, Harold Macmillan, to the South African parliament on 3 February 1960 in which he spoke of the 'wind of change' blowing through the continent, has been a subject of speculation for historians. In 1971 David Goldsworthy attributed the change to the 'new style of colonial policy' set 'irreversibly in motion' by Iain Macleod after he took over as secretary of state for colonies and made his first speech on the subject to the house of commons on 2 November 1959. Goldsworthy offers Macleod's own explanation, given in 1965, that the paramount aim was the avoidance of 'bloodshed': Britain could not afford to fight in Africa. Goldsworthy goes further: Macleod's policy, particularly in regard to settler territories, was inspired by the secretary's own 'egalitarianism'.[1] Robert Holland, in a work published in 1991, expands Macleod's 'egalitarianism' to include an 'inchoate' 'social grouping' which helped to underpin a bias in government policy 'towards the concentration of public expenditure at home...rather than spending "overseas" under one label or another'.

---

* I wish to thank: Stephen R. Ashton for drawing my attention to documents in the Public Record Office, London, on the Eden government's colonial policy and on Macmillan's interest in the Gold Coast; Majorie Nicholson and David Steeds for providing me with information on David Stirling and the Capricorn Africa society; Dr Peter Lyon for leads on the South African response to the 'wind of change' speech; and to Dr Robert Holland for inviting me to deliver a preliminary version of this paper to the institute of commonwealth studies, university of London.

[1] David Goldsworthy, *Colonial issues in British politics 1945–1961* (Oxford, 1971), pp. 360–3. J. D. B. Miller, *Survey of commonwealth affairs. Problems of expansion and attrition* (London, 1974), pp. 112–4, argues a similar case.

Holland does, however, concede that not 'all the roots of British decolonization were to be found, as it were, in Surbiton', and suggests that it was events in Central Africa, particularly Lord Devlin's 'police state' report on Nyasaland which prompted Macmillan to move to ensure that 'he controlled the pace and direction of affairs in British colonial Africa, rather than the intransigent European communities and their frequently die-hard leaders'.[2]

John D. Hargreaves, however, in an overall survey of decolonization in Africa published in 1988, places Macmillan's policy in the context of the need to maintain a special relationship with the United States which 'could be jeopardized if Britain remained too closely identified with the residues of her colonial empire in eastern and southern Africa'. Considering the international context Hargreaves suggests further that colonial commitments could prejudice any appeal for membership of the European Economic Community, and with the increasing demands on British financial and military resources, 'Africa seemed a region where many commitments could safely be contracted'. Hargreaves sees Macleod as being chosen by Macmillan to implement a change in Africa policy.[3] Also concentrating on the international perspective John Darwin, in a book which appeared the same year as Hargreaves's study, suggests that: 'It is too facile to see the accelerated colonial withdrawal after 1960 as a direct consequence of the humiliation of 1956 [at Suez].' A.N. Porter and A.J. Stockwell agree.[4] Darwin attributes the changes in British policy to the growing evidence that there would be disturbances in Africa similar to those in Asia at the end of the Second World War. He argues, secondly, that Britain had to take into account the activities of the other colonial powers in Africa, particularly France in Algeria and Belgium in the Congo. Darwin suggests further that the British policy makers in the period 1959–60 were influenced more by the 'constraints of the local situation on the African continent than by the new international considerations'. But Darwin does concede that: 'The causes of this decisive shift in the approach of the British towards the political development of their African possessions will remain obscure until the archives for the 1960s are opened up.'[5]

The documents that have been opened in the Public Record Office, London, suggest that the interpretation of the school of commentators identified by Holland as attributing the winding-up of the empire to the reaction of the Macmillan government to the Suez crisis and its immediate assessment of a 'profit and loss account' for the colonies[6] is challenged in that there is evidence that in investigating this question the Macmillan government was merely carrying through a reassessment of policy initiated by the Eden administration. The documents partially substantiate the case of those who

---

[2] Robert Holland, *The pursuit of greatness. Britain and the world role, 1900–1970* (London, 1991), pp. 296–8; see also Robert Holland, 'The imperial factor in British strategies from Attlee to Macmillan, 1945–63', *The Journal of Imperial and Commonwealth History*, XII (1984), 165–86;

[3] John D. Hargreaves, *Decolonization in Africa* (London, 1988), pp. 186–7.

[4] John Darwin, *Britain and decolonisation. The retreat from empire in the post-war world* (London, 1988), p. 223; A. N. Porter and A.J. Stockwell, *British imperial policy and decolonization*, II, 1951–64 (London, 1989), 29–32.   [5] Darwin, *Britain and decolonisation*, pp. 222–78.

[6] Holland, *The pursuit of greatness*, pp. 295–6.

have attributed Britain's decision to quit in Africa to its international considerations and the emphasis placed on the need to sustain the revived Anglo-American relationship. There is, however, also great emphasis in the archival material on cold war politics, the need for the West to maintain a common front in Africa to prevent Soviet penetration, as well as strategic calculations in relation to the protection of Middle Eastern oil. The Africa official committee argued, on the issue of Soviet expansion, that withdrawal from dependent territories would be the way to ensure a pro-Western or politically neutral Africa. The origins of the change in British policy in Africa from an emphasis on 'multi-racialism' or reserving rights to different racial groups, to 'non-racialism' and the concept that the qualifications had to be the same for all and even an emphasis on 'one man one vote', can now be traced to the influence of the commonwealth relations office under Lord Home, and an initiative from the founder of the Special Air Services and then a leader of the Africa Capricorn society, David Stirling. That policy was largely already in place before Macleod with his egalitarian approach became colonial secretary. The emphasis on the need for Britain to pursue the same policy in all of Africa rather than having different policies for West, East and Central Africa can also be attributed to the commonwealth relations office. That body further argued that unless the French succeeded in Algeria Britain would be faced with the choice of imposing multi-racial solutions by force, or acquiescing to one man one vote. It also emerges that it was the forthcoming general election of 1959 and a concern for the 'middle voters'' sensitivity about Africa at a time of the Hola camp massacre in Kenya and the Devlin 'police state' report on Nyasaland, that focussed Macmillan's attention on Africa. Macmillan himself, though sceptical of universal suffrage, appears in the end to have been most influenced by the moral aspect and its effect on young people of all parties, outlined by Enoch Powell in his speech to the house of commons in which he attacked his own government and said that Britain could not apply different standards in Africa to those at home. That consideration prompted Macmillan to visit Africa. The prime minister was also swayed by the policies pursued by the other colonial powers, particularly the Belgians in the Congo, but above all by the failure of the French policy in Algeria. The immediate idea of his making a general policy statement on Africa can be traced to a suggestion from Kwame Nkrumah, the Ghanaian leader, to Home in May 1959, as well as one from David Stirling.

I

On 4 June 1956 the secretary of the cabinet, Norman Brook, drew the cabinet's attention to the formation of a policy review committee of five ministers headed by the prime minister, Anthony Eden, and including the foreign secretary, Selwyn Lloyd, the chancellor of the exchequer, Harold Macmillan, the minister of defence, Sir Walter Monckton, and the lord president of the council, Lord Salisbury. The review was to take into consideration the adjustments to be made in British policy in the light of the changes in the 'methods, if not the objectives, of the Soviet Union'. The consideration of Britain's economic and financial circumstances was to 'cover changes in domestic and overseas policy and adjustments in our defence programmes'.[7] The committee outlined assumptions for future planning on 15 June: these gave priority to maintaining North American involvement in Europe, developing closer co-operation with the United States and Canada, and maintaining the cohesion of the commonwealth. It had to be borne in mind that the threat to Britain's position and influence in the world was political and economic rather than military. There had to be a change in emphasis from military preparations to the maintenance and improvement of Britain's political and economic position. The period of foreign aid was ending and Britain had to find means of increasing by £400 millions the credit side of its balance of payments.[8] In a minute of 5 July 1956, Sir H. Poynton wrote to the secretary of state for colonies, Alan Lennox-Boyd, speculating on the reasons for Britain's financial and economic difficulties in regard to colonial development as being mainly a 'result of adversities to which there can be no quick cure'. Poynton further raised the fundamental question of whether Britain could continue 'to afford Colonial development on the present scale at all'. He referred to the school of thought which held that if the resources were too small to go around, Britain 'may have to begin to have a deliberate policy of shedding some of our Colonial burdens'.[9]

On 10 January 1957 Anthony Eden resigned as British prime minister. Harold Macmillan took over. The new government reassessed Britain's interests and commitments in the aftermath of the Suez crisis. Before Macmillan's accession, the cabinet on 8 January, had discussed whether Britain should pursue a closer military and political association with Western Europe. The lord president, the Marquess of Salisbury, was distressed: such a policy could be inconsistent with the maintenance of the Anglo-American alliance; Britain should rather, particularly in the nuclear field, continue its co-operation with the United States which was 'the better course and one which was more in accordance with the fundamental basis of our foreign policy'. He was supported by the Earl of Home, the secretary of state for commonwealth relations, who felt that closer moves towards Europe would also need prior consultation with the older members of the commonwealth.[10] In April, from Paris, Sir Gladwyn Jebb warned that Britain would be unable for long to avoid the choice between a close association, political as well as economic with Europe, and increased dependence on the United States, becoming 'a sort of glorified 49th State'.[11] From Bonn Sir Christopher Steel

---

[7] P.R.(56)1, note by secretary of cabinet on cabinet policy review, secret, 4 June 1956, London, Public Record Office (P.R.O.), CAB. 134/1315.

[8] P.R.(56)11, note by Eden on assumptions for future planning, top secret, 15 June 1956, P.R.O., CAB. 134/1315.

[9] Minute from H. Poynton to Lennox-Boyd, 5 July 1956, P.R.O., C.O. 1025/76.

[10] C.M.(3)57, secret, 8 Jan. 1957, P.R.O. CAB. 128/30 pt. 2, fos. 788–91.

[11] Jebb to Lloyd, tel. no. 102, confidential, 27 Apr. 1957 r. 28 Apr. 1957; de Zulueta to Macmillan, 29 May 1957, P.R.O., PREM. 11/1844.

opposed Jebb: Britain could belong to an economic and defensive system in Europe while still being allowed sufficient independence to maintain its essential overseas interests.[12] The Macmillan government chose to emphasize the American link: when he met President Eisenhower at Bermuda in March 1957 Macmillan concluded that the president was 'genuinely anxious to restore the traditional relationship between the two countries'.[13] Following the Russian launch of sputnik Macmillan, during his visit to Washington in October 1957, finally succeeded 'in regaining the special relationship with the US which we had previously enjoyed'.[14] It was this relationship which enabled Britain to implement the revised defence policy outlined in April 1957 but first mooted by the Eden cabinet in June 1956, based on nuclear deterrence, limited commitments and personnel necessitated by the need to reduce expenditure.[15]

Macmillan, when he became prime minister, was probably not particularly interested in colonial or African affairs. In October 1956, as chancellor of the exchequer, he had resisted the suggestion of the colonial secretary, Lennox-Boyd, that the £1 million grant from the colonial development and welfare allocation be continued to be paid to the Gold Coast after independence: Macmillan argued that this could not be justified 'on financial or political grounds'. In the end the chancellor was persuaded that the money could be made available in some form or another.[16] Colonial and African affairs, however, did form part of Macmillan's cost-cutting exercise, one which had been investigated during Eden's premiership. On 28 January 1957 Macmillan wrote to the chairman of the reconstituted colonial policy committee, the Marquess of Salisbury, asking for an estimate of the probable course of constitutional development in the colonies, and also 'something like a profit and loss account for each of our Colonial possessions, so that we may better able to gauge whether, from the financial and economic point of view, we are likely to gain or lose by its departure'. The prime minister emphasized that this was to be weighed against the political and strategic considerations. What he wanted was 'the balance of advantage, taking all these considerations into account, of loosing or keeping each particular territory'. He suspected that there were places, not of vital interest to Britain, where there would be no interest in resisting constitutional change and even secession from the commonwealth. Viscount Kilmuir, the lord chancellor, took over as chairman of the committee in April 1957.[17] This report was presented in June 1957 to

[12] WU 1072/288, Steel to Lloyd, tel. no. 188, confidential, 17 July 1957, P.R.O., PREM. 11/1844.   [13] C.C.22(57), secret, 22 Mar. 1957, P.R.O., CAB. 128/31 pt. 1, fo. 171.
[14] C.C.76(57)2, secret, 28 Oct. 1957, P.R.O., CAB. 128/31 pt. 2, fo. 526.
[15] *Cmnd. 124, Defence: outline of future policy* (Apr. 1957).
[16] *British documents on the end of empire*, series B, I, *Ghana*, pt. II, *1952–1957*, Richard Rathbone ed. (London, 1992), 346–50, 370–4.
[17] C.P.C.(57)6, colonial policy committee and future constitutional development in the colonies, secret, 25 Feb. 1957, enclosing Macmillan to Salisbury, 28 Jan. 1957, P.R.O., CAB. 134/1555; D.J. Morgan, *The official history of colonial development*, v, *Guidance towards self-government in British colonies, 1941–1971* (London, 1980), 58–60, 96–7.

460   RITCHIE OVENDALE

the cabinet official committee on colonial policy, chaired by Norman Brook
and including Mr P.H. Dean of the foreign office, Sir Gilbert Laithwaite of the
commonwealth relations office and Sir John Macpherson of the colonial office,
and circulated for reference rather than being discussed by the full cabinet.

The report's authors regretted that Britain would not have time to complete
its civilizing and unifying mission in Nigeria. A realistic goal for Sierra Leone
was internal self-government, provided that the economic resources of the
country could be developed. Vital British economic interests need not be
endangered by these changes provided Britain left behind stable and friendly
governments. If the 'pipe-dream of a few African politicians' of a federation
of West African states were possible Sierra Leone, as a small state, might secure
its independence within this. Because of its size, its limited economy and
precarious financial position it was thought that the Gambia could never
aspire to full independence. In contrast the report suggested that a British
withdrawal from East Africa 'would bring to a shabby conclusion an
important and hopeful experiment in race relations, with repercussions locally
on the Central African Federation and a decline in UK prestige much more
significant and enduring than the self-congratulatory applause of the anti-
colonial, anti-Western world'. Furthermore, 'African gratitude would be felt
only by the self-seeking and expressed by none.' British financial interests
would be badly affected: an expanding market for British goods would
contract; British business connections would probably not survive 'the chaotic
mismanagement of successor States'. Even Uganda, thought by some to be as
advanced as West Africa, had less than a dozen civil servants above the
subordinate grades. The Middle East air barrier would be extended
southwards, and 'the flank of Africa would be thrown open to subversive
penetration from the Soviet Union and others hostile to the West'. The place
of Belgium and Portugal in Africa would be 'cruelly undermined'. It was
thought that a strengthening of British interests in East Africa would pay
dividends. Even during the Mau Mau disturbances the Kenyan economy had
grown. Aid might be necessary to develop Tanganyika's resources. But
provided the financial conditions could be satisfied, Britain might achieve its
objectives in East Africa.[18]

The cabinet official committee on colonial policy asked the colonial office to
reconsider aspects of its assessment of the financial position of the colonies.
This was done in consultation with the treasury and the board of trade. The
revised version suggested that Canada might be persuaded to share the British
financial burden. The colonies had helped to strengthen the sterling area: in
1956 they had had a current account surplus in their balance of payments and
had helped to free non-sterling capital. If, after independence, any of these
territories, and particularly those that were large dollar-earners, left the
sterling area the consequences for Britain could be serious. But the colonial

---

[18] GEN. 174/012, future constitutional development in the colonies, colonial office print,
secret, May 1957; C.P.(O)(57)2nd. mtg., cabinet official committee on colonial policy, secret, 5
June 1957, P.R.O., CAB. 134/1552.

office felt that none of the immediate candidates for independence were likely to do this. There were fears, however, that a premature grant of independence could lead to a serious deterioration in economic and political conditions and result in a serious loss to the sterling area's dollar reserves. The paper concluded that 'the economic considerations tend to be evenly matched, and the economic interests of Great Britain are unlikely in themselves to be decisive in determining whether or not a territory should become independent'. While Britain still exercised control, however, it should ensure that British standards and methods of business and administration permeate the whole life of the territory.[19]

The considered reply to Macmillan's request of 28 January for a profit and loss account of the colonies was given in a report by Norman Brook, the chairman of the official committee on colonial policy, to the colonial policy committee on 6 September 1957. It outlined those territories likely to obtain independence and become candidates for membership of the commonwealth within the next ten years. These included: Nigeria in 1960, 1961 or soon thereafter; the Central African Federation after 1960. It was thought that there could be demands for self-government in Uganda in 1961 and independence in 1967. But Uganda was unlikely by then to have developed the racial harmony that would justify Britain's relinquishing its authority and Britain might be forced to retain this in the face of opposition and criticism. Sierra Leone could be in a similar position. During the next ten years the African countries likely to achieve self-government were Kenya, Uganda, Tanganyika, Zanzibar, Sierra Leone, the Gambia, Somaliland Protectorate and Mauritius.

It was envisaged that Somaliland might join with its neighbour in a 'United Somaliland' which would be an independent state outside the commonwealth. It was felt that in the East African territories, particularly Kenya, the devolution of responsibility would largely depend on the growth of inter-racial confidence. How long that would take could not be predicted. In all these instances strategic and economic considerations need not inhibit the orderly development towards internal self-government. The colonies did, however, contribute to Britain's world-wide communications, certain areas provided bases, and East and West Africa were the greatest potential sources of military manpower. Nigeria and East Africa were included in the territories considered important for military reasons. The occupation of the Somaliland protectorate by an unfriendly power could be detrimental to British interests. The 'emergence of the potential air/sea barrier in the Middle East' emphasized the significance of the reinforcement route through West Africa and the need to deploy ground forces in East Africa. British military requirements should not be prejudiced by 'foreseeable political developments' in East Africa. The issue of Nigerian independence could force a decision on Britain's strategic needs. Kano was essential for the Central African air-route. The two

[19] C.P.(O)(57)6, cabinet official committee on colonial policy, note by the secretaries on future constitutional development in the colonies, secret, 4 July 1957, P.R.O., CAB. 134/1556.

462   RITCHIE OVENDALE

alternatives, via the Gambia or Sierra Leone, Ascension Island and South Africa, or alternatively across French West and Equatorial Africa would not give Britain freedom of action. While Britain should not delay artificially moves towards self-government, Britain stood 'to gain no credit for launching a number of immature, unstable and impoverished units whose performance as "independent" countries would be an embarrassment and whose chaotic existence would be a temptation to our enemies'.

The report pointed out that in many territories it was only 'British authority and administration which enables peoples of different racial or tribal loyalties to live in peace with one another'. Britain also bore a responsibility for encouraging the immigration and settlement of non-indigenous peoples. Britain had a responsibility to persuade the races to 'tolerance and co-operation'; this would be a slow process. In East Africa and Mauritius 'it would be irresponsible to remove jurisdiction and control before the process had been carried well beyond the present stage'. Responsibility for some of the smaller territories could be transferred to other commonwealth countries but there were dangers in this: South Africa could intensify its claims to the High Commission territories. Brook's conclusion was that Britain had been 'too long connected with its Colonial possessions to sever ties abruptly without creating a bewilderment which would be discreditable and dangerous'.[20]

II

On 28 October 1957 Macmillan, just returned from Washington where he had gone after the Russians had launched 'sputnik', reported to the cabinet that the United States and Britain had made in effect a declaration of 'inter-dependence'.[21] The commonwealth secretary, Lord Home, was anxious lest this new Anglo-American inter-dependence endanger the nature of the commonwealth with its neutral members: 'it works in such a way that the emerging countries of Asia and Africa feel they can enjoy close relationship with us under the umbrella of the Commonwealth without necessarily being obliged to adopt a policy of alignment in the cold war'. This characteristic of the commonwealth was a valuable asset to Britain, the United States and the West generally. But Home did emphasise that Britain should feel free to discuss with the United States the situation in new and emerging commonwealth countries and the best policy to adopt towards them.[22]

In October 1958, at Brize Norton, Selwyn Lloyd, the British foreign secretary, and John Foster Dulles, the American secretary of state, agreed that their two countries should take a joint look at Africa. Britain had agreed to discuss Africa with the French, and Dulles conceded that it would be a good idea to bring in the Belgians and the Portuguese. After this the Africa official

---

[20] C.P.C.(57)30(revise), report by chairman of the official committee on colonial policy to the colonial policy committee on future development in the colonies, secret, 6 Sept. 1957, P.R.O., CAB. 134/1556.

[21] C.C.76(57), secret, 28 Oct.1957, P.R.O., CAB. 128/31 pt. 2, fo. 525.

[22] Home to Lloyd, top secret, 21 May 1958, P.R.O., PREM. 11/2689.

committee, under the supervision of Burke Trend, prepared a paper entitled 'Africa: the next ten years' giving what Lloyd considered 'the first comprehensive picture of "Black Africa" as a whole', a paper [AF(59)-28(Final), 3 June 1959] still 'retained by the Department' and not available to researchers.[23] On 14 January 1959 Trend told the Africa official committee, made up of H. T. Bourdillon and C. G. Eastwood of the colonial office, and W. Hughes of the board of trade, with officials present from the ministry of defence, the commonwealth relations office, the colonial and foreign offices, and the treasury, that this study was the result of a concern that Africa was the next likely area of Soviet expansion, and that Britain and the United States should decide how best to defend their interests there over the following ten years.

The Africa official committee decided that the study could also be broadened to formulate Britain's own policy towards those territories for which it was responsible against the background of a comprehensive policy for Africa generally. The Americans should not be allowed to determine Britain's policies towards its colonial territories, and Britain should decide what it wanted to do before talking to the Americans. In a preliminary discussion it was emphasized that the withdrawal of control from the dependent territories would be the way to ensure a pro-Western or politically neutral Africa. East Africa, in particular, was singled out: as there was as yet no reasonably educated middle class, British withdrawal would lead to administrative chaos and a dangerous vacuum which would open the way to anti-Western influences; the repercussions in Northern Rhodesia and Nyasaland would also be serious. Britain, however, could not keep control indefinitely: the aim should be to stay long enough to build up an adequately educated middle class able to administer the territory after independence; and to promote measures such as the reform of land tenure. Doubts were expressed about the value of a middle class being an insurance against the spread of anti-Western influence. Some thought that education could assist the spread of hostile propaganda. The existence of an educated middle class had not prevented the development of an authoritarian government in Ghana, but maybe authoritarian government was preferable to administrative chaos.

There was also the problem of European settlement, encouraged by the British government; Britain could not just withdraw control. In East Africa, however, the European population was too small relative to the African to maintain a multi-racial form of government over a long period. Mr C.W. Wright of the ministry of defence advised that Britain's strategic interests in Africa hinged on whether Britain wanted to safeguard its oil supplies in the Persian Gulf by force: that necessitated the stationing of the strategic reserve in Kenya and over-flying and staging rights in certain African territories. At that time the matter was under review, and he felt that the requirement could be met by other means though that would be expensive. On the economic side

[23] P.M./59/72, Lloyd to Macmillan, secret, June 1959, P.R.O., PREM. 11/2587.

the committee felt that Africa would remain an important market, and would want to continue to trade with the West. Success in this field could be achieved if Africa were stable and a pro-Russian attitude did not develop.[24]

While 'Africa: the next ten years' was being drafted, the Africa official committee considered developments in Britain's African territories. Eastwood of the colonial office pointed to the importance of Nigeria for West Africa: it was the largest single unit; it had great strategic significance; and it showed the most goodwill towards the West. The dilemma the committee faced was summed up by Trend: Britain could encourage the forces making for federation and stability and risk being denied strategic facilities; alternatively it could support fragmentation. If Britain favoured keeping the country together, should it concert its policy with the other colonial powers in Africa?[25] When considering Sierra Leone Eastwood pointed out the developments elsewhere, particularly in French Africa, which were accelerating the pace. Britain in promoting recent constitutional advances in Sierra Leone had made no commitment to grant independence and had hoped that there would be 'a period of stability and consolidation'. But Sierra Leone ministers were now left with little alternative other than to press for further advance and the prime minister, Sir Milton Margai, intended in 1960 to ask Britain to say when his country would be independent, and that that should be no later than 1963. If the opposition came to power in Sierra Leone such a considered attitude was unlikely. Eastwood thought that Margai's request would have to be met and that at the end of five years Sierra Leone would be independent. The Gambia, made up of a small colony of 29 square miles and a large protectorate of 3,974 square miles, might also be difficult to retain as a dependent territory, but the strategically important airfield at Yumdum could be a reason for retaining control over the colony area and a little of the protectorate.

In its discussion the Africa official committee concentrated on the dangers of Soviet penetration in West Africa. Sierra Leone seemed the most likely target: it had the best port; the Creole population had no cohesive background; in the interior the Sierra Leone police controlled the illicit diamond mining in the interests of a British company. There was the example of Guinea immediately to the West, recently independent and wanting to build up its prestige.

Although a report by the joint intelligence committee suggested that the United Arab Republic had not shown an interest in Sierra Leone, it could be anticipated that the Muslim element of the population, as well as the Syrian and Lebanese traders would become a target for subversion by the United Arab Republic, particularly as that state had established an embassy in Accra. This had to be qualified: Accra was some way from Sierra Leone and many of the Lebanese concerned were Christian and not likely to sympathise with Cairo.[26] When it discussed Islam the Africa official committee felt that the

---

[24]   A.F.(59)1st. mtg., cabinet Africa official committee, secret, 14 Jan. 1959, P.R.O., CAB. 134/1353.   [25]   A.F.(59)2nd. mtg., secret, 21 Jan. 1959, P.R.O., CAB. 134/1353.
[26]   A.F.(59)5th. mtg., secret, 20 Feb. 1959, P.R.O., CAB. 134/1353.

foreign office had perhaps underestimated the potential influence of Islam as a political force in Africa: 'It had proved a potent force in the Arab world, and circumstances had shown that it could become a unifying force between nations which did not otherwise see eye-to-eye.'[27]

A colonial office memorandum considered by the Africa official committee on the pace in East Africa was particularly cautious. The colonial secretary, Alan Lennox-Boyd, hoped to ask for a reaffirmation of the prevailing policy in Uganda and Zanzibar. Referring to East Africa generally, F. D. Webber of the colonial office warned that if Britain 'permitted the pace of constitutional advance in the area to be set by African nationalist opinion, even in its more moderate forms, administrative chaos could not be avoided.' In Tanganyika, for example, few Africans could hold responsible posts and 'the likely result of premature independence and the withdrawal of the British would be a reversal to tribalism'. The commonwealth relations office representative, G. E. B. Shannon, welcomed the proposed policy of 'gradualism': he thought that this would help to stabilize the situation in the Central African Federation and throughout Africa. But he did want Britain to assist in speeding up the education programme, as well as the Africanization of senior administrative posts.[28]

On 7 April 1959 the Africa official committee was able to consider a draft of the report on the next ten years in Africa. A note by the commonwealth relations office dated 9 January 1959, and circulated to the Africa official committee, was highly influential in forming this report, and indeed the wind of change of the British policy in Africa.

At this time the commonwealth relations office estimated that even though there were only six independent countries in Africa south of the Sahara, by 1964 the majority of the inhabitants of Africa would be in independent countries. By 1969 there could be more than 15 independent states south of the Sahara. Ghana's independence in 1957 had alerted the imagination of the world to the 'process of emancipation' in Africa. 1960 would be more crucial: that year Nigeria would become independent as well as the Trust territories of Somalia, French Togoland and the French Cameroons. This would affect the remaining dependent African territories. Ghana and Nigeria had set the pace for British dependencies in Africa; Guinea was doing the same for the French. The commonwealth relations office pointed to a common feeling developing among Africans all over the continent: this had found focus in Nkrumah's Pan-African organization: 'Like peace, Black Africa is rapidly becoming indivisible.' In ten years time it would be difficult to pursue different policies in Central Africa from those pursued in West Africa. With the example of West Africa before them, as the Congo was already showing, the African populations of East and Central Africa, if not of South Africa would have become 'increasingly turbulent'.

The note suggested that economic questions were not likely to be to the fore

[27] A.F.(59)6th. mtg., secret, 2 Mar. 1959, P.R.O., CAB. 134/1353.
[28] A.F.(59)7th. mtg., secret, 6 Mar. 1959, P.R.O., CAB. 134/1353.

466   RITCHIE OVENDALE

in the next decade in Africa. But Britain and the Western democracies had an obligation to improve the living standards of the peoples of Africa otherwise there would only be a widening of the political and economic gaps between the privileged countries of the West and the African peoples.

It was the racial question that was likely to be the fundamental issue. Africans, better educated, would over the next ten years find themselves in a better position to demand 'one man one vote'. This would test Britain's multi-racial policies in East and Central Africa. Britain, and other imperial powers, could be faced with the choice of imposing multi-racial solutions by force, or acquiescing to one man one vote which could be resisted with arms by the European settler communities. But with the advance of the Africans towards European and Asian standards, the multi-racial solution with its guarantees and special privileges for European and Asian minorities was going to be less and less easy to justify. Unless the French were unexpectedly successful in imposing a multi-racial solution in Algeria, the force of example could be against Britain. But acquiescence in the 'one man one vote' solution would 'sentence the European and Asian communities in East and Central Africa to dependence on the toleration of Africans in the same way as the less numerous European communities in most countries of Asia have, since 1947, depended on Asian toleration; though it is on their "know how" technical and political, and the capital they contribute or can attract, that economic and political progress are essentially based'. It was thought that paradoxically, given the development of an African 'personality', the newly independent states, governed by the black majority would be likely 'to combine only to a small degree in loose local groupings involving a minimal surrender of sovereignty'.

The possible spread of communism had to be watched. Moscow and Cairo could capitalize on issues such as Britain's attitude to apartheid at the United Nations. There was the danger that hostility, or even neutrality, in the strategic parts of Africa could expose the southern flank of NATO, and endanger British sea communications in the Atlantic and the air routes to the Far East.

The commonwealth relations office also offered predictions. By 1964 it thought that there would have been no reaction in Ghana to the existing authoritarian control. While flirting with the Soviet Union Accra would suppress communist cells at home. Nigeria would have an authoritarian central government. By 1969 Nigeria would be the unquestioned leader of Black Africa. It was thought that because of African opposition the Federation of Rhodesia and Nyasaland could not survive without backing from Britain of the Europeans there. Provided the Federation survived until then, by 1964 it was thought that the Europeans would still dominate Southern Rhodesia, the Africans would control the legislature in Nyasaland, and in Northern Rhodesia would make up a substantial part. But if the Federation broke up Southern Rhodesia would drift into South Africa's orbit and perhaps amalgamate with it; Afrikaner racial policies would be extended to the Zambesi. If the Federation survived until 1969 the Europeans would still

MACMILLAN AND AFRICA 467

provide the driving force in the federal government, even though African influence at the ballot box would have strengthened. If it failed the prospect was gloomy: the Europeans would follow increasingly illiberal policies, and could even try to force the issue by declaring the Federation, or at least Southern and Northern Rhodesia fully independent. There was unlikely to be any change in the relationship between black and white in South Africa by 1964. There would be increasing bitterness between the independent black states and South Africa. But continued economic expansion would mean that the material welfare of the African population would improve faster in South Africa than elsewhere in Africa. Possibly by 1964, and most likely by 1969, South Africa would have become a republic within the commonwealth. Economic growth could enable the Nationalist government to resettle the African population which would then have 'both less chance and less desire to rise against his masters'. Even with the example of West Africa a violent uprising against the Europeans was not to be expected. South Africa could have left the United Nations, and while adopting more and more isolationist policies would retain close links with Britain and Portugal, two of the remaining friendly countries. It was thought that up to 1964 economic dependence on South Africa would limit demands for independence on the part of the High Commission territories.

The commonwealth relations office thought that there would not be sufficient constitutional progress in East Africa by 1964 to raise the issue of independence either inside or outside the commonwealth. Demands for independence were likely by 1969 from Kenya, Uganda and Tanganyika. Britain, if it wanted to keep British East Africa within the commonwealth, would have to decide soon whether to work towards the federation of the three territories, or their independence as separate states.[29]

The Africa official committee pointed out that tropical African countries were unlikely to develop along lines similar to those followed by the European countries in the eighteenth and nineteenth centuries.[30] It also moderated the commonwealth relations office's speculations about the Central African Federation and refused to discuss the merits of the different possible developments there.[31] Philip de Zulueta, Macmillan's private secretary who handled foreign affairs, described 'Africa: the next ten years' as being 'permeated by the unimaginative spirit of colonial administration in decadence'. He thought that it would result in the wrong policies being adopted, or, at best, in no policy. De Zulueta thought that Britain might consider reversing its policy of indirect rule through native chiefs and try to build up politicians well disposed towards Britain. That could be practicable in Nigeria. In Buganda the Kabaka remained Britain's best bet. The experience of Ghana suggested that democracy would not survive the end of

[29] A.F.(59)6, note by commonwealth relations office for the Africa official committee on the next ten years in Africa, secret, 9 Jan. 1959; annex, memorandum, secret, P.R.O., CAB. 134/1353. [30] A.F.(59)8th. mtg., secret, 7 Apr. 1959, P.R.O., CAB. 134/1353. [31] A.F.(59)9th. mtg., secret, 9 Apr. 1959, P.R.O., CAB. 134/1353.

468   RITCHIE OVENDALE

colonial rule. Britain, he thought, should decide what it would like to see in
its place rather than go on pretending. He was suspicious of American interest
in exploiting Africa's mineral resources and argued that the Americans had no
direct experience of colonial administration. Britain really shared with the
French the closest interest in Africa.[32] The chiefs of staff endorsed the need to
examine a long term strategy which did not involve reliance upon particular
African territories.[33]

   The final version of 'Africa: the next ten years' pointed to apartheid in
South Africa as contributing to the growth of 'Africanism' in the North. The
pan-African concept promoted by Accra had led to a reaction of Europeans
in Africa, particularly in the Federation and talk of 'independence'. But the
paper argued that in East Africa, in the Belgian Congo and, to a lesser extent
in part of the Federation, Europeans were becoming reconciled to the idea
that there would eventually be African majorities in the governments, and
were hoping that the Africans would recognize the permanent value and
importance of the non-African communities. Referring to prevailing British
policy the paper argued that the tribal chiefs would have an important role to
play for many years in maintaining stability and law and order in many parts
of Africa. It predicted that in ten years time there would be a 'balkanised'
Black Africa, a large number of nominally independent states, authoritarian
in outlook, but commanding popular support. British East Africa might have
advanced by peaceful and constitutional means to their ultimate status of
mainly African states largely controlled by the African majority. South Africa
would remain an apartheid state. If the Federation of Rhodesia and
Nyasaland worked it could constitute by 1970 'a primarily multi-racial
community interposed, as a shock-absorber, between the European-dominated
Union at the southern extreme of Africa and the predominantly black societies
which will be emerging in the central part of the continent'. If the Federation
had disintegrated, and the resulting separation had brought about white
domination by force 'the whole of the Western position in black Africa, even
in those territories (such as Nigeria) which are at present well-disposed
towards us, will be gravely shaken'.

   It was conceded that in British East Africa the future of the non-African
minorities needed to be safeguarded: it was their skill and enterprise that
generated much of the wealth of the territories. The Belgians were faced with
a similar problem in the Congo: white settlement was responsible for the
wealth in the copperbelt there. But the Belgian government and the leading
companies were moving to the conclusion that Belgian interests would best be
served by fairly rapid moves towards self-government on the principle of 'one
man one vote' without any attempt to achieve a defined basis for partnership:
'Indeed, Belgian policy now tends to regard the non-alienation of the native
majority and their moderate leaders as the only effective safeguard for the

[32] P.F. de Zulueta to T.J. Bligh, 1 July 1959, P.R.O., PREM. 11/2587.
[33] A.F.(59)37, comments by the chiefs of staff on 'Africa: the next ten years', secret, 10 July
1959, P.R.O., CAB. 134/1355.

future.' This policy would have major repercussions in British East Africa, especially in territories where the white minority was less important than in the Congo.

In the Federation the problem was more pronounced: Britain did not control the whole area and in Southern Rhodesia the numerical disparity between Africans and non-Africans was less pronounced. But the problem was the same: that of securing time to allow the African peoples to develop and for the 'gradual evolution of the right kind of relationship between the African and non-African inhabitants'. The handling of Central Africa was critical for Britain and the West: it was here that the stresses of European and African racialism met. If the experiment of partnership failed Southern Rhodesia could be forced into South Africa's orbit, and the northern territories would join the African bloc in the North. But to maintain the Federation by force without the consent of the African inhabitants would seriously weaken the Western position in Africa.

After Nigeria became independent in 1960 the period of British leadership of the advance of African colonial territories towards independence would appear to be over, and unless Britain could solve the problem of East and Central Africa 'our past record of benevolent government will be forgotten and it will be the French and perhaps the Belgians who will be regarded by world opinion as the leaders, while we may be classed with the Portuguese as the obstacles to further advance'. The growth of pan-Africanism would make it increasingly difficult for Britain to pursue policies which to the African mind seemed to differentiate between West, and East and Central Africa: 'If we fail to solve the problems of East and Central Africa in a manner which will satisfy all reasonable aspirations and will demonstrate that we are not seeking to perpetuate an unqualified white supremacy, we may lose West Africa as well.'

There was the difficulty that if the British territories in Central and East Africa, as well as Sierra Leone and the Gambia became members of the commonwealth, some would be small and all would be immature and hypersensitive. Other members of the commonwealth might think twice about admitting all of them as full members. The Federation would be a viable unit, as would Kenya, Uganda and Tanganyika especially if it came together in some sort of association. Overall the authors were impressed with two considerations: the lead the West, after a century of association, enjoyed over the Soviet Union in Africa; secondly, 'the rapidity with which the African scene is changing under the impact of new political and social pressures'. The West needed to present a common front to the problems of Africa, and to approach them with patience, imagination and courage.

Although France recognized that the existing constitutional links between metropolitan France and the dependent territories would weaken, it expected to keep the area economically and culturally linked to France and also to attract other African territories into the orbit. The Belgians had accepted the rapid advance of the Congo into a self-governing state. The Portuguese would want to maintain for at least the following ten years the dependence of their

470   RITCHIE OVENDALE

'Ultramarine Provinces' on Europe and Portugal. The American interest in
Africa, mainly to ensure that it remained associated with the West, was
increasing. While American public attitudes 'may still be somewhat anti-
colonial and affected by the negro vote', Washington was becoming
increasingly aware of the real problems of Africa and anxious to co-operate
with Britain. British interests included the maintenance of a pro-Western
sentiment, trade and investment, and 'the safety and welfare of white settlers
and other minorities in present or former British territories'.[34]

III

The rapidly emerging new British policy towards Africa which acknowledged
that it would be difficult to distinguish between the approaches in West, and
East and Central Africa, that there would probably have to be acceptance of
the one man one vote principle by the settler population which would have to
hope to survive as an essential element of the new states's economies, that it
would be difficult to follow a different policy in East Africa from that the
Belgian government was pursuing in the Congo which was based on universal
suffrage, and that the nature of the future of independent British Africa would
depend very much on whether the French succeeded in their experiment of
linking their African territories to metropolitan France, was given a jolt by
events on the continent itself, and the Labour opposition's attitude towards
policy on Africa before the October 1959 general election.

Against the background of rumours of a plot by Dr Hastings Banda and his
Congress supporters to murder prominent whites in Nyasaland, the governor
declared a state of emergency, brought in Southern Rhodesian troops to keep
order, and arrested Banda on 3 March 1959. Alan Lennox-Boyd, the colonial
secretary, told the house of commons that he had information that a massacre
had been planned. Macmillan decided to appoint a commission of inquiry
and the lord chancellor, Lord Kilmuir, and the deputy prime minister, R.A.
Butler, chose Sir Patrick Devlin, a judge, to head it. Macmillan confided to
his diary that he thought this choice 'naive': Devlin was 'Irish' and so anti-
government on principle, a lapsed Roman catholic, and had been bitterly
disappointed that Macmillan had not made him Lord Chief Justice. He was
not surprised that Devlin's report was 'dynamite', and 'may well blow this
Government out of office'.[35] Lord Perth, the minister of state for colonial
affairs, saw Devlin towards the middle of July and was told that the justice's
report would emphasize that 'it was necessary for this country, or any other
colonial power, to choose between benevolent despotic rule or else be prepared

---

[34] This summary of 'Africa; the next ten years' is based on the versions given to the French and
the Americans. See A.F.(59)41, secret, 30 Oct. 1959 attaching 'Africa: the next ten years', May
1959, for the version shown to the Americans which omitted two paragraphs and amended a
further six out of 105, P.R.O., CAB. 134/1355. See also J1079/38, 'Africa: the next ten years',
version handed to the French, secret, undated (file dated 8 Dec. 1959), P.R.O., F.O. 371/137974.
[35] Brian Lapping, *End of Empire* (London, 1985), pp. 478–83; Alistair Horne, *Macmillan
1957–1986* (London, 1989), pp. 180–1.

to release responsibility to the natives'.[36] The Devlin report found that Nyasaland was 'no doubt only temporarily, a police state'. The cabinet refused Lennox-Boyd's offer to resign.[37]

At the same time as considering the Devlin report the cabinet discussed the significance of the report on the deaths in the Hola camp in Kenya in February 1959 of 11 Mau Mau detainees who had been beaten to death by their black guards for refusing to work. The governor of Kenya, Sir Evelyn Baring, explained to members of the cabinet that the camp superintendent, Mr Sullivan, had failed to carry out instructions properly. The governor did not feel able to criticise the actions of the African warders.[38] The cabinet again refused Lennox-Boyd's proffered resignation. On 27 July, from the floor of the house of commons, J. Enoch Powell attacked his own government:

Nor can we ourselves pick and choose where and in what parts of the world we shall use this or that kind of standard. We cannot say, 'We will have African standards in Africa, Asian standards in Asia and perhaps British standards here at home.' We have not that choice to make. We must be consistent with ourselves everywhere. All Government, all influence of man upon man, rests upon opinion. What we can do in Africa, where we still govern and where we no longer govern, depends on the opinion which is entertained of the way in which this country acts and the way in which Englishmen act. We cannot, we dare not, in Africa of all places, fall below our own highest standards in the acceptance of responsibility.

Iain Macleod later recorded that the Hola camp killings were even more decisive than the Devlin report in influencing the British cabinet's policy towards Africa.[39]

Macmillan was also forced to consider African policy in relation to the forthcoming general election. The Labour opposition was capitalizing on difficulties in Africa and refusing to co-operate with the setting up of a royal commission to look into the difficulties of the Federation of Rhodesia and Nyasaland. Macmillan chose his friend, Walter Monckton, to chair the commission, and on 22 August briefed him: the Africans could not be dominated permanently as in South Africa; on the other hand the Europeans could not be abandoned.[40] On 30 August Macmillan told President Eisenhower: 'We have our Algerias coming to us – Kenya and Central Africa'.[41] Around this time de Gaulle offered the Algerians self-determination.[42] As Iain Macleod wrote to Macmillan on 25 May, Black Africa,

[36] T164/59, T. J. Bligh to D. L. Cole, 14 July 1959, enclosing note for record of mtg. between Macmillan, Lennox-Boyd, Perth, and Brook on 13 July 1959, P.R.O., PREM. 11/2783.

[37] Nigel Fisher, Harold Macmillan (London, 1982), p. 218.

[38] GEN. 688/2nd mtg., Kenya Hola detention camp, secret, 9 June 1959, P.R.O., CAB. 130/164; C.C.43(59)1, secret, 20 July 1959, P.R.O., CAB. 128/33, fos. 278–80.

[39] Fisher, Harold Macmillan, p. 218; Porter and Stockwell British imperial policy and decolonization, II, 513; W.P. Kirkman, Unscrambling an empire. A critique of British colonial policy 1956–1966 (London, 1966), p. 51.

[40] Harold Macmillan, Pointing the way 1959–1961 (London, 1972), pp. 135–9; Horne, Macmillan 1957–1986, pp. 182–3.

[41] Harold Macmillan, Riding the storm 1956–1959 (London, 1971), p. 748.

[42] Horne, Macmillan 1957–1986, p. 177.

perhaps, remained the Conservative party's most difficult problem in relation to the vital middle voters. It was the only policy on which the Conservatives were under severe criticism, and the universities felt more strongly on this than any other single matter.

Macleod suggested that Macmillan consider a memorandum by David Stirling whom he described as having 'a genius for leadership in war' and as being 'a dreamer in peace'. Stirling, the founder of the Special Air Services, after the Second World War had become fascinated by the situation in Africa. He instigated the foundation in 1949 of the Capricorn Africa society the constitution of which argued that a policy for Africa had to come from within Africa, and that it needed to be acceptable to and supported by all races on the continent. The society's premiss was that there had to be a common citizenship which could be subject to qualifications but had to be open on the same basis to members of all races. Stirling wanted all the political parties to join in a declaration on 3 June that self-government would be granted to all territories under British protection as soon as general conditions that would make possible a smooth transfer of power existed. Macleod favoured Stirling's policy that 'the rights of the individual should be secured to him by virtue of his position as a citizen rather than because of the colour of his skin or his membership of a particular community'. Macleod thought that this went further than Michael Blundell's policy in Kenya of conceding a great many rights to Africans, but was no different from Cecil Rhodes's idea of equal rights for all civilized men. It would mean the end of separate electoral rolls, African majorities on the unofficial side, and during the period of tutelage fairly stiff qualifications for the right to vote which would be the same for everyone.

Macmillan and Home saw Stirling on 11 June and discussed his proposals. Stirling later recalled that Home backed the ideas of the Africa Capricorn society in his argument with Macmillan. The prime minister doubted whether it was necessary for everyone to have a vote: in Britain the franchise had been comparatively narrow until recent times. Home pointed to the difficulty of the demand for one man one vote, made by Nkrumah and supported by the Labour party as an objective. Macmillan said that he favoured a written constitution on American lines; if the British system of simple majority vote were followed there would be greater instability. Home pointed to the difficulty of giving any date for the transfer of power: the governor of Nyasaland had told him that he could not find one African fit for appointment as a district officer. Home wondered how a predominantly black parliament could maintain competent administrative standards. Macmillan felt that the white people in Africa would have to recognize that one day the black majority would have to make itself effective, although not necessarily right away. But there were two forces capable of bringing about a civil war: if the franchise were extended too fast the reactionary white people might try to join South Africa; if Britain did not move fast enough the Africans would lead the disturbances. The prime minister insisted: 'It would have to be understood that the Constitution would be written and the rules of the Constitution would be imposed from outside, so that they could not be changed by a simple majority vote in the legislative assembly.'[43]

Home was also impressed with the idea of making a statement. While on a visit to Ghana between 15 and 20 May, Nkrumah had impressed on the commonwealth secretary that he would go on campaigning for independence in Africa based on one man one vote. Home argued that conditions in Central Africa were not the same as they had been in Ghana and to campaign for one man one vote would just invite bloodshed. Nkrumah said that he was genuinely anxious to find a way 'to stop the flood which could so easily be loosed against the white man and which could turn to hatred'. Nkrumah wondered whether Britain might not agree on a declaration of principles to which he and others could subscribe. He favoured Britain indicating a date for independence for each territory. Home suggested to Macmillan that an African committee should be set up to look into a 'declaration of intention' on the future of Britain's African territories.[44] On 3 June Home drafted a statement on colonial policy in Africa. It included reference to the need for leaders to have enough political maturity to exercise their new powers with respect for the rights of minorities and individuals. The principle of one man one vote had to be seen against that background. It referred to the inalienable rights of both Europeans and Africans and to the need for the two races to work together in governing. Universal suffrage could not come until the sense of responsibility of the leaders was sufficiently developed not to misuse the vast majorities they might control. A sentence about it taking 600 years for one man one vote to be reached in Britain, and then only a generation after universal education, was deleted.[45] After the meeting with Stirling Home changed his draft. The commonwealth secretary referred to British policy aiming to achieve a common roll where any individual of any race might exercise his political right on a basis of complete equality. Britain had taken 600 years to achieve one man one vote: 'Today no one suggest (sic) such a lengthy apprenticeship but if democracy is to be secure education in its broadest sense must underpin the franchise.'[46]

[43] Macleod to Macmillan, 25 May 1959; David Stirling to Macmillan, 26 May 1959 enclosing memorandum by Stirling on a policy for East and Central Africa, 20 May 1959; Note for record by T.J. Bligh, confidential, 10(?) June 1959 of mtg. between Macmillan, Home and Sterling, 11 June 1959, P.R.O., PREM. 11/2583. See Alan Hoe, *David Stirling. The authorised biography of the founder of the SAS* (London, 1992), pp. 284–8, 318–9.

[44] 38/59, Home to Macmillan, 29 May 1959; record by Home of conversation between Home and Nkrumah during Home's visit to Ghana, 1 June 1959, P.R.O., PREM. 11/2588.

[45] 41/59, Home to Macmillan, 3 June 1959 enclosing outline of statement on colonial policy in Africa, P.R.O., PREM. 11/2588.

[46] 50/59, Home to Macmillan, 22 June 1959, P.R.O., PREM. 11/2583; GEN. 688/5, memorandum by Home on constitutional development in Africa, 25 June 1959, P.R.O., CAB. 130/164.

474   RITCHIE OVENDALE

IV

The Conservatives won the general election. Lennox-Boyd left the cabinet for personal reasons and was succeeded as colonial secretary by Iain Macleod. Home had worked well with Lennox-Boyd, but found it difficult to establish the same understanding with Macleod. Macleod at 46 was regarded as a potential prime minister and had served as minister of labour, but his political experience was restricted to home affairs.[47] He told the house of commons on 2 November 1959:

In the colonial territories at the present time, there is a state of emergency which has lasted seven years in Kenya; there is a state of emergency which has lasted seven months in Nyasaland; there are persons in Northern Rhodesia living in restriction by order.... Here clearly are my first tasks.[48]

Following the suggestion of Home, a cabinet African committee was set up by direction of the prime minister with himself as chairman, and comprising the lord chancellor, and the foreign, commonwealth, colonial and home secretaries.[49] The first issue it dealt with was the request of Sir Edgar Whitehead, the prime minister of Southern Rhodesia, for Britain to remove from the Southern Rhodesian constitution all the existing restrictions on full self-government. Home argued that if Britain announced, before the Monckton commission had reported, that it was relinquishing its remaining powers to intervene in Southern Rhodesian affairs, the Africans would assume, however effective alternative safeguards might appear, that Britain was handing over power to the European minority and that was its intention for the federation as a whole.[50]

On 10 November Macleod told the cabinet that that day the governor of Kenya was announcing the end of the state of emergency and the release of 2,500 prisoners. The new colonial secretary hoped for a steady improvement in conditions in Kenya.[51] On 26 November Macleod reported to the cabinet that the colonial policy committee had approved his proposed plan for an announcement on constitutional advance in Tanganyika. This would mean an unofficial (i.e. black) majority in the council of ministers in 1960, and a substantial extension of the franchise. Because of the likely repercussions in Nyasaland and Northern Rhodesia the franchise would be more limited than had been recommended, and it was hoped that the constitutional conference that would work out the details could be postponed until April or May 1960.[52]

Macmillan himself, by 1 November, had decided to visit Africa. Apparently influenced by Powell's attack in the house of commons he wrote to Norman Brook:

...young people of all Parties are uneasy about our moral basis. Something must be

[47] Kenneth Young, *Sir Alec Douglas-Home* (London, 1970), p. 113; Nigel Fisher, *Iain Macleod* (London, 1973), pp. 141–2.   [48] Goldsworthy, *Colonial issues in British politics*, p. 362.
[49] A.F.(M)(59)1, cabinet Africa committee, 21 Oct. 1959, P.R.O., CAB. 134/1362.
[50] A.F.(M)(59)2, note by Home of a discussion with Whitehead on constitutional changes, 13 Nov. 1959, P.R.O., CAB. 134/1362.
[51] C.C.57(59)2, secret, 10 Nov. 1959, P.R.O., CAB. 128/33, fo. 359.
[52] C.C.60(59)8, secret, 26 Nov. 1959, P.R.O., CAB. 128/33, fos. 383–4.

done to lift Africa on to a more national plane, as a problem to the solution of which we must all contribute, not out of spite... but by some really imaginative effort.[53]

Between 20 and 27 November British officials discussed 'Africa: the next ten years' with their American and Canadian counterparts. The Canadians thought that South Africa could only end in disaster; the Americans hoped that the participation of the Afrikaner community in the economic life of the country could lead to a modification of apartheid. Britain tried to say as little as possible about South Africa's policies. The British pointed to the purely African nationalism in Kenya as one of the obstacles to building up a multi-racial community in Kenya. The Americans urged the need for the speedy building-up of a multi-racial community in Kenya.[54]

Macleod went to East Africa. He reported to Macmillan on 29 December:

The one common factor in the four East African territories is that in each of them something is happening about constitutional advance, but this is almost the only point they have in common and our approach to them will have to differ very widely.

Elections were due in Zanzibar in July 1960. There was little representative government but Macleod expected that Britain 'would have to move a short distance but that we need not contemplate anything drastic'. In Tanganyika Macleod encountered criticism of Britain's franchise proposals but after talking to Julius Nyerere decided that there was little need for a conference in London in the spring as Nyerere's ideas coincided with what Britain intended to offer. Macleod recommended a major measure of constitutional advance for Uganda, but was worried by the Buganda problem. The colonial secretary thought that Kenya posed the real problem, and was critical of views like those in the *Economist* that settlers in Kenya should accept the same position as those in Tanganyika. Kenya, he argued, was just emerging from seven years of terror. Its political parties were not united. And the problem of the settlers and the European and Asian businessmen was more formidable in Kenya than in any other colonial territory. Many thought that the Kenya conference due to be held in London was doomed to failure. Macleod insisted that the Kenya administration was good at all levels. The colonial secretary also saw the governor of Nyasaland, Sir Robert Armitage, at Dar-es-Salaam, and was worried that no real lead was being given in that country. The colonial secretary was convinced that, whether the Federal authorities liked it or not, an imaginative offer of constitutional advance at a fairly early date was the best, and perhaps the only hope of holding the position.[55]

V

On 5 January 1960 Macmillan left London and over the following six weeks visited Ghana, Nigeria, the Federation of Rhodesia and Nyasaland, and South Africa. Norman Brook recorded that the prime minister was conscious of the

[53] Macmillan to Brook, 1 Nov. 1959, quoted by Horne, *Macmillan 1957–1986*, p. 185.

[54] A.F.(59)42, report on a visit to Washington and Ottawa to discuss African affairs, confidential, 21 Dec. 1959, P.R.O., CAB. 134/1355.

[55] P.M.(59)65, Macleod to Macmillan, 29 Dec. 1959, P.R.O., PREM. 11/2586.

rising tide of nationalism in Africa and wanted to inform himself at first hand. Macmillan also recognized the specific challenge to Britain of the problem of constitutional advance in multi-racial societies in Africa. In Ghana, Macmillan found that opinion was scarcely disturbed by the suppression of the opposition, the declining effectiveness of parliament, and the domination of all aspects of public life by a single party. On 9 January at Accra Macmillan said: 'the wind of change is blowing right through Africa'. While in the Federation Macmillan reached the same conclusion as Macleod that the only way to save it was a rapid advance to self-government in all matters of territorial interest in Nyasaland; Macmillan 'jolted' European opinion. In a conversation at Groote Schuur in Cape Town with Dr H. Verwoerd, the South African prime minister, Macmillan explained how the two world wars had forced the pace of the transfer of colonial territories to the inhabitants. For Britain the problem was acute in East and Central Africa where there were many European settlers who had no other home. Rather than following South Africa's policy of separate development Britain thought it right to work for a non-racial state in which all communities would have a share in the government. Macmillan made a comparison with Algeria, 'a white country in North Africa, with about a million French settlers'. It looked as if the French had lost the struggle, and not for lack of courage or material strength and expenditure. If the French experiment did fail, it was likely to do so because they had tried to hold down an indigenous population by force.[56]

Addressing both houses of the South African parliament on 3 February 1960 Macmillan said:

In the twentieth century, and especially since the end of the war, the processes which gave birth to the nation states of Europe have been repeated all over the world. We have seen the awakening of national consciousness in peoples who have for centuries lived in dependence upon some other power. Fifteen years ago this movement spread through Asia. Many countries there of different races and civilisations pressed their claim to an independent national life. Today the same thing is happening in Africa, and the most striking of all the impressions I have formed since I left London a month ago is of the strength of this African national consciousness. In different places it takes different forms, but it is happening everywhere. The wind of change is blowing through this continent, and, whether we like it or not, this growth of national consciousness is a political fact. We must accept it as a fact, and our national policies must take account of it.[57]

VI

Macmillan in delivering this speech was, in effect, following Nkrumah's suggestion that Britain should make a declaration of policy, an idea pursued by Home, and also proposed by David Stirling. The policy that Macmillan outlined in Cape Town has been seen as the British abdication in Africa and the cynical abandonment of the white settlers. In Britain right wing Conservatives formed the Monday club to mark 'Black Monday' the day

---

[56] C.(60)66, note by Norman Brook on Macmillan's African tour, secret, 5 Apr. 1960, P.R.O., CAB. 129/100. Detailed accounts can be found in Macmillan, *Pointing the way*, pp. 116–77; Horne, *Macmillan* 1957–1986, pp. 186–200.   [57] Macmillan, *Pointing the way*, p. 156.

Macmillan spoke in Cape Town.[58] But on 18 March 1960, in a discussion by the colonial policy committee on constitutional advance in Nyasaland, Macmillan suggested that thought should be given to the franchise arrangements in countries like Kenya where there were significant European minorities: 'The one man one vote franchise was not necessarily the most appropriate for such societies and there might be advantage in some more indirect form of voting, designed to prevent the complete subjection of minority interests by the majority'.[59] But Macmillan did reflect the view that had increasingly emerged during 1959 in the commonwealth relations office, to some extent the colonial office, and the Africa official committee that British policy might have to move towards looking at the Asian example after independence for a guide as to the position of the European settlers who stayed on.

The Stirling memorandum was influential in getting across the idea that people could only have rights in societies as individuals, and not as privileged members of a particular race. The bold initial views of the commonwealth relations office in January 1959 that formed the background to the key document 'Africa: the next ten years' were moderated in the final version, but they probably sowed an important germ.

Macmillan, initially absorbed with reviving the Anglo-American special relationship, showed an interest in Africa only in so far as it showed a profit or loss to Britain. By May 1959 the Labour stand over the forthcoming general election, the emergency in Nyasaland, and the Hola camp killings in Kenya forced the prime minister to pay attention to Africa. Macmillan, personally, seems to have been largely influenced by the French experience in Algeria. Indeed the policies of the European powers in Africa did a great deal to determine the pace of British policy: Britain thought Belgium's moving towards the one man one vote solution in the Congo had obvious ramifications for British East Africa; Britain was also influenced by French policy in Algeria, and by the French granting independence to states in sub-Saharan Africa.

There is little evidence of any direct American influence: on the whole the Americans refrained from criticising British policy in Africa at a time when the policy of mutual inter-dependence was being pursued. Macleod's initial impact was perhaps not as dramatic as he later made out: his report on his visit to East Africa in December 1959 did not suggest any significant change in British policy, except possibly in the case of Nyasaland, a view Macmillan confirmed when visiting the Federation the following month.

The 'wind of change', to some extent initiated by the 'profit and loss' account of 1957 and even by the Eden cabinet's reassessment in June 1956 of Britain's position in the world, was possibly moved by French moves in Algeria in 1958, but really began to gain momentum with the internal policy debates in Britain starting with the initial considerations of 'Africa: the next ten years'.

[58] Fisher, *Harold Macmillan*, p. 237.
[59] C.P.C.(60)2nd mtg., secret, 18 Mar. 1960, P.R.O., CAB. 134/1559.

Part IV
Decolonization, Counter-Insurgency and Wars of Liberation

[13]

"Iron Claws on Malaya": The Historiography of the Malayan Emergency[1]

KARL HACK

Nanyang Technological University

This article addresses the historiography of the Malayan Emergency (1948–60). It does so by challenging two archetypal works on the conflict: those of Anthony Short and Richard Stubbs. These argue the Emergency was locked in stalemate as late as 1951. By then, a "population control" approach had been implemented — the so-called Briggs Plan for resettling 500,000 Chinese squatters. The predominantly Chinese nature of the Malayan National Liberation Army (MNLA)[2] had also ensured that most Malays — who constituted nearly half the 1950 population of five million — opposed the revolt. The several thousand strong Communist-led guerrillas thus laboured under severe limitations.

Nevertheless, incidents remained frequent and, according to Short, resettlement areas ineffective. Some lacked wire and lighting. By late 1951 the Emergency was, according to Short and Stubbs, still at stalemate. It was "the worst of times". The murder of the High Commissioner, Sir Henry Gurney, on 6 October 1951, was "a fitting epitaph on the muddled policy" pursued, and that month saw the highest security force casualties for a year. One resettlement area was abandoned on 19 October.[3] Malaya, according to Stubbs, seemed "condemned to a chronic state of fairly intense guerrilla warfare for years to

---

[1]The title is from a captured communist booklet, which talks of Britain setting "iron claws on Malaya" to monopolize its postwar wealth. See Rhodes House, Oxford, Hamer Papers, Box 2, "Lesson 4", "Aims of the Revolution on Malaya" (c1949, p. 74). The title phrase of my "Screwing down the People: The Malayan Emergency, Decolonisation and Ethnicity" (in *Imperial Policy and SE Asian Nationalism: 1930–1957*, ed. Hans Antlov and Stein Tonnesson [London: Curzon Press, 1995], pp. 83–109) is taken from a 1956 quotation from the Director of Operations (DOO).

[2]The MNLA originated in the communist-led, wartime Malayan People's Anti-Japanese Army. This stood down in 1945–48, as the Malayan Communist Party (MCP) sought power through politics and unions. It was reconstituted in June 1948, when relations between an increasingly violent MCP and an increasingly restrictive government broke down, and the Emergency was declared. Initially, the re-formed guerrillas called themselves the Malayan Peoples Anti-British Army. In 1949 it switched to "Malayan *National (Min-tsu)* Liberation Army"; the term *min-tsu* was unsatisfactorily translated as "Races" by Special Branch. Thus most works on the Emergency use MRLA. See C.C. Too, *New Straits Times*, 3 December 1989; and Lee Ting Hui, *The Open United Front: The Communist Struggle in Singapore, 1954–1966* (Singapore: South Seas Society, 1996), pp. 38–39, endnotes 100–101.

[3]See Anthony Short, *The Communist Insurrection in Malaya 1948–1960* (London: Frederick Muller, 1975), pp. 305–306 for "worst of times"; John Coates, *Suppressing Insurgency: An Analysis of the Malayan Emergency* (Boulder: Westview, 1993), p. 108, for the death being "symptomatic of a losing cause"; p. 186 for "epitaph", p. 110 for "worst of times"; and Richard Stubbs, *Hearts and Minds in Guerrilla Warfare: The Malayan Emergency 1948–1960* (Singapore: Oxford University Press, 1989), pp. 133–40. Gurney was ambushed in a flag-flying car, with inadequate escort. Yet as short a time before the assassination as 12 Sept. 1951, one J. Jones wrote to the *Straits Times* about officers suicidally riding in cars with "Flags but no Armour".

come".[4] Both Short and Stubbs therefore argue that an extra ingredient was required to turn stalemate into victory. Where they differ is in what this ingredient was.

For Anthony Short, in *The Communist Insurrection in Malaya 1948–1960*, the decisive factor was Templer's coordinating position, consequent to his appointment in early 1952 as both Director of Operations and High Commissioner. The key was Templer's ability, stemming from his absolute control in Malaya, to overcome previous red tape and inertia, energise the campaign, and so ride a favourable tide — a tide which otherwise might have been missed.[5] However, Richard Stubbs's *Hearts and Minds in Guerrilla Warfare: The Malayan Emergency 1948–1960* paints a different picture. For him, the crucial change was the intensification of a "hearts and minds" approach in 1952 to 1954.[6] This had to be added to a pre-existing and insufficient, "coercion" approach. Most works taking the Emergency as their central theme use some blend of these "stalemate", "Templer" and "hearts and minds" theses in explaining how insurgency was defeated and to specify a turning point in 1952–54.[7]

---

[4]Stubbs, *Hearts and Minds*, p. 126.

[5]Why does Short use hydraulic metaphors, and thus the still influential idea of Templer alone having the skills required to ride the "tide"? Born in Singapore and educated in England, having done his National Service in Johore during the period 1947–49, he taught in the University of Malaya from 1960 to 1966. His book, written with access to official records in Malaya, was submitted to the Malaysian government in 1968. He eventually had to find another publisher, possibly because his comments about race relations and policy were sensitive after the May 1969 Kuala Lumpur riots. How far did Short share the Anglo-centric, World War Two perspective of C. Northcote Parkinson (1950–58 Raffles Professor of History at the University of Malaya)? The latter's *Templer in Malaya* (Singapore: Donald Moore, 1954) was almost hagiographical (he also co-wrote a book on *Heroes of Malaya*). Short (p. 387) distances himself from Parkinson, yet they share the argument that 1951 saw stalemate, which Templer's leadership transformed. Short also adopts Parkinson's tide imagery. Parkinson entitled Chapter 4 of *Templer in Malaya* "Turn of the Tide". Short (p. 387) suggested that a quotation from Shakespeare's *Caesar* — not Parkinson's favoured *Henry V* — best fits Templer: "There is a tide in the affairs of men which if taken at flood leads on to fortune". Short drops Parkinson's lectures on the value of Britain's war-trained generals, along with his multiple quotations from *Henry V*. It seems strange that the difference between two historians of Malaya can be reduced to which Shakespeare to quote, until one realises that Short was a teenager during the war, while Parkinson served in wartime military education. Do their interpretations emerge not from Malaya, but from wartime England? From its images of military leadership, of Montgomery turning the World War Two "tide" at El Alamein? See Institute of Southeast Asian Studies (Singapore) biographical cuttings, filed at DS510 B61 Ref; and *Who's Who in Scotland 1992–93* (Irvine: Carrick Media, 1992). For World War Two and Western historiography, see R.J. Bosworth, *Explaining Auschwitz and Hiroshima: History Writing and the Second World War* (London: Routledge, 1993).

[6]Stubbs suggests "coercion", but he fails to make explicit the distinction between coercion *per se* and "population control". The latter is an integrated attempt to survey and control a population, using proportionate and directed force. By "hearts and minds" Stubbs means political concessions and providing amenities: a votes-and-piped-water approach. In a wider sense, it could also include military hearts and minds measures, such as payments for information, or psychological warfare.

[7]A few examples blending the three theses include: John Cloake, *Templer: Tiger of Malaya* (London: Harrap, 1985); Coates, *Suppressing Insurgency*; Noel Barber, *War of the Running Dogs* (London: Arrow, 1989), chs. 12–14. Malaysian works often share these interpretations, e.g. Dato' J.J. Raj, *The War Years and After* (Petaling Jaya: Pelanduk, 1995), ch. 13. However, two types of

By contrast, this paper argues the Emergency began to change in nature and direction as early as 1951–52 and that the necessary local and counter-insurgency ingredients were already in place by that time. This was happening even though "hearts and minds" measures were embryonic at this point, and despite the fact that Templer arrived only in late February 1952. This paper thus suggests the critical conditions had existed before Templer and "hearts and minds", and that in the most important policies there was, and was always likely to be, continuity not change around 1952.[8] It rejects the traditional view that the leadership and policy changes of one British general were both necessary and sufficient to transform the campaign.

In order to explain this, the article uses a two-stage interpretation. Stage One argues that British policy succeeded in "screwing down" Communist supporters, rather more than in wooing "hearts and minds". Stage Two then suggests how such a "population control" approach could work because of local ethnic, social and political patterns. In other words, Britain could "screw down" the fraction of the Chinese community which supported the Communists — and the small percentage of the Malay and Indian communities which did likewise — only because of Malaya's particular social and demographic structure. The outcome of insurgency and counter-insurgency can thus only be explained by integrating British "colonial records history" with texts written from the perspective of the communists, and of the Malaysian Chinese in general.

The first part of the article will now trace the critical years of the campaign, giving a new interpretation; the second will summarize the local terrain which made those events possible.

British works are slightly different. Those which sell the idea of British counter-insurgency as a particularly effective paradigm emphasize "population control" as part of an overall "British" model, downplaying Templer's personality slightly. See Robert Thompson (a British adviser in Vietnam), *Defeating Communist Insurgency: Experiences from Malaya and Vietnam* (London: Chatto and Windus, 1972); and Richard Clutterbuck, *Riot and Revolution in Singapore and Malaysia: 1945–1983* (Singapore: Graham Brash, 1984). Some more junior figures in the British "Establishment", especially those in Malaya before Templer, also see him in a more equivocal way. See, for example, Victor Purcell, *Malaya: Communist or Free* (London: Gollancz, 1954), and Leonard Rayner, *Emergency Years: (Malaya 1951–1954)* (Singapore: Heinemann Asia, 1991). (Leon Comber, who formerly served as a Special Branch officer in Johore, made this point about junior/senior establishment differences in a generous e-mail correspondence.) Malaysian-focused works more critical of British policy tend to be written by Malaysian Chinese — such as the following from Universiti Sains Malaysia (USM) staff — and focus on Chinese communities or shorter periods of time: Loh Kok Wah, *Beyond the Tin Mines: Coolies, Squatters and New Villagers in the Kinta Valley, Malaysia, c. 1880–1980* (Singapore: Oxford University Press, 1988); and Cheah Boon Kheng, *Masked Comrades: A Study of the Communist United Front in Malaya, 1945–1948* (Singapore: Times, 1979). It would be interesting to compare the output from USM — in the mainly Chinese state of Penang which, along with Singapore, was a part of the Straits Settlement Colony until 1946 and which had a secessionist movement in the 1940s and 1950s — with those of the Universiti Kebangsaan Malaysia in the capital.

[8]Thus while A.J. Stockwell argues for continuity in colonial policy through 1945–57, I argue that a similar continuity existed in Emergency policy between 1950 and 1960. The major discontinuity was the introduction in 1950 of the Briggs Plan and its population approach. For Stockwell's views see, for instance, *Malaya*, ed. A.J. Stockwell (London: HMSO "British Documents on the end of Empire" series, 1995), i, Introduction.

The Course of the Emergency in the Critical Years: 1949–54

Initial British counter-insurgency policy (1948–49) amounted to a "counter-terror".[9] Mass arrests, deportations, massive expansion of security forces and acts of arson against the homes of communist sympathizers, together disrupted large MNLA units. But they also increased support for the communists. After the MNLA reorganised its civilian supporters, the Min Yuen,[10] to survive despite such measures, it was able to strike back with increased effectiveness. Between mid-1949 and 1950 monthly incidents more than tripled. The MNLA also displayed an intimidating ability to eliminate "running dogs" (as it labelled informers). By 1950 the High Commissioner was pleading that he could not expect unprotected Chinese to support the government. He wrote that recently "a Chinese who was elected Chairman of [a] village by secret ballot wept on learning of his election".[11] A disconcerted British Chiefs of Staff stressed that ultimate victory now depended not on reinforcements, but on reasserting civilian control over the population.[12]

To this end, Lieutenant-General Sir Harold Briggs was appointed to the new post of Director of Operations (DOO). As such, he was given authority to coordinate the operations of the police (who had previously been responsible for coordination) and services on behalf of the High Commissioner. Taking up his post in April 1950, he drew up the first systematic plan for resettling the half a million jungle-fringe squatters. The aim was to deprive the communists of their main support, and so force them out of the jungle and into the open.[13] Beginning in June, large numbers of "resettlement areas" were created, ideally to be surrounded by barbed wire and lighting, and later renamed "New Villages". The aim was to undermine the communists' support network, the Min Yuen, by a combination of resettlement and a strengthening of civil administration, communications and police posts in populated areas.

Briggs also created a committee system which brought together the top military, police and administrative officers at all levels, allowing prompt, coordinated action. A Federal War Committee considered policy, leaving execution to State and District War Executive Committees. Combined military and police operations centres were set up. His tenure also saw a shift of emphasis from large army sweeps towards imposing a framework of small units across the country.

The "Briggs Plan" also aimed to clear the way for increased administrative control of the populated areas by concentrating striking forces in each state in turn, so as to roll the communists up from south to north. Since the communists were particularly strong in Johore — the southernmost state — this aspect of the plan failed. By the end of 1951, however, the other elements were becoming increasingly effective. The resettlement of nearly 350,000 squatters (over 70 per cent of the ultimate total) and the ongoing regrouping

---

[9]The term is used by both Short, *Communist Insurrection* (p. 160) and Stubbs, *Hearts and Minds* (pp. 66–93).

[10]Min Yuen was short for *Min Chung Yuen Tung*, or "People's Movement".

[11]DEFE11/34, High Commissioner to Secretary of State, 15 Feb. 1950.

[12]For the quotation, see Prem8/1406, MAL. C(50)6, 21 Apr. 1950, "Military Situation in Malaya".

[13]A Government Squatter Committee advised resettlement in Jan. 1949, but this was left up to the initiative of each individual state. They moved slowly because of cost, reluctance to give land to Chinese and a feeling that uncoordinated resettlement would simply displace insurgents; Stubbs, *Hearts and Minds*, p. 101.

of 600,000 plantation and mine workers caused a crescendo of activity. Resettlement drove more communist supporters into the jungle, even as the MNLA saw its supply and intelligence sources endangered.[14] Planters, security forces and communists alike came under pressure as incidents and casualties peaked.[15]

As insurgent recruiting continued apace, it might be argued that Briggs's "law and order" and population control approach had failed. The stemming of the early British tendency towards "counter-terror", however, shows the MCP failure to force counter-insurgency into a downward spiral of insurgent and government terror.[16] The insurgents now faced the dilemma of how to extract continuing support from a weary population. From 1951 the ratio of insurgents eliminated for every security force loss began a steady improvement.[17]

With the prospect of outside assistance receding as the Korean War stabilised, and the vast majority of the Malays opposed to a predominantly Chinese insurgency, the campaign faltered. As early as 1949 Siew Lau, a senior party official in the Johore-Malacca area, criticised the MNLA for excessive reliance on coercion. His complaints were echoed by lower ranking members, such as the political organiser Liew Thian Choy. In November 1949 the latter forlornly told a MCP labour leader at Batu Arang "that we coerced the people too much" and taught them too little. These criticisms are echoed in the statements of surrendered insurgents, and in the high-level defector Lam Swee's pamphlet, *My Accusation* (1951).[18] MNLA exactions of "justice" by summary shooting, executions in front of families, or tossing grenades into the shops of alleged collaborators, were probably no more vicious than Viet Minh or FLN (Algerian insurgent) tactics. The MNLA, however, had difficulty sustaining support while using both these methods and widespread economic

---

[14]Institute of Southeast Asian Studies (Singapore) (henceforth "ISEAS"), Tan Cheng Lok Papers, note dated 22 May 1950 from a "subscription collector" to Tan Cheng Lok, for the hatred caused by initial resettlement, and swelling MRLA numbers in 1948–50.

[15]For the "Briggs Plan", see Short, *Communist Insurrection*, pp. 231–53; and Air20/7777, "Report on the Emergency in Malaya from April 1950 to Nov. 1951", by Lt-General Harold Briggs. "Regroupment" meant moving workers' huts short distances to concentrate them in more easily defended groups.

[16]It was this erosion of the distinction between civilian and insurgent which fuelled Vietnam's cycle of state counter-terror and peasant alienation. See G. Kolko, *Vietnam: Anatomy of a War* (London: Allen & Unwin, 1986), pp. 92–96, 107–108, 131–37; and Milton Osborne, *Strategic Hamlets in South Vietnam* (Ithaca: Cornell University Southeast Asia Program, 1965), for the failure of "strategic hamlets" because Vietnamese peasants were settled farmers.

[17]After a low of 2.5 in 1950 the insurgent:security force elimination ratio climbed to 3 in 1951, 6 in 1952, and 15 in 1953. See Coates, *Suppressing Insurgency*, p. 76 (note 76), for MCP strength; pp. 190–202, for monthly figures; p. 202, for the ratio. See also Richard Clutterbuck, *Riot and Revolution in Singapore and Malaya, 1945–63* (London: Faber & Faber, 1973), pp. 183–86; and AIR20/10377, "Report on Emergency Operations", DOO, Sept. 1957, para. 11. The latter estimates average yearly CT strengths at 7,292 in 1951 and 5,765 in 1952, numbers falling roughly 20 per cent a year from 1951–57.

[18]Lam Swee was pre-Emergency Secretary-General of the Pan-Malayan Federation of Trade Unions. On the excessive use of fear and hardening public opinion, see Rhodes House, Oxford, Walker-Taylor Papers, "Statements" of SEP, p. 1, and Liew Thian Choy file, pp. 25–29. See also Rhodes House, Young Papers, MS British Empire s486/2/1, (N), "Surrender of CTs", pp. 29, 35–39, and (B); Coates, *Suppressing Insurgency*, pp. 63–65; and Lucian Pye, *Guerrilla Communism in Malaya: Its Social and Political Meaning* (Princeton: Princeton University Press, 1956), pp. 95, 104–105.

disruption.[19] Defectors and Surrendered Enemy Personnel (SEP) alike were emphasising that, by placing too much of the burden of supply on the poor and rural Chinese, the MCP was weakening its economic and ethnic base.[20]

Even before resettlement began to become effective, therefore, the MNLA's methods of securing support, and its difficulty in sustaining large groups, constituted an Achilles heel. Unable to dominate populated areas, lacking logistical links to other countries, and with the jungle offering only subsistence support to small groups, the MNLA had made itself reliant on its umbilical cord to the squatters. The 1950–51 Korean War Boom — caused by Western stockpiling pushing up the prices of Malaya's tin and rubber exports — was also important. Stubbs shows that by increasing government revenue, the boom financed resettlement while also boosting employment and wages. This development seems to have exacerbated MNLA difficulties in extracting cooperation. By late 1951 the movement was facing problems maintaining popular support, heightening military pressure from the government, and the prospect of diminishing supplies as resettlement areas slowly became more effectively protected and policed.[21]

Unable to seriously disrupt resettlement — only a handful of resettlements were ever abandoned — the MCP Central Executive Committee issued new orders in late September and early October 1951: the so-called "October Resolutions", referred to by the Government as "October Directives".[22] These announced that the armed struggle was now relegated to second priority in the MCP's "seven urgent tasks", behind building up mass organizations and support.[23] The aim was to fortify popular support, and so enable the military campaign to be sustained if not ultimately increased again. This cannot, however, be presented solely as a change in political tactics, despite the references in the decisions to the Chinese model of revolution, especially the early Maoist tactics of constructing a very broad "united front". The new measures were, to a significant degree, also aimed at avoiding the slow garrotting of supply-lines which the Directives otherwise

---

[19]Distinguishing between insurgent violence as policing and as terrorising the population into support is difficult, since the MNLA did not have the luxury of a secure prison system. For "random" atrocities, including the murder of a Chinese girl by driving a nail into her head: Rhodes House, Young, MS British Empire s486/2/1, Federation Police Hq — Misc.: "Short History of the Emergency", 21 Oct. 1952.

[20]Tim Harper, "The Colonial Inheritance: State and Society in Malaya, 1945–1957" (Cambridge: D. Phil thesis, 1991), pp. 190–93, on MCP difficulty maintaining support. Harper mentions the fear in late 1951 that ex-supporters of the SEP would be betrayed, leading to a 'confessional kind of politics'.

[21]For the Korean War boom, Stubbs, *Hearts and Minds*, p. 107. For MCP worries about *future* supply difficulties intensifying, see CO1022/187, High Commissioner to Colonial Office, 31 Dec. 1951, Oct. Resolutions, pp. 84–85 and 144. The seventh urgent task was to "strive to put food and material supplies on a sound basis", and increase farming, "even if it reduces the combatant action of the armed forces".

[22]For the terminology, Lee Ting Hui, *The Open United Front*, p. 34, endnote 43.

[23]An English-language copy (*not* a British translation) of the Directives, in the form of seven documents, is in CO1022/187, pp. 62–158, enclosed with High Commissioner (Malaya) to Colonial Secretary (from J.P. Morton, Director of Intelligence), 31 Dec. 1952. The "Directive of the Central Politburo on Clearing and Planting" specifically dealt with the present and *future* dangers posed by resettlement. For the "seven urgent tasks", CO1022/187, "Captured MCP Documents", FO memorandum, 27 Nov. 1953.

foresaw.[24] Several of the changes decided upon clearly seem to indicate a declining ability to sustain large guerrilla groups, especially the decisions to move to smaller units, to increase jungle cultivation, and to foster relations with the *orang asli* (the indigenous tribespeople of the interior).[25]

These changes suggest that, though as yet only partially effective, squatter resettlement was already taking its toll on insurgent logistics. The implementation of a federal food denial plan from June 1951 was slowly increasing pressure on MNLA supplies.[26] The Resolutions' concern with supply matters confirms this and is not easy to square with Short's claim that given "the primacy of political considerations in the October directives, the military decisions seem to be largely derivative". Indeed, though the Resolutions did increase the salience of political work *per se*, the injunction to make "mass organization" the number one "Urgent Task" was more precisely a supply measure, for "mass" organizations meant *Min Yuen* and other supply and intelligence units. The Resolutions linked the need to make these "mass" organizations the number one "urgent task" to the supply question and government "starvation policy".[27] A Selangor State Secretariat Document (issued in January 1952) added that "the broad mass base has been narrowed down to pockets by the enemy's resettlement policy. This new factor is of grave importance for us".[28] Urgent Task Number Seven was, therefore, "*to put food and material supplies in a sound basis*", and there was a separate directive on "Clearing and Planting". The Resolutions also admitted the previous policy of resisting resettlement up to the last moment had caused "doubts about the Party's leadership". The disadvantages of this

---

[24]It is also difficult to believe the MCP were not aware that the prospects for a "united front" strategy were poor. Political difficulties were part of the reason for the revolt, and Special Branch control of the population was now tighter than in 1948.

[25]For the directives being caused by pressure, Rhodes House, MS British Empire s486/2/1, Misc., p. 53, paras 33–35, "Short History of the Emergency", by Operations Branch, Federal Police Headquarters, 21 Oct. 1952, paras 33–34; and (F), "Aim and Strategy of the MCP". These are filed in the Young Papers for 1952–53 as lecture notes. For MCP difficulties with support, see Harper, "Colonial Inheritance", pp. 190–93. See also *Annual Report on the Federation of Malaya: 1951* (Kuala Lumpur: Federal Printers, 1952): "Evidence from captured documents corroborated that measures to control food seriously disrupted the terrorist food supply system. These measures, coupled with the Security Forces success in finding a large number of reserve food dumps, caused no little concern to the Malayan Communist Party leaders and forced the merging of their armed units and supply organization into small mobile gangs — a continuation of the trend which had become apparent during the latter part of 1950".

[26]AIR20/10377, DOO Report 1957, p. 18, "One of the Chief weaknesses of the CTO has been its inability to live off the jungle"; and p. 18, para. 68 (a) for measures including rationing, food movement restrictions, licensing shops, etc. See also Hack, "Intelligence and Counter-Insurgency", for the point that intelligence was best secured by combined and protracted food/Special Branch operations.

[27]The Resolutions' origins are too complex to discuss in full; see Hack, "Intelligence and Counter-Insurgency: The Example of Malaya", *Intelligence and National Security* 14,2 (1999). "Mass organization" is often wrongly interpreted as being mainly or solely political. See CO1022/187, Oct. Resolutions, p. 72, which introduces the "Urgent Tasks" for connections between "starvation policy" and mass organization becoming "Urgent Task" number one. It said: "owing to the enemies' concentration of and rigid control over the masses the party is confronted with numerous difficulties ... [with mass organizations] ... At present, certain difficulties in our procurement of supplies are closely connected with these weaknesses". For clearing, planting and supplies see also Oct. Resolutions, pp. 65–66, 85, 141–50.

[28]CO1022/187, "Extract from Weekly Intelligence Summary" no. 110 (no date).

policy outweighed the advantages, and so it was to be replaced by an emphasis on building up the mass movements in resettled areas.[29]

Even some supposedly "political" aspects of the Directives concerned questions of the first military importance, those of supplies and of sustaining popular support. Hence the MCP placed new emphasis on avoiding actions which harmed the people, such as shooting up buses and trains, destroying people's livelihood, or indiscriminate fire when "running dogs" mingled with crowds. Along with the failure to attract broader support, these were now labelled "left deviation". Previous failure to take adequate account of "concrete" conditions in Malaya and the "extant" interests of the masses now necessitated a re-examination of way Marxist-Leninist thinking was applied on the ground. The MCP recognised that their support was also being undermined by the degree of economic sabotage they were inflicting, by their attacks on resettled areas, and by excessive and ill-directed violence.[30] At the same time, economic sabotage was failing in its main aim of destroying Malaya's economic value to Britain and so the latter's will to fight. Rubber production in Malaya peaked in 1950 despite terrorism, and the Korean War boom saw government receipts from rubber and tin companies balloon in 1950–51.[31]

The October 1951 Directives thus show the MCP forced to admit that resettlement threatened its survival, that its economic strategy and handling of violence were counter-productive, and that it therefore needed to change tactics. Nor is this to deny that they also encouraged courting of the "medium national bourgeoisie" — local capitalists — and upgrading political and subversive work in general.[32]

This interpretation is shared by important contemporary British documents. In October 1952 the Malayan Combined Intelligence Staff (CIS) presented the communist change in tactics as a reaction to the maturing of the Briggs Plan and its resettlement of the Chinese. These had "robbed the M.C.P of the initiative" and resulted in its suffering "a steadily increasing casualty rate", so that "the situation clearly called for a drastic revision of tactics".[33]

---

[29]CO1022/187, High Commissioner to Colonial Office, 31 Dec. 1951, Oct. Resolutions, pp. 65–66.

[30]See CO1022/187, sheets 62–158, enclosed with High Commissioner to Colonial Secretary, 31 Dec. 1952, 63–69, 89–90, 116, 120–21; and "Captured MCP Documents", FO memorandum, 27 Nov. 1953. The quotation is in Short, *Communist Insurrection*, p. 321. Short is targeting Purcell's claim that "Templer's predecessors had succeeded in subjecting the Communists to such pressure that they had virtually called off the shooting war four months before his arrival ..." (Purcell, *Communist or Free*, quoted in Short, p. 318.) It is possible to argue for military causes and consequences without assuming an intention to call off the shooting. On "left deviation", see Stubbs, *Hearts and Minds*, pp. 147–51.

[31]Nicholas White, *Business, Government and the End of Empire* (New York: Oxford University Press, 1995), pp. 97, 121–23; "Capitalism and Counter-Insurgency", *Modern Asian Studies* 32,1 (1998): 149–77.

[32]There may be a direct line between the easing of the Malayan campaign from 1951–52 and the increasing prominence of strikes and demonstrations in Singapore by 1954–55. For an interpretation which also sees the October directives as forced on the MCP and yet identifies this link between 1951 and Singapore events, see Lee Ting Hui, *The Open United Front*, pp. 13–16, 34 (endnote 43).

[33]Rhodes House, Young Papers, MS British Empire s486/2/3, CIS(52)(7)(Final), "Combined Intelligence Staff Review of the Emergency as at 30th September 1952", 10 Oct. 1952, paras. 6–7. This examined reasons for changes in the Emergency in the six months to Sept. 1952. The CIS

A review on the "Aim and Strategy of the MCP", which is filed with the lecture notes of Police Commissioner Colonel Young for 1952 and 1953, also described the change of tactics as partly the result of "the success of the Government's resettlement in New Villages of the Chinese". This had increased the need for MNLA work amongst the Malays and Indians, "whose importance from the supply point of view had been enhanced...." The switch in emphasis towards political effort and more selective use of violence did not indicate any intention to call off the shooting war, nor any admission of defeat. It was "because a reverse policy had alienated mass support". The aim of the directives was to buttress popular support by increasing the emphasis on "united front" action.[34]

The Director of Operations' "Review of the Emergency" for 1957, by contrast, stated that the 1951 directives were also "based on instructions published in the Cominform Journal". Short counters this by arguing that "the advice that was offered by both China and Russia to Malayan Communists was at best uncertain". Perhaps the most that can be said is that changes in the international communist "line" towards placing more emphasis on "united front" tactics in insurgencies may have contributed to the MCP's October decisions. At the least, if stalemate in Korea made outside help decreasingly likely, it was best to prepare the political ground for a long haul by appealing to the broadest spectrum

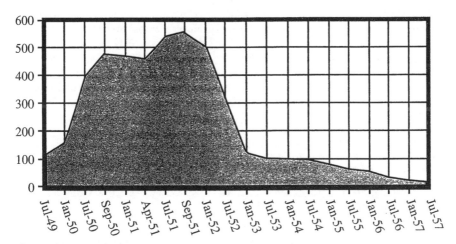

Source: AIR20/10377, DOO Report, 1957, Appendix A.

Figure 1
Emergency Incidents — Monthly Rates Calculated as Averages for 6-month Periods, and Plotted at the Mid-point

---

comprised civil service, police, army and RAF members who produced appreciations for the Director of Intelligence; see AIR20/10377, "Review of Emergency", 1957, p. 15, para. 54, (c); and Short, *Communist Insurrection*, p. 360.

[34]For the quotations, Rhodes House, Young Papers, MS British Empire s486/2/1, (F), "Review of the Security Situation in Malaya: Aim and Strategy of the MCP", paras. 5 and 6, pp. 35–36; and (I).

of support.[35] Neither of these factors, however, should detract from the MCP's domestic military, logistic and politico-military difficulties.

The MCP's October 1951 Resolutions were reaching State Committees by April 1952, though urgent sections were sent earlier. According to one British estimate, the resulting increase in Cultivation Units and in Armed Work Forces — especially the latter, to give added protection to the Min Yuen and those engaged in political work — implied a net reduction in mainstream MNLA strength of around 1,500. This represented 25 per cent of the average 1952 MNLA strength of approximately 6,000. MNLA comrades had to be sternly reminded that wielding the *"changkol"* (hoe) was not inferior to fighting, but rather 'glorious work conducive to the Revolutionary enterprise'. In other words, the MCP's change in tactics not only was an early symptom of the success of the Briggs Plan, but also implied a reduction of military operations. The October Resolutions and the statements by SEP and defectors, internal debates within the MCP, some British documents of 1952, and the MCP's inability to challenge tightening resettlement all suggest MCP fortunes were on the wane by the beginning of 1952.[36]

Meanwhile, in 1951 and 1952 the security forces continued to eliminate near-peak monthly levels of the MNLA, partly because of improving intelligence. With the communists engaged in Korea and Indochina, and the Briggs Plan maturing, the flow of information from the public slowly began to improve. In spring 1952 a pattern of uneven improvements in Emergency indicators (incidents, and security force and civilian casualties) gave way to a sustained improvement. In 1951 incidents averaged over 110 a week, while in the second, third and fourth quarters of 1952 they fell to weekly averages of 90, 56, and 31 respectively. Sabotage of rubber trees, running at 70,000 a month in February 1952, declined every single month thereafter, dropping to 600 in December. Attacks on buses likewise trailed off, reflecting the October Resolutions' orders to avoid undermining public support. By the second half of the year a general reduction in communist activity was increasingly obvious.[37]

---

[35]See Hack, "Intelligence and Counter-Insurgency". Short, *Communist Insurrection*, p. 318, argues the Cominform line was unclear. For the quotation, see AIR20/10377, "Review of the Emergency", DOO, 1957, p. 3. Ralph Smith stresses the world context and international communist "line" (not instructions) in, "China and SE Asia: The Revolutionary Perspective, 1951", *Journal of Southeast Asian Studies* 19,1 (1988): 97–110.

[36]For reductions in MNLA strength, Rhodes House, Young Papers, MS British Empire s486/2/ 1, item I, "Review of the Security Situation", para. 5. For the Directives' diffusion, see para. 4. Para. 3 suggested that "too forward a policy had alienated mass support and prejudiced Party Security". See also CO1022/187, sheet 168–69, "Secret Abstract of Intelligence" for 17 Nov. to 16 Dec. 1952. Pye, *Guerrilla Communism*, pp. 105–106, suggests the directives reduced the aggressiveness of MCP commanders, leading to orders in late 1952 to increase activity. These failed, because MNLA units were now too weak to increase activity significantly. For planting as "glorious", CO1022/187, High Commissioner to Colonial Office, 31 Dec. 1951, Oct. Resolutions, p. 144.

[37]See Figs. 1, 2 and 5; and DEFE11/47, "Malaya Report", Mar. 1952, (C), Average weekly incidents by months, (1576B). By the fourth quarter of 1952 incidents were at 1949 levels. For rubber trees, Richard Stubbs, *Counter-Insurgency and the Economic Factor: The Impact of the Korean War Prices Boom on the Malayan Emergency*, Occasional Paper No. 19 (Singapore: ISEAS, 1974), pp. 43–44. AIR20/10377, "Review of the Emergency", DOO, 1957, p. 9, para. 34, dates improved information to late 1951–52. Rhodes House, MS British Empire s486/2/3, CIS(52)7(f), "Combined Intelligence Staff Review", 10 Oct. 1952, para. 4(a), and appendices, for statistics

The Historiography of the Malayan Emergency 109

Number/Year

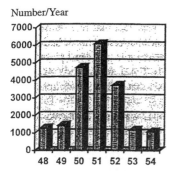

Number/Year

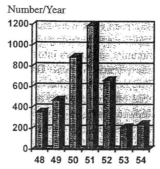

Source: Director of Operations Report dated Sept. 1957.[38]

Figure 2
Yearly Emergency Incidents

Figure 3
Yearly Total Security Casualties

With improvements in resettlement likely to have a ratchet effect on MCP supplies, the change in fortunes was probably decisive, even if it could be exploited only through sustained security force action.[39] How far the change was caused by the MCP's Resolutions themselves — as the dramatic falls in economic and transport sabotage obviously were — and how far by the "population control" which provoked them, is impossible to tell. All that can be said with certainty is that one of two things happened: either "population control" genuinely forced the MCP to change tactics, or the MCP had miscalculated in thinking it needed to make such a change. If the latter, then it was the MCP *belief* that it *had* to change its tactics which provided the security forces with a slackening campaign, the window of opportunity in which Stubbs argues they made the MNLA decline irreversible by implementing policy changes.[40] If the former, as this study suggests, then it was specifically population control which had broken the back of the campaign.

Ironically, just as the campaign approached the crest of the hill, High Commissioner Gurney's assassination on 6 October 1951 had spread a sense of gloom. With the MCP perhaps given a momentary boost by Gurney's death, a series of major incidents and spectacular train derailments gave the impression that the communist campaign was steady or even increasing. In particular areas, such as Johore, the MCP appeared to be

steadily improving from Feb.–Mar. 1952. Thus when Short notes (p. 306) that a week after Gurney's death security forces suffered the heaviest weekly total of casualties for a year, this is not representative of any deterioration or trend, but rather one of the erratic peaks within the pattern for 1951 to early 1952, which at best could be read as incipient but very slow, erratic improvement.

[38] AIR20/10377, "Review of the Emergency", DOO, 12 Sept. 1957.

[39] Short, *Communist Insurrection*, p. 381, stresses resettlement deficiencies in 1951 (e.g., insufficient barbed wire). He thereby downplays gradual improvement and the way the Resolutions reflected communist reaction to resettlement. The main test of resettlement must be empirical not theoretical, that is, based on *communist documents* or reactions, not on theorizing about the state of British operations.

[40] Stubbs sees the October Resolutions as MCP miscalculation. Together with Gurney's death, which Stubbs feels provided a personnel change vital to allow policy modifications, the resulting lull gave the chance to introduce the winning "hearts and minds" policy (Stubbs, *Hearts and Minds*, pp. 191, 249–54).

maintaining its effort despite the early completion of resettlement, even though successes against Min Yuen cells were increasing even there.[41] The very fact that resettlement and food control were threatening to become more effective and that resettlement had forced more communist supporters into the jungle, ensured this moment was not just pivotal, but also still desperately violent. On 5 September the *Straits Times* announced, under the banner "Briggs Steps Up 'Starvation War' Against Bandits", that further restrictions were being placed on the transport of food.

Churchill, returning to the premiership in October 1951, was thus dismayed to discover that the Emergency was still costing £56 million a year. His Conservative government sent its Colonial Secretary, Oliver Lyttelton, to Malaya in December 1951, and concluded drastic action was required. He chose General Gerald Templer to be both Director of Operations and High Commissioner (February 1952 to May 1954). Malaya had a supremo.[42]

With previous hopes of an early turn in the Emergency having been repeatedly dashed, Britain was understandably slow to realize that the Emergency was approaching a watershed. Likewise, most historians have been slow to realize that the Emergency was now not so much at a high-level stalemate — virtually requiring Gurney's death and Templer's arrival to break it — as at a murderous climax and turning point.

Short reinforces this case for a stalemate (accepted by most authors) by using counterfactuals. He suggests conditions would have deteriorated but for Gurney's death and Templer's arrival. He asks: "How would Gurney have dealt with the Chinese?"; "Would resettlement have continued?" Yet well over 70 per cent of squatters were moved before 1952. On 3 October 1951 Gurney wrote to Sir T. Lloyd (Permanent Under-Secretary of State, Colonial Office, 1947–56), saying that consolidation of resettlement areas could now begin and that he was attempting to increase Chinese cooperation. On 1 December the government announced it would grant land titles in New Villages.

Short also uses Gurney's so-called 'political will' — in fact a note or *aide-mémoire* of 4 October 1951 — to argue Gurney would have become tougher with the Chinese. The note severely criticized the Chinese failure to help more, and warned of extreme dangers if this attitude persisted. Yet it was probably written not as a prelude to a significantly harsher policy, but as part of Gurney's campaign to pressure Tan Cheng Lok and his coleaders into more action. Short seems unaware of Gurney's long letter to Lloyd of 3 October, and he omits the will's positive suggestions from an otherwise lengthy quotation. The "political will" in fact concluded by suggesting Tan Cheng Lok's Malayan Chinese

---

[41]See CAB129/C(51)26, "The Situation in Malaya", Colonial Secretary, 20 Nov. 1951, for a BDCC telegram of 15 Nov., describing the communist hold as being "as strong as ever"; CO1022/13 and 14, "Security Forces' Weekly Intelligence Summary", 1951–52; and Stockwell, *Malaya*, ii, pp. 302–355. For Johore, DEFE11/46, "Progress Report", DOO, Nov. 1951, Conclusions; and Malcolm MacDonald Papers, 25/2/86–87, "A note found in the handwriting of the late Sir Henry Gurney", c. 4 Oct. 1951, states that the MNLA in Johore increased from 700 (1950) to a peak of around 2300 (1951) as resettlement pushed communists into the jungle and sorted the sheep from the goats.

[42]For Gurney's death as a necessary development, see Coates, *Suppressing Insurgency*, p. 186; and Rhodes House, Granada End of Empire, Malaya, vol. 2, pp. 98–99, and vol. 4, p. 70. For British frustration, the change of government, and changes in personnel but not in the thrust of policy, see Stockwell, "British Imperial Policy and Decolonization in Malaya", *Journal of Imperial and Commonwealth History* 13,1 (1984): 79–83; and Stockwell, *Malaya*, ii, pp. 306–353.

Association (MCA) should put men into every settlement, raise $2,000,000 and develop a full-time central organization. Short and Stockwell thus accept a document harshly critical of the Chinese but motivated by the desire to secure more Chinese help, as evidence of dangerously hardening attitudes.

Gurney's policies had in any case always mixed ruthless "population control" of Chinese who supported insurgents (he favoured large-scale deportation), and pressure on neutrals, with the courting of potential Chinese allies. Admittedly, some extra measures against recalcitrant Chinese were suggested in late 1951, such as confiscating property. But overall Gurney and Templer *both* continued the policy of balancing harshness toward recalcitrants (including deportation, resettlement and group punishment) with encouraging more MCA help and improving New Villages. This basic policy continuity was confirmed in both London and Singapore in November 1951.

In line with this drive to increase Chinese assistance, Tan Cheng Lock got MCA approval to form a re-organizing committee on 16 September. Tan met Gurney about this matter on 3 October. Gurney wrote back on the 5th (the day *after* the so-called 'will'), arranging to meet Tan's new committee on 28 October. The Government kept the appointment, and on 26 November Tan read the will's positive parts to his re-organising committee. In accepting Short's interpretation, most works thus miss the point that the period 1951/52 was critical to MCA's development into a full-fledged political organization and so to the future of the Alliance and Malay[si]an politics. Equally important is the fact that the Emergency and political formation were in this way intimately intertwined.[43]

Most authors thus follow Short and Coates in seeing late 1951 as "the worst of times". And the October Resolutions are usually treated not as clear symptoms of change, and as contributors to that change, but with equivocation. Noel Barber calls the decisions "a document that was to change the course of the war", representing the MCP's partial admission of defeat and the failure of terrorism. But he also says the subsequent killing of Gurney paved the way for the appointment of a supremo, which alone could bring victory. Stubbs, meanwhile, argues that the Directives, by reducing incidents and relieving pressure, gave the government a window of opportunity to reorganize and improve all-important "hearts and minds" measures. Gurney's death and Templer's appointment supposedly ensured that this opportunity was grasped.[44]

---

[43]Tan Cheng Lok was President of the MCA. See Short, *Communist Insurrection*, pp. 303 and 306, for quotations on counter-factuals. For Gurney's policy, see Durham University, Malcolm MacDonald Papers [henceforth MMP] 25/2/56–62, Gurney to Lloyd, 3 Oct. 1951; 25/2/86–87, "A note found in the handwriting of the late Sir Henry Gurney", c. 4 Oct. 1951 (also slightly less complete version in Stockwell, *Malaya*, ii, p. 300f); MMP25/2/85; 19/7/40; 25/2/54. For continuity in Chinese policy in London and Singapore, see CAB129/C(51)26, Nov. 1951. For Gurney's attitudes to Chinese, see Stockwell, *Malaya*, ii, pp. 77, 88–91, 114–17, 195; for additional measures, see p. 300. For the MCA, see ISEAS, Tan Cheng Lok Papers 3/271, "Memorandum submitted to the Rt Honourable Oliver Lyttelton" MCA Delegation, 2 Dec. 1951; ibid., 11/11, passim; and MMP25/2/85, 22 Nov. 1951, Del Tufo to MacDonald. See also Stubbs, *Hearts and Minds*, pp. 207–213.

[44]Noel Barber, *The War of the Running Dogs: Malaya 1948–1960* (London: Arrow, 1992), pp. 157–59, 161 for quotations. Stubbs, *Hearts and Minds*, pp. 148–51, presents the Directives as attempting to breathe new life into the campaign, but (like Short) portrays MCP motivation as dealing with political shortcomings, internal dissent and the need to win more support. Unlike Short, however, he links the decisions to the dramatic statistical changes which followed in 1952. See Stubbs, p. 191, for the argument that the Resolutions were a mistake.

In November 1951, Oliver Lyttleton gave the Cabinet a report in which the top British generals in South East Asia concluded that "the communist hold is as strong as ever. This fact must be faced".[45] This impression was reinforced by a spate of bad ambushes around October, partly reflecting the MCP's annual boost to "celebrate" the anniversary of Russia's "October" (or "November" according to one's choice of calendar) Revolution.[46] Besides, there was a crisis in command. Briggs' term in Malaya had ended. Colonel Gray (Commissioner of Police and an ex-commando) had not yet retrained the hastily expanded police and was only reluctantly allowing them the armour necessary to protect them from ambush in Malaya's jungle terrain. There was room for improvement in the direction of intelligence, and the Malay States were still reluctant to grant citizenship to more Chinese.[47]

Templer thus arrived in February 1952 with the turning tide, but before it was obvious this was in fact what it was.[48] Energising the administration, he brought the campaign to peak efficiency.[49] Special Branch was reorganised, with the attachment of additional Military Intelligence Officers to quickly produce "hot" intelligence for the troops. Gurney's "New Villages" began to receive more amenities (schools, medical assistance, councils) and perimeter lighting. Colonel Young, seconded from London as the new Commissioner of Police, retrained the Malayan force to emphasise normal policing and service to the public.

Since Short suggests Templer only began to have a major impact from March, however, we may suspect that improvements before summer 1952 were due more to cumulative progress in New Village security and to changing MCP tactics and strengths than to Templer, unless it is thought that charismatic leadership can have instant, transmogrifying effects on complex and dispersed campaigns.[50] Indeed, for communist changes in tactics in 1951–52 to be interpreted as a Templer-induced turn-around, his effect on the insurgents, whose communications were slow, would need to have been both instant and cataclysmic. Security Force weekly reports showed increasing successes against the Min Yuen in and before February 1952. Extracts from two private communist letters, captured in Kedah

---

[45]Barber, *War of the Running Dogs*, says what others imply: "For the British the murder of Gurney would pave the way to victory. It had needed his death…" to get Templer appointed (pp. 158–59). See also Rhodes House, Oxford, Granada End of Empire, Malaya volumes, for Madoc's (Head of Special Branch, 1952–54) similar opinions. See Stockwell, *Malaya*, ii, p. 324. CAB129/ C(51)26, "The Situation in Malaya", 20 Nov. 1951, for Lyttelton and Malayan officers pitching for equipment for Malaya (wire, armoured cars, etc.) in the middle of Korean War rearmament. He probably overdrew the picture to maximise claims for priority. Yet Briggs' departing report in Nov. 1951, on the other hand, argued things were improving. One report was optimistic, the other gloomy, each for its own reason.

[46]For the point about the "celebration", see CO1022/249, "Translation of a cyclostyled document entitled 'Workers Express' Issue No. 6, 25 December 1951".

[47]Cloake, *Templer*, pp. 197–98, 228–29.

[48]Continuing Short's favoured hydraulic imagery, high tide — the moment before a change — is by definition precisely that time when things are at their peak, whether in terms of water-level or of incidents.

[49]For Templer's undoubted efficiency and the term "energized", Short, *Communist Insurrection*, pp. 342–43. For peak efficiency, AIR20/10377, DOO Report 1957, pp. 25–26. Nevertheless, how far were morale and activity "energized" by the improving situation? Given new MRLA orders, the partly consequent decline in incidents, and near completion of resettlement, to what extent would resources and energy be freed at this time, anyway?

[50]Short, *Communist Insurrection*, pp. 336–37, discusses the initially equivocal response to Templer.

around January 1952 and chosen to illustrate an emerging trend, read as follows: "the situation has changed since the beginning of the month" due to "the aimless fury of the mad dogs [British]" ... "the public are so frightened they even refuse to open the door when we visit them" ... "They ... begged us not to come to the village. So you see we have completely lost the co-operation of the public."[51]

In addition to such increasing incidences of local Min Yuen units suffering problems, and to the October 1951 Resolutions themselves, in 1952 the MCP began what developed into its version of the Chinese Communist Party's "Long March": a "Little Long March". In 1952 the MCP's Secretary General, Chin Peng, moved from Pahang to the Cameron Highlands; in mid-1953 he began moving with the 12th Regiment towards the Betong region in the Thai-Malaya border area.[52] These dramatic 1952 changes — notably in

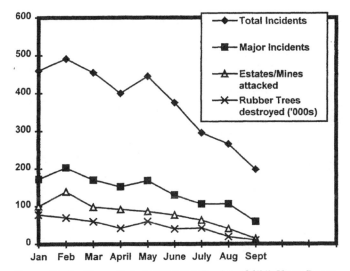

Source: Rhodes House, Oxford, MS British Empire s486/2/3: Young Papers,
Combined Intelligence Staff (Malaya) Report of October 1952,
Appendices A to G.

Figure 4
Emergency Monthly Statistics for 1952

---

[51]CO1022/14, SF (WIS) 7 Feb. 1952. Increasing Min Yuen troubles seem to constitute a theme, though of course some weeks could show bad figures, especially if a few big ambushes pushed up security force casualties, as they did in Oct. 1951 and Mar. 1952 (see SF WIS for 27 Mar.).

[52]The Betong border area — the MCP's Yenan — became their main base until a 1989 agreement ended hostilities. See Leon Comber, "'The Weather ... Has Been Horrible', Malayan Communist Communications during the "Emergency'", *Asian Studies Review* 19,2 (1995): 49, note 6. The 10th and 8th Regiments moved in 1954. Against this, a Frontier Intelligence Bureau was set up by Aug. 1953. I am grateful to C.C. Chin for confirming the "Little 'Long March'" idea, but see also Lee Ting Hui, *The Open United Front*, p. 36, endnote 52.

statistics and communist policy — are more likely to have been caused by what preceded them chronologically (the October Resolutions and "population control") than by what happened simultaneously (Templer's early months and new initiatives). Continuity can be seen, rather than the drastic change depicted in much of the traditional historiography.

In so far as Templer did have a significant additional impact on the MNLA in this period, it might be seen more as a result of his perfection of military tactics and population control than of "hearts and minds" measures. Even then, Templer's "energising" impact produced only a marginal increase in security force pressure. "Contact rates" — the number of times security forces initiated contact rather than being ambushed — attained near-peak levels after mid-1951, even increasing in early 1952 (see Figure 5 below)[53]. But they fell thereafter, with a timing that seems to correlate well with the MCP's change of tactics and reduction of activity.[54]

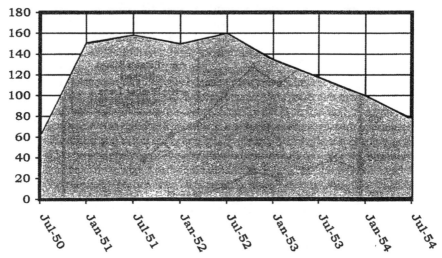

Source: AIR20/10377, DOO Report, 1957, Appendix A.

Figure 5
Emergency Contacts — Monthly rates calculated as averages for 6-month periods, and plotted at the mid-point

---

[53]Figs. 1 and 5 are from AIR20/10377, DOO Report 1957. They were constructed by reading figures from originals, then replotting. They are thus accurate for trends, but not precise numbers. The fact that these graphs use *averages* evens out fluctuations around the trend. For precise figures on incidents and some other indicators, however, see Coates, *Suppressing Insurgency*, Appendices.

[54]Many policies continued to develop across the Briggs-Gurney and Templer periods with little alteration, e.g. resettlement and increasing citizenship opportunities for Chinese. How quickly did changes made in mid-1952, such as reorganizing intelligence and police, become effective? Police retraining, for instance, involved 10 per cent of the force per month in 1952, and the opening of a Special Branch Training School. In both cases the impact would be cumulative over several months from May 1952 to 1953, not sudden.

By 1953 the Emergency was much improved. The government could thus increasingly afford to concentrate forces for intensified operations in selected areas, lasting up to three months. Tins would be punctured, and sometimes rice pre-cooked or served from central kitchens. Such combined Special Branch and food operations would bring population control to a climax at the local level. With insurgent supplies running short, mass arrests would sweep up committed Min Yuen, their less skilful replacements being more easily compromised and "turned" to become agents. This grip might be relaxed briefly, but only at selected points, to create "honeypots" where insurgents could be drawn and ambushed or more suppliers discovered. Success in these operations produced accurate intelligence, and intelligence bred success, thus creating a virtuous circle.[55]

In 1953 an area of Malacca was declared "white", with all restrictions removed. The inducement to maintain an area trouble-free proved effective, and white areas slowly increased. By mid-1954 there were as few as 3,500 insurgents in the jungle. The main threat was increasingly from subversion, and this was increasingly more pronounced in urban Singapore than in rural Malaya.

The Historiography and the Role of Inter-Ethnic, Intra-Ethnic and Social Factors

Why was a counter-insurgency technique centred on population control so effective? The predominant historiographical answer is that the turning of the Emergency was a victory for Templer's leadership and combined politico-military power, and for British "hearts and minds" tactics.[56] According to "hearts and minds" interpretations, there was an early, clear commitment to independence, and from 1952 resettled Chinese received medical, educational and social facilities. Elections were introduced from the village level up in 1951–52, and citizenship extended to increasing numbers of non-Malays, particularly from September 1952. By 1953 non-Malays were allowed to join the senior administrative service in a ratio of one for every four Malays. SEP were used for tours of villages. Surrender was made as easy as possible, with financial rewards for helping to secure other insurgents. As the British-directed "hearts and minds" strategy took effect between 1952 and 1954 — adding the carrot of political concessions and practical amenities to the stick of coercion — the Emergency turned for good.[57]

By contrast, this article argues the tide in the Emergency began to turn between summer 1951 and summer 1952, before most New Villagers enjoyed more than rudimentary facilities to compensate for being uprooted from their homes. Often villagers' new houses were located further from jobs or from vegetable plots and livestock. Farmers found themselves enclosed in barbed wire, sometimes with inadequate farming land.

Han Suyin — Belgian-Chinese autobiographer and novelist, doctor, then wife of a Special Branch officer and sympathizer of the new China, captures the feel of some of the worst resettlement conditions in 1952, as seen by someone sympathetic to villagers: "The dirt road was a red gash across the jungle. There, at the edge of a fetid mangrove swamp ... the barbed wire manned by a police post, was the 'new village', spreading

---

[55]For a detailed account of these techniques, see Hack, "Intelligence and Counter-Insurgency".

[56]See Stubbs, *Hearts and Minds*, pp. 1–2, 125–27, 248–49; Cloake, *Templer*, pp. 224–27, 262–94; and Short, *Communist Insurrection*, pp. 301–306.

[57]For "hearts and minds" as adding the "carrot" to the "stick", see Stubbs, *Hearts and Minds*, ch. 6.

itself into the swamp. Four hundred beings, including children, foot-deep in brackish mud ... there was no clean water anywhere".[58] Curfews and food controls were intensified precisely when the security forces stepped up operations in an area. One of the first things Templer did on arrival was to descend on the unfortunate Chinese village of Tanjong Malim, harangue the villagers and impose a 22-hour curfew in retribution for their unwillingness to supply information on nearby ambushes.[59] Chin Kee Onn's novel *The Grand Illusion*, written by a government information officer, also has its MNLA hero Kung Li say around 1952 that "the Government still had a long way to go to win the hearts of the squatters. Squatters were essentially people of the open spaces. They wanted to farm land. They would never be happy cooped up in fenced-in villages, no matter how well managed ...."[60] With the Emergency changing face rapidly in 1952, it can hardly have been due to winning the hearts and minds of recently uprooted inhabitants.

Over 12,000 Chinese, meanwhile, were deported, while many more were repatriated by request. Indeed, the intensification of resettlement from 1950 should be seen partly as a reaction to the closing off of outlets for deportation — Britain's favoured option for detainees — as China fell under communist control.[61] In May 1952 the Australian Commissioner's Office in Singapore reported that the police were still often haughty, allegations of assault too common, and improvements in the police only just beginning to show.[62]

At the end of 1952 constitutional advance was also unlikely to impress sceptical Chinese. The vast majority of citizens, and more so registered electors, remained Malay. Despite the 1948 Federation Agreement having called for elections as soon as possible, there had been no elections above municipal level. There was also no guarantee that with the vast majority of electors being Malay, UMNO (the United Malays National Organization) would not secure all the real power. Britain's previous willingness in 1946 to dilute proposals for generous citizenship measures in order to appease Malay anger hardly suggested Chinese would be able to gain an equal place. In 1954 Victor Purcell

---

[58]Han Suyin married Special Branch officer Leon Comber and acted as doctor to one New Village. Her autobiography, *My House Has Two Doors* (London: Granada, 1982), pp. 77–79, 81, 232–33; and semi-factual novel *...And the Rain my Drink* (London: J. Cape, 1956) depict New Villagers pounded between insurgents and government. For the quotation, see *My House*, p. 81.

[59]Short, *Communist Insurrection*, pp. 340–41, 343; Stockwell, *Malaya*, ii, p. 424.

[60]Stubbs, *Hearts and Minds*, p. 168. Chin Kee Onn, *The Grand Illusion* (London: G.G. Harrap, 1961), p. 144. After writing a book on the MPAJA, Chin — an English-educated teacher and Malayan tennis champion — was made research officer in the Psychological Warfare Unit for a year, afterwards working in the federal Information Department. While interviewing SEPs, he had the idea for the book, which traces the disillusionment of "good" communist Kung Li. (This background information is courtesy of Mr. Lee Liang Hye.) As late as 1957, the DOO Report on the Emergency (AIR20/10377), p. 17, noted the loss of villagers' land or interference with their farming as a major minus point in resettlement.

[61]AIR20/10377, "Review of the Emergency", DOO, 1957, pp. 13, 17. Also Rhodes House, Oxford, Granada End of Empire series, Malaya, vol. 2, pp. 17–19, for Hugh Humphrey, Secretary for Defence and Internal Security, 1953–57. His 1983 interview described deportation as "ruthless" but "necessary".

[62]Commonwealth Records, Australia: A5954/1, 2294/4, "The Police", 26 May 1952, Australian Commissioner's Office (Singapore) to DEA. For a more sympathetic account, see A.J. Stockwell, "Policing During the Malayan Emergency", in *Policing and Decolonisation*, ed. David Anderson and David Killingray (Manchester: Manchester University Press, 1992), pp. 105–126.

(who visited Malaya as a guest of the MCA in 1952 and quarrelled bitterly with Templer) described Malaya as a "police state". Tan Cheng Lok, chairman of the moderate, collaborationist Malayan Chinese Association (MCA), could say as late as December 1953 that "the government has struck no root in the heart of the people". Purcell's book *Malaya: Communist or Free*, embittered as it appears to be, drew on the genuine frustrations of less than radical Chinese.[63]

On a more negative note, Judith Strauch notes one Chinese New Village felt the stick had been more important than the carrot. Many resettled Chinese did not receive long-term land titles until long after 1952, or did not understand what rights they had received.[64] A study by Loh Kok Wah, based partly on participant-observation in four New Villages in Kinta, Perak, also confirmed that New Villagers remained frustrated agriculturalists. They received insufficient farming land; consequently there was recurrent pressure after resettlement for a return to the squatting which they had traditionally used to escape low wages, unemployment and poor conditions.[65]

Despite obvious improvements, with some New Villages developing into thriving communities, many of them posed a public health menace even in 1954.[66] As late as 1956

---

[63] Victor Purcell, *Malaya: Communist or Free*, pp. 5–14. Purcell was a Chinese scholar, a member of the pre-war Chinese Protectorate and post-war military administration in Malaya. For critical views of him, see Short, *Communist Insurrection*, pp. 379–87. For more radical and Marxist accounts of the Emergency, see *Malaya: The Making of a Neo-Colony*, ed. Mohamed Amin and Malcolm Caldwell (Nottingham: B.R. Peace Foundation, 1977); and Asoka Giukon, *A People's History of Malaya: the New Emergency* (Oldham: Bersatu, 1980), pp. 3–6. The Tan Cheng Lok Papers confirm Purcell accurately reflected Chinese anger at the harshness of population control, though his serious lack of tact and balance caused problems; see ISEAS Tan Cheng Lok Papers, 3/158–158j, 5/304–7, 6/1–3, 10/passim. Tan refused to disavow Purcell despite severe government pressure (3/271). For Purcell on New Villages, see 6/1 passim. TCL9/2/15–16 has Tan's threat to poll the MCA's '200,000 members' on whether they agreed with Purcell's views on villages point by point — in order to stop the Acting Secretary for Chinese Affairs from demanding MCA disavowal.

[64] Judith Strauch, *Chinese Village Politics in the Malaysian State* (Cambridge, MA: Harvard University Press, 1981), pp. 63–72.

[65] Loh Kok Wah, *Beyond the Tin Mines*, pp. 127–28, 139, 144–47, 154, 161, 178–81, 192–99. Donald Nonini's review in *Kajian Malaysia* 10,1 (1992): 96–99, argues Loh "demolishes the myth" of "hearts and minds", depicting a "Foucaultian nightmare" of control and alienation. Yet if most New Villages had (for instance) schools by late 1952, this was a gain for squatters who had previously had minimal facilities. The hope of more might have encouraged acquiescence, especially since Loh argues the squatters' mode of mobilization was socio-economic. Loh and Harper also present the Emergency as a crisis on the agricultural frontier, see Harper, "Colonial Inheritance", Chs. 4 and 5.

[66] Short, *Communist Insurgency*, pp. 400–401. For the good example of Sungei Boleh (near Sungei Siput, site of the three 16 June murders which provoked the declaration of Emergency), see Vernon Bartlett, *Report from Malaya* (London: D. Verschoyle, 1955), pp. 50–51. By 1954 it had a metalled central road, bean factory, all-important pig farm (the government later provided access to better pig breeding stock), fish-pond, elected town council, and visits from medical and veterinary services. Pigs and vegetables might make good guides to New Villagers' experiences and 'hearts and minds'. Vegetable production plummeted with resettlement in 1950–52. Foodcrop acreage almost recovered 1948 levels by 1954–55. In 1952, the proportion of agriculturalists amongst squatters/resettlers had plummeted by 60 per cent to just 27 per cent (see Stubbs, "Counter-Insurgency and the Economy", pp. 31–32). Not surprisingly, the October Resolutions were then desperately calling on the MNLA to step up its own farming, including pumpkins and melons (see CO1022/187, Oct. Resolutions, p. 124).

the Director of Operations could talk of one area where, "in spite of the sullenly hostile population, we are making very good military progress by screwing down the people in the strongest and sternest manner". The Chief Minister of Malaya, Tunku Abdul Rahman, then reportedly saw "no hope whatsoever of changing the Chinese mind", which he felt was wedded to China.[67] These views echoed earlier British attitudes that most Chinese would support the government only when "forced into giving practical assistance",[68] and that even rural Chinese were mostly "wind-blown", giving verbal support to whoever brought the greatest pressure to bear upon them.[69] Cheah Boon Kheng has thus argued that, "the Chinese memory of Templer's reign is probably one of fear and resentment, a most unhappy experience in which Templer used tough language and tactics to intimidate them ... the Malay memory of the Emergency was equally unpleasant — one of government indifference and neglect of Malay rural areas..." tempered by appreciation of Templer's tough approach to the Chinese.[70] In so far as there is direct evidence of Malayan Chinese attitudes, it seems to suggest Chinese squatters were not won over by a "hearts and minds" approach so much as they were acquiescing in firm control.

It is therefore difficult to see the slow maturing of "hearts and minds" measures — real as these were — as critical in the crucial period of 1951 to 1952, especially in relation to the recently resettled Chinese "squatters".[71] No doubt Britain's repeated commitment to guiding Malaya towards eventual self-government did help avoid alienating local opinion, but the change of tide which occurred then, before decolonisation picked up speed, demands further explanation. The key seems to have been the Briggs Plan's "law and order" and resettlement — its population control approach — in which "hearts and minds" tactics played an auxiliary role. Yet why should this have worked in Malaya, and not Vietnam, Palestine or Algeria? Why were the insurgents unable to step up guerrilla or terror activity and so win the battle over the legitimacy of force?[72] Why was it possible to arm increasing numbers of Chinese "New Village" Home Guards from 1952, without them turning these weapons back on the security forces?

One answer lies in the complexity of the fractures *within* Malaya's "Chinese community", where an over-abundance of possible identities and choices reduced the potential number of communists and multiplied the communists' potential enemies. These choices and fractures included: Malaya-centred versus China-centred identity; communist versus Kuomintang allegiance; participation in modern, ideological political organizations versus the protection of Chinese identity through communally organized clan groups or chambers of commerce; Chinese- versus English-language education; first- or second-generation immigrants versus long-established, pro-British and well-integrated 'Straits Chinese' such

---

[67]WO216/901, 15 Mar. 1956, DOO (Geoffrey Bourne) to Templer.

[68]This view dates from an Apr. 1949 paper enclosed with a letter from Gurney to Creech Jones, see Stockwell, *Malaya*, ii, pp. 129–33 (132 for the quotation).

[69]For the "wind-blown" Chinese, see CO1022/148, R.P. Bingham, Secretary for Chinese Affairs, Federation of Malaya, paper on Chinese for Secretary of Defence, Malaya. This is attached as Appendix B to a memorandum for the Malaya Borneo Committee, MBDC (51) 74, 16 June 1951.

[70]Cheah Boon Kheng's review of Stubbs' *Hearts and Minds*, in *Journal of Southeast Asian Studies* 22,2 (1991): 427–30.

[71]In other low-intensity conflicts that Britain won for instance Kenya (beginning in 1952) and Oman (1957–59 and the 1960s), "hearts and minds" tactics were even less salient.

[72]Alistair Horne, *A Savage War of Peace: Algeria 1954–62* (London: Macmillan, 1977), pp. 131–36, 170–72. What made the Viet Minh and FLN level of "terror" ineffective in Malaya?

as Tan Cheng Lok; and, of course, class differences. Malaya's Chinese community, because of its immigrant and entrepreneurial origins, had a large middle class: traders, shopkeepers, estate owners.

An extreme example of this is the Kuok brothers. Their father arrived in Malaya, opened a grocery store and engaged in commodity trading. Sons Robert and Philip went on to develop multi-billion dollar interests in sugar, hotels and property. Much of their wealth was made in Malaysia and Hong Kong, especially the Malaysian Sugar Company, with links to Indonesian-Chinese Liem Sioe Liong. The Kuoks are thus a classic "Overseas Chinese" entrepreneurial, Malaysian success story. Yet one brother — "Willie" — was killed fighting for the MNLA. This sort of family split is also reflected in Suchen Christine Lim's historical novel *Fistful of Colours*. Its central narrator is surprised to find that the son and daughter of a *towkay* (Chinese businessman) — both Chinese-educated, idealistic and the narrator's relatives — as well an uncle had joined the MCP — the son during the war and the daughter in the 1950s. The Emergency could thus be reconceptualized as part Malay battle to maintain Malay political dominance, part Chinese civil war, and part search for identity and focus by individual Chinese presented with a bewildering array of choices — a search in which even individual family members sometimes took different roads.[73]

Furthermore, put in this way, the Emergency becomes central to the process by which the business-dominated MCA emerged as the dominant Chinese political party and was integrated into the UMNO-MCA Alliance as a junior partner. The MCA's ability to convince the British that it was a sufficient representative of Chinese views, and the dominance within the Association of people willing to seek independence without first getting more concrete guarantees of Chinese power-sharing, must be related to Emergency conditions. These conditions helped ensure that the MCA gave priority to anti-communism over particularistic Chinese interests and accepted the entrenchment of Malay rights in 1957. How far the Emergency also removed from politics capable but more China-centred and Chinese-speaking Chinese, is open to question. The Emergency, decolonisation and the formation of the postcolonial political landscape can in these ways be rejoined as one, integrated process, rather than being told as separate stories.

What is here proposed, then, is a *two-part explanatory model* for the Emergency. Britain won the Emergency by "screwing down the people", by "population control" tactics. But these could and did succeed largely because of local conditions, namely both the inter-communal and the less noted but equally important intra-communal characteristics of Malaya's population. Success can thus be only partly explained by the racial situation of the MNLA, reliant on Chinese for over 90 per cent of its fighters.[74] The leadership's persistent calls for its ranks to be "Malaya-minded" made little impression. Insurgent

---

[73]Yet the *towkay* and another son — in this fictional example — provided the Japanese with mechanical services, being dubbed "wipers of Japanese bottoms". See Suchen Christine Lim, *Fistful of Colours* (Singapore: EPB, 1993), pp. 253–79.

[74]The 90 per cent figure is corroborated by communist sources. Rhodes House, Indian Ocean s251, Malayan Security Service, Political Intelligence Journal 9/1947, report for 15 June 1947, cites the communist *Freedom News*. According to this there were then 11,800 top grade communists (full Party members): 11,000 Chinese, 760 Indian, 40 Malay and Indonesian. More Malays, of course, would have been low level members of front organizations and farmers' unions. The largest numbers of communists were in Johore (2,650), Perak (1,800) and Selangor (1,700).

caps may have sported three stars (*tiga bintang* — one for each main race), but the units wearing them were too frequently of one race.[75] Chinese was often used as the lingua franca in units, where small attachments of Malays might find themselves in an alien cultural milieu. Malay nationalism had its origins partly in a fear of being swamped by the Chinese. Clashes between Malays (some of whom had been wartime collaborators in the guise of police and administrators) and Chinese MPAJA units during and after the war limited the MNLA's ability to recruit Malays.

As late as May 1952, the MCP Central Committee was still wrestling with these problems. It then proposed to set up Departments of Indian Work and of Malay Work within existing structures, from Central Committee to State Committee level. But it warned against entirely separate racial organizations or criticism of "essential" Chinese leadership. The document noted "past failure ... to influence and organize the Malay and Indian mass". It insisted Marxism was trans-national but denied this meant that "the party intends to try and weld all such different races into one Malayan nationality", recognising instead that race-specific cadres were best for each community. Yet it also acknowledged continuing language problems, and warned the party must "give up belittling" Malays and Indians (which it nevertheless described as backward culturally and politically!).[76]

The racial-social factor can also be plotted quantitatively. On a 1957 security force map, overwhelmingly Malay States such as Trengganu (fourteen guerrillas left) and Kelantan (thirty-eight guerrillas) are shown to be relatively free of insurgency. But with just 1,830 insurgents still listed, almost 1,200 were concentrated in two of the states with the highest percentage of Chinese: Perak (754), where there were a large number of Chinese tin miners; and Johore (435).[77] MCP Secretary-General Chin Peng — who came from Sitiawan himself, near the Perak tin-mining districts, has emphasised the centrality of this racial factor, and the MCP's failure to surmount it, as recently as June 1998.[78]

What Chin Peng did not acknowledge was the fracturing within the Chinese community suggested above, and the fact that the Chinese base of his MNLA may have suffered from adulterated and poorly focused nationalism. According to one British estimate, only around one million of Malaya's five to six million people (the population was growing fast in

---

[75]Rhodes House, Malayan Security Service, Political Intelligence Journals, 1947/6, MCP 'Freedom News', 15 Jan. 1947.

[76]CO1022/187, Precis of MCP document in English, "Central Committee's Resolution on the Question of Policy in Regard to Malay and Indian Work", 15 May 1952. See William Roff, *The Origins of Malay Nationalism* (Singapore: University of Malaya Press, 1967), for the roots of Malay nationalism. Up to 10 per cent of the MRLA were non-Chinese, often radicals or recruited through unions. The MRLA 10th Regiment was formed from Pahang Malays in 1949, though government action soon crippled it. See also Cheah Boon Kheng, *Red Star Over Malaya*, pp. 63–73; and Tan Chee-Beng, "Ethnic Relations in Malaysia", *Kajian Malaysia* 6,1 (June 1987): 99–119. Diaries of MNLA Malays can be found in Rhodes House, Brewer Papers, box 1, file 4, "Interrogations, Johore, 1948–49".

[77]AIR20/10377, DOO Report 1957, Appendix D. The small but heavily Chinese populated island of Penang, which was dominated by urban Georgetown, had 40 guerrillas. In fact, Johore and Perak also suffered two-thirds of the total "incidents" for 1951, see DEFE11/46, "Progress Report on the Emergency in Malaya", DOO, 15 Nov. 1951. There were roughly 444,000 Chinese in Perak and 738,000 in Johore, meaning that around half the total Chinese population of Malaya lived in just two states (ISEAS, Tan Cheng Lok Papers, D.H. Sinclair to Tan, 31 Sept. 1952).

[78]See the television broadcast "Malaya: The Undeclared War" (BBC2, 19 June 1998), and its review in *Straits Times*, 18 June 1998.

the 1950s) were potential communist sympathizers.[79] Chinese loyalties were torn between Nationalist and Communist China, traditional Chinese societies and the modern political organization of the MCP, between cultural introversion and participating in the nascent Malayan state.[80] It is suggested that the MNLA could never hope to command the breadth and depth of emotional commitment that the Algerian insurgents could against France, or the Viet Minh from Vietnamese. The origins of the Chinese presence in Malaya, stemming as it did from relatively recent economic migration, also resulted in a particularly large and important pro-business group in Chinese society, with strong interests in the defeat of the insurgents.[81] Considerable Chinese business interests and ex-KMT supporters opposed communism.[82]

Many Chinese thus joined the MCA — for which local shopkeepers, traders and Chinese Chambers of Commerce formed the backbone — despite the danger that they would be labelled "running dogs" and suffer attacks.[83] Minor MCA officers risked losing shops and families. Take the town of Kuala Pilah as an example. Its first MCA President fled after his shop was attacked with a grenade, and then an MCA Working Committee member lost three of his children in another grenade attack. Tan Cheng Lok himself, as MCA President, survived having a grenade thrown onto the platform during an address at Ipoh in April 1949, after which he reported losing two to three pints of blood.[84] It is no surprise then, that the MCA found it a struggle to persuade Chinese to join as *twa kau* (derogatory Hokkien for "big dog") or police inspectors.[85] Besides, the Chinese saying was that you don't make soldiers from good men (or nails from good iron). The same went for police.

MCA help to the government included social welfare in New Villages, screening detainees, and forming a legitimate focus for Chinese political activity. From the beginning the MCA was also asked to give assistance in promoting surrenders.[86] MCA Liaison

---

[79]For the figure, see AIR20/10377, "Review of the Malayan Emergency", DOO, Sept. 1957, para. 11.

[80]This analysis stems partly from sources such as Wang Gungwu, *Community and Nation: Essays on Southeast Asia and the Chinese* (Singapore: Heinemann, 1981). However, UK officials also saw the Chinese community as fractured; see Gurney to Lloyd, 8 Oct. 1948, in Stockwell, *Malaya*, ii, pp. 73–77.

[81]This point should not be taken too far, given that Chin Peng's father ran a bicycle repair shop. Were perhaps shop, workshop and moderate plantation owners those whom the MCP had in mind in wanting to court the "medium national bourgeoisie" from Oct. 1951? For Chin Peng, see John Coe, "The *Rusa Merah*: Reflections on a Revolutionary", in *The Beagle, Records of the Northern Territory Museum of Arts and Sciences* 5,1 (1988): 163–73. Stubbs, "Counter-Insurgency", p. 51, also cites Tan Cheng Lok as saying most Chinese were overwhelmingly economically motivated. In a December 1946 memorandum, talking of the lack of interest in political developments among the majority of Chinese, Tan Cheng Lok stated that "it has been said that ... 'the Chinese in Malaya don't care a damn who owns Malaya so long as they get to milk the cow'" (ISEAS, Tan Cheng Lok Papers 1/3, Memorandum of Dec. 1946).

[82]The Penang KMT's *Blood News* of 10 Oct. 1951 specifically instructed members to support MCA work (CO1022/198, extract from PMR10/1951). There were an estimated 40–50,000 KMT members in Malaya (ibid.).

[83]ISEAS, Tan Cheng Lok Papers, 3.266.

[84]Tan Cheng Lok to Thio Chan Bee, May 1949, in ISEAS, Tan Cheng Lok Papers, 3.145.

[85]I am grateful to Leon Comber for his comments on this, and much else besides.

[86]Short, *Communist Insurrection*, p. 266.

committees were also supposed to suggest individuals who might penetrate the MCP.[87] By 1951 *ad hoc* MCA consultative committees were being established for these purposes, meeting the police at circle and contingent levels.[88] In the critical states of Perak (13.2 per cent) and Johore (7.9 per cent) the MCA already had respectable proportions of the Chinese as members by mid-1952, when it was expanding its organization.[89] Despite its inability to encourage large numbers of Chinese into the police, the understandable reluctance of many of its officers to take public actions which would brand them as "running dogs", and the distance between its wealthy, business elite and the squatters, the MCA played important auxiliary roles.

Wang Gungwu, meanwhile, argues that most Chinese wished to retain their traditional communal organizations rather than follow mainland Chinese politics or seize the initiative locally. According to him, the MCA thus ran with the grain of Chinese politics while the MCP, with its modern political organization, went against the grain.[90] Arguably, the war had only temporarily disrupted the Chinese trade guilds, clan houses and associations, whose focus was on achieving economic success through the existing system of government and whose leaders later underpinned the MCA.

The nature of the Chinese community might also help to explain the willingness of many SEP — which so puzzled British officers — to work with the state, some joining the security forces in hunting down old comrades. Lucien Pye has argued that for many, communism did not represent a commitment to an ideology or to a cause such as nationalism, but rather was more a means of adapting to a changing and modernizing world, a potential avenue of advancement or a personal commitment.[91] For others, it was

---

[87]ISEAS, Tan Cheng Lok Papers, folio 11, (11b). By early 1952 the MCA was reorganizing as a more mass-based party and specifically planning to recruit a paid Secretary-General for Emergency matters, an Intelligence officer with CID experience and a corps of "intelligence men" country-wide.

[88]ISEAS, Tan Cheng Lok Papers, folio 11, (7a), message from Police HQ (KL) to all Chief Police Officers, 10 Feb. 1951. Membership was to include three or four MCA and civil representatives. The relevant CID officer was to chair these meetings, and a Special Branch representative was to attend.

[89]ISEAS, Tan Cheng Lok Papers, D.H. Sinclair to Tan Cheng Lok, 31 Sept. 1952. Of Perak's 444,000 Chinese (out of a total population of 953,000), 60,000 or 13.2 per cent were MCA members. Johore had 354,000 Chinese out of 738,000 inhabitants; 28,000 or 7.9 per cent of the Chinese were in the MCA. Among Selangor's 362,000 Chinese (out of a total of 710,000 inhabitants), 8.5 per cent or 31,000 Chinese were MCA. Another salient point is that the period from the 1940s to early 1950 was, in Malaya as elsewhere in Southeast Asia, a time of *pemuda* (youth). Forty-seven per cent of the Federation of Malaya's population was under twenty, while MRLA fighters tended to be mostly around 20 to 30 years old.

[90]See Wang Gungwu, *Community and Nation*, pp. 142–90, especially 188–90; and Harper, "Colonial Inheritance", pp. 152–54, 199–203. See also Heng Pek Koon, *Chinese Politics in Malaysia: A History of the Malaysian Chinese Association* (Singapore: Oxford University Press, 1988). Heng may be too uncritical in assuming MCA influence in New Villages; see Loh Kok Wah's review in the *Journal of Southeast Asian Studies* 22,1 (1991): 200–201.

[91]Pye, *Guerrilla Communism*, pp. 128–60, 225–47, 331–32. We should not exaggerate negative Chinese "hearts and minds" factors: just over 20 per cent surrendered (1948–60), 67 per cent were killed and most of the rest captured. For the MCP's recognition that damaging the populace's economic livelihood was undermining support, see, CO1022/187, High Commissioner of the Federation of Malaya to the Secretary of State for the Colonies, 31 Dec. 1952 [from J.P. Morton], sheets 63–67, containing the October 1951 Resolutions' comments on "The Party's Main Achievements and Their Significance".

simply the most prestigious pro-Chinese, anti-Japanese body of the war, or for still others, a means of addressing social and economic grievances. In all these cases, the motivating force may have been less powerful than that involved in nationalism *per se*. A comparison between SEP behaviour and motivation in Malaya and the Philippines, and in Vietnam, Cyprus and Algeria, might here prove instructive.[92]

Divisions between and within communal groups thus fatally undermined the MCP's "revolutionary space", limiting its choice of targets.[93] Had the insurgents concentrated attacks on the mainly Malay police rather than Europeans, the military and estates, for instance, they would only have reinforced the "Chinese" nature of the insurgency.[94]

Conclusion

This paper has argued that population control was central to the policies which won the Emergency. The turning point came with the switch from poorly directed counter-terror and coercion in 1948–49, to tightly organized population control from 1950. This approach was one of massive control and intimidation. The ratio of Security Forces (including Home Guard) to insurgents ranged from 5:1 to 12:1. Around ten per cent of the population was resettled, more if labour regrouping is included. This was accompanied by curfews, food control and large-scale arrests, with the right to detain without trial. In addition, over 12,000 were deported.[95] This approach initially, and almost inevitably, increased insurgent numbers and incidents as a battle for the New Villages intensified. But by late 1951 the MCP had been persuaded to change tactics. Resettlement had not yet made life impossible, but the MCP recognised that current supply difficulties would inevitably multiply as the noose tightened. Its October 1951 decisions then contributed to an accelerated decline in incidents in 1952. This foundation was strengthened under Templer in 1952–54, who brought counter-insurgency to peak efficiency.

---

[92]Philippine insurgency was vulnerable to surrenders when concerns about the 'moral economy' (land, justice, fair elections) were addressed but would recover when these problems resurfaced (Edward Lansdale, *In the Midst of Wars...* [London, 1972], p. 51.) Ideological-nationalist motives, by contrast, may have led peasants to support the Viet Minh when rational self-interest did not, Hy V. Luong, *Revolution in the Village: Tradition and Transformation in North Vietnam* (Honolulu: University of Hawaii, 1992), p. 167. For Loh, *Beyond the Tin Mines*, p. 90, the squatters' mobilization was socio-economic. The MRLA also suffered leadership problems: in Sept. 1942 a key meeting was ambushed near Batu Caves, and more leaders were arrested by the British by July 1948. As early as Oct. 1949 one SEP admitted he did not think the MCP would win, because of its lack of experienced leaders. For SEP doubts, Rhodes House, Walker-Taylor Papers, "Statements" of SEP, pp. 29–32. Coates, *Suppressing Insurgency*, pp. 49–76, is excellent on MNLA weaknesses. See also, Stubbs, *Hearts and Minds*, pp. 248–49.

[93]For radical politics dividing along communal lines, see Muhammed Said, "Ethnic Perspectives of the Left", in *Fragmented Vision: Culture and Politics in Contemporary Malaysia*, ed. Joel Kahn and Francis Loh Kok Wah (Sydney: ASAA and Allen & Unwin, 1992), pp. 254–81, especially 275. Frank Furedi, "Britain's Colonial Wars: Playing the Ethnic Card", *Journal of Commonwealth and Comparative Politics* 28,1 (Mar. 1990): 70–89, argues, by contrast, that Britain precipitated "emergencies" in Kenya, Malaya and British Guiana in order to control radical nationalism.

[94]At one point in 1949 Gurney told the Colonial Office "the bandits" had orders not to kill Malays, and to fire only three rounds at police posts (DEFE11/32 (242), 22 Jan. 1949).

[95]AIR20/10377, DOO Report 1957, p. 7, para. 21. Stubbs, "Counter-Insurgency", p. 45 suggests 650,000 were regrouped.

But this is a two-part, not a uni-dimensional, explanation. Population control could succeed only because of favourable local and international conditions. Locally, Malaya's communal patterns ensured neutrality or support for the government from Malays. Within the "Chinese community", many of the commercially orientated and pro-KMT elements were hostile to communism, even if a significant number paid communist "subscriptions" when the MNLA was strong in their area. Many more wanted simply to protect their communal identity, a task for which the MCA seemed appropriate. As the MNLA's wartime role as a popular anti-Japanese force became more distant and British coercion more effective, the communists' ability to command Chinese support waned.[96]

Internationally, stalemate in the Korean War from 1951 and Malaya's isolation from any external communist sources of *matériel*, both exercised positive effects. In short, given propitious local and international circumstances, Britain was able to "screw down" that fraction of the Chinese community which was willing to die for communism, and to avoid the likelihood of too many Chinese concluding communism was the logical route to modernity and *Merdeka* (independence).

"Hearts and minds" tactics were an important, but auxiliary, part of the "population control" paradigm. British propaganda, for instance, tried to "win hearts" by persuading Chinese minds that support for Communism, or loyalty to Communism once captured, could mean just one thing — death.[97] Nevertheless, British traditions of "minimum force" did — albeit belatedly and imperfectly — help prevent coercion from spiralling into self-defeating oppression, and army action from producing excessive and alienating "collateral damage". Political concessions from 1951 — leading to independence by 1957 — also ensured that few Malays, and fewer Chinese than might otherwise have been the case, were tempted by the MCP's anti-colonialist rhetoric. Finally, social welfare in New Villages must have had some impact on rural Chinese, though many sources suggest Chinese "New Villagers" were — in 1952 if not later — at best resigned, at worst hostile.[98]

---

[96]Even the moderate, English-speaking teacher Chin Kee Onn (later a government information officer) saw the wartime MPAJA as heroes, an unseen force causing Japanese soldiers to temper brutality lest revenge be taken. See his *Malaya Upside Down* (Kuala Lumpur: Kuala Lumpur Federal Publishers, 1976, first published 1946). Early insurgent propaganda and diaries made use of the idea that the British were like, or worse than, the hated Japanese, see Rhodes House, Oxford, Brewer Papers, box 1, File 4, Insurgent Diary, entry for Nov. 6, "The British are operating in the same way as Japanese — torturing the people ...", and p. 39, documents recovered on 17 Nov. 1948, on police searches: 'Their tactics were worse than the Japanese'.

[97]Kings College London Archives, Stockwell Papers, Stockwell 7/1–7, 1953 propaganda leaflets (in Chinese and Tamil). Leaflet 1534 mentioned consequences including deportation, arrest, being shot by security forces or communist liquidation as a suspected traitor. It concluded: "So any action in helping the bandits will lead to only one end — death". This message — betrayal means life and possibly rewards, while loyalty means death — was reinforced by using deportation or the death penalty for insurgents who remained loyal. For only a one-month period, see *Straits Times*, 16, 23, 24, 30 Aug. 1951.

[98]See above and Han Suyin, *My House Has Two Doors*, pp. 77–79, 81, 232–33; Loh Kok Wah, *Beyond the Tin Mines*, Ch. 3–4; and *Observer*, 4 Jan. 1953, for a Johore Resettlement Officer thinking 75 per cent of New Villagers were "choking with animosity against us", as quoted in Susan L. Carruthers, *Winning Hearts and Minds: British Governments, the Media, and Colonial Counter-Insurgency, 1944–1960* (London, New York: Leicester University Press, 1995), p. 121.

These conclusions have been made possible by a tentative integration of works which focus on Malaysian sub-national stories and communities — Loh Kok Wah, Wang Gungwu and even literature and autobiography such as Han Suyin's — with the predominant Emergency historiography, the latter being more a "Colonial Records" narrative. Also, part of the approach has been to take seriously as evidence the relevant communist documentation, and sources such as the Tan Cheng Lok papers. Ideally, more space would have been devoted to the Emergency as an essentially Malayan process, but the claims of the dominant historiography had to be addressed first.[99]

This article is, therefore, offered as a comment on the historiography of the Emergency. It is also a small contribution towards explaining the course of the Emergency not just as a "Colonial Records" account or a small part of a larger, supra-national story about "British policies" and "British success" in the Cold War, decolonization and counter-insurgency, nor as a minor part in a sub-national story of one social or ethnic group, but as one of the central integrating processes in "Malayan", or "Malaysian", history which was both shaped by, and in return shaped, most communities as well as the emerging post-colonial state.[100]

---

[99]More work is still needed in a number of areas, including: Malay-language sources and especially the *Jawi* script newspaper *Utusan Melayu*; Chinese-language newspapers; and oral and documentary work on communist organizations, members and sympathizers.

[100]T.N. Harper's thesis ("Colonial Inheritance") attempted to relate the Emergency to politics and the post-colonial security state. In revised form, it is forthcoming as *The End of Empire and the Making of Malaya* from Cambridge University Press. See also Zakaria Haji Ahmad and K.S. Sandhu, "The Malayan Emergency: Event Writ Large", in *Melaka: the Transformation of a Malay Capital, c. 1400–1980*, ed. Kernial Singh Sandhu and Paul Wheatley (Kuala Lumpur: Oxford University Press, 1983), vol. 1. The effect of the post-colonial Malayan "security state" on its history-writing is hinted at in Cheah Boon Kheng, "Writing Indigenous History in Malaya: A Survey on Approaches and Problems", *Crossroads* 10,2 (1996): 49–52.

[14]

DECOLONIZATION, THE COLONIAL STATE, AND CHIEFTAINCY IN THE GOLD COAST

RICHARD C. CROOK

THE PURPOSE of this article is to suggest a reinterpretation of the relationship between the colonial state and chieftaincy in the Gold Coast, looking in particular at the interaction between land law, class formation and the structure of indirect rule. The need for such a reinterpretation is prompted by the implausibility (in my view) of much of the very large standard literature on the subject, when viewed from the perspective of the decolonization period of the 1950s. During the 1950s, the colonial chieftaincy in the British African colonies was abandoned by colonial governments, together with the structure of administration known as 'indirect rule'. The change was ostensibly part of a programme of devolution of power to a new elite of 'educated' Africans, either elected to local or central government bodies, or recruited into an Africanized administration. By the end of the decade—beginning with the Gold Coast in 1957—local self-government by these new groups formed the basis for a new policy of granting sovereign independence to all of the colonial territories, large or small. The demise of the chieftaincy has, therefore, been seen as inextricably linked to this process of decolonization, not simply because it preceded decolonization chronologically, but because it was an integral part of the reforms which determined the political form of independence—the so-called 'Westminster model'. With historical hindsight it has been easy to accept the inevitability of progress, to see the chieftaincy as a doomed institution which made sense in the context of high colonialism, but had to go when colonialism itself, for whatever reason, came to an end.

Such assumptions, however, continue to beg a number of questions. First, why was it that the policy which the British had always maintained was at the heart of their colonial trusteeship—encouraging the development of the African 'along his own lines', including forms of self-government—*why* was this policy changed so radically after the Second

The author is Lecturer in Politics at Glasgow University. This article began life as a seminar paper presented at the Centre of West African Studies, University of Birmingham in 1984. It was subsequently presented at the York Conference of the ASAUK in September 1984, and discussed at the Institute of Commonwealth Studies, University of London in October of the same year. The author is grateful to all those who made comments and suggestions at those seminars; he remarks that 'some will find in the footnotes at least a partial acknowledgement of their help, others will notice the corrections in the text!'

76   AFRICAN AFFAIRS

World War? Secondly, did the reforms implemented in the late 1940s and early 1950s actually lead to independence, in the form and at the time at which it occurred—or were there intervening variables? And thirdly, how was such a radical change in the political basis of the colonial state carried out without any apparent costs in terms of political or administrative control? The Gold Coast is especially important in this argument because, 'as every schoolboy knows', it was the first 'black' African colony to be given independence.

The vast body of scholarly research, both historical and anthropological, which exists on the subject of the chieftaincy and the transition from Indirect Rule to democratic forms of self-government and independence, has changed quite considerably in the kinds of answers it currently gives to these questions. In the historiographical review which follows, a dividing line is drawn between 'pre-revisionist' literature, i.e. that written before around 1975–6, and 'revisionist' history, i.e. research based on the newly-opened post-1945 British imperial archives.

Historiographical Review

(i) Pre-revisionist literature In this literature the centrality of the chieftaincy, as it became incorporated into the colonial state through the NA system, is firmly established.[1] Many of the detailed studies, particularly in anthropology, focus on the 'problems' of the colonial chief's role in relation to his subjects, the contradictions in authority and values, the impact of commercialization and so on. Nevertheless, historians agree that following the creation of the Colony Provincial Councils in 1925, and the Ordinances of 1927 in the Colony and 1932 and 1935 in the NTs and Ashanti respectively, the power and authority of the chiefs in Gold Coast colonial society was consolidated and strengthened. The colonial government's commitment to the chiefs was seemingly unshakeable, and bolstered by an increasingly elaborated ideology which sought political legitimation through a romantic notion of cultural trusteeship—Kimble quotes Guggisberg's book of 1929 (*The Future of the Negro*)—'we must aim at the

---

1. A selection of the main sources would include: R. S. Rattray, *Ashanti Law and Constitution* (Oxford, 1929); Lord Hailey, *Native Administration in the British African Territories, Part III* (London 1951) and *General Survey, Part IV* (London, 1951); K. A. Busia, *The Position of the Chief in the Modern Political System of Ashanti* (London 1951); M. Fortes and E. E. Evans-Pritchard, *African Political Systems* (London 1940); D. Apter, *The Gold Coast in Transition* (Princeton, 1955); D. Kimble, *A Political History of Ghana, 1850–1928* (London 1963); W. Tordoff, *Ashanti under the Prempehs, 1888–1935* (London 1965); M. Crowder and O. Ikime, (eds), *West African Chiefs* (New York, 1970); D. Brokensha, *Social Change at Larteh, Ghana* (London, 1966); L. H. Gann and P. Duignan, (eds), *The History and Politics of Colonialism, 1914–1960* (Cambridge, 1970), especially chapters by K. W. J. Post, M. Crowder and M. Kilson; M. Owusu, *Uses and Abuses of Political Power* (Chicago, 1970); J. Dunn and A. F. Robertson, *Dependence and Opportunity: Political Change in Ahafo* (Cambridge, 1973); and M. Staniland, *The Lions of Dagbon: Political Change in Northern Ghana* (Cambridge, 1975).

development of the people along their own racial lines, and not at the wholesale replacement of their ancient civilizations by our own ...'.[2] Apter, writing in 1955, quotes similar sentiments: 'These Provincial Councils are really the breakwaters defending our [*sic!*] native constitutions, institutions and customs against the disintegrating waves of Western civilization'.[3] In retrospect, not unworthy ideals, and ones with which an African nationalist of the 1980s might well agree. But in the 1920s, they justified not only the colonial administration's acceptance of the chiefs as the true representatives of their people, but also the corollary—the administration's contempt for and dismissal of educated African politicians.[4] Even the reformed Burns Constitution of 1946 gave a majority voice to the NAs at the central level of politics. In interpreting the post-1951 period, therefore—the period when the chieftaincy was abandoned by its former masters and power handed over to nationalist politicians—the standard literature points to such factors as the rise of mass anti-colonial movements led by educated Africans of a 'new generation' and changes in imperial policy in the 1950s.[5] These factors have to be assumed to be very powerful, insofar as they overthrew the apparently immutable alliance of chiefs and administration with which the period opened.

(ii) Revisionist literature With the opening of the archives of the post-war Imperial government, historians and political scientists such as Hargreaves, Flint, Gifford and Louis, Lee and Pearce have amended the above picture in a number of ways, the two major shifts being (a) a switch of emphasis away from mass nationalist movements back to imperial policy—even to the extent of asserting that imperial policy was the prime mover or independent variable—and, (b) a pushing back of the timing of changes in imperial policy, on such matters as indirect rule, or self-government, to the early 1940s or, in Flint's case, to 1938–9.[6] The current historiography tends to give a common answer to the first

2. Kimble, *Political History*, p. 486.
3. Apter, *Gold Coast*, p. 134.
4. See Post in Gann and Duignan, *op. cit.*, p. 37.
5. *ibid.*, p. 54; see also Apter, *Gold Coast*, pp. 170–2; D. Austin, *Politics in Ghana, 1946–60* (London, 1964), p. 27.
6. See J. Flint, 'Planned decolonization and its failure in British Africa', *African Affairs* **82**, 328, (1983); J. Gallagher, *The Decline, Revival and Fall of the British Empire* (Cambridge, 1982); P. Gifford and W. R. Louis (eds), *The Transfer of Power in Africa: Decolonization 1940–60* (New Haven and London, 1982); R. F. Holland, *European Decolonization 1918–1981* (London, 1985); A. H. M. Kirk-Greene (ed.), *The Transfer of Power: the Colonial Administrator in the Age of Decolonization* (Oxford, 1979); J. M. Lee and M. Petter, *The Colonial Office, War and Development Policy* (London, 1982); D. J. Morgan, *The Official History of Colonial Development* (5 vols) (London, 1980); W. H. Morris-Jones & G. Fischer (eds), *Decolonisation and After* (London, 1980); and R. D. Pearce, *Turning Point in Africa: British Colonial Policy 1938–48* (London, 1982); 'The Colonial Office in 1947 and the transfer of power in Africa' *Journal of Imperial and Commonwealth History* **10**, 2, (1982), and 'The Colonial Office and Planned Decolonization in Africa' *African Affairs* **83**, 330 (1984).

question—*why* the change in policy on Indirect Rule—and recent contributions by Flint and Pearce, whilst making some important new points, are no exception.   The explanation for the demise of the chieftaincy, they say, is to be found in London.

According to Flint, as early as 1938–9, and according to Pearce not until 1947, imperial policy makers decided to replace Indirect Rule with a democratic form of self-government which would appeal to the new African educated classes.   They, and other historians, point to a scepticism about the chieftaincy in London circles epitomized by such comments as: 'Africans cannot be preserved as interesting museum exhibits' indefinitely[7] and (in relation to the Governor of Sierra Leone) that the Governor 'ought to get off his high horse and remember that you can't do the 'Sanders of the Rivers' stuff in Freetown'.[8]   Why were such changes being contemplated? Because the British were planning decolonization and the aim of self government required the cooperation of these new Westernized Africans. Decolonization as a policy rested either on an 'unspoken assumption' that self-government required democratic legitimacy for central government which only these African elites could deliver (Flint) or, that a deliberate pre-emption of nationalist demands was required to avoid making the mistakes of the Indian Empire (Pearce).[9]   In both variants of the argument, decolonization is a policy adopted for imperial reasons, rather than the acknowledgement either of the intrinsic failures of Indirect Rule, or of the power of nationalist movements.   Particularly in Flint's arguments, the *reasons* for a decolonization decision in 1938–9 remain obscure.   Pearce's case rests more solidly on the widely acknowledged significance of the 1947 Report on African Policy produced for the Colonial Office by Cohen and Caine.   He asserts that 1947 must be seen as a turning point, when Indirect Rule was abandoned and a 'consistent and conscious strategy of decolonization emerged.'[10]   The reason was simply a recognition of the political inevitability of independence; only the timing remained to be determined, and for this the British were prepared to respond to the fledgling nationalists' successes at building mass support for independence. Flint's argument, on the other hand, is more in line with that of historians such as Gallagher; the decision to decolonize and the end of Indirect Rule are not permitted any connection with so-called 'nationalism', even of a pre-emptive kind.   Hence Gallagher's comment that imperial policy was the 'Frankenstein' which called forth the 'monster' of anti-colonial nationalism.[11]

7.   Pearce *Turning Point*, p. 47.
8.   J. Hargreaves in Morris-Jones and Fischer, *Decolonisation and After*, p. 86.   This was written in 1939.
9.   Flint, 'Planned decolonization', p. 397; Pearce, in *African Affairs* 83 (1984), p. 92.
10.   Pearce, *Ibid.*, p. 86.
11.   Gallagher, *Decline, Revival and Fall*, p. 148.

Whatever the reasons given for a decolonization decision, whether in 1938 or 1947, the assertion that such a decision existed performs a clear function in relation to explanations of the end of Indirect Rule. The direction of causation has been reversed; the outcome—independence in 1957 or 1960—has been used to explain the political reforms of the 1940s. By imputing an 'intention to decolonize' in 1940s policy making, an explanation of the end of Indirect Rule is derived from what happened a decade later. Of course both Flint and Pearce are aware of this problem, and are careful to disclaim the existence of an imperial plan which was actually implemented in its original purity. Indeed Flint argues that the plan for decolonization had 'failed' as early as 1951–2, insofar as the substantive reforms envisaged as necessary preludes to independence never came to fruition.[12] (Flint's argument rests crucially upon what he *means* by decolonization, as will be seen further on in the discussion.) Pearce, too, admits that the 'ideas of 1947' were never realised. Nevertheless the logic of the argument is unshaken; plans that fail, or plans that are liberal and response-oriented are still intentions which, once imputed, can be used to explain what was being done in the 1940s.

The circularity of these arguments about the meaning of 1940s reforms is only broken by considering the alternative possibility; instead of assuming that Indirect Rule went because of the plan for decolonization, let us suppose—as many historians now argue—that the reforms of the 1940s, whatever their precise date, did not intend decolonization in its minimum sense of self-determination for the colonies within a foreseeable or proximate time period. This argument points to Britain's continuing military power in the post-war world, and to the apparent determination of the Attlee government to revive and deepen the African empire even after the loss of India. The plans for political reform were, it is argued, an adjunct to the main thrust of policy, which was to develop the imperial estates to the 'mutual benefit' of colonial and metropolitan interests. 'Self-government' meant finding new collaborating elites who would, by accepting voluntarily a new form of association with Britain, help to preserve the British connection.[13] The doctrine of viability was crucial to this policy, combining social welfare elements (particularly education) with a programme of economic development geared as far as possible to individual territories.[14] This early form of autarchic developmentalism was based on the supposition that stable self-government of the Dominion type was

12. Flint, 'Planned decolonization', pp. 410–1.
13. D. Fieldhouse and D. Austin in Gifford and Louis, *Transfer of Power*, p. 490 and p. 232; Gallagher *op. cit.*, p. 144; Morgan *op. cit.*, vol. 5, p. 21; M. Cowen, 'Early years of the CDC: British state enterprise overseas during late colonialism', *African Affairs* **83**, 330 (1984), pp. 63–4.
14. Lee and Petter, *Colonial Office*, p. 217.

80 **AFRICAN AFFAIRS**

impossible without an industrial and agricultural base capable of sustaining the more ambitious social and political structures planned. Some colonies, it was felt, were self-evidently incapable of ever sustaining such a development which in any case would take many generations even in the most promising situations.[15] In this view of imperial policy, therefore—an establishment version of 'neo-colonialism' theory—the real end of empire and the decision to scuttle is marked by the abandonment of 'viability' at the end of the 1950s.[16] The decolonization decision, then, is pushed forward, with very important consequences for our understanding of the imperial or metropolitan dimension of policy-making. Attempts to situate the decolonization policy in the 1940s can be seen to suffer from either the improbable piety or determined ambiguity of official thinking. Morgan and Lee also show in convincing detail how the post-war plans for African social and economic development turned out to be, quite simply, beyond Britain's capabilities, at least within an imperial framework.[17] It then becomes quite plausible to argue, even without the benefit of archival data, that by the late 1950s the British political elite had decided that empire was finished. And it was only in this later period that the belief that political developments could be controlled through judicious reforms and timely concessions—a belief at the heart of 1940s policy-making—came to be seen as naively optimistic.

What the British themselves meant by 'self government' is at the heart of the current debate. The evidence now being presented by historians shows that 1940s policies were, at the very least, ambiguous. Questions concerning the significance of British economic plans for the colonies, the role of colonial dollar earnings, the priority assigned to 'viability' in social and economic terms and the degree to which the rhetoric of self-government concealed as much as it revealed about imperial intentions cannot be disposed of by proving that there was no neo-colonial conspiracy to fix up a 'false independence'. Nor can the ambiguity be resolved as a problem of 'timing'; self-government meaning the achievement of reformed or modernized forms of African local administration within a few generations is qualitatively different from handing over sovereign independence within ten years and without conditions. The more extreme versions of the 'plan that failed' argument come close to admitting this. Sceptics such as Gallagher and Low now argue that the attempt at political engineering was a 'sorry delusion', and that control over the 'pace and

15. Morgan, *op. cit.*, vol. 5, p. 33.
16. *ibid.* p. 96 and p. 307; Holland, *op. cit.*, pp. 191 and 200; Austin in Gifford and Louis *op. cit.*, p. 236. See also B. Schaffer 'The concept of preparation', *World Politics* 18, (1965) and H. Tinker's review of M. Lee, *Colonial Development and Good Government*, in *Government and Opposition* 3, 2, 1968, for percipient prerevisionist anticipations of this argument.
17. Lee and Petter, *op. cit.*, p. 215 and p. 243; Morgan *op. cit.*, vol. 2, pp. 182–96; vol. 5, pp. 88–93.

DECOLONIZATION IN THE GOLD COAST 81

form' of change was quickly lost.[18]   If this was so, then we have once again to understand what this 'political engineering' was supposed to be about, and why Indirect Rule was considered eventually to have no part to play in the reforms contemplated but never fully implemented.

Once the problem of explaining the reforms of the 1940s is separated from the explanation of decolonization in the late 1950s, it also becomes much easier to give plausible answers to the second and third questions posed earlier: the nature of the historical connection between those reforms and the later decolonization policy, and the issue of political control.   A simple first step is to acknowledge that decolonization can arguably be seen to *follow on* from the failure of reform and attempts at socio-economic development without necessarily arguing that decolonization was always the intention of those reforms.   To discuss the sequence of events between 1940 and 1960 in terms of a plan that failed serves only to divert attention from a more difficult and interesting set of questions.   A more fruitful conceptualization of the problem would have to acknowledge that what took place was an interaction between a bewilderingly rapid series of policy changes at the London level with a varied set of responses to crises at the level of individual colonies.   It is difficult to envisage a Colonial Office master plan which can explain the change from policies of 'modernizing the NAs' to 'neo-colonialism using educated Africans' to 'independence without viability' all (in the Gold Coast) within seven years *and* simultaneously explain the changing power relationships between colonial government and colonial society.   The rapidity of change has served to conceal the significance of the changes themselves.   The assumption that the chieftaincy, for instance, was swept away in order to prepare for decolonization is an illusion produced by the shortness of the interval, particularly in the Gold Coast, between the inauguration of the chiefs' replacements and the coming of independence with Parliamentary-style constitutions.   The speed of the transition is made even more startling when it is realized that the policy of reforming or modernizing the Indirect Rule system lasted well into the 1950s in some cases, and until 1951–2 in the Gold Coast.

It is important to insist, therefore, that there were three quite separate sets of policies in the period 1940 to 1960.   The distinction between them is often blurred by the revisionist historiography, particularly the difference between the policy for modernizing the Native Authorities, and its successor, the policy of creating democratic institutions which would accommodate the educated 'nationalist' African elites.   For an explanation of these stages both Flint and Pearce return to the plan for decolonization,

---

18.   D. Low in Gifford and Louis, *Transfer of Power*, p. 27; Gallagher, *Decline, Revival and Fall*, p. 153.

which in its 1940s guise is made to be the prime cause of the decision taken for clearly quite different reasons in the late 1950s. The reluctance to admit other explanations of those earlier transitions in policy is, of course, governed by the obsession with proving imperial initiative as the prime mover in the pre-nationalist period. As will be shown below, however, the nationalist pressure denied by the revisionists may be something of a straw man. One can deny the significance of the nationalists without necessarily accepting that an imperial plan for decolonization is the principle explanation of the 1940s reforms as they actually occurred in the individual colonies.

The perspective offered, then, by the revisionist historiography presents many new and interesting insights, particularly concerning the extent to which reformist thinking gathered pace during the Second World War, and the extent to which a yawning gap existed between London scepticism about the value of Indirect Rule, and the apparent determination of colonial administrations to continue along the lines set by that policy. But the new research also reveals the ambiguity of much of the reform mooted in the 1940s, in terms both of its goals and its motivations; and it seems to point quite clearly to the fact that decolonization, defined as independence, was a decision taken in the late 1950s for reasons quite different from those considered relevant in the 1940s. The main explanation for both the attempt to modernize Indirect Rule and its abandonment remains a circular one; both developments are seen as part of the plan for decolonization, an imperial initiative which, because the outcome in sequential terms was decolonization, is interpreted as having intended that outcome, however imperfectly.

Any attempt to explain the demise of the chieftaincy and its place in the decolonization process in one particular colony must, therefore, adopt a framework of analysis which specifically separates the explanatory factors relevant at each stage in the sequence of events between 1940 and 1960. In the analysis of the Gold Coast which follows, it is argued that the explanation for both the policy of reforming the NAs and its abandonment after 1951 is to be found in the nature of the colonial state, in particular its weakness and 'externality' or lack of rootedness in colonial society. This juridical, economic and political crisis of the colonial state was cumulative, and was revealed by the popular upheavals of the 1940s and their aftermath which, whether or not they were led by 'nationalists', did cause a rethinking of colonial policy. The initial response to these upheavals was to continue reforming the NAs, a policy abandoned as a result of the ineffectiveness and lack of cooperation of the chieftaincy itself. The revelation that the chiefs could be abandoned without significant loss of control was a lesson, perhaps not fully appreciated at the time, in the lack of rootedness of an institution which had always been thought to be the crucial link between colonial state and society. The brief period of evolutionary democracy which followed should not, therefore, be seen as an experiment which got out of control, and hence forced a decolonization decision; on the contrary, it was a successful accommodation to the demands of a group which, admittedly, had even weaker links with rural society than the chiefs but which nevertheless was easier to satisfy than the urban mobs and farmers' movements of the 1940s.

The nationalists presented themselves as the obvious 'solution' to the crisis. But the change was not a solution, insofar as the abandonment of the chieftaincy in favour of the nationalists did not affect the fundamental character of state-society relations. The oddity of the decolonization decision, then, is that it followed so rapidly on this successful accommodation, but before it had had time to fill the political vacuum revealed (but not caused) by the demise of the chieftaincy. In other words, decolonization in the late 1950s did not follow either from the failure of reform or from loss of control. The nationalists were simply easier to persuade—indeed did not need to be persuaded—that political independence was the solution to the economic and social problems of colonial society. In this sense, the revisionist historians are correct to emphasize the imperial factor, but for the late 1950s not the late 1940s. For it is only by reference to this factor that one can explain the precipitous abandonment of the unfinished experiment with evolutionary democracy. On the other hand the revisionist historians miss the crucial point in regard to the 1940s, which is that whilst 'nationalism' may not have forced the British to adopt a decolonization policy, a more fundamental crisis in relations between the colonial state and society in the 1940s did lead to first the radical modification and then the abandonment of Indirect Rule. There is no need to discover a Whitehall plan for decolonization in 1943, or 1947, to explain these changes.

The End of Indirect Rule in the Gold Coast

Between 1944 and 1954 there was an attempt to turn the Indirect Rule system in the Gold Coast into a form of 'modern' local government. It was not finally abandoned until a few years after the role of the chieftaincy in the central political institutions of the colony was formally ended in 1954. Revisionist historians who, as indicated above, see the 1950s rather than the 1940s as the key period, would still interpret these changes as a cunning piece of metropolitan *dirigisme,* a neo-imperial ploy to replace one set of colonial collaborators with another. The problem with this interpretation is twofold: first, it does not fit the local reality of policy as conceived and implemented in the Gold Coast itself, and secondly it does not explain the very rapid abandonment of the policy of reform, much later than would have been anticipated by those who emphasize the 1940s, without any apparent loss of control. How could the colonial state so easily abandon an ideology and a set of institutions which it had spent 30 to 40 years building up, and which it had always maintained was its central rationale?

First, closer examination of the Gold Coast reforms of 1951 shows them to have been a long way short of the Cohen–Caine vision of 1947. (The same is true *a fortiori* of other colonies.) And local policy in the years 1947–1951 seems in fact to have been pointing in the opposite direction. Whilst Burns had, as a reforming Governor, pushed the Colonial Office into accepting an African unofficial majority in the Legislative Council in 1946, this new Constitution was based firmly on the Joint Provincial Council and Ashanti Confederacy Council as electoral colleges.[19] And it followed on the 1944 comprehensive reform of the NAs and Native Courts in the Colony, a reform which in every sense embodied the high point of Indirect Rule. Under the 1944 Ordinances, the government at last regularized the appointment of chiefs, established Treasuries with regular tax income (thus dramatically increasing the revenue of the NAs) and rationalized the system of Native Courts.[20] In Ashanti too Finance Committees and NA Advisory Committees had been in operation since 1940, in pursuance of a policy of encouraging greater 'interest' on the part of educated Africans in NA affairs.[21] Even the 1951 Constitution itself, under which Nkrumah and the CPP took power, provided for 37 of the 75 seats in the new Assembly to be elected by the chiefly Territorial Councils.[22] The 1952 local government reforms in the Gold Coast, whilst separating for the first time chiefly or traditional councils from the new local government authorities, retained for the chiefs a one-third representation on the latter bodies.[23] The constitution of the local Native Courts, moreover, was not secularized until 1958, after independence.[24] And it was not until 1954 that the chiefs were ousted from the central legislature and a directly elected assembly of 104 members set up.[25] The dramatic changes did not occur, then, until 1954, a fact which reemphasizes the rapidity of change after 1951, a change apparently unthought of in 1950 and not, except with hindsight, necessarily prefigured in the 1951 constitution.

In truth, the new London-inspired policy of preparation for 'self-government' did not seem to have prepared anybody for the idea that the government would be handed over to people despised only the previous

19. Hargreaves in Gifford and Louis, *op. cit.*, p. 128.
20. Hailey, *Native Administration*, pp. 206–8.
21. Busia, *Position of the Chief*, pp. 158–60.
22. The Coussey Commission whose recommendations were reflected in the Constitution was packed with chiefly representatives: Apter, *Gold Coast*, p. 176 and p. 180.
23. D. Austin, *Politics in Ghana* (London, 1964), p. 158.
24. See R. Crook, 'Local elites and national politics in Ghana', unpublished PhD, thesis, University of London (1978), p. 54 and pp. 152–3.
25. Austin, *op. cit.*, p. 202.

year as unrepresentative and irresponsible agitators; the paradox was deepened by the intensification of the colonial relationship in both political and economic terms during the 1950s, to a peak which it had never achieved during the colonial period proper.[26]

How did the Gold Coast colonial administration itself see its policy in this period? Clearly there was a tension between London and Gold Coast government appreciations of what was desirable or feasible in the way of reform, as we shall see. Yet if we assign primacy to the Gold Coast government it is still difficult to understand what it *thought* it was doing, other than facing both ways at once. Those at the top clearly continued to believe that reforming the chieftaincy was a viable option; and it seems implausible to assume that British colonial administrators experienced a Pauline conversion which enabled them suddenly to see the merits and virtues of Nkrumah's 'Standard 7' boys. Indeed, we have the evidence of many officers who lived through this period that they, especially the DCs at the grass roots, were sceptical of the pace of change, and felt that 'at the bottom level . . . it's all a fraud'.[27] Attitudes to the new political class differed, of course; as former Governor Turnbull said 'The man who read the Economist [or New Statesman] wouldn't behave exactly the same toward a politician as a man who gained his entry through stroking the Jesus First Eight'.[28] And by no means all Governors, even the most reformist, were of the 'Economist-reading' variety!

Nevertheless in spite of local attitudes the changes *were* made, in a remarkably rapid way. And this raises the second problem of interpretation; how did the colonial government come to abandon its long standing policies and its erstwhile key collaborators in the local population so easily and so rapidly—albeit later in the day than has hitherto been assumed? No doubt in the Gold Coast the prodding of a 'liberal' Governor (Arden-Clarke) after 1949 was a local factor of some importance; we do not know whether he read the 'Economist', but clearly he pushed a sceptical and in some cases hostile administration as far as he was able. Metropolitan direction was too weak and contradictory to be other than an indirect and general influence on local reform. The Governor himself was only an 'agent' of Whitehall in a very tenuous sense; we do not need to posit a dictatorial Colonial Office which, even after the war-time experience constantly reminded impatient ministers of its persuasive rather than executive role.[29] The *Journal of African Administration,* which during the 1950s

---

26. Hargreaves in Gifford and Louis, *Transfer of Power*, p. 134. The new emphasis on combining political reform with socio-economic development had been prefigured in the Colonial Development and Welfare Acts of 1940 and 1945.
27. Kirk-Greene, *Colonial Administrator*, p. 87.
28. *ibid.*, p. 157.
29. Lee and Petter, *Colonial Office*, pp. 194–9. On Arden-Clarke's role see: R. J. A. R. Rathbone, 'The Transfer of Power in Ghana, 1945–57', unpubl. PhD thesis, University of London, 1968,. pp. 111, 141 and 242.

preached the Office line that representative local government was what colonialism was all about, was hardly the equivalent of an imperial *ukase*.[30] In any event, officers in the field had barely got used to the idea that they were patiently building the foundations of African self-government, when full independence was decreed.[31] Nor, on the other hand, do we need to resurrect the former 'nationalist' explanation. As shall be shown in greater detail, the upheavals of the 1940s were important in causing certain responses by colonial governments, but they did not necessarily have much to do with the nationalist elites, and do not in themselves explain the decision to abandon attempting to reform the chieftaincy. Above all, neither of the above explanations, whether it is the 'pressure from below' thesis, or 'pressure from above', in the shape of liberal Governors and Whitehall, helps to explain how it was possible for such changes to be made, and made as rapidly and as smoothly as they were. Understanding the influences on policy-making is not the same as understanding what actually happened, as an historical and social process. For this, one must return to an analysis of the crisis in colonial state-society relations which emerged most starkly in the Gold Coast of the 1940s and pose the question: was the colonial state *ever* quite what it seemed, both to contemporary official apologists and to latter day historians?

The Colonial State, Chieftaincy and Land Law

One of the basic characteristics of the Gold Coast colonial state has long been known, but only recently remarked upon. It is a characteristic which it shared with many other African colonies, namely that it was and remains (as Ghana does today) a mercantilist or 'customs post' state, deriving its revenues from the surplus of an externally-oriented trading economy.[32] In 1938, 98·5 per cent of tax revenues in the Gold Coast came from indirect taxes; before 1926 import and export duties were the only forms of indirect taxation, with 75 per cent of revenues in 1930–31 coming from import taxes alone.[33] The Gold Coast, moreover, was singled out by generations of

30.   See Ronald Robinson's 'retrospective' on the role of the Journal: 'The Journal and the transfer of power, 1947–51' *Journal of Administration Overseas* 13, 1, (1974); also Lee and Petter *op. cit.*, p. 254, on the formation of the African Studies Branch of the CO.
31.   The comments of an official reviewer in the *Journal of African Administration* 8, 2 (1956) p. 107, neatly encapsulate the conventional wisdom of the time: 'More and more Americans [now] admit that the African question is not one of how to end European rule but one of building something to take its place.'
32.   See R. Crook 'Bureaucracy and politics in Ghana: a comparative perspective', in P. Lyon and J. Manor (eds), *Transfer and Transformation: Political Institutions in the New Commonwealth* (Leicester, 1983), p. 186. C.f. Lonsdale's comments on the low degree of 'statishness' of the colonial state, and its reliance on the 'peasant marketing chain'; 'State and Peasantry in Colonial Africa', in R. Samuel (ed.) *People's History and Socialist Theory* (London, 1981), pp. 107 and 111, and 'States and Social Processes in Africa' *African Studies Review* 24, 2/3, (1981) pp. 190–1.
33.   Lord Hailey *An African Survey* (London, 1956) p. 682; G. B. Kay *The Political Economy of Colonialism in Ghana* (Cambridge, 1972) p. 348; W. P. Holbrook 'The impact of the Second World War on the Gold Coast, 1939–45', unpublished PhD thesis, Princeton University, 1978, p. 19.

colonial government advisers and despairing Governors for its failure to impose *any* form of direct taxation on the native population.[34] Only the Northern Territories had a formal NA tax, established in 1932, but this was wholly retained by the NAs themselves.[35] It was not until 1943 that an income tax was collected, mainly from the mining companies and employees, and in 1944 the first formally established NA rate in the Colony.[36] Of course, colonial governments conveniently overlooked the extent to which the population was taxed by arbitrary levies and collections made by the NAs for the purposes of supporting the stools; nevertheless the fact remained that the Gold Coast government did not have to use its intermediaries in local society as tax farmers or agents in even the most limited sense. That this was made possible by the emergence of the cocoa economy in southern Ghana need not be rehearsed here; the significance of the happy fiscal position of the colonial government is best appreciated through comparative analysis.

In India under East India Company rule, the colonial state 'latched on' (as Washbrook puts it), to the agrarian class structure, allocating the patronage of the state land revenue system to those whose traditional status conveyed rights to avoid or apportion revenue. Landed property was, therefore, not emancipated from political institutions; rather, it was incorporated into the state, which supported the particular property rights e.g. serfdom, of its revenue-collecting gentry.[37] In Africa, perhaps only the Kano lands of Northern Nigeria and the pre-1928 Buganda chieftaincy formed the basis of a similar system.[38] In other areas, including the Gold Coast colony and Ashanti, political statuses existed which had the potential for development from 'tribute' forms of land claims into more regular forms of land tax, although not, of course a land revenue system proper. When the commercialization of land in southern Ghana began in earnest at the turn of the 19th century, it is clear that the chiefs were already attempting this kind of a conversion.[39] But the oddity of the Gold Coast colonial

34. See Kay, *op. cit.*, p. 109.
35. Hailey, *African Survey* (1956) p. 666.
36. Hailey *op. cit.* (1951) p. 198 and p. 208; see also M. Wight, *The Gold Coast Legislative Council* (London, 1947), p. 189.
37. D. A. Washbrook, 'Law, state and society in colonial India', *Modern Asian Studies* 15, 3 (1918), p. 664. Land revenue accounted for nearly half of total Government of India revenues at the end of the 19th century and remained the largest single source until the early 1920s; see D. Kumar (ed.) *The Cambridge Economic History of India*, vol. 2 (Cambridge 1983), pp. 916–9.
38. Hailey, *Native Administration*, p. 77; see Wrigley in L. Fallers, *The King's Men* (London, 1964), p. 42. The comparison with Uganda and also with Kenya is instructive, since it may be argued that the 'partiality' of the post-colonial state in both these countries, and its greater involvement in civil conflict, is directly related to the state's greater degree of rootedness during the colonial period. Cf. Londsale, 'States and Social Processes', p. 204.
39. See Dunn and Robertson, *op. cit.*, pp. 52–3; and W. Birmingham, I. Neustadt and E. N. Omaboe, *A Study of Contemporary Ghana, vol. 2, Some Aspects of Social Structure* (London, 1967), Chapter 8, for a good general survey.

state was that it never engaged directly with agrarian society, in the sense of incorporating and supporting either a landlord class or a landed 'gentry' (that is, land owners with political statuses or functions); it did not even support, or need, tax collectors or tax farmers.   On the contrary, when wealthy commercial farmers began to emerge who also happened to be chiefs, the colonial state tried to *prevent* their consolidation into a 'gentry', when it became clear that chiefs were attempting to amalgamate Stool and family land revenues utilizing the legal and political powers afforded them by the state.   In other words, the colonial state was not prepared to under-write or incorporate an incipient and as yet private landlordism.   It did not enforce laws which would facilitate the conversion of the private wealth accumulated by chiefs into landed property.   If this seems an argument which smacks of functionalism ('the mercantilist state did not need a landed gentry, therefore one did not emerge'), it should be emphasized that such an outcome was also a paradoxical and partially unintended conse-quence of the ideological and legal orthodoxies which came to dominate the colonial state.[40]

For an explanation and justification of the above assertion, one must return to the development of the so-called Indirect Rule system and its effect on relations between the chieftaincy and the state.   The key to this development is undoubtedly the failure of the Lands and Forestry Bills of 1894, 1897 and 1912.   These Bills were attempts by the colonial govern-ment to take over the administration and allocation of land rights, particu-larly of so-called unoccupied or 'waste' lands, and to make 'absolute' ownership of land more certain through a land certification scheme.   The underlying purpose of the legislation was to control the current concessions boom and its attendant abuses, and, in the case of the 1911 Bill, to give the government power to establish publicly owned and controlled Forest Reserves.   The legislation was abandoned in the face of considerable opposition from both the chiefs and their lawyer/intelligentsia allies of the ARPS and the local press, together with European commercial interests.[41] The argument of the opposition, which was to become elaborated in legal textbooks and treatises on land tenure, was that 'there is no land without an owner', and that land apparently unused was 'community' land which the local Stool, as the embodiment of the community, held in trust for the

---

40.   I agree with Lonsdale that 'To obtain an historical engagement between African peasantry and colonial state, one must . . . concentrate more on the conditions of reproduction for both'.   Lonsdale, 'State and Peasantry', p. 110; but this is only a starting point.   One cannot 'read off' the Gold Coast state's venture into the politics of Indirect Rule from its need to secure its tax base.   The introduction of Native Treasuries in the 1930s was in fact counter-productive for the economic interests of both state and chiefs.   But this did not become clear until the 1940s.
41.   See Kimble, *Political History*, pp. 330–70 and *passim*.

living and future generations.[42] As Luckham (and Kimble before him) have observed 'there was at least temporarily a coincidence of interest between these local groups [chiefs, merchants and professional men] and foreign concessionaires who also preferred to negotiate their concessions with a minimum of interference from the colonial government'.[43] Nevertheless the acceptance of this principle of community ownership of land had profound and far-reaching consequences.

First, insofar as colonial rule accepted that indigenous customary law was to remain in force and be enforced—for native subjects—then it came to accept the codifications of that law produced by lawyers such as Mensah-Sarbah, Casely-Hayford, or Danquah, legal judgements in Court and, later, the work of anthropologists such as Rattray.[44] Hence it came to be accepted, as an unshakeable legal—and sociological—fact, that there was no such thing as absolute individual ownership in customary law; the land belonged to the community, meaning the dead, living and yet to be born. The irresoluble ambiguity in this doctrine was—*which* community? Whilst it was recognized that stools, families and even individuals could separately hold land, the question of whether a particular stool or family held the reversionary or communal right depended on vexed questions of historical precedent and jurisdictional claims.

Most important, the doctrine was quickly turned by the paramount chiefs, the heads of pre-colonial political entities recognized by the government, into a claim that the land of the *whole state* was vested in the paramount stool, all other rights being usufructory—including those of subordinate stools. This was the root of the infamous Asamankese dispute in Akyem Abuakwa, which lasted from around 1902, when the Okyeman Council issued a law prohibiting alienation of land in the state without the consent of the Okyenhene, to 1934.[45] In Ashanti, too, the powerful *amanhene* pressed similar claims to absolute or reversionary rights against both subordinate stools and, of course, against the weakened Kumasi chiefs until 1935.[46] The work of Rattray in particular was crucial in showing that the customary land tenure system was similar throughout the Akan territories of both Colony and Ashanti. He also linked it to an

42. See J. E. Casely Hayford, *Gold Coast Native Institutions* (London, 1903); *The Truth about the West African Land Question* (London, 1913); J. Mensah Sarbah, *Fanti National Constitution* (London, 1906), and the extended discussion by A. N. Allott in 'Akan Law of Property', unpublished PhD thesis, University of London, 1953, pp. 60, 83 and 287.
43. R. Luckham, 'Imperialism, law and structural dependence', *Development and Change* 9, 2 (1978), p. 238; cf. J. Forbes Munro 'Monopolists and speculators: British investment in West African rubber, 1905–14', *Journal of African History* 22, (1981), p. 272.
44. Rattray, *Ashanti Law*; J. B. Danquah, *Akan Laws and Customs* (London, 1928); the impact of Rattray's work is discussed in Kimble, *op. cit.*, p. 486.
45. R. Addo-Fening in P. Jenkins (ed.), *Akyem Abuakwa and the Politics of the Inter War Period in Ghana: Basel Africa Bibliography no. 12* (Basel, 1975), p. 66.
46. Allott, *op. cit.*, p. 313; Tordoff, *Ashanti*, p. 309.

understanding of the matrilineal family structure, to the laws of succession and inheritance, and to indigenous religion. In short, such a powerful array of legal, political and intellectual arguments surrounded the topic of customary land tenure by the end of the 1920s that it is small wonder that the government itself began to take them seriously; this was a consequence which was to be embodied in the Indirect Rule system.

In pursuit of both political legitimation and of a strategy of local government, the doctrine of Indirect Rule emerged in the late 1920s, as has been indicated, as a form of romantic cultural conservationism. African institutions were to be preserved but also encouraged to develop along progressive lines. In the Colony, however, the chiefs consistently resisted all attempts at reform legislation which (a) attempted to make chieftaincy a legal status conferrable only by the government, albeit that the government wanted only to support customary procedures for selection and enstoolment; (b) attempted to enforce procedures for accounting for revenues, particularly land revenues, through Native Treasuries, and (c) attempted to establish administrative supervision of Native Court procedures, income and membership.[47] Although the 1927 *Native Jurisdiction Ordinance* was welcomed by Nana Ofori Atta and the JPC chiefs—partly because it bolstered the position of the JPC and Paramount Stool in Akyem Abuakwa—it did not establish Treasuries or supervision of Tribunals.[48] It was not until 1939 that government took the power to compel NAs to establish a Treasury, and it was 1944 before a complete package of reforms was introduced (see above).[49] In Ashanti and the NTs reforms came earlier, 1935 and 1932, but in Ashanti, as in Colony, the British were most concerned with 'the disinclination of Divisional chiefs to agree that monies received from the sale or lease of communal lands or similar sources should be brought to account in the Native Treasury. . .'.[50]

Nevertheless, in spite of the tardiness of the legislation, it may be argued that British persistence on these matters had a very important outcome. By the time of the 1927 NJO, the British had come to interpret community ownership of land as meaning that the Stool particularly the Paramount Stool should be viewed as a public corporate body, holding community resources in trust, as it were, and quite distinct from the 'private' interests of families or individuals. The British were also willing to uphold the 'customary' laws of tenure and succession in the local courts and if necessary in the Supreme Court, and hence consistently resisted what they regarded as the self-interested and hypocritical attempts of lawyers to bring themselves—and English legal concepts—into the customary Courts

47. See Hailey, *Native Administration*, p. 226.
48. Addo-Fening, *op. cit.*, pp. 71–8.
49. Hailey, *Native Administration*, p. 204.
50. Hailey, *op. cit.*, Part IV, p. 30.

through amalgamation into the Supreme Court system. The British attitude was influenced in particular by what they regarded as the mischievous activities of lawyers in the Asamankese case.[51] This, together with British insistence on upholding 'customary law and practice', both in the courts through the exclusion of lawyers and politically in stool disputes, meant that the chiefs were caught in traps partly of their own making.

As their former allies, the educated politicians and lawyers began to criticize the Indirect Rule system in the 1930s, the chiefs had to accept the close cooperation offered by the British, particularly when the British seemed ready to bolster up the claims of the Paramount Stools (no doubt in the interest of more rational local government units). But the price of acceptance was a more rigid British insistence on the principles of customary law which the chiefs had thrown at them since 1900. Thus, while the chiefs were incorporated into the colonial state as a political status group, agents of a governmental system which wanted to portray itself as *legitimate* to the rural dwellers, their attempts to convert themselves into a landlord group, waxing rich from a state-supported system of rent extraction, were deliberately excluded from the bargain.[52] Instead, in its paternalistic way, the colonial government was acutely sensitive to its duties as protector of the innocent peasantry from the evils of landlordism and moneylenders; as elsewhere, the Indian experience fed into the African Empire. After the re-creation of the Ashanti Confederacy in 1935, the Ashanti administration was horrified at the attempts of the Kumasi clan chiefs to reimpose their authority in the Ahafo area, particularly through the extraction of 'cocoa tribute', and tried to stop it. Two rules were enunciated: (i) Kumasi citizens and local inhabitants should not pay tribute; (ii) money collected should be treated as public money, to be accounted for either by the ACC or the NA in its local governmental expenditure.[53] Hailey recorded the fears of the Gold Coast administration when he wrote that: 'Whereas a move to individual land tenure might please the agricultural expert, the administration must have regard to its other implications. In an agricultural community there is no greater source of unrest than a system of tenure which may subject the peasantry to exploitation by a landlord or moneylender.'[54] He also pointed out the damaging effects of cocoa commercialization 'which led some chiefs to seek independence from their Councillors and Elders by increasing their personal incomes through the sale or leasing of unoccupied lands'.[55] Clearly, as a glance at any of the

---

51. See B. M. Edsman, *Lawyers in Gold Coast Politics* (Uppsala, 1979), pp. 36, 48 and 143.
52. cf. Kay's view that the colonial state was weak and cautious and relied on at least passive popular acceptance: Kay, *op. cit.*, p. 9, and A. B. Holmes in P. Jenkins, *Akyem Abuakwa*, p. 21; 'Government [in the 1930s] was both paternalistic and cautiously accommodating'.
53. Dunn and Robertson, *Dependence*, p. 53.
54. Hailey, *Native Administration*, Part IV, p. 57.
55. Hailey, *op. cit.*, Part III, p. 199.

local studies of colonial administration shows, the government's attempts to stop the chiefs pocketing Stool Land revenues were never wholly effective. Nevertheless, it may be argued that they did prevent the consolidation of the chieftaincy as a landlord class incorporated into the state, with its interests articulated within the state and its property laws enforced. The laws which *were* enforced served only to *hinder* the growth of large-scale landed property, although of course big farmers did emerge. It was also very difficult, however, for a chiefly family to convert the resources of the colonially-recognized Stool into hereditary landed property because of another facet of customary law, namely the large number of shifting matrilineal segments from which the chief might be drawn.[56] (The degree to which matrilineal family property really was communal can also be exaggerated; the Asantehene's dynasty was perhaps one of the exceptions.)[57]

A further consequence of the preservation and development of customary law under colonial rule may be seen in the pattern of class formation in agrarian society, particularly in the relation between these classes and the state. Here I differ from Luckham who argues that the 'superstructure' of customary law did not affect the development of capitalist relations in commercial agriculture, e.g. the consolidation of individual property and the emergence of land as a commodity.[58] Undoubtedly the commercialization of agriculture produced certain forms of accumulation; but in southern Ghana we have an instance of the effects of the introduction of a commercial crop which was primarily an export commodity dependent on world markets. This meant that not only did agro-commercial small towns grow up, foci of that typical interpenetration of rich peasant money with trading, transport and property, but also that agricultural producers became peculiarly enmeshed with those who *marketed* the crop—brokers, buyers, and moneylenders.[59] Studies of these kinds of agricultural economies, e.g., West Canada, or the populists of America, show the emergence of similar kinds of political mobilization against the buying interests, the 'banks' or 'middlemen'.[60] But in two respects, I would

---

56. See M. Fortes in A. R. Radcliffe-Brown and D. Forde (eds), *African Systems of Kinship and Marriage* (London, 1950), p. 257; I. Wilks in D. Forde and P. M. Kaberry (eds), *West African Kingdoms in the Nineteenth Century* (London, 1967), p. 214.
57. R. Crook, 'Colonial rule and political culture in modern Ashanti', *Journal of Commonwealth Political Studies* 11, 1, (1973), p. 7.
58. Luckham, *op. cit.*
59. See B. Beckman, *Organising the Farmers: Cocoa Politics and National Development in Ghana* (Uppsala, 1976), pp. 37–38, and p. 46: '[The Nowell Report of 1938] implies that perhaps as much as every tenth farmer may have been engaged in cocoa trading'.
60. cf. S. M. Lipset *Agrarian Socialism* (Berkeley, 1967), p. 71; J. D. Hicks, *The Populist Revolt* (Minneapolis, 1931), p. 76. A vague concept of 'populism' has frequently been advanced as a common feature of these movements; in my view, however, the crucial variable is involvement in a cash-crop, export economy.

argue, the Gold Coast was different; land never became a class issue, and an agrarian interest was never properly formulated and represented at the level of the state. Why was this?

Various arguments have been advanced; Hopkins, for instance, sees the lack of a fully-fledged landlordism as connected to the scattered pattern of landholding, the lack of a competitive market in land and the extensive use of family and share cropper labour.[61]   The conditions of access to land are emphasized by many others, including Hill, who emphasizes in addition the reciprocal or non-antagonistic character of relations between 'rich' and 'poor' farmers involved in the networks of rural debt.   This she attributes to the peculiar importance of 'finance' rather than access to land as such in the growth of the cocoa industry.[62]   I would rather point to the fact that such landlordism as did exist was never properly consolidated either at the legal or political level.   Just as the colonial government never completely prevented chiefs appropriating Stool land revenues, so chiefs' levies themselves were more often avoided than paid—and the colonial state by the 1930s was not in the business of helping such enforcement.   Thus any grievances which the cocoa farmer had about debts, foreclosures or availability of land were focussed on moneylenders and brokers, and land itself was not *tied* to any set of feudal or rigid tenant relations; grievances were not therefore against the land-owning gentry backed up by the state. Similarly, insofar as the chiefs particularly during the JPC era were the nearest the Gold Coast ever got to the representation of an agrarian interest, and are often viewed as representing in particular the interests of large farmers, they did not behave like a 'gentry'.   As investors in produce buying and transport, property and education, the chiefs articulated more the general grievances of export farmers against the buyers—the foreign companies—and, for themselves, those of indigenous agro-commerce.[63] Thus, the conditions of land ownership did not become a class issue because of the peculiar position of the state in relation to property; and neither did land owners themselves (in the modern sense)—i.e. farmers, rich or poor—represent themselves as such at the political level.   It was only when the state became associated with the marketing system that

61.   A. G. Hopkins, *An Economic History of West Africa* (London, 1973), pp. 239 and 233; cf. J. Saul, 'African peasants and revolution', *Review of African Political Economy*, **1**, (1974) p. 49.
62.   P. Hill *Migrant Cocoa Farmers of Southern Ghana* (Cambridge, 1963), pp. 183 and 186; *Studies in Rural Capitalism in West Africa* (Cambridge, 1970), p. 25; cf. K. Post, 'Peasantization and rural political movements in West Africa', *European Journal of Sociology* **13**, 3, (1972), p. 251; G. Hyden, *Beyond Ujamaa in Tanzania* (London, 1980), pp. 10 and 17; F. R. Bray, *Cocoa Development in Ahafo, West Ashanti* (Achimota, 1959, mimeo), pp. 51–2; J. Tosh, 'The cash-crop revolution in tropical Africa: an agricultural reappraisal', *African Affairs* **79**, 314(1980), pp. 91–2.
63.   Crook, 'Ashanti', pp. 18–9; Dunn and Robertson, *Dependence*, p. 82; Bray *op. cit.*, pp. 36–7.

farmers could be mobilized against the *state*—as in the cocoa hold-ups—by those who represented a commercial interest.[64]

Indirect Rule and the Crisis of the 1940s

Now our initial question may be posed; what is the significance of these consequences of the preservation of customary law for our understanding of the relation between the reform of Indirect Rule and decolonization?

At the very time when Indirect Rule was being introduced formally into the administrative system, there was an increasing gap between ideology and reality both in terms of political practice and socio-economic relations. Not only were the chiefs resisting the administration's best-intentioned endeavours to uphold customary law and practice, and to regularize the basis of NA finances; the chiefs were also failing to deliver on the central core of the bargain. They were supposed to represent legitimate rule, guarantors of the acceptability of colonial rule. But the cocoa hold-ups, particularly of 1937–8, revealed the critical ambivalence of the chiefs' position. Recent work on the cocoa hold-ups reveals the extent to which the chiefs right down from Nana Ofori-Atta to the village levels in Eastern Province and Ashanti were involved in the formal organization and enforcement of the hold-ups.[65] In Central Province, Stone has noted the greater caution of the chiefs produced by the vigorous action of DCs in actually prosecuting chiefs who helped enforce the hold-ups.[66] Whatever the commercial ambitions of the chiefs and their merchant friends, Miles argues forcefully that they did have the support of the farmers generally, and in that sense represented a dangerous form of mass mobilization. In the past, both the neo-traditional elite and the educated reformers to be found in the Gold Coast Youth Conference had kept their distance from 'radical' agitational groups such as Wallace-Johnson's West African Youth League; the mere thought of the elite–mass alliances suggested by the events of the cocoa hold-up must have sent far greater shockwaves through

---

64.　cf. Lonsdale, *State and Peasantry,* p. 113; 'the state took into itself the contradictions within peasant economy, the contradictions between peasants and settlers, the contradictions between producers and trading houses'. See also Lonsdale, 'States and Social Processes', p. 193.

65.　R. Howard, 'Differential class participation in the Ghana cocoa boycott, 1937–8', *Canadian Journal of African Studies,* **10,** 3 (1976); J. Miles, 'Cocoa marketing in the Gold Coast, 1919–39, with special reference to the hold-up movements', unpubl. PhD thesis, University of London, 1978; J. E. Milburn, *British Business and Ghanaian Independence* (London, 1977); S. Rhodie, 'The Gold Coast Cocoa Hold-up of 1930–31', *Transactions of the Historical Society of Ghana* **9,** 1968. See also Tordoff, *op. cit.,* p. 273, and Kimble *op. cit.,* pp. 50–1, for the 1921 and 1930 hold-ups; A. B. Holmes and P. Jenkins (ed.) *op. cit.,* p. 26.

66.　R. Stone, 'Colonial administration and rural politics in South-Central Ghana, 1919–51', unpubl. PhD thesis, University of Cambridge, 1974, p. 133; cf. Hailey's cryptic comment on the need for reform of the NA police: 'As the "cocoa hold-up" of 1937 showed, they are liable to be used for objects other than the maintenance of law and order or the purposes laid down in the NA Ordinance' (*Native Administration,* p. 210).

the administration than any of the ineffectual campaigns of the WAYL during the 1930s.

The paradox of Indirect Rule is that many officers in the colonial service had always known, or felt, the hollowness at the centre of the policy. One can always find quotations in the archives illustrating the despair and even cynicism of DCs faced with the task of implementing Indirect Rule in the face of the daily realities of their knowledge of the local chiefs.[67] But it was in the 1930s, with the contradiction between the administration's interpretation of how NAs should collect and use land revenue and the chiefs' landlordish ambitions, that the doubts really began to emerge—although never at the top level. Stone has noted the progress of these feelings in Central Province, and in Colony generally; in 1938 for instance the JPC petitioned the King that the colonial government was not listening to their advice, and the SNA and other senior officials began to distrust even Ofori Atta, because of his opposition to the establishment of Native Treasuries, as well as his role in the hold-ups.[68] The lack of progress in the 1940s meant that the 1944 Ordinance was regarded by at least the CP administration as a last chance—a reform accepted by the chiefs perhaps because they too felt the pressures from other quarters. But, as Stone notes, 'By 1944 the government was evidently unwilling to seek the assistance of the chiefs of the CP in either the planning or implementation of local development'.[69] Feelings of disillusion with official policy on the chiefs were compounded during the Second World War by other problems of staff shortage, low pay, lack of leave and lack of promotion prospects; by 1945 the government had experienced the unprecedented—a petition of junior administrative officers (38 out of 90 signed) complaining particularly about lack of communication between senior and junior officers.[70]

It is in this context of low morale, and a simmering disillusion with official policy on Indirect Rule, that the post-war crises of the swollen-shoot disease and the boycott must be understood. At the very moment when elements in the administration were beginning to wonder whether even the 1944 reforms would work, and when the chiefs themselves were losing faith in the government, the chiefs were faced with a new set of challenges to their loyalty. Should they side with their people or support the government? The importance of the swollen-shoot disease is difficult to exaggerate insofar as it led to the government's cutting-out campaign which decimated the cocoa industry in Eastern Province and aroused the countryside to a state of near-insurrection over both the methods used

67. Crook, 'Ashanti', p. 18; Dunn and Robertson, *Dependence,* p. 169; Staniland, *op. cit.,* pp. 104–16; Stone, *op. cit.,* p. 185.
68. Stone *op. cit.,* p. 167.
69. *ibid.,* p. 165.
70. *ibid.,* p. 194; cf. Pearce, *Turning Point,* p. 70.

and the lack of a compensation programme. Both the JPC and the ACC argued that cutting-out should be voluntary, that notice should be given and compensation paid.[71] The government then twisted the arm of the Asantehene and got the ACC to issue an order supporting compulsory cutting-out in Ashanti—where the disease was not too bad.[72] The reaction against the chiefs was, nevertheless, fierce and in 1948 the ACC memorandum of evidence to the Watson Commission argued that the Agricultural Department's policy of cutting-out was *mistaken*, and complained bitterly of the historic failure of the colonial government ever to give proper help to the cocoa farmers.[73]

By early 1948 the rise of the campaign to boycott expatriate and Syrian firms' 'high priced' imports, organized by Nii Bonne in Accra, made the government fear a repeat of 1938. There is clear evidence that chiefs throughout Ashanti and Colony, frightened by the upheavals caused by swollen-shoot, sided with the boycott and helped enforce it with all the resources of the NAs.[74] Dennis Austin's later reflections on this period hint that the ACC's displeasure with Krobo Edusei *after* the riots had less to do with the government's hardline, than with Edusei's attempt to use the boycott to run a protection racket.[75] The Boycott Committees in southern Ghana clearly attracted groups of local African small traders—of whom Edusei was a typical example—with a grievance against foreign, particularly Syrian business, as well as those who saw the financial potential in the enforcement of such a ban on other traders. Enforcement had only become socially possible, however, because of the involvement of the chiefs and the local 'small town' elites of big farmers, brokers, schoolteachers and company clerks so accurately described in Austin's accounts of the Improvement or Youth Associations of the 1940s.[76] The local studies which followed on Austin's and Apter's work have shown that it is virtually impossible to distinguish, at least in class terms, between chiefs, local elites and so-called 'nationalists', that is, those who supported or who claim to have supported the UGCC and then its CPP faction before 1951.[77] They were one and the same; as argued above, the structure of southern Ghanaian commercial agricultural society was such that those who represented cocoa farmers' resistance to the cutting-out campaign were

71.   Austin, *Politics in Ghana*, pp. 59–66.
72.   See *Interim Report of the Committee of Enquiry to Review Legislation for the Treatment of Swollen Disease of Cocoa* (Beeton), Appendix VI (Gold Coast Sessional Papers, 1, 1948).
73.   *Report of the Commission of Enquiry into Disturbance in the Gold Coast* (Watson) (Great Britain, 1948, C.O. 231)—see 'Resolution of the Ashanti Confederacy Council in connection with the recent disturbances'—memo of evidence submitted to Commission of Enquiry.
74.   *Watson Report* para 170; Stone, *op. cit.*, p. 208.
75.   cf. D. Austin, *Politics in Ghana*, pp. 78–9, and *Ghana Observed* (Manchester, 1976), p. 180.
76.   Austin, *Politics in Ghana*, pp. 92–102 and *Ghana Observed*, passim.
77.   See next page.

DECOLONIZATION IN THE GOLD COAST 97

also those who demanded—and had demanded since the 1930s—a marketing system not dominated by a monopsony whether private or public. Such a demand had always been linked with the attack on expatriate monopoly control of the import trade, and with the allegation that this control kept prices high.   There was thus a coincidence of general and particular interests; the popular demands for a better deal for all producers (on price and marketing), the resistance to cutting out and for lower prices to urban (and rural) consumers coincided with the 'agro-commercial' (as opposed to 'agrarian landlord') interests of African traders, produce brokers and large cocoa farmers.   In this movement, it was the Ghana Farmers Congress, the chiefs and local Youth Associations (which often overlapped with the Boycott Committees), the trade unions in Accra and Takoradi, and ultimately the urban mobs who were the real instigators of the urban and rural upheavals which so shocked colonial and metropolitan opinion in 1948.[78]

The argument as to whether or not it was 'nationalism' which, in the aftermath of 1948, 'forced' colonial reform in the direction of decolonization is, therefore, something of a straw man.   Clearly the UGCC, which can be taken to embody nationalist organization between 1947 and 1949, gained a retrospective credibility from the arrest of its leaders after the 1948 riots; but, as Austin originally acknowledged, it was an infamy which they did not deserve.   In spite of the Watson Commission's Communist scare stories, the UGCC had had little or nothing to do with the farmers' movement and the boycott committees or with the ensuing riots.   It is true that it claimed the support of Youth Associations and other groups across the country, but in the absence of electoral politics the concept of 'support for the UGCC' in 1947–8 was decidedly abstract and tenuous.   Neither is it necessary to accept the CPP version of history, put about later by Nkrumah

77.   See Dunn and Robertson, *Dependence*, p. 317; M. Owusu, *Uses and Abuses of Political Power* (Chicago and London, 1970), pp. 172–91; Crook, *op. cit.* (1978); Stone, *op. cit.*, A Cawson, 'Local Politics and Indirect Rule in Cape Coast 1928–57', unpublished DPhil thesis, University of Oxford 1975; J. Simensen, 'Commoners, Chiefs and Colonial Government; British Policy and Land Politics in Akim Abuakwa', unpublished PhD thesis, University of Trondheim, 1975; D. Brown, 'Politics in the Kpandu Area of Ghana', unpublished PhD thesis, University of Birmingham, 1977.   (In the Northern Territories the elite character of local politics, as it emerged in the late 1940s and early 1950s, was even more strongly marked; see Staniland, *op. cit.*, p. 137; P. A. Ladouceur, *Chiefs and Politicians: the Politics of Regionalism in Northern Ghana* (London, 1979), pp. 83–5.)   In some cases, particularly in Akim Abuakwa, the CPP was associated from a very early date with groups in opposition to the NA chiefly establishment; but such opposition was predominantly factional or communal in character rather than 'class' based.   As argued above, there was little basis for a class-type hostility to chiefs or big farmers *qua* landlords, although the system of marketing could clearly lead to assymetric relations between 'money lender' farmers and debtors.   But there is no evidence that the CPP ever mobilized or represented *that* kind of grievance; the nearest it ever came to it was the use of the CPP-sponsored Cocoa Purchasing Company to give out loans to small farmers (or even non-farmers) in the mid-1950s—see Crook *op. cit.* (1978), p. 129.   In Akim, of course, the big migrant farmers were initially in the anti-Ofori-Atta camp.
78.   Beckman, *op. cit.*, pp. 52–5.

and indeed any CPP activist one cares to interview, which attributes the
mass protests to the influence of the CPP's linear precursors—radically
minded 'youth' who were *'later to become* CPP cadres'.   Whilst it may be
true that many of those who emerged as CPP leaders both at local and
national level after 1951 had participated in the 1947–50 events, it is
anachronistic to explain the class character or political motivation of the
earlier events by reference to the character of the CPP as it was after taking
office in 1951.   In this respect the debate over the origins and social
character of the nationalist party is of little help.

One cannot approach the events of 1947–50 armed with one's explanation of what nationalism was 'really' about without also making the
assumption that these events were proto-nationalist, that is, that the social
movements were led and the issues were set by those who later crystallized
into the radical nationalist party, the CPP.   Whilst Rathbone has convincingly laid to rest the idea that the CPP can be understood as an expression
of the interests of either an educationally defined group or of that catch-all
pseudo-class, the 'petty bourgeoisie', is it any more convincing to apply the
concept of an 'aspirant small business' interest to the events of 1948?[79]
The small businessmen described by Rathbone as the core element of the
CPP were undoubtedly to be found on the Boycott Committees and the
Youth Associations of the 1940s; but insofar as such individuals did participate in these groups they were less 'aspirants' than members of the local
elites formed by the commercialized agrarian society of southern Ghana.
The leading elements in these elites were the chiefs and big farmers,
together with the local establishment of educated employees of mercantile
companies, teachers, produce brokers and traders who usually formed the
core of the slightly incongruously named Youth Associations.   As argued
above, such groups whatever criticisms they may have had, as 'educated'
men, of the Indirect Rule system, were firmly tied in with the elite network
of agro-commercial interests so powerfully represented by the chieftaincy.
The issues with which they were engaged in 1947–48 have already been
described and it is difficult to discern or differentiate, at that time, within

---

79.   See R. J. A. R. Rathbone, 'Businessmen in Politics: Party Struggle in Ghana, 1949–57',
Journal of Development Studies **9**, 3, 1974, and 'Parties' Socio-Economic Bases and Regional
Differentiation in the Rate of Change in Ghana', in P. Lyon and J. Manor (eds), *Transfer and
Transformation: Political Institutions in the New Commonwealth* (Leicester, 1983), pp.
143–5.   Rathbone's concern is, of course, with the nature of the party itself and the degree to
which its radicalism can be explained by differences in its social character from the UGCC on
the one hand and the Ashanti-based National Liberation Movement of the 1950s, on the
other.   He does not attempt to interpret the whole range of social discontent involved in the
1948 crisis through the prism of the CPP's precursors.   He does claim, nevertheless, that
CPP radicalism, derived from these interests, was what mobilized and gave force to the
coalition of southern-based social groups brought under the banner of nationalist or anti-
colonial protest in the lead-up to 1951.   What is being argued below is that, even if the CPP
was formed by aspirant small businessmen, the radicalism of the anti-colonial protest 1948–51
did not derive its force or relevance from the interests of such a group.

the dominant themes of the grievances against expatriate and Lebanese business, the urban price issue and the incipient farmers' revolt, a sub-theme representing the hard-edged grudge of 'aspirant' businessmen *against* these local African elites. Only in Accra, perhaps, as a result of the expansion and boom conditions created by the war-time military operations, was there a sufficiently large urban white collar and commercial lower-middle class which was not tied in to the chiefly agro-commercial elites, and was therefore more independently vociferous on the typically 'nationalist' themes of Africanization and political reform. But the UGCC still at this time adequately articulated their economic grievances, although the Boycott Committee had brought in the street-traders. Only by recognizing the dominance of groups and interests other than those which may have characterized the CPP at a later date can one comprehend the evidence that the CPP—seen as a radical faction of the nationalist movement—was *supported* by many chiefs, rich farmers, local elite youth associations and the farmers' movement, as well as the urban workers, up until 1951. More accurately, the CPP supported these groups, and echoed the issues which they defined as important. The evidence simply cannot support a view of the CPP as simultaneously a broad-based aggregator of the range of demands described, and as 'really' being about the interests of aspirant businessmen with a grudge either against the local establishment or against the 'merchant princes' of the UGCC. The solution to the puzzle is very simple; after 1951, the CPP *did* become a party with distinctive, and narrower, interests—which is why it turned against the chiefs, the cocoa farmers and the trade unions who had set in motion the events which had so frightened the colonial government, and which in turn had enabled the CPP to appear as an answer to the crisis so caused.[80]

The government in 1948 therefore faced what appeared to be a united opposition of farmers, urban dwellers and chiefs; the chiefs, at the moment of test, had failed to provide what had been the core rationale of Indirect Rule: effective political leadership which kept the population loyal to the government. As is well known, the riots and the arrest of leading nationalists eventually frightened the chiefs back into more or less supporting the government. But the damage had been done. The crisis, and the government's response to it, had not been caused by nationalism, as such. But neither was it the product of a Whitehall plan. The initial response of the government was to hope that continuation of the reform of the NAs would work, and it was only the revealed unreliability and lack of cooperation of the chieftaincy which set them looking for alternatives.

The crisis of the colonial state between 1948 and 1951 was, then, very

80. After 1951 the CPP emerged as clearly associated with a modernizing, statist, and hence centralizing, ideology which brought it into conflict with chiefs, farmers and unions.

much a crisis of political institutions, a crisis which emphasized above all the 'externality' of the colonial state—its lack of dependence on and hence lack of deep support in the 'conditions of existence' of local society.[81] A 'revolutionary' opportunity was presented when social and economic unrest appeared at that moment to be dangerously out of control;[82] the administration itself was weak and divided, with low morale and extensive disillusion with policy;[83] its main and supposedly solid political support group in colonial society had been giving cause for concern since at least the hold-up of 1937–8, and had now shown itself to be a broken reed in the far more dangerous swollen-shoot and boycott affairs. The development of the economy under war-time controls had also made clear the role of the state in collecting the surplus of the cocoa economy and the chiefs themselves were more willing than ever to distance themselves from this state, following on the demands of Ashie Nikoi and other farmers' leaders for producers' control over the marketing of cocoa.[84] There was, therefore, a drawing apart of government and society which revealed to the chiefs (amongst other things) the extent to which they were, in effect, dispensable; if they had no political role to play, what was to stop them siding with the farmers in pursuit of their private economic interests? They did not need the state for that; on the contrary, the state now appeared as antagonist. It had never accepted their aspirations to become landlords, but instead had tried to force NA Treasuries on them. For its part, the colonial state was also forced by this open confrontation to see that what was *important* was to maintain its control over the cocoa economy; and *it* didn't need the chiefs for that.[85]

One of the most interesting revelations of the revisionist literature on decolonization, however, concerns the extent to which the highest official circles covered up the extent of the criticism of chiefs presented in the evidence to the Watson Commission, and to the Coussey Committee of 1949. Whilst both Committees received numerous attacks on Indirect Rule from junior staff, both the Gold Coast government in its official statement, the British Government in its 1948 White Paper on the Watson Commission, and Lord Hailey in his published work rejected—as late as 1951—any idea that the NAs were finished.[86] As the Chief Commissioner of the Colony, T. O. Mangin, wrote: 'Such untold damage can be done by

81. cf. Hyden, *op. cit.*, p. 16.
82. cf. T. Skocpol *States and Social Revolutions* (Cambridge, 1979), p. 29 and 'What makes peasants revolutionary?' *Comparative Politics* 14, 3, (1982), p. 373.
83. See R. J. A. R. Rathbone 'The Government of the Gold Coast after the 2nd World War', *African Affairs*, **67**, 268, 1968, where it is argued that the interregnum between Burns's departure in June 1947 and Arden-Clarke's arrival in August 1949 was crucial.
84. See Beckman, *op. cit.*, pp. 42 and 57–8.
85. cf. Lonsdale, 'States and Social Processes', pp. 192–3 on the new need to administer markets, and 'State and Peasantry', p. 107, on the state's fear of the cocoa farmers.
86. Stone, *op. cit.*, pp. 194 and 204.

enthusiastic officers trying to obtain quick results in native administration. Satisfactory results will only be obtained long after we have disappeared.'[87] Burns, the 'reforming' Governor who had secured an unofficial majority for Africans on the Legislative Council, continued to believe that this was no more than a price to be paid for greater central control of reformed NAs, a control necessary for the NAs to be turned into more effective agencies of social and economic development.[88] Not only did the 1951–1954 Constitution offer the chiefs a continuing role, but even the local government and local court reforms of 1952–8 did not bring about the destruction of chiefly power which might have been contemplated either in Whitehall or nationalist circles. The significance of a continuing official refusal to accept that Indirect Rule was finished is undeniable, for it underlay the continuing double-think in Gold Coast policy referred to earlier. In 1951, when power was actually being handed over to the CPP, the policy of reforming the NAs was still extant; the presence of the CPP government merely accelerated the implementation of the Coussey Commission's proposals for a new local government system in which the chiefs would continue to have a role. Was it a case of Whitehall dragging a reluctant colonial government into the decolonization era? In fact, it is easier to reconcile the caution of the Gold Coast government at certain points with the view from Whitehall than might be thought; the core of the contradiction is best explained as a local phenomenon. As argued above, the official caution of the Colonial Office is less surprising once the Cohen–Caine plans are placed in their 1940s context of reform of local government—the foundation for 'training in self-government'—rather than seen as components of a radical plan for decolonization. In 1947–8 it was agreed that the chiefs needed to be 'retained but democratized', not done away with.[89] The British Government's response to the Watson Commission 'closely reflected the views of the [Colonial] Office', according to Morgan.[90] But in the Gold Coast itself, the debate was already more polarized. 'Diehard' officers such as Mangin and Scott, the Colonial Secretary, played a key role during the crucial period 1947–9, when for many months (13 altogether) there was no Governor and, in between, a weak Governor, Creasy, whose appointment did not long survive the 1948 riots.[91] They continued to believe in the chiefs as viable representatives of an 'old order' and were perhaps ideologically incapable of seeing the very real links which

87. *ibid.*, p. 185.
88. cf. Hargreaves in Gifford and Louis, *Transfer of Power,*. pp. 124–8; see also A. Burns, *Colonial Civil Servant* (London, 1949), pp. 200–4.
89. Pearce, *Turning Point,* p. 153.
90. Morgan, *op. cit.*, Vol. 2, p. 14.
91. D. Rooney, *Sir Charles Arden-Clarke* (London, 1982), pp. 87–8; Rathbone, 'Government of the Gold Coast'.

existed between the chiefs, local elites, Youth Associations (and by extension the so-called 'educated' politicians) and the farmers' movement. It was their views which must have shaped the response of the Gold Coast government itself to the events of 1948. Arden-Clarke, on the contrary, once having established control of the government machine and removed some of the old guard, saw that winning back the chiefs from their flirtation with sedition was no longer a sufficient condition for progress. His initial aim was to incorporate the much broader elements involved in the post-war upheavals, whilst isolating what was then thought of as the hooligan element in the CPP; in this he was not significantly out of tune with Colonial Office policy, shorn of its utopian elements. The new Governor played a determining role, then, in liberating that climate of opinion in the Gold Coast which had already recognized the ultimate logic of the chiefs' weak and ambivalent position. The Colonial Office had a vague idea that the chiefs ought to be 'democratized'; they were thinking, in the old cliché, of 'bringing in the educated African'. On the ground it was more complex than that, as Arden-Clarke recognized, and it was this, perhaps, which accounted for his occasionally over-zealous determination after 1951 to make the world see that a CPP administration could work, and that it was the only feasible policy for the colony. Even then, he was opposed by elements in the Ashanti administration throughout the 1950s who still failed to see the significance of the *new* role which the chiefs had adopted as a consequence of throwing in their lot with popular anti-government forces.

Continuing ambivalence in Gold Coast policy towards the chiefs, particularly during 1947 to 1949, but continuing into the 1950s, had less to do with Whitehall reformism, therefore, than with a conflict in the administration dating back to the 1930s, a conflict deepened by the 1947–9 crises in both government–chief relationships and in the unstable direction of the administration itself. The ambivalence was highly significant in that it made the chiefs, at a crucial point, the victims of a 'false message' from the highest authorities. It was false because it represented the views of those in the administration whose days were numbered, and whose ideology was being undermined by the fudge which passed for a policy in the Colonial Office. Although the policy of 'democratizing the NAs' crumbled within a few years of attempts at its implementation, it was this, on top of the apparent stand of both Gold Coast and British governments which led the chiefs into their final trap. After 1948, they decided reluctantly to co-operate with the colonial government in order to head off the nationalists. It was an ambivalent kind of cooperation which at the local level was often contradicted by either support for or benevolent neutrality towards the nationalists. Too late they discovered that they were no longer needed—particularly when the nationalists achieved a successful dyarchy with the colonial government in the 1950s. Ironically enough, it was the die-hards' view of the chiefs which the CPP government found to be a convenient political myth for attacking those social forces which opposed it in the 1950s.

Conclusions

The essentially cautious and fragile nature of the Gold Coast administration meant that, once faced with a united and mass-based opposition to the core of the state's economic basis—its control over the cocoa economy—it quickly accommodated to maintain that base. There is no need to discover an imperial plan for self-government in 1943 or even 1948 to explain this shift. The accommodation, initially intended to reform the chieftaincy, turned into an unceremonious ditching of the NA system after 1952. The change was concealed at the time with false appearances of continuity with the past, the rhetoric of the new partnership with educated Africans notwithstanding. Deeper study of this crisis of the colonial state, focussing on how and why such a rapid and seemingly self-destructive course could have been taken, has been the main task of this article. Why did the necessary accommodation to the challenge from the cocoa industry take the form that it did? All policy up to then had pointed in the direction of consolidation of and, if necessary, concessions to, the power of the Native Authority elites, viewed as they were as the genuine representatives of the farming communities. It has been argued, however, that the post-1951 reversals, which were critical in that they destroyed the existing power structures without fulfilling the aim of consolidating a new local elite committed to working with the British, are inexplicable unless rooted in a set of more long-standing and fundamental characteristics of state–society relationships.

The apparatus of Indirect Rule, both juridical and political, embodied an essentially romantic conception of the chieftaincy's role in the various societies of the Gold Coast. The continuing consolidation of this concept in formal institutions and legal processes, well into the 1940s, sustained the ideology of chiefs as 'communal trustees' at the same time as the enforcement of the law prevented the emergence of an agrarian interest led by a powerful land-owning rural bourgeoisie. Some of the weaknesses and contradictions in the chiefs' position had always been recognized by colonial officials, and the solution was, by the 1940s, thought to lie in making the chieftaincy a more fully integrated part of the state machinery. Such a development was bound to emphasize—and deepen—the chiefs', and hence the state's, lack of an organic connection with emerging socio-economic structures in the countryside. This was especially so when the mercantilist nature of the state had been reinforced rather than modified by the impact of war-time produce controls and the setting up of the Cocoa Marketing Board. The weakness of the chiefs was only fully revealed when in the crises of the 1940s they appeared incapable of either leading or suppressing the various upheavals. If they had genuinely articulated an agrarian interest the colonial government would have had to have dealt with them; but in the eyes of the government they had merely revived an unholy alliance of brokers, moneylenders (the *bêtes noires* of all DCs) and local commercial interests riding on the backs of middle peasant grievances. In a rural economy dominated by export crops, the government saw itself as the best mediator of populist grievances vis-a-vis relationships with the world market. And with the CMB it felt that it had a powerful mechanism for simultaneously ensuring justice for the peasantry and meeting metropolitan needs. If the chiefs had cooperated earlier and more wholeheartedly with the state's political project they could have been used, as Hailey and other reformists intended, to outflank and suppress the urban nationalists' efforts to pose as the leaders of the rural malcontents. But here too, local realities had constantly undermined the formal and legal purposes of the NAs; resistance to both modern local government functions and the corporate conception of land responsibilities had made the NAs a byword for corruption and inefficiency in government circles. From the local point of view the NA chiefs remained powerful and (in Ashanti and EP), wealthy patrons, a neo-traditional elite, as they have been called;[92] but their abuses of governmental power and their economic roles vitiated their potential as popular leaders. The only weapon they did have was the ability to call on a reservoir of traditional loyalties and sentiments—a power used later to good effect in Ashanti in particular, when the chiefs threw in their lot with the agro-commercial interests they had supported in 1938 and 1948, but this time in an unambiguously anti-government mood.

Overall, however, it is not surprising that this set of relationships between the state and its seemingly indispensable collaborating elites in local society crumbled rapidly in the crises of 1945 to 1950. The challenges coming from both rural and urban groups did force an accommodation or, at least, an attempt to maintain the momentum of reform. It was the chiefs who failed the goals set up by those reforms. The nationalists—UGCC, and then CPP—did not cause either the upheavals or the failure of NA reforms. But they did benefit in 1951, insofar as colonial government came to see them as a 'solution'—a more amenable and perhaps more legitimate group than the chieftaincy. But because of their lack of a class basis in rural society, the nationalists became very quickly a co-opted group, reproducing the externality of the colonial state. To these structural weaknesses of the colonial state were added the messages from the Colonial Office reformers, and the situational weaknesses of the

92. Kilson in Gann and Duignan, *op. cit.*, p. 374.

DECOLONIZATION IN THE GOLD COAST 105

period such as disunity and low morale within the administration. Thus in spite of the attempt to maintain a facade of continuity in the 1950s, the search for a new, more secure and more acceptable form of colonial rule was already on by the end of the 1940s. That it failed (insofar as early independence can be seen as 'not what was intended' in 1947) was, it may be argued, very largely a product of the unchanged 'externality' of the state from local society. The nationalists were very much the weak last—or unfinished?—act of the play, not the first. They inherited, with their 'statist' aspirations, this weak state with its potential for conflict with the rural economy yet to come; a state which had not succeeded in moving beyond a mercantilist form of taxation to a more organic relationship with the local economy, and which had left substantial 'unfinished business' in the crucial area of land law and tenure.[93] The imperial dimension as an explanatory factor only takes on its critical significance in the mid-1950s, with the economic failure of the 'new empire' and the rediscovery in the metropole of convenient political ideologies derived from the old Dominions' experiences.

93. As early as 1926 the Ormsby Gore report, whilst recognizing the political need to support the chieftaincy, had pointed out the fundamental confusions caused by the preservation of 'customary' land law, and recommended comprehensive reform in the shape of land courts, registration and legislation. In 1951, Hailey was still recommending the same measures. Nothing was ever done. See Kay *op. cit.*, pp. 212–4; Hailey *op. cit.* (1951) p. 223 and *Part IV*, p. 57.

[15]

School Wars: Church, State, and the Death of the Congo

by PATRICK M. BOYLE*

Two conventions tend to shape appraisals of the Belgian Congo and the manner of its decolonisation. The first describes the colonial power structure as an alliance of state, church, and large corporations.[1] This trinity was 'not only...a virtually seamless web', writes Crawford Young, 'but each component, in its area of activity, was without peer in Africa in the magnitude of its impact'.[2] The second convention typically portrays decolonisation as tumultuous, chaotic, bungled, or simply 'gone awry'.[3] Indeed, the mutiny and secession movements that followed hard upon the proclamation in June 1960 of the Republic of the Congo (renamed Zaïre in October 1971) resulted in the rapid internationalisation of responses to them, thereby demonstrating the fragility of domestic political arrangements.

However convenient, conventions such as these – of seamless colonial rule and chaotic decolonisation – prove inadequate when applied to specific dimensions of the political realities they seek to characterise. This is especially true when new research seeks to understand the impact of colonial practices on contemporary African realities.[4] This article argues that the link between late colonial church–state relations and the relatively smooth decolonisation of the education sector suggests a different political analysis of the period than these conventions lead us to expect.

Two interrelated claims comprise the argument. First, struggles between church and state for control over the direction of education demonstrate that this wing of the triple alliance was much weaker than has been presumed.[5] The so-called 'school wars' in the 1950s actually

---

* Assistant Professor of Political Science, Loyola University Chicago, Illinois.

[1] Kita Kyankenge Masandi, *Colonisation et enseignement: cas du Zaïre avant 1960* (Bukavu, 1982), p. 27. [2] Crawford Young, *Politics in the Congo* (Princeton, NJ, 1965), p. 10.

[3] J. D. Hargreaves, *Decolonization in Africa* (London and New York, 1988), pp. 179–83.

[4] Crawford Young, *The African Colonial State in Comparative Perspective* (New Haven and London, 1994).

[5] Nzongola-Ntalaja, 'National Liberation and Class Struggle in Zaïre', in *Contemporary Marxism* (San Francisco), 6, 1983, p. 61.

452   PATRICK M. BOYLE

threatened to destroy the colonial web, even if specific incidents did not
by themselves end the alliance. Second, these same conflicts generated
changes in colonial policy such that the 1960 move to 'independence
education', unlike transitions in other administrative and political
sectors, occurred with relative ease. This claim underscores views of
decolonisation as a fundamentally uneven process, varying according
to the sector.[6]

Part I presents the development of collaborative relations between
church and state in education before 1939, and the serious differences
that surfaced after World War II over which kinds of schools to
promote in the colony. Part II re-examines a number of such conflicts
in the 1950s. Specifically, when the newly appointed Minister of
Colonies in the *Parti libéral belge* (PLB) and *Parti socialist belge* (PSB)
coalition Government in Brussels challenged Roman Catholic predominance in the education sector in 1954, a church–state entente
foundered and then collapsed. The ensuing crisis drew local leaders
into political activities which hastened the death of the Congo, and
deeply divided colonists among themselves.

Part III outlines the implications of the ensuing unprecedented
scrutiny of the educational services provided by the church. When
combined with international pressures for reform and growing demands
from the indigenous population, the crisis stripped the official colonial
policy of 'adapted' education of its political acceptability, and set the
stage during the last five years of the colonial period for the
development of one of sub-Saharan Africa's most fully elaborated post-
independence élite school systems.

In contrast to views stressing the colonial unity of church and state,
therefore, this article argues for recognition of the real disintegration of
that wing of the colonial alliance.[7] But that is not all. The radical re-
orientation of education policy that has been either overlooked by
scholars, or dismissed by them as a defunct colonial power's eleventh-
hour posturing, actually anticipated the sector's transition to independence and thus prepared a smooth passage in the early 1960s.
The priorities arising from the conflict, including the mandate for the

---

[6] Crawford Young and Thomas Turner make this point in *The Rise and Decline of the Zaïrian State*
(Madison, WI, 1985).

[7] Adrian Hastings views the school conflicts as inconsequential, because 'in practice in the eyes
of Africans the union of church and state was probably little impaired'. *A History of African
Christianity, 1950–1975* (Cambridge, 1979), p. 19.

rapid development of a system of élite education based on Belgian models, established a strikingly prominent place for the sector in the post-colonial era, despite the contentious environment in which they were implemented.[8]

I. MISSIONS, STATE, AND EDUCATION, 1880–1954

Education for the Congolese was rarely the focus of political or social conflict in the colony or in Belgium before 1946. Partly through their efforts on behalf of a nascent education sector, colonial agents, missionaries, and congregations helped to forge key political relationships in the colony, to create and then solidify administrative structures in both church and state, and to set the orientations for colonial social policy. Not surprisingly, it was precisely the close collaboration in education between missionaries and administrators, and their divergent views about how and when to form an indigenous élite, that eventually became the focus of late colonial conflicts. But relations between the missions and the colony's Belgian rulers, despite their difficult beginnings, had steadily improved until the 1950s.

Léopold II's *État indépendant du Congo* (EIC) was marked by considerable church–state conflict. At issue was the respective status of Catholic and Protestant missionaries in the territory, as well as the practice among EIC agents of placing Congolese children in military camps called *colonies scolaires*.[9] Roman Catholic missionaries won a major rôle in Léopold II's *mission civilisatrice* as a result of the 1906 Concordat between the Vatican and the King that not only responded indirectly to charges levelled against the kind of treatment many were receiving at the hands of Léopold's agents, but also established the basis for subsequent church–state relations.

The 1906 Concordat gave administrative protection and a grant of land for each mission station established in the interior by the Catholics. In so doing it also contributed to their 'struggle against English and American protestant missionaries',[10] effectively excluding

---

[8] See Patrick M. Boyle, 'The Politics of Education in Zaïre', Ph.D. dissertation, Princeton University, 1991.

[9] Mukadi Luaba Nkamba, 'Aperçu historique de l'enseignement au Zaïre, 1880–1960', in *Zaïre-Afrique* (Kinshasa), 134, April 1979, p. 199. Mostly English-speaking missionaries from Britain and the United States reported abuses by Léopold's agents, and seem to have provoked the King's anger against foreign (non-Belgian) operatives in the territory. See Richard Dodson, 'Congo–Léopoldville', in David G. Scanlon (ed.), *Church, State, and Education in Africa* (New York, 1966), p. 67.

[10] Barbara Yates, 'The Triumph and Failure of Mission Vocational Education in Zaïre, 1879–1908', in *Comparative Education Review* (Chicago), 20, 2, June 1976, p. 200.

454 PATRICK M. BOYLE

them from 'national missions', defined as those established by Catholic religious congregations based in Belgium. Such a pro-church policy continued long after Belgium annexed the EIC in 1908: the state encouraged Catholics in the Congo and created conditions favouring the spread of their missions, as well as any activities associated with them. However, Protestants also created *écoles libres* (private schools) aimed at evangelisation and education, albeit placing particular emphasis on basic literacy and bible training.[11] Colonial administration reports claim that over 100,000 indigenous children were receiving rudimentary instruction by the early 1920s in either Protestant or Catholic schools.[12]

The 1922–4 educational commission set up by the Minister of Colonies, Louis Franck, recommended that administrators collaborate with the missions in standardising a programme of education genuinely 'adapted to the rural milieu', that used African languages for instruction, stressed agricultural practices, and included education for girls.[13] The Belgians made 'adapted' education one of the defining characteristics of 'national mission' *écoles libres*, as well as state financing for their construction and maintenance.[14] Although such legislation brought most Catholic schools under the nominal control of the colonial administration, in effect, it gave the Catholic missions what René Lemarchand termed a 'semi-official role that allowed them to extend their action far beyond the limits of evangelization'.[15] Indeed, according to Richard Dodson, Belgian missionaries considered state assistance 'at first as a favor, then as common sense, and finally as an obligation of the Government'.[16]

Notably absent from educational reforms during the 1920s was any provision for an 'élite track', an idea recommended in a study of education in Africa conducted by the Protestant-supported Phelps–Stokes Fund.[17] The frequently repeated preference for giving the indigenous population moral rather than academic instruction reflected

[11] Barbara Yates, 'Knowledge Brokers: books and publishers in early colonial Zaïre', in *History in Africa* (Waltham, MA), 14, 1987, pp. 311–40.

[12] Albert DeJaeger, 'De Protestanche Zendingen in Kongo', in *Congo* (Brussels), 2, 4, April 1921, pp. 580–1, and 'Les Missions catholiques au Congo belge', in ibid. 2, 3, August 1921, p. 413.

[13] Congo belge, *Projet de l'enseignement libre au Congo belge avec le concours des sociétés de missions nationales* (Brussels, 1925).

[14] Bureau de l'enseignement catholique, *Où en est l'enseignement au Congo?* (Léopoldville, 1960), pp. 8 and 31.

[15] René Lemarchand, *Political Awakening in the Belgian Congo: the politics of fragmentation* (Berkeley and Los Angeles, 1964), p. 125.   [16] Dodson, loc. cit. p. 69.

[17] Thomas Jesse Jones (ed.), *Education in Africa* (New York, 1922). See Barbara Yates, 'Comparative Education and the Third World: the nineteenth century revisited', in *Comparative Education Review*, 28, 4, 1984, p. 452.

a common concern that uprooted rural dwellers, the *déracinés*, congregating in urban and mining centres, would become violent.[18] Colonial assemblies only slightly muted growing fears that training indigenous personnel would 'put colonials at their mercy and lead to insurrection'.[19]

None the less, even before the conflicts of the 1950s, certain colonial schools trained a small but 'non-traditional' élite, the first generation of which comprised soldiers, preacher-teachers, and artisans.[20] Later, administrative clerks and medical assistants joined their ranks, along with an important cadre of indigenous clergy – arguably at the top of the modern social hierarchy. During World War II, many of these *évolués* were able to exercise responsibilities previously reserved for colonial officials. Their insistent demands for higher education,[21] however, may have played a smaller rôle in stimulating post-war change and conflict in the colony than the arrival of Belgian expatriates who demanded schools for their children.[22] The Minister of Colonies during 1946–7, Robert Godding, a PLB member in a post-war PSB coalition, sought to respond by supporting the creation of three 'lay' or secularist schools for European children.

Although Godding drew fire from Catholics for supporting non-religious education, his policy embodied the Government's new commitment to fashion Belgium – and its colony – into a modern welfare state. Such a new perspective as well as growing *évolué* discontent and newly arrived expatriates, created pressure to extend health and education services for the African population. Thus, in 1946 the state started subsidising up to half the operating costs of Catholic schools in urban centres.[23] In addition, Godding advocated the formation of an indigenous élite to further the aspirations of low-level cadres and aid economic development. His assimilationist approach called for expansion of secondary and higher education opportunities for the African population, a view that enjoyed support among certain

[18] 'Rapport de la Commission pour l'étude du problème de la main-d'oeuvre au Congo belge (Suite)', in *Congo*, 2, 1, June 1925, p. 6.
[19] Congrès colonial national, *Compte rendu des séances. Bruxelles 18–20 décembre 1920* (Brussels, 1921), pp. 123 and 331.
[20] Barbara Yates, 'Educating Congolese Abroad: an historical note on African elites', in *International Journal of African Historical Studies* (New York), 14, 1, 1981, p. 63.
[21] See Léon Georges Ilunga, 'L'Enseignement dans le Congo de demain', in *La Voix du congolais* (Léopoldville), 5, 1945, p. 175.
[22] See 'Nos écoles', in *L'Essor du Congo* (Elisabethville), 1 December 1942. The non-African population increased from 18,683 to 36,080 in 1954, surpassing 100,000 expatriates by 1958. Office de l'information et des relations publiques pour le Congo belge et le Ruanda-Urundi, *Belgian Congo* (Brussels, 1960), Vol. 2, p. 12.
[23] Bureau de l'enseignement catholique, op. cit. p. 31.

456   PATRICK M. BOYLE

influential missionary and administration authorities in the colonial capital, but not always among expatriates or rural missionaries.[24] The return to power in 1948 of the Belgian *Parti social chrétien* (PSC), known as the *Parti catholique* until 1946, blunted Godding's initiative.

Although the PSC's *Plan décennal* for economic and social development in the Congo only opened the door to élite education, it drew disparate programmes into a single, more amply funded system and committed the Belgian state to 'adapted' education on a mass scale.[25] Spending on the sector more than tripled from 1949 to 1950.[26] In exchange for a reduction in their autonomy over curriculum, missionary groups won re-affirmation of the principle of teaching indigenous languages, added French to certain programmes, and received larger school subsidies (extended to the Protestant network in 1948).[27] While opportunities grew almost exclusively at the primary level, a commitment to expand élite education had become part of Belgium's official plans for development.

Post-war proposals for the creation of a colonial university significantly raised the political stakes for the PSC which, in the face of vociferous PLB and PSB opposition, had to contend with the overlapping demands of deeply divided linguistic, cultural, and religious elements in Belgian society. The absence of any budgetary provision in the 1948 *Plan décennal* for higher education suggests a governmental lack of commitment.[28] Not surprisingly, pressures mounted when faculty from the Université de Louvain and Belgian Jesuits combined professional institutes for medical and agricultural assistants in 1947 to form the *Centre universitaire congolaise Lovanium* (CUCL) at Kisantu, and added a division for commercial, legal, and administrative education. The CUCL's promotional literature argued that only a university-trained African élite could check the political

---

[24] Chambre des représentants, *Rapport sur l'administration de la colonie du Congo belge pendant les années 1945 et 1946* (Brussels, 1948), p. 147. Supporters included André Ryckmans, former Governor-General (1934–46), missionaries in the *Conseil colonial*, bishops in the *Conseil des Ordinaires du Congo*, and some local newspapers. See 'L'Enseignement supérieur pour les indigènes du Congo', in *Le Courrier d'Afrique* (Léopoldville), 18 June 1946, p. 1. Guy Mosmans discusses opposition to élite formation in 'Les Impératifs de l'action missionaire en Afrique belge', in *La Revue nouvelle* (Brussels), 24, 7–8, July–August 1956, p. 15.

[25] Ministère des colonies, *Plan décennal pour le développement économique et social au Congo belge* (Brussels, 1949), pp. 62–3 and 67.

[26] Spending on education rose from 237,396,000 Belgian francs in 1949 to 961,991,000 in 1950. Dodson, loc. cit. p. 83.

[27] The churches successfully argued that in the 1940s their schools had saved the state 6,000 million Belgian francs. *Plan décennal*, p. 63.

[28] In contrast, the British Colonial Office contemplated higher education expenditures in 1943. Hargreaves, op. cit. pp. 63 and 95.

advance and ambitions of semi-intellectual *évolués*.[29] This reasoning, however, did little to create enthusiasm from colonial administrators or comfort expatriates who saw in the creation of a university the seed-bed of revolution and insurrection. Moreover, the PSC's weakness hindered it from ever translating its public support for CULC into substantial state funding for construction.[30]

II. *LA LUTTE SCOLAIRE*

The decade of the 1950s opened with bright prospects for educational development in the Belgian Congo. Representatives of the missions and the administration completed the 1948 reforms of primary and secondary school programmes and structures by signing a Convention in 1952 that regulated the operation of all subsidised schools. Neither internal conflicts over the management and rural location of CULC nor lack of financial support from Brussels deterred Catholic educators from opening *L'Université Lovanium* near Léopoldville in 1954.[31] These two developments and the creation of the *Bureau pour l'éducation catholique* (BEC) in 1951 clearly enhanced the Catholic position in an expanding educational system managed almost entirely by missionaries.

News of secret negotiations in 1953 between the PSC and the Vatican to replace the 1906 Concordat made the topic of colonial education a volatile political issue in Belgium. The new treaty, signed in December 1953 by the Belgian Minister of Foreign Affairs and a Vatican representative, fixed fresh financial terms for church–state relations, and reduced the authority of the Catholics in Belgium over the administration of the church in the Congo.

If the treaty met the new demands of a rapidly growing colonial church, it none the less sparked controversy in Belgium, not least since the PSC's desperate attempt to secure parliamentary approval just before the elections gave opposition party members powerful campaign material. They argued that most of the treaty's provisions could be accomplished unilaterally or were already provided for in the law, that it gave special privileges to the Catholic church, which might have legal grounds for demanding that salaries of missionary school personnel be raised to the much higher levels paid in the state network.

---

[29] Marvin D. Markowitz, *Cross and Sword. The Political Role of Christian Missions in the Belgian Congo, 1908–1960* (Stanford, CA, 1973), p. 71.   [30] Ibid. p. 72.
[31] Romain Yakemtchouk, *L'Université Louvanium et sa faculté de théologie. L'action éducative de l'Université Catholique de Louvain en Afrique Centrale* (Chastre, Belgium, 1983), pp. 35–7.

458   PATRICK M. BOYLE

PSC support for the treaty only strengthened opposition to it, and diminished room for political compromise or accommodation with a powerful Liberal Party minority. Although being approved by the lower house in a vote taken before the April 1954 elections, the treaty never came to the Senate for ratification under the Socialist–Liberal coalition that replaced the PSC Government.[32]

The treaty issue fed an already acrimonious *guerre scolaire* in Belgium over subsidies to parochial schools. Pitched and even vituperative parliamentary battles over their administration and funding had been commonplace in Europe, particularly in France and Belgium, since the nineteenth century.[33] But the Congo, despite its legal and sentimental status in Brussels as the 'tenth Belgian province', had escaped such bitter struggles.[34] Thus, the *lutte scolaire* was unique, not only because it focused on educational policy appropriate for a colony, but also because it sowed mistrust among three groups: the colonial administration, the missionaries, and the population. At a crucially important moment for the Congo's future, the *lutte scolaire* set church against state in an unprecedented conflict over colonial social policy.

Auguste Buisseret, the new Minister of Colonies (1954–8), opened his first press conference with statements about the priority he intended to give to education, and to the insistent demands in the Congo for the creation of 'non-missionary' schools. Suggesting that missionaries had 'scant competence to organize and teach all the Congolese want to learn', and that they may well have over-extended themselves in the educational sphere, Buisseret articulated his intention to challenge their predominance in education because it raised 'liberty of conscience' issues.[35] He also proposed a government review of the activities and degree-granting process at the Catholic-sponsored Lovanium University, reminding his audience that its budget was now almost entirely subsidised by the state.

Such comments reflected the perspective of a Government that was quite 'anxious to diminish the clerical appearance of its colonial system'.[36] The parliamentary commission sent to evaluate mission schools in the Congo enumerated many deficiencies: both Congolese

---

[32] Markowitz, op. cit. pp. 78–9.

[33] Vernon Mallinson, *Power and Politics in Belgian Education, 1815 to 1961* (London, 1963).

[34] André Schöller, *Congo, 1959–1960: mission au Katanga. Intérim à Léopoldville* (Brussels, 1982), p. 218.

[35] See Buisseret's comments in 'Belgium's Colonial Policy', in *The Belgian Congo Today* (Brussels), 3, October 1954, pp. 126–7. Expatriate demands for state-operated secular schools seem also to have figured in his priorities. Markowitz, op. cit. pp. 77 and 83.

[36] Hastings, op. cit. p. 19.

and Belgian teachers lacked training; some religious congregations were making profits from the sale of work done by their students in state subsidised technical schools; students were directed towards academic or seminary programmes to the neglect of technical education; and the missions actually saved the state many fewer billions of francs than they had claimed earlier.[37] In short, the report suggested that missionary education was an economic and political liability: it cut into the sales of expatriate entrepreneurs, and its literary and humanist character was doing more to develop political agitators than to supply industry with skilled labour.[38]

The commission proposed as an antidote the expansion of 'lay' or secular primary and secondary schools in urban and rural areas.[39] Except for military institutions run by the *Forces publique,* secular education was practically inaccessible to the Congolese before 1954. Many greeted the news of a possible expansion of the network of official state schools with enthusiasm, especially in urban settings where the socio-economic benefits of an education were highest. The commission set a goal: make available to the Congolese exactly the same kind of schools created for expatriate children in 1946, including a standard Belgian curriculum and instruction given in French.

The report was leaked to the public before being submitted for parliamentary approval. More disturbing to Catholics than proposals for lay schools or criticisms of their own was the provocative description of the nature of missionary activity:

It is not without reason that since the disappearance of ancient Paraguay, some consider the Congo to be the one remaining theocratic state. Incontestably, on both the religious and political level at least, the missionary deals with people as a sovereign with his vassals; respected by some, feared by others, but always obeyed, always making the rules in a way that brings to mind... his own narrow self-interest [rather] than the greater interest of the population as a whole.[40]

The attempt to discredit the missionary, to portray his behaviour as something less than selfless in the service of a grand colonial 'civilising mission', struck at the heart of the Catholic church's self-understanding of its ministry.

Reaction to the report was swift and vehement. Critics questioned the quality of data collected in haste by persons mostly unfamiliar with the colony, and allied with its most determined opponents. Church

[37] Ministère des colonies, *Mission pédagogique Coulon-Deheyn-Renson: la réforme de l'enseignement* (Brussels, 1954).   [38] Markowitz, op. cit. pp. 84–5.
[39] *Mission pédagogique*, p. 230.   [40] Ibid. p. 207, my translation.

460   PATRICK M. BOYLE

authorities, missionaries, and members of the PSC reacted strongly to what they saw as thinly veiled attacks on Catholicism by anti-clerical elements in the Government.[41] If in Belgium the 'report became a domestic issue on par with the *guerre scolaire*', in the colony it stirred missionary fears that years of Catholic work in education would be undone through the laicisation and secularisation of schools.[42] Some bishops, like Félix Scalis of Léopoldville, did not oppose the idea of state-sponsored education, but wanted to safeguard the church's right to have schools.[43]

Polemicists exchanged recriminations over the question that implicated them all: who was the more responsible for hindering the emancipation of the Congolese? Was it backward missionaries who opposed upgrading school programmes, or was it the Government that cut budgets and developed norms that stifled missionary efforts to open new schools?

To the dismay of a traditionally Catholic staff in the colonial administration, Buisseret appointed anti-clericals to posts with supervisory power over mission schools.[44] They began to shift allocations in favour of governmental projects, such as the construction of state-sponsored schools and the creation of a state university at Lubumbashi. Although Buisseret generally supported the provision of education in the colony at all levels, the sudden creation of a second university drew him into controversy over Belgium's policy of prohibiting the Congolese from studying abroad.[45]

In late 1954, the colonial administration announced that it would have to reduce subsidies for African teacher salaries and for boarding school operations, and end those for first-level primary education programmes for boys. This provoked the Catholic episcopacy in the Congo to issue an ultimatum. The Governor-General, Léon Pétillon, was told that implementation of the measures would force bishops to close all Catholic schools because such measures clearly violated the 1952 Convention.[46] The Minister of Colonies met with Pétillon and episcopal representatives to express Belgium's willingness to reconsider its position, and to offer a communiqué to that effect. But after the bishops had rejected the text as too vague, Buisseret capitulated by

[41] Joseph Van Wing, *Objectivité 'sur mesure'* (Brussels, 1955).
[42] Markowitz, op. cit. p. 86.   [43] Ibid.
[44] A. A. J. Van Bilsen, 'Quatre années de politique congolaise', in *La Revue Nouvelle*, 27, 1958, p. 462.   [45] See *The Belgian Congo Today*, op. cit. and Markowitz, op. cit. pp. 92–3.
[46] Cinquième conférence plénière des ordinaires du Congo belge et du Ruanda-Urundi, *Compte rendu des séances. Textes et documents* (Léopoldville, 1956), p. 58.

reaffirming the Government's strict adherence to the 1952 Convention, pledging continuation of subsidies, and promising 'a real equity between government and mission education'.[47]

The acrimonious exchanges through which the Catholic bishops in the Congo forced Buisseret to change course introduced real antagonisms into church–state negotiations over many dimensions of colonial education policy.[48] Eventually a kind of uneasy truce ensued when Buisseret and the president of the *Bureau de l'éducation catholique*, Abbé Moermans, agreed that the three main providers of schools in the Congo should be subsidised according to a new formula: Protestants would receive 10 per cent, as against 45 per cent for both Catholic and official state networks.[49]

Protestants generally resisted involvement in this 'Belgian' political and religious conflict. Some of them supported the creation of state schools (with an option for religious education), because these would relieve them of demands from their adherents for more and better facilities, and would provide the churches with the chance to sell some buildings to the colonial administration for reconversion into state schools. Protestants expressed surprise at the Moermans–Buisseret agreement on subsidies and objected to the Government's failure to consult them. Characteristically, however, they demanded only to be included in future negotiations.[50] Nor were they enthusiastic about state support for the Catholic-sponsored Lovanium University. Wary of associating themselves with the project for a state university at Lubumbashi because they feared that this would be given an anti-religious orientation by its proponents, they waited until 1963 to open a Protestant university at Kisangani in the hope that it would be 'neither financially nor academically dependent on any one sector of national or international politics or confessional opinion'.[51]

III. IMPLICATIONS OF *LA LUTTE SCOLAIRE*

Given the 'intimate link between Belgian domestic politics and colonial policy and practice',[52] the *lutte scolaire* demonstrated the danger of bringing a controversy between Europeans into the colony. Despite its origins in the Belgian *guerre scolaire*, the Congo's *lutte scolaire*,

---

[47] Markowitz, op. cit. p. 101.

[48] For example, Buisseret required the missions to issue public bids for the construction of new schools, even in remote areas. Ibid.   [49] Cinquième conférence, op. cit. p. 61.

[50] When not choosing to avoid confrontation with state officials, Protestants tended to lend *post-facto* support to Catholic initiatives. Markowitz, op. cit. p. 102.

[51] Dodson, loc. cit. p. 90.   [52] Yates 'Educating Congolese Abroad', p. 37.

462   PATRICK M. BOYLE

because of its unique setting and timing, had far-reaching consequences. First, the charges and counter-charges tore apart a previously collaborative church–state relationship. Church supporters reminded all concerned of the years they had laboured to provide education in remote areas without state support, while the Government blamed missionaries for low school standards, untrained teachers, and inadequate facilities. At the heart of the conflict were questions that could no longer be avoided: How well were the Congolese being prepared to assume positions of responsibility within and for the colony? What kind of social and economic promotion was available to the inhabitants as a result of their education? More was at stake than the relative merits of 'élite' over 'adapted' education.[53]

Caught in a contentious struggle, both sides tried to articulate and defend the magnitude of their efforts to help the indigenous population. Since the founding of the United Nations, the Belgian Government had been in a defensive posture over colonial policy, generally. Education was a particularly sensitive issue because much early UN criticism focused on the lack of intellectual formation for the Congolese.[54] The Catholics, who had worked so hard to develop an indigenous church, had everything to lose and much to gain from the way their activities were presented to the local inhabitants, to Belgian donors, and to the outside world. Therefore, the objective that had previously united church and state – the defence of colonial policy and practice – now threatened to drive these two members of the colonial alliance apart. Indeed, in 1956, Guy Mosmans, later to become secretary of the Congolese episcopacy, publicly advocated the complete disassociation of the Catholic church from the colonial administration and its policies.[55] As the prospects for a colonial future dimmed, church workers attached themselves more closely to local populations, and to certain nationalist movements.

Second, the conflict encouraged the Congolese to think more seriously about their own welfare and future. Unlike previous issues of social policy, where administrators and missionaries argued for their respective interpretations of the needs and desires of the population, this conflict saw them appeal directly to the population. Buisseret

[53] Gaetan Feltz, 'Une Introduction à l'histoire de l'enseignement en Afrique Central (XIXe–XXe siècles): idéologies, pouvoirs et sociétés', in *Bulletin de l'Institut historique belge de Rome* (Brussels and Rome), 51, 1981, p. 393.

[54] Part of Belgium's response to international pressure was the use of English language media to publicise progressive colonial policy. See, for example, Pierre Ryckmans's speech, 'Belgium and the UNO', in *The Belgian Congo Today*, 2, 2, April 1953, pp. 45–51.

[55] Mosmans, loc. cit. p. 14.

apparently failed to understand that the anti-clericalism encouraged by his attack on the missionaries, was, in reality, anti-colonialism and nationalism.[56] By taking the case for a particular form of colonial education to the people, whether through the Belgian parliament or media, or through the colonial press and pulpit, Belgians, at first unwittingly, and then very consciously, drew the Congolese into the fray.[57] Future Prime Minister Patrice Lumumba, writing in 1956 in defence of Buisseret, argued that the school wars were used by some as propaganda 'to stir up indigenous populations – particularly in *évolué* circles – against the government in power'.[58]

Indeed, the conflict politicised more Congolese as missionaries and government officials sought local support for their positions. For the first time many discovered the depths of cleavages in Belgian society and the possibilities that these offered. According to Jean Stengers:

[The Congolese] learned a lesson from all this: if the Europeans were appealing to them, this meant that they constituted a political force in the eyes of the Europeans themselves. Their self-confidence and belief in their own capabilities emerged stronger from this battle.[59]

To supporters of the colonial status, the administration's loss of support from the church could not have come at a worse time – just when they were floating a new scheme to 'integrate' the metropole and the colony in a 'belgo-congolese community'.[60] The inhabitants, however, were beginning to advance specific, even antithetical demands, like political independence. Therefore, the *lutte scolaire* gave them the perfect opportunity not only to participate in Belgium's reassessment of the colonial relationship, but also to begin to find their own version of the nationalism sweeping the continent.

The 1956 publication of Van Bilsen's plan for the timing of independence focused the debate among *évolués* concerning the future of the colony.[61] In an atmosphere permeated with church–state tension, young Congolese articulated a nationalist manifesto in the

---

[56] Van Bilsen, loc. cit. p. 466.

[57] See, for example, Albert de Vleeschauwer's remarks in *Annales parliamentaires: Chambre des représentants* (Brussels), 1954, p. 115; Markowitz, op. cit. pp. 70 and 90; and the editorial, 'Controverse sur l'enseignement au Congo', in *La Voix du congolais* (Léopoldville), 107, February 1955, pp. 204–5.

[58] Patrice Lumumba, *Le Congo – terre d'avenir – est-il menacé?* (Brussels, 1961), p. 189.

[59] Jean Stengers, 'Precipitous Decolonization: the case of the Belgian Congo', in Prosser Gifford and Wm. Roger Louis (eds.), *The Transfer of Power in Africa: decolonization, 1940–1960* (New Haven and London, 1982), p. 322.

[60] Zala L. N'Kanza, *Les Origines sociales du sous-développement politique au Congo belge* (Kinshasa, 1985), p. 282.

[61] A. A. J. Van Bilsen, 'Plan de trente ans pour l'émancipation de l'Afrique belge', in *Dossiers de l'action sociale catholique* (Brussels), February 1956.

464   PATRICK M. BOYLE

journal *Conscience africaine* (Léopoldville). Only a few supporters of colonialism could fathom the significance of the document, much less the speed with which pressure was building for political independence.[62] In retrospect, Pétillon recognised the importance of the *lutte scolaire* as the beginning of the end. Acknowledging the extent to which the controversy revealed deep divisions between Belgians and aroused the political interests of the Congolese, the former Governor-General noted that it was in the wake of the *lutte scolaire* that the 'Congo belge – presque sans rémission, avançait vers sa perte'.[63]

If the controversy played some rôle in destroying the unstable façade of Belgian colonialism, it was surely a catalyst for growth in education. The Congolese realised that there was much to gain from the struggle. Although they were at first astonished to see the church and state at odds, they soon came to support the side which seemed to offer the greatest advantages,[64] and the competition unleashed between the networks benefited thousands of students. State spending on education rose from 10 to 15 per cent of the ordinary colonial budget between 1954 and independence in 1960, largely in order to create 67 new state schools – including primary (47), teacher assistant (6), mixed race (4), professional secondary (3) – as well as a university at Lubumbashi.[65] Students in state schools numbered 50,000 by the end of the decade, albeit only 3 per cent of the Congo's total. Some 1,011,800 students were enrolled in the Catholic network, as against 128,000 in Protestant schools.[66]

The scholastic conflict highlighted the paternalistic character of a system designed primarily to provide schools in rural areas, and discredited the earlier policy goal of raising all levels of education in the colony in gradual steps. A final set of reforms during 1958–9 adopted élite education as the general standard, and aligned colonial programmes with those in Belgium. These actions secured Belgian parliamentary recognition of the equivalency of academic degrees.[67]

Among the charges frequently levelled against late colonial policies were the reactionary and 'eleventh hour' character of preparations for independence. Looked at from the perspective of the minimal political

[62] Zala N'Kanza, op. cit. pp. 282–3.

[63] Léon A. Pétillon, *Récit. Congo, 1929–1958* (Brussels, 1985), pp. 324 and 329.

[64] Ibid. p. 329.   [65] Feltz, loc. cit. p. 392.

[66] William M. Rideout, Jr., David N. Wilson, and M. Crawford Young, *Survey of Education in the Democratic Republic of the Congo* (Washington, DC, 1969), American Council on Education, Overseas Liaison Committee, p. 14.

[67] Kazadi-Mwepu, 'Le Point sur les réformes de l'enseignement au Zaïre', in *Problèmes sociaux zaïrois* (Lubumbashi), 128–9, 1985, p. 107.

requirements for a timely and smooth transfer of power, and for the creation of a well-trained Congolese cadre in the public and private sectors, Belgian colonialism was a singular failure. However, the record is more nuanced from the standpoint of the developing school system, which benefited from being caught between two objectives: that of adapting the curriculum to what authorities believed were the primary needs of a rural population, and that of assimilating the Congolese to Belgian models of education in order to create an élite. But in 1954 the end of colonialism was not in sight, nor, when it did come to be debated, was there any anticipation of independence in so short a time.

Despite imbalances, Congo's educational record compares favourably with that of other African countries simultaneously reaching independence. In all cases the school systems were imbalanced because enrolments were concentrated at the initial years of primary education, and among males from urban centres in the most economically developed regions. A few African states distinguished themselves for their cadre of pre-independence college graduates. But even on this score, it ought to be remembered that the first university in Central Africa had been started in the Congo, where 763 students were enrolled in 1959, with 445 highly trained technicians having earlier 'graduated' from specialised institutes.[68]

Most students, however, were enrolled in a standard two-year elementary programme. Assuming that four years of schooling is an accepted proxy for functional literacy, the estimate that 31 per cent of the adult population was literate in 1959 strains credulity.[69] It is none the less the case that primary-school enrolments in 1960 included over 70 per cent of the relevant age group, twice the average for sub-Saharan Africa, and were reportedly growing faster than anywhere else on the continent.[70] The Congo's 1960 enrolment rates were bested only by Cameroon and Zimbabwe among more populous African states.[71]

Moreover, the *lutte scolaire* considerably strengthened the admin-

[68] Young, *Politics in the Congo*, p. 200. The educational status of the colony's 350 indigenous priests, 3,000 seminarians, numerous Protestant ministers, and over 3,000 former seminarians (including Joseph Kasavubu, the Congo's first President), has been dismissed by some scholars as politically insignificant, or used by others as an explanation for the lack of better trained intellectual élites. See, for example, Stengers, loc. cit. pp. 307–8.

[69] World Bank, *Accelerated Development in Sub-Saharan Africa: an agenda for action* (Washington, DC, 1981), p. 181.

[70] Barbara Yates, 'Structural Problems in Education in the Congo (Léopoldville)', in *Comparative Education Review*, 8, October 1963, p. 153, and *Bureau de l'enseignement catholique*, op. cit. p. 11.

[71] Cameroonian and Zimbabwean 1960 primary-school enrolment rates were 65 and 95 per cent, respectively. Some countries with small populations reported higher rates: Gabon 85, Lesotho 83, and Congo 78 per cent. World Bank, op. cit. p. 181.

istrative structure and governance of the school system. The church gained not only increased credibility from having learned how to negotiate with 'a rather less than compliant government' in Brussels after 1954, but also from having established the *Bureau de l'enseignement catholique* to co-ordinate its educational work.[72] State officials and church representatives came to anticipate negotiations over subsidies and the expansion of schools. Unlike the permutations of personnel that occurred in other parts of the colonial apparatus in 1960, missionaries in education stayed on. Thereafter, while much of the administration experienced 'semi-paralysis', the educational sector continued to expand, suffering only minor setbacks in the period of rebellions.[73] At the end of the 1960s, as many as 3.5 million students were enrolled in the Congolese school system, the second largest in Africa (after Nigeria) and among the biggest in the developing world.[74]

CONCLUSIONS

This analysis of church–state relations in the Congo has sought to highlight the rôle played by education conflicts in the political dynamics leading to independence, and better to understand how they set the groundwork for the rapid expansion of education. By probing the limitations of the widely accepted 'triple alliance' and 'chaotic decolonisation' scenarios, this article has attempted to sharpen our understanding of the realities they try to describe. The Catholic church struggled to become disassociated from the colonial administration in the late 1950s only to find itself always deeply involved with – and, at times, closely identified with – the régime headed by Mobutu Sese Seko.[75] Thereafter, the spectacular development of the Zaïrian education system during a period of fundamental political instability gave rise to a genuine contradiction: élite education flourished in response to an unquenchable thirst for social promotion through schooling,[76] but its relevance to the socio-economic needs of the general population was increasingly challenged.

The system of mixed control over schools and their financing worked well so long as church and state shared similar perspectives and a

[72] Hastings, op. cit. p. 259.
[73] 'Rapport de la commission consultative économique et sociale sur la politique d'austérité', in *Congo 1961* (Brussels, 1962), p. 146.   [74] World Bank, op. cit. pp. 125–6.
[75] 'Les Relations entre l'église et l'état au Zaïre', in *Études africaines du CRISP* (Brussels), 145, 3, 28 December 1972.
[76] Benoît Verhaegen, 'L'Enseignement supérieur: vers l'explosion', in *Politique africaine* (Paris), 41, March 1991, pp. 49–55.

willingness to collaborate. The Catholic bishops, far more secure as regards their status and influence than any of the political leaders during the First Republic, 1960–5, won recognition for their understanding of the educational formula in the 1964 constitution, and successfully negotiated a pre-eminent place for their church in year-to-year budgeting and expansion. But the Mobutu régime, consolidating its forces in the late 1960s, felt strong enough in 1974 to announce that all schools would be exclusively managed by the state. This attempted 'nationalisation' of education, part of Mobutu's programme of 'Zaïrianisation', proved disastrous for the school system. It convulsed under the pressure for instantaneous administrative transformations mandated from above. Its very size and complexity opened the doors for abuses, and made it even more of a financial burden for a state beginning to be crushed under the weight of its debt.

Continuing conditions of economic scarcity, administrative break-down, and international meddling, have brought Zaïre's educational sector into a period of major decline.[77] The 1980 national goal of enrolling every school-age child in a primary school was almost achieved, but has long since slipped from view. Enrolment and population estimates in an official report suggest that in the year 2000 only about half of Zaïre's 8 million primary school-age children will find a class to attend.[78] Government attempts to revive the system by employing (mostly Belgian) expatriate education experts in the 1980s only revived church fears for its own autonomy in the sector, and stimulated resentment among less-well paid Zaïrian school administrators.[79] Although the children of urban élites began to attend private schools after legislation in 1986 had facilitated their creation, these institutions only served a small minority and did little to ease conditions in overcrowded and under-funded urban schools. By the end of the 1980s Zaïre was among the countries in Africa spending the smallest percentage of its national budget on education.[80]

The problems and possibilities of a school system that had failed to keep up with demographic growth for almost a decade and a half were confronted by the representatives of church and state, as well as

[77] University conditions exemplify the decline. See Steve Askin, 'Amid Stench and Decay, Professors and Students in Zaïre Struggle to Keep Their Impoverished University Alive', in *Chronicle of Higher Education* (Washington, DC), 27 January 1988, pp. A1 and 42–3.
[78] République du Zaïre/Unesco, 'Le Secteur éducation et son financement, volume I: rapport provisoire (Badouin Duvieusart) 14 juin 1989', Kinshasa, p. 1.
[79] Gasibirege Rugema, 'Dans le concret de la coopération au Zaïre', in *Pile et face. Bilan de la coopération belgo-zaïroise* (Brussels, 1989), pp. 126–30.
[80] Jean Claude Michel, 'L'Enseignement au Zaïre', in ibid. p. 225.

468   PATRICK M. BOYLE

multilateral organisations, who gathered in Kinshasa in 1991. It is too
early to be sure of even the short-term outcome of their plan of action
for the development of education in the whole country,[81] even though
the issues separating them over school administration and curricula are
obviously manageable when compared with the magnitude of the ongoing difficulties that constrain so many families from turning their
attention and resources to the education of their children. These young
Zaïrois, especially, are the unfortunate victims of the political and
economic impasse that has brought the school system to its present sad
condition.

[81] Ekwa bis Isal, 'Premier plan d'action pour la promotion de l'éducation pour tous au Zaïre',
in *Zaïre-Afrique* (Kinshasa), 253–4, March–April 1991, pp. 141–8.

[16]

People's War, State Formation and Revolution in Africa: A Comparative Analysis of Mozambique, Guinea-Bissau, and Angola[1]

by

Patrick Chabal

University of East Anglia

What can revolution imply for Africa? In the following discussion I take my cue from the compassionate Guinean who relieved me of the growing anxiety which I had developed at being labelled a 'redfoot' when, in 1979, I was doing research in Guinea-Bissau. I had worried a great deal about this, echoes of red terror in mind, until the tale of 'redfeet' was unravelled for me by this kind soul who had given me a lift. 'You see', he said like a schoolteacher, 'since we had to gain independence through armed struggle and since we are committed to socialism, we have attracted the attention of all of you, Europeans and Americans. Can't manage a revolution at home so you're looking for one in the Third World. First, it was China, then Vietnam, then Cuba, then Algeria. Today it is us. In a few years you will tell us that our revolution has failed and you'll move on to some other place: Western Sahara perhaps?' I protested, but to no avail, that I was no 'redfoot' but an academic. 'Yes, of course', he said, grinning.

To what extent and in which ways do wars of national liberation usher in new post-colonial states substantially unlike those born of constitutional decolonisation? Political independence in Angola, Guinea-Bissau, and Mozambique (hereafter referred to as lusophone) came by way of armed conflict. Zimbabwe followed. Namibia is also at war. The success of the lusophone nationalists was seen by many to redraw the political map of independent Black Africa. The supporters of the lusophone nationalists as well as their opponents recognised the historical significance of what came to be labelled the second wave of African independence. The governments of the three lusophone countries, and later that of Zimbabwe, claimed and were perceived to be committed to socialist development. The socialism of which they spoke did not echo earlier claims of African socialism, a socialism which the new regimes disowned, and from which they derived little inspiration.

More significantly, the political organisation of these three countries, based on the structures of the parties as they evolved during the long decade of armed struggle, was in many respects more akin to revolutionary parties outside of Africa than to the first wave of African nationalist parties.[2] It was scarcely credible that this was so only because the lusophone parties had received the bulk of their financial aid and equipment from Eastern countries. War, then, had mattered. Or had it? Could it be that we were just being dazzled, all political 'redfeet', by the glitter of the firmly held Kalyishnikov as the new flag unfurled – socialist brotherhood and revolutionary fervour?

The argument implicit in the claims of many Africanists sympathetic to the new regimes is that the process of a people's war causes fundamental changes in the political, social, and economic structures of the colony, changes which did not obtain in countries which decolonised constitutionally and which now open the door to further revolutionary changes.[3] For them, a successful people's war leads, first, to the emergence of a 'revolutionary class alliance' of radical *petits bourgeois*, workers, and peasants which had hitherto not existed in Africa. The war requires total commitment and thus weeds out those *petits bourgeois* unprepared to move towards socialism. Political mobilisation demands the ability to forge an alliance between *petit bourgeois* leadership and peasants. The gap between elite and mass is closed. The post-colonial state is, therefore, in the hands of true revolutionaries.

Secondly, it is argued, a successful people's war is predicated on the creation of a well organised, united, and ideologically homogeneous political party. In practice such parties are more radical in their socialist orientation and more committed to socialist changes than any of their constitutional predecessors in Africa. Thus, it is claimed that the lusophone nationalist parties evolved structures, policies, and an ideology which can be used as effective instruments of revolutionary change after independence.

The third argument put forward by those who view the revolutionary potential of the three lusophone countries with optimism is that the nationalist parties had already achieved significant political, social, and economic changes in the liberated areas before independence. New forms of political institutions had been created from below, new forms of collective production and distribution had been introduced, new social and economic priorities had been defined. New bonds of national identity and solidarity were now at hand. People's war would succeed, where constitutional decolonisation had failed, in bringing revolution to Africa and thus in laying the foundations for a non neo-colonial path to development: a transition to socialism. What is claimed, then, if only implicitly, is that, like the Chinese Communist Party or the Vietminh, the three lusophone parties possess the apparatus, the men, the skills, the ideology, and the experience to see the revolution through.[4]

Many historians of Africa, however, are dubious about these claims.[5] They reject the contention that a successful nationalist struggle is a sounder basis for revolution (which, in any case, they doubt is about to occur in Africa) than the previous less violent and less spectacular forms of decolonisation characteristic of the 1950s and 1960s. They put forward three broad counter-arguments. First, revolution is the cant of modern nationalism. Nationalists fighting a war utter the slogans which will get them the material and political support they require. The aim of nationalists is independence, not revolution: heed not their rhetoric. Secondly, even assuming that this new generation of nationalists somehow *is* dedicated to revolution, it is naive to suggest that the political and military campaign designed to force a colonial power to negotiate independence heralds a new revolutionary dawn. The one has historically little to do with the other. Finally, and perhaps most crucially, the experience of other so-called African socialist states dedicated to revolution has shown that the social and economic under-development of African societies, and the constraints imposed by the world market economy from which they cannot expect to detach themselves, foreclose any hope of emulating the Russian or Chinese examples. There is, therefore, no reason to believe that, simply because they were successful in the prosecution of nationalist wars, the leaders of the lusophone countries can be more successful in achieving a revolutionary transformation of society than their equally ambitious predecessors in Africa.

These claims and counter-claims can only be sorted out by means of a sharper and more explicit conceptual apparatus than has hitherto been available. I propose to initiate the process of conceptual clarification by addressing the two questions which are implicit in the debate on the political significance of the nationalist struggles in the three lusophone countries. In what ways did it matter, firstly, that the post-colonial state in Angola, Guinea Bissau, and Mozambique was born of an armed struggle (or what I shall call a people's war)? Does the process of people's war usher in the establishment of radically distinct post-colonial states in Africa? More generally, is there a correlation between the nature of the post-colonial state and the success of the people's war which preceded independence? Secondly, is it either legitimate or even meaningful to infer that the emergence of a distinct post-colonial state is causally related to the development of a revolutionary process in the three lusophone countries? Does the creation of a 'people's state' lead to the transition to socialism? Or to put it more bluntly, when, if ever, is a nationalist waving a gun a revolutionary?

Usefully to discuss these two questions requires conceptual clarification in respect of the assumptions made in the usage of notions such as revolution, state, and, crucially, people's war.[6] Although there is no firm consensus on the subject, most political scientists and historians would agree that a revolution requires not only the overthrow of the existing political state – whether indigenous or foreign – by a counter-elite but more importantly the ability by the new political masters, the new elite, to establish a radically distinct social and economic order. A successful revolution can be seen to have occurred when the initial phase of 'political' revolution is followed by a 'social' revolution. Historically, most modern revolutions have undergone a period of civil or people's war and have been, in most instances, carried out by Marxist professional revolutionaries who, through the agency of a well organised and politically efficacious party, have aimed at establishing a socialist state. What sort of society they have envisaged and whether they can be said to have succeeded need not impinge on the conceptualisation of the process of revolution.

Since the Vietnamese revolution, however, the issue of nationalism has been paramount in the political process of what are generally recognised as the more recent revolutions. That this has been so is historically linked with the end of colonial rule and the struggle in much of the non-Western world to move away from ever sharper neo-colonial relations. Nationalism has been broadened to imply economic independence, that is some degree of autonomy from the constraints of the world-market economy. It is clear, therefore, that the meaning as well as the concept of revolution has changed in the second half of the twentieth-century – Vietnam and Cuba emerging as the two poles of the most relevant 'model', much as China and Russia had been earlier.[7] It may well be that the failure of most revolutionary attempts in Latin America and the apparent consolidation of the Ethiopian revolution point to the next historical step in the development of new forms of political and social revolutions. Whether the Ethiopian revolution, however, is a 'model' for what African revolutions would look like is not altogether very convincing given the peculiar and in many ways unique features of the country's social and economic structures.[8] It is simply not clear what revolution in lusophone Africa (or anywhere else in Africa) would mean. What follows, therefore, is no more than a cockshy.

The political component of an African revolution would imply, minimally, the acquisition and establishment of political power in a post-colonial state whose structure, personnel, and policies would derive not from its colonial predecessor but from the legitimacy of a vanguard mass party rooted in the countryside. Social revolution in Africa would mean the development of policies leading to a form of autonomous economic development in which agriculture would be modernised through the establishment of new structures of production and distribution and in which industrial advance would be tailored to the economic needs of the country and to its potential for self-sustained growth. In short, revolution in Africa (and here the lusophone revolutionaries rejoin their earlier counterparts on the continent) must mean the establishment of a state capable of breaking with the all too familiar pattern of neo-colonial development common, in its successful or failed version, to most African countries. Historically, therefore, although not causally, the formation of such a state must come before revolution.[9]

What of the state, then, that all too elusive monster which so fascinates social scientists and, of late, historians as well? Like all monsters it is more useful unseen but present. About the state one can ask a number of questions and any conceptualisation must ultimately depend on the ques-

108   STATE AND CLASS IN AFRICA

tions asked. Here, I follow Lonsdale who, in his extraordinarily catholic paper, has given us some hope as well as some means of understanding, *historically*, the notion of state in Africa. As he pithily writes:

> Otherwise than in myth, states do not have origins; they are formed. Origins are magical events; formation is slow, often very slow, social and political process .... Only states without a past look like the simple instrument of their dominant class; and even revolutionary states have pasts .... There are periods when states do appear to have origins, to take on new forms, autonomously to exert or instrumentally to transmit power more inclusively in a burst of law making. Historical eras do come to an end, new ones do begin; even people living at the time can be aware of that.[10]

Decolonisation appeared to be one such period, so that the formation of the post-colonial state matters.

How it matters is a question for analysis and analysis requires some conceptualisation. Lonsdale's gallant efforts at unpacking the layers of meaning attached to the notion of the state are not in vain. The state can be conceptualised through its four inter-connected structures: its apparatus, its representative estates, its ideology, and its material base.[11] At any one time in history, the state is the resultant of the conflict extant in the process of relationships between these structures. By definition, therefore, the state is not an a-historical hydra nor is it simply the political instrument of a given class but, like other concepts, a code-word for the analysis of the connection between historically specific processes and structures. The merit of this approach, beyond its obvious coherence, is to make it possible to conceptualise the state, that is to ask the right questions about it, in its relation to social processes and over time. State formation becomes amenable to analysis in the complexity of the transition between two historical eras. Questions can be asked which make possible comparisons between the process of state formation in different areas of the world, under different historical circumstances. It also becomes possible to ask whether state formation in eighteenth or nineteenth-century Europe is conceptually relevant to state formation in Africa in the second half of the twentieth century.[12]

Here I am essentially concerned with state formation in Africa, the key question of the epoch of decolonisation. The issue is whether historically different forms of decolonisation lead to the formation of significantly distinct post-colonial states. By now the liberal and radical post-mortems of the death of the dream of socialist states on the morrow of the first wave of independence rejoin, though for opposite reasons, in their conclusions: 'revolutionary nationalists' become bulwarks of conservatism once in power. Because the post-colonial state was essentially unchanged after independence, the argument is made, radical leaders were able to use revolutionary rhetoric to conceal, in most cases not very effectively, private plundering and the social reproduction of their privileges. Fanon was right![13] Or to put it another way, these radical nationalists inherit a

PEOPLE'S WAR, STATE FORMATION, AND REVOLUTION   109

post-colonial state which it is in their interest to make prosper as a neo-colonial state.[14] To liberal and radical critiques alike, then, the independence of these countries was nothing but the Africanisation of the colonial state. Independence did not imply a radical re-definition of the state, much less therefore a revolution.

The argument implicit in much of the writing on Angola, Mozambique, and Guinea-Bissau is that, to follow Lonsdale's conceptualisation, the post-colonial state of these countries is significantly different in its apparatus, representative estates, ideology, and material base *because* of the nationalist wars.[15] What this means is that the structures of the post-colonial states in these countries (though like most other African countries they are one-party states) are new. They do not derive from the colonial apparatus as it was inherited at independence but from the political and administrative organisation which sustained the party's effort in the liberated areas. The nature and legitimacy of these new political structures are determined by the experience of political mobilisation not by colonial white papers. The representative estates of the new state have joined in what is referred to as a 'revolutionary class alliance' of *petits bourgeois*, workers, and peasants. Such a political coalition, it is argued, was not to be found in countries which underwent constitutional decolonisation. The process of war has enabled the most radical section of the *petite bourgeoisie* to assume the leadership of the party. The requirements of massive peasant participation in the political process of mobilisation gives them a powerful political voice in the party. The balance of political forces in the state is thus subtantially different from what it was in the earlier wave of independent African countries.

Similarly, the ideology of the new states has, through the political process of war, evolved squarely towards the more radical end of socialism. More importantly, it is contended, this ideology was born of political mobilisation and, because it is congruent with the structure of the party, it can be used for revolutionary purposes. In other words, it is no longer rhetoric but the ideal fashioned out the blood, sweat, and tears of a truly popular political movement. It is also an indigenous ideology because the harsh reality of the war has eliminated the political clichés picked up in London, Paris, Lisbon, or Moscow.

Finally, it is argued, even the material base of the new states has changed in ways which were not possible for those other African nations which inherited the economy, as well as the administration, of the colonial state. The point here is not that the material resources of the lusophone states were somehow altered by the war (in fact they were; agriculture, in particular, was badly damaged) nor that the dependent economic position of lusophone Africa differs from other African states, but rather than the wars have led to changes in the aims as well as in the organisation of economic production and distribution. The economic priorities of the new states have been redefined and means are now at hand to implement them. The experience of political mobilisation, the necessity to become economically self-sufficient in the liberated areas and the existence of a popular party to affect economic change at the local level, all re-define the potential action of the new state on its material base. The Chinese and Vietnamese cases are implicit 'models' here. The claim, in effect, is that the material base of the liberated areas (the image of the society to be) has already been re-shaped during the armed struggle.[16]

These are impressive claims – particularly when earlier assertions about the radical nature and revolutionary promise of the post-colonial state in Africa have disappeared without echo.[17] Meaningfully to assess these claims in the case of lusophone Africa demands that we understand the process of nationalist (or people's) war. Simply to *assume* that a people's war leads *ipso facto* to the formation of a radical post-colonial state which holds the key to a successful transition to socialism is not good enough.

The argument, as I see it, involves two steps. First, how successful was the nationalist war in each case? How do we gauge the success or failure of people's wars? Secondly, is there a correlation (and if there is what is its nature) between the success of a nationalist war, the distinctiveness of the post-colonial state, and the potential for revolution in Angola, Mozambique, and Guinea-Bissau?

I proceed, then, with what I take to be the process of people's war in Africa in the third quarter of the twentieth century, using the three lusophone countries as my source material.[18] Historically, people's wars have assumed the form of a guerilla war in which the indigenous nationalist movement has sought to mobilise the largest possible section of the predominantly rural population to challenge and eventually eliminate foreign political and military control. Although very much a military conflict, the nature of a people's war is, to my mind, essentially political and cannot, therefore, be reduced to military parameters.[19] There are three broad areas of enquiry relevant to my first concern, the assessment of the success of a people's war, and to its potential for revolutionary change. First, to what extent has the nationalist party achieved effective political control over the territory it claims and what degree of political legitimacy has it acquired in the country as a whole? Secondly, to what extent does the party represent the political articulations of social forces during the anti-colonial struggle – that is, what is its political complexion and its potential as an agency for societal transformation? Thirdly, with what success has the party managed to promote meaningful political, social, and economic changes in the liberated areas *before independence*?

The key to the success of a people's war lies in the party's ability to achieve effective political mobilisation, that is, the ability to generate sufficient *active* political support for its aims and actions. In concrete terms, success here means not only to be able to operate freely in the countryside, receiving food, shelter, and protection, but also, and crucially, to be able to recruit members locally. This requires the mobilisation of the rural population, an extremely difficult task under any circumstances, however ill-disposed it may be towards the established colonial state.[20] Villagers are suspicious of outsiders, justifiably 'parochial' in their concerns, and, if anything, millenarian rather than socialist. Thus, the gains of political mobilisation are always likely to be fragile and reversible. Mobilisation depends ultimately on the ability of party cadres to convince individuals and communities that their interests will best be served by the nationalists.[21] Although such mobilisation can be achieved by various means (and it has been achieved by various means in different settings), the methods used are not politically neutral. The use of ethnic hostility (as in Angola) or of terror (as in Algeria) has obvious consequences and may become self-defeating. Finally, however successful political mobilisation has been, the coalition of interests between villagers and party is relatively unstable. Once independence is achieved, the party's political ambitions may clash with the demands of the villagers.

Successful political mobilisation is predicated on the party's capacity to overcome three internal contradictions. The first concerns one of the most essential components of successful political mobilisation in Africa, that is the creation of over-arching ties of supra-ethnic loyalties and a sense of national identity. The paradox is that successful mobilisation demands, not the abolition of ethnic sentiments (if that were possible), but rather the politicisation of ethnicity for nationalist purposes.[22] Here the role of the party is crucial: it is both the agency through which ethnic mobilisation is channelled and the organisation through which ethnic particularisms are transcended into a new state. The party must reconcile its conflicting interests between the need to achieve national unity and the use of local and parochial issues for purposes of mobilisation. In Africa, all nations had to be created out of colonies through some form of political mobilisation, but a successful people's war requires far more unambiguous commitment to national unity if the armed struggle is not to be jeopardised. Ethnic nationalism, of course, has no such dilemma.[23]

The second contradiction inherent in the process of a people's war is that the party needs to maintain *political control* of the war in a period when military efficiency is at a premium, when the dynamics of war favour the military men and when the requirements of a successful political campaign do not always coincide with those of military effectiveness. Here I am assuming, on the basis of most people's wars (the most significant exception being Cuba) that military success is dependent on the success of political mobilisation. There seems, in fact, little doubt that in Africa at least (and probably elsewhere as well) the development of successful people's war is determined by the extent to which the party has secured *active* political support. The failure of the UPC in Cameroon illustrates the point.[24]

The third contradiction is that the party must maintain a balance, and avoid a split, between the internal and external wings of the party in a situation where the lack of effective communication channels tends to isolate the fighting men from the external leadership. Here two observations can be made. First, a people's war is unlikely to be successful so long as it is conducted from outside the country: a strong and autonomous internal party organisation is essential. Second, exile politics are likely to be detrimental to the party's overall effectiveness.[25] The aim of any nationalist party engaged in a people's war must be to reduce its dependence on external bases and to become politically self-sufficient in the interior.

People's wars, by their very nature as anti-colonial struggles, are international in character. Both the rulers of the colonial state and the nationalists seek to legitimise their action internationally and to acquire allies, if not active support. Successful diplomacy of national liberation movements, therefore, is essential.[26] Broadly, such diplomacy must manage, first, to gain the support of neighbouring countries and to procure the necessary bases. Secondly, it needs to create, and preferably to maintain, nationalist unity in order to win international recognition as the sole legitimate nationalist organisation. Thirdly, the party must secure financial aid and military equipment. Finally, the nationalists must generate the largest and most vocal metropolitan and international opposition to the colonial war in order to obtain, ultimately, the widest and most prompt recognition of the independent government of the country. Hence, the importance of remaining non-aligned.

The ultimate significance of people's wars, however, does not lie in the nationalists' ability to mobilise villagers into bands of guerillas. The lusophone parties claimed, like their predecessors elsewhere in the world, that their aim was to construct a new society, not merely to expel the colonial forces. The measure of their success in doing so must initially be gauged by an examination of their achievements in the liberated areas.[27] Here, three inter-related issues are of particular significance: (i) the extent of effective party control in the liberated areas and the rate of progress in extending these areas; (ii) the effectiveness of the party in creating a genuinely popular leadership; and (iii) the nature and extent of socio-economic reconstruction in the liberated areas. The legitimacy of each nationalist party and the validity of its claims to form the first independent government depend largely upon success in the liberated areas.

*   *   *

The different outcomes of the three people's wars in lusophone Africa are best understood through an analysis of the degree to which each party managed successfully to mobilise the countryside and the extent to which it overcame the contradictory demands made on it by the process of war.[28] The conclusion which emerges is that there are broad similarities between the PAIGC and FRELIMO but that the MPLA is a party with substantially different political experience and achievements.[29] The PAIGC was the most adept in its prosecution of a people's war. It was most successful in achieving nationalist unity, in carrying out political mobilisation and in establishing new political structures in the liberated areas. At independence it had achieved the largest degree of control over its territory and its

PEOPLE'S WAR, STATE FORMATION, AND REVOLUTION   113

overall political legitimacy was high. The PAIGC certainly was a popular party as it integrated the historic nationalist leadership and the next generation of cadres who had emerged during the war. The party had also managed to advance the reorganisation of the liberated areas and was active in their reconstruction. Not surprisingly, it posed the most serious political and military threat to the Portuguese.

FRELIMO, despite serious difficulties throughout the 1960s, eventually managed to follow the same route as the PAIGC. Once it had overcome the weaknesses which threatened to split the Mozambican nationalists further and once it had assimilated the lessons of the failure of the early military campaigns, it developed a successful strategy of political mobilisation which, by 1974, had borne fruit.[30] Because of the size of the country (and other contextual factors) and because of the political costs of the early mistakes, FRELIMO had not achieved control over as high a proportion of the country as the PAIGC.[31] Where it had, however, it had done so by a similar process and its achievements in the liberated areas compared favourably with those of the Guinean party. FRELIMO was certainly a military force to reckon with and posed a serious military threat to the colonial armed forces. Colonial rule was not in immediate danger, however, as there was *de facto* military stalemate.

The MPLA, on the other hand, never overcame the ethnic, political, and military obstacles which stood in the way of its nationalist and socialist ambitions. Without Cuban support from 1975, the MPLA might have been eliminated whereas there was little doubt that both the PAIGC and FRELIMO would take power at independence. Briefly, the MPLA had little success in the development of a people's war because it could not progress either effectively or substantially with political mobilisation in the countryside.[32] It was the least successful of the three lusophone parties in overcoming the three central contradictions which are the most damaging to the success of a people's war.[33] The outcome of the Angolan nationalist conflict was therefore more the result of strictly military factors and outside intervention than the product of the political process of mobilisation which is so essential to the strength of the post-colonial state and to its distinctiveness as a new, more independent, and radical instrument of political change. To my mind, then, the Angolan state at independence was not only weaker but also less structurally distinct from the colonial state than either Mozambique or, even more, Guinea-Bissau.[34]

Furthermore, my analysis clearly indicates why and how the political process of people's wars differs in kind from that of constitutional and legal decolonisation. Although it is often argued that nationalist wars are nothing more than the pursuit of nationalist goals by military means, the process of political mobilisation ensures that this is not really the case. People's wars differ from constitutional decolonisation in three fundamental respects: (i) successful political mobilisation requires a form of political collaboration between a modern party and the rural population which was not necessary, and thus did not obtain, during constitutional decolonisation; (ii) the demands of a guerilla war lead to the development of political parties whose organisation, leadership, ideology, and political effectiveness are in fact more akin to parties committed to revolution than to those political organisations which negotiated independence in the rest of Africa; (iii) successful people's wars usher in the establishment of states the legitimacy and structure of which owe little to their colonial predecessors.

The PAIGC, FRELIMO, and to a much more limited extent the MPLA, were thus the first African nationalist parties in a position to replace, rather than simply inherit, the colonial state. Thus, it would appear that the potential role of the new states as instruments for revolution is greater in those three countries (although less in Angola) than it ever was in any other African colony – much as it was greater in Vietnam than in India.

Whether revolution is thereby more likely in any or all of the three lusophone countries is an entirely different and essentially empirical question. The issue is clear, if not easily resolved. Even if we assume that the leadership of the three states is genuinely committed to revolutionary change, are they in a better position than their equally ambitious nationalist predecessors elsewhere in Africa to carry out such a revolution? I return to an assessment of the claims of those who view the revolutionary potential of the three countries with optimism, and examine in turn the three arguments which they put forward. However, the generalisations I make on the basis of a comparison of the three nationalist movements must always be seen in the context of the significance of the differences between the three cases. It is difficult, in some instances, to argue that the MPLA can be usefully compared to the other two parties.[35]

The Nature of the 'Revolutionary Class Alliance'

The 'optimists' (as I shall call them) put forward two arguments. First, they contend that the process of war itself has enabled the most radical section of this class alliance to assume the leadership of the party. Secondly, they believe that the requirements of massive peasant participation in the political process of mobilisation gives them a 'passive veto' over the party and thus ensures that their voice will be heard. This, it is argued, fundamentally distinguishes the process of a people's war from any other form of decolonisation.[36]

Leaving aside the problem raised by the definition of these various classes (peasants, workers, and *petits bourgeois*) and by the meaning of 'passive veto', a few observations can be made.[37] In Guinea-Bissau and Mozambique, the process of political mobilisation did indeed lead to the development of parties which differed greatly from earlier African nationalist parties. Although the original leadership of the PAIGC and FRELIMO did not differ in either class origin or social status from their counterparts elsewhere in Africa (assimilated, educated, professional, middle class), the process of war saw the emergence of a 'second genera-tion' of cadres who rose to the top because of their political skills and, in both instances, this new leadership ultimately displaced the first generation.[38]

It is equally true that this new leadership owes its political status to the party and not to 'traditional ethnic' affiliation or to the urbanised middle classes which took power in most of Africa. These 'party men' see themselves as, and in many instances indeed are, the representatives of those who did not have a voice under colonial rule and who still have no say in most African countries. Their 'natural' constituency is in the countryside where the party is most popular. Their commitment lies with the construction of a new social order which is not to be found in Africa today, rather than in the maintenance of the neo-colonial *status quo*. To that extent the leadership of the PAIGC and FRELIMO is radical, albeit in different ways. By contrast, the leadership of the MPLA, although socialist in ideology, is more akin to previous nationalist parties precisely because the process of war did not lead to the same degree of political mobilisation in the countryside. The party's 'natural' constituency remains in the cities (primarily Luanda).[39]

But, however distinct the leadership of the three lusophone parties is seen to be, there is no structural reason why this radical *petit bourgeois* leadership, as Cabral himself pointed out, should 'commit suicide as a class' in order to pursue a revolutionary path after independence.[40] Whether they do so cannot meaningfully be determined by the nature of the class alliance which the party is supposed to embody. Nowhere in Africa have the workers, as a class, shown great proclivity towards revolution. Nor, and that is more damaging to the case, is there any evid-ence that the peasants are revolutionary or even that their voice, if it is to be heard after independence, will necessarily radicalise the leadership.[41]

There are two fallacies in presuming an active political role by the peasants.[42] In the first instance, although it is true that the requirements of political mobilisation gave the rural population a *de facto* political veto during the war, there is no reason to believe that such veto can be maintained after independence when the party leadership assumes con-trol as the new government. During the war the power of the villagers lay in the party's dependence on their cooperation. But, unless specific political structures have been created which ensure villagers a voice commensurate with their numbers, their participation in the war does not automatically guarantee them power after independence.[43] A crucial factor in lusophone Africa is likely to be the economic potential of the country.[44] Where there are virtually no other resources but agriculture, as in Guinea-Bissau, the countryside will have to be placated if production is to increase. On the other hand, Angola's immense oil and mineral wealth may well persuade the government to initiate a 'forced march' forward towards industrialisation – of which the countryside will inevitably be the main victim.

Secondly, and again to quote Cabral, the 'peasantry is not

revolutionary'.[45] Thus, even if the countryside should retain a passive veto after independence, there is no reason to believe that this would favour a revolutionary transformation of society. The history of revolutions seems to indicate that peasants (villagers) do not, and perhaps cannot, share the political aims of a modern socialist party. There are many historical precedents for thinking that a socialist leadership tends to favour forms of economic development which may not be to the benefit of the country-side. In such cases it is more likely than not that conflict will arise between party and villagers.[46]

In sum, then, it is not certain that the nature of the class alliance embodied in any or all of the lusophone parties is necessarily favourable to revolution. Independently from the question of whether it is possible to define a 'revolutionary class alliance' in the context of Africa, it seems causally simplistic to suggest that the process of class coalition which obtained during the nationalist wars is structurally more revolutionary than in other forms of decolonisation. What weakens the argument of the 'optimists'' here is their assumption that the radical ideological commit-ment of the leadership reflects the revolutionary nature of the existing nationalist class alliance rather than the greater need to utilise ideological mobilisation to move such a class alliance towards a more revolutionary project.[47]

The Nature of the Party

In the twentieth century the party has visibly been the driving force of most revolutions. The 'optimists' argue here that it is politically of the greatest significance that the wars in lusophone Africa have led to the emergence of political parties which are structurally different from their earlier nationalist counterparts in Africa. Three arguments are most commonly put forward to show why the PAIGC, FRELIMO, and the MPLA are now in a position to pursue a revolutionary course. First, their ideology, leadership, and policies are 'revolutionary'. Secondly, their organisation of and their integration into local political life provides them with the tools to affect change. Thirdly, the parties have acquired legi-timacy not only as nationalist organisations but, crucially, as instruments of socio-economic change.

There is a *prima facie* case in favour of these arguments, with the proviso (rarely made) that the MPLA differs greatly from the other two parties. The political requirements of a successful people's war – the development of effective political mobilisation and the need to adminis-ter the reconstruction of the liberated areas – have created parties which have acquired a vastly different political experience from that of Congres-ses lobbying for constitutional reform. The obstacles which the PAIGC and FRELIMO had to overcome, the relative failure of the MPLA, the difficulties of ZANU and ZAPU in Rhodesia, all point to the uniqueness of political organisations capable of succeeding in war.[48]

In structure, leadership, and ideology, the three lusophone parties do

differ from earlier African nationalist parties. All three are firmly com-
mitted to modern (as opposed to Africa) socialism. The party leadership
has had to evolve a form of socialist ideology adapted to the country.[49]
Consequently, a form of socialist ideology, understood and accepted by
the party cadre and available for further mobilisation, emerged early.
This experience differs significantly from those African countries, such as
Guinea (Conakry), Tanzania, Uganda, or the Congo, which turned to the
Left in the mid-sixties, a few years after independence.

The ideology of the lusophone parties is more pragmatic and their
socialist objectives more suitably modest than those adopted, for example, in Ghana or Guinea (Conakry). More importantly, the process of
war created a party apparatus based on the experience of implementing
policies which, at the outset, did not look promising. The party organisation was severely tested and the war itself carried out a ruthless selection
of the most competent political cadres. In short, the PAIGC and FRE-
LIMO (unlike the MPLA) emerged at independence as toughened,
effective, and self-confident political organisations with a clear sense of
political identity, realistic ambitions, and considerable political experience.

It is equally true that the PAIGC and FRELIMO (more than the
MPLA) had acquired political legitimacy as instruments of change at the
local level in the liberated areas unlike other African parties.[50] War forced
the three parties to create local political structures integrated in some way
to indigenous village administration. This required not only collaboration
in village and regional committees but also the creation of local party
structures capable of reconciling local demands with party directives.
Councils of elders or other so-called traditional forms of local government combined or fused with local party committees and some villagers
themselves assumed important positions in the party hierarchy. Finally,
the party's legitimacy depended on what it did rather than, as in much of
Africa, on what it promised to do.

There were, however, vast differences between the three lusophone
territories, differences which will undoubtedly affect their political evolution and which considerably reduce the value of generalisations about the
three cases. The PAIGC could reasonably claim at independence to have
acquired full legitimacy and to be in control of a national party organisation extending all the way down to the local level. The 1972 and 1976
elections have clearly indicated that the PAIGC's constituency was in the
countryside and that, although not universally popular, it had support in
all areas of the country.[51] FRELIMO was at independence less advanced
in that it did not control the southern half of the country where, in any
case, political mobilisation had not been as extensively carried out as
FRELIMO would have wished.[52] However, the party's national legitimacy was not seriously in dispute and its political experience enabled it
rapidly to extend the new party structures to the whole country. In
Angola the situation was different. At independence the MPLA controlled little of the country beyond a small Mbundu base and some liberated

areas along the Eastern border. The tripartite nationalist division along ethnic lines and the lingering war against UNITA robbed the MPLA of much of its national legitimacy. Finally, the MPLA had far less political experience in the countryside, much of which was without party organisation at independence.

There is thus little to dispute the argument that the PAIGC, FRELIMO, and (to a much lesser extent) the MPLA differed from their earlier African nationalist counterparts. There is, however, equally little to suggest that such significant political differences as exist either amount to or are a prelude to revolution in lusophone Africa.[53] Scepticism must remain, not because these parties could not be used as instruments of revolution – clearly they could insofar as they do not differ in structure, leadership, personnel, or ideology from parties which did carry through the hoped-for revolution – but because revolutions are rare and their occurrence cannot be anticipated either on the basis of the pronouncements of party leaders or from an examination of the nature of the party as such. Self-proclaimed revolutionary leadership and effective party machines are essential to the process of revolution. They are, however, far from sufficient, unless, that is, one believes in the ability of any revolutionary party to carry out a revolution from above, under any circumstances. Most political scientists (whether Marxist or not) would argue that revolutions rarely occur unless there are *social and economic*, as well as political, factors which are favourable to revolutionary change. Whether in the case of the three lusophone countries, as in the case of other nationalist revolutions, there are sufficient structural (as distinct from political) forces helping the revolutionaries is not altogether clear.

The three lusophone parties were initially set up as nationalist, not revolutionary, parties and their success as such cannot form a reliable guide to their potential as agencies of socio-economi change. The course of development followed in the three countries since independence would suggest, if anything, that there is no obvious correlation between the two. The PAIGC, ostensibly the most successful of the three parties, has pursued the most moderate and pragmatic path since independence. The MPLA and FRELIMO, although vastly different, have both opted for 'scientific socialism' and a 'Marxist-Leninist path to development'.[54] The political orientation of each party is not, therefore, necessarily a result either of the process of war or of the party's achievements in the liberated areas.

Reconstruction in the Liberated Areas: A New Society?

It is here that the claims of the 'optimists' are most ambitious and far reaching. To them, the achievements of the three lusophone parties in the liberated areas provide the foundations of the future revolution. In order to assess these claims it is best to discuss separately the three main areas of party policies: political, economic, and social. In the political sphere two questions require examination: the degree and significance of political mobilisation in the country and the nature of the political institutions established *before independence*. As concerns the parties' economic policies, it is necessary to assess the degree to which structural changes have actually occurred in agriculture and whether such changes can form the basis of a socialist economy. Finally, a consideration of the social implications of people's wars must include a brief (and probably impossible) evaluation of the claim that a 'new man' has emerged in the liberated areas.[55]

Briefly, the development strategy pursued with varying success by the three parties aimed at creating a popular leadership and a party organisation capable of integrating local socio-political structures (like councils of elders) into a new political system. The key to their efforts was the village committees designed to work in collaboration with the local party. On the whole, the three parties found it more convenient to utilise rather than replace pre-existing political structures. People's stores, health clinics, schools, security forces, and 'agricultural brigades' were set up locally. Every effort was made to improve agricultural methods and to increase production by developing new cooperative forms of production. Finally, the three parties sought to impart a new political ethos to the population of the liberated areas. These were their aims.[56] What have they in fact achieved?

a. *Political Change:* Political mobilisation was most complete and thorough in Guinea and northern Mozambique. In Angola, the MPLA was not really in a position to 'develop' the liberated areas. In Angola, as in Mozambique, the Portuguese had set up 'strategic hamlets', thereby restricting the impact of the party's attempts at reconstruction.[57] Where political mobilisation succeeded, however, the three parties relied heavily on existing local political structures (traditional authorities). In most instances, anti-colonial sentiments in the village amounted to a desire for a return to 'traditional' socio-political institutions rather than for integration into a modern socialist party organisation. The extent to which the three parties actually managed to change the structure of local political institutions must have been limited.[58]

Although village committees did form the linchpin of local administration in the liberated areas and although they enjoyed a certain degree of autonomy in their dealings with the party, it is unlikely that they acted as instruments of socio-political change.[59] There is thus little ground to suggest that the experience of political mobilisation and of war-time collaboration between villagers and party turned village committees into 'revolutionary cells'.

However, in Guinea-Bissau and Mozambique, such experience does represent a political resource which was never available to other African nationalist parties at independence. Undoubtedly, the most original and significant political innovation occurred in Guinea-Bissau, where the PAIGC held elections before independence to establish independent representative political institutions.[60] Whether this attempt to institutionalise popular participation in the emergent party-state is revolutionary cannot be determined at this point. What is clearer is that the political changes which were achieved in the liberated areas of Guinea-Bissau and Mozambique did not (perhaps could not) fundamentally alter local socio-political structures. In most twentieth-century revolutions, revolutionary parties were able to set up new forms of political organisations largely *because* the socio-political order was in the process of disintegration and a new one was wanting.[61] This does not seem to have been the case in lusophone Africa.

b. *Economic Change:* Similarly, the economic context within which the lusophone nationalists launched their armed struggles differed substantially from that of most other countries where revolutions have taken place. The existing structure of land ownership, the degree of economic exploitation and misery, and the social organisation of village life were not similar to those of, for example, Russia, China, or Vietnam. With few exceptions, there was no private African ownership of land and, in the lusophone countries, food was readily available. The villagers' grievances did not question 'traditional' patterns of agricultural production but only attacked the most obvious abuses of the colonial economy, most notably plantation labour and taxation.[62]

Thus successful political mobilisation in the countryside did not require an 'economic programme' nor did it require significant reforms, much less revolutionary change. As a result, the lusophone parties merely sought to sever the liberated areas from the colonial economy and to increase production; they did not innovate much. This was largely achieved by a return to traditional methods of cultivation and an increase in labour input rather than by the implementation of structural change. Despite the efforts of a leader like Cabral, who was more aware than most of the necessity to transform agriculture, little was achieved.[63] For example, there is no evidence to suggest that much progress was made in Guinea-Bissau towards some form of collective agriculture during the war. The structure of agricultural production remained essentially unchanged in the liberated areas.

Although the people's stores fulfilled their role during the war, state control of marketing which has derived from it since independence has not proved effective.[64] In fact, the disastrous effects of the wars compounded with the very serious economic difficulties faced by the three governments have led to a collapse of agricultural production and consequent food shortages. There is precious little here to cheer those who envisage a form of socialist development based on the Chinese, rather than the Soviet, model. Although the primary resources of Angola might make the Soviet option more feasible there, Guinea-Bissau and Mozambique cannot expect to follow that route.

c. *Social Change:* Has the war led to new forms of socio-political consciousness? In the absence of reliable data, speculation would be otiose. All that can be said is that the more successful political mobilisation was, the greater the social consensus it achieved. In Guinea-Bissau and Mozambique, political unity has been attained; ethnic, regional, and racial divisions have, for the time being, been neutralised and non-particularistic institutions are operating effectively.[65] The same cannot be said of Angola. There is some ground for hoping, although no more than that, that the nature of the political institutions which have been established in Guinea-Bissau and Mozambique will make it possible to avoid the politicisation of ethnic, religious, racial, or other potentially divisive forms of social identity.[66] In these two countries there is support for the 'socialist ideals' put forward by the government and a commitment to social goals which is rarely found in Africa. But clearly, such socialist commitment is an eminently evanescent commodity which may facilitate the party's attempt to transform society in the short run but which cannot replace new forms of political mobilisation in the long term. Revolutions do succeed in part because they have fired the imagination of many and because they are perceived as pursuing legitimate goals. But only structural change can consolidate the political gains of the war.

*   *   *

I think it clear that the drama of armed struggle did matter in Guinea-Bissau, Angola, and Mozambique. It was more than a mere trick of the light. The requirements of a successful people's war helped in the formation of a post-colonial state which differed substantially from those born of constitutional decolonisation. But what of revolution, then?

The wars in the three lusophone countries were launched because the nationalists could not achieve their aims through peaceful negotiations. The political, economic, and social context within which these were launched was not in any sense 'revolutionary', as it is plausible to argue that it was in Russia, China, or Vietnam.[67] The existing political order, the colonial state, was not crumbling. Colonial rule had not led to massive economic exploitation and wide-spread social disruption, as it had in Vietnam for example. Nor was there, as there was in Russia and China, a collapse of the agricultural system and famine. There were not, in short, many of the 'revolutionary pre-conditions' which students of revolution have identified in other instances.[68] In a real sense, therefore, the nationalists were not in any position to mobilise the population on the basis of the economic and social grievances which have been paramount in most twentieth-century revolutions.

Moreover, and perhaps more discouragingly for the 'optimists', the international economic context within which most African countries must develop is not favourable to socialist revolution. Short of the barbaric extremes which total 'socialist autarky' (on the Cambodian model) imposes on third world countries, there is little scope for an African country to control the nature of its economic links with the world market. Paradoxically, from the viewpoint of underdevelopment theory, Guinea-

Bissau, the most successful politically, is in the weakest economic position because it is entirely dependent on the export of agricultural products, whereas Angola may be one of the few countries in Africa with the resources to exercise a large degree of control over its economic development. In Guinea-Bissau it is very unlikely and in Mozambique improbable that industrialisation can serve as the engine of socialist development. The range of choices open to these two countries, especially Guinea, is not auspicious for development outside the world market and without outside financial aid.[69]

But the sceptics' mirth at these apparently gloomy conclusions could well be premature. There may not be a causal relationship between people's war and revolution in lusophone Africa but there is no sound reason for thinking that revolutions *cannot occur*. Revolutions are only defined as such in hindsight. The creation out of armed struggle of novel post-colonial states in lusophone Africa can be seen as a *political* revolution. It may be, although the odds are not very favourable, that hard ideological labour, dedicated revolutionary leadership, and an efficient party machine will move one (or more) of these countries through a *social* revolution.

NOTES

1. A preliminary version of this article was presented at the panel on 'The Nature of the State in Africa', Twenty-fifth Annual Meeting of the African Studies Association, Washington, DC, 4-7 November 1982. I am grateful to the members of the panel, especially Nelson Kasfir, Frank Holmquist, and Richard Joseph, for their useful comments. The material used for this article largely derives from the research done for the last chapter of my book: *Amilcar Cabral: Revolutionary Leadership and People's War* (Cambridge, 1983), henceforth referred to as *Cabral*.
2. For a discussion of the first and second waves of African socialism, see, for example, Carl Rosberg and Thomas Callaghy (eds), *Socialism in Sub-Saharan Africa* (Berkeley, 1979).
3. In what follows I have drawn on the arguments of many. See more particularly, Bonnie Campbell, *Libération nationale et construction du socialisme en Afrique* (Montreal, 1977); John Saul, *The State and Revolution in Eastern Africa* (London, 1979); Basil Davidson *et al.*, *Southern Africa: The New Politics of Revolution* (Harmondsworth, 1977); Thomas Henriksen, 'Marxism and Mozambique', *African Affairs*, 77 (1978), 441-62; Basil Davidson, 'African Peasants and Revolution', *Journal of Peasant Studies*, 1 (1974) and 'Questions about Nationalism', *African Affairs*, 76 (1977); James Mittelman, *Underdevelopment and the Transition to Socialism: Mozambique and Tanzania* (New York, 1981).
4. Bonnie Campbell writes, for example: 'La poursuite et les impératifs de la lutte armée ont transformé de manière fondamentale le contenu idéologique de l'indépendance nationale en substituant au nationalisme "traditionnel" un nationalisme révolutionnaire – phénomène qui se concrétise par la transformation radicale de la pratique et donc des structures en place'. Campbell, *op. cit.*, 15.
5. They have not, however, cared to put their arguments in writing. I am grateful to John Lonsdale for talking me through these arguments.
6. For a cogent review of theories of revolution, see Theda Skocpol, *States and Social Revolutions* (Cambridge, 1979); on people's wars, see Eric Wolf, *Peasant Wars of the Twentieth Century* (New York, 1969).

7. For a useful discussion of the concept of modern revolutions, see John Dunn, *Modern Revolutions* (Cambridge, 1972) and 'Understanding Revolutions', *Ethics*, 92 (1982).
8. For a controversial account of the Ethiopian case, see Fred Halliday and Maxine Molyneux, *The Ethiopian Revolution* (London, 1981).
9. For an argument in favour of such causality, see Mittelman, *op. cit.*, 7.
10. John Lonsdale, 'States and Social Processes in Africa: a Historiographical Survey', *African Studies Review*, 24 (1981), 154.
11. *Ibid.*, 156.
12. See Thomas M. Callaghy, 'External Actors and the Relative Autonomy of the Political Aristocracy in Zaire' in this collection.
13. Frantz Fanon, *The Wretched of the Earth* (New York, 1968).
14. See, among many, Colin Leys, *Underdevelopment in Kenya: the Political Economy of Neo-Colonialism* (London, 1975), 207-12.
15. This is what I take to be the most coherent of these arguments, although they have not been expounded in this form.
16. See, for example, Campbell, *op. cit.*, 33-8.
17. See Thomas Callaghy, 'The Difficulties of Implementing Socialist Strategies of Development in Africa: The "First Wave" ', in Rosberg and Callaghy, *op. cit.*, 112-30.
18. On Guinea-Bissau, see *Cabral* and Lars Rudebeck, *Guinea Bissau: A Study of Political Mobilisation* (Uppsala, 1974). On Mozambique, see Thomas Henriksen, *Mozambique: A History* (London, 1978) and Luis Serapiao and Mohamed El-Khawas, *Mozambique in the Twentieth Century: From Colonialism to Independence* (Washington, 1979). On Angola, see John Marcum, *The Angolan Revolution*, I and II (Cambridge, 1969, 1978) and Douglas Wheeler and René Pélissier, *Angola* (London, 1971).
19. A point which Henriksen, for example, seems to have overlooked in 'People's War in Angola, Mozambique and Guinea Bissau', *Journal of Modern African Studies*, 14 (1976).
20. For a comparative perspective, see Wolf, *op. cit.*
21. For a comparison with China and Vietnam, see Mark Selden, 'People's War and the Transformation of Peasant Society: China and Vietnam' in Edward Friedman and Mark Selden (eds), *America's Asia: Dissenting Essays of Asian-American Relations* (New York, 1971).
22. For the most comprehensive discussion of ethnicity and politics in the context of Africa, see Nelson Kasfir, *The Shrinking Political Arena* (Berkeley, 1976), chapters 2 and 3.
23. For a discussion of ethnic nationalism in Angola, see Réne Pélissier, *Le Naufrage des Caravelles* (Orgeval, 1979), 99-140.
24. For a revealing account of the UPC rebellion, see Richard Joseph, *Radical Nationalism in Cameroun: Social Origins of the UPC Rebellion* (Oxford, 1977).
25. On this point, see Marcum, *The Angolan Revolution*, II, 3.
26. For a discussion of what I mean by diplomacy of national liberation in the context of Guinea-Bissau, see *Cabral*, chapter 3, section E.
27. Which in the case of Guinea-Bissau is assessed in *Cabral*, chapter 4, and Rudebeck, *op. cit.*, chapters 4-6.
28. *Cabral, op. cit.*, chapter 7.
29. The comparative analysis of the people's wars in the three countries is to be found in *Cabral, op. cit.*, chapter 7. Contrast with Henriksen, 'People's War in Angola, Mozambique and Guinea Bissau'.
30. See Walter Opello, 'Pluralism and Elite Conflict in an Independence Movement: FRELIMO in the 1960s', *Journal of Southern African Studies*, 2 (1975).
31. Henriksen, *Mozambique*, 226-7.
32. For a sympathetic account of their success, see Basil Davidson, *In the Eye of the Storm: Angola's People* (Garden City, 1972).
33. See my discussion of the MPLA's difficulties in *Cabral*, chapter 7.
34. See Marcum, *The Angolan Revolution,* II, conclusion.
35. It is, however, necessary to examine the three parties comparatively not only because, on paper, they are very similar but also because in most of the literature it is often assumed that they in fact were.

36. See, among many, Saul, 'Free Mozambique' in *The State and Revolution in Eastern Africa*, 79-92.
37. There is little agreement on the definition of these classes in the context of Africa. For a review of the arguments, see, *inter alia*, Stephen Katz, 'Marxism, Africa and Social Class: A Critique of Relevant Theories', Occasional Monograph Series, 14, Centre for Developing Area Studies, McGill University, 1980.
38. For a discussion of this process in Guinea-Bissau, see Patrick Chabal, 'Party, State and Socialism in Guinea Bissau',' *Canadian Journal of African Studies*, forthcoming; in Mozambique, Barry Munslow, 'Leadership in the Front for the Liberation of Mozambique' in *Collected Papers*, Centre for Southern African Studies, University of York, Part I, pp.139-66, Part II, pp.114-27.
39. David Birmingham, 'The Abortive Coup in Angola, 1977', *African Affairs*, 77 (1978).
40. Amilcar Cabral, *Revolution in Guinea* (London, 1969), 89.
41. A somewhat naive view which Cabral did not hold, *ibid.*, 50.
42. There is a vast literature on the political role of the peasants. See, among others, John Lonsdale, 'State and Peasantry in Colonial Africa', in R. Samuel (ed), *People's History and Socialist Theory* (London, 1981); Ken Post, ' "Peasantization" and Rural Political Movements in West Africa', *Archives Européennes de Sociologie*, 13 (1972); John Saul and Roger Woods, 'African Peasantries' in Teodor Shanin (ed), *Peasant Societies* (Harmondsworth, 1971).
43. Even in Guinea-Bissau, where such political structures were set up (through elections) before independence, there occurred in the five years after independence a gradual but significant loss of power on the part of the countryside. This was one of the factors which precipitated the November 1980 coup in Bissau. On the coup, see my articles in *West Africa* (15 December 1980), 2554-6; (22/29 December 1980), 2593-4; and (12 January 1981), 62-3.
44. A point generally valid for most African countries. See, for example, John Dunn, *West African States: Failure and Promise* (Cambridge, 1978), 11.
45. Amilcar Cabral, *Revolution in Guinea*, 50.
46. Wolf writes about the role of peasants in modern revolutions: '... the peasant is an agent of forces larger than himself .... The peasant's role is thus essentially tragic: his efforts to undo a grievous present only usher in a vaster, more uncertain future'. Wolf, *op. cit.*, 301.
47. See Campbell's reasoning here: 'Ces nouvelles relations sociales rendues nécessaires par la dynamique de la lutte impliquent une transformation radicale des structures et souvent le création de structures tout à fait nouvelles .... Le lutte de libération est donc un processus cumulatif, et génère sa propre dynamique. Les conditions nécessaires pour son avancement deviennent en fait les moyens de l'approfondissement du contenu idéologique de la lutte et la meilleure garantie de sa consolidation et de son succès'. Campbell, *op. cit.*, 37-8.
48. For a relevant comparison with Vietnam and China, see Selden, *op. cit.*
49. For a useful comparison see the analysis of the last three party congresses in Luis Moita, *Os Congressos de FRELIMO, do PAIGC e do MPLA: una analise comparativa* (Lisbon, 1979).
50. In the case of Guinea-Bissau, see Rudebeck, *op. cit.*, 146.
51. See my discussion of the 1972 elections in *Cabral*, chapter 4, section E.
52. Henriksen, *Mozambique*, 226-7.
53. As John Saul seemed to imply in 1975: A revolutionary nationalism which has broken through the barrier of Portuguese "ultra-colonialism" now stands poised to confront the more subtle dangers of a threatened neocolonialism'. *The State and Revolution in Eastern Africa*, 55.
54. See Molita, *op. cit.*
55. Generally, there has been too little research done here to provide enough comparative material. For a beginning on Guinea-Bissau, see James Cunningham, 'Guinea Bissau 1956–74: A Re-Assessment', *African Affairs*, forthcoming.
56. For a discussion of the Guinean case, see *Cabral*, chapter 4.

57. See Gerald Bender, 'The Limits of Counter-Insurgency: An African Case', *Comparative Politices*, 4 (1972).
58. This, however, is almost never discussed in the literature even though the experience of other 'rural revolutions' shows that it is a crucial point.
59. See Rudebeck's cautious conclusions about Guinea Bissau. Rudebeck, *op. cit.*, 248-52.
60. *Cabral*, chapter 4, section E.
61. See Skocpol, *op. cit.*
62. For two different views on the relevance of the plantations of northern Angola, see René Pélissier, *La Colonie du Minotaure* (Orgeval, 1978) and Mario de Andrade and Marc Ollivier, *La guerre en Angola: étude socio-économique* (Paris, 1971).
63. Cabral was an agronomist and, earlier, had conducted the first agricultural survey of Guinea. See his comments in 'Le rôle social de la paysannerie', in *Unité et Lutte*, 1 (Paris, 1975).
64. In both Guinea-Bissau and Mozambique there have been moves to return to some form of private trading and commerce.
65. By neutralised I mean that they are not, at the moment, politically salient. I am not implying, however, that they may not become politically salient in the future. I do not subscribe to the view that such forms of social identity 'disappear' with modernity. I am simply concerned here to analyse under what historical circumstances they become more or less salient.
66. These forms of social identity need not necessarily be divisive but, historically, they have often been so during the end of colonial rule and the first few years of independence in Africa. Revolution itself is no guarantee that such forms of social identity will not become politically salient again as quite clearly they have become in some countries which underwent a revolution.
67. See here Dunn, *Modern Revolutions*, and Skocpol, *op. cit.*
68. Wolf's comparative analysis is most relevant here.
69. All three countries have established, or seek to establish, close economic links with the West and with such economic agencies as that set up by the Lomé Convention.

Part V
The Internationalization
of Decolonization

China and the First Indo-China War, 1950–54*

Chen Jian

Despite its obvious significance, the involvement of the People's Republic of China (PRC) in the First Indo-China War has long been an under-researched and little understood subject in Cold War history. Because of lack of access to Chinese or Vietnamese sources, few of the many publications in English deal with China's connections with the war. In such highly acclaimed works as Marilyn B. Young's *The Vietnam Wars, 1945–1990*, Jacques Dallaoz's *The War in Indo-China, 1945–1954*, Anthony Short's *The Origins of the Vietnam War*, R. E. M. Irving's *The First Indo-China War*, Ellen Hammer's *The Struggle for Indo-China, 1946–1955*, Edgar O'Ballance's *The Indo-China War, 1945–1954*, and Bernard Fall's *Street Without Joy: Insurgency in Vietnam, 1946–1963*, the PRC's role is either discussed only marginally or almost completely neglected.[1] King Chen's *Vietnam and China, 1938–1954*, using information from contemporary newspapers and radio, gives the most detailed and generally plausible treatment of the PRC–Viet Minh relationship, but even this is restricted by its sources and fails to provide a comprehensive picture of the strategic co-operation between the Chinese and Vietnamese Communists, which leaves a crucial lacuna in judging the extent and nature of exchanges between the respective leaders.[2] This article uses recently-released Chinese sources, especially memoirs and diaries by key Chinese figures, telegrams from top Beijing leaders, and information attained through interviews, and offers some new insights into the PRC's policy towards the First Indo-China War.[3]

*This article was originally prepared for the fifth annual convention of Chinese Historians in the United States, held in August 1991 at Clark University. The author benefited greatly from comments and suggestions by Michael Hunt, Zhai Qiang, William Turley, Marilyn Young, Marc Trachtenberg, William Stueck and James Somerville. He is also grateful for Raymond Mayo's help in preparing the map and for the financial support of a 1991 SUNY–Geneseo Presidential Summer Fellowship.

1. Marilyn B. Young, *The Vietnam Wars, 1945–1990* (New York: Harper Collins, 1991); Jacques Dallaoz, *The War in Indo-China, 1945–1954* (Savage, MD: Barnes and Noble, 1990); Anthony Short, *The Origins of the Vietnam War* (London & New York: Longman, 1989); R. E. M. Irving, *The First Indo-China War* (London: Croom Helm, 1975); Ellen Hammer, *The Struggle for Indo-China, 1946–1955* (Stanford: Stanford University Press, 1966); Edgar O'Ballance, *The Indo-China War, 1945–1954* (London: Faber & Faber, 1964); and Bernard Fall, *Street Without Joy: Insurgency in Vietnam, 1946–1963* (Harrisburg, PA.: Stackpole, 1964, 4th ed.).

2. King Chen, *Vietnam and China, 1938–1954* (Princeton: Princeton University Press, 1969).

3. Since the mid-1980s, several major Chinese sources have been available for studies of China's involvement in the First Indo-China War, which release for the first time a series of previously unknown telegrams, directives and inner-Party documents of the Beijing leadership. The most valuable among these sources are *Jianguo yilai Mao Zedong wengao* (*Mao Zedong's Manuscripts since the Founding of the People's Republic*, hereafter *Mao Zedong's Manuscripts*), Vols. 1–5 (Beijing: Central Historical Documents Press, 1987–1991); The Editorial Group for the History of Chinese

(footnote 3 continued on page 86)

86   The China Quarterly

The Indo-China area (Vietnam, Cambodia and Laos) and China are neighbours and the Chinese Communist Party (CCP) and Vietnamese Communists have historically had close connections. Early in the 1920s, Ho Chi Minh and other Vietnamese Communists initiated contacts with their Chinese comrades. Ho himself often came to China and could speak fluent Chinese; in the late 1930s and early 1940s he was even a member of the CCP-led Eighth Route Army.[4] After the end of the Second World War, Ho's Indo-China Communist Party[5] led a national uprising and established the Democratic Republic of Vietnam (DRV) with Ho as president. When the French returned to re-establish control, Ho and his fellow Communists moved to mountainous areas to fight for independence, without support from the outside between 1946 and early 1950.

The Chinese Communist victory in 1949 offered Vietnamese Communists a golden opportunity to be backed by a friendly PRC. Both sides were eager to establish close co-operation. In late 1949, the Indo-China Communist Party sent Hoang Van Hoan, a member of its central committee, to China to strengthen ties between the two parties. (Hoang later became the first DRV ambassador to the PRC, defected to China in the late 1970s and died there in 1991.[6]) In early

---

(footnote 3 continued from page 85)

Military Advisers in Vietnam (ed.), *Zhongguo junshi guwentuan yuanyue kangfa douzheng shishi* (*A Factual Account of the Participation of Chinese Military Advisory Group in the Struggle of Assisting Vietnam and Resisting France*, hereafter *The CMAG in Vietnam*) (Beijing: People's Liberation Army Press, 1990); Luo Guibo, "Comrade Liu Shaoqi sent me to Vietnam," in He Jinxiu *et al.* (eds.), *Mianhuai Liu Shaoqi* (*In Commemoration of Liu Shaoqi*) (Beijing: Central Historical Documents Press, 1988); Chen Geng, *Chen Geng riji* (*Chen Geng's Diaries*), Vol. 2 (Beijing: People's Liberation Army Press, 1984); and Han Huanzhi and Tan Jinjiao *et al.*, *Dangdai zhongguo jundui de junshi gongzuo* (*The Military Affairs of the Contemporary Chinese Army*, hereafter *Contemporary Chinese Army*) (Beijing: Chinese Academy of Social Sciences Press, 1988). Although the Chinese authorities obviously allowed the declassification of these sources, usually on a selective basis, under the politically sensitive circumstance of a total confrontation between Beijing and Hanoi, the scholarly value of this fresh information should not be ignored. While a better scholarly balance could of course be reached with the releasing of the Vietnamese side of the story as well as a more complete declassification of Chinese documents, these new Chinese materials, combined with information from other sources, have created the basis for a new, though not conclusive, study of the PRC's involvement in the first Indo-China War.

4. For a Chinese account of Ho Chi Minh's connection with the Chinese Communist revolution from the 1920s to early 1940s, see Huang Zheng, *Ho Zhiming he zhongguo* (*Ho Chi Minh and China*) (Beijing: People's Liberation Army Press, 1987), chs. 1–4; see also Hoang Van Hoan, *A Drop in the Ocean: Hoang Van Hoan's Revolutionary Reminiscences* (Beijing: People's Liberation Army Press, 1987), chs. 3 and 4.

5. The Indo-China Communist Party was established in 1930; after February 1951, its name was changed to the Vietnamese Worker's Party (VWP or Dang Lao Dang Viet Nam).

6. Hoang Van Hoan, *A Drop in the Ocean*, pp. 247–253.

China and the First Indo-China War, 1950–54   87

Figure 1: **Indo-China, 1950–54**

January 1950, Liu Shaoqi, who was next to Mao in the CCP leadership, decided to send Luo Guibo, then director of the Administrative Office of the Central Military Committee of the CCP (CMCC), to be the CCP's liaison representative in Vietnam. Liu made it clear that Luo's appointment was approved by Mao and the CCP Central Committee. His task in Vietnam was to establish good communications between the two parties as well as to provide the CCP Central Committee with first-hand information for their plans to assist the Vietnamese Communists in their struggle for independence. Liu stressed to Luo that "it is the duty of those countries which have achieved the victory of their own revolution to support peoples who are still conducting the just struggle for liberation," and that "it is our international obligation to support the anti-French struggle of the Vietnamese people."[7] In mid-January 1950, the PRC granted formal

7. Luo Guibo, "Comrade Liu Shaoqi sent me to Vietnam," pp. 233–34; interview with Luo Guibo, 22 August 1992.

diplomatic recognition to the DRV so that it could participate in international society.[8]

Before Luo actually went to Vietnam, however, Ho Chi Minh, after walking for 17 days, secretly arrived in China in late January. Liu Shaoqi immediately received him and reported his visit to Mao Zedong, who was then in Moscow. Meanwhile, the CCP Central Committee established an ad hoc commission composed of Zhu De, vice-chairman of the Central People's Government and commander-in-chief of the People's Liberation Army (PLA), Nie Rongzhen, acting general chief of staff of the PLA, and Li Weihan, director of the United Front Department of the CCP Central Committee, to discuss with Ho his mission in China.[9] Ho made it clear that he came to obtain a substantial Chinese commitment to support the Vietnamese Communists.[10] He also wished to meet Stalin and Mao in Moscow and obtain Soviet and Chinese military, political and economic assistance. Through arrangements by the CCP and the Soviet Communist Party, Ho arrived in Moscow in early February.[11]

Ho's secret trip to Moscow brought mixed results. While the Soviet Union decided to recognize Ho's government, Stalin had international priorities in Europe and was unfamiliar with, and to a certain extent even suspicious of, Ho's intentions. He was therefore reluctant to commit the strength of the Soviet Union directly to the Vietnamese Communists and turned Ho to the Chinese.[12] To Ho's great satisfaction, Mao and Zhou, first in Moscow then Beijing (to where Ho

8. Mao Zedong to Liu Shaoqi, 17 and 18 January 1950, *Mao Zedong's Manuscripts*, Vol. 1, pp. 238–39; see also Zhou Enlai's statement recognizing the Democratic Republic of Vietnam, 18 January 1950, *Xinhua yuebao* (*New China Monthly*), February 1950, p. 847. When deciding to recognize Ho's government, CCP leaders understood that this would inevitably make an early French recognition of the Chinese Communist regime unlikely. They still believed, however, that recognizing the DRV was in the fundamental interests of revolutionary China. Following the example of China, the Soviet Union and other Communist countries quickly recognized the DRV. The DRV government later named 18 January as the day of "diplomatic victory." See Hoang Van Hoan, *A Drop in the Ocean*, pp. 255–56; *Renmin ribao*, 7 February 1951.

9. Luo Guibo, "Comrade Liu Shaoqi sent me to Vietnam," pp. 234–35; see also Hoang Van Hoan, *A Drop in the Ocean*, pp. 254–56 (in his memoir, Hoang recalls that Mao held a banquet in Ho's honour after Ho reached Beijing, but as Mao was then in Moscow, this was impossible); *The CMAG in Vietnam*, pp. 1–2; Han Nianlong *et al.*, *Dangdai zhongguo waijiao* (*Contemporary Chinese Diplomacy*) (Beijing: Chinese Academy of Social Sciences Press, 1988), p. 55.

10. Hoang Van Hoan, *A Drop in the Ocean*, pp. 254–55; Huang Zheng, *Ho Chi Minh and China*, p. 125.

11. Luo Guibo, "Comrade Liu Shaoqi sent me to Vietnam," p. 235; Hoang Van Hoan, *A Drop in the Ocean*, pp. 254–55.

12. For a plausible analysis of Stalin's attitude towards Ho Chi Minh and the Viet Minh in the early period of the First Indo-China War, see Gary Hess, *Vietnam and the United States: Origins and Legacy of War* (Boston: Twayne Publishers, 1990), p. 37. For Stalin's attitude toward Ho during Ho's visit to Moscow, see Li Ke, "Chinese military advisers in the war to assist Vietnam and resist France," *Junshi lishi* (*Military History*), No. 3 (1989), p. 27; Wu Xiuquan, *Huiyi yu huainian* (*Recollections and Commemorations*) (Beijing: Central Party School Press, 1991), pp. 242–43; my interviews with Chinese researchers who had access to archives in May 1991 and August 1992 also confirmed that during Ho's visit to Moscow Stalin refused to offer direct military and financial support to the Viet Minh.

returned), promised that the CCP would do its best "to offer every military assistance needed by Vietnam in its struggle against France." When Ho returned to Vietnam he was certain that he could now rely on China's support.[13]

The CCP's attitude towards Vietnam was first and foremost the natural result of the Chinese Communist perception of an Asian revolution following the Chinese model. During the Chinese Communist revolution, Mao and other CCP leaders had consistently seen it as part of a world proletarian revolutionary movement initiated by the Russian Bolsheviks. As it progressed, however, and differed from the Russian Revolution by concentrating largely on rural instead of urban areas, Mao and the CCP leadership had second thoughts on the nature and significance of their revolution. During 1948–49 they began to talk in terms of a much broader anti-imperialist Asian and world revolution. First, their model of revolution transcended China and offered an example of universal significance to other peoples struggling for national liberation. Secondly, the victory of the Chinese revolution represented the beginning of a new high tide of revolution movements of oppressed peoples in Asia and the world. Consequently, they believed it their duty to assist Communist revolutionaries and national liberation movements in other countries in order to promote an Asia-wide or even world-wide revolution.[14]

The CCP's policy of supporting the Vietnamese Communists was also consistent with Mao's "leaning to one side" approach, one of the corner-stones of the CCP's domestic and international policy in the early years of the PRC. Materials available now reveal that during Liu Shaoqi's secret visit to the Soviet Union in July and August 1949, Stalin strongly encouraged the Chinese to take a larger role in promoting revolutionary movements in East Asia.[15] When Mao visited Moscow, the Chinese and the Soviets may have further divided the sphere of responsibility between them, leaving the support of Communist revolutionaries in Vietnam as China's duty.[16]

13. Huang Zheng, *Ho Chi Minh and China*, pp. 125–26; Hoang Van Hoan, *A Drop in the Ocean*, pp. 254–55; *Contemporary Chinese Army*, pp. 520, 576.

14. Liu Shaoqi, "Internationalism and nationalism," *Renmin ribao*, 7 November 1948; Liu Shaoqi's address on the Conference of Union of the Asian-Pacific region, *Xinhua yuebao*, No. 2, Vol. 1, p. 440. See also Jin Zhonghua, "China's liberation and the world situation," *Shijie zhishi* (*World Affairs*), Vol. 20, No. 1, 17 June 1949; Du Ruo, "China's liberation and South-east Asia," *World Affairs*, Vol. 20, No. 4, 8 July 1949; "China's revolution and the struggle against colonialism," *People's China*, 16 February 1950, pp. 4–5.

15. For a more detailed discusson of Liu Shaoqi's visit to Moscow, see Chen Jian, "The Sino-Soviet alliance and China's entry into the Korean War," (Washington, D.C.: The Cold War International History Project of the Woodrow Wilson International Center for Scholars, December 1991), pp. 9–15; see also Shi Zhe, "Random reflections of Comrade Liu Shaoqi," *Geming huiyilu* (*Revolutionary Memoirs*), supplementary issue, No. 1 (October 1983), pp. 110–11; Zhu Yuanshi, "Liu Shaoqi's secret visit to the Soviet Union in 1949," *Dangde wenxian* (*Party Historical Documents*), No. 3 (1991), pp. 76–77.

16. Interviews with Chinese researchers in May 1991; see also Li Ke, "Chinese military advisers," p. 27.

China's commitment to Ho's struggle in Vietnam was apparently compatible with the Sino-Soviet strategic alliance.

CCP leaders also believed that standing by their Vietnamese comrades would serve their goal of safeguarding China's national security interests. Mao, though a Marxist–Leninist revolutionary, demonstrated interestingly an approach similar to many traditional Chinese rulers: the safety of the "Middle Kingdom" could not be properly maintained if its neighbouring areas fell into the hands of hostile "barbarian" forces. In 1949–50, while considering potential threats to China's national safety, Mao and the CCP leadership were particularly concerned with the prospect of a military confrontation with imperialist countries and their acolytes in the Korean Peninsula, Indo-China, and the Taiwan Strait. Convinced that events in these areas were closely interrelated, they viewed supporting Vietnamese Communists as an effective means of strengthening their position against the threat to China's national security interests by the United States.[17] This view was supported by the fact that some Chinese Nationalist units who were still loyal to Chiang Kai-shek had fled to the Chinese–Vietnamese border area, making it a source of trouble for the newly-established CCP regime.[18] After the outbreak of the Korean War, although Mao and the CCP leadership placed the emphasis of their strategy vis-à-vis the United States on Korea, they continued to view the Vietnamese Communist struggle against the French as part of the overall anti-imperialist struggle in the Far East.[19]

When the decision to support the Vietnamese Communists was made, the CCP moved forward immediately. On 13 March 1950, Liu Shaoqi telegraphed Luo Guibo, who had arrived in the Viet Minh's Viet Bac (northern Vietnam) base four days earlier, instructing him to start his work in two stages. He was first to deal with urgent problems, including providing the CCP Central Committee with a clear idea about the way in which Chinese military, economic and financial aids

---

17. In the autumn and winter of 1949, the CCP leaders believed that China should now prepare to confront the American threat in three inter-related areas: Vietnam, Korea and the Taiwan Strait. They also believed, as later pointed out by Zhou Enlai, that a conflict between Communist China and the United States was inevitable. Accordingly, in the spring of 1950, CCP military planners decided to deploy their central reserves (three armies under the Fourth Field Army) along a railway within easy reach of Shanghai, Tianjin and Guangzhou, so as to be able to move in any of the three directions. For a detailed analysis of the CCP's military preparations under the "three fronts" assumption, see Chen Jian, "China's road to the Korean War," Ph.D. dissertation, Southern Illinois University, 1990, ch. 6; see also Zhang Shuguang, "Deterrence and Sino-American confrontation, 1949–1958," Ph.D. dissertation, Ohio University, 1990, pp. 78–79.

18. From late 1949 to early 1951, Mao and the Chinese military planners paid close attention to the annihilation of remaining Nationalist troops in areas adjacent to the Vietnamese border. See Mo Yang and Yao Jie *et al.*, *Zhongguo renmin jiefangjun zhanshi* (*The War History of the Chinese People's Liberation Army*), Vol. 3 (Beijing: Academy of Military Sciences Press, 1987), pp. 394–98.

19. Chen Geng, *Chen Geng's Diaries*, Vol. 2, p. 7; Yao Xu, *Cong Yalujiang dao Banmendian* (*From the Yalu River to Panmunjom*) (Beijing: The People's Press, 1985), pp. 21–22.

China and the First Indo-China War, 1950–54 91

should be given to the Vietnamese and how these aids could reach Vietnam. Secondly, Luo was instructed to make careful investigations to enable him to understand the overall situation in Vietnam so that he could offer the CCP Central Committee suggestions about how to prepare long-term conditions for beating the French colonists.[20] The CCP obviously took the cause of the Vietnamese Communists as if it were their own.

In April 1950, the Central Committee of the Indo-China Communist Party formally asked for military advisers from the CCP. The CCP leadership responded immediately. On 17 April, the CMCC ordered each of the PLA's Second, Third and Fourth Field Armies to provide advisers at battalion, regiment and division levels for a Vietnamese division. The Third Field Army organized the headquarters of the Chinese Military Advisory Group (CMAG) while the Fourth Field Army set up a military school for the Vietnamese. On 26 April, the CMCC instructed the PLA North-western, South-western, Eastern, and South-central Headquarters to offer another 13 cadres over battalion level to join the CMAG to work with the Vietnamese Communists at the top commanding positions of their forces.[21] The military advisers gathered in Beijing during May and received indoctrination courses for the CCP's international policy. They also met top CCP leaders to receive instructions. General Wei Guoqing, political commissar of the Tenth Army Corps of the Third Field Army, was assigned to take charge of the preparation work.[22]

However, before training was completed, the Korean War started on 25 June 1950. The United States responded swiftly and firmly. Within 36 hours, American policy-makers decided to dispatch military forces to assist South Korea. Meanwhile, President Harry Truman ordered the Seventh Fleet to enter the Taiwan strait to neutralize the area. The Korean War quickly changed into an international crisis.

The North Korean attack on the South should not have greatly surprised Chinese leaders because of their close contact with North Korean leaders. Mao Zedong and others in Beijing, however, were certainly shocked by the quick and unyielding American reaction. They viewed it not as an isolated event, but as the reflection of an overall American plot of aggression in the Far East, including China, Korea, Vietnam and the Philippines.[23] Accordingly, Mao and the CCP leadership decided to push forward their support to the Viet Minh.[24]

20. Cited from Luo Guibo, "Comrade Liu Shaoqi sent me to Vietnam," p. 238.
21. *Contemporary Chinese Army*, pp. 518–19; *The CMAG in Vietnam*, p. 3.
22. *The CMAG in Vietnam*, p. 3.
23. See the PRC Information Bureau's instruction, 29 June 1950, in the Research Department of the Xinhua News Agency (eds.), *Xinhuashe wenjian ziliao xuanbian* (*A Selected Collection of Documents of the Xinhua News Agency*), Beijing, n.d., p. 50.
24. For a more detailed discussion of the overall change of the CCP's strategy vis-à-vis the United States after the outbreak of the Korean War, see Chen Jian, "China's road to the Korean War," pp. 180–82.

On 27 June, two days after the outbreak of the Korean War, Mao
Zedong, Liu Shaoqi, Zhu De and other top CCP leaders received the
Chinese military advisers who were preparing to work in Vietnam.
Stressing that supporting Vietnamese Communists was the "glorious
internationalist duty" of the Chinese revolutionaries, Mao assigned
the advisers two major tasks: to help the Vietnamese organize and
establish a formal army, and to assist them in planning and
conducting major operations to defeat the French colonists. Liu
Shaoqi explained the reasons for the decision to support the Viet
Minh. He emphasized that Vietnam was an important area and that
sending Chinese military advisers there would have world-wide
significance. If they failed to support the Vietnamese revolutionaries
and allowed the enemy to stay there, Liu stated, this would cause
more difficulties and trouble for the Chinese.[25] The CMAG, composed of 79 experienced PLA officers, was formally established in late
July, with General Wei Guoqing as the head, assisted by Generals Mei
Jiasheng and Deng Yifan, both army-level commanders from the
Third Field Army. To maintain secrecy, they were known publicly as
the "Working Group in Southern China." They finally arrived in
Vietnam in early August, and started to serve with the Vietnamese
Communist forces.[26]

Meanwhile, the CCP leadership had decided to send General Chen
Geng, one of the most talented high-ranking PLA commanders and a
member of the CCP Central Committee and commander of the PLA's
20th Army Corps, to Vietnam to help organize a major military
campaign along the Chinese–Vietnamese border so that the Viet
Minh would be directly backed by the PRC. This idea was first put
forward by Ho during his visit to China in early 1950 and was
received with much interest by the CCP leadership. Ho himself had
suggested Chen Geng, whom he had known since the 1920s.[27] General
Chen travelled to the Viet Bac bases in mid-July. After a series of
meetings with Ho Chi Minh, General Vo Nguyen Giap and other Viet
Minh leaders, he suggested that the Vietnamese–Chinese border
campaign should follow the line of "concentrating our forces and
destroying the enemy troops by separating them," a principle that had
proved effective for the Communists during China's civil war. Ho and
the Vietnamese accepted this plan.[28] On 22 July 1950, Chen reported
by telegraph to the CCP Central Committee that he had reached a
consensus in the general strategy of the forthcoming border campaign.
They would first annihilate some mobile units of the enemy in mobile

25. *Contemporary Chinese Army*, pp. 519–520; *The CMAG in Vietnam*, pp. 5–6.
26. *Contemporary Chinese Army*, p. 520; *The CMAG in Vietnam*, p. 4.
27. Xu Peilai and Zheng Pengfei, *Chen Geng jiangjunzhuan (The Biography of
General Chen Geng)* (Beijing: People's Liberation Army Press, 1988), pp. 580–81; Mu
Xin, *Chen Geng dajiang (General Chen Geng)* (Beijing: People's Liberation Army Press,
1988), pp. 581–599.
28. *Contemporary Chinese Army*, pp. 521–33; Chen Geng, *Chen Geng's Diaries*, Vol.
2, pp. 9, 11; interview with Luo Guibo, 22 August 1992.

operations and destroy a few small enemy strongholds. This would allow the Vietnamese to gain experience, stimulate and consolidate the momentum of their soldiers, and win the initiative, so that they would be ready for large-scale operations. Then they would start an offensive against Cao Bang, a small town on the Vietnamese–Chinese border, by adopting a strategy of "besieging the enemy to annihilate its relief force": instead of attacking the town directly, they would surround it and sweep out enemy strongholds in the peripheral areas one by one while at the same time attracting and destroying the enemy's reinforcements from Lang Son, and then seize Cao Bang. Chen believed that this strategy would guarantee the occupation of Cao Bang, "thus thoroughly changing the balance of power between the enemy and us in north-eastern and northern Vietnam." The CMCC approved Chen's plan in a telegram to him on 26 July.[29] To guarantee that the strategy would be fully followed by Vietnamese units, Chinese military advisers were sent to the battalion, regiment and division levels of Vietnamese troops, with the approval of Ho.

The Chinese also offered assistance in military equipment and other war materials to support the border campaign. In late March 1950, Luo Guibo asked the CCP Central Committee for military equipment, ammunition and communication equipment for 16,000 soldiers, to be used in military operations against Cao Bang and Lao Cai.[30] From April to September 1950 the Chinese delivered more than 14,000 guns, 1,700 machine guns, about 150 pieces of different types of cannons, 2,800 tons of grain, and large amounts of ammunition, medicine, uniforms and communication equipment.[31]

The border campaign started on 16 September. After 48 hours of fierce fighting Vietnamese troops seized Dong Khe, a strategically important spot on Route Colonial Four which linked Cao Bang with the inner land of Vietnam, in the early morning of 18 September. The French command was surprised and dispatched a mobile army corps to Dong Khe while sending five battalions to attack Thai Nguyen, the location of the Viet Minh centre. Chen judged that their real purpose was to rescue their isolated units in Cao Bang. Instead of withdrawing troops from the Dong Khe–Cao Bang area to defend the Viet Minh centre, he strengthened pressure over Cao Bang. On 3 October, as he had predicted, French troops retreated from the Dong Khe and Cao Bang area and moved south, to fall into his trap in nearby mountains. In response to Chen's report about the situation, Mao sent him a telegram on 6 October to give him clear instructions on the final stage of the campaign:

It is correct for you to plan first to concentrate your main forces on eliminating the enemy troops south-west of Dong Khe who have now been surrounded by us and then, according to the situation, surround and

29. *Contemporary Chinese Army*, pp. 522–23.
30. *The CMAG in Vietnam*, p. 44.
31. *Ibid.* pp. 44–46; Mu Xin, *General Chen Geng*, pp. 590–93.

94   The China Quarterly

annihilate the enemy troops escaping south from Cao Bang. If the enemy
troops south-west of Dong Khe can be annihilated in a few days, the enemies
from Cao Bang can be held, and the enemy reinforcements in Lang Son and
other places will dare not come out; or we can use part of our troops to stop
the enemy's reinforcements, defeat the enemies both in Cao Bang and Dong
Khe and thus win two victories. So, you have to annihilate the enemy troops
south-west of Dong Khe swiftly, resolutely and thoroughly; your determination should not waver even in the face of heavy casualties (and you must
anticipate that some cadres may start to waver). Meanwhile, you have to hold
the enemies escaping from Cao Bang and make due preparation for the enemy
reinforcements from Lang Son and other places. If you can properly solve
these three problems, victory will be yours.[32]

Ho also read this telegram, and then ordered the final assault on 6
October. By 13 October, seven battalions of French troops, about
3,000 men, were destroyed, and the French were forced to give up the
blockade line along the Vietnamese–Chinese border which they had
held for years.[33] General Chen Geng left Vietnam in early November
1950 to take up commanding responsibility in Korea.[34]

The Viet Minh's victory in the border campaign changed the
balance of power in the Indo-China battlefield. With the vast territory
of the PRC backing them, Ho Chi Minh and the Vietnamese
Communists were now in an unbeatable position. Encouraged by the
victory, Giap and other Viet Minh military leaders, together with
members of the CMAG, planned to lead the war to the Tonkin Delta
area. They hoped that a series of victories against the weak links of the
French defensive system on the Delta would create the conditions for
a total Viet Minh victory in Indo-China.[35] The CMCC and the Central
Committee of the Indo-China Communist Party both endorsed the
plan.[36]

At almost the same time as this plan was made, General Jean de
Lattre de Tassingny, former commander-in-chief of the land forces of
Western Europe, was appointed by the French government as high
commissioner and commander-in-chief in Indo-China. Immediately
after his arrival in Saigon, he started a programme to strengthen the
French defensive system in the Delta area. By integrating into his
defensive planning every means available, including the French air
force which was now equipped with new American techniques, he
called French soldiers to stick to, and if necessary, to be destroyed in,

32. Cited from *The CMAG in Vietnam*, p. 22.
33. *Contemporary Chinese Army*, pp. 524–27.
34. Chen Geng, *Chen Geng's Diaries*, Vol. 2, pp. 39–42; *The CMAG in Vietnam*,
p. 25.
35. Giap even boasted that he would be able to put Ho Chi Minh back in Hanoi by
the end of 1950. See O'Ballance, *The Indo-China War*, p. 121. It is interesting to note
that Chinese sources fail to provide as detailed a coverage of the period in early 1951
when the Viet Minh forces suffered several setbacks as they do of the border campaign,
the north-west campaign and the Dien Bien Phu siege.
36. *The CMAG in Vietnam*, p. 27.

China and the First Indo-China War, 1950–54 95

the Delta.[37] The Viet Minh's new offensive plan was now encountering a difficult French general.

From late December 1950 to June 1951, Viet Minh troops initiated three campaigns respectively in the Vinh Yen area, about 20 miles north of Hanoi (the "Tran Huong Dao" campaign), the Mao Khe area next to Hai Phong (the "Hong Hoa Tham" campaign), and the Ninh Binh area (the "Quang Trung" campaign). General Giap used Viet Minh's best units, including the "iron division" (the 308th Division), in these operations, hoping that the "general counter-offensive" would bring the Viet Minh closer to a final victory. However, Viet Minh forces suffered from heavy casualties from firm French defence supported by superior artillery fire, without making any significant strategic gains. General Giap had to give up plans for head-on attacks against fortified positions in the Red River Delta area by mid-1951,[38] and the Viet Minh high command and their Chinese advisers had to reconsider the whole strategy. The CMAG was now convinced that it was premature for Viet Minh forces to wage the "general counter-offensive" aimed at seizing the Delta area, and they must instead shift the direction of their operations.[39]

Meanwhile, the French hoped to extend their victory. While continuing to consolidate their control over the Delta area, they began a counter-offensive against Hoa Binh, the key point in the Viet Minh's north–south line of communications. If they occupied this area they would, among other things, be in a favourable position to establish a corridor from Hai Phong through Hanoi and Hoa Binh to Son La, thus totally cutting off the connection between the Viet Minh forces in the north and south.[40]

General Giap asked advice from Luo Guibo and Deng Yifan (both Wei Guoqing and Mei Jiasheng were then taking sick leave in China). Following the instructions of the CMCC, Deng suggested the Viet Minh forces should cope with the French attack with medium or small-scale mobile wars. Luo further proposed that Viet Minh forces should not only focus on defending the Hoa Binh area, which they could not afford to lose, but also dispatch some units to the rear of the French-occupied zones to conduct guerrilla operations aimed at harassing the enemy and restoring guerrilla bases. The Vietnamese Workers' Party (VWP) Central Committee and the Viet Minh high command carefully studied these suggestions and decided in late November to start an all-out effort aimed at smashing the French offensive. They would deploy four divisions in defending the Hoa Binh area and send the 316th and 320th Divisions into areas behind the enemy lines.[41] The Viet Minh forces' counter-offensive began in

37. Phillip B. Davidson, *Vietnam at War: The History 1946–1975* (Oxford: Oxford University Press, 1988), p. 102.
38. *Ibid.* pp. 105–127.
39. *The CMAG in Vietnam*, p. 30.
40. Davidson, *Vietnam at War*, pp. 129–130.
41. *The CMAG in Vietnam*, pp. 31–32; interview with Luo Guibo, 22 August 1992.

early December 1951. After three months of difficult efforts, General Giap and his troops successfully repulsed the French, maintained their position in Hoa Binh, and strengthened their overall strategic status.

Chinese military advisers were now more convinced than ever of the necessity of waging guerrilla warfare in the rear of the enemy zones. Luo Guibo, who was then also in charge of the CMAG during the sick leave of General Wei Guoqing,[42] recommended that the Viet Minh should consider leading the war into the vast north-west so that the overall military situation in Indo-China could be changed in the Viet Minh's favour.[43]

Early in 1952, after several months of investigation of the situation on the battlefield, the CMAG sent two reports, "A study of the conditions between the enemy and us in Northern Vietnam and our tasks and policy lines in the future" and "Tasks and policy lines for 1952," to the Vietnamese, proposing to start a new campaign – the north-west campaign. Chinese military advisers believed that this would further consolidate the Viet Minh's liberation zone in north-western Vietnam, and form the basis for a general strategic counter-offensive in the future.[44] On 16 February 1952, the CMAG proposed to the Viet Minh high command that that year they should focus on guerrilla tactics and small-scale mobile wars to gain time for their main formations to go through political and military training and preparation for conditions for combat tasks in the north-west. The same day, Luo Guibo stated in a report to the CMCC that in the first half of 1952 Viet Minh troops would focus on rectification and training; in the second half of 1952 they would try to eliminate enemies in Son La, Lai Chau and Nghia Lo, all in north-western Vietnam, and consolidate their control of these areas; and then in 1953 they would take north-western Vietnam as a base to initiate operations in upper Laos.[45] This plan was quickly approved by the CMCC. Liu Shaoqi commented that "it is very important to liberate Laos."[46] The Vietnamese Communists also gave their approval. On 18 March, the Viet Minh high command decided to include the organization of the north-west campaign as one of its three major tasks of 1952 (the other two being conducting political rectification of Viet Minh troops and guerrilla operations in the rear of the enemy forces). In April 1952, the VWP Politburo formally decided to initiate the north-west campaign, and Chinese military advisers were authorized by Ho himself to command it.[47]

42. The CCP Central Military Committee assigned Luo to head the CMAG in early 1952. In May 1952, he was formally appointed by the CMCC as the head of the CMAG. See *The CMAG in Vietnam*, p. 53.
43. *Ibid.* and interview with Luo Guibo, 22 August 1992.
44. *Contemporary Chinese Army*, pp. 527–28.
45. *The CMAG in Vietnam*, pp. 52, 56.
46. *Ibid.* p. 56.
47. *Ibid.* pp. 56–57; *Contemporary Chinese Army*, p. 528.

On 14 April, Luo reported to the CMCC on the CMAG's initial plan for the campaign. Offensive operations in north-western provinces would begin in mid-September. Viet Minh troops would first attack Nghia Lo, the province closest to the Viet Minh's Viet Bac bases, and then march toward Son La. After the liberation of most of the north-west region in 1952, Viet Minh troops would attack Lai Chau in 1953. The CMCC approved Luo's plan in a telegram to him on 19 April. They anticipated fierce fighting in seizing Nghia Lo, and the telegram stressed the importance of making proper preparations before the start of the campaign.[48]

Luo and Mei Jiasheng, then the second deputy chairman of the CMAG, analysed the military situation in the north-west further, and sent a telegram to the CMCC on 11 July suggesting two stages to the north-west campaign. In the first stage, they would use two divisions to seize Nghia Lo and at the same time annihilate the enemy's paratroopers, if used as reinforcements. In the second stage, they would dispatch three regiments to enter Son La, while using the other three regiments, together with two regiments in Phu Tho, to march towards Lai Chau. They would thus be able to occupy all of north-western Vietnam by the end of 1952. In accordance with the demands of the Vietnamese, they also asked the CCP to send Chinese troops from Yunnan province to take part in attacking Lai Chau.[49]

On 22 July, the CCP Central Committee replied that the PRC would not send troops directly into fights in Vietnam, because this had long been an established principle. Chinese troops, however, could be deployed along the Chinese–Vietnamese border, in the Hekuo and Jinjie area in Yunnan province. The telegram also instructed Chinese military advisers to adopt the strategy of "concentrating our own forces" and "the easiest first and the most difficult last," seizing Nghia Lo province before considering occupying the entire north-west. The CMCC reminded the CMAG that Viet Minh troops lacked experience of offensive operations and asked the CMAG and the Viet Minh high command not to pursue the total occupation of the north-west by the end of 1952, but to prepare for a protracted war.[50] In early September, the VWP politburo decided to conduct the north-west campaign following these suggestions.[51]

In late September, Ho Chi Minh secretly visited Beijing. The CCP leadership and Ho agreed on the grand strategic design that the Viet Minh would first concentrate their main attention in the north-west (including north-western Vietnam and upper Laos), then march southward from upper Laos, and finally compete for the Red River Delta. In terms of the concrete plan of the campaign, following the

48. *The CMAG in Vietnam*, p. 57.
49. *Ibid.* pp. 57–58.
50. *Ibid.* p. 58; see also *Contemporary Chinese Army*, p. 528.
51. Ho Chi Minh, "Instructions on the cadres' meeting for preparing the north-west campaign, 9 September 1952," *Selected Works of Ho Chi Minh* (Hanoi: The Foreign Language Press, 1962), Vol. 2, pp. 232–36; *The CMAG in Vietnam*, p. 59.

suggestions of CCP leaders, (especially Mao Zedong and Peng Dehuai), the CMAG and Viet Minh high command decided to concentrate on Nghia Lo. After seizing Nghia Lo, Viet Minh troops would not attack Son La immediately but focus on establishing revolutionary bases around Nghia Lo and constructing the highway linking it with Yen Bay. General Giap may have had different opinions about the narrowing down of the campaign goals, but as the Chinese emphasized the importance of winning a steady victory he finally yielded.[52] General Wei, after almost a year's sick leave, returned to his post in mid-October to participate in commanding the campaign.

It began on 14 October 1952. The Vietnamese Communists concentrated eight regiments in attacking French strongholds in Nghia Lo. In ten days, they annihilated most enemy bases. After a short period of readjustment, Viet Minh troops continued to attack enemies in Son La and Lai Chau. By early December 1952, Nghia Lo, Son La, southern Lai Chau and western Yen Bay, all in north-western Vietnam, had been liberated by Vietnamese Communists.[53]

After this victory the VWP Central Committee, having consulted the CCP several times, decided in February 1953 to develop further to the west by organizing the Xam Neua campaign in upper Laos. This would connect the "liberation zone" in north-western Vietnam with Communist-occupied areas in northern Laos, thus imposing greater pressure on the French.[54] On 23 March 1953, Wei Guoqing and Mei Jiasheng led some members of the CMAG to Laos to organize the campaign. It started in late March and lasted until early May. The Viet Minh troops annihilated three battalions and 11 companies of the enemy, seizing control of the entire Xam Neua province and part of Xiang Khoary and Phong Sali provinces. The Viet Minh base in north-western Vietnam was now linked with these areas and its military position was further enhanced.[55]

By the summer of 1953, the confrontation between Vietnamese Communists and the French on the Indo-China battlefield had reached a point of dramatic change: the Viet Minh's gains in the past two years put them in a position to pursue other major campaigns aimed at establishing an overriding superiority in the war. Meanwhile the end of the Korean conflict in July 1953 meant that the Chinese were able to give more attention to their southern neighbour. Vietnamese Communists and the CMAG therefore began to formulate military plans for the autumn and winter of 1953 and spring of 1954.

At this stage there were changes on the French side. In the face of a series of setbacks under the pressure of the Viet Minh offensives, in May 1953 General Henri Navarre replaced General Raoul Salan (who had succeeded General de Lattre in 1952) as the commander of the

52. *The CMAG in Vietnam*, pp. 58–59.
53. *Contemporary Chinese Army*, p. 529.
54. *The CMAG in Vietnam*, p. 63.
55. *Ibid.* pp. 64–65.

French forces in Indo-China. Supported by the United States, Navarre immediately adopted a new strategy aimed at winning back the initiative on the battlefield over a three-year period. He divided Indo-China into northern and southern theatres along the 18th parallel, and aimed to eliminate Viet Minh guerrillas in southern and south-central Vietnam by spring 1954 and then, by spring 1955, concentrate the main formation of French forces to fight a decisive battle with the Communist forces in the Red River Delta.[56] To carry out this plan, the French began to send more troops to Indo-China. The United States, released from its heavy burden in the Korean conflict and worried about the serious consequences of French losses in Indo-China, dramatically increased its military and financial support (by an additional $400 million) to France in order to check "Communist expansion" in another key part of East Asia.[57]

The VWP Central Committee asked the CCP Central Committee on 13 August 1953 "to help offer opinions" concerning "the understanding of the current situation as well as strategies for operations in the future."[58] The VWP politburo, following the initiative of General Giap, decided on 22 August that they would transfer the emphasis of their future operations from the mountainous north-western area to the Red River Delta. The former would be maintained but not as a priority. Luo Guibo attended the meeting of the VWP politburo and reported this strategic change to the CCP Central Committee.[59]

The CCP Central Committee sent messages to Luo and the VWP Central Committee on both 27 and 29 August, opposing the change of strategic emphasis and insisting that the original plan of focusing on the north-western battlefield should be continued. In the 29 August telegram the CCP Central Committee emphasized:

We should first annihilate enemies in the Lai Chau area, liberating northern and central Laos, and then extend the battlefield gradually toward southern Laos and Cambodia, thus putting pressure on Saigon. By adopting this strategy, we will be able to limit the human and financial resources of the enemy and separate enemy troops, leaving the enemy in a disadvantageous position . . . . The realization of this strategic plan will surely contribute to the final defeat of the colonial rule of French imperialists in Vietnam, Laos and Cambodia. Of course, we need to overcome a variety of difficulties and prepare for a prolonged war.[60]

The VWP politburo met in September to discuss this. Ho favoured the opinions of the Chinese, and the politburo decided that the strategic emphasis of the Viet Minh's operations would be kept in the north-western area.[61] On 10 October, the CCP Central Committee

56. Davidson, *Vietnam at War*, pp. 162–67.
57. Hess, *Vietnam and the United States*, p. 43.
58. *The CMAG in Vietnam*, p. 87.
59. *Ibid.* p. 88; see also *Contemporary Chinese Army*, p. 529.
60. *The CMAG in Vietnam*, p. 88; see also Li Ke, "Chinese military advisers," p. 28.
61. *Contemporary Chinese Army*, p. 529; *The CMAG in Vietnam*, pp. 88–89.

informed the VWP Central Committee that Wei Guoqing had been appointed as the general military adviser and Luo Guibo the general political adviser, representing the CCP in all military and political decision-making in the future. Wei came back to Beijing to report the situation in Indo-China personally to the CCP Central Committee. Mao received him and emphasized again that emphasis upon the north-western area should be maintained.[62]

In late October and early November 1953, Wei and the Viet Minh high command made the operation plan for winter 1953 and spring 1954. According to this plan, Vietnamese Communist forces would continue to focus on Lai Chau. They would try to seize the entire Lai Chau province in January 1954, and then attack various places in upper and central Laos. At the same time, Viet Minh troops would march from the mountainous areas in central Vietnam toward Laos, making lower Laos the target for attacks from two directions. The VWP politburo approved this plan on 3 November 1953,[63] and in the middle of that month five regiments of Viet Minh forces headed toward Lai Chau.

General Navarre received intelligence reports about Viet Minh troop movements and, following the spirit of his original plan, decided on 20 November to drop six parachute battalions to Dien Bien Phu, a strategically important village in the north-western area. If the French controlled Dien Bien Phu, Navarre believed, they would be able to prevent the Communist forces from occupying the entire north-western region and attacking upper Laos, and it would also form a "launching point" for offensives to destroy Viet Minh forces. The French quickly reinforced their troops at Dien Bien Phu, constructed airstrips, and started building defences, making the village a real fortification. Dien Bien Phu thus became the focus of the whole Indo-China battlefield.

General Wei Guoqing learned that French paratroopers had landed at Dien Bien Phu on his way from Viet Bac to the north-western area. After consulting other members of the CMAG, Wei suggested to the CMCC that Viet Minh troops should start a campaign to surround French forces in Dien Bien Phu while still sticking to the original plan of attacking Lai Chau. The CMCC approved, and instructed Wei to convey the idea to the Viet Minh high command. They also stressed that in addition to its military and political importance, the Dien Bien Phu campaign would have enormous international influence.[64]

The CCP's emphasis on the international significance of the Dien Bien Phu campaign should be understood in the context of the Communist negotiation strategy which took shape in late 1953 and early 1954. With the end of the Korean War, the Communist world launched a "peace offensive" in late 1953. On 26 September, the

62. Li Ke, "Chinese military advisers," p. 28; *The CMAG in Vietnam*, p. 89.
63. *The CMAG in Vietnam*, pp. 89–90.
64. *Contemporary Chinese Army*, p. 530.

Soviet Union proposed in a note to the French, British and American governments that a five-power conference (including China) should be convened to discuss ways of easing international tensions. On 8 October Zhou Enlai issued a statement supporting the Soviet proposal, followed by another two months later, on 9 January 1954, asserting that international tensions in Asia needed to be solved through direct consultations by big powers. The Berlin four-power conference at the end of January finally endorsed the Soviet-initiated plan to convene an international conference at Geneva to discuss the restoration of peace in Korea and Indo-China.[65] A victory at Dien Bien Phu would greatly help to strengthen the Communist position at the forthcoming conference.

The Viet Minh high command responded favourably to the CMAG's Dien Bien Phu campaign proposal. The VWP Central Committee and the CMAG decided on 6 December to start the campaign, and a headquarters with General Giap as the commander-in-chief was established. General Wei was the top Chinese military adviser. Ho Chi Minh called on the whole VWP, Vietnamese people and army "to use every effort to ensure the success of the campaign."[66] Thousands of peasants had been mobilized to build roads and carry artillery and ammunition over almost impassable mountains. From mid-December Viet Minh troops gradually concentrated in the areas around Dien Bien Phu to encircle the French forces. General Navarre sent more troops: by the end of 1953, French forces at Dien Bien Phu reached 16 battalions.

The CMAG were determined that the campaign efforts should continue, and were supported by policy-makers in Beijing. On 24 January 1954, the CMCC gave Wei Guoqing instructions on the strategy for the Dien Bien Phu siege:

While attacking Dien Bien Phu, you should avoid making assaults of equal strength from all directions; rather, you need to adopt the strategy of separating and encircling the enemy forces, and annihilate them bit by bit.[67]

This strategy was accepted and adopted by the Viet Minh high command.

At the same, the PRC accelerated its military delivery and other support to the Viet Minh. To cut Dien Bien Phu off from French airborne support, China sent back to Vietnam four Vietnamese anti-aircraft battalions which had been receiving training in China. During the Dien Bien Phu campaign, more than 200 trucks, over 10,000 barrels of oil, over 100 cannons, 3,000 pieces of various types of guns,

---

65. For a Chinese account of the process of the Communist "peace offensive," see Han Nianlong *et al., Contemporary Chinese Diplomacy,* pp. 56–57.
    66. *Contemporary Chinese Army,* pp. 530–31; *The CMAG in Vietnam,* p. 90.
    67. Cited from *The CMAG in Vietnam,* p. 98.

2,400,000 gun bullets, over 60,000 artillery shells, and about 1,700 tons of grains were rushed to the Viet Minh troops.[68]

By March 1954, Vietnamese Communist forces had encircled Dien Bien Phu for three months. The Geneva Conference about Korea and Indo-China was scheduled for April, so Zhou Enlai instructed Chinese advisers in Vietnam: "In order to achieve a victory in the diplomatic field, you may need to consider if you could follow our experiences on the eve of the Korean armistice to win several battles in Vietnam."[69] Chinese military advisers consulted the Viet Minh high command and decided to start the offensive in Dien Bien Phu in mid-March.

On 13 March Communist forces began to attack French strongholds in the northern part of Dien Bien Phu. By 17 March, they had overrun three strongpoints there and temporarily knocked out two French airstrips. The French, suddenly realizing that "the stronghold of Dien Bien Phu was a deadly trap,"[70] rushed another three battalions into the area. General Paul Ely, France's chief of staff who was visiting Washington at the time, asked for a more active American involvement in Indo-China.[71] But the Communist offensive went ahead. On 30 March Communist forces attacked the central part of Dien Bien Phu, where the French frontal command was located. When their advance was hindered by strong French defensive barriers, the CMCC, after receiving reports from Chinese advisers in Vietnam, urgently summoned several engineering experts of the Chinese Volunteers in Korea to teach the Vietnamese to dig trenches and underground tunnels.[72]

Mao Zedong was eager for the Viet Minh to win an overriding victory in Dien Bien Phu, and thus lay the basis for a future victory in northern Vietnam. In a letter dated 3 April 1954 to Peng Dehuai, then vice-chairman of the CMCC in charge of its daily affairs, formerly commander-in-chief of Chinese forces in Korea, Mao stated that the Vietnamese needed to form four additional artillery regiments and two new engineering regiments, who should complete their training in six months. If the Chinese did not have enough cannons to equip these new Vietnamese units, Mao suggested, they could transfer the equipment from their own units to the Vietnamese. The Chinese should also supply the Vietnamese with instructors and advisers selected from the Chinese troops that had fought in Korea,

68. *Contemporary Chinese Army*, p. 532; *The CMAG in Vietnam*, p. 114. According to one Chinese source, China even sent an artillery division to participate in the Dien Bien Phu Campaign: see Ye Fei, *Ye Fei huiyilu* (*The Memoirs of Ye Fei*) (Beijing: People's Liberation Army Press, 1988), pp. 644–45. For understandable reasons, no Chinese source mentions that, as the standard Vietnamese account alleges, the Chinese high command or Chinese advisers to Vietnam urged "human wave" tactics on the Vietnamese during the initial stage of the Dien Bien Phu siege – though no Chinese account rejects the Vietnamese allegation.

69. *The CMAG in Vietnam*, p. 99.

70. Georges Bidault (trans. Marianne Sinclair), *Resistance* (London: Weidenfeld and Nicolson, 1965), p. 195.

71. Melanie Billings-Yun, *Decision Against War: Eisenhower and Dien Bien Phu, 1954* (Columbia: Columbia University Press, 1988), ch. 2.

72. *Contemporary Chinese Army*, p. 532; *The CMAG in Vietnam*, p. 101.

including some division and army level officers. The best training site for these units would be in Vietnam, but somewhere in Guangxi province was also acceptable. Six months was a short time for the realization of this plan, so Mao asked Peng, together with the General Staff and Artillery Command of the PLA, to contact the Viet Minh immediately to seek their agreement. Mao believed that with these new artillery units, together with another artillery division already under the command of the Viet Minh, and by concentrating five infantry divisions, the Vietnamese would be able to launch direct attacks against Hanoi and Hai Phong. Mao asked Peng to start immediately to prepare sufficient artillery shells and engineering equipment for these units while at the same time offering more anti-aircraft guns to the Viet Minh. Concerning the current fighting in Dien Bien Phu, Mao stressed: "Dien Bien Phu should be conquered resolutely, and, if things go smoothly and success is certain, the final attack [against Dien Bien Phu] should start ahead of the previous schedule." In this letter, Mao mentioned that the Viet Minh, after their victory in Dien Bien Phu, should quickly mobilize 5,000–8,000 new soldiers to supplement their forces and prepare to attack Hanoi no later than early 1955.[73]

When the Viet Minh's assaults at Dien Bien Phu encountered tough French resistance, the CMCC sent telegrams to Wei Guoqing twice on 9 April, promising him that artillery ammunition supplies would be guaranteed to the Vietnamese so that they could use as many shells as they wanted. The CMCC also instructed Wei to adopt the following strategies in attacking Dien Bien Phu: to cut off the enemy's front-line by attacking in the middle; to destroy the enemy's underground defences one section after another by using concentrated artillery fire; to consolidate position immediately after seizing even a small portion of ground, thus continuously tightening the encirclement of the enemy; to use snipers widely to restrict enemy activities; and to use political propaganda against the enemy.[74]

Under the fierce offensive of the Communist forces, by late April French troops in Dien Bien Phu were confined to a small area of less than two square kilometres, with half their airstrips occupied by the Communists. At this stage the United States threatened to interfere. In a speech to the Overseas Press Club of America on 29 March, the American Secretary of State, John Foster Dulles, had issued a powerful warning that the United States would tolerate no Communist gain in Indo-China and called for a "united action" on the part of western countries to stop it.[75] One week later, President Eisenhower uttered the "falling domino" theory to state the necessity of a joint military operation against the plot of Communist expansion in Indo-

73. Mao Zedong to Peng Dehuai, 3 April 1954, *Mao Zedong's Manuscripts*, Vol. 4, pp. 474–75.
74 *The CMAG in Vietnam*, p. 101.
75. *The Pentagon Papers: The Defense Department History of United States Decisionmaking on Vietnam*, Vol. 1 (Boston: Beacon Press, 1971), p. 98.

China.[76] Policy-makers in Washington even considered the possibility of using tactical nuclear weapons to stop a Communist victory in Dien Bien Phu.[77]

With hindsight it can be seen that, without the support of either Congress or the allies, the Americans were not ready to interfere in Indo-China in 1954. The threat of direct intervention was primarily used for diplomatic reasons during the Dien Bien Phu crisis and at the Geneva Conference.[78] It, as will be seen, eventually worked, though in a complicated way, against the Communists. But it did not save the remaining French resistance in Dien Bien Phu. Chinese advisers in Vietnam insisted on continuing the campaign efforts. General Wei believed that the American warning was just an empty threat to make the Vietnamese Communists give up the current offensive. As the Vietnamese had achieved a superior position in the battlefield, General Wei stressed, they should not yield to the American threat and lose the golden opportunity. The Viet Minh high command, after carefully weighing the arguments, decided to go on and start the final offensive in early May. To facilitate this the Chinese transferred large amounts of military equipment and ammunition to the Vietnamese. Two Chinese-trained Vietnamese battalions, equipped with 75mm recoilless guns and six-barrel rocket launchers, arrived at Dien Bien Phu on the eve of the final assault. The CMCC promised once again to the CMAG:

To eliminate the enemy totally and to win the final victory in the campaign, you should use overwhelming artillery fire. Do not save artillery shells. We will supply and deliver sufficient shells to you.[79]

To guarantee the final victory in the campaign, top CCP leaders carefully considered every possible problem which might endanger the prospect of a total Viet Minh victory. On 28 April, Mao Zedong instructed Peng Dehuai and Huang Kecheng, two leading members of the CMCC, to guard against the possibility that the French might send paratroopers to land at the rear of the Vietnamese and cut off their supply line. Mao emphasized that this should be taken as the "most possible danger," which, if it occurred, could force the Vietnamese to give up the campaign. Mao instructed Peng and Huang to "ask the Vietnamese to deploy immediately more troops in proper areas" so

76. U.S. Government, *Public Papers of the President of the United States: Dwight D. Eisenhower, 1954* (Washington, D.C., 1958), pp. 381–390.

77. John Newhouse, *War and Peace in the Nuclear Age* (New York: Alfred A. Knopf, 1988), pp. 99–101.

78. For a plausible brief analysis of America's stand toward the Dien Bien Phu crisis, see Hess, *Vietnam and the United States*, pp. 46–48; for a more detailed analysis of the Eisenhower administration's attitude toward involving American forces in the Indo-China War in 1954, see Billings-Yun, *Decision Against War*.

79. Cited from *Contemporary Chinese Army*, pp. 533–34.

that the French parachute landing could be prevented.[80] On 30 April the CMCC, obviously following Mao's instruction, instructed Wei Guoqing to advise the Vietnamese to take pre-emptive measures against such an attack. On 3 May, General Su Yu, the Chinese general chief of staff, again contacted General Wei, reiterating the importance of preventing a French airborne landing.[81]

The final offensive of the Communist forces began on the evening of 5 May. The newly-arrived Chinese rocket launchers played an important role by destroying the French defences in minutes. By the afternoon of 7 May, French troops had neither the ability nor the willingness to fight and announced surrender. The Dien Bien Phu campaign ended with a glorious victory for the Vietnamese Communists.

As has happened on many other occasions in history, the First Indo-China War was fought on the battlefield but would conclude at the negotiation table. Evidence shows that the thinking of CCP leaders about Indo-China was strongly influenced by the American warning. This in turn brought the Chinese Communists into dispute with their Vietnamese comrades.

On 8 May, the day after the end of the Dien Bien Phu campaign, the Geneva Conference, which had started on 26 April, began its discussion of the Indo-China problem. It was at this moment of victory, ironically, that sharp divergences emerged between the Vietnamese and Chinese Communists who had co-operated to win on the battlefield.

In retrospect, the close relationship between the CCP and their Vietnamese comrades offers no support to the theory of a unified international Communist movement. Even at the height of co-operation between Vietnamese and Chinese Communists, there were signs of contradictions and, in some cases, conflicts between them. Chinese military advisers complained that the quality of Viet Minh troops was too poor to realize some of their strategic designs. General Chen Geng mentioned in his diary that General Giap and some other Vietnamese Communists lacked the "Bolshevik-style self-criticism" and were unhappy with the Chinese criticism of their "shortcomings." On one occasion, General Chen even described General Giap as "slippery and not very upright and honest" to his Chinese comrades.[82] The Vietnamese, on the other hand, were not satisfied with some of the Chinese advisers' suggestions, especially those concerning land reforms and political indoctrination following China's experiences.

80. Mao Zedong to Peng Dehuai and Huang Kecheng, 28 April 1954, *Mao Zedong's Manuscripts*, Vol. 5, p. 91. (The editors mistakenly date this telegram 28 April 1955. This is probably because Mao only put day and month on the letter and, for reasons unknown, the document was misplaced in Mao's 1955 files. As there was no real fighting in the Dien Bien Phu area in 1955 and as the content of this letter is compatible with the CMCC's 30 April 1954 telegram and Su Yu's 3 May 1954 telegram, which I also cite here, I believe that 1954 is the correct date.)
81. *The CMAG in Vietnam*, pp. 103–104.
82. Chen Geng, *Chen Geng's Diaries*, Vol. 2, pp. 22, 31.

The Vietnamese discontent was shown most explicitly in the 1979 official review of Vietnamese–Chinese relations, where the Chinese were called "traitors" even during the First Indo-China War.[83] Seeing signs of Chinese–Vietnamese friction, the CCP leadership stressed in several telegrams to Chinese advisers in Vietnam that they should avoid "imposing their own opinions on Vietnamese comrades."[84] The Chinese did not feel easy dealing with the Vietnamese, a people who had struggled against Chinese control for centuries and who had so vigorous a nationalist tendency.

With victory in hand, the differences between the Chinese and Vietnamese surfaced, focused on the final settlement of the Indo-China problem. The Vietnamese hoped for a solution which would leave clear Communist domination not only in Vietnam but also in Laos and Cambodia, while the Chinese, supported by the Soviet Union, were eager to reach a compromise.

Sino-Soviet relations were still very close. In the first three weeks of April, before the opening of the Geneva Conference, Zhou Enlai visited the Soviet Union twice. According to the recollections of Shi Zhe, who was Zhou's interpreter during these visits, the Chinese and the Soviets agreed to co-operate with each other at the forthcoming conference. Zhou's views seemed to be greatly influenced by those of V. M. Molotov. In his meeting with Zhou, Molotov stressed that it was possible for the Geneva Conference to solve one or two problems, but the imperialist countries would certainly stick to their own interests. So the Communists should adopt a realistic strategy which was compatible with this situation. It was the first time the Chinese had attended an important international conference, and Zhou made it clear that they would try their best to co-operate with the Soviets.[85]

In the first three weeks of discussions about the Indo-China problem at the Geneva Conference little progress was achieved. The Viet Minh delegation, headed by Pham Van Dong, the prime minister of the DRV government, were encouraged by the Vietnamese victory at Dien Bien Phu and tried to ask for the maximum from their adversaries. Their stand on Vietnam was to pursue an on-the-spot truce, then, with some adjustment, to hold a nation-wide plebiscite (which they were certain they would win) to settle the war. On Laos and Cambodia, the Viet Minh delegation refused to admit the existence of Vietnamese Communist combat units in these countries,

83. The Foreign Ministry of the Socialist Republic of Vietnam, "The truth about Vietnam–China relations in the past 30 years," FBIS (Asia and Pacific), Supplement, 19 October 1979.

84. Mao Zedong to Wei Guoqing, 29 January 1951, *Mao Zedong's Manuscripts*, Vol. 2, p. 90.

85. Shi Zhe, *Zai lishi juren shenbian: Shi Zhe huiyilu* (*Together with Historical Giants: Shi Zhi's Memoirs*) (Beijing: Central Historical Documents Press, 1991), pp. 539–544. According to Khrushchev, Zhou Enlai told him in one of his visits to Moscow prior to the Geneva Conference: "We've already lost too many men in Korea – that war cost us dearly. We're in no condition to get involved in another war at this time." Nikita S. Khrushchev, *Khrushchev Remembers* (London, 1971), p. 481.

insisting that they should be treated in the same way as Vietnam. Zhou Enlai, the head of the Chinese delegation, wanted the Geneva Conference to reach an agreement on the Indo-China problem which would allow China to return to the international scene after almost five years of total isolation since the formation of the PRC. He believed that Dong's stand was unrealistic. In his opinion, the Vietnamese Communists should accept the solution of dividing Vietnam into two areas, the north belonging to the Communists and the south to the French and pro-French Vietnamese, while waiting for a national plebiscite. Zhou tried to convince Dong that this would give the Viet Minh all northern and central Vietnam with the prospect of gaining back the south after the plebiscite. On the Laos and Cambodia problems, Zhou favoured a separate solution, which, he believed, would simplify the situation and make the total settlement of the Indo-China problem possible.[86] In order not to jeopardize the prospect of reaching an agreement at Geneva, on 20 June Mao instructed the CMAG not to expand military operations in Vietnam in July.[87]

China's stand at the Geneva Conference reflected its immediate strategic considerations. First, with the end of the Korean War the CCP leadership was now more willing to focus on domestic problems. In 1953 and 1954 they were contemplating the introduction of the first Five-Year Plan as well as "liberating" the Kuomintang-controlled Taiwan either peacefully or, if necessary, by military means. After five years of sharp confrontation with the United States and the west, China needed a settled outside environment. Secondly, in the crisis situation created by the Dien Bien Phu siege, CCP leaders did believe in the possibility of direct American military intervention. Their reaction was based on their experience in the Korean War: they would try everything possible, including pursuing a compromise at Geneva, to prevent an American intervention; only if the Americans directly entered the war in Indo-China would they consider sending troops there to prevent American forces from approaching the Chinese border, while at the same time maintaining the momentum of the Vietnamese revolution.[88] Thirdly, a moderate Chinese stand at the Geneva Conference, Zhou and other CCP leaders believed, would contribute to the PRC's new claim on peaceful co-existence while at the same time creating for the PRC new channels of communication with France, Great Britain and other western countries. Before the

86. Qu Xing, "On Zhou Enlai's diplomacy at the Geneva Conference of 1954," Pei Jianzhang *et al.*, *Yanjiu Zhou Enlai – waijiao sixiang yu shijian* (*Studying Zhou Enlai's Diplomatic Thought and Practices*) (Beijing: The World Knowledge Press, 1989), pp. 255–56.

87. Mao Zedong to the CCP Guangxi Province Committee, 20 June 1954, *Mao Zedong's Manuscripts*, Vol. 4, p. 509.

88. Interview with Chinese researchers who have access to archival sources in May 1991; for the Chinese assessment of the American intention at the Geneva Conference, see Han Nianlong *et al.*, *Contemporary Chinese Diplomacy*, p. 65; see also Xu Yan, "The outstanding contribution to extinguishing war flames in Indo-China," *Party Historical Documents*, No. 5, 1992, pp. 22–23.

Chinese delegation left Beijing for Geneva, the CCP leadership instructed them to "strengthen diplomatic and international activities," "break the American blockade and embargo" against the PRC, as well as "open new ways for solving international disputes through big power consultations."[89] Zhou wasted no opportunity at the conference to establish contacts with French and British delegates.[90] Moreover, CCP leaders also believed that Vietnamese Communist control of the whole Indo-China area (though unlikely at that particular time) would not necessarily serve the PRC's interests: Vietnam would thus emerge as another centre of Communist activity in East Asia, probably overshadowing the influence of the Chinese revolution. On 18 May, ten days after the start of the conference, one of Zhou's deputies explained to a French delegate over dinner that "we are here to re-establish peace, not to back the Viet Minh."[91]

The United States, a superpower which believed itself to have important strategic interests in South-east Asia, did not want to see the Geneva Conference reach a compromise. Dulles, the head of the American delegation, followed a line of blocking any Communist initiatives at the conference. He truly believed that an inconclusive result was better than reaching any agreement which would provide the Communists with even minimal gain. Dulles' uncompromising stand was matched by Dong's, leading to a deadlock by mid-June.

At this stage a major change occurred in France: the French parliament, reflecting public impatience with the immobility at Geneva, ousted Prime Minister Laniel and replaced him with Pierre Mendes-France, a long-standing critic of the war in Indo-China, who promised that he would lead the negotiation to a successful conclusion by 20 July, or would resign. Zhou seized the opportunity to push negotiations at Geneva forward. On 15 June, the Chinese, Soviet and Vietnamese delegations held a crucial meeting. Zhou pointed out that the key to the deadlock lay in the Vietnamese refusal to admit the existence of their forces in Laos and Cambodia. He believed that this would make any negotiations fruitless, and would lose the Vietnamese Communists an opportunity to win a possible peaceful solution of the Vietnam problem. Zhou suggested that the Communist camp adopt a new line in favour of all foreign forces, including the Viet Minh troops, withdrawing from Laos and Cambodia. This would mean that the Communists would now agree to settle the Indo-China problem on a separate basis. Zhou's stand was strongly supported by the Soviets, and under the heavy pressure of both, Dong finally yielded.[92] On 16 and 17 June, Zhou communicated the change of Communist

89. Wang Bingnan, *Zhongmei huitan jiunian* (*Recollections of the Nine-Year Sino-American Talks*) (Beijing: The Press of World Affairs, 1985), pp. 5–6.

90. For a summary of Zhou's contacts with the British and French at the Geneva Conference, see Ronald C. Keith, *The Diplomacy of Zhou Enlai* (New York: St Martin's Press, 1989), ch. 3.

91. Stanley Karnow, *Vietnam: The First Complete Account of Vietnam War* (New York: The Viking Press, 1983), p. 201.

92. Qu Xing, "On Zhou Enlai's Diplomacy," p. 257.

attitude to the French and British. The foreign ministers' meeting on the Indo-China problem at Geneva adjourned for three weeks from late June.

In order to co-ordinate with the Chinese, Ho Chi Minh, accompanied by General Giap, visited China and met Zhou Enlai from 3 to 5 July in Liuzhou, a city in the south. Zhou, by emphasizing the serious consequences of a possible direct American intervention, convinced Ho that it was in the interests of the Vietnamese Communists to pursue an agreement with the French. The two sides reached a consensus on their stand for the next phase of the conference: on the Vietnam problem they would favour dividing the country temporarily along the 16th parallel, but as Route Colonial Nine, the only line of transport linking Laos to the sea port, was located north of the 16th parallel, they would be willing to accept some slight adjustment of this solution; on the Laos problem they would try to establish Xam Neua and Phong Sali, two provinces adjacent to China, as the concentration zone for pro-Communist Laos forces; and on the Cambodia problem they would allow a political settlement which would probably lead to the establishment of a non-Communist government.[93] When Ho returned to Vietnam, the VWP Central Committee issued an instruction on 5 July containing all these agreements with the CCP.[94] The Soviets also shared the Chinese view.[95] In mid-July, the VWP Central Committee held its sixth meeting. Ho Chi Minh endorsed the new strategy of solving the Indo-China problem through a cease-fire based on "temporarily" dividing Vietnam into two areas, which would supposedly lead to the unification of the whole country after the withdrawal of French forces and a nation-wide plebiscite. Ho criticized the "leftist tendency" among the Party which ignored the danger of American interference as well as the importance of struggles at international conferences.[96] Ho's report, especially, his stress of the danger of American interference, clearly demonstrated Zhou's influence.

The foreign ministers' meeting at Geneva resumed on 12 July. Zhou found that Dong was still reluctant to accept the new line of negotiation and had an overnight meeting with him to try to persuade him of the necessity of reaching a compromise. He used America's interference in the Korean War as an example to emphasize the tremendous danger involved in direct American military intervention in Indo-China. Zhou promised, "with the final withdrawal of the French, all of Vietnam will be yours." Dong finally yielded, probably, to Zhou's logic, if not to his pressure.[97]

93. *Ibid.* pp. 257–58; Huang Zheng, *Ho Chi Minh and China*, pp. 140–41; Wang Bingnan, *Recollections*, p. 13.
94. Qu Xing, "On Zhou Enlai's Diplomacy," p. 257.
95. Han Nianlong *et al.*, *Contemporary Chinese Diplomacy*, pp. 66–67.
96. Ho Chi Minh, "Report to the sixth meeting of the VWP Central Committee," 15 July 1954, *Selected Works of Ho Chi Minh*, Vol. 2, pp. 290–98.
97. Qu Xing, "On Zhou Enlai's Diplomacy," p. 258; Shi Zhe, *Together with Historical Giants*, p. 557.

Zhou dominated the final stage of the Geneva Conference. Mendes-France stated that the 17th parallel was the final line of his concession, otherwise he had to resign, and Zhou made the decision to change the Communist line from the 16th parallel to the 17th to meet this stand. The Geneva Conference reached a settlement of the Indo-China problem in the early morning of 21 July, leaving Mendes-France's deadline officially unpassed.[98]

The real winner at the conference was Zhou. He left Geneva with nearly everything he could have anticipated before he came. The creation of a Communist-ruled North Vietnam would serve as a buffer zone between Communist China and the capitalist world in South-eastern Asia (in this respect, the difference between the 16th and the 17th parallels did not matter to China). The opening of new dialogues between China and such western powers as France and Great Britain would help break the PRC's isolated status in the world; and, much more important, the crucial role played by China at the conference implied that for the first time in modern history (since the 1840 Opium War) China had been accepted by international society – friends and foes alike – as a real world power.

The First Indo-China War ended with the signing of the Geneva Agreement of 1954, but the confrontation in this region was far from over. Only two years later, when the United States and the State of Vietnam broke the agreement about the national plebiscite in Vietnam, the Second Indo-China War was begun, which lasted until the mid-1970s. More surprisingly – and ironically – Communist China and a unified Communist Vietnam entered the Third Indo-China War in 1979 as hostile adversaries. The origin of the confrontation between them, however, could be traced back to their co-operation during the First Indo-China War.

98. Although the agreement was signed at 3.00 a.m. on 21 July, it was dated 20 July, so that Mendes-France could still allege that his deadline had been kept.

[18]

American Attitudes Toward Decolonization in Africa

STEVEN METZ

Many writers consider U.S. policy toward decolonization, at least under John F. Kennedy, as an extension of Americans' traditional support for self-determination, and argue that without judicious prompting from the U.S., Europe would have dragged out the decolonization process for the rest of the century.[1] Radical and Third World authors, on the other hand, claim that in those very rare instances in which U.S. foreign policy was conducive to decolonization, it simply fostered the transition from formal control under European masters to informal control under the aegis of American corporations.[2] What little real change occurred, this group argues, was the result of protest and rebellion on the part of the Africans. These conflicting interpretations and dis-

---

[1] Strangely enough, most "radical revisionists" remain silent on the American role in African decolonization. In three of the better known works in the genre—David Horowitz's *The Free World Colossus* (New York: Hill and Wang, 1971), Gabriel Kolko's *The Roots of American Foreign Policy* (Boston: Beacon Press, 1969), and William Appleman Williams's *The Tragedy of American Diplomacy* (New York: Delta, 1969)—there are a total of two indexed references to Africa plus two additional references to the more specific issue of the Congo crisis.

[2] For a range of approaches utilizing this approach see: E. A. Tarabin, ed., *Neocolonialism and Africa in the 1970s* (Moscow: Progress Publishers, 1978); Samir Amin, *Neo-Colonialism in West Africa* (New York: Monthly Review Press, 1973); idem, "Underdevelopment and Dependence in Black Africa: Origins and Contemporary Forms," *Journal of Modern African Studies* 10 (1972): 503–524; I. William Zartman, "Europe and Africa: Decolonization or Dependency?" *Foreign Affairs* 54 (1976): 325–43; and Timothy M. Shaw and M. Catherine Newbury, "Dependence or Interdependence: Africa in the Global Political Economy," in Mark M. DeLancey, ed., *Aspects of International Relations in Africa* (Bloomington, Ind.: University of Indiana African Studies Program, 1979).

STEVEN METZ is assistant professor of political science at Virginia Polytechnic Institute and State University. He is at work on a book entitled *The Anti-Apartheid Movement and American Foreign Policy*.

agreements leave the essential questions concerning the American role in decolonization unanswered.

It was pointed out in a report prepared in 1959 for the Senate Foreign Relations Committee that postwar American policy towards Africa could be divided into three distinct phases.[3] During the Truman administration, Africa was viewed as an appendage of Europe, and there was very little Africa policy separate from European considerations. The residue of this emphasis on the European aspects of African problems remained throughout the 1950s. During the period from 1952 to 1956, attention was riveted on Korea and again on Europe, and thus interest in Africa declined to a new low. But in the years after this low, African issues once again surfaced in American foreign policy.

Given the emphasis placed on nation-building and Third World problems by Kennedy, it is often assumed that the shift in favor of a more rapid decolonization process, which was undoubtedly an aspect of U.S. foreign policy by 1962, arrived with the Kennedy administration.[4] This shift is often considered to have culminated in the transition from a Eurocentric Africa policy to an Afrocentric policy. But, as a closer examination will show, there was no radical shift in American attitudes towards African decolonization in 1961.[5] In fact, American perceptions of the decolonization issue underwent a gradual evolution during the entire period from 1952 to 1962, with 1958 generally representing a watershed.

In this article, I will examine this evolution of American attitudes toward the decolonization of Africa during the decade from 1952 to 1962.[6] Although the real roots of the decolonization debate can be traced back much further, the issue was a crucial one during World War II.[7] The 1950s saw the culmination of the issue. The focus of the paper will fall on what can be termed the opinions of the foreign-policy elite, with official policy statements, scholarly publications, and the news media providing the bulk of the evidence. The body of the paper will comprise four sections: an overview of the position of Africa in the

[3] U.S. Senate Committee on Foreign Relations, *United States Foreign Policy: Africa* (A study prepared by the Program of African Studies, Northwestern University), 86th Cong. 1st sess., October 1959, 49–50.

[4] For example, Waldemar A. Nielsen, in *The Great Powers and Africa* (New York: Praeger Publishers, 1969), points to 1960 as the "hinge year." While the great number of African nations reaching independence in 1960 undoubtedly marked a watershed for U.S. policy, the change in attitude which set the stage for this policy change can be found earlier.

[5] For a detailed discussion of this point see, inter alia, George Liska, "The Third World," in Robert E. Osgood, et al., *America and the World From the Truman Doctrine to Vietnam* (Baltimore, Md.: Johns Hopkins University Press, 1970).

[6] The term "Africa" when used here actually refers to Sub-Saharan or "Black" Africa.

[7] See William Roger Louis, *Imperialism At Bay* (New York: Oxford, University Press, 1978). Evidence for the gradual growth of support for decolonization is also found in the League of Nations mandate system and the U.N. trusteeship system. See also: Henry Gilchrist, "The United Nations: Colonial Questions at the San Francisco Conference," *American Political Science Review* 39 (1945): 982–92; Ernst B. Haas, "The Attempt to Terminate Colonialism: Acceptance of the United Nations Trusteeship System," *International Organization* 6 (1953): 1–21; and *The Mandate System: Origin, Principles, Application* (Geneva: League of Nations Publishing Office, 1945).

emerging American world view during this period; a sketch of the evolution of official attitudes toward decolonization; a corollary outline of non-official thinking on the issue; and a synthesis and conclusion.

AFRICA AND THE DILEMMA OF POWER

Foreign policy can in the broadest sense be broken down into two constituent elements — goals and means. This simple typology can provide some basic insight into the problems faced by the U.S. on the decolonization issue. There was in the long run very little debate over the goal of the policy; after World War II, the inevitability of decolonization was an accepted fact in nearly every corner.[8]

The actual debate centered on three aspects of the implementation of decolonization. First was the actual method for decolonization and the role that the United States should play. Issues dealing with the proper role of the United Nations in decolonization can also be classified here. Second was the timing and speed of decolonization. This later became the key issue in the debate, and thus was the point that exhibited the greatest degree of change over the period examined here. Third was the issue of the actual stake or interest of the United States in Africa, an issue that would determine the approach to the other two.

Hans Morgenthau began a 1955 essay on the U.S.'s Africa policy by stating that "the United States has in Africa no specific political or military interests" and that nearly every observer agreed that actual American interests were "somewhat marginal."[9] Although this type of attitude may have overstated the case for the lack of interests in Africa, and is certainly not true today, the real security interests of the United States were beyond a doubt minimal.[10] U.S. interests in Africa during this period can be broken into three categories. First were the economic and what can be termed "Open Door" interests. Although the degree of actual trade and investment was limited, as is true in most cases of Open Door thinking, it was the pure potential of the African market that awed American businessmen. But the African market was the most underdeveloped in the world, and since most American attention was concentrated on rebuilding Europe and on fostering the postwar transition to mass consumerism in the United States, economic interests in Africa played only a minor role in policy formulation.

The second category comprises ideological or altruistic interests. Strains of Wilsonian idealism were still important in many debates over U.S. foreign policy,

---

[8] A major exception that is discussed below is Philip W. Bell, "Colonialism as a Problem in American Foreign Policy," *World Politics* 5 (1952): 86–109.

[9] Hans J. Morgenthau, "United States Policy Toward Africa," in Calvin W. Stillman, ed., *Africa in the Modern World* (Chicago: University of Chicago Press, 1955), 317–28. See also Donald Rothchild, "Engagement Versus Disengagement in Africa," in Alan M. Jones, Jr., ed., *U.S. Foreign Policy in a Changing World* (New York: David McKay, 1973).

[10] For an excellent evaluation of current U.S. interests in Africa see Gordon Bertolin, "U.S. Economic Interests in Africa: Investment, Trade and Raw Materials," and Geoffrey Kemp, "U.S. Strategic Interests and Military Options in Sub-Saharan Africa," in Jennifer Seymour Whitaker, ed., *Africa and the United States: Vital Interests* (New York: New York University Press, 1978).

and the longstanding American dedication to self-determination was often mentioned in discussions of the decolonization issue. Paul Nitze illustrated this strain of thinking in 1955 when he argued that support for colonialism was "abhorrent to American sensibilities."[11] But as was often the case, this type of interest proved more valuable as a mechanism for mobilizing support behind policies created through other motives than as an actual instigative factor in policy formulation.

The third type of American interest was undoubtedly the most important — cold war considerations and the global containment of communism. As late as 1960, candidate Richard M. Nixon argued that "in the struggle with the Russians, Africa is the most critical area in the world," while a few months later President-elect Kennedy claimed that Africa was the objective "of a gigantic communist offensive." Every defector from the Soviet Union came complete with a copy of the "blueprint" for the Soviet takeover of Africa.[12] It had gradually become clear to American policymakers that instability and chaos in Africa, which was increasingly the result of the continuation of the colonial relationship, would foster Soviet expansionism.

The intense desire for stability in Africa that resulted from this led to the first of several dilemmas that faced U.S. policymakers. The primary goal of American policy during this period was the strengthening of the North Atlantic Treaty Organization (NATO) alliance and the continued prosperity of the recovering West European economy. The exploitation of the resources of Africa was considered essential to this recovery. But as the 1950s wore on, two facts became increasingly obvious. The link between African resources and political stability in Western Europe was not as strong as had been expected earlier.[13] After 1948 no new European states fell to Communist control. By the mid-1950s, as pressure for decolonization mounted in Africa, it was obvious that the West European economic and political systems had withstood the challenges that had seemed so dire in the immediate postwar period. Secondly, the European empires were not stabilizing factors in Africa, but rather served to generate growing waves of repression and rebellion. This left the U.S. in the face of a tremendous paradox in which the support of European economic growth created conditions conducive to the expansion of Soviet influence. This was a problem that American policy never successfully overcame, but one that was eventually alleviated by the

[11] Paul H. Nitze, "The United States and Africa: An American View," in C. Grove Haines, ed., *Africa Today* (Baltimore: Johns Hopkins University Press, 1955), 475–69.

[12] See, for example, *Newsweek*, 28 November 1956.

[13] The economic benefits of colonies had been hotly debated in Britain at least since the publication of J.A. Hobson's *Imperialism* in 1902. By the end of World War II common opinion was that, contrary to the Leninist thesis, colonies were more an economic burden than a benefit. On this debate see Nielsen, *The Great Powers and Africa*, 28; L. H. Gann and Peter Duignan, *Burden of Empire* (New York: Praeger Publishers, 1967), 55ff.; and Leonard Woolf, *Empire and Commerce in Africa* (London: Labour Research Department, 1920). Ronald Robinson and John Gallagher argue in *Africa and the Victorians* (London: MacMillan, 1969) that the motives for African colonization were almost exclusively geostrategic and political.

pure rush of events in Africa and by a reevaluation of the economics of colonialism.

A second dilemma resulted from the debate concerning the proper role of the United States in the decolonization process. The postwar world situation had left the United states with an imbalance between the means of projecting power and the proper ends for this extension.[14] The U.S. was like an ungainly adolescent boy who suddenly finds himself strong, but yet is without the guiding constraints on the use of the strength. Thus, the United States found itself with a tremendous degree of influence in a sphere where no material interests guided the proper use of the influence. Later, with the growth of what Robert W. Tucker and George Liska have called an "imperial" foreign policy, in which American security and world stability were congruent, the effects of this dilemma would diminish.[15] By the 1960s the value given to global stability—the defining characteristic of an imperial power—had become a major theme of U.S. foreign policy.

In discussing the role of the United States in African decolonization, Vernon McKay argued in 1963 that by the early 1960s American interests in Africa had become "an integral part of [a] broader interest in American security, prosperity and freedom," while Chester Bowles noted as early as 1956 that on African issues "wealth and power have inescapably committed the United States to world policies and world responsibilities."[16] G. Mennen Williams, the assistant secretary of state for African affairs in the Kennedy administration, probably expressed this position best when he wrote in 1962: "Our self-interests in Africa stem from acceptance of the idea that there can be no peace for our children or our children's children unless there is stability and satisfaction around the world."[17]

Both of these dilemmas—the wavering between a Eurocentric and an Afrocentric policy and the transition from a national to an imperial definition of security—led to a policy of indecision and inaction on issues concerning African decolonization. The usual U.S. policy consisted of vague rhetoric about the right of self-determination coupled with insistence on the benefits of colonialism and abstention on U.N. votes on decolonization problems. American policymakers not only waited until it was entirely clear exactly which side change was on, but very nearly waited until the winds of change had blown the roof from the house.

[14] George Liska argues in the "Coda" to *Russia and World Order* (Baltimore, Md.: Johns Hopkins University Press, 1980) that this imbalance between foreign policy means and ends is a defining characteristic of the modern world system.

[15] For more on this point see Robert W. Tucker, *Nation or Empire?* (Baltimore, Md.: Johns Hopkins University Press, 1969); idem, "The American Outlook," in Osgood, et al., *America and the World From the Truman Doctrine to Vietnam*; or George Liska's *Imperial America: The International Politics of Primacy* (Baltimore, Md.: Johns Hopkins University Press, 1967) and idem, *Career of Empire* (Baltimore, Md.: Johns Hopkins University Press, 1978).

[16] Vernon McKay, *Africa in World Politics* (New York: Harper and Row, 1963), 273; Chester Bowles, *Africa's Challenge to America* (Berkeley and Los Angeles: University of California Press, 1956), 3.

[17] G. Mennen Williams, "American Foreign Policy and the Emerging Nations of Africa," State Department Press Release 241, 4 November 1962.

OFFICIAL ATTITUDES: FROM EUROCENTRISM TO GLOBAL STRATEGY

Other than in the brief period following the Spanish-American War, U.S. attitudes had always been decidedly anticolonial. Before World War II, however, isolationist sentiment and America's status as a minor power had limited this anticolonialism to a strictly rhetorical level. During the war, however, support for the worldwide expression of American values was whipped to a fervor in order to solidify public support for the war effort. According to the popular view, the war was not fought in order to prevent the aggrandizement of German or Japanese national power, but for the global promulgation of American ideals. This great belief that the war represented the victory of American ideals, when combined with the preponderance of American power, led to a new wave of foreign-policy idealism best expressed in the creation of the United Nations. This belief also formed the embryo of American support for African decolonization. Even during the war, Franklin Roosevelt "repeatedly and insistently . . . made clear to the European allies his conviction that the Age of Imperialism was over." Secretary of State Cordell Hull was an especially vigorous proponent of decolonization.[18]

At the beginning of the 1950s, however, many American policymakers felt that decolonization could at least be postponed if not avoided altogether. It was thought that when the European metropoles had recovered enough from the war to turn their attention to the construction of their proposed imperial unions, the unrest and burgeoning nationalism in the colonies would prove transitory. It did not. By the late 1950s, it was found that nationalism did not disappear when suppressed, but tended to surface with increased vigor, increased popularity, and increased violence. Thus, there was a slow and incremental growth in the attitude among U.S. policymakers that change could not be stemmed, and that somehow the U.S. should throw its weight with the trends of the future.

But the problem arose in this evolution of discovering exactly which side change was on. The lack of trained and knowledgeable Africa experts was appalling—there was no Africa Bureau in the State Department until 1958, so all information about the continent was handled by the thinly stretched Bureau of Near Eastern, South Asian and African Affairs. The crucial decade of 1952–1962 was not only a period of transformation of American policy towards Africa, but was also a period of learning for the foreign-policy elite. For the first time, Africa was not merely an appendage of Europe, but had become a policy problem in its own right.

The leitmotif of foreign policy during the first years of the Eisenhower administration, both towards Africa and towards the rest of the world, was the cold war. The perceptions generated by this struggle pervaded policymaking. Within this context, the American experience with the new states of Asia and Africa in

---

[18] See Hull's speech reprinted in Leland M. Goodrich and Marie J. Carroll, eds. *Documents on American Foreign Relations* (Boston: World Peace Foundation, 1944), 5:6. For more detail, see the first volume of Hull's *Memoirs* (New York: Macmillan, 1948).

the period directly following World War II tainted opinions on other aspects of the decolonization issue. As John Foster Dulles so repeatedly expressed, decolonization and the other problems of the new states were to be viewed through the prism provided by the cold war, and thus strategic and tactical considerations molded attitudes towards further decolonization. It was felt that decolonization was to proceed only when the allegiance of the new states to the Western alliance could be ensured. Often in Africa this criterion could not be met.

This fact led to the two primary aspects of U.S. policy towards African decolonization before 1958: a Eurocentric policy that placed the growth and stability of the European economies at the top of the priority list in the colonial relationship; and a repeated warning that in the long run colonialism had benefited the African states and that the detrimental results of an independence granted before the African state was "fully prepared" would outweigh any possible benefits. These two aspects of the U.S. Africa policy are evident in nearly all official statements during this period.

The assessment of the situation in Africa as the 1950s began had been radically different. Africa at that time, according to one State Department official, was "not a crisis area"; there had been "no significant inroads" by communism, and the political situation across the entire continent was "relatively stable and secure."[19] The general recommendation was that the United States should not pursue the decolonization issue too strenuously, and when action was required, it should be strictly through the auspices of the metropole. There was a widespread feeling that this "stable and secure" area, replete with the "happy" colonial relationships that Philip Bell described, should be left alone. Colonialism was "progressive"; it had led to the modernization of Africa and would eventually generate stable and economically viable states.[20]

The only obvious result of severing the colonial relationship before the sufficient development of the economy and political system would be chaos, a situation conducive to Communist penetration. It was felt that Britain and France, at least, were making the minimum acceptable movements toward decolonization. Warnings of the dangers of premature independence pervaded statements on Africa policy during the first Eisenhower administration. George C. McGhee, the assistant secretary of state for Near Eastern, South Asian and African affairs, stated in 1951 that "the United States government has always maintained that premature independence for primitive, uneducated peoples can do them

[19] George C. McGhee, "United States Interests in Africa," State Department Press Release 469, 5 June 1950, 2. McGhee was assistant secretary of state for Near Eastern, South Asian and African affairs.

[20] The emphasis on the beneficial nature of colonialism was standard in policy statements of this period. See, for instance, Julius C. Holmes, "The United States and Africa: An Official Viewpoint," State Department Press Release 235, 1 May 1958; George V. Allen, "United States Foreign Policy in Africa," State Department Press Release 206, 21 April 1956; and George C. McGhee, "Africa's Role in the Free World Today," State Department Press Release 564, 27 June 1951.

more harm than good."[21] Two years later, McGhee's successor, Henry A. Byroade, echoed this viewpoint when he argued that "premature independence can be dangerous, retrogressive and destructive."[22] Even in the later years of the decade, Julius C. Holmes, a special assistant to the secretary of state, argued that "premature independence and lack of appreciation of the interdependence of the world community may be as dangerous for Africa as the denial of independence."[23]

The problem with thinking of this type is obvious. As premature independence became a stock anathema in U.S. policy, the tendency was great to categorize all moves towards independence as premature. When premature independence grew to a phobia for policymakers, the ability to accurately discern the phenomenon diminished. And likewise, the ability to "get on the side of change" was eroded.

In the larger struggle that represented the cold war, Europe was, of course, the first line of defense. Thus, all policy considerations tended to become sublimated to European concerns. U.S. policymakers were seldom bothered by the fact that the use of African resources as a tool for European economic recovery and the simultaneous economic development of the African economies were, in the long run, antithetical. The United States had been stung by the post-independence neutralism of India and others, and wanted to be certain that Africa would not join this desertion of the West. The Asian-African Conference, held in Bandung, Indonesia in April 1955, had heightened American fears that the newly independent nations, although operating under the guise of "non-alignment," were, in fact, inching toward the Communist camp.[24]

Therefore, the brunt of American policy was composed of support for slow, orderly progress towards some faraway state of independence, or preferably, of autonomy within a colonial league—all instigated and controlled by the metropole. What, Americans desired, in fact, was the preservation of a facade of Wilsonian-type support for self-determination while carefully avoiding any affront to the European metropoles.[25]

---

[21] McGhee, "Africa's Role," 3.

[22] Henry A. Byroade, "The World's Colonies and Ex-Colonies: A Challenge to America," State Department Press Release 605, 30 October 1953, 3.

[23] Julius C. Holmes, "Africa: Its Challenge to the West," State Department Press Release 32, 27 January 1958, 6.

[24] For an analysis of the Bandung Conference see George McTurnan Kahin, *The Asian-African Conference* (Ithaca, N.Y.: Cornell University Press, 1956). For more on Dulles' reaction to the non-aligned movement, see Michael A. Guhin, *John Foster Dulles: A Statesman and His Times* (New York: Columbia University Press, 1972), 252–64. Richard Goold-Adams argues in *The Time of Power: A Reappraisal of John Foster Dulles* (London: Weidenfeld and Nicolson, 1962) that Dulles's inability to adjust to neutralism sometimes leaned him toward support for the continuation of colonialism. See, inter alia, 310.

[25] But it must be remembered that Woodrow Wilson too could jettison self-determination when other calls beckoned. Wilson's original mandate plan was used as a bargaining chip with the British and French on other issues. See, for instance, Ernst B. Haas, "The Reconciliation of Conflicting Colonial Policy Aims: Acceptance of the League of Nations Mandate System," *International Organization* 5 (1952): 521–30.

The total bankruptcy of this position gradually became evident. As Senator John Kennedy noted in a 1956 speech in Kansas City, Missouri, the U.S. position on decolonization issues had "frequently been characterized by indecision, confusion, haste, timidity and an excessive fear of giving offense."[26] But the growing rapidity of change, as crucial event piled on crucial event in Africa, forced a reevaluation of the U.S. position on decolonization and in a broader sense, came to illustrate the changing perception of America's role in the world.

These changes in the United States Africa policy were not the result of large-scale alterations in policy strategy or content, nor were they entirely the result of personality differences between the Kennedy and Eisenhower administrations. The most significant of these changes, in fact, took place within the Eisenhower administration. *New York Times* columnist James Reston noted that by 1956, U.S. foreign policy was "in its tone and procedure . . . quite different from what it was at the beginning of the Eisenhower administration," and that one of the most important of these changes was "a new emphasis on working with the rising nationalistic forces of Asia, the Middle East and Africa."[27] Reston accredited the bulk of this shift to a growing involvement of Eisenhower himself in the foreign-policy decision-making process.

The first hints that the American policy of promulgating glacial change was ineffective had come not from Africa, but from Asia. There was a feeling among American policymakers that communism had gained dominance over nationalism in many of the new states of the region.[28] The drawn-out rebellions in Malaysia, the Philippines, and Indochina seemed to illustrate the results of futile attempts at stopping the tide of decolonization.

Although the Suez crisis in 1956 represented the first great divergence of American and European thinking on events in the Third World, most of the shift in Africa policy that took place between 1952 and 1960 can be traced to the climactic ruse of events in Africa itself. Even though violent uprisings had been crushed in Madagascar, Kenya, Cameroon, Ivory Coast, and Guinea, there was a feeling among both Africanists and policymakers that perhaps revolution in Africa was not as far in the future as had been expected.[29] The growing strife in Algeria provided stark evidence for this.

[26] Reprinted in *Congressional Record*, 6 June 1956, 9,614–15.

[27] James Reston, "U.S. Diplomacy," *New York Times*, 19 November 1956.

[28] Paul M. Kattenburg, *The Vietnam Trauma in American Foreign Policy 1945–75* (New Brunswick, N.J.: Transaction Books, 1980), 10. For a good thumbnail sketch of decolonization in India, Pakistan, Burma and Malaysia see *Britain and the Process of Decolonization*, pamphlet R.F.P. 5865/70 (London: Reference Division, Central Office of Information), 10–16.

[29] Crawford Young, "Decolonization in Africa," in Peter Duignan and L.H. Gann, eds., *Colonialism in Africa*, 2 vols. (Cambridge: Cambridge Press, 1970), 2: 461. For a good discussion of the political events surrounding the rebellions in the French colonies see Edward Mortimer, *France and the Africans 1944–1960* (New York: Walker, 1969). On the Mau-Mau revolt in Kenya see Robert Buijtenhuijs, *Le Mouvement "Mau-Mau"* (The Hague: Mouton, 1971); Carl G. Rosberg, Jr., and John Nottingham, *The Myth of "Mau Mau": Nationalism in Kenya* (New York: Praeger Publishers, 1966); and Fred Majdalany, *State of Emergency: The Full Story of Mau Mau* (Boston: Houghton-Mifflin, 1963).

Political events in Africa also added to the feeling of great and imminent change. 1958 proved to be an especially crucial year in this respect. The independence of Sudan in 1956 and, even more importantly, the creation of Ghana in 1957 had had far-reaching consequences in the rest of Africa. The imminence of continent-wide independence could be sensed by the remaining African colonies. In 1958, a series of conferences and meetings, beginning with the Afro-Asian Peoples Solidarity Conference, illustrated both the ability of African peoples to speak for themselves in the world arena and the importance which this group placed on speedy decolonization.[30]

In addition, gradual changes in the intensity and tone of the cold war could finally be felt in the years following Josef Stalin's death in 1953. Waldemar Nielsen noted:

> President Eisenhower took office early in 1953 in an international atmosphere still dominated by the confrontation with the Soviet Union. By the beginning of his second term, however, profound changes had begun to take place within the Soviet Union and the Communist world and throughout the less developed areas, which led to the emergence of a new and more intricate world balance and, in the case of Africa, called for far-reaching revisions of American policy. The adequacy and the timeliness of the Eisenhower administration's response to the new requirements led to great disputes and eventually made Africa for the first time a major issue in American politics.[31]

In 1959, Joseph C. Satterthwaite, the first assistant secretary of state for African affairs, recognized that 1958 was a landmark year and noted that "the political situation in Africa can be described as vibrant if not effervescent."[32] Given these events, U.S. policymakers began a frantic re-evaluation of the decolonization issue.

The changes that emanated from this reevaluation were again more transitions of tone than of content. A type of Aristotelian ethics predominated, as moderation remained the password for policy proposals. In May 1958 State Department official Julius Holmes summed up the attitudes toward decolonization as "support for progressive tendencies in the metropole and moderate leaders in Africa."[33] This distillation of U.S. policy illustrated two overwhelming problems. First, while everyone supported "progressive" actions by the metropole, it was much more difficult to garner consensus as to the definition of progress. A major source of irritation with African leaders was the American satisfaction with any action professing movement towards independence; what interested the Africans was the speed with which this movement proceeded. Thus the African

---

[30] For a discussion of the impact the events of 1958 had on U.S. policy see Vernon McKay, *Africa in World Politics*, 399–442.

[31] Nielsen, *The Great Powers and Africa*, 259.

[32] Joseph C. Satterthwaite, "The United States and the New Africa," State Department Press Release 38, 17 January 1959.

[33] Julius C. Holmes, "The United States and Africa." Holmes repeated this point later in the same month in the speech "Africa's Challenge to the Free World," State Department Press Release 292, 29 May 1958.

leaders called on the United States to foster movements that were both progressive and rapid. Second, "moderate" African leaders were often merely whoever both had power and was anti-Communist. As was illustrated after a slate of military coups swept Africa in the mid-1960s, "moderation" often equaled pro-Westernism.

But policy rhetoric did change after 1958 and by 1960 on the verge of the great wave of African independence — administration spokesmen did begin the call for a stronger degree of support for decolonization.[34] But in the long run, Eisenhower policy towards Africa remained Eurocentric and avoided direct involvement in the decolonization process. It was found that it was easier and politically expedient to avoid taking sides altogether in decolonization conflicts. As late as 1959, Dana Adams Schmidt, a foreign correspondent for the *New York Times*, wrote in an article entitled "U.S. Still Seeking an African Policy" that the United States had no coherent and clear Africa policy.[35]

But change in Africa had begun to flow at a breakneck pace even without U.S. support. The growing importance of Africa could be sensed in policy-making circles. The 1959 study of the U.S. Africa policy made for the Senate Foreign Relations Committee was highly critical of the apathy of the policy. The report opened with the contention that "the United States has never had a positive, dynamic policy for Africa."[36] It was noted that the rapidity of change in Africa had eroded the validity of the Eurocentric policy of the pre-1958 period, and that the retention of any degree of influence in Africa required the relinquishment of the "negative, ad hoc approach that has marked . . . [U.S.] policy."[37] Among the recommendations of the report were the creation of a policy that would emphasize three main features: the realization that Africa was a major policy area in its own right and not merely an appendage of Europe; the acceptance of non-aligned and neutral positions by the new African states; and support in the United Nations for a definite timetable for decolonization, especially for the trusteeships.

There were two other very important themes of this study, one of which represented a radical break with past policy and one of which represented a continuation of earlier policy. First, the report stated that "evidence of effective penetration by Russia or her satellites is light and spotty," thus opposing the cold war considerations that had and would continue to determine much of the American Africa policy.[38] Second, although the report did call for a more intense degree of support for decolonization, it continued to stress the emphasis on the mechanisms of the metropole in this process. Thus, the U.S. continued to favor moderation in all changes.

[34] See, for example, Joseph C. Satterthwaite, "The United States and the Continent of Africa," State Department Press Release 610, 24 October 1960.

[35] Dana Adams Schmidt, "U.S. Still Seeking an African Policy," *New York Times*, 2 February 1959.

[36] Senate Foreign Relations Committee, *United States Foreign Policy: Africa*, 1.

[37] Ibid., 12.

[38] Ibid., 11.

Kennedy had beeen an early vocal supporter of decolonization. In 1956 he had
called for increased pressure for decolonization on the European metropoles and
for an end to the American practice of abstaining from U.N. votes on decolonization issues.[39] But like Dulles and other members of the Eisenhower administration, the primary rationale behind this position was cold war considerations,
thus illustrating that a schism in tone but not in content existed between the
Kennedy and Eisenhower positions. The actual decolonization issue played a
smaller part in Kennedy's Africa policy than in Eisenhower's since the majority
of Africa states were independent by the time Kennedy took office in 1961. There
were three aspects of the Kennedy approach to the issue that set it off from earlier methods.

First was the great emphasis placed on the internal nature of the threats to the
African states, including those that were approaching independence. G. Mennen
Williams noted in an important policy speech soon after Kennedy's inauguration
that the revolution of rising expectations, and its ensuing chaos and instability,
was the greatest threat to peace in Africa and not Soviet intervention.[40] Even ear-
lier, Williams had emphasized that a basic change in American relations with
Africa would have to be predicated on a slate of domestic changes in the United
States, including a solution to civil rights problems, an increasing study of
Africa and African issues, and the growth of cultural exchange programs with
African states.[41]

As an aspect of the nation-building policy, Williams argued that the creation
of stable economies in Africa would prove a greater deterrent to Communist intervention that would other cold war tactics. It was proposed in a State Department pamphlet that as African nations develop "the opportunities for communism to establish quick or easy footholds on the continent will diminish."[42]
Williams furthered the exuberant optimism of the nation-building mentality
when he announced that "we can compete with the Communists on equal terms,
and I think we need have no fear of comparison with them."[43]

When a newspaper in Kenya quoted Williams as advocating "Africa for the
Africans," many black Africans felt that a real change in the American position
was imminent.[44] Economic development through the local leaders appeared to
be the order of the day. But contrary to a trend that appeared to have emerged
in the last Eisenhower years, cold war considerations were again the paramount
rationale of U.S. policy; nation-building was, in the end, merely a new tactic in

---

[39] See the speech reprinted in *Congressional Record*, 6 June 1956, 9,614–15.

[40] G. Mennen Williams, speech to National Press Club reprinted as State Department Press Release 156, 24 March 1961.

[41] G. Mennen Williams, speech reprinted as State Department Press Release 41, 30 January 1961.

[42] U.S. Department of State, Office of Public Service, "The United States and Africa," Department of State Publication 7710, African Series 40, July 1964, 15.

[43] G. Mennen Williams, "American Foreign Policy and the Emerging Nations of Africa."

[44] For a discussion of this event see McKay, *Africa in World Politics*, 351–53. It later turned out
that this quotation was printed out of context, but because of the furor that it created among the
white settlers in Kenya, Williams later explained that he meant all Africans, black and white.

the strategy of global containment.[45] Tactics and tone had changed, but policy content, whether verbal or real, changed very little from the Eisenhower to Kennedy administrations.

A second major aspect of the Kennedy policy was a concerted attempt to separate the African and European aspect of the problem. Decolonization was no longer considered a zero-sum game in which the independence of an African state meant the weakening of a European state. This change was due to two developments. First, the resurgent European economy had proved that it could function quite well without attached empires. Second, national liberation movements in Africa had raised the costs of colonialism to the point where the benefits of empire were far outweighed by the costs.

A third important aspect of the Kennedy policy was the growth of imperial-type interests in the evaluation of American security concerns in Africa. When G. Mennen Williams wrote that "there can be no peace for our children or our children's children" without world stability, he expressed this trend of changing U.S. attitudes. Other U.S. officials, while noting the lack of American material interests in Africa, stressed that Africa was part of an indivisible security system based on global containment and world stability.[46]

In sum, the official line in U.S. policy towards decolonization exhibited a gradual evolution in tone from 1952 to 1962, with a growing acceptance of eventual African independence and the role that the U.S. would play in the post-independence period. There was a parallel shift from a strictly Eurocentric policy in which the benefits of colonialism to the NATO countries was the primary motive of our Africa policy to a position that attempted to separate the European and the African aspects of the problem. There was a shift from the perception that African independence was a threat to the West to the perception of an opportunity for the establishment of stable, pro-Western states. But in the long run, the changes in U.S. policy were often frantic attempts to catch up with the tremendous pace of change, and this meant that the actual impact of U.S. policy was often small.

NON-OFFICIAL OPINION: DEVELOPING CRITIQUES AND PROPOSALS

While most issues in U.S. foreign policy inspire criticism in academia and journalism, the U.S. Africa policy during the 1952–1962 period showed an amazing lack of discussion. This was due in part to a widespread ignorance of African

---

[45] Two important policy statements by the deputy assistant secretary of state for African affairs in 1959 and 1960, for example, made no mention of the cold war aspects of U.S. policy in Africa. See James K. Penfield, "The Role of the United States in Africa: Our Interests and Operations," State Department Press Release 325, 19 May 1959; and "Africa: A New Situation Requiring New Responses," State Department Press Release 246, 5 May 1960.

[46] G. Mennen Williams, "American Foreign Policy and the Emerging Nations of Africa"; J. Wayne Fredericks, acting assistant secretary of state for African affairs, "The Impact of the Emergence of Africa on American Foreign Policy," State Department Press Release 291, 4 May 1962.

affairs in the United States and in part simply to the lack of African experts in the universities and the press. When the need arose in the early 1950s for a cadre of African experts in the State Department, few could be found among career Foreign Service officers. Africa had traditionally been a very low-status area that was often avoided by the most highly skilled professionals. This meant that many of the State Department's Africa experts were drawn from the universities. Prior to the 1950s, American policy had relied on European sources, both diplomatic and academic, for African information. A small number of African studies programs had been established at American schools in the 1950s but the number of available scholars, and thus the number of Africa experts in the State Department, was limited. This meant that there was an astonishing dearth of appreciation for the long-range implications of events transpiring in Africa. Because of the interconnectedness of policymakers and students of African affairs — with several key figures such as Chester Bowles and Vernon McKay having written both as policymakers and as scholars — the academic discussion of the U.S. Africa policy closely followed the contours of the official line.

An early discussion of the decolonization issue is found in a 1952 article in *World Politics* by Philip W. Bell.[47] In an extreme example of realpolitik logic, Bell decried the "general moral-political attitude" that led the U.S. at least verbally to support decolonization even in instances where the decolonization process would have run counter to American interests. Bell pointed out that the primary goal of U.S. foreign policy was the continuation of the European economic recovery. Since decolonization would have ostensibly have damaged or slowed this recovery, he argued, the United States should foster what Bell called "happy" colonial relationships, while allowing decolonization where resistence was strong.[48] Thus, the U.S. should support colonialism as long as it did not clash with other vital interests or become "morally corrupting to our own culture or institutions." There are two very obvious shortcomings in these proposals. First, Bell did not clarify the order of priority of his various proposals. For example, what should the U.S. do in a case in which the metropole practices repressive policies to the point that support for the metropole is contrary to American "culture and institutions"? Which is the higher goal, American culture or Europe's economy? Second, Bell did not discuss the means by which "happy" colonial relationships are to be preserved in the face of growing nationalism and widespread dissatisfaction with the colonial relationship. As resistance and nationalism grew in Africa, arguments such as Bell's tended to disappear, but the idea that European economic recovery depended on the survival of colonialism persisted well into the late-1950s.[49]

In a 1955 article, Hans Morgenthau focused on the problems which arise when the interests of the metropole states clash with those of the United States on

---

[47] Bell, "Colonialism as a Problem."

[48] Ibid.

[49] See, for example, "Africa Makes a Start Toward a Better Day," *New York Times*, 8 February 1953.

decolonization issues.[50] Morgenthau realized that "the United States has in Africa no specific political or military interests," which meant that the major interest in the continent were those associated with global containment and world stability.[51] Because of the tendency to subordinate American to European interests in U.S. Africa policy, Morgenthau argued that the United States "subordinated its long-range interest in the autonomous development of the native population in short-range considerations of strategy and expedience."[52] Morgenthau proposed the abandonment of the Eurocentric aspects of the Africa policy and an attempt to "internationalize" the decolonization issue by increasing the role of the United Nations. In this way, Morgenthau argued, the United States could hurry the decolonization process and increase its influence in Africa without tarnishing its image either in Africa or in Europe. Whether the gradual erosion of the ability of the U.S. to control the General Assembly and the ensuing radicalization of the body on decolonization issues would have altered Morgenthau's position remains unknown.

In stark opposition to the realpolitik of Bell and Morgenthau, Paul Nitze argued in a 1955 essay that colonialism was completely incompatible with "American sensibilities," and in a somewhat Hegelian vein, proposed that the "historic development of world forces" would force the United States to take a stronger stand on decolonization.[53] Nitze felt that since unequivocally supporting all instances of decolonization could lead to chaos (and to Communist penetration), a middle course should be found that consisted of "throwing our weight behind the acceleration of self-determination for all peoples under conditions which will see preserved these precious freedoms one attained."[54] This proposition was obviously simply a rehash of the Eisenhower administration's warnings of the dangers of premature independence with an added dose of bombast.

One of the most influential discussions of the American role in Africa to emerge from this period was Chester Bowles's *Africa's Challenge to America*.[55] Bowles argued that the Eurocentric nature of American foreign policy had led to a perception of containment that stressed only the military aspects of the policy, thus creating an African policy constructed of "negativism," which actually eroded the potential influence of the United States in Africa. Like Morgenthau, Bowles favored a more Afrocentric policy in which the goal of the American policy was to be an increase of U.S. influence rather than the stabilization of the European situation. But again, the policy positions of Bowles did not differ substantially from official policy, since he favored the "orderly evolutionary approach" to decolonization. But in one respect Bowles was slightly ahead of the official line, in that he favored the establishment of a specific

---

[50] Morgenthau, "United States Policy Toward Africa."

[51] Ibid., 317.

[52] Ibid., 321.

[53] Nitze, "The United States and Africa," 477.

[54] Ibid., 478.

timetable for decolonization rather than the open-ended procedure then in practice.

This emphasis on a gradual decolonization continued throughout the 1950s, often surfacing even after the events of 1958 had proven the inevitability of decolonization. An editorial in the 27 January 1959 *New York Times* stated that "in many, if not most, cases it can be argued that the native people are not yet capable of organizing a democratic, efficient, economically viable state," and thus "progress should be controlled and measured."[56] But one year later, C. L. Sulzberger pointed out that U.S. policy towards Africa adapted to change much too slowly, and thus a transformation of American attitudes was needed.[57]

This admixture of conflicting approaches, divergent interpretations, and jumbled policy proposals was as typical of American comments on African decolonization as it was an official policy. But the actual differences in content were small. The view that pictured decolonization as a minor struggle between an intransigent Europe and an equally intransigent Africa persisted throughout the decolonization period. The need to preserve the image of the United States as the altruistic champion of liberal causes lent weight to those who supported the African position, but the spectre of Communist gains in Europe created a policy that could not sever the support for any European policies, however hopeless and misdirected. What resulted was a widespread desire to avoid the issue completely and to remain aloof from the decolonization process.

But this approach too proved hopeless. As Rupert Emerson has pointed out, for the U.S. during this period, hegemony precluded apathy on an issue as important and as inflammable as decolonization. Emerson noted that "the softening of the attitude toward colonialism is . . . one phase of the general American turn toward conservatism in world affairs."[58] And this was a conservatism bred by superpower status. As Vernon McKay argued, world hegemony had caused American attitudes towards Africa decolonization to swing from an "unthinking support of the abstract principle of self-determination" to the exact opposite — an overwhelming fear of "the dangers of premature independence."[59]

Rupert Emerson's *From Empire to Nation*, written in 1959, perhaps came the closest to expressing the attitudes of a nearly mature U.S. attitude toward decolonization.[60] While warning of the ominous — and inevitable — struggles that accompany the rise to nationhood, Emerson noted also the unstoppable nature of decolonization. Part of imperialism was the diffusion of culture and ideas, he argued, and a major portion of the ideas borne by European imperialism consisted of a high value for nationalism. As Emerson wrote: "Imperialism forged

[55] Bowles, *Africa's Challenge*.

[56] "Africa on the Move," *New York Times*, 27 January 1959.

[57] C. L. Sulzberger, "When the Cold War Reaches Africa," *New York Times*, 6 January 1960.

[58] Rupert Emerson, "American Policy in Africa," *Foreign Affairs* 40 (1962): 309.

[59] McKay, *Africa in World Politics*, 322.

[60] Rupert Emerson, *From Empire to Nation* (Boston: Beacon Press, 1960).

the tools with which its victims could pry it loose."[61] In Emerson's work, as in the policy of the Kennedy administration, there was a pervasive feeling that whether to support or oppose decolonization was no longer the issue—the real question was how best to tap the currents of change that decolonization brought.

As Donald Rothchild has noted, by the late 1950s the United States had "emerged as a key force for stability, not transformation."[62] America attempted to "get on the side of change," but all too often it was change which had already occurred rather than change which was about to happen, and "as a result, the United States stands out prominently as a status quo power in a rapidly changing African context."[63]

CONCLUSION

Americans' attitudes toward decolonization, like their perceptions of many other facets of world politics, underwent a drastic evolution during the crucial decade from 1952 to 1962. The United States had begun to feel comfortable with the hegemony which had been thrust upon it, and had begun to explore the resulting consequences and nuances. It was found that hegemony was not merely a source of unwanted responsibility and unnecessary fear, but was also a potential vehicle for the enactment of practical change. The evolution of U.S. perceptions towards African decolonization during this period is illustrative of many of these changes.

The African policy of the U.S. exhibited the growth of an imperial-type array of interests. No longer were the limited bounds of physical security the only, or even the major, parameters of U.S. interests. Although the argument can be made that the increasing costs of repression in Africa would have offset the economic benefits, Philip Bell may very well have been right when he argued that the continuation of the African empires would have contributed to containment as it was originally construed. But for the first time stability—world stability—was a central goal of U.S. foreign policy. It is this broadening of the concept of national interests that is the first indication of an imperial-type policy. But even as American interests became imperial, it was imperialism of an adolescent type in which the ideological and moralistic considerations indicative of a minor power continually infringed on the more amoral analyses of a true empire.

This situation created a paradox in which the traditional cry for world self-determination, which had been a useful rallying point when American attitudes actually mattered very little in world politics, was mixed with the difficulties of world leadership. Americans discovered that one must be more careful of what one says when people listen. As an imperial power, America's interests and world stability had become more congruent. But perhaps the major problem of many

[61] Ibid., 18.
[62] Rothchild, "Engagement versus Disengagement," 217.
[63] Ibid., 221.

imperial powers, as Henry Kissinger has pointed out, is the paradox of promulgating stability in a revolutionary world system.[64] And the world of the 1950s and 1960s was nothing if not revolutionary. This paradox led to many attempts to remain detached and aloof from the events that transpired in Brussels or Accra, though the total bankruptcy of this position was quickly evident. However much Americans wanted to, they could not both create stability and ignore potential instability. This led to frantic attempts to "get on the side of change," often with mixed results.

Thus the United States attempted to mold what was considered a "moderate" policy that would foster decolonization only when a slate of crucial criteria were met. To a casual reader of statements on African decolonization during this period, it would appear that even though the boundries of moderation were never seriously challenged, there was a gradual shift from a strongly Eurocentric policy to a strongly Afrocentric one. In fact, this was not true. What actually happened was an attempt to solve this paradox through the separation of the European aspects of world stability from the African aspects. The U.S. claimed that it could both wholeheartedly support decolonization and continue to place the highest priority on the European alliance. In effect, Americans came to realize (somewhat later than Europe itself) that Europe did not really need Africa, and that by fostering political independence within the framework of economic dependency, Europe could come very close to preserving the benefits of colonialism without the onerous costs.

At some time during this period, essential American attitudes about the meaning of national liberation and decolonization were changed. Independent Africa was no longer a "threat" to the West, and decolonization was no longer synonymous with the collapse of the European economy and a new Communist onslaught. Africa was considered an eager laboratory for the experiments in nation-building. It was realized that somehow, through sheer luck and in spite of frequent bungling, we had won the battle for men's minds in Africa, since, for the time being, most of the new African nations had rejected Marxism/Leninism. Even the "worst-case" situations—the Nkrumahs, the Tourés and the Nyereres—were not Fidel Castro or Ho Chi Minh. In effect, the United States decided that decolonization was not so bad after all. It would take more time and some real instances of "premature independence" (the Congo and the Portugese colonies) to seriously challenge this new euphoria. While the Congo did bear out the fact that the granting of independence "prematurely" could augment Soviet influence in Africa, the American answer to the problem had changed since 1952. Rather than attempting to bolster European rule during the period of political development in Africa, the U.S. itself stepped in to fill the political void. The problems remained the same, but the answers were different.[65]

[64] See Henry Kissinger, *A World Restored* (New York: Grosset and Dunlap, 1964).

[65] On the impact that the Congo crisis had on U.S. policy toward Africa see Henry F. Jackson, *From the Congo to Soweto: U.S. Foreign Policy Toward Africa Since 1960* (New York: William Morrow, 1982), 21–52; Arnold Riukin, *Africa and the West* (New York: Praeger Publishers 1962),

Racism and ethnocentrism were still intricately interwoven in U.S. Africa policy; it was, however, racism of a different type. Africans were no longer considered intractable primitives in need of perpetual (or at least long-term) tutelage, but rather as people who, given economic assistance and an occasional well-placed shove, might possibly prove able to govern themselves. American leaders, however, remained blind to the fact that aid and shoves given in an imperial context cannot destroy colonialism, but only serve to make it slightly less onerous and marginally more bearable. The residue of this blindness remains an element of American Africa policy today. U.S. policymakers have yet to learn that decolonization is not merely an exchange of flags, but is a transformation of both attitudes and actions.

110-25; and Steven R. Weissman, *American Foreign Policy in the Congo* (Ithaca, N.Y.: Cornell University Press, 1974).

[19]

RETHINKING THE COLD WAR AND DECOLONIZATION: THE GRAND STRATEGY OF THE ALGERIAN WAR FOR INDEPENDENCE

Matthew Connelly

October and November 1960 were two of the coldest months of the Cold War. Continuing tensions over Berlin and the nuclear balance were exacerbated by crises in Laos, Congo, and—for the first time—France's rebellious *départements* in Algeria. During Nikita Khrushchev's table-pounding visit to the United Nations, he embraced Belkacem Krim, the foreign minister of the Gouvernement Provisoire de la République Algérienne (GPRA). After mugging for the cameras at the Soviet estate in Glen Cove, New York, Khrushchev confirmed that this constituted de facto recognition of the provisional government and pledged all possible aid. Meanwhile, in Beijing, President Ferhat Abbas delivered the GPRA's first formal request for Chinese "volunteers." U.S. President Dwight D. Eisenhower asked his National Security Council "whether such intervention would not mean war." The council agreed that if communist regulars infiltrated Algeria, the United States would be bound by the North Atlantic Treaty to come to the aid of French President Charles de Gaulle and his beleaguered government. After six years of insurgency, Algeria appeared to be on the brink of becoming a Cold War battleground.[1]

What are scholars to make of such episodes? Even without knowing its particular origins or outcome, numerous studies would suggest that little good could result from bringing the Cold War into a colonial conflict. Historians have long been critical of how the United States imposed its global priorities regardless of local contexts, confused nationalists with communists, and supported colonial powers rather than risk instability.[2] With the opening of Soviet archives, scholars have also begun to document how Moscow subordinated revolutions in Asia to its own security interests and exploited conflicts in China and Korea for material advantage.[3] But comparatively little attention has been paid to how anti-colonial nationalists, for their part, approached the superpower rivalry. Some scholars assume that they were inevitably losers—even pawns—in that larger game; that it was at best a distraction.[4] But even without access to their archives, others have surmised that leaders such as Mohammed Mosaddeq and Gamal Abdel Nasser found opportunities as well as risks in the Cold War compe-

Matthew Connelly is Assistant Professor of History and Public Policy, University of Michigan, Ann Arbor, Mich., 48109, USA. E-mail: mattconn@umich.edu

tition.[5] The question, then, is not whether the Cold War was a "good" or a "bad" thing for anti-colonial nationalists. Rather, it is how they dealt with the challenges it posed in the formulation of their foreign policies.

With the opening of the Algerian archives—along with those of France, the United States, and the United Kingdom—it is now possible to document elite decision-making during the Arab world's most bitter anti-colonial conflict. How, it is asked, did Algerians relate their independence struggle to superpower rivalries, and how did the strategies they pursued influence international politics and contribute to their eventual victory? Although much work remains to be done, it is already clear that the Algerian perspective places episodes such as the one described earlier in an entirely new light. Thus, even while Abbas was warning Western journalists that a communist intervention would be a "disaster for the whole world," Krim worked with his North African allies to exaggerate the danger and drive France to the negotiating table.[6] Indeed, years before the Algerians launched their fight for independence, they had planned to harness the Cold War to their cause. Exploiting international tensions was part of a grand strategy that backed diplomatic lobbying with demonstrations of mass support, attracted foreign media with urban terror, and used U.N. debates to inspire peasant revolutionaries. But the boldest stroke came in 1958, when the Algerians established a provisional government and demanded diplomatic recognition despite the fact that they could not control any of the territory they claimed. The precedents they set would show the way and smooth the path for other national liberation movements. This article will show how, rather than being mere pawns of the great powers, the Algerians rewrote the rules of the game.

The origins of the grand strategy of the Algerian War can be traced to the last day of World War II in Europe. Nationalists had associated themselves with American anti-colonialism and organized celebratory marches. These quickly turned into bloody clashes in which French forces massacred from 6,000 to 45,000 Algerians—mass graves and an official cover-up made an exact accounting impossible.[7] Algeria's leading opposition figure, Messali Hadj, then turned to electoral politics. His new party, the Mouvement pour la Triomphe des Libertés Démocratiques (MTLD), won municipal offices across Algeria. But in the 1948 elections, Interior Minister Jules Moch had the MTLD's candidates arrested while local authorities stuffed ballots for "*Beni oui-ouis*"—Muslim yes-men.[8]

Later that year, the MTLD asked the head of its paramilitary wing, Hocine Aït Ahmed, to advise on how the party might win Algeria's independence through force of arms. Aït Ahmed was only 27 years old at the time and had never been formally educated in matters of strategy. Even so, he displayed considerable erudition in his report. He analyzed both earlier rebellions against the French and examples from abroad—the 1916 Easter uprising in Ireland, the Yugoslavian resistance, Mao's Long March, and Indochina—while incorporating insights from Carl von Clausewitz, Ernst Jünger, and B. H. Liddell Hart. All this led him to a sobering conclusion: "[i]f one considers dispassionately contemporary military history . . . one would search in vain even among the fights of colonized peoples against the European powers as great a disproportion in the forces facing each other." Algeria was only 400 miles from France, and, unlike any other colony, it was constitutionally an integral part of the republic. Moreover, unlike Indochina, most of Algeria was arid, exposed terrain ideal for the employment of air power. Above all, virtually no other anti-colonial movement had had to deal with such a sizable and politically powerful settler population—the 1 million *pieds noirs,* who exercised a virtual right of veto over French Algerian policy through their lobby in the National Assembly. For all of these reasons, Aït Ahmed ruled out a popular uprising, a liberated zone, or mass demonstrations. He prescribed nothing less than *une grande stratégie* for a truly revolutionary war, relating finances, logistics, morale, propaganda, and foreign policy. This article focuses on this last aspect: the foreign policy of national liberation.[9]

If Algerians had to "integrate the people's war in the international context," it was only because Aït Ahmed did not think they could hope to prevail otherwise. Thus, their "vital force" was "the historic movement which leads the peoples of Asia and Africa to fight for their liberation. . . . They will follow our example as we follow the example of other peoples who liberated themselves by force of arms or who are fighting still." But Aït Ahmed stressed that this was a "dogmatic and sentimental" principle, practical only to the extent that it would cause France to disperse its forces. Instead, their foreign policy would be independent and eminently flexible: "placing the good on one side and the bad on the other would be to ignore the complexity and ambiguity of elements that determine the interest of each country or group of countries." He knew that the United States, in particular, would never allow North Africa to pass under Soviet influence.[10]

Yet the Americans' interest created potential leverage, as Aït Ahmed pointed out. Even if the Americans would never be allies, he would exploit their rivalry with the Soviets to undermine their alliance with France. "Our strategy will follow this guideline in diplomatic matters: When we intend to put on our side of the scale an act of support from a Socialist country we will think at the same time of removing from the colonial side of the scale the weight of Western support." In December, the MTLD Central Committee approved the report in near-unanimity.[11]

In the following years, the MTLD would more often be divided, as younger militants such as Aït Ahmed chafed under Messali's autocratic rule. After six years, they finally broke away to form the Front de Libération Nationale (National Liberation Front; FLN) and launch the war for independence. It was soon apparent that Aït Ahmed's report had either inspired the FLN's strategy or reflected the views of its other leaders. The FLN's 1 November 1954 proclamation declared among the front's aims the "internationalization of the Algerian problem" and accorded it the same emphasis as the struggle's internal, military dimension.[12]

Aït Ahmed joined with his brother-in-law Mohammed Khider, a former National Assembly deputy, and Ahmed Ben Bella, a twice-decorated veteran of the Italian campaign, to form the FLN's first external delegation. Aït Ahmed and Khider's orders were to defeat French efforts to define Algeria as an internal affair and to take the FLN's case to the United Nations. Aït Ahmed would represent the FLN in New York and at international conferences, while in Cairo Khider was responsible for the overall direction of FLN diplomacy. Meanwhile, Ben Bella traveled throughout the Middle East and North Africa arranging arms shipments to the forces fighting in the interior.[13]

At the time, anti-colonialism was only beginning to emerge as a coordinated, international movement, and recently emancipated states were still a small minority at the United Nations. Consequently, the Algerians found it difficult to make headway. In

December 1954, neutral Asian countries meeting in Colombo, Sri Lanka, refused even to mention them in their final communiqué, explaining that it was up to the Arab states to take the lead.[14] On Khider's urging, Saudi Arabia did petition the U.N. Security Council. But most Arab League members were unwilling to challenge French claims that Algeria was juridically an internal affair. The Iranian representative who held the council's rotating presidency declared the whole business to be "perfectly absurd."[15]

Nevertheless, the Quai d'Orsay noted that the Saudi petition had "revealed the supposed existence of an Algerian question to American public opinion, which had been totally unaware of it before." The Interior Ministry was therefore asked to provide information on the number of rebels and the scale of their operations to help "reduce the present events to their exact proportion."[16] In fact, initially the FLN consisted of fewer than 2,500 mujahedin possessing no more than 400 rifles.[17] But the French were already concerned that diplomatic and military actions, however ineffectual in isolation, could together amplify Algerian demands through international organizations and the media, redounding to their disadvantage in world, and especially American, opinion.

The tensions the Algerian war would create in Franco-American relations were already apparent in a National Security Council meeting held three weeks after it began. Admiral Arthur Radford, chairman of the Joint Chiefs of Staff, pointed to the central dilemma facing American policy: "the possibility of either losing our whole position in the Middle East by offending the Arabs, or else risking the rupture of our NATO position by offending the French." While Radford advocated "outright support of the Arabs," Secretary of State John Foster Dulles prevailed on President Eisenhower to allow him quietly to urge his French counterparts to implement reforms leading to greater autonomy.[18]

The Bandung conference of Asian and African states in April 1955 exacerbated the Americans' apprehensions. Learning the lessons of the earlier conference, the Algerians prepared the ground by sending propaganda missions to the Colombo countries and joined representatives of the French protectorates of Morocco and Tunisia in a united North African delegation. They obtained a resolution recognizing that all had a right to independence.[19] Almost immediately there was a sharp increase in the number of FLN attacks in Algeria, from 158 in April to 432 in May.[20]

Philippe Tripier has attributed the escalation to the conference, marking the start of a pattern: "every important international event affecting the allies or sympathizers of the Algerian uprising would immediately have an effect on Algerian opinion and on the morale of the rebels themselves." Conversely, every reported exploit of the rebels within Algeria aided the FLN's allies and irritated the friends of France. "One noticed a phenomenon of resonance and reciprocity," Tripier concluded, "a natural interaction between the Algerian event and its global context." Indeed, in September 1958 the French delegation to the United Nations ordered a chart showing the correspondence between General Assembly debates on Algeria and the incidence of FLN attacks in Kabylia.[21]

Although many different factors determined the level of rebel activity, Tripier's account does reflect the perception of French security forces that the FLN's campaign abroad kept the rebellion alive—not surprisingly, because he served as an intelligence officer during the war. There is also ample contemporary evidence. In September 1955, for instance, the director-general of security in Algiers complained that "it would be difficult to restore calm as long as the nationalists felt they were going to get help from outside."[22] The French therefore concluded that they could not avoid doing battle with the FLN in the international arena, waging the Algerian war as a kind of world war—a war for world opinion.

The most fiercely contested terrain would be the United States and the United Nations. The French counted on U.S. military and especially diplomatic support, assuming it could easily command a majority in the General Assembly.[23] But in 1955, seventeen states—most of them Eastern bloc or Afro-Asian—were to gain membership. Even so, Aït Ahmed doubted that he had the votes to place the Algerian question on the agenda. Hoping to influence the outcome, shopkeepers in Algiers staged their first general strike on the opening day of the debate while the French deployed troops at strategic points around the city. Once again, an FLN diplomatic campaign coincided with a sharp increase in armed attacks.[24]

On 30 September 1955, the delegates voted in "an electrified atmosphere," as Aït Ahmed later recalled, with his deputies "counting on their toes." They won by a single vote, provoking thunderous applause and an abrupt walkout by the French foreign minister, Antoine Pinay.[25] At a dinner party in New York that evening, Pinay launched what a startled British ambassador described as "a ferocious attack" on his Soviet counterpart's support for the FLN.[26] Absent primary evidence, one can only surmise that this vote was part of Khrushchev's new Third World strategy. He had scored his first major success earlier that month by supplying arms to Egypt, breaking a Western monopoly in the Middle East. After it was announced that Krushchev would visit India, Burma, and Afghanistan—where he promised additional aid—Dulles concluded that "[t]he scene of the battle between the free world and the communist world was shifting."[27]

In November, the United States helped the French U.N. delegation adjourn discussion of the Algerian question. But at the same time, American diplomats began a series of meetings with the FLN. They were particularly impressed with Aït Ahmed, whom they described as "silken in tone and marble-hard in content." Aït Ahmed warned that "the attitudes of an independent North Africa toward the West would depend on the circumstances in which she won her independence."[28] Ben Bella, for his part, claimed that the FLN had "closed the door" to the communists. Still, he subtly played on American anxieties, criticizing U.S. support for France not only because it hurt its image in North Africa, but also because it "weakened the defenses of Western Europe against the Soviet Union." Indeed, the Americans were increasingly concerned about the shift of French forces from NATO to Algeria. Ben Bella was equally astute in suggesting what they might do about it:

There was no thought, he said, that the United States should exert public pressure on France. Such a move would be bound to fail. He hoped however that the United States, behind the scenes, would continually urge the French in the direction of finding a peaceful solution through negotiations with the Algerian Nationalists.[29]

In fact, behind the scenes the United States did urge the French to make concessions and seek a negotiated settlement.[30] In Paris, everyone from communists to conservatives accused Washington of playing a "double game"—pretending to back France while secretly favoring the rebels.[31]

In February 1956, a new French government under Prime Minister Guy Mollet resolved to grant Tunisia and Morocco "independence within interdependence," calculating that with aid and advisers France could retain these countries as allies, or at least prevent their aiding the FLN. But Mollet complained to U.S. Ambassador Douglas Dillon that the Moroccans "are constantly telling [the] French that they can obtain [aid] more easily and in greater quantities from [the] U.S. than they can from France." The prime minister insisted that the United States not allow North Africans to play the allies off against each other.[32]

In March, a series of reports arrived in Washington indicating a "dangerously sharp rise in anti-American sentiment." Without a strong, public statement of U.S. support for France in North Africa, Dillon predicted "an explosion."[33] Conversely, the new foreign minister, Christian Pineau, pledged that his government "was really determined to reach [an] agreement with [the] Algerian nationalists," though they could succeed only with U.S. support.[34] Washington finally extended only token aid to the former protectorates, prompting the Tunisians to joke that they would use the money to build an embassy in Moscow.[35] At the same time, Eisenhower approved a qualified but well-publicized endorsement of French policy in Algeria.[36]

Undeterred, Aït Ahmed simply redoubled his efforts, pressing the Afro-Asian caucus to convene a special session of the General Assembly and petition the Security Council. "[T]he more we push the U.S. to implicate itself with colonialism," he predicted, "the closer will be the day when they will see themselves obliged to bail out." He urged his allies to make *démarches* to all the NATO capitals, especially to Washington and London. At the same time, he called on Khider to obtain "the most extreme positions possible" from the Arab League. These efforts were interconnected and mutually reinforcing: "extreme" positions by the league would lend urgency to the *démarches* of even "moderate" states such as India, while the collective weight of the Afro-Asian world would compel France's allies to press for a compromise peace.[37]

The one weak link was Nasser, heretofore the Algerians' most valued supporter. Worried about French arms shipments to Israel, he was now exploring a possible rapprochement. The bargaining began in March 1956, when Pineau paid a surprise visit to Egypt. Nasser promised not to oppose any settlement in Algeria that had the support of its Muslim population and agreed to arrange a meeting between a French representative and the FLN.[38] In the next three weeks, there was a significant decline in the size of Egyptian arms shipments, which the FLN attributed to the Pineau–Nasser meeting.[39] Both Aït Ahmed and Khider also noted a weakening of Egypt's diplomatic support at the United Nations and the Arab League.[40]

Nasser's point man on North Africa, Mohamad Fathi al-Dib, suggested that he make a deal with France. Noting France's ability to destabilize the region, he would require that country to limit both military aid and Jewish emigration to Israel; to assist in the settlement of the Palestinian problem; and to continue opposing British efforts to form a regional defense organization, the Baghdad Pact. Thus, at the same time a political solution in North Africa was beginning to seem possible, Egypt would make it contingent on these and other French concessions that had nothing whatever to do with Algerian independence—but everything to do with Egypt's problem with Israel.[41]

Yet even if Pineau had wanted to make this deal, he probably would not have been able to pull it off. Both Mollet and Defense Minister Maurice Bourgès-Maunoury had a deep, sentimental attachment to the Israelis and might have been repulsed rather than tempted by the offer. Moreover, the French government had been powerless to stop the Defense Ministry from sending the Israelis tanks and planes.[42] The Israelis, for their part, were pushing hard from the other direction. As early as June 1955, Shimon Peres, then director-general of the Israeli Defense Ministry, had observed that "[e]very Frenchman killed in North Africa, like every Egyptian killed in the Gaza Strip, takes us one step further towards strengthening the ties between France and Israel."[43] Israel's Mossad assisted France's Service de Documentation Extérieure et de Contre-Espionnage (SDECE) with intelligence on Nasser's aid to the FLN, which made a French–Egyptian rapprochement even more unlikely.[44] So, too, did a statement by Israeli Prime Minister David Ben-Gurion praising France as the only country to supply Israel with weaponry. On 15 May, the Paris daily *Le Monde* reported that the Israelis had contracted for another dozen Mystère IVs, the latest generation of French jet fighters.[45] That same day, Nasser asked Dib to re-evaluate Egypt's policy. Quickly reversing course, he decided to step up support for the FLN.[46]

Egypt's increasing aid encouraged the French tendency to view the FLN as a mere instrument of Nasser's ultimate ambition "to re-create the empire of Islam around Egypt," as Mollet explained it to Anthony Eden. When Egypt nationalized the Suez Canal in July 1956, Pineau vowed to respond with force, even without allied support.[47] The French finally brokered the agreement that would bring Britain and Israel into the war together. But, ironically, France was preparing to strike at Nasser at precisely the moment the FLN was repudiating Egyptian influence.[48]

On 20 August, the FLN's leadership within Algeria met secretly in the Soummam valley to compose a common platform.[49] None of the external delegation attended, so Ben Bella could not counter criticism that he was too close to Nasser and had not provided enough arms. The congress's platform openly criticized "the Arab states in general, and Egypt in particular":

Their support for the Algerian people's struggle was limited and was subjected to the fluctuation of their general diplomacy. France exerted a special form of pressure on the Middle East by means of her economic and military aid and her opposition to the Baghdad pact.

The platform denied any role to Algerian communists and condemned the equivocal position of the French Communist Party. Conversely, it downplayed "the rather embarrassed declarations forced out of the representatives of the United States, Great Britain, and NATO" in support of France.[50]

Most significantly, the Soummam congress did not envisage a military victory. Instead, it looked for "the total weakening of the French army to make victory by arms impossible." Equally important, the FLN would work for "the political isolation of France—in Algeria and in the world."[51] Toward that end, the platform foresaw a permanent office at the United Nations and in the United States, as well as a delegation in Asia. In fact, by October 1956 there would be eight FLN bureaus: in Cairo, Damascus, Tunis, Beirut, Baghdad, Karachi, Djakarta, and New York. The Soummam congress also called for "mobile delegations" that would visit various capitals and international cultural, student, and trade-union meetings. The FLN had already formed

228 *Matthew Connelly*

a labor affiliate, the Union Générale des Travailleurs Algériens, and would create a commercial association the following month, the Union Générale des Commerçants Algériens. While forming links with their counterparts abroad, these organizations would coordinate labor and commercial strikes during the next U.N. debate. They also facilitated indirect contributions to the FLN, including important sums from the CIA, which thereby hedged the public U.S. position behind France.[52]

Thus, the FLN's international strategy—particularly the campaign to undermine U.S. support for France—was a sustained effort that withstood temporary setbacks and had the support of the party's top leaders. The Soummam platform did establish the principle that the interior leaders would have primacy over the exterior, but only because FLN foreign policy was deemed too important to be delegated. The most influential among these leaders, Ramdane Abbane, had already dispatched a personal envoy—Dr. Lamine Debaghine—with nominal authority over the rest of the external delegation. Although Debaghine soon quarreled with his new colleagues—Ben Bella "almost strangled him on several occasions," according to Khider—the clash was of personalities rather than policies.[53]

The proof came in October 1956, when the French intercepted a plane carrying Khider, Aït Ahmed, Ben Bella, and Mohammed Boudiaf (who had served as liaison to Algeria's Western front). The French introduced their captives as "Ben Bella and his associates," reflecting both his close ties to Cairo and the French view that they all worked for Nasser. But once officials read their papers, they admitted that the internal leadership was in charge, not the FLN diplomats, and certainly not Ben Bella (though he benefited enormously from the publicity).[54] The internal leaders simply dispatched new representatives abroad to continue their policies under Debaghine's direction.

The arrest of the external delegation and the Suez fiasco only heightened American doubts about Paris's ability to contain the conflict and conclude a compromise peace. Indeed, by this point the best-known Algerian moderate, Ferhat Abbas, had gone over to the FLN. In his first State Department meeting in November 1956, he warned that the war increased the danger of communist infiltration. If the French succeeded in actually decapitating the FLN, "red Maquis" would take over.[55]

Abbas was exaggerating, as there were now close to 20,000 armed regulars in the Armée de Libération Nationale (ALN). In January 1957, the ALN executed almost 4,000 attacks around the country, including more than one hundred within the capital itself—a nearly tenfold increase since May 1955.[56] But the FLN leaders continued to direct their efforts at defeating the French abroad. As Abbane put it:

Is it preferable for our cause to kill ten enemies in some riverbed in Telergma, which no one will talk about, or rather a single one in Algiers, which the American press will report the next day? Though we are taking some risks, we must make our struggle known.[57]

On 2 January, the FLN's new representative in New York, M'Hammed Yazid, called for U.N. sponsorship of renewed negotiations based on a recognition of Algeria's right to independence.[58] That same day, the head of ALN forces in Algiers, Larbi Ben M'Hidi, began to prepare for a general strike. "As the UN session approaches," he explained, "it is necessary to demonstrate that all the people are behind us and obey our orders to the letter." This would negate the French government's argument against negotiating—that is, that the FLN represented no one if it did not actually represent Nasser. The rest of the leadership agreed unanimously, and leaflets announced and explained the action as directed at the U.N. debate.[59]

In what became known as the Battle of Algiers, French paratroopers marched into the Algerian capital, broke the strike, and systematically dismantled Ben M'Hidi's organization. In the following months, the French would send 24,000 Muslims from the city to internment centers, where torture was systematically practiced. This was more than four times as many as the entire FLN organization there, and almost 10 percent of the city's total Muslim population. By the end of the year, nearly 4,000 people had disappeared without a trace.[60]

Meanwhile, Abbas and Yazid struggled to win support for a forceful U.N. resolution, but they were outgunned and outspent. Mollet met with no fewer than thirty-six ambassadors in Paris, while in New York Pineau personally lobbied most heads of delegations.[61] When diplomacy did not suffice, SDECE agents distributed outright bribes.[62] The French Information Center, for its part, delivered propaganda films to American television stations that were shown more than 1,500 times to an estimated 60 million viewers. The $450,000 that the French Information Center was estimated to have spent on a full-page advertisement in the thirty-one largest U.S. newspapers was more than ten times the FLN office's entire budget.[63]

The Algerians were finally forced to settle for a compromise resolution that merely called for "a peaceful, democratic, and just solution . . . conforming to the principles of the United Nations charter."[64] With the sacrifices being made in Algiers, this could only disappoint the FLN leadership. That same day, they decided to abandon the city and direct the rebellion from Tunis. Even before they arrived, Ben Bella's representative was attacking their record. "We have risked the dismantling of the revolutionary organization to make a noise at the United Nations," he exclaimed. "It's stupid and ridiculous!"[65]

Yet as Abbane had anticipated, the risks the FLN ran were repaid with media attention in France and around the world. Indeed, as French methods came to light, the Battle of Algiers began to appear as a Pyrrhic victory. Authorities banned articles and books about torture, but this merely lent these works cachet and did not stop FLN publicists from citing them to argue that France had violated the U.N. resolution. Translations of Henri Alleg's *La Question* became best-sellers elsewhere in Europe and in the United States.[66] Censorship also made "the worst impression abroad," as the French Director of Information and Press Pierre Baraduc pointed out in March 1958.[67] Even writers who condemned the FLN, Ambassador Hervé Alphand reported, "observed that the persistence of terrorism implicitly attests to the fact that France cannot take the situation in hand. . . . [L]ittle by little, [this] prepares American public opinion for the idea that the Algerian question is on the way to becoming an international problem."[68]

French propagandists therefore began to ignore the war and emphasize their efforts to "develop" Algeria. As Baraduc argued, "Each time that one can speak of something other than blood in Algeria . . . this is progress for pacification because it represents a return to normal."[69] Yet a "return to normal" did not interest newsmen attracted to a story with strong visuals and plenty of violence. Although the FLN could not equal France in its propaganda output, the FLN gained a decisive advantage in "free media."

The radio and television formats rewarded the FLN for creating controversy and providing combat footage, whereas the French would not even dignify their adversary with a debate. The host of a CBS radio program, Blair Clark, resorted to letting an FLN spokesman sitting in the studio debate the network's correspondent in Algiers.[70] Similarly, Chet Huntley of NBC TV's *Outlook* program showed clips taken by mujahedin using a portable camera. Perhaps the scenes of children crying beside their parents' corpses and French soldiers falling to the ALN were staged, as the French maintained, but they obviously made a greater impact than propaganda films such as *Water, Crops, and Men.*[71] And what did it matter if, as Paris complained, Italian and German correspondents who thought they were accompanying FLN raids never really left Tunisia? By making the rebels appear to control parts of Algeria, these reports buttressed the FLN's claims to international recognition. As one French diplomat later remarked about FLN visits to the State Department, "It's not the reality of what they say or do, but the way it is represented in the radios of Tunis and Cairo and the myth that it gives life to in [Algeria]." Indeed, this "myth" of a conquering army and diplomats with entrée to every chancellery would gradually help to transform reality within Algeria itself, inspiring nationalists to persist in their struggle and making the once unassailable notion of *Algérie française* itself seem illusory.[72]

In the near-term, the FLN focused on inciting international opposition to the Algerian war and using Tunisia as a safe haven in which to regroup its forces. The French, for their part, began to fortify the border with electrified fences, minefields, and radar-directed artillery. This led to a series of clashes that drew in Tunisia's own small army, leading President Habib Bourguiba to threaten to turn to Egypt or the Eastern bloc for arms that France now refused to supply.[73] The Tunisian arms crisis, as it came to be known, culminated in November 1957 with an Anglo-American decision to provide a small but symbolic shipment, despite the vociferous objections by the new French government led by Prime Minister Félix Gaillard. As Eisenhower described it, Gaillard had threatened "a complete breakup of the Western alliance."[74]

Yet the worst crisis came in February 1958, when the French bombed a Tunisian border village that they alleged to be an ALN base, inflicting scores of civilian casualties. Within hours, Bourguiba had brought foreign correspondents and cameramen to the scene, and the resulting articles and images created a public-relations fiasco for Paris. After barricading French troops in their bases, Bourguiba threatened to petition the U.N. Security Council before accepting American and British mediation. All through the talks, Bourguiba sought to expand their mandate to include a settlement of the Algerian war while rejecting any measures that might have hindered the ALN.[75] Meanwhile, the rebel command sent whole battalions against the French border fortifications, leading to some of the most intense fighting of the war.[76]

By word and deed, passivity and aggressivity, the Tunisians and Algerians together were forcing each of the foreign powers to weigh in on the future of North Africa. Virtually all had struggled to avoid an unqualified commitment to either French Algeria or independence—America playing a "double game," Germany conducting a "double strategy," Italy pursuing a "two-track" policy, Britain publicly supportive but privately skeptical[77]—because none, not even the USSR, wanted to see French influence eradicated in the region. Thus, the Soviet deputy foreign minister urged Paris to undertake "an 'audacious' initiative" or risk being replaced by the United States.[78] Indeed, Dulles had already told Alphand that it was "indispensable that you look for a political solution while there is still time." He warned, "[W]hatever may be the French determination to continue the fight, . . . financial conditions could, at some point, stand in their way." Only two months before, France had narrowly averted a balance-of-payments crisis thanks to loans from the United States, the International Monetary Fund, and the European Payments Union. Dulles noted that certain, U.S. senators had asked him to go back on the decision. With a new financial crisis looming, and France ever more isolated, his words carried considerable weight.[79]

A week later, the American member of the "good offices" mission, Robert Murphy, sought British support in demanding that France accept a cease-fire and an international conference on Algeria. If Paris did not agree, the United States would be forced to provide political, economic, and military support to Tunisia and Morocco—thus placing America behind France's adversaries in a public and definitive fashion.[80] The perception that the United States was unfairly pressuring Paris caused the downfall of the Gaillard government. But leading candidates to succeed him were prepared to work with the Americans. On 1 May, René Pleven told U.S. Ambassador Amory Houghton that he "would hope that we would be willing to use our contacts with [the] FLN, if good enough, to try to get it to discuss a cease-fire." Mollet, for his part, favored sending a negotiating team to meet with the Algerians.[81] Their long and patient efforts to secure U.S. support for a negotiated settlement appeared to be on the brink of success.

But rather than submit to a "diplomatic Dien Bien Phu," the *pieds noirs* rose up on 13 May, and, under the leadership of the local army commanders, demanded the return of de Gaulle. Assuming full powers on 1 June, de Gaulle quickly settled the border conflict with Tunisia and restored confidence in France's ability to end the war. Yet it soon became clear the general would make peace only on his own terms, which did not include political negotiations with the FLN or full independence for Algeria.[82]

De Gaulle's return was a massive setback for the FLN's international strategy. "We've settled into the war, the world has also gotten used to it," the FLN's chief of armaments and logistics, Omar Ouamrane, bitterly observed two months later. The world would "continue to turn to the Algerian war as long as it lasts, if necessary until the last Algerian." The ALN had suffered demoralizing losses in assaults on the French border fortifications. Soon they would become all but impenetrable as French forces set to work stamping out the insurgents of the interior. Diplomatically, de Gaulle could "permanently bar the way to the West and neutralize the Eastern bloc," Ouamrane wrote. "He has already succeeded in partially cutting us off from our own brothers." After making a separate deal with de Gaulle, the Tunisians joined the Moroccans in urging the FLN to accept less than full independence.[83]

Instead, Ouamrane called for a "truly revolutionary political and diplomatic action"—though it was an action that Aït Ahmed had already suggested nearly two years before. In fact, Ouamrane was inspired by a study he had written in his prison cell in the Santé.[84] Here is how Ouamrane summarized Aït Ahmed's critical insight:

Our whole policy consists of requesting, of demanding our independence. We demand it from the enemy. We want that our brothers, our friends, the U.N. recognize it. We ask it of everyone except ourselves, forgetting that independence proclaims itself and is not given.[85]

Aït Ahmed argued instead that by unilaterally declaring independence and establishing a provisional government, the FLN could drive France to the negotiating table. First, re-establishing the *dawla*—or state—was the dream of generations of Algerian

232   *Matthew Connelly*

Muslims; it would now inspire them to persist in their struggle. The Arab and Asian states would be "forced, by their public opinion and by mutual competition for interests and prestige, to conform their actual policy to their profession of faith." By obtaining their recognition, Algeria would be perceived as an integral part—rather than merely as an outward sign—of the Afro-Asian movement, which was the object of increasing superpower competition. And if the provisional government won recognition from the communist states, the Americans might be led to end their "complacency and capitulations" to French blackmail. Finally, a campaign for recognition could be conducted continuously, unlike the once-a-year test of strength in the U.N. General Assembly. Each success would galvanize the energy of the Algerian people and help convince Paris that the process was irreversible.[86]

So on 19 September 1958, Ferhat Abbas called a press conference in Cairo to announce the formation of the GPRA, with himself as president. Despite having discouraged this initiative, Morocco and Tunisia immediately extended diplomatic recognition, explaining to Paris that they would otherwise be subject to attack from more militant states such as Egypt and Iraq—just as Aït Ahmed had anticipated. Indeed, every Arab state except Lebanon immediately joined them.[87] China's recognition came within the week, followed shortly by North Vietnam, North Korea, and Indonesia. All together, thirteen of some eighty-three states recognized the GPRA within ten days of its creation.[88]

While the GPRA sent delegations to the communist states, its forty-five representatives abroad—accredited and not—were initially concentrated in Middle Eastern and Western European countries, twenty in total.[89] In theory, they reported to Debaghine, now designated foreign minister. But given the circumstances in which they worked, all of the GPRA's ministries had to deal with other governments—or evade them—in order to carry out their functions. By June 1960, French intelligence counted 177 GPRA officials in thirty-eight countries, not counting Tunisia and Morocco. But this figure included—and doubtless excluded—dozens working clandestinely as recruiters or money collectors in emigrant communities.[90] Although all of this was inimical to rational organization, it would have been impossible for the Foreign Ministry's small staff to oversee the entirety of Algerian activities abroad.[91] Rather than implying the insignificance of foreign affairs for the GPRA this attested to its all-encompassing importance. With a Ministry of Armaments dealing with everyone from German arms dealers to communist China, and a Ministry of General Liaisons running bagmen and agents across Europe and the Middle East, nothing was "foreign" to the new government. Indeed, in 1960 even the "minister of the interior," Lakhdar Bentobbal, concluded that "each one of our agencies, military, political, diplomatic, social, associational or otherwise should act in its area according to the same objective: *INTERNATIONALIZATION.*"[92] In that year, the French estimated, the GPRA's expenditures abroad—for arms purchases, maintenance, support for refugees, and so on— had nearly equaled expenditures in the five Algerian *Wilayat*. The GPRA was like a state turned inside out.[93]

De Gaulle's strategy was to reverse this process of internationalization and isolate the GPRA. Like his predecessors, he believed that the provisional government would not otherwise acknowledge defeat.[94] His main concern was that the Algerians and their allies would exploit the competition between the United States and the USSR, observing that "the Arabs were past masters in playing off one white power against another."[95] He therefore called for a tripartite organization that would divide the world into French, British, and American spheres of influence. In September 1958, he warned that such an organization was "indispensable," and that France "subordinates to it as of now all development of its present participation in NATO." Thus, both sides escalated their international campaigns without fundamentally altering their strategies.[96]

During the U.N. debate on Algeria in December 1958, three GPRA ministers toured China, North Vietnam, and North Korea. Soon the press was reporting that they had requested economic and military aid—even volunteers. Yet this visit did not provoke a violent reaction from the West, as a GPRA official noted. Indeed, the United States refused to vote with France's supporters at the United Nations. More than half of the U.N. General Assembly explicitly recognized the GPRA, though a resolution calling for "negotiations between the two parties" failed by a single vote to obtain the requisite two-thirds majority. The U.S. abstention was "incontestably a success" from Abbas's standpoint, encouraging the Algerians' efforts to exploit the escalating "war of nerves" between the putative allies.[97] The French U.N. representative, for his part, observed that "[i]f the FLN has lost ground in Algeria, there is little doubt that it has gained a good deal on the international level and in all the countries of the world where it has sent missions, especially the United States and the United Nations."[98]

There were a number of reasons for the American abstention, but the main one remained Dulles's and Eisenhower's determination not to alienate Third World opinion. It is indicative of this attitude that what worried the secretary about de Gaulle's tripartite proposal "was not so much its impact on NATO countries but the disastrous effects it would have on countries in Africa and the Middle East."[99] De Gaulle retaliated by withdrawing the French Mediterranean fleet from NATO command.[100] His new prime minister, Michel Debré, instructed French ambassadors that Algeria was now the "first priority" of the government and its foreign policy. "[I]t is imperative that the rebellion lose the support and complacence that it currently benefits from," he asserted, "and that it feel abandoned and asphyxiated."[101]

Denying the GPRA diplomatic recognition was therefore critical to French strategy. Since September 1958, Lebanon and Mongolia had joined the group of states that recognized the provisional government. French spokesmen privately suggested that a Muslim or Arab country could not do otherwise. But if de Gaulle was not unduly exercised by anything Ulan Bator said or did, he warned in April 1959 that Paris would sever ties with any "responsible" state that followed suit. Nevertheless, nothing was done to Ghana after it accorded de facto recognition that summer, thus extending the zone of French tolerance to all of Africa. Otherwise, in trying to isolate the GPRA, France risked isolating itself.[102]

Algeria's evident importance to Paris encouraged unfriendly states to turn the war to their advantage. In August 1959, Soviet Foreign Minister Andrei Gromyko warned his French counterpart, Maurice Couve de Murville, that Moscow would drop the restraint it had displayed on Algeria if Paris continued to back West Germany on Berlin.[103] Conversely, German Chancellor Konrad Adenauer's support for French Algeria—including tolerance for SDECE operations against arms traders and GPRA officials in West Germany—mitigated the credit de Gaulle hoped to obtain for his uncompromising stance, even if Adenauer was too skilled a statesman to link these issues explicitly.[104] Francisco Franco, on the other hand, called on de Gaulle to end tolerance toward dissident Spanish emigrés, as Madrid had already done vis-à-vis the Algerians. De Gaulle flatly refused, denying any equivalence between the Spanish republicans and the Algerian provisional government, but the whole conversation must have been distasteful to him.[105] It was from such episodes that de Gaulle concluded that Algeria "undermines the position of France in the world," as he said at the time. "As long as we are not relieved of it, we can do nothing in the world. This is a terrible burden. It is necessary to relinquish it."[106]

So on 16 September 1959, de Gaulle declared: "[t]aking into account all the givens—Algerian, national, and international—I consider it necessary that the principle of self-determination be proclaimed from today." After peace was restored, Muslims would decide their own future in a referendum to which de Gaulle would invite "informants from the whole world." At first some actually dismissed the speech as intended only for foreign consumption. De Gaulle himself privately explained that he hoped "to defuse the debate at the U.N. at the end of September."[107]

Yet despite de Gaulle's acceptance of self-determination, the Americans still refused to associate themselves with his Algerian policy. "How could we say that we support the French and still not damage our interests?" Eisenhower asked in an August 1959 National Security Council meeting. Interpreting a proposed policy statement, he stated that "a solution 'in consonance with U.S. interests' meant that we should avoid the charge that we were one of the colonial powers." He would not openly side with de Gaulle, no matter what he proposed, as long as it was not immediately accepted by the Algerians.[108]

Eisenhower's reasoning shows why, as the French representative Armand Bérard wrote in July 1959, "the evolution of the situation in North Africa and that of our position at the U.N. are going in exactly opposite directions."[109] Indeed, by that point the number of ALN regulars within Algeria had declined by a third from its peak, while a quarter of their weapons lacked parts or ammunition. Moreover, morale was suffering: the proportion of prisoners to killed rose from 27 percent to 42 percent over the same period, and there was a doubling in the monthly rate of rebels voluntarily rallying to the French.[110] The impossibility of breaching the border fortifications without staggering losses prevented reinforcement while creating disciplinary problems in the armies left idle on the frontier, problems that contributed to a deterioration in relations with Tunisia and Morocco.[111]

The evolution Bérard traced was not inexorable. In fact, the U.N. General Assembly resolution calling for negotiations barely missed the required two-thirds majority. But after having achieved virtually the same result as in 1958 despite making a maximum effort to win over world opinion, it was now clear that de Gaulle could not domesticate the Algerian question. The cause of Algerian independence had taken on a life of its own at the United Nations and around the world. And this, in turn, had begun to help sustain loyalty to the provisional government within Algeria despite the reversals suffered by the ALN. French officials touring Algeria in January 1960 discovered that "the successes, even relative, of the FLN in the international arena seem to have deeply affected Muslim opinion."[112]

Yet de Gaulle would have to overcome the opposition of the *pieds noirs* and his own military, who did not see why they had to concede to the GPRA what it could not win in the field. That same month, another settler uprising once again forced de Gaulle to rule out political negotiations. Debaghine's successor as foreign minister, Belkacem Krim, therefore embarked on the risky strategy that culminated in the episode described at the outset of this article. Debaghine had already provided the rationale in an October 1959 memorandum. Noting that U.S. support for France weakened the moment it was rumored that China might back the Algerians, he proposed that they continue to escalate. De Gaulle's difficulties increasingly affected the West, Debaghine noted, and "[t]he process is going to intensify":

The Arab states will commit themselves further, and so too will the Afro-Asian countries. On the French side it will be necessary to involve the West even more. The radicalization of the war, with the co-belligerence of the Arab countries and the participation of Chinese volunteers, will lead in the end to a confrontation between the West and the East. . . . The final stage is the intervention of China. This will lead the West to put a stop to the war in Algeria. If not this would be world war.[113]

Krim confirmed this shift in Algerian strategy in "Our Foreign Policy and the Cold War," one of the first memoranda he wrote as foreign minister. The Algerians would no longer present themselves as potential allies of the United States or limit themselves to threats to turn to "the East." Although the goal remained the same—to exacerbate divisions in the West and thereby exert indirect pressure on Paris—they would pursue it through a policy of brinkmanship, confronting France's allies with actual and increasing communist support.[114] This aid might also help militarily, but for Krim that was secondary. Thus, when he formally called for foreign volunteers— initially limited to the Arab and African states—there was no discussion of how they might actually be used. "The modalities of putting this into practice will be discussed and debated later," he explained in an internal note. "Right now what matters is to conduct a vigorous propaganda [campaign] around the principle of volunteering and above all to demonstrate, if the war continues, de Gaulle alone will be responsible and world peace will be directly threatened." For Krim, both African and Arab support were alike a "means of pressuring the East and the West."[115]

Thus, even while the Algerians' international strategy came to encompass East and West, North and South, it remained interdependent and essentially political in nature. Support by African and Arab states sought after by the superpowers would compel the communists to provide more active assistance, while the threat of increasing communist influence or even direct intervention would cause France's allies to compel a settlement. Yet, as in the earlier phase, a weak link could cause the whole plan to unravel. That weak link was now located in Moscow.

The Soviets had always been reluctant to give the Algerians more than their General Assembly votes. In addition to their solicitude for French communists and fear that the United States would fill any vacuum in North Africa, more forthright support would cost them a valuable bargaining chip in relations with de Gaulle—especially while the Berlin question was unsettled and a summit in Paris was imminent. Indeed, Krim was nervous about a rapprochement between the great powers, as he made clear during a conversation in Beijing on 1 May 1960. He told the Chinese vice premier that he "would have loved to see . . . the Soviet Union adopt very firm positions like those of the government of the People's Republic of China" and asked him to make certain that Khrushchev acted as an advocate for colonized peoples.[116] Considering their divide-and-conquer strategy, the Algerians had reason to fear that a relaxation in superpower tensions "would materialize on our backs," as they had told Indian Prime Minister Jawaharlal Nehru two years before.[117] But that same day, the Soviets shot down Gary Powers's U-2 spy plane. De Gaulle backed Eisenhower in the midst of the collapsing summit, and, in retaliation, Khrushchev condemned his "war against the Algerian people that has lasted five years and for which France needs American support." This ended the danger that détente posed to Algerian diplomacy.[118]

When the Soviets extended de facto recognition to the GPRA in October, Yazid demanded a meeting with a high-level U.S. State Department official to warn that the pro-Western faction was losing power.[119] Later that month, Abbas formally appealed for Chinese "volunteers." At the same time, Morocco's Crown Prince Hassan told the British ambassador that the Algerians had delivered a written request to admit them. He warned British Prime Minister Harold Macmillan that he could not delay their entry more than two months, urging progress toward peace talks before the U.N. General Assembly debated the question. Macmillan called it "a very dangerous" proposal and urged Hassan not to force the Western powers to choose between Paris and the GPRA. Bourguiba tipped off the Lebanese ambassador—who quickly passed the tip on to his French colleague—that soon "Chinese hordes" would sweep across North Africa.[120]

In fact, Hassan and Krim concocted this request for the express purpose of "putting pressure on Macmillan," as Krim noted at the time. "Result: Macmillan felt the pressure." The GPRA's foreign minister was equally pleased with Hassan's self-imposed deadline, "[w]hich leaves the Anglo-Americans two months to make their move and avoid letting Algeria become a theater of the Cold War." Little did they know that Krim and Hassan were talking about only forty technicians, hardly the makings of a horde. Even so, the Moroccans were genuinely reluctant to admit the Chinese, with the minister of the interior suggesting instead that they might join the GPRA as co-belligerents. But Krim insisted, explaining that "Chinese and Russian intervention has a much greater political effect because it constitutes a more immediate danger for the West."[121]

The British and the Americans quickly rose to the bait. On 26 October, London pressed de Gaulle to declare his peaceful intentions or risk defeat in the U.N. General Assembly. A week later, the U.S. State Department stepped up the pressure, warning that it would not otherwise defend the French position. The very next day, de Gaulle declared that he was prepared to negotiate with the GPRA over a referendum in Algeria that he admitted would inevitably result in an independent republic.[122]

Nevertheless, the GPRA continued to press for a resolution that called for a U.N.-supervised referendum. There was no chance that the French would allow it, but they continued to fear that diplomatic victories strengthened the Algerian bargaining position.[123] Ironically, by this point the Algerians themselves would have opposed a U.N. intervention, mindful of the chaos then occurring in the Congo. But, as they explained to Yugoslavia's Marshal Tito, "we also knew, on the one hand, that General de Gaulle was frightened by the idea of an internationalization of the Algerian problem and that, on the other hand, our proposition would deepen the divisions that reign among France's allies."[124]

Yet while neither Paris nor the GPRA considered the United Nations capable of halting hostilities, the U.N. General Assembly debate had taken on a life of its own in Algeria. In August 1960, a meeting of top French officials in Algiers found that most Muslims increasingly thought that only the United Nations could end the conflict. The French Delegate General's monthly report for September agreed. Similarly, in October de Gaulle's adviser on Algeria found that Muslims were showing increasing interest in the provisional government's activities abroad and the upcoming U.N. General Assembly debate. Indeed, Bentobbal urged them "not to place too much hope in the decisions of the U.N. so as not to be disappointed." But they appeared not to listen, even placing hopes in the outcome of the American presidential election because of its potential impact in Algeria. Thus, a correspondent who visited an ALN camp high in the Atlas mountains at the time was astonished to find grizzled mujahedin asking what John F. Kennedy's chances were against Richard M. Nixon, doubtless recalling a 1957 speech in which Kennedy had called for Algerian independence. On the night of the election, ALN fighters listened to transistor radios as the returns came in, cheering whenever Kennedy pulled ahead, cursing when Nixon threatened to overtake him.[125]

In December 1960, as the debate was about to begin in New York, de Gaulle decided to go to Algeria. In five days he faced four separate assassination plots and innumerable mobs of angry *pieds noirs*. But while this was fully expected, no one was prepared for the Muslims of Algiers and Oran to mount a massive counter-protest. Marching in the thousands from the Casbah, they waved homemade Algerian flags and chanted "long live the GPRA!"—much to the surprise of the provisional government itself. It was all the more shocking for rioting *Algérie française* activists, forcing them to wheel around and close ranks with the police.[126]

Meanwhile, the demonstrations in Algiers led France's supporters in New York to waver. Once moderate delegations, such as India's, violently attacked the repression. Even normally friendly representatives from Francophone African states such as Mali and Togo defected.[127] The paragraph calling for an internationally supervised referendum failed by a single vote. But a majority of sixty-three to eight demanded guarantees for self-determination for the whole of Algeria—de Gaulle had floated rumors of a possible partition—and insisted on a U.N. role. As a French army report noted, "Nearly all the nations of the world have thus proved their will to end the Algerian conflict, if need be by foreign intervention."[128]

Once again, Algerians had paid a heavy price for a diplomatic victory. Yet perhaps the most significant casualties were three political myths, as the *New Yorker* magazine's Paris correspondent, Janet Flanner, wrote at the time: the myth that Algeria was French, that only a handful of rebels wanted independence, and that de Gaulle alone could impose peace.[129] It also marked the moment at which another "myth" became reality: the once mythical notion that a national liberation movement could triumph without having liberated any of the national territory. It was the culmination of the strategy Aït Ahmed had first articulated more than a decade before, a strategy that all along aimed at establishing a mutually reinforcing relationship between the Algerians'

238   *Matthew Connelly*

diplomatic campaigns abroad and manifestations of popular support at home. Although more than a year of negotiations remained—during which the Algerians would continually threaten to invite direct intervention by their Soviet and Chinese supporters—independence was at hand.[130]

This article can only begin to suggest the kinds of research made possible by the opening of the GPRA archives, which will doubtless enrich our understanding of the social, cultural, and military aspects of the Algerian war. But one can offer some tentative conclusions about its international history, especially because we can compare the Algerian archives with those of France and its two main allies, the United States and the United Kingdom. For instance, the inverse relationship between France's military strength and the progressive weakening of its hold on Algeria has been called the "supreme paradox" of this long struggle.[131] This paradox now appears to be a matter of perspective. Even before the war began, the FLN leaders did not consider winning a conventional victory to be possible. At the peak of their military strength, they continued to conduct operations for the purpose of achieving diplomatic and propaganda victories. And even when they invited outside intervention, it was intended to compel France's allies to force de Gaulle to negotiate.

From the point of view of French governments, on the other hand, the problems this strategy presented were indeed paradoxical and ultimately insuperable. Concentrating on the war within Algeria—the initial response of both the Fourth and Fifth Republics—allowed the nationalists to develop diplomatic, military, and economic resources abroad with which to harry the French on every front. But engaging them in the external arena made the war even more of an international struggle, one in which France had to deliver and receive blows and risk becoming vulnerable to its adversaries and dependent on its allies. French attempts to isolate the Algerians led to crises in which the French themselves were isolated, and their own efforts to win over international opinion led them to move steadily toward conceding independence. Where once holding on to Algeria appeared like "the last chance for French power," the GPRA's international campaigns finally convinced French leaders that they had no chance of restoring their stature without relinquishing Algeria.[132] We cannot know when and how the Algerians might have won without pursuing this strategy. But it is altogether clear that their adversaries always considered their support abroad to be their main strength and ultimate refuge.

Just as Algeria's independence is impossible to explain without placing it in an international context, the war had an equal if not opposite impact on the outside world—what Elie Kedourie called "prodigious peripeties."[133] It accelerated decolonization in Morocco, Tunisia, and Sub-Saharan Africa; it contributed to France's decision to back Israel and confront Nasser; it triggered the fall of the Fourth Republic and the return of de Gaulle; and it provoked de Gaulle into beginning the withdrawal of French forces from NATO commands. And although the Algerians never sent foreign volunteers into combat, their example attracted and influenced key figures in the next generation of national liberation movements. Thus, when the ALN marched in a victory parade through its main base in Morocco, Nelson Mandela was there to see it, having come to learn revolutionary strategy and tactics. The mujahedin appeared to Mandela like an apparition of the future ANC forces. And when the FLN finally entered Algiers in triumph, Yasir Arafat was in the crowd cheering. He would consciously model Fatah after the FLN. Soon Algiers became known as the "Mecca of the revolutionaries."[134]

In fact, other revolutionary movements would have to develop their own strategies, though the Algerians had shown that it was not enough simply to play off the super-powers. Instead, they exploited every international rivalry that offered potential lever-age—revisionist against conservative Arab states, the Arab League against Asian neutrals, China against the USSR, the communist powers against the Western allies, and, above all, the United States against France itself. To that end, the Algerians projected a more or less "moderate" or "pro-Western" image according to the tactical needs of the moment, encouraging outsiders to view personal rivalries among Algerian leaders through their own geo-political and ideological preconceptions. Consequently, a less-ening of international tensions was potentially disastrous, as in the case of France and Egypt and, still more, the United States and the USSR. Yet the Algerians did not need to win support from both sides in all these different struggles. As Aït Ahmed had predicted, it was no less effective to use aid from the communist powers to undermine France's position among its allies.

No amount of diplomatic virtuosity would have sufficed if the GPRA's activities abroad had not visibly resonated with the people it represented. The genius of the provisional government's grand strategy was to ensure that political, diplomatic, and military campaigns were mutually reinforcing, so that Algiers and New York, Beijing, and Paris, became theaters in the same struggle. By thinking and acting globally to attain their goals at home and abroad, the Algerians revealed how even a stateless and embattled people could be authors of their own history, a history in which the Cold War was a small but essential part.

NOTES

Author's note: I am grateful to all those who commented on earlier versions of this article, especially Daniel Byrne, Charles Cogan, Juan Cole, Jeffrey Herbst, Martin Thomas, and the anonymous reviewers of *IJMES*. I am also indebted to Hocine Aït Ahmed, Mabrouk Belhocine, and Rédha Malek for granting interviews, and to Daho Djerbal, Samer Emalhayene, William Quandt, and Fadila Takour for advice and assistance in organizing a research trip to Algiers. This work was made possible through the financial support of the Center for Middle Eastern and North African Studies and the Office of the Vice President for Research at the University of Michigan.

[1]"Note," 5 October 1960, Ministère des Affaires Etrangères (hereafter, MAE), Paris, Europe 1944–60, URSS, dossier 271; La Grandville to Couve de Murville, 7 October 1960, MAE, Mission de liaison algérien (hereafter, MLA), Action Extérieure, URSS, dossier 88; Abbas to Zhou Enlai, 24 October 1960, Moham-med Harbi, ed., *Les Archives de la révolution algérienne* (Paris: Editions Jeune Afrique, 1981), 527–28; 466th meeting of the National Security Council, 7 November 1960, *Foreign Relations of the United States* (hereafter, *FRUS*, with year and volume) 1958–60, vol. 13 (Washington, D.C.: Government Printing Office, 1992), 706.

[2]William Appleman Williams, *The Tragedy of American Diplomacy: United States Foreign Policy 1945–1980* (New York: W. W. Norton, 1959, 1988); Robert J. McMahon, "Eisenhower and Third World Nationalism: A Critique of the Revisionists," *Political Science Quarterly* 101 (1986): 453–73; Gabriel Kolko, *Confronting the Third World* (New York: Pantheon, 1988). More recently, scholars have credited the Eisenhower administration with an appreciation for the force of anti-colonial nationalism, particularly in the Middle East and North Africa, while emphasizing the dilemmas it presented for U.S. policy. See H. W. Brands, *The Specter of Neutralism: The United States and the Emergence of the Third World, 1947–1960* (New York: Columbia University Press, 1989); Peter Hahn, The *United States, Great Britain, and*

240   *Matthew Connelly*

Egypt, 1945–1956: Strategy and Diplomacy in the Early Cold War (Chapel Hill: University of North Carolina Press, 1991); Egya N. Sangmuah, "Eisenhower and Containment in North Africa, 1956–1960," *Middle East Journal* 44 (1990): 76–91; Irwin M. Wall, "The United States, Algeria, and the Fall of the Fourth French Republic," *Diplomatic History* 18 (1994): 489–511.

³See, for instance, Vladislav Zubok and Constantine Pleshakov, *Inside the Kremlin's Cold War: From Stalin to Khrushchev* (Cambridge, Mass.: Harvard University Press, 1996), 54–62; Chen Jian, "The Sino-Soviet Alliance and China's Entry into the Korean War," Cold War International History Project (hereafter, CWIHP) Working Paper No. 1 (1993), 8–9; Kathryn Weathersby, "Korea 1949–50: To Attack, or Not to Attack? Stalin, Kim Il Sung, and the Prelude to War," CWIHP *Bulletin*, no. 5 (1995), 3.

⁴Paul Gordon Lauren, *Power and Prejudice: The Politics and Diplomacy of Racial Discrimination*, 2nd ed. (Boulder, Colo.: Westview Press, 1996), 220–21; Thomas Borstelmann, *Apartheid's Reluctant Uncle: The United States and Southern Africa During the Early Cold War* (New York: Oxford University Press, 1993), 195.

⁵Zachary Karabell, *Architects of Intervention: The United States, the Third World, and the Cold War, 1946–1962* (Baton Rouge: Louisiana State University Press, 1999), 65–67; Fawaz Gerges, *The Superpowers and the Middle East: Regional and International Politics, 1955–1967* (Boulder, Colo.: Westview Press, 1994), 38–39, 245–46.

⁶Waverly Root, "Offer of Massive Chinese Aid Hangs over Algerian Talks," *Washington Post*, 20 July 1960, A8, and see later for an analysis of the episode. The GPRA archives are quite accessible—especially when compared with some of those in France—*pace* Charles-Robert Ageron, "A Propos des Archives militaires de la Guerre d'Algérie," *Vingtième Siècle* 63 (1999): 128–29.

⁷Charles-Robert Ageron, *Modern Algeria: A History from 1830 to the Present*, trans. Michael Brett (London: Hurst, 1991), 98–102; John Ruedy, *Modern Algeria: The Origins and Development of a Nation* (Bloomington: Indiana University Press, 1992), 147–50. For evidence of the cover-up, see Bergé to Bringard, 17 June 1945, Archives d'Outre-Mer (hereafter, AOM), Aix-en-Provence, Ministère des Affaires Algériennes (MAA), dossier 586, and Barrat, "Additif à mon Rapport sur les événements de Guelma," 27 June 1945, ibid.

⁸Moch to Schuman, 31 January 1948, AOM, MAA, dossier 18; Charles-André Julien, *L'Afrique du Nord en Marche. Nationalismes Musulmans et Souveraineté Française* (Paris: Julliard, 1952), 284–88.

⁹"Rapport d'Aït Ahmed," December 1948, in Harbi, *Les Archives*, 15–49. Harbi's collection has long been virtually the only source of internal documents from the nationalist movement. It still serves as a valuable supplement to the state archives.

¹⁰Ibid., 43–44.

¹¹Ibid., 44; Hocine Aït Ahmed, *Mémoires d'un combattant: L'esprit de l'indépendance, 1942–1952* (Paris: Sylvie Messinger, 1983), 156–58. The Moroccans and Tunisians also emphasized the international aspect of their independence struggle, and they, too, sought to exert pressure on France's allies by pointing to the danger of communist expansion in North Africa. See Allal al-Fassi, *The Independence Movements in Arab North Africa, 1948* (New York: Octagon Books, 1970), 381–94, and Habib Bourguiba's July 1946 letter to Ferhat Abbas, reprinted in Samya El Méchat, *Tunisie, Les Chemins vers l'Indépendance, 1945–1956* (Paris: L'Harmattan, 1992), 259–63.

¹²The proclamation is reprinted in Harbi, *Les Archives*, 101–103.

¹³M'Hammed Yazid, "Rapport," July 1957, in Harbi, *Les Archives*, 172–73.

¹⁴Ibid. See also Hocine Aït Ahmed, "Bandoeng Trente Ans Après," *Jeune Afrique*, no. 1272 (1985), 18.

¹⁵Khider to Djouad Zakari, 14 December 1954, Centre National des Archives Algériennes (hereafter, CNAA), Algiers, Le Fond du GPRA, MAE, dossier 1; Hoppenot to Mendès France, 5 January 1955, MAE, Série ONU, dossier 546; Mendès France to Mitterrand, Service de l'Algérie, 13 January 1955, no. 189, ibid.

¹⁶Mendès France to Mitterrand, 13 January 1955, no. 327, MAE, Série ONU, dossier 546; Gillet to Mendès France, 11 December 1954, ibid.

¹⁷Mohamad Fathi al-Dib, *Abdel Nasser et la Révolution Algérienne* (Paris: L'Harmattan, 1985), 23.

¹⁸225th Meeting of the NSC, 24 November 1954, *FRUS 1952–54*, vol. 2, 792.

¹⁹Yazid, "Rapport," 173; El Méchat, *Tunisie, Les Chemins vers l'Indépendance*, 231–33; Aït Ahmed, "Bandoeng," 18–19.

²⁰Philippe Tripier, *Autopsie de la guerre d'Algérie* (Paris: Editions France-Empire, 1972), 211; John Talbott, *The War Without a Name: France in Algeria, 1954–1962* (New York: Knopf, 1980), 53.

[21]Tripier, *Autopsie,* 210–12; Langlais to Algiers, 4 September 1958, MAE, Série ONU, dossier 557.

[22]Clark to Dulles, 19 September 1955, U.S. National Archives (hereafter, USNA), College Park, Md., RG59, Central Decimal Files, 751S.00. For other examples, see Dillon to Dulles, 25 July and 16 November 1956, ibid.

[23]Lodge to Dulles, 1 November 1955, *FRUS* 1955–57, vol. 18, 230. U.S. military aid was rapidly winding down in the aftermath of the Indochina war, though Paris sought approval for the transfer of previously supplied equipment.

[24]Clark to Dulles, 23 September 1955, USNA, RG59, Central Decimal Files, 751S.00; Slimane Chikh, *L'Algérie en Armes, ou, Le Temps des Certitudes* (Algiers: Office des Publications Universitaires, 1981), 421.

[25]Aït Ahmed to Margaret Pope, 15 October 1955, Aït Ahmed personal papers; Guiringaud to Pinay, 4 October 1955, MAE, Série ONU, dossier 546; Aït Ahmed, interview, Lausanne, August 1998.

[26]Dixon to Macmillan, 1 October 1955, Public Record Office (hereafter, PRO), Kew, U.K., PREM 11/902.

[27]267th Meeting of the NSC, 21 November 1955, Dwight D. Eisenhower Library (hereafter, DDEL), Abilene, Kans., Ann Whitman File (hereafter, AWF), NSC Series.

[28]Memorandum of Conversation (Memcon) Root, Bovey, Looram, and Aït Ahmed, 5 December 1955, USNA, RG59, Central Decimal Files, 751S.00; Memcon Aït Ahmed, Bovey, 16 May 1956, ibid.

[29]Memcon Nes, Allen, Ben Bella, Ali Hawazi, 6 December 1955, USNA, RG59, Central Decimal Files, 751S.00; Chase to Dulles, 25 February 1956, USNA, RG59, Central Decimal Files, 751S.00.

[30]See, for instance, Dulles to Dillon, 27 May 1955, *FRUS* 1955–57, vol. 18, 219–20.

[31]Dillon to Dulles, 4 October 1955, *FRUS* 1955–57, vol. 18, 222–24. On the double game, see Pierre Mélandri, "La France et le 'Jeu Double' des États Unis," in *La Guerre d'Algérie et les Français,* ed. Jean-Pierre Rioux (Paris: Fayard, 1990), 429–50.

[32]Dillon to State, 21 February 1956, USNA, RG59, Central Decimal Files, 751S.00. On Morocco's and Tunisia's use of U.S. aid to win greater autonomy from France, see I. William Zartman, *Morocco: Problems of a New Power* (New York: Atherton Press, 1964), 27, and Carol Mae Barker, "The Politics of Decolonization in Tunisia: The Foreign Policy of a New State," (PhD. diss., Columbia University, 1971), 240–41, 349.

[33]Dillon to Dulles, 2 March 1956, *FRUS* 1955–57, vol. 18, 115–16.

[34]Dillon to Dulles, 4 February 1956, USNA, RG59, Central Decimal Files, 751S.00.

[35]Thomas Brady, "Tunisian Rebukes U.S. on Aid Policy," *New York Times,* 11 May 1957, 1, 6.

[36]"Text of Address by Ambassador Dillon on North Africa," *New York Times,* 21 March 1956, 4.

[37]Aït Ahmed to Khider, 7 April 1956, CNAA, GPRA, dossier 1.

[38]Pineau to Mollet, 14 March 1956, MAE, Secrétariat Général, dossier 56; Keith Kyle, *Suez* (London: Weidenfeld and Nicolson, 1991), 116; *L'Année Politique, 1956* (Paris: Presses Universitaires de France, 1957), 279–80.

[39]Al-Dib, *Abdel Nasser,* 120–21; Harbi, *Le FLN: Mirage et Réalité* (Paris: Editions Jeune Afrique, 1980), 174.

[40]Khider to Aït Ahmed and Yazid, 9 May 1956, CNAA, GPRA, dossier 2.

[41]Al-Dib, *Abdel Nasser,* 123–32. It is not clear whether the Egyptians actually offered this deal. But Mollet did publicly reaffirm his opposition to the Baghdad Pact, betraying a commitment to Anthony Eden: Kyle, *Suez,* 116; see also Chauvel to Massigli, 15 March 1956, MAE, René Massigli Papers, vol. 95.

[42]Charles G. Cogan, "The Suez Crisis: Part I, The View from Paris," paper presented at a conference on the Suez Crisis and Its Teachings, American Academy of Arts and Sciences, Cambridge, Mass., 15–16 February 1997, 18.

[43]Matti Golan, *Shimon Peres,* trans. Ina Friedman (London: Wiedenfeld and Nicolson, 1982), 36.

[44]Zachary Karabell, "The Suez Crisis: Part I, The View from Israel," paper presented at a conference on the Suez Crisis and Its Teachings, 14–15; Cogan, "The View from Paris," 18–19. For French intelligence reports that would suggest new—and well-informed—sources, see the unsigned "Note" by Sous-Direction de Tunisie, 5 March 1956, MAE, Cabinet du Ministre, dossier 157, Tunisie; "Note sur les ingérences egyptiennes en Afrique du Nord," 20 October 1956, MAE, Cabinet du Ministre, dossier 155, Algérie, Loi Cadre.

[45]Cogan, "The View from Paris," 17–18; Kyle, *Suez,* 117–18.

[46]Al-Dib, *Abdel Nasser,* 145–49.

242 Matthew Connelly

[47]Memcon Mollet, Eden, 11 March 1956, *Documents Diplomatiques Français*, 1956, vol. 1, no. 161 (Paris: Imprimerie Nationale, 1988) (hereafter, *DDF*, with year and volume); Cogan, "The View from Paris," 3. See Matthew Connelly, "Taking off the Cold War Lens: Visions of North-South Conflict During the Algerian War for Independence," *American Historical Review* 105 (2000): 739–69, for how images and ideas about Africa and Islam helped to shape French policy.

[48]Bernard Droz and Evelyne Lever, *Histoire de la guerre d'Algérie (1954–1962)* (Paris: Editions du Seuil, 1982), 103.

[49]The platform was released in November 1956 and is reprinted in Tripier, *Autopsie*, 571–601.

[50]Ibid., 578–79, 598–600.

[51]Ibid., 583.

[52]Guy Pervillé, "L'insertion internationale du F.L.N. algérien," *Relations Internationales* 31 (1982): 374, 377; Richard J. Barnet, *Intervention and Revolution: The United States in the Third World*, rev. ed. (New York: Mentor, New American Library, 1972), 316–17.

[53]Tripier, *Autopsie*, 600; Khider to Aït Ahmed; 1 August 1956, CNAA, GPRA, dossier 1; Mabrouk Belhocine, interview, Algiers, December 1999.

[54]Dillon to Dulles, 31 October 1956, USNA, RG59, Central Decimal Files, 651.71.

[55]Memcon Bovey, Abbas et al., 29 November 1956, *FRUS* 1955–57, vol. 18, 255–58; Wall, "The United States, Algeria," 493–94.

[56]Tripier, *Autopsie*, 78–79.

[57]"Directive number 9" (fall 1956), as quoted in Jacques Duchemin, *Histoire du FLN* (Paris: La Table Ronde, 1962), 263–64.

[58]Georges-Picot to Pineau, 4 January 1957, *DDF* 1957, vol. 1, no. 17.

[59]Yves Courrière, *Le Temps des Léopards, La Guerre d'Algérie* (Paris: Fayard, 1970), 2:448–50, 473. See also Tripier, *Autopsie*, 130.

[60]Courrière, *Le Temps des Léopards*, 2:516–17; Henri Alleg, *La guerre d'Algérie* (Paris: Temps actuels, 1981), 2:466–69; Gilles Manceron and Hassan Remaoun, *D'une rive à l'autre: La Guerre d'Algérie de la mémoire à l'histoire* (Paris: Syros, 1993), 177–78.

[61]"Minute" from the Secrétariat des conférences to Georges-Picot, 23 January 1957, MAE, Série ONU, dossier 549.

[62]Douglas Porch, *The French Secret Services: From the Dreyfus Affair to the Gulf War* (New York: Farrar, Straus and Giroux, 1995), 366.

[63]Bureau de New York, "Rapport d'Activité," 18 February 1957, CNAA, GPRA, dossier 4.5; Vaurs to Langlais, 15 March 1958, MAE, MLA, propagande, dossier 1; "Le Cabinet du Ministre Résident et les titres d'ouvrages et de brochures qu'il a diffusé depuis 15 mois" (n.d., but c. early 1957), Archives Nationales, Paris, Bidault Papers, 457AP, box 110.

[64]"Note: La Question Algérienne à la XIeme Session de l'Assemblée Générale," 9 March 1957, MAE, Série ONU, dossier 551.

[65]Alistair Horne, *A Savage War of Peace: Algeria, 1954–1962*, rev. ed. (New York: Penguin, 1987), 224.

[66]De Guiringaud to Pineau, 3 April 1957, *DDF* vol. 1, no. 290; Pineau circular, 13 April 1957, ibid., no. 312.

[67]Baraduc to Gorlin, 22 March 1958, AOM, 12/CAB/234.

[68]Alphand to Pineau, 14 June 1957, MAE, MLA, vol. 23 bis. (provisoire), Action extérieure, Etats-Unis, December 1956–December 1957, Cote EU.

[69]Baraduc to Gorlin, 22 March 1958.

[70]Vaurs to Pineau, 6 October 1958, MAE, Série ONU, dossier 559.

[71]Alphand to Baraduc, 14 June 1957, MAE, Direction Amérique 1952–63, Etats-Unis–Afrique du Nord, dossier 32.

[72]"Note sur le rôle réservé par le F.L.N. à la Presse, au profit de sa propaganda," 11 May 1957, MAE, Série ONU, dossier 544; "Exploitation de la Presse par la Propagande du FLN," n.d., MAE, MLA, propagande, dossier 2; Lebel to Langlais, 16 June 1959, MAE, MLA, vol. 24 (provisoire), Action extérieure, Etats-Unis, January 1958–June 1959, Cote ML 4.

[73]Jones to Dulles, 4 September 1957, *FRUS* 1955–57, vol. 18, 679–80.

[74]Diary entry, 14 November 1957, *FRUS* 1955–57, vol. 18, 758–61. Both the French and the Americans were influenced by their experience with Egypt, which first turned to the Soviets after Washington refused

to deliver new weaponry. For a more extended analysis, see Matthew Connelly, "The Algerian War for Independence: An International History" (Ph.D. diss., Yale University, 1997), 289–311.

[75] Accounts of the Sakiet crisis can be found in Wall, "The United States, Algeria," 503–11, and Matthew Connelly, "The French–American Conflict over North Africa and the Fall of the Fourth Republic," *Revue française d'histoire d'outre-mer* 84 (1997): 20–27.

[76] Tripier, *Autopsie,* 163–66; *L'Année Politique, 1958* (Paris: Presses Universitaires de France, 1959), 249–50.

[77] Mélandri, "La France et le 'Jeu Double'," 429–33; Müller, "Le réalisme de la République fédérale," 418–21; Rainero, "L'Italie entre amitié française et solidarité algérienne," 394–95, all in Rioux, *La Guerre.* Regarding Britain, see Martin Thomas, *The French North African Crisis: Colonial Breakdown and Anglo-French Relations, 1945–62* (New York: St. Martin's Press, 2000).

[78] Dejean to Pineau, 17 March 1958, MAE, Europe 1944–60, URSS, dossier 271.

[79] Alphand to MAE, 5 March 1958, Direction Amérique 1952–63, Etats-Unis–Algérie, dossier 33 (provisoire). On U.S. economic leverage, see Connelly, "French–American Conflict," 9–27.

[80] Beeley to Lloyd, 12 March 1958, PRO, PREM 11/2561.

[81] Houghton to State, 1 May 1958, USNA, RG59, Central Decimal Files, 751.00.

[82] For a discussion of de Gaulle's Algeria policy, see Connelly, "Algerian War," chap. 7.

[83] Ouamrane to the Comité de Coordination et d'Exécution (or CCE, the FLN's highest decision-making body), 8 July 1958, in Harbi, *Les Archives,* 189–93. Regarding Tunisia and Morocco, see the *procès-verbaux* of the June 1958 Tunis conference, reprinted in Harbi, *Les Archives,* 414–26.

[84] The study is reprinted in Hocine Aït Ahmed, *La Guerre et l'Après-guerre* (Paris: Editions de Minuit, 1964), 9–57. In his Introduction, Aït Ahmed doubts that his study ever reached the CCE, but Ouamrane attached it to his report, and its influence is evident in the "Rapport de la Commission gouvernementale sur la Formation d'un Gouvernement provisoire de l'Algérie libre," 6 September 1958, reprinted in Harbi, *Les Archives,* 210–14. Aït Ahmed first suggested forming a provisional government in August 1956: see Khider to Aït Ahmed, 17 August 1956, CNAA, GPRA, dossier 1.

[85] Ouamrane to CCE, 8 July 1958, 191–92; Aït Ahmed, *La Guerre,* 25.

[86] Aït Ahmed, *La Guerre,* 25–29, 33–36, 55.

[87] Parodi to MAE, 18 September 1958, MAE, MLA, Action Extérieure, Maroc, dossier 48.

[88] "Liste des Etats Ayant Reconnu le G.P.R.A.," 22 November 1961, MAE, Secrétariat d'Etat aux Affaires algériennes (hereafter, SEAA), dossier 6.

[89] "Les Animateurs de la Rebellion Algérienne," 16 October 1958, MAE, Série ONU, dossier 560.

[90] See SDECE note number 23754/A in MAE, SEAA, dossier 6, and the "Condense des Renseignements" for Debré, Division Renseignement, Etat-Major général de la défense nationale, 10 November 1959, MAE, MLA, Action Extérieure, R.F.A., dossier 4.

[91] Pervillé, "L'insertion internationale," 375–77. See also Chikh, *L'Algérie en Armes,* 418–19.

[92] The emphasis is in the original: Lakhdar Bentobbal, "Plan d'organisation pour l'Organisation politique," 12 November 1960, CNAA, GPRA, dossier 8.2.

[93] "Les Dépenses du FLN a l'Extérieur de l'Algérie," Delegation Générale du Gouvernement en Algérie, Bureau d'Etudes, 2 May 1960, AOM, 14/CAB/193; "Les Dépenses du FLN a l'Intérieur de l'Algérie," 16 April 1960, AOM, 14/CAB/48.

[94] Jebb, "Record of conversation with General De Gaulle," 20 March 1958, PRO, PREM 11/2339.

[95] "Mr. Dillon's Interview with General de Gaulle on January 10th," attached to Jebb to Lloyd, 18 January 1957, PRO, PREM 11/2338.

[96] De Gaulle to Eisenhower, 17 September 1958, *FRUS* 1958–60, vol. 7, 81–83. Regarding the Algerian motive behind de Gaulle's tripartite proposal, see Connelly, "Algerian War," 380–86, and Irwin M. Wall, "Les Relations Franco-Américaines et la Guerre d'Algérie 1956–1960," *Revue d'Histoire diplomatique* 110 (1996): 79–80.

[97] Mostefai, "Quelques idées sur les tâches actuelles," 22 December 1958, CNAA, GPRA, dossier 5.3; Abbas, "Rapport de Politique Générale," 20 June 1959, idem; "L'Algérie et l'Actualité internationale," c. January 1959, ibid., dossier 8.2.

[98] "Question Algérienne," n.d. (c. January 1959), MAE, Série ONU, dossier 557; Georges-Picot to Couve, 16 December 1958, ibid.

[99] Caccia to Lloyd, 25 October 1958, PRO, PREM 11/3002. For other reasons that the United States would not support de Gaulle on Algeria, see Mélandri, "La France et le 'Jeu Double'," 440–42.

244   *Matthew Connelly*

[100]Memcon Herter, Alphand, 3 March 1959, USNA, RG59, Records of the Policy Planning Staff 1957–61, lot 67D548, box 136, France; Lyon to Herter, 6 March 1959, *FRUS 1958–60*, vol. 7, 185–86.

[101]Memcon Debré, Couve et al., 14 March 1959, MAE, Cabinet du Ministre, Cabinet de Couve de Murville, dossier 212bis, Algérie confidentiel. See also "Instruction: Lutte contre les activités du F.L.N. à l'étranger," 2 April 1959, AOM, 14/CAB/177.

[102]Mohamed Bedjaoui, *La Révolution algérienne et le droit* (Brussels: International Association of Democratic Lawyers, 1961), 124–27.

[103]"Note," 8 August 1959, MAE, Secrétariat Général, dossier 60.

[104]Memcon Verdier, Ritter von Lex et al., 18 November 1958, MAE, MLA, Action Extérieure, R.F.A., dossier 2; Seydoux to Couve, 16 April and 22 April 1959, ibid., dossier 3; Porch, *French Secret Services*, 371–72; Müller, "Le réalisme de la République fédérale," 424–28.

[105]Memcon de Gaulle, Castiella, 5 September 1959, MAE, Secrétariat Général, dossier 60.

[106]Alain Peyrefitte, *C'était de Gaulle* (Paris: Fayard, 1994), 59.

[107]Charles de Gaulle, *Discours et Messages: Avec le Renouveau, Mai 1958–Juillet 1962* (Paris: Plon, 1970), 117–23; Jean Lacouture, *De Gaulle: 3. Le Souverain, 1959–1970* (Paris: Editions du Seuil, 1986), 69–71.

[108]417th Meeting of the NSC, 18 August 1959, DDEL, AWF, NSC Series.

[109]"Note: la question à la XIVème session . . . ," 23 July 1959, MAE, Série ONU, dossier 561. See also "Schéma d'un plan d'action," 5 June 1959, ibid.

[110]Tripier, *Autopsie*, 331–38; Harbi, *Le FLN: Mirage*, 244–50; Commandement en Chef des Forces en Algérie, "Evolution de la situation militaire en Algérie," July 1959, Service Historique de l'Armée de Terre (hereafter, SHAT), Paris, 1H, 1751, dossier 2.

[111]Abbas, "Rapport de Politique," 20 June 1959 CNAA, GPRA, dossier 5.8; Yazid to Krim, Bentobal, and Boussouf, "La Politique Nord-Africaine," 6 September 1959, CNAA, GPRA, dossier 17.2.

[112]Essig to Delouvrier, 13 January 1960, AOM, 14/CAB/142.

[113]Debaghine to GPRA, 27 October 1959, CNAA, GPRA, dossier 5.3; Debaghine to GPRA, 17 November 1959, in Harbi, *Les Archives*, 272–74.

[114]Krim, "Notre Politique extérieure et la Guerre froide," 13 March 1960, CNAA, GPRA, dossier 5.3.

[115]Krim, "Note sur Notre Politique Actuelle," "Notre Politique à Moyen Orient," "Note sur Notre Politique dans le bloc Afro-Asiatique," all dated 13 March 1960, CNAA, GPRA, dossier 5.10.

[116]Memcon Krim, Boussouf, Francis, and Ho Long, 1 May 1960, CNAA, GPRA, dossier 5.12.

[117]Ibid. Adda Benguettat and Cherif Guellal, "Rapport," c. March 1958, CNAA, GPRA, dossier 3.3.

[118]Dejean to Couve, 28 May 1960, MAE, MLA, Action Extérieure, URSS, dossier 87.

[119]Dillon to Houghton, 11 October 1960, USNA, RG59, Central Decimal Files, 651.51s.

[120]Abbas to Zhou Enlai, 24 October 1960, in Harbi, *Les Archives*, 527–28; Chauvel to Couve, 27 October 1960, *DDF 1960*, vol. 2, no. 186; Macmillan to Lloyd, 28 October 1960, PRO, FO 371, 147351; Memcon Macmillan, Home, Hassan, 28 October 1960, PRO, PREM 11/3200; Raoul Duval to Couve, 17 November 1960, MAE, Asie-Oceanie 1956–67, Chine, dossier 523.

[121]"Entrevue avec Moulay El Hassan," 21 October 1960, CNAA, GPRA, dossier 8.4; "Rapport du Ministre des Affaires Extérieures sur son Séjour au Maroc," c. October 1960, ibid.

[122]"Note pour le Ministre," 26 October 1960, MAE, Cabinet du Ministre, Cabinet de Couve de Murville, dossier 212bis, Algérie 1959–62; Bérard to Couve, 1 November 1960, ibid.; Alphand to Couve, 3 November 1960, ibid.; De Gaulle, *Discours*, 257–62. It is, of course, difficult to prove that international pressure accounts for this particular decision, and Couve de Murville was at pains to correct the impression that the timing had created—even while admitting to his American counterpart that the policy shift was "in line with your concern": Couve to Herter, 7 November 1960, MAE, Cabinet du Ministre, Cabinet de Couve de Murville, dossier 212bis, Algérie 1959–62. For a more detailed discussion of the importance of international, and especially American, pressure on de Gaulle's policy, see Connelly, "Algerian War," chap. 7 and 8.

[123]Lacouture, *Le Souverain,* 136; Carbonnel to Bérard, 6 October 1960, MAE, Cabinet du Ministre, Cabinet de Couve de Murville, dossier 212bis, Algérie 1959–62.

[124]Memcon Tito, Abbas et al., 12 April 1961, in Harbi, *Les Archives,* 509; Bentobbal, "Directives Générales."

[125]Comité Central de l'Information, "Procès-Verbal," 19 August 1960, AOM, 14/CAB/177; Delegation Générale du Gouvernement en Algérie, Affaires Politiques, "Rapport Mensuel sur l'évolution de la situation générale," 13 September 1960, AOM, 15/CAB/74; Bernard Tricot, *Les Sentiers de la Paix: Algérie 1958/*

Rethinking the Cold War and Decolonization 245

1962 (Paris: Plon, 1972), 194; Bentobbal, "Directives Générales"; Richard Mahoney, *JFK: Ordeal in Africa* (New York: Oxford University Press, 1983), 22.

[126]Lacouture, *Le Souverain,* 137–41.

[127]"Note: a/s l'Inde et la question algérienne," 10 March 1961, MAE, Asie 1944..., Inde 1956–67, dossier 248; Bérard to Couve, 21 December 1960, AOM, 15/CAB/149.

[128]Lieutenant-Colonel Thozet, "La Politique du GPRA de la 15o session de l'Assemblée Générale des Nations Unies a l'ouverture des pourparlers d'Evian," 14 June 1961, SHAT, 1H, 1111/3.

[129]Janet Flanner, *Paris Journal,* ed. William Shawn, vol. 2: 1956–65 (New York: Harcourt Brace Jovanovich, 1988), 162.

[130]See, for instance, Joxe to de Gaulle, 3 June 1961, MAE, Cabinet du Ministre, Cabinet de Couve de Murville, dossier 212bis.

[131]Jean Lacouture, *Algérie, La Guerre est finie* (Brussels: Editions Complexe, 1985), 11.

[132]Charles-Robert Ageron, "'L'Algérie dernière chance de la puissance française,' Etude d'un mythe politique (1954–1962)," *Relations internationales* 57 (1989): 113–39.

[133]*Islam in the Modern World and Other Studies* (London: Holt, Rinehart and Winston, 1980), 213–14.

[134]Nelson Mandela, *Long Walk to Freedom* (New York: Little Brown, 1995), 259–60, and testimony at the Rivonia Trial, 1963–64, track 11.1 *Apartheid and the History of the Struggle for Freedom in South Africa,* CD-ROM (Bellville, South Africa: Mayibuye Center, University of the Western Cape, 1993). On Arafat, see Alan Hart, *Arafat: A Political Biography* (London: Sidgwick & Jackson, 1994), 102–104, 112–13, 129–30; Barry Rubin, *Revolution Until Victory? The Politics and History of the PLO* (Cambridge: Harvard University Press, 1994), 7, 10. On Algiers as a Mecca, see John P. Entelis, *Algeria: The Revolution Institutionalized* (Boulder, Colo.: Westview Press, 1986), 189.

Part VI
Forgotten Constituencies?
Women and Returnees

[20]

The Mau Mau Rebellion, Kikuyu Women, and Social Change

Cora Ann Presley

Résumé

Remarquablement absents dans la littérature historique sur la révolte Mau Mau et le nationalisme kényan, sont à la fois l'affirmation de la participation féminine et des renseignments sur cette participation. De représenter la révolte comme une lutte entre hommes africains et européens, ignore l'initiative des femmes et leur souci de changement, en dissimulant les effets néfastes du colonialisme sur les femmes, les changements dans leur statut et leurs protestations contre les changements économiques et culturels. En outre, d'ignorer l'activisme politique féminin obscurcit le processus qui a élargi la participation politique pour permettre l'inclusion de politiciennes dans le Kenya moderne. Cette article critique les études actuelles sur le nationalisme Kikuyu, en révélant la force cachée mais puissante du nationalisme féminin indépendant et parallèle. Il examine l'importance du rôle des femmes dans le nationalisme militant et suggère que ces activités ont donné lieu à une lutte pour un leadership féminin dans le Kenya post Mau-Mau.

Introduction

In his 1982 work, *Essays on Mau Mau: Contributions to Mau Mau Historiography*, Robert Buijenthuis surveys the state of scholarship on the Mau Mau rebellion in Kenya from the 1950s to the 1980s. Buijenthuis, an early scholar of the Mau Mau rebellion and Kenyan nationalism, ably assesses the questions that researchers and participants in Mau Mau have addressed. Some of the fundamental questions explored are: What were the origins of Mau Mau? What were its patterns of recruitment and definition of membership? A second level of questions attempts to delineate the political, ideological, and personal connections of Mau Mau to nationalist associations in the pre-1948 period. Third, the historiography has focused on the different phases of the Mau Mau rebellion. A fourth concern has been how the colonial state and the British government marshalled their forces to counter and defeat Mau Mau. These questions were widely explored from the 1950s to the 1970s. Beginning in the 1970s, questions of class and local level analysis came into vogue. Typical questions were: Which of the Kikuyu districts in the Central Province contributed members to the rank and file as opposed to

503 Presley: The Mau Mau Rebellion

the Mau Mau leadership? Was Mau Mau a conflict or civil war between rural / urban populations and elite mass / sectors of society? Or was it best understood as labor conflict which evolved between the lumpenproletariat and the skilled workers in the trade unions?

All of these questions have deepened our understanding of the multifaceted nature of Mau Mau and have revealed cleavages in Kikuyu society. Some cleavages began in the pre-colonial period. Others were introduced under the colonial regime. While debate rages over some of these issues, in particular over local level and class differences in Mau Mau participation, scholars still exclude from consideration women's contribution to the rebellion and to Kenyan nationalism in general. The earlier Mau Mau studies did not examine women's participation. (See Rosberg and Nottingham 1966; Tignor 1976; Kilson 1955; Buijenthuis 1973, 1982; Kanogo 1987; Barnett and Njama 1966; Clayton and Savage 1975; Furedi 1973; Furedi 1974; Kanogo 1977; Tamarkin 1978; Coray 1978; Newsinger 1981; Stichter 1975; Tamarkin 1976; Leakey 1952, 1954; Majdalany 1963; Ogot 1972; Sorrenson 1967). With the exception of a few works, such as Tabitha Kanago's recent book on Mau Mau and squatters in the Rift Valley, 1980s scholarship accords women only token acknowledgement as participants in the "passive wing" of Mau Mau (Kanogo 1987). By not questioning women's contribution to Kenyan nationalism and Mau Mau, analyses continue to project a view that Mau Mau was a conflict among males. The following dyads were created:

Africans *versus* Europeans

nationalists *versus* loyalists

mass *versus* élites

rural *versus* urban

lumpenproletariat *versus* trade union members

Research has ignored an important aspect of Kenyan nationalism: the development of nationalist sentiment and activity among women since the 1920s; and the colonial state's response to women's nationalism.

The Government's response was to alter social policy. The center-piece of this was the development of a department whose policies and programs were directed specifically to wean women away from Mau Mau. These policies were developed in response to two needs. The first was to isolate the military force of Mau Mau and to defeat it by attacking and cutting off its popular support, which the British called the "passive wing," composed largely of women. Their function was to supply information, to smuggle arms, food, clothing, and medicine to the guerilla army, and to maintain the lines of transit for recruits travelling from the urban and rural sectors of the Central Province to join the military forces in the forest.[1] The phrase "passive wing" hides the importance of this type of activity. The women and men who were the support troops of Mau Mau should more aptly be termed the non-combatant forces. They were treated as a serious force by the British.

The second part of the Government's policy was a program aimed at capturing the loyalty of the Kikuyu. This involved villagization and a full-blown propaganda program whose major purpose was to detach women from Mau Mau. The Government paid special attention to women's activism since key officials believed that women were "far more rabid and fanatical than the males" and more violent in their support of Mau Mau.[2] In response to women's "fanaticism" institutions designed to address such unmet needs as education, health care, access to a clean and reliable water supply, and child-care were created. The policy acknowledged, perhaps for the first time, that the colonial government had a primary responsibility for the welfare of rural populations. The Community Development Department, which was created in 1954, addressed these problems. It was given a large annual budget of £250 000 and a staff which included Africans as well as Europeans (Great Britain 1954, 80).[3]

This Department was part of the British struggle to control women. Before the 1920s, the contest over who would control women, African or European males, revolved around jural issues: chiefly the marriage laws. The colonial state, of course, won the contest (Presley 1986, 149-200).[4] Other conflicts of this nature revolved around female circumcision and women's wage labor.[5] Women's massive participation in Mau Mau contributed to the rebellion's initial psychological, if not military successes. A total of 34 147 women were sentenced to prison for violation of the Emergency Regulations from 1952 to 1958 (see Table 1). Thousands of these women were repeat violators of the regulations, which included taking oaths and aiding the forest fighters through supplying food, guns and information. Thus, from the standpoint of both the British and the nationalists, wooing women's loyalty was an essential ingredient in winning the war.

The Image of Women Nationalists

When women's activities are described in the pro-colonial histories, two pictures of women emerge. Women are seen either as victims of Mau Mau or as prostitutes who, through personal contact with male nationalists, were drawn to Mau Mau while resident in Nairobi. The view of women as victims of Mau Mau originates from the colonial record. Women are presented by officials as the physical and psychological victims of atavism. The first

505   Presley: The Mau Mau Rebellion

type of victimization characterizes women as being forcibly compelled to take the oath of allegiance to Mau Mau. A 1952 Special Branch report on intimidation in oathing recounted the forced oathing of a Catholic Kikuyu woman. She was stripped naked, severely beaten to the point of unconsciousness, and upon her revival compelled to "drink blood from a bottle, and perform the other disgusting rites constituting the Mau Mau ceremony" (Corfield 1960, 155-156.) Another 1952 incident contributed to the view of women as victims. In Nyeri, the District Commissioner reported that forcible oathings of women and children were widespread (Corfield 1960, 134). Further fuel was added to this image of women by writers who were openly antagonistic to Mau Mau. In *State of Emergency*, F. Majadalany portrayed women's attraction to Mau Mau as being caused by a misdirected hero-worship of nationalists, described as "young thugs and criminals." According to Majadalany, however: "When the fighting gangs were formed each included its quota of women, and though their first function was to act as pack transport (with some concubinage on the side) many of them became ferocious and implacable fighters too" (1963, 60).

Both F. D. Corfield and Majadalany ascribe irrationality and bestiality to Mau Mau. One measure of its supposed fanaticism was the repeated attacks on Loyalist women (Corfield 1960, 101). In the Lari Massacre (26 March 1953) eighty-four Loyalists were killed, two-thirds of the victims women. During 1952 Mau Mau military actions killed twenty-three loyalists of whom two were women and three were children (Corfield 1960, 157; Majadalany 1963, 137-147). While the rebellion was in progress, a popular British tactic was to portray women as Mau Mau's principal victims. However, only ninety eight of the 1 024 Kikuyu killed by Mau Mau were women (Buijenthuis 1982, 184). This figure represents actual deaths and does not include threats, beatings, and other intimidation.

The image of women nationalists as prostitutes originates from district and provincial reports. Women nationalists began to be described as prostitutes when the Kenya African Union (KAU) successfully staged mass rallies. For example, a rally in Nyeri on 26 July 1952 was described by the District Commissioner: "Over 20 000 men, women and children attended. KAU insinuated over 40 bus loads of Nairobi thugs and prostitutes, who were clearly under instructions to excite the crowd" (Corfield 1960, 136-137). In describing the participation of the Meru in Mau Mau, J.T. Kamunchulah repeats the theme of a connection between prostitution and women's activism. He attributes the success of the Mau Mau in acquiring arms from government soldiers from 1950 to 1952 to "a network of communication with prostitutes, who lay 'tender traps' for African askaris, of ambushing the African askaris in dark streets and abducting and later suffocating them to death" (Kamunchulah 1975, 193).

Women, Nationalism, and the Colonial Infrastructure

These views suggest that women were attracted to Mau Mau for other than political reasons and that, moreover, only those women who were pariahs in European and African society were likely to be seduced by Mau Mau nationalism. These images of detribalized women as the initial female contingent of Mau Mau are counter-factual. In the first year of the Emergency, local level British officials noticed that large numbers of women were actively involved in Mau Mau. The accepted explanation for women's attraction to Mau Mau was that they had had less exposure to British institutions such as the missionary schools, fewer opportunities for employment in the settler economy, and were more "primitive" than males who had become westernized.[6] Indeed, Kikuyu women were not as tied to the day to day structures of colonial rule as were their men. Nonetheless, they were affected by colonialism. In the pre-colonial period women farmed land which was later alienated by the Crown Lands Act (1902). Loss of land produced scarcity. Consequently, women as well as men were affected by overpopulation and land pressures which the introduction of the settler economy and state had induced. In the areas dominated by the settler economy, women were an important part of the labor economy, used extensively as seasonal laborers in the production of coffee, the country's leading export. During the harvest season, female and juvenile labor made up sixty percent of the labor force (Presley 1986, 108-119).[7] Missionaries intensively recruited women. They viewed themselves as champions of the alleviation of women's misery through stamping out customs they perceived as devaluing and harmful. From the European standpoint, these included the payment of bridewealth, prohibitions on remarriage of widows, and female circumcision. Though mission efforts at educating girls always received a lower priority than those directed toward boys, the rural schools and churches focused on persuading women to accept western mores, customs, and values (Temu 1972, 106-107; Presley 1986, 149-164).

Colonial laws also were directed toward women. The effect of land alienation has already been mentioned. Other colonial laws such as communal labor (1908) and the hut and poll taxes (1910 and 1934) were also assessed against women. These laws caused resentment, and combined with the issues of female circumcision, unfair labor practices, taxation, lack of adequate education, and exclusion from politics, they drew women to the nationalists' ideology.

Affected by colonial laws, women, long before Mau Mau, had registered their protest against these laws. Colonial officials did not, however, treat women's resistance as an integral part of the rising tide of protest dating to the 1920s. Several indicators of women's activism were dismissed as being instigated by others. Women had organized labor strikes over the conditions on the coffee estates. These strikes, notably one in 1947, were dismissed as being caused by male agitators (Presley 1986a, 129-148).[8] Another major incident occurred in 1947 and 1948, when women of Fort Hall District participated in what was termed "The Revolt of the Women." This was a protest against a scheme to compel women to dig terraces in their fields for the purpose of soil conservation. According to the Corfield report, this protest was initiated by the Kenya African Union. At a large meeting, an agreement was reached that women would not participate in the government scheme. The women's unanimous support for this agreement meant that none of them showed up for the communal labor, and "by the end of August all communal labour was virtually at a standstill" (Corfield 1960, 67). The Corfield Report consistently interpreted women's agitation as aberrant:

> During the earlier part of the year [1948] agitation against soil conservation continued in Fort Hall district and led to a minor political upheaval known as "The Revolt of the Women" in two locations of that district. Disruptive elements outside the district continued to agitate against the co-operation of women in soil conservation work, and this later led to a full-scale descent of the women themselves to district headquarters. This as the District Commissioner commented, marked a growing tendency which was entirely alien to normal Kikuyu custom, indicating that agitators had been at work (1960, 77).

Women in the Mau Mau Rebellion

Women's participation in public arena politics was indeed alien to Kikuyu custom. Colonialism changed women's political roles. This change did not originate in the decade before the State of Emergency was declared but predated Mau Mau by twenty years.[9] Small groups of women became nationalists in the 1930s. Over the next twenty years, they recruited thousands of other women to the nationalists' cause.[10] Women gained recognition from the major nationalist associations, the Kikuyu Central Association (KCA) and the Kenya African Union (KAU) before these organizations were proscribed by the government.[11] Their roles in the Mau Mau rebellion were as multifaceted as the revolt itself. Women had primary responsibility for the organization and maintenance of the supply lines which directed food, supplies, medicine, guns, and information to the forest forces. They also recruited for Mau Mau. They officiated at and participated in oathing ceremonies (Corfield 1960, 84). In 1950 the Kiambu District Commissioner reported to his superiors that men were no longer administering oaths of loyalty to Mau Mau:

> Women, however, were proceeding with the work of oath-giving.... For a woman to administer a Muma oath would be utterly contrary to Kikuyu custom, although it must be admitted that until the Dedan oaths were started it was also unknown for a woman to have a Muma oath (Corfield 1960, 90).

A break with custom in giving and taking oaths was one of the many changes in gender roles nationalism introduced for women.[12] They also joined the forest forces and served as combat troops. They were so important to the movement that the British rounded them up in the military sweeps, aimed at arresting the leaders and the more active Mau Mau adherents who were not in the forests. Their high visibility in the movement is indicated by their mention in colonial records. In 1953 women's activism caused the District Commissioner of Kiambu to pass on this observation to his superiors:

> In September, the Chura location appeared to become a centre of the Mau Mau central committee, and every Itura had its own sub-committee, nor did they lack a women's section. the latter throughout may well be described as the "eyes and ears of Mau Mau."[13]

The 1953 *African Affairs Report* notes:

> The part played by women to aid the terrorists was considerable. They not only fed them but carried food to gangs in the forest, and some were caught dressed as Mau Mau "askari" [soldiers]. The attitude of the women of the tribe towards the Emergency was, in general, particularly distressing ... the primitive and indigenous cult of Mau Mau has had for many a powerful appeal. There have been instances of female relatives being privy to the murder of their loyal menfolk.[14]

Kikuyu women joined the nationalist associations to improve their economic status, to gain access to the political process, to further their education, and to abet the return of alienated land. Muthoni wa Gachie was a member of KCA and KAU in the 1940s. She recounted women's motives as being political in origin:

> Q: When did you join?
> A: I joined in April of 1945.
> Q: Why did you become a member?
> A: So that I could be a politician of the country.
> Q: Were there other women who were members?
> A: Yes, there was a group of us.
> Q: How many?
> A: The whole of Central Province.
> Q: Were women already members when you joined?
> A: Yes, very many were already members.
> Q: What did KCA want?
> A: We wanted only to make the Europeans to go from the country.
> Q: What were your responsibilities as a member?
> A: I was cooking for visitors and I contributed for Mzee [Kenyatta] to go to Europe. We were fighting so we would know how to become independent....

Q: Were you a leader?

A: Yes, even I was taken to prison. When the war started we thought of some people going to the forest. We were cooking food and taking it to the forest. We were carrying guns, if we would give it to her and she would take it to the forest. We went during the night, During the day the Homeguards came to collect us. We were brought here to dig the ground with our hands. Some were killed. Others were jailed for some years. Then from there the war slowly came to an end.

Q: How long did you spend in jail?

A: In one year I was jailed three times. This was in 1958. Then I was detained in 1959 for one year. I was detained at Athii River, then I was taken to Embu.[15]

Wagara Wainana also described herself as a leader of Mau Mau. Unlike Muthoni wa Gachie, she was able to avoid being placed in detention.

Q: When did you take your first oath?

A: About 1948.

Q: How many did you take?

A: Only two.

Q: Were you a member of the Mau Mau committee?

A: I was a committee member of KAU and of Mau Mau.

Q: Which area did you represent?

A: I represented Karura (Muthurura) Kiambaa.

Q: Was your husband involved in politics?

A: Yes.

Q: How was it that you were not put in prison?

A: I was not detained because my husband was beaten. My co-wife's son was also detained. The co-wife was sick so that there was no one left so that the Europeans left me to care for the sick.

Q: Did they know that you were an active Mau Mau?

A: They knew [there were Mau Mau in the area] but not who the actual person was unless the other Kikuyu told them.

Q: Did you get put into the villagization program?

A: Yes, we built the villages.

Q: Did you carry on the work of Mau Mau from the villages?

A: Yes, we continued after that. We women were taken to a place and forced to do work for nothing. This place was called Kianjogu.... We did digging and we didn't know the reason we were doing this digging. We dug all around the camp, sweeping and clearing the camp. Then we were taken to another camp. We stayed in Kianjogu for seven months. Then we were taken to a village for four years and then I went to my farm. This was in 1955. We were only fighting and in the end we were helped by God. In the 1930s the women started the Mumbi Central Association and when Kenyatta came back from England he called us all together and organized us. I took food to the Mau Mau. We also took guns. When I was taking food, I was hiding from the Europeans when another one of us saw the police, she started screaming and ran down to the river. I grabbed her by the throat so that we could not be heard. When the soldiers came near, I ran away and the other one was screaming again. Then the other one was caught and put into detention.[16]

Wangui wa Gikuhiu joined KCA when it was first organized. Though an active supporter of Mau Mau, she described herself as "only a member." Women leaders "did the work of talking about how to get the land."[17] Priscilla Wambaki, a leader before Mau Mau and a KANU (Kenya Africa National Union, the ruling party) leader in her division in the independence period, recalled the beginning of women in politics:

Q: Were you a member of a political party?

A: Yes, I was a member of KAU.

Q: Did you belong to KCA?

A: KCA was the one before KAU, but I was only a member of KAU.

Q: Did you ever hear of an organization called Mumbi Central Association?

A: I was a member of Mumbi Central Association. I was also a member of KAU.

Q: When did you join Mumbi Central Association?

A: I can't remember the year but I joined it with Wambui Wangaram and I worked with Rebecca Njeri....

Q: What did Mumbi Central Association want to accomplish?

A: Kiama kia Mumbi had the aim to preserve the customs, to not allow them to dissolve. But before we went further the war started.... First women were not invited to join Kikuyu Central Association. We met together and decided we didn't like this so we asked the pastor of the church to help us. He did and we raised money and started Mumbi Central Association. We would have dances to raise money and the men could not matter. It was only Mbiyu Koinange who was allowed. After a while we joined the men again.

Q: How much money did you raise for Kiriri?[18]

A: I don't know since the books were destroyed, but it was much more than 100 000 shillings.

Q: How many oaths did you take?

A: ... Only children did not take the oath. I won't talk about that. I want to tell how Mbiyu helped to build the dormitories so that you can understand the role women played when Mzee [Kenyatta] came from Europe. We met with him. We had not completed the dormitories. We had no windows. He helped us, he was on our side. From that time on he was on our side. If there were no women, then the war would not have been carried on. And the women were mostly girls, because if the men were beaten, they would tell the secrets and the girls would not. Even Mzee knew that the girls played a great part and that is why he gave us Madaraka....[19]

511 Presley: The Mau Mau Rebellion

TABLE 1
Women Admitted to Prisons, 1952–1958

Year	Number	Number Sentenced	Recidivists	First Offenders
1952	347	n / a	n / a	n / a
1953	4 415	3 132	55	3 077
1954	9 609	8 494	290	3 204
1955	13 265	11 467	1 506	9 961
1956	8 900	7 906	1 627	6 279
1957	8 854	7 472	2 068	5 404
1958	7 295	5 976	1 873	4 103

SOURCE: Kenya Colony and Protectorate, Kenya Prisons. *Annual Report*, 1953, 8; Kenya Prisons, *Annual Report*, 1956, 8-9; Kenya Prisons, *Annual Report*, 1958, 10.

TABLE 2
All Africans Admitted to Detention Camps,
1948–1957

Year	Number
1948	16 369
1949	16 637
1950	18 037
1951	18 257
1952	23 201
1953	32 862
1954	25 979
1955	30 247
1956	41 441
1957	53 080

SOURCE: Kenya Colony and Protectorate, *Annual Report on the Treatment of Offenders*, 1957, 2.

Women's activism sparked a response from the Government. They were arrested, detained, and interrogated in large numbers. When the Emergency officially ended in 1956, of the 27 841 Kikuyu who were still in the detention camps, 3 103 were women (*Daily Chronicle* 7 September 1956). Tables 1 and 2 reveal the number of women imprisoned during the Mau Mau period compared to the total number of Africans detained in the camps. Of the 13 265 females admitted to prison in 1955, 1 714 were discharged from prison custody, 11 467 were sentenced to imprisonment (9 961 of these were first offenders, the balance were repeat offenders).[20] Virtually all women imprisoned were suspected of Mau Mau involvement.

Before the Emergency, there was so little female crime that no particular prison facilities had been built. To the surprise of the colonial government, when Mau Mau activities became pronounced, women's participation was on such a large scale that a facility had to be built to house them. The Kamiti prison was extended to accommodate the upsurge in women prisoners and detainees; the camp included 1 335 women prisoners and 1 010 women detainees by the end of 1954.[21] Women were also detained in other facilities. The Athii River detention camp which was built in 1953 to contain violaters of the Emergency Regulations had ten compounds containing 1 429 detainees. One of the compounds was reserved for twenty-seven female detainees.[22] Most women prisoners were sentenced for violations of the Emergency regulations.[23] A large proportion of the women sentenced were first time offenders. Sentences ranged from short terms of one or two months to the full duration of the Emergency, with a majority sentenced to terms of six months or less – twenty percent (1952) and twenty-seven percent (1953) were sentenced to six months to two years. As Mau Mau became more threatening, the length of sentences increased.

The camps were not merely holding facilities. Prisoners were required to work and also to go through a re-socialization process whose goal was to get them to renounce Mau Mau and be "cleansed."[24] The Community Development organization was involved in rehabilitating prisoners.[25] At Kamiti, the Department was given some control over the detainees' "leisure time."[26] Nearly three hundred female detainees attended classes. They received instruction in animal husbandry, hygiene, health, agriculture, and local government.[27] However, these classes were not the most important aspect of the organization's work in the struggle to defeat Mau Mau. The Department also ran child-care facilities.[28]

Most of the apparent success the Government achieved in converting Mau Mau detainees in 1955 and 1956 was among female prisoners in Kamiti prison. Several facilities for women were maintained around the colony, but Kamiti was for the "hardcore" Mau Mau women.[29] The number of women released from the Kamiti facility in 1956 was 1 194 leaving 1 384 women in the camp. In 1957 4 220 women were released and 174 remained in detention. Many "hardcore" women were not released until 1960. The rehabilitation efforts among women were so "successful" that by 1957 Mau Mau women detainees were:

> ... processed straight to their homes on release and have not passed through the pipe line camps in their own areas as is the case with men. This is a tribute to the thorough and successful rehabilitation work undertaken at the camps.[30]

Community Development officers were aided in their work of detaching women from Mau Mau by the missionaries. The Christian Council of Kenya sent representatives to the camps to hold Christian services and "cleanse" women prisoners of their radical beliefs.[31] The Department categorized prisoners according to the strength of their attachment to Mau Mau and response to rehabilitation. The "Y" category were those who were responding to re-socialization.[32] Kamiti women prisoners were considered to be in the "Y" category of rebels. Confession was stressed. When word circulated that those who confessed could gain an early release, the number of penitents rapidly soared (Wipper 1977, 255).

Conditions in the Prisons

Former women prisoners at Kamiti described conditions of terror, physical punishment, and forced labor. They received inadequate food and clothing. Conditions for women Mau Mau and / or Mau Mau suspects were similar to those for males who were arrested and detained. Interviews with former Mau Mau female prisoners reveal a prison system which meted out harsh treatment.[33] Women in Kamiti were required to work for the prison system.[34] Light work of raising vegetables and fruit was given as a reward for co-operating with the rehabilitation program, another impetus to confess.[35] This co-operation usually took the form of taking a pledge renouncing Mau Mau and giving information about Mau Mau activity in the prisons and elsewhere. The more intransigent were required to work on road-building and quarrying stone. The prison commandant reported in 1955 that 199 000 running feet of stone was quarried by Kamiti prisoners.[36] Once the stones were quarried and dressed, women prisoners transported them on their heads. In 1954 women helped to terrace the thirty-five acre prison farm. The value of the labor extracted from these women through the cultivation of the 197 305 pounds of vegetables they raised in 1956 was £1 973.[37] Other forms of punishment included solitary confinement, the withholding of food, and corporal punishment.[38] Harsh and inhuman treatment was the rule in the prisons and detention camps according to former Mau Mau prisoners. The following is from an interview with one of them, Priscilla Wambaki:

Q: Were you detained?

A: Yes.

Q: Where were you taken?

A: I was taken to Kajado in Maasailand.

Q: When was this?

A: It was in 1952. That was the time when Mzee [Kenyatta] was detained with Rebecca Njeri.... [Njeri was the most prominent woman nationalist, detained at the same time as Kenyatta]. I was in detention for one year then I was taken to the Athii River [camp].... At Kajado only the women leaders were detained. Men were there also but the women were kept separate. We were not forced to work but kept locked in our rooms. There we were beaten but not too much. But when we were taken to the Athii River, we were beaten very much. All of the members of KAU, men and women were detained. Women were not many at Athii River, we were about two hundred, but the men were uncountable. Those who were involved in politics or any other movement but not the church were taken to Kamiti. This was in 1954, and only women were there. We were beaten and very many died. During that time people were hanged in great numbers and we buried many there. We were not afraid of the corpses, even if we were doing this job we were still beaten. We could see some corpses with the blood from the beating still on them. During the time of getting food in the prison the young girls would pull the carts, they were tied three by three to the carts in order to pull them to where they were to get the food and then they had to pull the carts back to Kamiti. Even now, I remember what was done when I see a young girl like you.... We would leave the prison to dig the terraces. We took breakfast at 5:00 a.m. We had *uji* [boiled ground maize meal]; the girls would bring it from two miles away; then we took the *jembes* [hoes] and basins to dig the terraces; we were only women.... We got *ugali* [boiled ground maize meal] with boiled beans or boiled cabbage. We worked up to three then we took supper at four. After that we were locked in the house and one could go to wash. We were fed *ugali*, and it was not well cooked. If there were no beans or cabbage, we got only one boiled potato with the *ugali*.

Q: Was there any meat, eggs, milk or tea?

A: No! Even the children couldn't get these things. I am disappointed to hear that many people believe that women did nothing in the war; we buried the bodies. The children of Kamiti were tied with ropes together to be guarded while we women worked. They gradually died off. It was due to hunger. We suffered a lot from hunger.... Kamiti was a hell prison. Some were dying, some were beaten to death, sometimes they died after work. We were happy when someone died because we said "Now she is free!" I was still in Kamiti in 1956.[39]

Muthoni wa Gachie was detained in 1959. Her experiences were consistent with those recounted by other respondents. She talked of torture inflicted by the Homeguards.

515   Presley: The Mau Mau Rebellion

Q: Were you a leader?

A: Yes, even I was taken to prison.... When we were in detention the work was only to be beaten, given hard work and not enough food. We spent one week digging trees with other women.

Q: Why were you detained?

A: Because I was speaking about the Government.

Q: What did you say?

A: I was saying that Europeans should be taken to their homes and our children should be given education.

Q: How did the European know about you?

A: Other people reported me.

Q: Were you married then?

A: Yes.

Q: Did your children go to detention with you?

A: No, they were not in detention with me but they suffered because they lacked food, clothing and education.

Q: Was your husband involved?

A: He was also jailed but not put into detention.

Q: Who took care of the children while you were in jail and detention?

A: Only God. Our homes were burnt, cattle were taken, we were left with no clothing and wore banana leaves. Even that women gave birth on the way. We had nothing to help the child. We removed the headscarf to carry the child. Bottles were put in our private parts as a punishment.

Q: Where were you detained that they did these things?

A: Just here at Githunguri. The Homeguards were doing this.

Q: Were they doing this to make you admit Mau Mau?

A: They were doing this so that the Europeans could give them something.[40]

The fact that women were a significant portion of the prison population and that they were not accorded any special treatment because of gender is little known and rarely mentioned in the historiography of Mau Mau, although these facts were not hidden from public view during the Emergency. Indeed, the treatment of women prisoners caused a minor scandal in 1956 in Kenya and England. Eileen Fletcher, a former member of the Kamiti Prison staff, revealed the poor conditions and abuse by officials at Kamiti in her testimony before members of the House of Commons in London and in statements and interviews with the British press. She recounted that under-age girls were wrongfully detained. In the course of several House of Commons debates on the subject, an official inquiry into the prison system was initiated (Presley 1986, 256-264; *Tribune* [London] 16 November 1956; *Daily Chronicle* [Nairobi] 31 May and 7 September 1956]. After the inquiry, annual reports on the conditions in the prisons included detailed information on the treatment of prisoners and the punishment or dismissal of wardens and staff for their mistreatment of prisoners.

Greater administrative attention to reporting on prison conditions was not enough, however, to ensure the end of abuse. The scandal involving the murder of eleven male detainees at the Hola Camp in 1959 finally brought an end to the detention system and the "pipeline" process of gradually releasing detainees from high to ever lower security facilities until finally they were released to their home villages.[41]

The Impact of Social Policy on Women's Nationalism

When the remaining women detainees were released and returned to their villages in 1960, they discovered that the Government had radically altered village life as a part of its war against Mau Mau. The campaign against women was a major part of this. This change was achieved through the villagization program. Initially begun as a punitive measure, the project became a centerpiece of social policy.[42] The turning point in defeating Mau Mau on the home front was achieved when activists or those suspected of being activists were rounded up. The entire Kikuyu population was semi-imprisoned in guarded villages. The importance of the villagization program in the defeat of Mau Mau was recognized in official circles. Addressing the Legislative Assembly in 1955, the Governor, Sir Evelyn Baring stated:

> ... it has been possible in many areas to arrange a system of movement control by which villagers going to work on their *shambas* [farms], or herding their cattle, do so under escort from either the Tribal Police or the Watch and Ward Units. It is the establishment of this system which in many areas has broken the physical contact with the gangs. The individual gangsters must often have hidden in a hole in a sisal hedge and have slipped out for a few minutes to tell a woman working in her field that food must be left at a certain place at a certain time or else there would be trouble. In this way the fear of the terrorist was maintained. Now, there can be no absolute certainty, but it appears probable that the new system has in most areas broken that physical contact and dissipated that fear.... As a result too, the flow of information from the villagers has greatly improved.[43]

The breaking of contact between villagers and Mau Mau fighters meant that women who were not imprisoned during the Emergency had their own intensive encounters with the regime. The object of these encounters was, of course, to defuse nationalism and curtail their Mau Mau activities. Just as in the prisons and detention camps, the main plank of the policy was the withholding and granting of benefits to sway the non-combatant wing away from radical nationalism. One of the consequences of being identified as Mau Mau was loss of land. The Government confiscated the land of Mau Mau members and reallocated it to "deserving Loyalists." The instrument

517 Presley: The Mau Mau Rebellion

for this policy was the Community Development Department. It was thought to have the potential for creating a true social revolution in the villages, its major goal being:

> ... to teach the women in the new villages a new way of life and to show them that the possibilities of community life in a smaller area offer better opportunities for improved homes than the old scattered villages – as indeed they do.[44]

The relocation scheme was begun in 1954 and began to be phased out in 1958.[45] It involved the forced relocation of the entire Kikuyu population of the three Kikuyu districts in Central Province. More than eighty thousand Kikuyu households were uprooted in Kiambu District in 1954 and 1955. Also, more than seventeen thousand squatters who were ejected from the Rift Valley by settler farmers joined the Kikuyu who were required to live in the new villages.[46] For Kiambu District, the focus of my research, this involved over 300 000 men, women, and children. They were compelled to build new villages and tear down or abandon their homesteads. They lived under guard behind barbed-wire fences. To farm, women were escorted to their fields by the Homeguard. Everyone had to be back behind the barbed-wire fences by the 4:00 p.m. curfew.[47] In 1955 threats of the confiscation of land and the imposition of a twenty-four hour curfew were used in Kiambu District to break the "passive wing."

Abuse of villagers under the authority of the Homeguard was reported. Milka Ngina who spent the Emergency in the guarded villages recalled:

> A: We were beaten and forced to dig the terraces. They beat us very much and it was the Homeguard who did the beating.
> Q: Did you take the oath?
> A: Yes, I took very many, and we were beaten when we took the oath.
> Q: Were you put into detention?
> A: Some women were detained but not all of them.
> Q: Did Kenya become independent because of Mau Mau?
> A: Yes, because they bought the freedom with blood.
> Q: Did others in your family take the oath?
> A: All the Kikuyu took the oath at that time.
> Q: Was there any fighting around your home?
> A: Yes.
> Q: What happened?
> A: We were beaten by the Homeguard because the Mau Mau passed through our homes. I myself was almost beaten to death.
> Q: Why did the Homeguard help the British?
> A: We were beaten by the Homeguard because the Mau Mau were not on good terms with the Homeguard and those who were giving food were on good terms with the Mau Mau.[48]

Catherine Wajiru, who lived in Embu during the Emergency, was also exposed to the civil war between Mau Mau supporters and the Loyalists (Kikuyu seen as loyal to the colonial regime).

Q: Did you help the freedom fighters?

A: Yes.

Q: How did you help?

A: I gave them cooked food.

Q: Does that mean that there were freedom fighters in Embu?

A: Yes, they were there because they were living in the forest near us.

Q: Were you happy to give them food?

A: We gave them food because we had no security and if we refused to give them food, they could beat us.

Q: Were you living near Embu people?

A: Yes, we were mixed. We built the homes in the same place and we worked on the *shambas* with other groups.

Q: Did the Embu give food?

A: Yes, they did. They stopped giving them food when the villages were built but before that the Mau Mau would take goats and even cows by force. Also we were beaten by the colonials if they found that we were giving food. There were spies called Homeguard who would tell when you helped.

Q: Were you beaten?

A: Yes, I was beaten very much and my husband died during that time because of the beating.[49]

Villagization was successful in demoralizing the non-combatant wing. The African Affairs Department recorded:

> The withdrawal of the surrender terms on 10 July was combined with local propaganda, so that at the end of June and the beginning of July the volume of confession swelled to such a degree that the teams were unable to cope. A very great deal of Mau Mau funds was handed in as well as guns and ammunition. The threat of confiscation of land, together with the imposition of 24-hour curfews also had a considerable effect in breaking the last efforts of the *Mau Mau* to conceal information. The confession teams in the settled areas ... had an extremely difficult job to begin with ... they subsequently achieved remarkable and effective results in breaking the passive wings on the farms and discovering the main gang bases or food depots.[50]

The major point of contact under these semi-concentration camp conditions was through the Community Development Department. Initially, most of the Department's annual budget of 250 000 pounds was spent on the work of rehabilitation.[51] The Department focused on women:

519   Presley: The Mau Mau Rebellion

> In view of the large numbers of women and children to be found in these villages whose husbands are either serving sentences, detained, working in the home guard, operating in the forests or living in the towns, the accent of rehabilitation must be on women.[52]

The Department's major vehicle for influencing women was through the Maendeleo ya Wanawake (Progress among Women) clubs. The clubs had begun in the late 1940s but did not have a significant membership until the Emergency. Membership in the organization expanded tremendously during the Emergency years since it could be the crucial difference between survival and starvation under the villagization program. The work of the clubs included running day nurseries, making and supervising the distribution of soup, distributing milk to hungry children, and "caring for children whose parents were missing or dead."[53]

These humanitarian efforts were affected by the Emergency since the "Work of Maendeleo clubs [was] hampered by subversive propaganda and additional communal work necessary in the rehabilitation of and fortifying

TABLE 3
Maendeleo ya Wanawake Clubs

District	Clubs	Members
Army Camps	8	400
Kiambu	45	5 050
Fort Hall	35	3 250
Nyeri	100	7 500
Embu	25	1 250
Meru	1	20
Settled Areas	10	300
Naivasha	1	45
Thompson's Falls	1	85
Nairobi	5	400
Machakos	94	10 000
Other Districts	183	8 510
Total	508	36 810

SOURCE: Kenya Colony and Protectorate,
Community Development Department, AR /
1954, 13.

villages." The clubs were only able to meet after the four o'clock curfew.[54] The Department measured its success through the increase in membership. In 1954 the membership totalled 36 810 in 508 clubs (see Table 3). Kiambu women joined forty-five of the clubs with a membership of 5 050.[55] Forty-five percent of the members came from the three Kikuyu districts of Kiambi, Fort Hall and Nyeri, and Nairobi where Mau Mau activities were greatest.

In addition to administering to the needy, the Community Development programs were "responsible for internal broadcasting, libraries, the distribution of papers, classes, *barazas* [public gatherings], recreation and instruction in various forms."[56] The purpose of the education component of the program was to counteract Mau Mau by providing a course of "general knowledge."[57] Typically, this included bringing books, pamphlets, and a film truck to villages. This information stressed the positive benefits of colonialism and the evils of Mau Mau.[58] The Government viewed the clubs as "an effective instrument against subversive elements."[59]

In the guarded villages, the clubs were used to aid the security forces. Club members gathered information about Mau Mau activities and tried to persuade Mau Mau adherents to abandon the movement.[60] Women were told that they had to become allied with the Government rather than with Mau Mau. If they chose to remain publicly sympathetic to Mau Mau, they lost access to the services which the clubs offered.[61]

> In most areas where the backbone of Maendeleo clubs had been in existence since 1951-53, the club members have in many cases been of value to the Security forces giving information freely and persuading others to give up *Mau Mau*. In at least one case they played an important part in the capture of a *Mau Mau* general. The women realized that the ideals of *Maendeleo* and *Mau Mau* were incompatible and they would have to choose between them. It is very encouraging to note that the numbers of clubs and members in these areas are on the increase as more and more realize that *Mau Mau* has brought nothing but distress and sorrow.[62]

This persuasive message resulted in a tremendous growth in membership. By 1955 the number of clubs increased to 596 with a membership of 43 000.[63] The benefits of belonging or simply being associated with the clubs were particularly crucial in 1955 and 1956 when famine struck Kiambu District.[64] A scarcity of food was induced by the curfew, for women had fewer hours available to them in which to fetch water and fuel and to cultivate their fields.[65] During the famine, the 107 clubs in Kiambu District operated soup kitchens and increased their milk allotments.[66] In 1956 there were 34 500 fully paid members, in addition to 11 500 women who benefitted from the club services but were unable to pay the membership fees.[67] By the end of 1957, the number of clubs had grown to 986, but fully paid membership had declined to 33 613.[68]

One of the goals of the Community Development Department was to train Africans to be good citizens according to British standards. A byproduct of this was women's representation on the village and district councils. By 1955 "Maendeleo members [were] coming forward to take their place on locational and District Councils in greater numbers, so that in future there is hope that the voice of the women will be heard more and more."[69]

Conclusion

Viewing Mau Mau from the female perspective adds several important aspects to the understanding of the rebellion. It illuminates an often repeated statement that landless and less affluent Kikuyu were more likely to take part in Mau Mau whereas the better off Kikuyu publicly took sides with the British and joined the loyalist forces as Homeguards. In some families, women were deeply involved in Mau Mau while males publicly disassociated themselves from it. There are two possible explanations for this phenomenon. First, women's involvement with Mau Mau cut across "class" lines. Wives of prominent Kikuyu were jailed. At least one woman organizer was the wife of a chief. Second, women's involvement in radical nationalism expresses the ambiguity of prominent families' identification with Mau Mau. Males of such families might have silently supported Mau Mau while maintaining a public face as Loyalists. If men openly supported the rebellion, the consequence was loss of more land and privileges. This may have led to a perception that it was marginally safer for women to carry out the family's commitment to Mau Mau. The entire family need not then be impoverished by supporting it. A nationalist female, if arrested and detained, could be easily discredited and disowned. Whether this was deliberate family policy among a number of families is of course unknown. It may, however, explain some of the curious features of Mau Mau reported by the Government and uncovered in oral interviews. Specifically, it may explain the Government's contention that women were more rabid and fanatical, that men had stopped giving oaths, and that women were assuming these responsibilities. It may also explain the Government assertion that women of loyalist families were involved with Mau Mau. Mau Mau women reported to the author that their husbands, though considered loyal to the Government, knew of the aid they gave to the Mau Mau rebels and did not report them.

Women's participation in the violent Mau Mau revolt focused Government attention on the need to use some of its resources to develop programs to serve women and their needs. In order to defeat Mau Mau militarily, it was crucial for the British to isolate the guerilla fighters from their supplies. Mere isolation, however, was not sufficient. The non-combatant force, led and organized to a large degree by women, had to be engaged with force and persuasion. Thus, women were jailed in increasing numbers from 1954 to 1957. The increase occurred at the same time that the British victory over Mau Mau was assured. It is my contention that this was not mere coincidence, but that success in the war against women was a necessary ingredient in the war against Mau Mau. The campaign of propaganda and education was designed to convince women not already Mau Mau activists that disassociation from Mau Mau held positive rewards. First, the entire Kikuyu population was relocated to villages which were closely supervised by the Security Forces, the Homeguard, and the new Community Development Department. Within three years of this policy, a drop in Mau Mau activities occurred. The British government started a social revolution by providing an extensive social services program. Women were the first to be experimented upon since the Government recognized that they had to be detached from Mau Mau for final victory to occur. This had consequences for post-Mau Mau Kenya. The creation of the Community Development Department was the precursor of the Community Development Program in independent Kenya and, much later, the Women's Bureau. The contemporary Maendeleo ya Wanawake clubs also owe their origin to women's vigorous nationalism during Mau Mau. In the 1980s the Maendeleo clubs number over six thousand. Maendeleo is Kenya's largest women's organization (Ndumbu 1985, 86; Wipper 1975; Wipper 1975-76).

One reason for the lack of research on women's nationalism is that scholars followed the line taken by the colonial government. Until thousands of women were imprisoned for Mau Mau offenses, colonial administrators dismissed incidents which indicated that women were actively involved in resisting colonialism. In the case of labor stoppages and protests against terracing, district officers maintained that women's activism was caused by male agitators. Therefore, psychologically, the administrators were unprepared for women's protest. It seemed to them to be sudden, fanatical and unexpected.

Historians of Mau Mau have also treated women's nationalism as incidental to the main currents of nationalism. Their sources of data for the study of Mau Mau have been almost exclusively male, whether they were Europeans or Africans. The use of this data source and perspective has created the false paradigm that politics was mainly a male concern. Consequently, the questions posed to male respondents and the official records focus on the actions of men. When men did comment on women's involvement, it did not seem to be a major thread of the rebellion. In searching for answers to a political dilemma, scholars have naturally looked to those

523   Presley: The Mau Mau Rebellion

departments which had responsibility for political and economic issues.
The full story of the colonial battle against women's nationalism is not
revealed by political records, though important indicators occur there. In the
social services area, even more revealing data surface. Since the colonial
officials were trapped in their 1950s perceptions of women, they relegated
policies dealing with women to community development. As the Community Development report noted, the voice of women began to be heard during
the Mau Mau rebellion, although women had spoken out through their protest, be it on economic, political, or social issues, for over twenty years in
colonial Kenya. When they took up arms and supported violent rebellion,
their voices began to be heard. The legacy for contemporary Kenyans is to
acknowledge women as equal partners in politics.

Notes

1. For a more extensive treatment of women's roles and contributions to the rebellion see Presley 1986c.

2. Kenya National Archives (KNA), Native Affairs Department (NAD), *Annual Report (AR) 1953*, 25; Kenya Colony and Protectorate (KCP), Community Development Department (CDD),*AR 1956*, 4.

3. The original Community Development staff included twenty-four European Rehabilitation Officers and thirty-seven African Rehabilitation Officers.

4. KNA. *Political Record Book, Kiambu District 1912*, KBU / 109 / Part II(K), 10; KNA. *Political Record Book, Kiambu District 1908-1912*, KBU / 76, 85-87).

5. For female circumcision see: KNA. NAD. *AR 1929*, 11-12; Rosberg 1966, 106-125; Murray 1974; Presley 1986a. For women's wage labor see Presley 1986b.

6. KNA, NAD, *AR 1953*, 25; KCP, African Affairs Department (AAD), Central Province (CP), *AR 1953*, 27.

7. KNA, NAD, *AR 1926*, 79, 87; KNA, NAD, *AR 1925*, 64.

8. KNA, *AR 1946*, KBU / 38, 1-2.

9. There is well documented evidence that Kikuyu women's public political activity predated Mau Mau by at least thirty years going back to the Harry Thuku Riot in 1922 (see Wipper 1988).

10. Interviews with former women nationalists conducted in 1978. The main women who described the organization of the women's network are: Wambui Wagarama, Nduta wa Kore, Phillis Wanjiko (Margo) wa Mimi, Priscilla Wambaki and Mary Wanjiko. See Presley 1986, 222-227.

11. I interviewed Kikuyu women nationalists in 1978. They told me of the development of women's nationalism. In 1930 women of Kiambu district formed their own nationalist association because they were excluded from formal participation in the KCA. After three years of organizing other women, they approached the Kiambaa branch of KCA and were able to persuade the leaders that women's organizational talents were indispensable to it. From then onwards, each location had a women's wing. See Presley 1986c.

12. Oath-taking by Kikuyu women appears to have occurred in the Harry Thuku movement in the early 1920s (see Wipper 1988).

13. KNA. *Political Record Book, Kiambu District 1953*, KBU / 44, 1.

14. KNA. AAD. CP. *AR 1953*, 27.

15. Interview on 10 January 1979 in Githunguiri, Kiambu District.

16. Interview on 29 April 1978 in Kiambu.

17. Interview on 13 May 1979 in Ruiru, Kiambu.

18. Kiriri was the women's dormitory at the Githunguri Independent School which was established by nationalists after the break with church and government controlled education which resulted from the circumcision controversy. Mbiyu Koinange and his father Sr. Chief Koinange were the driving forces behind changing the Githunguri School into the Kenya African Teachers College, an institution for the higher education of all Africans in Kenya. When it formally opened in 1939, there was a feeling among nationalistic Kikuyu that education was the key to political power (Rosberg and Nottingham 1966, 179-180).

19. Interview on 23 May 1979 in Juja, Kiambu. Madaraka Day marks the granting of internal self-government in 1963, about half a year before independence.

20. KCP. *Treatment of Offenders Annual Report 1957*, 10.

21. KCP. "Report on the General Administration of Prisons and Detention Camps in Kenya," by G. H. Heaton 1953, 3; KCP. *Report on the Treatment of Offenders for the year 1953*, 4; KCP. *Report on the Treatment of Offenders for the Year 1954*, 4.

22. KCP. *Report on the Treatment of Offenders for the year 1953*, 16-17.

23. KCP. *Treatment of Offenders Annual Report 1956*, 8-9.

24. KCP. CDD. *AR 1954*, 21-24; KCP. CDD. *AR 1955*, 22-26.

25. KCP. *Treatment of Offenders Annual Report 1955*, 2.

26. KCP. *Treatment of Offenders Annual Report 1955*, 2.

27. KCP. *Treatment of Offenders Annual Report 1956*, 2.

28. KCP. CDD. *AR 1956*, 6.

29. KCP. CDD. *AR 1954*, 30.

30. KCP. CDD. *AR 1956*, 4.

31. KCP. CDD. *AR 1955*, 22-23.

32. There were four categories: (1) Z1 – Mau Mau leaders who refused to respond to the rehabilitation program; (2) Z2 – rank and file who refused to renounce Mau Mau; (3) Y – those who responded to rehabilitation; and (4) X – those who were rehabilitated and placed on parole. See KCP. CDD. *AR 1956*, 3-6.

33. Oral interviews: Tabitha Mumbi, Thika, 24 May 1979; Elizabeth Gachika, Kiambu Town, 7 January 1979; Nduta wa Kore, Tingang'a, 13 January 1979; Wambui Wangarama, Kabete, 29 April 1979. See Presley 1986c for extensive oral interviews with Mau Mau women.

34. KCP. *Report on the Treatment of Offenders for the year 1953*, 4-5; KCP. *Treatment of Offenders Annual Report 1955*, 16, 18.

35. Convict labor was an important source of both income and supplies for the Department of Prisons. In 1953 the value of the agricultural produce raised by prisoners totalled £10 220. The amount of revenue received from prison industries amounted to £150 595, and £15 897 was given to the system as payment for using convict labor on the East African Railway, Harbour Administration, and other authorities. See KCP. *Report on the Treatment of Prisoners for the year 1953*, 14-15. In Kamiti, the value of vegetables raised by female prisoners was £1 973 in 1956. See KCP. *Treatment of Offenders Annual Report 1956*, 14-15.

36. KCP. *Treatment of Offenders Annual Report 1955*, 15.

37. KCP. *Treatment of Offenders Annual Report 1956*, 14.

38. KCP. *Report on the Treatment of Offenders, Kenya Prisons for the year 1954*, 11.

39. Interview 23 May 1979 at Juja, Kiambu.

525   Presley: The Mau Mau Rebellion

40. Interview 10 January, 1979, Githunguri, Kiambu.
41. KNA. *Records of Proceedings and Evidence into the Deaths of Eleven Mau Mau Detainees at Hola Camp in Kenya,* 1959; Rosberg and Nottingham 1966, 335-344.
42. KCP. AAD. CP. *AR 1954,* 33.
43. KCP. *Legislative Council Debates* 18 October 1955, 4.
44. KCP. CDD. *AR 1954,* 31.
45. KCP. CDD. *AR 1958,* 7.
46. KCP. AAD. CP. *AR 1955,* 35, 51.
47. KNA. CDD. *AR 1957,* 33; KNA. AAD. *AR 1954,* 33.
48. Interview 11 May, 1979, Kiambu town.
49. Interview with Catherine Wajiru, Kitambaya, Kiambu, 11 May 1979.
50. KCP. AAD. *AR 1955,* 37.
51. KCP. CDD. *AR 1955,* 1.
52. KCP. CDD. *AR 1954,* 31.
53. KCP. CDD. *AR 1955,* 7.
54. KCP. CDD. *AR 1955,* 7.
55. KCP. CDD. *AR 1954,* 13.
56. KCP. CDD. *AR 1955,* 25.
57. KCP. CDD. *AR 1955,* 25.
58. KCP. CDD. *AR 1952,* 9; KCP. CDD. *AR 1956,* 1-10.
59. KCP. CDD. *AR 1954,* 12-13.
60. KCP. CDD. *AR 1955,* 7. These activities caused the Maendeleo movement to be severely stigmatized among the Kikuyu in the early period of independence. (See Wipper 1975-76, 199-204.)
61. KCP. CDD. *AR 1955,* 7.
62. KCP. CDD. *AR 1955,* 7.
63. KCP. CDD. *AR 1955,* 12.
64. KCP. AAD. CP. *AR 1955,* 48.
65. The connection to the Emergency conditions and the famine in the district is clear. No mention is made in the colonial records of famine in other parts of Kenya in 1956.
66. KCP. CDD. *AR 1956,* 13-14.
67. KCP. CDD. *AR 1956,* 10.
68. KCP. CDD. *AR 1957,* 8.
69. KCP. CDD. *AR 1955,* 6.

Bibliography

Barnett, Donald and K. Njama. 1966. *Mau Mau From Within: Autobiography and Analysis of Kenya's Peasant Revolt.* New York and London: Monthly Review Press.

Buijenthuis, Robert. 1982. *Essays on Mau Mau: Contributions to Mau Mau Historiography.* Leiden: African Studies Centre No. 17.

———. 1973. *Mau Mau Twenty Years After: The Myth of the Survivors.* The Hague-Paris: Mouton.

Clayton, Anthony. 1976. *Counter-Insurgency in Kenya, 1952-60.* Nairobi: TransAfrica Publishers.

Clayton, Anthony and Donald Savage. 1974. *Government and Labour in Kenya, 1895-1963.* London: Frank Cass.

Coray, Michael. 1978. "The Kenya Land Commission and the Kikuyu of Kiambu." *Agricultural History* 52, no. 1: 179-193.

Corfield, F.D. 1960. *Historical Survey of the Origins and Growth of Mau Mau*. London: HMSO (Cmnd 1030).

Furedi, Frank. 1974. "The Social Composition of the Mau Mau Movement in the White Highlands." *Journal of Peasant Studies* 1, no. 4: 486-505.

———. 1975. "The Kikuyu Squatters in the Rift Valley, 1918-1929." *Hadith* 5: 177-194.

Furley, Q.W. 1972. "The Historiography of Mau Mau," *Hadith* 4: 105-133.

Great Britain. 1954. *Colonial Office Report on the Colony and Protectorate of Kenya*. London: HMSO.

Kamunchulah, J.T. 1975. "The Meru Participation in Mau Mau." *Kenya Historical Review* 3, no. 2: 193-216.

Kanogo, Tabitha. 1987. *Squatters and the Roots of Mau-Mau 1905-1963*. Columbus: Ohio University Press.

Kilson, Martin. 1955. "Land and the Kikuyu: A Study of the Relationship Between Land and Kikuyu Political Movements." *Journal of Negro History* 40: 103-153.

Leakey, L.S.B. 1952. *Mau Mau and the Kikuyu*. London: Methuen & Company.

———.1954. *Defeating Mau Mau*. London: Methuen and Company.

Majdalany, F. 1963. *State of Emergency: The Full Story of Mau Mau*. Boston: Houghton Mifflin Company.

Mungai, Evelyn and Joy Awori. 1983. *Kenya Women Reflections*. Nairobi: Lear Publishing Co.

Murray, Jocelyn. 1974. "The Kikuyu Female Circumcision Controversy with Special Reference to the Church Missionary Society's 'Sphere of Influence.'" Ph.D. thesis, University of California, Los Angeles.

Ndumbu, Abel. 1985. *Out of My Rib: A View of Women in Development*. Nairobi: Development Horizons.

Newsinger, John. 1981. "Revolt and Repression in Kenya: The 'Mau Mau' Rebellion, 1952-1960." *Science and Society* 45, no. 2: 159-185.

Ogot, B. A. 1972. *Politics and Nationalism in Colonial Kenya*. Nairobi: East African Publishing House.

Presley, Cora. 1986a. "The Transformation of Kikuyu Women and their Nationalism." Ph.D. thesis, Stanford University, Stanford, California.

———. 1986b. "Labor Protest Among Kikuyu Women, 1912-1947." In *Women, Race and Class in Africa*, edited by Claire Robertson and Iris Berger. New York: Holmes and Meier Press.

———. 1986c. "Women in the Mau Mau Rebellion." In *In Resistance: Studies in African, Afro-American and Caribbean Resistance*, edited by Gary Okihiro. Amherst: University of Massachusetts Press.

Rosberg, Carl and John Nottingham. 1966. *The Myth of Mau Mau: Nationalism in Kenya*. New York-Washington: Frederick A. Praeger.

Sorrenson, M.P.K. 1967. *Land Reform in the Kikuyu Country*. London: Oxford University Press.

Spencer, John. 1974. "The Kikuyu Central Association and the Genesis of Kenya African Union." *Kenya Historical Review* 2, no. 1: 67-79.

———. 1985. *The Kenya African Union*. London: KPI Limited.

Stichter, Sharon. 1975. "Workers, Trade Unions and the Mau Mau Rebellion." *Canadian Journal of African Studies* 9, no. 2: 259-275.

527   Presley: The Mau Mau Rebellion

Tamarkin, M. 1976. "Mau Mau in Nakuru." *Journal of African History* 17, no. 1: 119-134.

———. 1978. "Loyalists in Nakuru During the Mau Mau Revolt and its Aftermath." *Asian and African Studies* 12, no. 2: 247-261.

Temu, A.J. 1972. *British Protestant Missions*. London: Longman Group.

Tignor, Robert. 1976. *The Colonial Transformation of Kenya: The Kamba, Kikuyu and Maasai from 1900 to 1939*. Princeton: Princeton University Press.

Wipper, Audrey. 1975. "The Maendeleo ya Wanawake Organization – The Co-optation of Leadership." *African Studies Review* 18, no. 3: 329-355.

———. 1975-76. "The Maendeleo ya Wanawake Movement in the Colonial Period: The Canadian Connection, Mau Mau, Embroidery and Agriculture." *Rural Africana*: 195-214.

———. 1988. "Kikuyu Women and the Harry Thuku Disturbance: Some Uniformities of Female Militancy." *Africa* 59, no. 3: forthcoming.

[21]

Decolonization: The Ultimate Diaspora

Anthony Kirk-Greene

In March 1997, a group of expatriate civil servants exercised their entitlement under Colonial Regulations to a sea-passage home on retirement and sailed from Hong Kong on board *SS Oriana*. After long years abroad, yet in many cases not having reached statutory retirement age, what did they come home to in terms of expectation of employment?

That snapshot symbolizes the last page in a 50-year album of similar occasions as Britain's imperial civil services, their latter-day mission of enabling independence in the colonial territories accomplished, progressively came to an end: the Indian Civil Service in 1947, the Sudan Political Service in 1955, and Her Majesty's Overseas Civil Service (up to 1954 the Colonial Service) in 1997. The dissolution of the three Services and the consequent dispersal of members who had not yet attained retiring age (variously a voluntary 45 to a compulsory 55) highlights a largely unexplored item in the jigsaw of imperial withdrawal and possibly the ultimate major event in the process of decolonization. What employment did the thousands of British overseas civil servants find whose permanent and pensionable (p. and p.) careers were cut short between 1947 and 1997 by premature retirement consequent on the end of colonial rule? Generally in their thirties or forties, and sometimes nudging fifty or under thirty, what kind of 'second careers' did they take up? Here, arguably, is the ultimate diaspora in the story of twentieth-century decolonization — the resettlement and [un]employment of at least 25,000 overseas civil servants. For some, of course, retirement was not so much a matter of looking for a second career as of deciding, to quote a nineteenth-century critic of the Indian Civil Service on the ultimate problem of where to retire to, 'whether to settle in a Cheltenham villa, or a Brighton Crescent, or at Rugby to educate his sons, or in London to dispose of his daughters'.[1]

Underlying the personal experience of this enforced relocation of (for the most part) mid-career civil servants, which in statistical terms is the focus of this article, runs the need for further research not only into the 'second career' phenomenon itself but also into the impact, both economic and social, of this large-scale absorption into postwar Britain of thousands of qualified and already experienced men and women. Conventionally, British society abroad was several years behind the fashion of the metropolis, whether in modes, manners or (Kenya's interwar 'Happy Valley' set arguably apart)[2] morals. The

---

1   G.O. Trevelyan, *The Competition Wallah* (London 1864), 217.
2   A classic exposé of Happy Valley society and its mores is to be found in James Fox, *White Mischief* (London 1982).

resultant culture-shock of this repatriation could be a two-way affair. In economic terms, too, the post-colonial era witnessed a further strain on the employment market, as over the first 30 years the armed forces reduced their wartime and later their regular strength, and then, during the next two decades, retrenchment, downsizing, ageism and early retirement became part of the standard vocabulary of Britain's industrial and business community. At the same time here was a reservoir of proven experience and expertise coming onto the labour market, admittedly not always *prima facie* relevant yet often of a quality which could be turned to advantage by redirection, retraining and 'retooling' or through straight integration. For the second half of the twentieth century the so-called 'retreads' became a standard element in Britain's professional labour force.

The study of decolonization has largely focused on the receiving end of imperialism, its process and effect on the new states of Asia, Africa, the Caribbean and the Pacific. In this article, the research transfers to the donor end, the thousands of imperial civil servants who found their careers prematurely terminated and themselves in search of a second one. Here is a fresh dimension to the metropolitan implications of decolonization as Britain divested itself of empire.[3] As an agenda for extended research, the article examines the diaspora of members of each of Britain's three overseas civil services between 1947, when the first of them (the Indian Civil Service) was terminated, and 1980, when the last of HMG's agencies established to help the resettlement of its imperial officials, the Overseas Service Resettlement Bureau, was closed on the grounds of 'mission accomplished'.

No attempt has been made to separate out the literal Colonial Service from Her Majesty's Overseas Civil Service (HMOCS): when the latter replaced the former in 1954, career (p. and p.) officers could apply to transfer and thus continue unbroken service.[4] Though by 1960 HMOCS was moving towards recruitment on contract terms and, wherever possible, on secondment from posts in the UK,[5] out of the 20,500 members of HMOCS two-thirds were still on p. and p. terms.[6] No attention has been paid to imperial civil servants who, before the second world war, retired early (but voluntarily) and then took up a second career in Britain — indeed, the Sudan Political Service maintained a voluntary retirement age of 48 expressly to enable this.[7] Here the emphasis is

---

3   The topic is hinted at (rather than treated) in M. Kahler, *Decolonization in Britain and France: The Domestic Consequences of International Relations* (Princeton, NJ 1984); more palpably in the special issue of the *Journal of Contemporary History*, 15,1 (January 1980); and suggestively in Ronald Blythe's socio-rural novel *Akenfield: Portrait of an English Village* (Harmondsworth 1969).
4   See Col. No. 306, *Reorganization of the Colonial Service*, 1954.
5   See Cmnd. 1193, *Service with Overseas Governments*, 1960; Cmnd. 1740, *Recruitment for Service Overseas: Future Policy*, 1962.
6   Anthony Kirk-Greene, *On Crown Service: A History of H.M. Colonial and Overseas Civil Services* (London 1999), 74.
7   On some notable pre-war ICS second careers, see L.S.S. O'Malley, *The Indian Civil Service 1601–1930* (1931, 2nd edn London 1965), chaps XI and XII; T. Honda, 'Indian Civil Servants,

on those who in the period 1947–80 left their respective Service prematurely in the run-up to or at independence as accelerated localization of the bureaucracy (Indianization, Sudanization, Africanization, etc.) overtook them. The Hong Kong experience of second careers has yet to be recounted, though, for many HMOCS officers who had started their career in Africa or the Pacific, Hong Kong was their second (and final) career.

With recruitment suspended during the war years 1939–45 (in the event, the extraordinary entry of 1940, which underwent its training course in Dehra Dun instead of the conventional Oxford or Cambridge, was to prove the last regular intake[8]), the strength of the Indian Civil Service (ICS) — including the post-1937 Burma Civil Service Class I cadre — when recruitment came to a halt in 1939 was 1299.[9] Of these, 540 were Indian officers, whose post-independence employment pattern does not form part of this research other than to note that the majority were absorbed into the Indian Administrative Service (IAS) or the Civil Service of Pakistan (CSP), often staffing their new diplomatic services.[10] In 1943 the Viceroy, Lord Wavell, had warned London that ICS recruitment from Britain should be formally closed, 'unless HMG are prepared to arrest the progress of constitutional reform and decide to continue British rule for at least fifteen to twenty years'.[11] The seriousness of the staff shortage in the critical field administration prompted the Governor of Bengal in 1946 to utter his memorable comment that 'the proverbial steel frame was now more like lath and plaster, and more plaster than lath'.[12] By the time the war ended the ICS Association, which sent a deputation to the Secretary of State in April 1946, and the Governors' conference held in July, were warning of a total collapse of morale and even a breakdown in administration unless the ICS received some definite reassurances about where and how its future lay.

Two White Papers were now published, setting out the options on offer.[13] Provided an officer was *persona grata* to the new administration, he could elect to continue in either of the two new Dominion civil services, in which case his existing terms of contract (which never included promotion) would be honoured. British officers were given the further guarantee that, when they left

---

1892–1937', chap. 5 (unpublished Oxford DPhil thesis, 1996); G.W. Bell and A.H.M. Kirk-Greene, *The Sudan Political Service: A Preliminary Register of Second Careers* (1989, privately published). A pre-war ICS character appears in George MacDonald Fraser's recollections, *Quartered Safe Out Here* (London 1992), as headmaster of a very minor public school in the West Country, 'who liked to imagine he was a house-master at a big public school' (150).

8   Sir Fraser Noble, *Something in India* (Bishop Auckland, Co. Durham 1997), chap. III.

9   Philip Woodruff [Mason], *The Guardians* (London 1954), 363.

10 See David Potter, *India's Political Administrators, 1919–1983* (Oxford 1986).

11 Quoted in Ann Ewing, *ICS and Burma CS (I): Post-Independence Careers Project* (1991, privately published), 1. Cf. Penderel Moon (ed.), *Wavell: The Viceroy's Diary* (London 1973), 33 and passim on ICS retirements and morale.

12 Quoted in Ewing, op. cit., 1.

13 Cmd. 7116 and Cmd. 7189, 1947.

either at independence or after a period of duty with the new Dominion government, they would be paid the proportional pension earned, together with compensation for premature loss of career calculated on a fixed scale. In due course, a modification allowed British officers temporarily to join the staff of the new British High Commission in Delhi or Karachi.[14]

An India and Burma Service Re-employment Organization office was set up in London to help officers find further employment. Table 1 shows the diaspora of the All-India Services (predominantly the ICS but also including members of the Indian Medical Service, the Imperial Police, the Indian Forest Service and the judiciary) in 1948, one year after independence. Little if any outside academic interest was taken in the ICS diaspora until the 1982 initiative of the Oxford Development Records Project (ODRP), which undertook a pilot project on the second careers of the Indian Civil, Sudan Political, and Colonial Services. With the co-operation of the ICS (Retired) Association, data was elicited from members of the Punjab Service (Commission).

The most complete collection of data in the ICS is the 'Post-Independence Careers Project' Survey undertaken by Dr Ann Ewing in collaboration with the ICS (Retired) Association, extending the ODRP pilot to eight Presidencies and Provinces.[15] This research was privately published in 1991. Although this is the fullest survey to date, by then more than 40 years had elapsed since the closure of the ICS and the number of respondents was only 347, under half the 759 on the books in 1947. Two supplementary provincial listings raised this to 370. The average length of service of the respondents was 17 years, with 5 years as the minimum (1 per cent), and 35 years as the maximum (approximately 20 per cent had more than 25 years service). The largest group (105) had 5–10 years service, followed by 90 in the 15–20 years bracket, together forming the very essence of the 'second career' problem. In her profile, Ewing admirably summarizes the second career track (for many it was also the third or even fourth career) of each named officer by provincial origin and under principal re-employment. Table 2 presents her 1991 data.

In interpreting this data, one needs to take care on two points. First, coming so long after the dissolution of the ICS, the corpus relates to 350 respondents rather than the 759 names on the books in 1947. That 40-year gap, with its natural wastage of potential respondents, is critical when it comes to attempting to construct any final profile of ICS second careers. Second, in describing a second career option as 'Colonial Service', the distinction is not always made between the Colonial Service/HMOCS, the Sudan Political Service and the Colonial Office.[16] Ewing succinctly sums up her invaluable findings in terms that could equally apply to the other Services under review here: 'The consistent themes that emerge are the concept of *service*: either government (e.g.

---

14   For a view of this arrangement from the first British High Commissioner in Karachi in 1947, see L. Grafftey-Smith, *Hands to Play* (London 1975), 88.

15   Ewing, op. cit., 64.

16   Interesting memoirs by ICS officers who then joined the CAS include J. Butter, *Uncivil Servant* (Edinburgh 1989), and J.C. Griffiths, *A Welshman Overseas* (privately published 1993).

Home, Civil, Diplomatic, Colonial Services) or public service (e.g. hospital, church, university administration) and of an international vision.'[17]

While the Indian Political Service (IPS) enjoyed a separate identity, two-thirds were recruited from the ICS and one third from the Indian Army. On its closure in 1947, the IPS had an authorized establishment of 170 officers, though the ban on recruitment during the war meant that only 124 were *en poste*. Of these, 107 were Britons.[18] As a supplement to the IPS names mentioned in the Ewing data, the biographical appendix to Chenevix Trench's history of the IPS is useful.[19] A number of IPS officers stayed on in contract jobs as Politicals in Pakistan under Sir George Cunningham, among them Pat Duncan who was the last of many British officers to be assassinated by Mahsuds.[20]

As with the relocation statistics of all three Services featured here, the tabulation refers only to paid institutional employment and not to the extensive and varied voluntary work undertaken by so many retired overseas civil servants in diverse and often multiple capacities. In all cases, the term 'second' career also subsumes subsequent careers.

For all the superficial similarity of the rationale and process of the closure of the three overseas civil services featured here, the case of the Sudan carries one feature unknown in the case of either the ICS or the Colonial Service. The final stimulus to localization of the bureaucracy — and hence its reverse face, the dismantling of the expatriate dominance of the public service — came not, as conventionally, from within but, uniquely in both direction and determination, from without. It was to be the programme of the international Sudanization Committee, set up as part of the Anglo-Egyptian Agreement of 12 February 1953[21] with a remit to 'complete the Sudanization of the Administration, the Police, the Sudan Defence Force, and any other Government post that might affect the freedom of the Sudanese at the time of self-determination' within just two years, which introduced the most deliberate of all the final localization procedures.[22] The Sudan government's own balanced programme of 1948, aimed at reducing the British presence through a bottom-up approach, of first speeding up the recruitment and promotion of Sudanese into the post of District Commissioner (DC), was completely undermined. Based on the premise of Sudanization without loss of efficiency, it had envisaged the enhancement of localized posts in the SPS from 14 per cent in 1948 to 21 per cent in 1952 and to 55 per cent in 1962. Such an 'ordered with-

---

17   Ewing, op. cit., 6.
18   T. Creagh Coen, *The Indian Political Service* (London 1971), 4.
19   C. Chenevix Trench, *Viceroy's Agent* (London 1987), 355–63
20   Ewing, op. cit., 63; Trench, op. cit., 349–50.
21   Cmd. 8904, 1953.
22   Douglas Johnson (ed.), *Sudan, 1951–56* (BDEEP series B, vol. 5) (London 1996), pt. I, lxxx; pt. II, 337. See also G. Balfour-Paul, *The End of Empire in the Middle East* (Cambridge 1991).

drawal'[23] was now totally negatived. Instead, Sudanization was to be instantly implemented at every level of the field administration, from DC to Provincial Governor. Senior posts which had hitherto required between 15 and 20 years' service were filled by Sudanese with sometimes less than 5, among them the latest intakes from the School of Administration.

British recruitment into the SPS was halted after 1952, when the last three probationers were appointed. Permanent and pensionable terms had already given way to mostly contract terms, with 38 appointments being made on long contract terms in 1947, supplementing the 26 made on permanent terms in 1945 and 1946. The SPS came to an end in 1954 when 'all but a handful of senior members of the Political Service had left'.[24] No British staff remained in the field, and the last few officers withdrew to the Palace to serve on the Governor-General's personal staff.[25] One remained as Financial Adviser, staying on until 1959.[26] By August 1955, when the Committee reported its task completed, a total of 647 out of the 1069 British officers working in the government had had their posts Sudanized or suppressed.[27] Of these, 144 were in the SPS when the Anglo-Egyptian Agreement had been signed in 1953. By the eve of independence, only 160 British officials were left out of the 1180 on the establishment in 1954. Unlike the case of the ICS or the Colonial Service, the option of staying on in the public service of the new government in Khartoum was not on the table for the SPS, though a number of departmental officers in the Sudan Civil Service were allowed to continue. Compensation paid for the loss of career was considered to be quite generous.[28]

The impact of this sudden and substantial surge of ex-DCs in search of a second career was so pressing that a Sudan Resettlement Bureau was opened in London. It was staffed by two former SPS officers.[29] For all its interest, David Sconyers's article 'Hurrying Home' does not answer its stated question of 'What happened to the Sudan Political Service after leaving the Sudan?'[30] As the SPS recruitment figures (Table 3) imply, the SPS rarely had more than 250 officers *in situ* at any one time and never exceeded 500 officers all told during the 55 years of its existence, so that the Sconyers figures (Table 4) of over one thousand officers must refer to the whole of the Sudan Civil Service and not to the SPS alone as claimed.

It is from two other sources, the ODRP initiative of 1983 (cited earlier) of a pilot scheme for researching the second careers of the SPS as a follow-up to its ICS project and the in-house compilation of a register of second careers, that

---

23   Sir Gawain Bell, *Shadows on the Sand* (London 1983), 214.
24   Ibid., 217–19.
25   Ibid., 217.
26   This was J. Carmichael.
27   Kenneth Younger, *The Public Service in New States* (London 1960), 68. See also David Sconyers, 'Hurrying Home' in Ismail H. Abdalla (ed.), *Perspectives and Challenges in the Development of Sudanese Studies* (Lewiston, NY 1993), 189–209.
28   Younger, op. cit., 67.
29   These were G. Hawkesworth and D.M. Evans.
30   Sconyers, op. cit., 208, note 32.

the most extensive SPS figures derive.[31] The register is not restricted to those who left prematurely because of independence and includes officers who left between the wars to take advantage of the Service's early retirement option and embarked on a second career in Britain. However, for the more specific purpose of this article, the data provided here (Table 5) relates to some 200 officers who left the SPS between 1946 and 1955.

The impact of the SPS, with its high degree of Arabic-speaking skills, on the diplomatic service and on employment with oil companies operating in the Middle East, is notable. Expectedly, too, a large proportion opted to continue to pursue their first career wish to be a DC and applied to the Colonial Administrative Service. Others became directors, etc., of business firms or personnel officers. Perhaps not surprisingly, given the strong Christian tradition of the British presence in the Sudan dating back to Wingate's lengthy governor-generalship and beyond to General Gordon, a sizeable number of the relocated SPS were closely involved in Church affairs, often in a voluntary capacity. At least three became ordained on retirement. As many as eleven took up farming. Among the miscellaneous group, three became MPs, two became Deputy Lieutenants (DL), two became game wardens in East Africa, one joined the Conservative Central Office staff, one was killed by Mau Mau after retiring to Kenya, two became antiquarian collectors and one became general manager of the Eton College Stores. One, Wilfred Thesiger, went on to confirm his reputation as a leading explorer. No less remarkably, W.G.R.M. Laurie, after a dozen years in field administration, qualified as a medical doctor. It is interesting that in the Ewing data on second careers, no fewer than five ICS men took up medicine.

Of the three overseas civil services considered here, an analysis of the Colonial Service — even of its component the Colonial Administrative Service (CAS) has a number of built-in problems not shared by its sister Services. First, there is the sheer size of the Colonial Service, exceeding 20,000 in 1957, distributed over 20 branches and located in some 40 territories.[32] In 1947 the CAS (the focus of this section) alone employed 1390 colonial administrators in Africa, 264 in South East Asia, and 140 in the other CO territories. Ten years later the figures had risen to 1782, 350 and 230 respectively.[33] Second, the colonial territories achieved independence not in a single year as in the case of India (1947) or the Sudan (1956), but at different times, from Ceylon and Palestine in 1948 to Ghana and Malaya in 1957, and on through the 1960s and 1970s to the culmination in the hand-back of Hong Kong in 1997 and the concurrent

---

31 The SPS questionnaires are now in the Sudan Archive, University of Durham (SAD). For the Register, see note 7. A summary article of the Register's contents, listing names and not just numbers, by A.H.M. Kirk-Greene and G.W. Bell, 'Survey of the Sudan Political Service', appeared in *Sudan Studies*, 6 (1989), 10–13, and 7 (1989), 20–3.

32 Jeffries's figure of 300,000 men and women include all the locally-recruited staff — Sir Charles Jeffries, *Partners for Progress* (London 1949), 28.

33 Sir Charles Jeffries, *Whitehall and the Colonial Service* (London 1972), 48.

closure of HMOCS. Third, while the Colonial Service did come to an end in 1954 when it was replaced by an HMOCS geared towards a system of short-term, contract appointments in lieu of the concept of a permanent and pensionable career service, many members of the Colonial Service were accepted for transfer to HMOCS and by 1960 they still made up two thirds of HMOCS, particularly in the Pacific and Hong Kong.[34] Finally, this in turn means it is as yet too early to be able to track right up to (and in some cases after) 1997, the very last year of the imperial diaspora.

Compensation schemes for premature loss of career had been part of the final constitutional negotiations on the independence of India (1947), Ceylon (1948), and the Sudan (1950) and were to loom large (too large, in the view of some local ministers) throughout the following decolonizing decades. The dismantling of the Colonial Service and the handling of the exodus of HMOCS officers at the end of the 1950s was a different story. The test case was Nigeria, the largest territory in the colonial empire, with lesser variants of the problem identifiable in Singapore, Malaya, Gold Coast and Tanganyika. While the two South East Asian colonies and the Gold Coast moved at a brisk pace to localize their administrative services and succeeded in doing so without provoking any special reaction in Whitehall, and Tanganyika's 'second wave' of enforced retirement[35] carried echoes of Singapore's so-called 'Sack Race', the case of Nigeria caused an anxious Colonial Office to press the Cabinet for the creation of a Special List of HMOCS officers in order to prevent what the governor-general warned of as a breakdown in government brought about by the rapid departure of administrative officers. When this Special List, offering a measure of employment and pension protection up to the age of 55 by the UK government, was announced in 1956, it failed to reassure Nigeria's expatriate civil servants, only 400 out of the eligible 2000 officers joining it.[36] The view generally prevailing was that since compulsory retirement was bound to come sooner rather than later, it made sense for the early and the mid-career officer to get out at once and test the employment market at home before it became saturated.

To abate the flood of resignations, tendered or threatened, two years later, HMG came up with a variant of its Special List.[37] This Special List 'B' (the original was now restyled SL 'A') was designed to slow down the rate of early retirements by means of improved terms for the payment of lump sum compensation so as to mitigate the financial attraction of immediate retirement. Although this revised scheme was promised to other territories should the need be felt to be imperative, in the event neither SL'A' nor SL'B' was ever imple-

---

34   Cmnd. 1193, 1960.

35   Cf. J. Lewis-Barned, *A Fanfare of Trumpets* (privately published 1993), Appendix 6; R. Sadleir, *Sunset and Sunrise in Tanzania* (London 1999).

36   Cmd. 9768, *Her Majesty's Overseas Civil Service*, 1956. See Younger, *Public Service*, op. cit., 7–8.

37   Cmnd. 497, *HMOCS: Statement of Policy Regarding Officers Serving in Nigeria*, 1958. See also Younger, op. cit., pt. II. For a discussion of both Special Lists, see Kirk-Greene, *On Crown Service*, op. cit., 71ff.

mented outside the four Nigerian governments. The complexities of the two Lists and the detailed statistics of posts unlocalized or unfilled because of accelerated expatriate retirement have been scrupulously recorded by Younger, while the in-fighting between the Colonial Office and HM Treasury forms the core of Sir Charles Jeffries's memoir.[38]

Perhaps because of the manifold complications outlined above, less research has so far been undertaken on the resettlement of the Colonial Service than on either the ICS or the SPS. In practice, the literature consists of little more than one survey of the Northern Nigerian Administrative Service;[39] an outline of the Western Nigerian Service (reproduced as Table 6), with valuable self-descriptive accounts;[40] and a wider survey of the diaspora of the CAS, including diplomacy (reproduced in Table 7).[41] All of these (other than that for Western Nigeria) were derived from an Oxford pilot research project implemented by means of sending a copy of the last territorial Staff List before independence to every tenth name (to ensure a generational spread) asking for information from personal or association knowledge of colleagues' post-retirement employment. Though no more than a sampling, the unpublished 1978 findings are presented in Table 8.

It is, however, now possible to provide further basic statistical findings generated by two more research schemes. One derives from the permission granted to the writer in 1973 to consult the non-personal files and reports of the Overseas Service Resettlement Bureau (OSRB). Because of the inevitably *ad hominem* nature of much of the data seen, an agreed condition of that privileged access was that nothing should be published until 15 years after the closure of the OSRB. This Bureau was established in 1957 to assist members of the Malayan Civil Service in their search for employment in the UK, and in 1958 it was renamed and extended to look after all members of HMOCS. Almost 1700 enquiries were registered in 1957–60, and by the time the Bureau closed in 1980 more than 15,000 names had been registered. Officers were under no compulsion to register, and several thousand found employment on their own.[42] Tables 9, 10, 11 present some of the OSRB statistics.

The second major source is the questionnaire sent out in 1984 to some 10,000 members of the Overseas Service Pensioners Association (OSPA) by the ODRP and with OSPA's generous co-operation as part of the research into the social history of the HMOCS, seeking *inter alia* information on second

38 Younger, op. cit., Annexes II-VII; Jeffries, *Whitehall*, op. cit., chaps 4–8.

39 Anthony Kirk-Greene, 'Where Did the DOs Go?', *West Africa*, 15 February 1987, 448–9.

40 M.C. Atkinson,*WRNA Careers After Nigeria* (privately published 1990).

41 Anthony Kirk-Greene, 'Diaspora of the DOs', *West Africa*, 8 February 1987, 368–9.

42 OSRB final *Newsletter*, 1/1980. para. 4. The Bureau earlier produced regular OSRB *Progress Reports*. Among its other publications was a series of *Notes for Guidance* on various career openings. On its closure, its parent ministry, the ODA, published a substantial *Guide for Returning HMOCS and Aid Personnel* (1980). The only analysis of the OSRB to date is Anthony Kirk-Greene's 'Resettling the Colonial Service', *West Africa*, 1987, 4 April, 552–3, and 11 April, 603. See also the brief reminiscence by N.F. Cooke in *Overseas Pensioner*, 77 (1999), 57 and the longer account by R.L. Peel, 'O.S.R.B.' in *Corona*, XI (1959), 141–2.

careers. Some 2000 of these 'HMOCS Data Project' forms were returned. It was agreed that this information, too, would be restricted, for a period of ten years. In 1996 the forms were made available to Nile Gardiner (Yale University) as primary data for his dissertation on the educational and family background of the Colonial Administrative Service. In return for this privileged access, Dr Gardiner extended his statistical research to include tables on second careers for use in the present article. These form the basis of Tables 12 and 13. They are important in that they present the first data available on the second careers of departmental officers as well as of the CAS. The 2000 completed forms of the HMOCS Data Project and Dr Gardiner's spreadsheets based on them will now be deposited in Rhodes House, Oxford, as part of its ongoing Colonial Service Archive.

In considering the diaspora of all these Services featured here, there is one aspect of the question of re-employment which exasperated members of the ICS, SPS and CAS at the time and which has continued to exercise students of the dispersal of Britain's overseas civil services. The Commonwealth Relations Office (CRO), which might have been thought to value the intimate overseas experience of Britain's imperial administrators as the territories in which they had served became independent and were transferred from the jurisdiction of the CO to that of the CRO (later the FO and later still, from 1968, the reconstructed FCO), was resolute in its refusal to accept any lateral transfer from HMOCS.[43] As with the ICS in 1947, and again in the case of the SPS, it was open to members of the CAS to apply for the CRO or FO, but they were required to sit exactly the same Civil Service Examination as the contemporary young entry. The only concession made was on the maximum age for entry, whereby applicants from the Services were allowed to deduct the time served from their age and so sit the Civil Service Commission Limited Competition, known as the Reconstruction Exam in 1947 and subsequently the Special Entry Competition.[44] For the ICS in 1947 alone, further flexibility — invaluable to an understaffed CRO — had been introduced to allow recommended officers to transfer to one of the two new British High Commissions on the continent, but at the end of their tour they were still obliged to sit the standard CSC examination in London before they could be confirmed in their appointment. The principle — or at least the thinking — behind this predisposition by the CRO and the FO to maintain, as it seemed to the ICS, SPS and CAS, a distinct distance from 'ex-colonials' may call for further enquiry into the success or disappointment of those who were admitted as well as those who failed to gain entry.[45] What is noticeable is the considerable number of those 'ex-colonials'

43 'I asked for the CRO but was told that they would not accept former Colonial Service people', unpublished memoir, 1999, by a former CAS officer (and the son of a Governor-General).
44 An appendix to Cmnd. 1193, 1960, included guidelines for retiring HMOCS personnel on the Special Entry Competitions for entry into the Home Civil Service and the Foreign Service.
45 In chap. 8 of his memoir *Lying Abroad* (London 1999), Harry Brind — who made the transfer from the CAS into the Diplomatic Service and held four High Commissionerships — has much of interest on this issue of the two careers compared. See also Joe Garner, *The Commonwealth Office, 1925–68* (London 1978), 406–9.

who accepted the need to sit the regular CSC examination they had sometimes spurned on graduation in favour of an overseas civil service career. Recent research has shown that frequently, in the end, the FCO did enlist that experience to man their new missions in the Third World.[46] In Africa, it allowed the FCO to introduce a new cadre of African specialists. What still remains to research is the fascinating question of how the 'ex-colonial' found his new 'diplomatic' work, often in the same or similar countries (and a fair proportion became ambassadors and High Commissioners, including postings back to 'their' original Khartoum or Nairobi), and how they perceived their new colleagues . . . and vice versa.[47]

Two further conspicuous second career directions for the CAS (which to a lesser extent also featured in the ICS and SPS cases) were academia and university/school administration. Among the academic stimuli for the CAS was the fact that a good number of them were, during their last years of service, seconded to the latterday Institutes of Public Administration established in most of the African colonies in the decade 1954–64 to accelerate training and localization. Many of these officers were able to transfer their skills to the new departments of public administration or development studies in the UK or the evolving Pacific. Notable, for example, was the high proportion of staff at Manchester University's Department of Public Administration, Birmingham University's Institute of Local Government Studies, and Sussex University's Institute of Development Studies drawn from CAS in the 1960s and 1970s.[48] Continuing a pre-war tradition, departments of anthropology and of exotic languages — in particular the School of Oriental and African Studies — also looked to the CAS for reinforcing their teaching capabilities. It so happened that the peak years of the CAS exodus coincided with the large-scale expansion of higher education in Britain in the early 1960s, and many successful second careers were taken up in university, college and school administration. Half a dozen ended up as Vice-Chancellors.

Keeping to their profession, other members of the CAS relocated in hospital, charity, New Town, Club, Society, etc., administration. While at least four became MPs (and one a Minister), few went into paid local government employ. This may reveal more about the trade union stance of NALGO than it does about the specialist skills of the CAS. Coming onto the market later than the second career-seekers from their sister services, some found a niche in the British Council and BBC. The Ministry of Defence welcomed many into MI5, a second career for the CAS wryly illustrated by the track record of Sir John Hargreaves in Graham Greene's novel, *The Human Factor*.

* * *

46   A.H.M. Kirk-Greene, 'Accredited to Africa: British Diplomatic Representation and African Experience, 1960–1995', *Statecraft and Diplomacy*, 11 (March 2000), 79–128.
47   Cf. the review of Brind, *Lying Abroad*, *Journal of African History* (forthcoming).
48   Cf. Anthony Kirk-Greene, 'Public Administration and the Colonial Administrator', *Public Administration and Development*, 19 (1999), 507–19.

'What happened to Y Sahib or Bwana X?' when he was faced with the realization that having been Deputy Commissioner Rawalpindi, Deputy Governor Darfur or DC Rift Valley was no longer a qualification *per se*, has so far remained a neglected aspect of decolonization. Yet the problem clearly reflects the reverse side of the coin of the much-analysed localization schemes. In this connection, preliminary insider soundings suggest that pension and retirement benefits were never as major a dimension to the 'second career' phenomenon as they may have appeared to the outsider. While overseas civil service compensation schemes for premature loss of career were regularly introduced shortly before each transfer of power, starting with India and Ceylon in 1947 and 1948 respectively, through the Sudan in 1954 and Malaya and Ghana in 1957, and throughout Colonial Service Africa in the decade 1958–68, the sums on offer were rarely sufficient to allow an officer under the age of 42 (maximum benefits eligibility) to retire and live — rather than survive — on his fresh capital without seeking other paid employment. The lump sum maximum fluctuated between approximately £8500 in the Sudan in 1954 and £9000 in Nigeria in 1960 to £11,000 in Malaya in 1957. Pension rates, too, varied between territories. In general they were calculated at 1/600 of the final year's salary for every month of service. Private means apart, the weight of evidence and of Service lore suggests that it would be a matter of purely personal preference rather than any financial self-sufficiency acquired from retirement benefits which might prompt a prematurely retired colonial civil servant under the age of 42 not to make at least one initial attempt to secure a 'second career' on his return to the UK. Such an assumption indeed underpinned the rationale of all three Resettlement Bureaux.

In a preliminary investigation of this nature, of raw data on a virtually unexplored topic, it is the next stage of research as much as any tentative conclusion that is the important feature. The sources used here can supplement consultation of the files of the three Resettlement Bureaux, although with such an emphasis on, inevitably, personal matters, restrictions are likely to be encountered.[49] Raising the whole research topic to the international level, it would be interesting to compare the second careers secured by Britain's overseas civil servant with those taken up by members of other colonial services, e.g. France, Belgium, Holland and Portugal. Findings so far suggest that the French government was far more willing to incorporate them into its 'home' government structures.[50]

At the end of the day, Britain's overseas administrators clearly demonstrated two qualities in their second careers. First, they showed that innate versatility which had stood them in such good stead throughout their colonial career: professionally trained in nothing, they consistently revealed a huge capacity for

---

49   The principal series are IOLR (in the India Office Library) and FO 371, CO 1017 and LAB 8 in the PRO. A short personal memoir of the work of the OSRB by J.S.A. Lewis is forthcoming in the *Overseas Pensioner*.

50   Cf. William B. Cohen, *Rulers of Empire: The French Colonial Service in Africa* (Stanford, CA 1971), chap. IX.

turning their hand to anything, often ending up as first-class public administrators. The result was that, come enforced retirement, it was often by shrewdly accepting a modest initial salary and a status post lower than that from which they had just come, that their very versatility enabled them to rise high — sometimes to the top — in their second career.[51] Second, the concept of service to others, which had generally led them into the ICS, SPS or CAS in the first place, remained a continuing priority in the second careers so many of them took up. Psmith Sahib, CIE and Senior Wrangler, or Bwana Bow, CMG and rowing Blue, may privately wonder as he reads of appointments secured: 'Good for A, I always thought he would go far!' or, less charitably, 'Good heavens! Fancy B an ambassador — I never thought he had it in him!', but the reality is that it was often the initial principle of *reculer pour mieux sauter* which allowed the Collector to end up in the embassy or in the executive dining-room and the generic DC to make his final mark as diplomat, director or don.

However elusive and exacting it will be to evaluate the impact of the dispersal of these 'returnees' on British society and its economy in the second half of this century, the relocation of at least 25,000 mature, experienced, qualified men and women who in mid-career suddenly found themselves in search of a second career is too prominent and too potentially influential a phenomenon for social historians to ignore. Their integration into a second career is at once the last diaspora in the end-game of Britain's imperial withdrawal and arguably, along with post-imperial immigration ('The Empire Strikes Back' syndrome), the final domestic legacy of empire.

TABLE 1
Relocation categories of registered officers of the All-India Services, 1948

Business	158
Home Civil Service	146
Continuing in government service of India, Pakistan, Burma	136
Foreign Service	51
Colonial Administrative Service	53
Colonial Service	21
Colonial police	7
Sudan Political Service	1
Sudan police	2
Other police forces	13
Control Commission/BMA	20
Dominions employment	70
Public boards	23
Intelligence services	23
Crown patronage and Church appointments	28
University and school administration	30
Hospital administration	1
Law	15
Medicine	8
British Council	2
Miscellaneous	106

51 An interesting account of the frustrations (and eventual success) in 'job-hunting' is to be found in Bruce Nightingale, *Seven Rivers to Cross* (London 1996), 67ff.

TABLE 2
Relocation of ICS (1991 Survey)*

Stayed on	59
Home Civil Service	62
Diplomatic Service	36
Colonial/Sudan Service	30
International organizations	15
Local government	5
Business	61
Public administration	6
Law	20
Clergy	6
Church administration	6
Medicine	5
Academia	10
Schoolteaching	20
University administration	14
School administration	2
Prison administration	1
Hospital administration	10
Politics	3
Farming	17
British Council	3
BBC	1

*The original figures are broken down by 8 Provinces.

TABLE 3
SPS Recruitment, 1899–1952

1899–1914	88
1915–1933	185
1934–1939	43
1940–1944	12
1945–1952	69

TABLE 4
Relocation of the Sudan Civil Service, 1955

Commerce and industry	263
Colonial Service and Persian Gulf	162
Public and academic	111
International organizations and foreign governments	43
Home Civil Service	25
Emigrated within Commonwealth	20
Self-employed	54
Remaining in Sudan government service	141
Miscellaneous	234

TABLE 5
Relocation of SPS (1989 Survey)

Chief Executive/Secretary of institutions	27
Directors, commerce and industry	23
Colonial Administrative Service	23
Diplomatic Service	20
Oil companies	13
Personnel management	13
Farming	11
Church	8
Home Civil Service	7
Middle East foreign government service	6
International agencies	6
Intelligence service (MOD)	5
College bursar	5
Law	4
Schoolteaching	4
University administration	3
Hospital/new town administration	3
University teaching	2
School bursar	2
British Council	2
Editorial	2
Chartered accountancy	1
BBC	1

TABLE 6
Western Region of Nigeria Public Service (1990 sample)

Commerce and industry	12
Colonial Service	8
Intelligence service (MOD)	5
Charity administration	4
Education administration	4
FCO	3
Local government	3
Law	2
Management consultancy	1
Financial consultancy	1
Diplomatic Service	1
Hospital administration	1
Civil defence	1

TABLE 7
CAS Second careers in the FCO (1985 Survey)

West Africa	Nigeria	19
	Ghana	6
	Sierra Leone	3
	Cameroons	1
East Africa	Tanganyika	24
	Kenya	17
	Uganda	13
	Somaliland	1
	Zanzibar	1
Central Africa	N. Rhodesia	9
	Nyasaland	3
High Commission Territories		3
Malaya		14
Palestine and Aden		3
Sarawak and N. Borneo		3
Cyprus		2
Ex-colonial police		35

TABLE 8
Diaspora of CAS (Africa) (1978 Survey)

	Gold Coast	N. Nigeria	Nigerian Fed.	N. Rhodesia	Nyasa-land	Kenya	Tanganyika	Uganda
Home Civil Service	4	4	11	7	3	6	6	1
ODA	1	7	1	6	1	2	2	9
Foreign Office	4	13	3	9	5	15	15	10
Intelligence service (MOD)	2	9	1	9	6	2	1	6
Overseas government service	21	27	11	9	5	8	8	10
University/school teaching	14	12	3	11	5	5	9	11
Law	4	5	3	11	3	4	4	4
Church	4	1	1	1	–	2	1	1
Local government/ corporations	2	12	6	4	4	1	–	8
Business	10	26	9	11	6	11	5	6
University administration	6	15	4	24	11	4	9	19
School bursar	2	9	1	2	2	3	–	1
Club/charity administration	3	9	6	6	3	9	6	1
Personnel management	1	2	3	15	1	2	1	1
Hospital administration	1	3	–	4	–	–	–	1

TABLE 9
Colonial Service officers on OSRB books, June 1962 (age groups)

Category	Under 35	35–45	Over 45
Accountants	3	16	18
Administrative officers	33	88	67
Administrative auxiliaries	7	50	75
Agriculture/forestry	19	34	35
Customs	2	6	8
Education	8	36	18
Engineering (professional)	6	25	27
Engineering (technical)	6	61	68
Legal	–	5	7
Medical	–	15	7
Police/prisons	22	64	82
Railways/marine	4	25	26
Storekeepers	1	9	5
Surveyors	3	9	5

TABLE 10
CAS officers on OSRB books, 1962–73

Year		Total	Nearest departmental total			Total on books
1962	(January–June)	188	Police and prisons		168	1235
	(July–December)	151	Engineering (technical)		135	–
1963		136	Police		140	935
1964	(January–June)	162	Police		155	738
	(July–December)	122	Police		128	–
1965	(January–June)	122	Police		99	475
	(July–December)	83	Police		60	–
1966		77	Police		75	434
1967		97	Police		76	543
1968		93	Police		52	469
1969		69	Police 64,	Education	60	510
1970		n/a			–	–
1971		57	Police 54,	Education	53	450
1972		41	Police 38,	Education	65	428
1973		35	Police 56,	Education	50	376

While the CAS was usually the largest group on the OSRB books, the police was often one of the hardest groups to resettle.

TABLE 11
Cumulative totals registered and resettled by OSRB, 1957–68

Year	Registered	Placed	To commerce and industry
1957–64	6508	5911	2381
1965	6981	6185	2623
1966	7719	6949	2939
1967	8543	7662	3191
1968	9194	8375	3447

TABLE 12
HMOCS data project resettlement summaries (1986), CAS

Second Career	Percentage (corpus = 580)
Business	14
Remained within Empire	12
Charity/voluntary work	7
Schoolteaching	6
Home Civil Service	6
University administration	5
Academia	4
FO/CRO	4
Local government	4
Bursar	3
Church	3
Diplomatic Service	3
Farming	3
Intelligence service (MOD)	3
Law	3
Accountancy	2
Education	2
International organizations	2
Public administration	1
Politics	1
NHS	1
Consultancy	1

TABLE 13
HMOCS data project resettlement summaries (1986),
Colonial Service (non-administration)

Second career	Percentage (corpus = 1155)
Remained within Empire	15
Business	9
Schoolteaching	8
Academia	7
Home Civil Service	6
Local government	6
Medicine/NHS	6
UN	5
Engineering	5
Farming	4
Charity/voluntary work	3
University administration	2
FO/CRO	2
ODA	2
Accountancy	1
Public administration	1
Bursar	1
Church	1
Consultancy	1
Education	1
Law	1
Police	1
Media	1
Intelligence service (MOD)	1
Scientific research	1
World Bank	1

Anthony Kirk-Greene

is Emeritus Fellow of St Antony's College, Oxford, where he held the
first lectureship in the modern history of Africa. His current research
focuses on the history of Britain's Overseas Civil Services, with which
his last two books have dealt: *On Crown Service* (1999), and
Britain's Imperial Administrators (2000).

Name Index